# COMPUTERS
## TOOLS
## FOR AN
## INFORMATION
## AGE

# COMPUTERS
## TOOLS
## FOR AN
## INFORMATION
## AGE

# H.L. CAPRON

**The Benjamin/Cummings Publishing Company, Inc.**

Menlo Park, California • Reading, Massachusetts
Don Mills, Ontario • Wokingham, U.K. • Amsterdam • Sydney
Singapore • Tokyo • Madrid • Bogota • Santiago • San Juan

*For the people who are there, even when I'm not: MEC, PLC, RED, BLH, DBJ, JDL, BMC, MMM, SJS, JZT, PTW*

Editor-in-Chief   **Sally D. Elliott**
Sponsoring Editor   **Jake Warde**
Developmental Editor   **Patricia S. Burner**
Production Management   **Wendy Earl**
Text, Cover, and Color Gallery Design   **Design Office Bruce Kortebein**
Art Direction   **Design Office Bruce Kortebein**
Buyer's Guide Design   **Victoria Philp**
Text Photo Research   **Tobi Zausner**
Color Gallery Photo Research   **InfoEdit**
Illustrations   **George Samuelson**
Copy Editor   **Toni Murray**
Production Assistants   **Elizabeth Robinson and Sharon Montooth**
Composition and Film   **York Graphic Services**

The programs presented in this book have been included for their instructional value. They have been tested with care but are not guaranteed for any particular purpose. The publisher does not offer any warranties or representations, nor does it accept any liabilities with respect to the programs.

**Library of Congress Cataloging-in-Publication Data**

Capron, H. L.
   Computers tools for an information age.
   Includes index.
   1. Computers.  I.  Title.
QA76.C358  1987      004      86-26420

ISBN 0-8053-2249-3

   DEFGHIJ-DO-898


The Benjamin/Cummings Publishing Company, Inc.
2727 Sand Hill Road
Menlo Park, California 94025

# The Capron Collection of Supplements and Software

## Supplements to the Text

- *Instructor's Guide* by H. L. Capron (32261)
- *Study Guide* by H. L. Capron (32262)
- *Test Bank* by R. E. Duffy (32264)
- Transparency Masters (32263)
- Transparency Acetates (32265)

*The Capron Collection of supplements is available in a convenient, reusable box.*

## Software for Students and Instructors

- *Using WordStar 3.3*—manual plus WordStar 3.3 Educational Version systems disk (36740)
- *Using dBASE III PLUS*—manual plus dBASE III PLUS Limited Use Version systems disks (36742)
- *Preview II Software and Lab Manual: An Introduction to Applications Software* (IBM manual 32405; IBM disk 32406; Apple manual 32407; Apple disk 32235)
- *Test Bank* available on *TestGen II* for IBM and Apple microcomputers and *Computerized Testing Service* for minicomputers and mainframes
- *University Gradebook*—manual plus disk (32268)

## Of Related Interest

- *Basic BASIC: A Structured Approach*, second edition, by M. Kittner and R. Northcutt; programs available on disk (32271)
- *Pascal: Programming with Style, A Brief Introduction*, by R. Lamb; programs available on disk (35835)
- *Learning to Use Lotus 1-2-3* by L. Metzelaar and M. Fox; data disk available (36736)
- *Learning to Use dBASE III* by L. Metzelaar and M. Fox; data disk available (36716)

For more information on any of the items listed on this page, see the Preface on pages xxv–xxviii, contact your Benjamin/Cummings sales representative, or call toll-free (800) 227-1936 or, in California, (800) 982-6140.

# BRIEF CONTENTS

## PART 1

## PART 2

## PART 3

**PART 4**

## MICROCOMPUTERS AND APPLICATIONS SOFTWARE  355

**PART 5**

## COMPUTERS IN THE WORKPLACE  475

# DETAILED CONTENTS

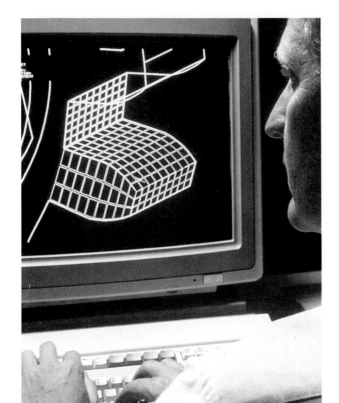

# PART 1
# THE BEGINNING
# OF COMPUTER
# LITERACY 1

*Chapter 3 continues*

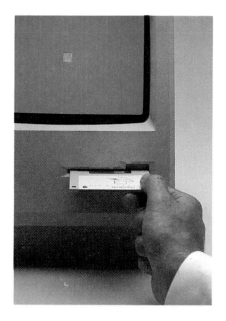

# PART 3
# SOFTWARE 211

*Chapter 13 continues*

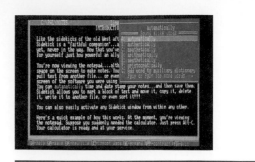

## PART 5
## COMPUTERS
## IN THE
## WORKPLACE  475

# THE GALLERIES AND BUYER'S GUIDE

7

The five full-color Galleries and the *Buyer's Guide* highlight topics in a photo-essay style, providing a look at some exciting uses of computers. The photos are accompanied by explanations of how computers are being used.

This Gallery takes a look at how silicon chips are made. We follow the process from design to manufacturing to testing to packaging to the final product, a microcomputer.

Computers are all around us, being used in ways that are practical, exciting, beautiful, helpful, and even fun. Gallery 2 examines some of the interesting uses of computers in our lives.

How are cultures around the world adapting to the Computer Revolution? To find out, take a look at this international Gallery.

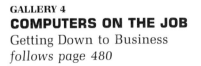

This special 16-page section presents issues and questions to consider before buying a personal computer. If you are thinking about buying a personal computer now or in the future, read this section carefully.

If you are not already working, someday you probably will be. This Gallery presents some everyday and not-so-everyday uses of computers in business and government.

What does the future hold in the world of computers? We can't say for sure, but in this Gallery we look at some of the cutting edge technologies that will impact the next stage of the Computer Revolution.

# / PREFACE

## / Why Adopt This Book?

*Computers: Tools for an Information Age* presents a complete introduction to computers in a very readable style. We think students will enjoy reading the book and retain a high percentage of what they read. In addition, instructors will find all the elements they have been asking for in this text, the accompanying software, and the supplements package.

## / The Text: A Complete Introduction to Computers

*Computers: Tools for an Information Age* covers all the topics needed for an introductory course in computers. The text emphasizes personal computers but does not ignore larger computer systems. In addition, we have especially strong coverage of graphics, communications, structured programming, operating systems, systems analysis and design, applications software, computer-integrated manufacturing, security, privacy, and ethics. Other features of this text include the friendly writing style, up-to-date coverage, the exciting art and photo program, five special topic Galleries, extensive student learning aids, and a comprehensive BASIC appendix. We will now introduce you to the organization of the book and then look at each of the features.

### Organization of the Text

The book is divided into five parts. Part 1, *You and Computer Literacy*, presents a strong case for universal literacy and provides the student with a foundation on which to build. Part 2 covers history and hardware. Part 3 includes chapters on structured programming, operating systems, and systems analysis and design. Part 4 provides a thorough look at microcomputers, including a complete chapter on the computers themselves and three separate chapters on word processing, spreadsheets and graphics, and database management systems. Part 5 offers information about computers in business, including office and factory automation, management information systems, decision support systems, and security and privacy issues. The text ends with appendices on BASIC programming and number systems.

The text is designed for maximum flexibility. For example, instructors who plan to give their students hands-on experience on personal computers may wish to cover the three software applications chapters sooner than the chapter order suggests.

Let us now look at the features of *Computers: Tools for an Information Age.*

### Extensive Microcomputer Coverage

Microcomputers are covered in four main ways in the text:

- **Four Chapters on Microcomputers and Applications Software.** Part 4 includes an entire chapter on microcomputers (Chapter 13) plus three chapters on word processing, spreadsheets and graphics, and database management systems (Chapters 14–16). These three chapters do not try to teach the student how to use specific software, but rather, they present the basic concepts of these types of applications packages. Extensive examples from WordStar, Lotus 1-2-3, and dBASE III PLUS are woven into a storyline that leads the student through the chapters.

- **The Microcomputer Corner.** Every chapter has a special topic box on microcomputers called

"The Microcomputer Corner." Topics range from practical "how to" information to unique microcomputer applications.

■ **Buyer's Guide: How to Buy Your Own Personal Computer.** This special 16-page four-color insert presents issues and questions to consider before buying a personal computer.

■ **Integrated Microcomputer Coverage.** Most chapters begin with a story about a microcomputer user and include specific, fully-integrated sections on microcomputers.

## Friendly Writing Style

This text speaks directly to the student in a manner that will make students want to read the book. Each chapter begins with a "grabber"—a story that gently leads students into the material. Before they know it, they are in the middle of the chapter. As we all know, when students enjoy what they read, they remember what they read.

To make reading the book even more enjoyable, 96 margin notes are carefully placed throughout the text. The margin notes expand on the material in the chapter and add interest to the text.

## Up-To-Date Coverage

We have made every effort to include the most up-to-date information possible. Some of the new developments discussed in this text include the Compaq Deskpro 386, the Apple IIGS, the IBM PC Convertible, the IBM PC RT, megabit chips, voice input and output, erasable optical disks, fourth-generation languages, natural languages, artificial intelligence, expert systems, and more.

## Exciting Art and Photo Program

This is a new book with a new look. Four-color photos are integrated into the text to motivate and teach the student. We have carefully chosen photos that not only provide information about computers but also convey the excitement of computers. The all-new art program has been designed to amplify the text discussion.

## Special Topic Galleries

Five four-color Galleries highlight special topics: Making Microchips, Computers in Our Lives, Computers Around the World, Computers on the Job, and The Cutting Edge. The Galleries include dynamic four-color photos showing computers in use with an explanation of how computers are being used in each photo.

## Extensive Student Learning Aids

We have included a variety of pedagogical features: a preview of each chapter, key terms bold-faced in the text, extensive summaries with key terms boldfaced, review questions, discussion questions, a complete glossary, and a thorough index.

## Comprehensive BASIC Appendix

The Appendix on BASIC programming stresses structured programming techniques and is compatible with Microsoft BASIC and other popular versions of BASIC. The 78-page Appendix provides enough material for most introductory courses. *Basic BASIC: A Structured Approach*, second edition, by M. Kittner and R. Northcutt is available for those instructors who wish to include greater coverage of BASIC in their course.

# The Software Packages

Benjamin/Cummings is proud to present our exciting software package. We offer educational versions of commercial software, a generic introduction to applications software, and software to assist the instructor.

### *WordStar 3.3 Educational Version*®

The *WordStar 3.3 Educational Version* systems disk is bound into *Using WordStar 3.3* by L. Metzelaar and M. Fox. This disk is a functional version of the popular *WordStar 3.3* software by MicroPro. The *Educational Version* allows a document size of four to five pages and includes all the functions needed to teach students how to use *WordStar*.

### dBASE III PLUS Limited Use Version®

The **dBASE III PLUS Limited Use Version** systems disks are bound into **Using dBASE III PLUS** by L. Metzelaar and M. Fox. These disks are fully functional versions of *dBASE III PLUS* software from Ashton-Tate—the standard of microcomputer database management systems. With the *Limited Use Version of dBASE III PLUS*, 31 records may be created per database.

### Preview II

**Preview II** provides an excellent starting point for beginning students, who may then go on to learn the educational versions of commercial software. This free, self-paced tutorial provides a hands-on introduction to generic word processing (*Wordsworth*), spreadsheets (*Calcworth*), graphics (*Graphicsworth*), and database management (*Dataworth*). The tutorial consists of independent lessons which a student can follow with no documentation and a minimum of supervision. Both IBM and Apple IIe/IIc versions are available. *Preview II Software and Lab Manual: An Introduction to Applications Software* by K. Thompson and J. Mock provides complete documentation and additional exercises.

### Software for the Instructor

The *Test Bank* is available on our **TestGen II** software for IBM and Apple microcomputers and the **Computerized Testing Service** for minicomputers and mainframes.

**University Gradebook,** developed by D. Herrick of the University of Oregon, is a complete class record-keeping system. Available for the IBM PC and compatibles, this comprehensive program calculates student grades using an instructor-defined scoring and weighting system. A variety of individual and class performance statistics can be generated.

### Software Support

If you have any questions regarding our software offerings, please contact your local Benjamin/Cummings Sales and Marketing Representative or call toll free (800) 227-1936 or, in California, (800) 982-6140.

## The Capron Collection: A Complete Supplements Package

The Capron supplements are an important part of the learning experience. They have been designed for the convenience of both students and instructors. The Capron Collection of supplements includes an *Instructor's Guide*, a *Study Guide*, a *Test Bank*, 100 color *Transparencies*, 200 *Transparency Masters*, and a reusable box to keep everything in. In addition, short BASIC and Pascal texts are available for those instructors who wish to include more extensive coverage of programming in their courses.

### Instructor's Guide

To ensure consistency with the main text, the **Instructor's Guide** has been written by H. L. Capron, whose extensive teaching experience makes this *Instructor's Guide* a superior instructional tool, particularly for part-time instructors.

For each chapter in the book, the *Instructor's Guide* presents learning objectives, a chapter overview, a lecture outline, key words, and additional lecture material.

### Study Guide

The **Study Guide,** also written by H. L. Capron, helps students solidify their knowledge. For each text chapter, the *Study Guide* presents learning objectives, an explanation of why this chapter is important, a chapter outline, a list of key words with blank lines for students to fill in the definitions, study hints, self-tests (multiple choice, true/false, matching, and fill-in), answers to self-tests, additional margin notes, and a description of how the chapter relates to the student's home or work environment.

### Test Bank

The **Test Bank,** by R. E. Duffy, includes over 2500 objective test questions. There are four types of questions: multiple choice, matching, completion, and true/false. The *Test Bank* is available on **TestGen II** software for IBM and Apple microcomputers and the **Computerized Testing Service** for minicomputers and mainframes.

### Transparencies and Transparency Masters

**100 four-color and two-color *Transparencies*** of artwork from the book are available to qualified adopters. In addition, a set of **200** *Transparency Masters* includes every piece of art in the book plus 47 additional pieces of art. This large number of transparencies should prove invaluable to instructors.

### BASIC Programming Text

For those instructors who wish to cover BASIC programming in greater depth than the BASIC Appendix in the text allows, the second edition of **Basic BASIC: A Structured Approach** by M. Kittner and R. Northcutt is ideal. The book stresses structured programming concepts throughout and is compatible with Microsoft BASIC and other popular versions of BASIC. Each chapter includes exercises with answers for immediate feedback to the student.

### Pascal Programming Text

For those instructors who wish to teach Pascal to their introductory students, we offer **Pascal: Programming with Style, A Brief Introduction** by R. Lamb. The text contains enough material for a normal four-week coverage of the language. Each chapter includes a discussion of common errors and debugging techniques, self-tests, and exercises. The answers to the self-tests are provided at the end of the book.

## Special Note to the Student

We have tried to speak directly to you, in ways that will prepare you to be a computer literate person. We think this book will give you needed knowledge, broaden your background, and raise your confidence level. We hope you will take every opportunity to learn more about computers.

We welcome your reactions to this book. Any comments, favorable or otherwise, will be read with care. Write in care of the publisher, whose address is listed on the copyright page. All letters that supply a return address will be answered.

## Acknowledgments

The success of a project of this magnitude is directly related to the contributions of many people. We would like to thank some key people now.

For significant material contributions to the book, thanks to Ralph Duffy and Marcy Kittner, who produced superior work on a timely basis.

Exquisite attention to detail is the hallmark of developmental editor Pat Burner. Her contributions produced a level of quality that could not otherwise have been achieved.

Production editor Wendy Earl lined up the finest people resources. She then used mirrors and sleight of hand and iron determination to keep myriad activities on a schedule that produced this book in record time. The net result is greater currency than is normally possible.

Editor-in-Chief Sally Elliott orchestrated the entire project with wisdom, finesse, and a horse-trader's eye on the schedule. She is the moving spirit and the key element in our success.

Reviewers and consultants from both industry and academia have provided valuable contributions that improved the quality of the book. We choose to name them individually, and they are so listed following this section.

# REVIEWERS

Kay Arms
Tyler Junior College
Tyler, Texas

Mark Aulick
Louisiana State University
Shreveport, Louisiana

Gary Brown
Santa Rosa Junior College
Santa Rosa, California

Jane Burcham
University of Missouri
Columbia, Missouri

Patricia Clark
Management Information Systems
Seattle, Washington

Carole Colaneri
Mid-Florida Technical College
Orlando, Florida

James Cox
Lane Community College
Eugene, Oregon

Janet Daugherty
Seton Hall University
South Orange, New Jersey

Ralph Duffy
North Seattle Community College
Seattle, Washington

Neil Dunn
Massachusetts Bay Community
College
Wellesley, Massachusetts

John Hamburger
Advanced Micro Devices
Sunnyvale, California

Sharon Hill
Prince George's Community
College
Largo, Maryland

Carey Hughes
North Texas State University
Denton, Texas

Marcy Kittner
University of Tampa
Tampa, Florida

Mary Kohls
Austin Community College
Austin, Texas

Cliff Layton
Rogers State College
Claremore, Oklahoma

Vicki Marney-Petix
Marpet Technical Services
Fremont, California

Spencer Martin
North Shore Community College
Beverly, Massachusetts

Doug Meyers
Des Moines Area Community
College
Ankeny, Iowa

Jeff Mock
Diablo Valley Community College
Pleasant Hill, California

Charles Moulton
Beaver College
Glenside, Pennsylvania

Linda Moulton
Montgomery County Community
College
Blue Bell, Pennsylvania

Mike Nakoff
Cincinnati Technical College
Cincinnati, Ohio

Robert Oakman
Le Conte College, University of
South Carolina
Columbia, South Carolina

Dennis Olson
Pikes Peak Community College
Colorado Springs, Colorado

James Payne
Kellogg Community College
Battle Creek, Michigan

Gordon Robinson
Forest Park Community College
St. Louis, Missouri

Gerald Sampson
Brazosport College
Lake Jackson, Texas

Fred Scott
Broward Community College
Ft. Lauderdale, Florida

Lenny Siegel
Advanced Micro Devices
Sunnyvale, California

Debbie Smith-Hemphill
AT&T Information Systems
Honolulu, Hawaii

Bruce Sophie
North Harris County College
Houston, Texas

Rod Southworth
Laramie County Community
College
Cheyenne, Wyoming

Sandra Stalker
North Shore Community College
Beverly, Massachusetts

Dave Stamper
University of Northern Colorado
Greeley, Colorado

Sandy Stephenson
Southwest Virginia Community
College
Richlands, Virginia

Greg Swan
Mesa Community College
Mesa, Arizona

Earl Talbert
Central Piedmont Community
College
Charlotte, North Carolina

J. Langdon Taylor
Ohio University
Athens, Ohio

Tim Vanderwall
Joliet Junior College
Joliet, Illinois

Kenneth Walter
Weber State College
Ogden, Utah

William Wells
Sacramento City College
Sacramento, California

# RESEARCH PARTICIPANTS

W. James Abbott
Broome Community College
Binghamton, New York

Joyce Abler
Central Michigan University
Mt. Pleasant, Michigan

Paulette Alexander
University of North
Alabama
Florence, Alabama

Gary Armstrong
Shippensburg University
Shippensburg, Pennsylvania

Lynn Averill
Los Angeles City College,
Santa Monica Community
College
Los Angeles, California

William Baker
Jamestown College
Jamestown, North Dakota

James J. Ball
Indiana State University
Terre Haute, Indiana

Larry Beck
Findlay College
Findlay, Ohio

Pamela J. Beer
Nevada Area Vocational
School
Nevada, Missouri

Robert F. Bergner
Rockford College
Rockford, Illinois

Leo Bishop
North Carolina Wesleyan
College
Rocky Mountain, North
Carolina

David S. Black
Liberty University
Lynchburg, Virginia

Jennifer Blair
Temple Business School
Alexandria, Virginia

Roy F. Bonnett, Jr.
American Technological
University
Killeen, Texas

Susan Brender
Boise State University
Boise, Idaho

John Breshears
Southeastern Community
College
Keolsuk, Iowa

Celeste Williams
Brockington
Aiken Technical College
Aiken, South Carolina

William E. Burkhardt
Carl Sandburg College
Galesburg, Illinois

Jerry F. Carlisle
Orangeburg-Calhoun
Technical College
Orangeburg, South Carolina

Bob Cassidy
Arizona Western College
Yuma, Arizona

James Chalfant
Midwestern State University
Wichita Falls, Texas

Paul A. Chase
Becker Jr. College
Leicester, Massachusetts

Terry W. Conley
Hazard State Vocational-
Technical School
Hazard, Kentucky

Sharon L. Cook
University of Alaska Juneau
Juneau, Alaska

James W. Cox
Lane Community College
Eugene, Oregon

Kevan H. Croteau
University of Dubuque
Dubuque, Iowa

Jerry DeMoss
Blue Mountain Community
College
Pendleton, Oregon

Richard A. Dilling
Grace College
Winona Lake, Indiana

Bob Dressel
Kent State University
Stark, Ohio

Jean Ettelson
Erie 1, Board of Cooperative
Educational Services
Lancaster, New York

Joyce Farrell
College of DuPage
Glen Ellyn, Illinois

Poonam Gahlawat
Fairleigh Dickinson
University
Rutherford, New Jersey

Jack Goebel
Montana College of Mineral
Science and Technology
Butte, Montana

Paul Goeller
Draughons Jr. College
Memphis, Tennessee

Leonard Goldman
Kingsborough Community
College of New York
Brooklyn, New York

Ken Griffin
University of Central
Arkansas
Conway, Arkansas

R. P. Haduch
Indiana Vocational
Technical College
Columbus, Indiana

Cindy Hanchey
Oklahoma Baptist
University
Shawnee, Oklahoma

Dwight Hazlett
Texas A & I University
Kingsville, Texas

James F. Holloway
Tennessee State University
Nashville, Tennessee

C. Brian Honess
University of South Carolina
Columbia, South Carolina

William J. Horne
Boston College
Chestnut Hill,
Massachusetts

Chang-Tseh Hsieh
Tennessee Technical
University
Cookeville, Tennessee

Carol E. Jackson
Pickens Area Vocational-
Technical School
Jasper, Georgia

Ronald D. Jenkins
St. Johns River Community
College
Palatka, Florida

Sherwood Jernigan
Nash Technical College
Rocky Mountain, North
Carolina

Robert G. Jerus
Northwestern College
Roseville, Minnesota

Hattie Russel Jones
Chowan College
Murfreesboro, North
Carolina

Gerry L. Jones
J. Sargeant Reynolds
Community College
Richmond, Virginia

Thaddeus A. Jones
Jefferson Community
College
Watertown, New York

Cynthia J. Kachik
Santa Fe Community
College
Gainesville, Florida

Anand S. Katiyar
McNeese State University
Lake Charles, Louisiana

David G. Kay
University of California at
Los Angeles
Los Angeles, California

Viola V. Kelsey
Indiana Business College
Indianapolis, Indiana

Gary L. King
New Mexico State
University
Almagordo, New Mexico

Marvin Kushner
Borough of Manhattan
Community College
New York, New York

Walter Lai
Maui Community College
Kahului, Hawaii

E. Jay Larson
Lewis-Clark State College
Lewiston, Idaho

David R. Lee
San Jose State University
San Jose, California

Philip A. Mackey
Delaware Technical and
Community College
Dover, Delaware

Robert W. Mammen
The School of the Ozarks
Point Lookout, Missouri

Spencer Martin
North Shore Community
College
Beverly, Massachusetts

Rhonda Mason
Hill College
Cleburne, Texas

Caroline Mazak
Southern Ohio College
Cincinnati, Ohio

Charles R. Mielke
University of Colorado at
Colorado Springs
Colorado Springs, Colorado

Donna R. Miller
Central Florida Computer
Institute
Orlando, Florida

Donald T. Mon
Rush University
Chicago, Illinois

Judy I. Murray
Clark Technical College
Springfield, Ohio

Lorrie O'Donovan
Trinity College of Vermont
Burlington, Vermont

William O'Hare
Prince George's Community
College
Largo, Maryland

Robert H. Orr
Purdue University at
Indianapolis
Indianapolis, Indiana

Teresa Peterman
Davenport College of
Business
Grand Rapids, Michigan

Guy W. Pollock
Mountain View College
Dallas, Texas

Earl Pratt
RETS Technical Center
Centerville, Ohio

Herbert F. Rebhun
University of Houston—
Downtown
Houston, Texas

Elaine Rhodes
Illinois Central College
East Peoria, Illinois

Charles Richards
Central Michigan University
Mt. Pleasant, Michigan

Larry G. Richards
University of Virginia
Charlottesville, Virginia

James Richardson
Pierce College
Tacoma, Washington

Thomas Roberts
Worcester State College
Worcester, Massachusetts

R. Waldo Roth
Taylor University
Upland, Indiana

Gene Sacha
Wayne County Schools
Career Center
Detroit, Michigan

Tom C. Scharnberg
Tarrant County Junior
College, Northeast
Ft. Worth, Texas

Judith Scheeren
Westmoreland County
Community College
Youngwood, Pennsylvania

John Seydel
Boise State University
Boise, Idaho

Cheryl Shearer
Oxnard College
Oxnard, California

JoAnn Shoemake
Hinds Junior College
Raymond, Mississippi

William Sloboda
Gall Audet College
Washington, D.C.

C. Donald Smith
Louisiana State University
Shreveport, Louisiana

Rod B. Southworth
Laramie County Community
College
Cheyenne, Wyoming

William J. Spezeski
North Adams State College
North Adams,
Massachusetts

Eugene F. Stafford
Iona College
New Rochelle, New York

Ellen Stanley
St. Mary's College
Notre Dame, Indiana

S. S. Stephenson
Florida Atlantic University
Boca Raton, Florida

Barbara Stevenson
Gloucester County
Vocational Technical School
Sewell, New Jersey

Andrew Suhy
Ferris State College
Big Rapids, Michigan

Renee Sundrud
Harrisburg Area Community
College
Harrisburg, Pennsylvania

Don Supalla
Rochester Area Vocational-
Technical Institute
Rochester, Minnesota

Ralph A. Szweda
Monroe Community College
Rochester, New York

Mohammed H. Alai Tafti
St. John Fisher College
Rochester, New York

Robert S. Tannenbaum
Hunter College of the City
University of New York
New York, New York

John J. Trifiletti
Florida Junior College
Jacksonville, Florida

Jerre L. L. Troutman
Lee College
Baytown, Texas

Alan Tucker
Everett Community College
Everett, Washington

John Turchek
Robert Morris College
Pittsburgh, Pennsylvania

George UpChurch
Carson Newman College
Jeff City, Tennessee

Sandra Ussia
Ohio Valley Business
College
East Liverpool, Ohio

Raymond F. Vogel
Schenectady County
Community College
Schenectady, New York

R. Kenneth Walter
Weber State College
Ogden, Utah

Dwight Watt
Swainsboro Tech
Swainsboro, Georgia

G. Craig Weaver
Savannah Tech
Savannah, Georgia

Janet S. Weber
McCook Community College
McCook, Nebraska

Frank Webster
Sawyer College of Business
San Diego, California

Leslie A. Weedon
Kankakee Community
College
Kankakee, Illinois

Carl Wehner
University of Northern Iowa
Cedar Falls, Iowa

Linda S. Whippo
J. Sargeant Reynolds
Community College
Richmond, Virginia

David Whitney
San Francisco State
University
San Francisco, California

John A. Willhardt
Alabama State University
Montgomery, Alabama

Bill Williams
Ouachita Baptist University
Arkadelphia, Arkansas

Tom Williams
Northwest Vocational-
Technical School
Springdale, Arkansas

Helen W. Wolfe
Post College
Waterbury, Connecticut

George Zaken
Lock Haven University
Lock Haven, Pennsylvania

Sue Zulauf
Sinclair Community College
Dayton, Ohio

## PART 1

# THE BEGINNING OF COMPUTER LITERACY

This book is about the future—your future. It is about your place in a technological revolution that will make—and is making—profound changes in your life. The instrument of this revolution is, of course, the computer. For many, the computer promises greater ease and an end to drudgery. For others, it is a source of dread. The key to survival in the computer age is computer literacy.

Computer literacy: This is what you seek and what we offer. In fact, you will travel a long way toward computer literacy in just these two opening chapters. The first chapter should raise your awareness of computers to a higher level. The second chapter forms the foundation for the technical chapters that follow. It is easier than you think.

# 1

# The Unfinished Revolution

## You and Computer Literacy

The Computer Revolution may well be far more sweeping than the Industrial Revolution—and certainly far more sudden. The effects of the computer are now seen in spectacular ways in many areas of our lives: in business, government, agriculture, robotics, education, science, graphics, our homes, and our personal lives. We cannot turn back the clock, nor would we want to. Liberation lies in computer literacy.

A recent Lou Harris poll asked this question: Do you believe that computers make life easier and better? Nine out of ten Americans answered "Yes." Harris reports a bright and optimistic mood in the country regarding the information age. Although they might not put it quite this way, people are joining the Computer Revolution.

# Don't Start the Revolution Without Me

The Industrial Revolution, which resulted from the development of the steam engine, the dynamo, and the factory system, took place relatively rapidly. In less than 100 years, human society was changed on a massive scale. To live between 1890 and 1920, for instance, was to live with the dizzying introduction of electricity, telephones, radio, automobiles, and airplanes— perhaps a more tumultuous period than the times in which we live. But the Computer Revolution is also irreversible and massive and will probably bring about dramatic shifts in the way we live, perhaps even in the way we think. This revolution, however, is happening a great deal more quickly than the Industrial Revolution.

The Computer Revolution is unfinished and will probably roll on to the end of the century. Let us see how far we have come—first in society, then on a more personal level.

**UP, UP, AND AWAY**

If the space program had moved as swiftly as the computer industry, you might be attending classes on the moon.

## Forging a New Society: The Information Age

Computers are not a fad like Hula-Hoops or pet rocks. Few fads result in hundreds of magazines and thousands of books. Only a major trend has the momentum to sustain these classic indicators of acceptance. But computers have gone beyond acceptance; they are shaping society in fundamental ways.

In traditional economics courses, professors taught that the cornerstones of an economy are land, labor, and capital. That tradition now is being challenged, and we speak of *four* key economic elements: land, labor, capital, and information. We are converting from an industrial society to an information society. We are moving from physical labor to mental labor, trading muscle power for brain power. Just as people moved from the farms to the factories when the Industrial Revolution began, so we must join the information age. You have already taken that first step. But should you go further and get your own computer? It certainly is a possibility.

## A Computer for You

Remember the ads? "A tool for modern times." "If you can point, you can use a computer." "A computer for the rest of us."

**Computers on stage.** Computer-controlled lighting systems get rave reviews from Broadway to the Met. Here, Ronald Bates, production stage manager of the New York City Ballet, checks lighting cues on his computer during a ballet company rehearsal.

The personal computer—the one small enough to sit on a desk top—came seemingly out of nowhere in the late 1970s. Names like Apple, Atari, Commodore, Radio Shack, and IBM were joined by dozens of others. Commercials featuring Bill Cosby, Alan Alda, and others filled TV screens. Personal computers were hustled like encyclopedias: "For the price of a bicycle, you can help your child's future. . . ."

For some, the opening wedge was playing computer games. But personal computers have moved into more intimate corners of our lives. In the home they are being used not only as playthings but also for keeping track of bank accounts, writing term papers and letters, learning a foreign language, designing artwork, turning on lawn sprinklers or coffee makers, monitoring temperature and humidity, teaching math and reading skills to children, and organizing Christmas card lists. Many people are also using computers on the job, whether they sit at a desk from 9 to 5 or run a farm. Personal computers are extremely useful for writing letters and reports, forecasting and updating budgets, creating and maintaining files, and pro-

**Figure 1-1   Personal computer users.**
All these people, whether at school, at
home, or at work, are making good use
of the personal computer.

ducing charts and graphs. Almost any job you hope to get in the
future will involve a computer in some way. Clearly, the computer
user no longer has to be a Ph.D. in a laboratory somewhere. We are
all computer users (Figure 1-1).

But just how happy are we with this newfound sophistication?

## Worry About Computers? Me?

Terms such as **computer anxiety** and **computer phobia**
have now entered the language. People often fear the unknown, and so they avoid it. Even people in the business community
who deal with computers on a daily basis may experience some form
of **cyberphobia**—fear of computers—which is characterized by such
symptoms as nausea, sweaty palms, and high blood pressure.

What are people afraid of? Some people are nervous about the
mathematical sound of the word *computer*. It seems to suggest that
only a person with strong analytical and quantitative skills can use
the machine. In fact, however, as we see all around us, computers are
becoming more and more accessible to more and more people.

## YOU KNOW MY NAME, LOOK UP THE NUMBER

People who are annoyed about depersonalization might insist that *names*, not numbers, make the world turn. But ever since automation began, just about any government organization or business that keeps personal information has demanded a person's Social Security number (SSN). Some people worry about this and, indeed, there is reason for concern. The principal purpose of the SSN is to link information in different data banks.

Think about it. Who's got your number? Chances are that your SSN is already in—or will soon be in—the files of credit bureaus, retail stores, banks, oil companies, supermarkets, check validation services, utilities, insurance companies, hospitals, motor vehicle departments, employers, schools and universities, state agencies, and contest promoters. Yes, contests. After all, the IRS wants to know about you if you win!

Some people are fearful of the whole environment of computing. The machinery looks intimidating to them. There is a notion that computers are temperamental gadgets, and that once a glitch gets into a computer system it may wreak all kinds of havoc, from fouling up bank statements to launching nuclear missiles by mistake. Indeed, computer billing and banking errors are a pervasive problem. You should note, however, that errors usually result from mistakes made by the people who put the data into the computer system, not by the computer itself. Even so, setting the record straight is often frustratingly slow.

People are also nervous that computers might be used to "get" them in some way—by the Internal Revenue Service, by credit bureaus, by privacy invaders of one sort or another. Some of these fears are justified. Think of all the forms we fill out: forms for schools, jobs, medical matters, credit, taxes, and so on. There is scarcely any data related to your daily life that is not in a computer file somewhere. Could unauthorized persons obtain this information? The computer industry has been trying to deal with the matter of privacy, but solutions are expensive and difficult.

Many people are worried about computers in relation to their jobs. Some people doubt they have the skills to find jobs and keep them in the technological labor market of the future. A good many present-day executives whose companies are installing computer terminals in their offices worry about typing—either they do not know how or they are afraid they will lose status if they use a keyboard.

Eventually, the number of people suffering from computer anxiety will decline. The availability of cheaper, easier-to-use personal computers will reduce the intimidation factor. But probably more important, a new generation is growing up that is perfectly comfortable with the computer.

Interestingly, the fear related to computers cuts two ways. The more obvious fear is of the machines themselves, but less obvious is the fear of being without computers. Some fear they will be left out or left behind.

## Computer Literacy for Everyone?

Yes. You know it, schools know it, the general public knows it. But it was not always so. The average person worried about the disadvantages of computers but failed to recognize the advantages. The situation was similar in the early 1900s when cars were first introduced. Historians tell us that the reaction to that newfangled contraption was much the same as the first reactions to computers. Today's traffic crush, however, is a good indication that attitudes changed somewhere along the way.

The analogy here is a good one. In the very near future, people who refuse to have anything to do with computers may be as inconvenienced as people who refuse to learn to drive.

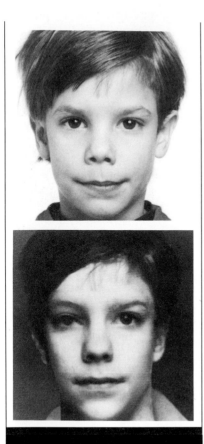

**THE AGE MACHINE**

How would you like to see what you will look like five years from now? Ten? Twenty-five? A computer-generated art process can do just that, based on a recent picture of you. The process, not neatly named, is called The Method and Apparatus for Producing an Image of a Person's Face at a Different Age. It uses complex computer graphics to simulate the aging process.

The case of Etan Patz illustrates a valuable application of this method. Six-year-old Etan disappeared in 1979 in New York City on his way to the school bus. The top photo above shows Etan's appearance in 1979. The lower photo is a combination of Etan's photo and a photo of an older sibling; it gives us a glimpse of what Etan might look like today. If you think you have seen Etan, call the National Center for Missing or Exploited Children at 1 (800) 843-5678.

## Computer Literacy Defined

Why are you reading this book? Why are you studying about computers? In addition to curiosity (and perhaps a course requirement), you probably recognize that it will not be easy to get through the rest of your life if you do not know anything about computers. But how much is enough? Do you need to actually be able to tell the computer what to do? The answer to the last question, fortunately, is "No!"

We offer a three-pronged definition of **computer literacy**:

- **Awareness.** As you study computers you will become aware of their importance, their versatility, their pervasiveness, and their potential for good and ill in our society.

- **Knowledge.** You will learn what computers are and how they work. This requires learning some technical jargon, but do not worry—no one expects you to become a computer expert.

- **Interaction.** Computer literacy also means learning to use a computer to do some simple tasks. By the end of this course, you should feel comfortable sitting down at a computer and using it for some suitable purpose.

Note that no part of this definition suggests that you need intimate knowledge of computers or that you must be able to form the instructions that tell a computer what to do. That would be akin to saying that everyone who plans to drive a car should become an auto mechanic. Someone else can write the instructions for the computer; the interaction part of the definition merely implies that you are able to make use of those instructions. For example, a bank teller can use a computer to see if an account really contains as much money as the customer wishes to withdraw. Computers can also be used by an accountant to prepare a report, a farmer to check on market prices, a store manager to analyze sales trends (Figure 1-2), or a teenager to play a video game. We cannot guarantee that these people are computer literate, but they have at least grasped the hands-on component of the definition—they can interact with computers.

Is it possible for everyone to be computer literate? That depends less on personal skills than on school budgets. Enter Senator Lautenberg.

## The Haves and the Have-Nots

Senator Frank Lautenberg of New Jersey has glimpsed the future, a future divided between the "haves" who are information-rich and the "have-nots" who are information-poor. The source of that information, of course, is the computer. The senator sees a growing chasm between the rich and the poor groups because children

**Figure 1-2   Milk, butter, cheese, and computers.** Stew Leonard's World's Largest Dairy Store in Norwalk, Connecticut, is a marketing wonder. Shoppers walk along one wide aisle that meanders through the entire store, passing by a plastic cow and a creamery on the way to the produce and meat departments. Over 100,000 people visit the store each week. Mr. Leonard conducts corporate planning, forecasting, and budgeting on nine personal computers. If we are to believe this picture, the chickens roam freely among them.

who grow up with advantages have better access to computers. These children live in school districts that have the money to promote computers and computer literacy. In addition, the children may have access to computers at home. Children in poorer areas, however, may never have the opportunity to deal with computers as part of their education. And so another social gap is defined at an early age.

Unlike many senators, who come to politics from the legal field, Senator Lautenberg comes from the computer industry. He proposes to alter the social equation by providing federal funds for computers in schools. In his very first speech in the Senate, he proposed a law that would provide federal funds to buy computers for the classroom. The law, the Computer Education Assistance Act, did not pass. But Lautenberg's proposal sparked controversy about the responsibility of the federal government to provide equal access to new technology. The debate goes on, and legislation representing various positions continues to come before Congress.

## And Now That You Are Taking a Computer Class

Federal assistance or not, you are now taking your first computer class. Is using a computer as simple as the TV commercials say? Is it as easy as pointing? Most students do not think so. Students are usually surprised when they take their first computer course. In fact, they may be surprised, confused, and frustrated.

They may be surprised by the subject matter, which was not what they thought it would be; they thought it would be fun, like video games. They might be confused by the special language used in computer classes; some feel as if they have entered a foreign culture. They may be frustrated by the hands-on experience, in which they have a one-to-one relationship with the computer. Their previous learning experiences, in contrast, have been shared and sheltered—they were shared with peers in a classroom and guided by an experienced person. Now it is just the student facing a machine, at least some of the time. So, this experience is different and maybe slightly scary. But others have survived and even triumphed. You can too.

Since part of the challenge of computer literacy is awareness, let us now look at what makes computers so useful. We shall then turn to the various ways computers can be used.

## Everywhere You Turn

It seems that everywhere you turn these days, there is a computer—in stores, cars, homes, offices, hospitals, banks. What are some of the traits of computers that make them so useful?

### The Nature of Computers

The computer is a workhorse. It is usually capable of laboring 24 hours a day, it does not ask for raises or coffee breaks, and it does the ten-thousandth task exactly the same way it did the first one—all without complaining of boredom.

There are at least six reasons why computers have become an indispensable part of our lives:

**Figure 1-3   Service means speed.** The speed of a computer helps provide the fast service that customers expect.

- **Speed.** By now it seems it is human nature to be resentful if service is not fast. But it is "computer nature" that provides that fast service. Thus, unless we are prepared to do a lot more waiting—for paychecks, grades, telephone calls, travel reservations, bank balances, and many other things—we need the split-second processing of a computer (Figure 1-3). The speed of a computer also makes it ideal for processing large amounts of data, as in accounting systems and scientific applications.

- **Reliability.** Computers are extremely reliable. Of course, you might not think this from hearing the stories about "computer mistakes." Unfortunately, what is almost never brought out in these

## THE MICROCOMPUTER CORNER

### Computers Come to Taos Pueblo

Computers would seem out of place in a town where the homes have no running water, no central heating, no electrical lighting, and no plumbing. Nevertheless, they have found a place in at least one such community, the ancient Tiwa Indian village of Taos Pueblo, New Mexico. A federally funded computer-assisted education program is benefiting the children at Taos Day School, many of whom are learning English twice as fast as they would have through regular instruction. For the first time in the school's history, 50% of the students are reading at or above grade level. This has been accomplished with the help of 13 Apple IIc microcomputers and a voice synthesizer. How have these machines made such a big difference at Taos Day School?

Each student from kindergarten through eighth grade has access to a microcomputer for about one hour a week. The computers reinforce learning in a number of ways. For instance, the five-year-olds enjoy learning English with the help of a voice synthesizer attached to the computer. When a child strikes a letter key on the computer keyboard, the letter appears on the computer screen and the voice synthesizer pronounces the letter. This instant reinforcement speeds up the learning process while making it more enjoyable. In many cases games provide the reinforcement. For instance, the computer rewards a correct math answer by giving the student an opportunity to build a video-game spaceship. The computers also aid learning in other areas, such as music, sociology, physical education, and technology.

The computers assist the teachers as well, although at first some of them experienced computer phobia—they thought the computers would eliminate their jobs. These teachers now see the computers as useful tools that provide drills and exercises so that instructors can concentrate on the more creative aspects of teaching. Many of the teachers are taking computer-education courses and looking for ways to benefit from computer-education programs at other schools.

The teachers and other members of the Taos Pueblo community are committed to preserving the Indian traditions. However, through using computers, they are also helping their children compete in the modern world.

**VOTING AT HOME**

They call it electronic democracy, and it is not some futuristic dream. It is, in fact, technologically possible right now. Imagine a nationwide network whereby each voter, using an individual secret password, could use his or her own home computer to vote in a national election.

Attractive? Maybe. Scary? Yes. The immediate results—not just for candidates but for national referendums—are attractive. The "scary" part is two-fold. First, how do we prevent fraud? Could someone tamper with the computer results? And just who assigns the passwords? Second, how do we guarantee computer access to all potential voters?

We noted that such a scheme is technologically possible today. But that does not mean it is socially or politically possible.

stories is that the mistakes are not the fault of the computers themselves. True, there are sometimes equipment failures, but most errors supposedly made by computers are really human errors. Although one hears the phrase "computer error" quite frequently, the blame usually lies elsewhere.

- **Storage capability.** Computer systems are able to store tremendous amounts of data, which can then be retrieved quickly and efficiently. This storage capability is especially important in an information age.

- **Productivity.** Computers, with their speed and accuracy, are able to perform jobs that humans cannot do. They can also perform boring, dangerous, or highly sensitive jobs that people should not do. Working with nuclear fuel rods is such a job. Granted, computers will eliminate some jobs; automation is a tough societal nut to crack and always has been. But computers free human beings for other kinds of productivity. We can also turn this idea around: If we were to abolish computers, we would have to hire millions of people to do what computers are now doing and ask them to perform some very tedious tasks.

- **Decision making.** Because of expanding technology, communications, and the interdependency of people, we suffer from an information deluge. Although this is in part brought on by the computer, it is also the computer that will help solve it. To make essential business and governmental decisions, managers need to take into account a variety of financial, geographical, logistical, and other factors. The computer helps managers sort the wheat from the chaff and make better choices.

- **Reduction in costs.** Finally, for all of these reasons, the computer helps reduce waste and hold costs down for labor, energy, and paperwork. Thus, computers increase productivity and reduce the costs of goods and services.

With all these wonderful traits to its credit, it is no wonder that the computer has made its way into almost every facet of our lives. Let us look at some of the ways computers are used to make our workdays more productive and our personal lives more rewarding.

## The Uses of Computers

The jobs that computers do are as varied as we can imagine, but the following are some of the principal uses.

- **Paperwork.** There is no doubt that our society runs on paper. While in some ways the computer contributes to this problem—as in adding to the amount of junk mail you find in your mailbox—in many other ways it cuts down paper handling. The techniques of

**Figure 1-4   Pastry process control.** Beth's Bakery runs smoothly with the help of her IBM Personal Computer, which you can see behind the croissants. The computer is used to plan production and track sales.

word processing, for example, allow a writer to make changes to letters, memos, and reports without retyping the entire document. Even Supreme Court justices use word processing, storing their opinions in draft form for future reference. Computerized bookkeeping, record keeping, and document sending have also made paperwork more efficient (Figure 1-4).

- **Money.** Computers have revolutionized the way money is handled. Once upon a time it was possible to write a check for the rent on Tuesday and cover it with a deposit on Thursday, knowing it would take a few days for the bank to process the rent check and debit it against your account. With computers, however, the recording of deposits and withdrawals can be done more quickly. Computers have also brought us the age of do-it-yourself banking, with automatic teller machines available for simple transactions. Computers have helped fuel the cashless economy, enabling the widespread use of credit cards and instant credit checks by banks, department stores, and other retailers. Some oil companies are using credit-card–activated, self-service gasoline pumps.

- **Commerce.** Products from meats to magazines are now packaged with zebra-striped symbols that can be read by scanners at supermarket checkout stands to determine the price of the products. This Universal Product Code is one of the highly visible uses of computers in commerce; however, there are numerous others. Modern-day warehousing and inventory management could not exist without computers. Take your copy of this book, for instance. From printer to warehouse to bookstore, its movement was tracked with the help of computers.

Figure 1-5  **Energy control center.** Pacific Gas and Electric Company, which serves northern California, operates these computers 24 hours a day to calculate the most economical way of providing electricity for their three million customers. The company uses several different sources of electricity—hydro, geothermal, fossil fuel, wind, and solar. Every four seconds the computers scan the entire electrical network to determine the most efficient mix of these resources.

### TALKING TO YOUR CAR

You have probably heard that some new car models come equipped with a computer. What you have probably not heard is that soon all cars will come with not one but as many as 14 computers. Ed Czapor of General Motors says that engineers are taking a new look at cars and trying to improve every function with on-board computers.

Some of these computers are out of sight and mind, busily regulating controls like the air-fuel mix fed to each cylinder. But the visible computers promise to captivate us in new ways. Computer screens on the dashboard can give you maps for your destination or flash *oil change* if needed. But even that capability seems routine compared with the car that listens to its master's voice.

Imagine walking up to the car and saying "This is me." The car recognizes your voice. The door opens, the seat and steering wheel automatically adjust, and the radio tunes to your favorite station. Just how far out can we get, talking to our cars? Well, you could talk to the computer as you drive and have it flash stock quotations on the dashboard screen. Or most anything else. The key question is this: Is it worth it?

- **Energy.** Energy companies use computers to locate oil, coal, natural gas, and uranium. Electric companies use computers to monitor their vast power networks (Figure 1-5). In addition, meter-readers use hand-held computers to record how much energy is used each month in homes and businesses.

- **Transportation.** Computers help run rapid transit systems, load containerships, keep track of railroad cars and send them rolling home again, fly and land airplanes and keep them from colliding, and schedule airline reservations. They are also used in cars and motorcycles to monitor fluid levels, temperatures, and electrical systems and to improve fuel mileage.

- **Government.** The federal government is the largest single user of computers. The Social Security Administration, for example, produces 36 million benefit checks a month with the help of computers. Computers are also used for forecasting weather, for managing parks, for processing immigrants, for running the military, for meting out justice, and—yes—for collecting taxes. The FBI keeps track of suspected criminals by compiling separate bits of information into elaborate dossiers. A veteran can walk into a local Veterans Administration office and get a rundown of his or her benefits in moments. The Department of Agriculture keeps track of the amount of snow in the winter, then uses computers to predict how much water farmers will have in the summer. As one bureaucrat said, the only way you can survive in the government is to learn to use computers.

- **Agriculture.** Are we ready for high tech down on the farm? Absolutely. Farming is a business, after all, and a small computer—which can be a lot cheaper than a tractor—can help with billing, crop information, cost per acre, correct feed combinations, and so on. As farming becomes less profitable, wise management—which can be aided by computers—becomes increasingly important. Cattle breeders can also use computers to store and analyze breeding and performance data about livestock. Furthermore, sheep can be sheared by a computer-run robotic shearing arm. The arm is guided by sensors and the dimensions of a typical sheep stored in the computer's memory. In addition to these specific uses, experts predict that computers will give people the option of working at home instead of in city offices. The promise of increased communication that computers provide may decrease the isolation of country living and the movement of younger people to the cities.

- **Robotics.** With the age of the computer has arrived the age of the robot. These are not human-shaped robots like C-3PO of *Star Wars*, but rather information machines with the manual dexterity to perform tasks too unpleasant, too dangerous, or too critical to assign to human beings. Examples of these dextrous machines are pattern-cutting robots in garment businesses, which are able to get the most apparel out of several bolts of cloth; robots used in defense to perform underwater military missions; robots used by fruit growers to pick fruit (Figure 1-6); and even robots that patrol jail corridors at night. Especially controversial are the robots that do tedious jobs, such as welding or paint spraying, better than human beings do. Clearly, these robots signal the end of jobs for many

**Figure 1-6  Robot fruit picker.** Unlike human pickers, robots have trouble telling an orange from a leaf or a branch. Researchers are "teaching" this machine to find the fruit under varying light conditions.

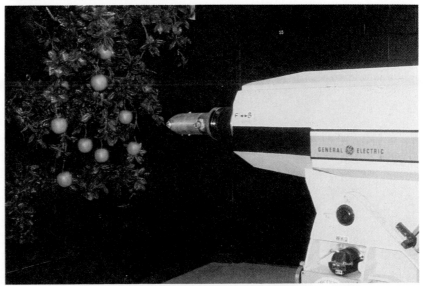

factory workers—a troublesome social problem. Robots are one more sign that we the people are moving away from industrial society and toward an information society.

- **Education.** Computers have been used behind the scenes for years in colleges and school districts for record keeping and accounting. Now, of course, they are rapidly coming into the classroom in elementary and secondary schools and colleges. Many parents and teachers believe that computer education is a necessity, not a novelty. Parents want to be sure that their children are not left behind in the computer age. The pressure is on school districts to acquire computers and train teachers and students in their use.

- **Training.** Computers are being used as training devices in industry and government. It is much cheaper and safer, for instance, to teach aspiring pilots to fly in computerized training cockpits or simulators than in real airplanes. Novice engineers can also be given the experience of running a train with the help of a computerized device.

- **Health and Medicine.** Computers have been used on the business side of medicine for some time; in addition, they are being used as part of the healing process. For instance, computers help produce cross-sectional X-ray views and ultrasound pictures, they help pharmacists test a patient's medications for compatibility, and they help physicians make diagnoses. In fact, it is estimated that computers diagnose disease with 85% accuracy. (The doctor, have no fear, makes the final diagnosis.) If you are one of the thousands who suffer one miserable cold after another, you will welcome the news that computers have been able to map, in exquisite atomic detail, the structure of the human cold virus; this is the first step to a cure for the common cold (Figure 1-7). Computers are also being used to promote health maintenance by providing information in weight-loss programs, by recording heart rates, and in many other ways.

- **The Sciences.** As you might imagine, computers are used extensively in the sciences to process research data. In many projects, however, scientists are using computers during the research phase as well. Consider the beleaguered mouse, that creature who has endured so much to further scientific research. The mouse will be spared exposure to suspected poisons, now that the Food and Drug Administration has a computer programmed to react in the same way as a mouse's digestive system. In England researchers have used computers to invent a bionic nose that can distinguish subtle differences in fragrance—an invention that could have major benefits for the food, perfume, and distilling industries. On another front entirely, the National Aeronautics and Space Administration has developed a computerized system to scan the heavens and listen in on eight million narrow-band radio frequencies in an attempt to find signs of communication from alien beings. (So far, no takers.)

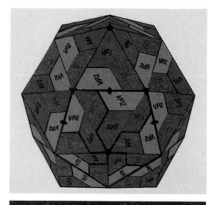

**Figure 1-7   Cold virus.** This computer-produced model of the cold virus culprit named HRV-14 raises hopes that a cure for the common cold may be possible after all. With the aid of a computer, the final set of calculations for the model took one month to complete. Researchers estimate that without the computer the calculations might have required ten years of manual effort.

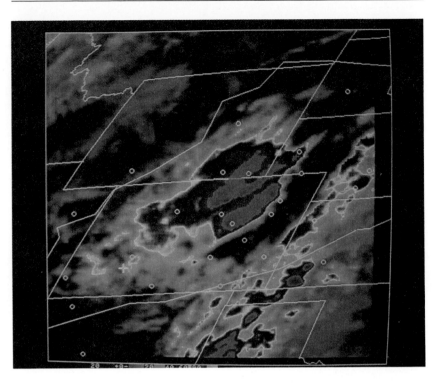

**Figure 1-8   Weather in color.** This computer-generated weather map combines a radar image of a thunderstorm with political boundaries (city limits). Purple indicates areas of maximum storm intensity.

■ **Graphics.** There is no better place to get a sense of the computer's impact than in the area of design and graphics. Breathtaking "photographs" of the rings of Saturn are beamed back over millions of miles of space. Color-coded portraits of solar flares and different gases reveal violent fireworks on the sun. Meteorological satellites photograph the births and deaths of hurricanes and other forms of weather (Figure 1-8). Technically, however, none of these transmissions from space is a photograph in the traditional sense; they are electronic impulses assembled by computers.

Closer to home, the graphic capabilities of the computer are evidenced in medicine, where brain scanners produce color-enhanced "maps" to help diagnose mental illness. Biochemists use computers to examine, in three dimensions, the structure of molecules. Architects use computer-animated graphics to give clients a visual walk-through of proposed buildings, to show possible exteriors, and to subject buildings to hypothetical earthquakes. Aircraft designers use computer graphics to create experimental aircraft and put them through simulated flights without having to resort to building models and wind tunnels. Business executives make bar graphs and pie charts out of tedious figures and use color to convey trends with far more impact than numbers alone can do. Finally, a whole new kind of artist has emerged, who uses computers to create cartoon animation, landscapes, television logos, and still lifes (Figure 1-9).

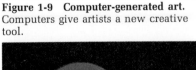

**Figure 1-9   Computer-generated art.** Computers give artists a new creative tool.

**Figure 1-10   Computers assist the disabled.** This quadriplegic is using a mouthstick to communicate with the computer.

- **The Home.** Are you willing to welcome the computer into your home? Many people already have. Some justify the computer as an educational tool for their children, but education is only the beginning. Adults often keep records and do word processing on their computers. The more adventurous hook up the family computer to control heating and air conditioning, answer telephone calls, and so on. The question about whether you *need* a home computer remains open to debate, but there is no question that it can make your life easier and more entertaining.

- **The Human Connection.** Are computers cold and impersonal? Look again. The disabled do not think so (Figure 1-10). Neither do other people who use computers in very personal ways—ways that assist humans in areas in which we are most human. Can the disabled walk again? Perhaps, with the help of computers. Can dancers and athletes improve their performance? Maybe they can by using computers to monitor their movements. Can we learn more about our ethnic backgrounds and our cultural history with the aid of computers? Certainly.

Now let us move to an early literacy check. Let us see what you believe.

## What Do You Believe?

With your current level of knowledge about computers, what do you believe the future of computers will be? Here is a brief set of statements for you to label *true* or *false*. We suspect that you already know the answers. Try your hand.

- There will be a computer on almost every desk by the mid-1990s.

- By the end of the century, there will be as many computers in homes as there are television sets.

- Computer-based word processing will be the means of recording and transmitting the written word; typewriters will be in museums.

- Blue-collar job losses will continue to rise due to increased use of robots in factories.

- The personal computer will lead the way to increased productivity.

- People will communicate more—and more effectively—through networks of computers.

Give yourself a perfect score if you labeled all statements *true*. Since we are talking about the future, however, we cannot guarantee truth. Perhaps the best we can say is that, if you answered "true," you agree with the experts.

You know more than you think you do. Even though you do not know a lot about computers yet, you have been exposed to computer hype, computer advertisements and discussions, and magazine articles and newspaper headlines about computers. You have interacted with computers in the various compartments of your life—at the grocery store, your school, the library, and more. The beginnings of computer literacy are already apparent.

## Toward Computer Literacy

The Computer Revolution is an unfinished revolution, one that will continue throughout our lifetimes. But its seeds are already sown. Throughout the rest of this book, we will describe the implications of the near future for the tasks we must learn today.

We have written this book with two kinds of readers in mind. If you are contemplating a computer-related career, you will find a solid discussion of technology, computer applications, and various jobs associated with computers. If you are not interested in a career in computers, this book will at least provide you with a foundation in computer literacy. If the computer is to liberate us rather than confound us or threaten us, we must assume some responsibility for understanding it.

## Summary and Key Terms

- A recent Lou Harris poll shows that nine out of ten Americans now believe that computers make life easier and better. There is an optimistic mood in the country regarding computers.

- Like the Industrial Revolution, the Computer Revolution is irreversible and is making massive changes in society. However, it is happening more quickly than the Industrial Revolution. Though unfinished, the Computer Revolution is well under way.

- Traditionally, we have thought of land, labor, and capital as the cornerstones of an economy. Now we are adding a fourth cornerstone: information. We are changing from an industrial society to an information society.

- The personal computer was developed in the late 1970s. Since then, dozens of manufacturers have joined the race to sell personal computers for home use and business use.

- Personal computers can be used in the home for playing games, tracking bank accounts, writing term papers and letters, learning a foreign language, teaching children, and many other uses. In businesses, personal computers are used for preparing letters, reports, budgets, files, and graphics.

- Some people suffer from **computer anxiety** and **computer phobia,** or **cyberphobia** (fear of computers). Some people feel intimidated by computers; others fear computer errors, invasion of privacy, job loss or change, and depersonalization.

- **Computer literacy** includes an awareness of computers, knowledge about computers, and interaction with computers. To use a computer, however, you do not need to be able to write the instructions that tell a computer what to do.

- Senator Frank Lautenberg believes that unless all students have equal access to computers, the gap between the "haves" and the "have-nots" will widen. He has proposed federal funding for computers in schools.

- There are at least six reasons why computers have become an indispensable part of our lives. (1)

They are fast. (2) They are extremely reliable. (3) Computer systems are able to store large amounts of data. (4) Computers can perform boring, dangerous, or highly sensitive jobs. (5) They can help us sort through the deluge of information and make better decisions. (6) They can help reduce waste and cut labor and paperwork costs.

■ Experts believe that in the future there will be a computer on almost every desk, that there will be as many computers in the home as there are television sets, that word processing systems will replace typewriters, that robots will continue to replace humans in blue-collar jobs, that the personal computer will lead to increased productivity, and that people will communicate through networks of computers. Computers are not machines of the future; they are very much a part of the present.

## Review Questions

1. In what ways are the Industrial Revolution and the Computer Revolution similar? In what ways are they different?

2. What are the four cornerstones of today's economy?

3. When was the personal computer developed? Name five manufacturers of personal computers.

4. List four uses of personal computers in the home.

5. List four uses of personal computers in businesses.

6. What are the fears people have about computers?

7. Name two reasons why computer anxiety will probably decline.

8. What are the three components of computer literacy?

9. Describe Senator Frank Lautenberg's concern about computers and education. How did he address this concern?

10. Give six reasons why computers have become an indispensable part of our lives.

## Discussion Questions

1. Do you believe that computers make life easier and better? Explain.

2. Do you feel any discomfort or anxiety about computers? Explain why or why not.

3. Why are you taking this class? What do you expect to learn from this class?

# 2

# Overview of a Computer System

## Hardware, Software, and People

The purpose of a computer system is to turn unprocessed data into usable information. This requires three main areas of data handling—input, processing, and output—plus secondary storage. The equipment associated with a computer system is called hardware. A set of instructions that tells the hardware what to do is called software. People, however, are the most important component of a computer system.

When Chris Wilson's father taught her to drive, he gave her several under-the-hood lessons first. Before she was allowed to slip behind the wheel, she endured lectures on valves and pistons and carburetors. Chris was not interested in how the car was put together, much less how to fix it. She surmised, correctly, that she did not need to know any of these things to make the car do her bidding.

Chris, of course, did need some training in driving a car, but she did not really need to know all its inner workings to make it start and stop and turn corners. We have used the car analogy before, and it fits pretty well. You can learn to use a computer without knowing all about its internal functions, too. As in learning to drive, the experience is new and a little scary at first, but the average person can learn quite readily.

There is a major difference, though, between learning how to drive a car and learning how to use a computer: familiarity. Most of us have been around cars all our lives, so before we even started taking driver training, we already knew what a steering wheel was, what the ignition key did, and where to put the suitcases when we went on a long trip. Most of us, however, have *not* been around computers all our lives. Thus, we need to start on the road to computer literacy by learning some basics. That is the purpose of this chapter—to introduce you to the vocabulary and ideas that will lay the foundation for your computer education. Once you absorb some of the basics, you will be better prepared to sit down "behind the wheel" and learn how to use a computer.

**COMPUTERS IN THE DOGHOUSE**

Has software gone to the dogs? In some cases, yes. Customized canine software is a reality. The Next Generation, for instance, is a special-purpose word processing program used to keep track of the pedigree of dogs or other animals. With this software breeders are better able to plan the breeding strategies they will use and are able to ensure greater accuracy in their recordkeeping.

Specialized software is also available for kennels, which have unique scheduling problems. Such software handles the scheduling of boarding, grooming, and training services for the furry clients, while simultaneously controlling inventory, work schedules, accounting, and other business needs.

## The Beginning of What You Need to Know

The computer and its associated equipment are called **hardware.** The instructions that tell a computer what you want it to do are called **software.** The term **packaged software** refers to software that is literally packaged in a container of some sort—usually a box or folder—and is sold in stores. There is a great assortment of packaged software to help us with a variety of tasks: writing papers, preparing budgets, drawing graphs, playing games, and so forth. The wonderful array of software available is what makes computers so useful.

Software is also referred to as programs. To be more specific, a **program** is a set of step-by-step instructions that directs the computer to do the tasks you want it to do and produce the results you want. A **computer programmer** is a person who writes programs. But most of us do not write programs—we use programs written by someone else. This means we are **users**—people who purchase and use computer software. We shall emphasize the connection between computers and computer users throughout this chapter and, indeed, throughout this book.

As we continue the present chapter, we shall first examine hardware, then software, then data. We shall then consider how these components work together to produce information. Finally, we shall devote a separate section to computers and people. As the title of this chapter indicates, what follows is an overview, a look at the "big picture" of a computer system. Thus, many of the terms introduced in this chapter are defined only briefly. Do not despair. In subsequent chapters we will discuss the parts of a computer system more leisurely and in greater detail.

# Hardware: Meeting the Machine

What is a computer, anyway? A six-year-old called a computer "radio, movies, and television combined!" A ten-year-old described a computer as "a television set you can talk to." That is getting closer but still does not recognize the computer as a machine that has the power to make changes. A **computer** is a machine that accepts data (input) and processes it into useful information (output). The processing is done by the software, but in this section we shall examine the hardware.

A computer system consists of three main areas of data handling—input, processing, and output—and is backed by a fourth, storage. The hardware responsible for these four aspects, diagrammed in Figure 2-1, operates as follows:

■ **Input devices** take data in machine-readable form and send it to the processing unit.

**Figure 2-1   The four primary components of a computer system: input, processing, output, and storage.**

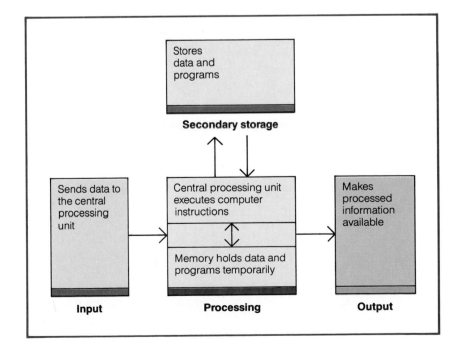

Stores data and programs

**Secondary storage**

Sends data to the central processing unit

Central processing unit executes computer instructions

Memory holds data and programs temporarily

Makes processed information available

**Input**            **Processing**            **Output**

## THE MICROCOMPUTER CORNER

### Computers on Campus

On college campuses, computers may soon be as common as pizza and dirty laundry. Many colleges, including Dartmouth, Carnegie–Mellon, Lehigh, and Drexel, require or strongly recommend that students purchase computers. Drexel, which requires each entering freshman to purchase a personal computer and software, has thoroughly integrated computers into its curriculum.

Drexel's ambitious development of a computer-assisted curriculum has received strong student and faculty support. Faculty members developed software with the help of student and pro-

fessional programmers. For instance, a chemistry professor designed software that helps students understand molecular structure by seeing arrangements of atoms displayed on the computer screen. A program written by a mathematics professor shows students how to solve complex algebra problems. An English professor created software that helps students write more coherently.

Drexel's integration of computers into its curriculum has had a positive effect on the school's morale. A study shows that as students and faculty be-

This college student is using the IBM PC Convertible.

come more adept at using computers, they tend to feel more optimistic about the future.

- The **processor,** more formally known as the **central processing unit** (CPU), has the electronic circuitry that manipulates input data into the information wanted. The central processing unit actually executes computer instructions. **Memory,** which is associated with the central processing unit, temporarily holds the data and instructions (programs) needed by the central processing unit.

- **Output devices** make the processed information available for use.

- **Secondary storage devices** are auxiliary units outside the central processing unit that can store additional data and programs. That is, they supplement memory.

Now let us consider the equipment making up these four parts in terms of what you would need on your own personal computer (microcomputer) or one to which you may have access.

### Your Personal Computer Hardware

Suppose you want to do word processing on a personal computer, using the hardware shown in Figure 2-2. Word processing software allows you to input data such as an essay, save it, revise and resave it, and print it whenever you wish. The *input* device, in this case, is a keyboard, which you use to key in the original essay and any changes you want to make to it. All computers, large and small,

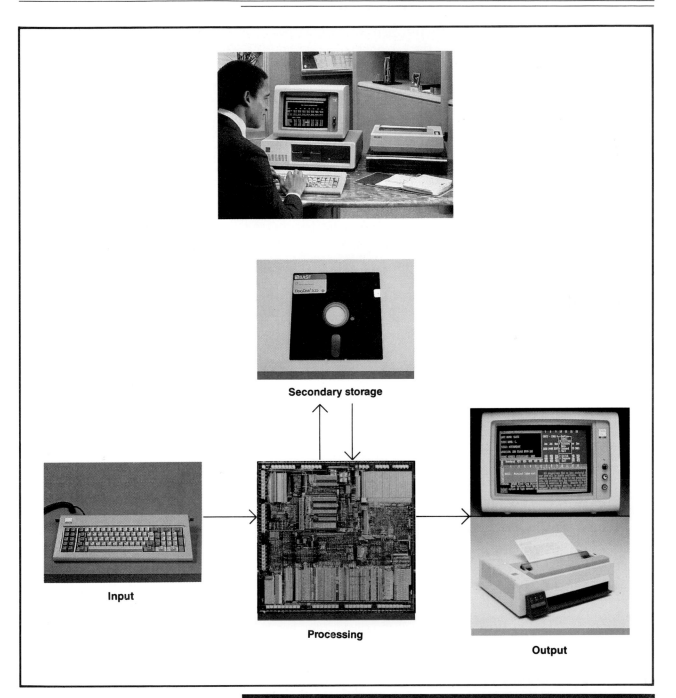

Secondary storage

Input

Processing

Output

**Figure 2-2   A personal computer system.** In this IBM PC microcomputer system, the input device is a keyboard, which feeds data to the central processing unit. The central processing unit is an array of electronic circuits located in the computer housing. The two output devices in this example are the screen and a printer. The secondary storage device is a floppy disk. These components of the system operate together to make the computer work for you.

**Figure 2-3　Input.** (a) The most widely used input device is the keyboard. (b) This wand reader scans data on price tags with special letters and numbers. Wand readers are often found in department stores. (c) Bar code readers are used in supermarkets to input the bar codes found on product labels.

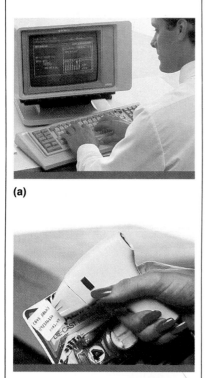

**(a)**

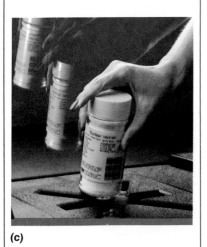

**(b)**

**(c)**

must have a *central processing unit,* so yours does too—it is within the personal computer housing. The central processing unit uses the word processing software to accept the data you input through the keyboard. Processed data from your personal computer usually is *output* in two forms, both a screen and a printer. As you enter the essay on the keyboard, it appears on the screen in front of you. After you examine the essay on the screen, make changes, and determine that it is acceptable, you can print the essay on a printer. Your *secondary storage* device is a floppy disk, a magnetic medium that stores the essay until it is needed again.

Now we shall take a general tour of the hardware for input, processing, output, and storage. These same components comprise all computer systems, whether small, medium, or large. In this discussion we will try to emphasize the types of hardware you are likely to have seen in your own environment. These topics will be covered in more detail in Chapters 4, 5, and 6.

## Input: What Goes In

**Input** is the data that is input—put in—to the computer system for processing. Some of the most common ways of feeding input data into the system are by:

- Typing on a **keyboard** (Figure 2-3a). Computer keyboards operate much the same way as electric typewriter keyboards, except that the computer can respond to what you enter; that is, it "talks" back to you.

- Reading with a **wand reader,** which can be used to scan the special letters and numbers on price tags in retail stores (Figure 2-3b).

- Reading with a **bar code reader,** which scans **bar codes,** the zebra-striped symbols now carried on nearly all products from meats to magazines (Figure 2-3c).

There are some other interesting ways to enter data into the system (such as by voice), but for the moment let us consider those just listed.

Wand readers and bar code readers are able to read data directly from an original document. Thus, they significantly reduce the cost and potential error associated with manually entering data on a keyboard.

An input device may be part of a **terminal** that is connected to a main computer. A terminal includes: (1) an input device—a keyboard, wand reader, or bar code reader, for instance; (2) an output device—usually a television-like **screen**; and (3) a connection to the main computer. The screen displays the data that has been input, and after the computer processes this data, the screen displays the results of the processing—the information wanted. In a store, for instance, the terminal screen displays the individual prices (the data) and the total price calculated by the computer (the desired information).

## The Processor and Memory: Data Manipulation

The **processor** is the computer's center of activity. The processor, as we noted, is also called the **central processing unit,** or **CPU.** The central processing unit consists of electronic circuits that interpret and execute program instructions, as well as communicate with the input, output, and storage devices.

It is the central processing unit that actually transforms data into information. **Data** is the raw material to be processed by a computer. Such material can be letters, numbers, or facts—such as grades in a class, batting averages, or light and dark areas in a photograph. Processed data becomes **information**—data that is organized, meaningful, and useful. Data that is very uninteresting to one person may become very interesting information to another. The raw facts of births, eating habits, and growth rates of calves, for instance, may mean nothing to most people. But the computer-produced relationships among feed, growth, and beef quality are critical information to a cattle breeder. Or, closer to home, consider the check amounts you write as the raw data that is processed into information such as account balance and service charge.

The computer's **memory,** also known as **primary storage,** is closely associated with the central processing unit but separate from it. Memory consists of electronic circuits that are similar to those in the CPU. The circuits temporarily hold the data after it is input to the system and before it is processed. They hold the data after it has been processed but before it has been released to the output device. Memory also holds the programs (computer instructions) needed by the central processing unit. Memory stores letters, numbers, and special characters such as dollar signs and decimal points. Computer memory can even store images in digitized form.

The central processing unit and memory are usually contained in a cabinet or housing. In the past the cabinets of medium or large computers also contained the computer **console**—a panel of switches, dials, colored buttons, and winking lights that inspired the control rooms of so many Hollywood-built spaceships. The console allowed the computer system to signal the operator when something needed to be done—for example, resupplying the printer with paper. Modern computers are less likely to have dials and lights— the operator mainly communicates with the computer system through a console terminal (Figure 2-4). For example, the operator can use the console terminal to determine which programs the system is executing.

**Figure 2-4   The computer console.** Through a console terminal, an operator can determine the status of processing occurring in the computer.

## Output: What Comes Out

The results produced by the central processing unit are, of course, a computer's whole reason for being; **output** is raw data processed into usable information. Some ingenious forms of output have been devised, such as music and synthetic speech, but the most common forms are words and numbers and graphics. Words, for example, may be the letters and memos prepared by office people using word processors. Other workers may be more concerned with numbers, such as those found in formulas, schedules, and budgets. And, as we shall see, numbers can be easily understood when output is in graphics form.

Two common output devices are screens and printers. Screens are the same as those described under input. However, they can vary in their forms of display: Some may produce lines of written or numerical display; others may produce a display of color graphics (Figure 2-5a).

**Printers** are machines that produce printed reports at the instruction of a computer program (Figure 2-5b). Some printers form images on paper as typewriters do; they strike a character against a ribbon, which makes an image on the paper. Other printers form characters by using heat, lasers, photography, or ink spray. In these types of printers there is no physical contact between the printer and the paper when the characters are being formed. Besides forming characters, some printers are able to produce graphic images.

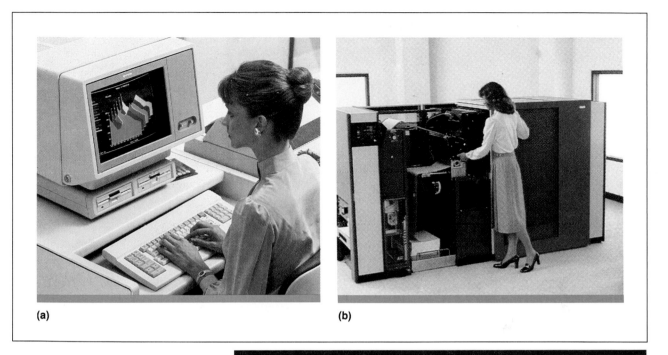

(a)                                                    (b)

**Figure 2-5  Output.** Screens and printers are two types of output devices. (a) The graphics displayed on this screen are one form of output. (b) This high-speed printer is typically used in businesses that produce a high volume of printed material.

## Secondary Storage

**Secondary storage** is additional storage for data and programs that is separate from the central processing unit and memory. For instance, it would be unwise for a college registrar to try to house the grades of all the students in the college in memory; if this were done the computer probably would not have room to store anything else. Also, memory only holds data and programs temporarily. Hence the need for secondary storage. Secondary storage is a safe place to store data on a permanent or semi-permanent basis.

The two most common secondary storage media are magnetic disk and magnetic tape. A **magnetic disk** is an oxide-coated disk like a phonograph record on which data is recorded as magnetic spots. A disk can be a diskette or hard disk. A **diskette,** also called a **floppy disk,** looks something like a small phonograph record. It is called floppy because it is somewhat flexible (Figure 2-6a). A **hard disk** is not flexible, and it holds more data and allows faster access than a floppy disk. Hard disks are usually contained in **disk packs,** and the data on them is read by **disk drives** (Figure 2-6b). On some medium-size or large computers, the disk packs can be removed from the drives. This permits the use of interchangeable packs, and the result is practically unlimited storage capacity.

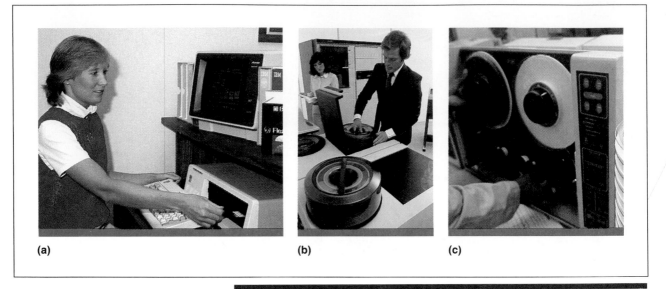

(a)                              (b)                              (c)

**Figure 2-6   Secondary storage.** (a) A floppy disk is being inserted into a disk drive. (b) Hard disks are contained within the round disk pack shown on the top of the cabinets containing the disk drives. A disk pack is lowered into the opened drawer when it is to be used. (c) Magnetic tape, shown here being mounted on a tape drive, travels off one reel and onto another.

**Magnetic tape,** which comes on a cassette, reel, or cartridge, is similar to cassette tape or reel-to-reel tape that is played on a tape recorder. Magnetic tape reels are mounted on **tape drives** when the data on them is ready to be read by the computer system or when new data is to be written on the tape (Figure 2-6c). Magnetic tape is usually used with medium-size or large computers.

## The Complete Hardware System

The hardware devices attached to the computer are called **peripheral equipment.** Peripheral equipment includes all input, output, and secondary storage devices. In the case of microcomputers, most or all of the input, output, and storage devices may be built into the same physical unit. In the IBM PC we saw in Figure 2-2, for instance, the CPU and disk drive are contained in the same housing; the keyboard and screen are separate.

In larger computer systems, however, the input, processing, output, and storage functions may be in separate rooms, separate buildings, or even separate countries. For example, data may be input on terminals at a branch bank, then transmitted to the central processing unit at the bank's headquarters (Figure 2-7). The information produced by the central processing unit may be transmitted to the bank's international offices, where it is output on a printer. Meanwhile, disks with stored data may be kept in the bank's headquarters,

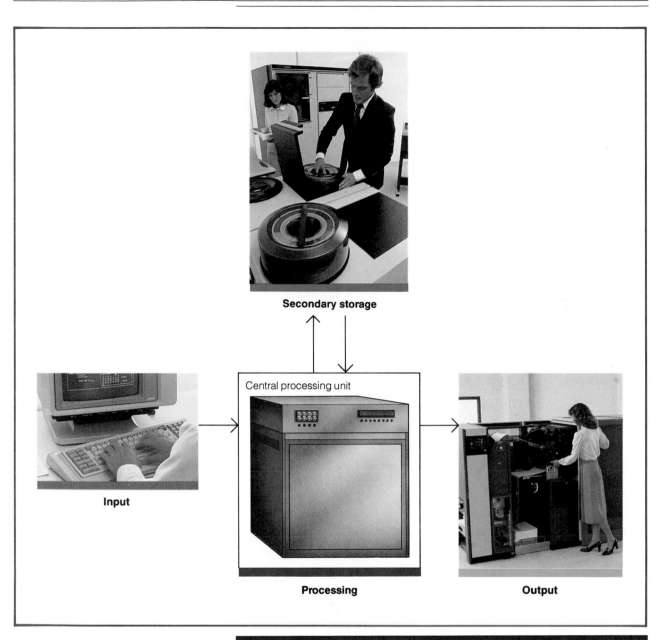

**Figure 2-7   A large computer system.** Data is input and then sent to the central processing unit, which may be at a different location. Information can be output on a high-speed printer. Secondary storage may take the form of magnetic tape or, as shown here, magnetic disk.

and duplicate disk packs may be in a warehouse across town for safekeeping.

Although the equipment may vary widely—from the simplest computer to the most complex—the four elements of a computer system remain basically the same: input, processing, output, and storage. Now let us look at the various ways computers are classified.

(a)

(b)

(c)

(d)

**Figure 2-8   Computer classifications.** (a) IBM announced the Sierra, the most advanced computer in its mainframe line, in 1985. Despite all the talk of the IBM Personal Computer in the trade press, mainframes remain IBM's most important business by far. Two thousand Sierras (also known as the IBM 3090 series) were ordered in the first week after it was announced, despite the machine's price tag. Depending on the amount of memory, a Sierra costs between $4.6 million and $9.3 million. (b) The Cray-2, the fastest computer in operation today, has been nicknamed Bubbles because of its bubbling, shimmering coolant liquids. You can own one for $17.6 million. The Cray-3, scheduled for delivery by 1989, will pack more processors, faster computing speed, and larger memory than the Cray-2 into a box "the size of a loaf of bread." (c) The VAX, a popular minicomputer system made by Digital Equipment Corporation (DEC). (d) This microcomputer is made by Hewlett–Packard.

## Classifications: Computers Big and Small

Computers range from tiny to monstrous, and the range of their capabilities is just as broad. The computer that a person or an organization needs depends on the computing requirements. Clearly, the U.S. Weather Bureau, which keeps watch on the weather fronts of many continents, has different requirements than a car dealer's service department, which keeps track of inventory. And both of them are even more different from the needs of a salesperson who uses a lap-top computer to record client orders on a sales trip.

### Mainframes and Supercomputers

In the jargon of the computer trade, large computers are called **mainframes** (Figure 2-8a). Mainframes have access to billions of characters of data and are capable of processing data very quickly—they can process millions of instructions per second. The price of a mainframe can vary from several hundred thousand dollars to $10 million. With that kind of price tag, you will not buy a mainframe to store your recipes. Because they process vast amounts of data quickly, some of the obvious mainframe customers are banks, insurance companies, and manufacturers. But this list is not all-inclusive; large mail-order houses, airlines with sophisticated reservation systems, government accounting services, aerospace companies that design complex aircraft, and other companies with sophisticated needs use mainframes too.

The mightiest of the mainframes—and, of course, the most expensive—are known as **supercomputers** (Figure 2-8b). Supercomputers process over one *billion* instructions per second—40,000 to 50,000 times faster than a personal computer. The price of one supercomputer can be over $17 million. There are about 150 supercomputers in use today. They are used for such mammoth data manipulation as worldwide weather forecasting and oil exploration and by the military for weapons research and analyzing surveillance data.

### Minicomputers

Computers smaller than mainframes in storage capacity are called **minicomputers** (Figure 2-8c). Minicomputers are slower and less costly than mainframes. Usually in the $10,000 to $500,000 range, they are affordable for many small businesses. The advent of the minicomputer greatly expanded the computer market.

Minicomputers were originally intended to be small and serve some special purpose. However, in a fairly short time, they became more powerful and more versatile, and the line between minicomputer and mainframe has blurred. In fact, the appellation *mini* no longer seems to fit very well. The term **supermini** has been coined to describe minis at the top of the size and price—up to $500,000—scale. Minicomputers are widely used by retail businesses, colleges, and state and city agencies.

### Microcomputers

The smallest computers, such as desk-top and personal or home computers, are called **microcomputers** (Figure 2-8d). For

## COMPUTER CHESS CHAMPION?

Chess, anyone? How about challenging a computer to a chess match? Well, unless you happen to be a grand master, you are likely to lose. For the past 20 years, computer programmers have been improving the software that turns computers into chess players. With their processing speed and memory capacity, computers can scan thousands of possible moves per second. In fact, supercomputers can scan over 100,000 moves per second—a clear advantage over human players. However, what happens when computers play each other?

In one computer chess match, the world computer chess champion, a $14 million Cray supercomputer, faced a challenger, a $20,000 Sun minicomputer—and lost. This clash revealed the most important factor in computer chess: the strategy provided by the software. Quite simply, the minicomputer's software was more effective. For Hans Berliner, one of the designers of the winning software, this was just a warm-up match. His ultimate goal is the Fredkin Prize, a $100,000 award offered to the programmer whose chess software defeats a human world champion.

## WHAT'S A "MICROSUPER"?

In days of old, say, back in 1970 when engineers sauntered through corridors with holstered slide rules swinging at their hips, large companies and universities had what they called "computers."

Those in the know, people who had access to locked, chilled, glass rooms, called their computer "the system." That was it: slide rules, systems and, of course, paper.

But all of that was before marketing people were invented. With marketing people came distinctions. One company sold mainframes, another minicomputers and, eventually, microcomputers and supercomputers. Perhaps, an argument could be made for each of those four labels.

Then, as technology progressed and the 1970s faded into distant memories, justification for some computer classifications became strained. Marketers for every generation of computers at each level weren't happy with using existing labels or even with having their products called "high-end systems." Thus, supermini, supermicro, and within the past year, minisuper drifted into press releases and sales pitches.

Who knows what sets a supermini apart from a mini? . . . How does a supermini differ from a supermicro? If it's the number of users, how do you tell a supermini from a mainframe? Who cares . . . ?

What computer buyers really want to know is whether a system will address their needs, how fast and reliably it will run their own applications and with what existing products it compares.

—from an article in *Computerworld*

many years the computer industry was on a quest for the biggest computer. The search was always for more power and greater capacity. Prognosticators who timidly suggested a niche for a smaller computer were subject to ridicule by people who, as it turned out, could not have been more wrong. Now, for a few hundred dollars, anyone can have a small computer. The subject of microcomputers is so important that we will return to them again and again in every chapter. In addition, we shall include Chapter 13 on microcomputers and Chapters 14, 15, and 16 on microcomputer software. You will also be interested in the Buyer's Guide, which describes how to buy a microcomputer. This guide appears later in the book on yellow paper.

Unfortunately, the definitions of *mainframe, minicomputer,* and *microcomputer* are not fixed because computer technology is changing so rapidly. One observer noted that looking at these three types of computers is like trying to take a picture of three melting ice cubes. However, since these categories are still used throughout the industry, they are worth keeping in mind.

## Data Communications: Processing Here or There

Originally, computer hardware was all kept in one place; that is, it was centralized in one room. While this is still sometimes the case, more and more computer systems are **decentralized.** In some cases the computer itself and some storage devices are in one place, but the devices to access the computer—terminals or even other computers—are somewhere else in order to serve users better. That is, the processing is still in one place, but various input and output devices may be scattered among the users. These devices are usually connected to the computer by telephone lines. For instance, the computer and storage that has the information on your checking account may be located in the bank headquarters, but the terminals are located in branch banks all over town so a teller anywhere can find out what your balance is. The subject of decentralization is intimately tied to **data communications,** the process of exchanging data over communications facilities, in particular, the telephone. The topic of data communications is so important that we shall study it in detail in Chapter 7.

Some systems decentralize processing as well, placing computers and storage devices in dispersed locations. This arrangement is known as **distributed data processing** because even the processing is distributed. There are several ways to configure the hardware; one common method is to place small computers in local offices but still do some processing on a larger computer at the headquarters office. For example, an insurance company headquartered in Denver with

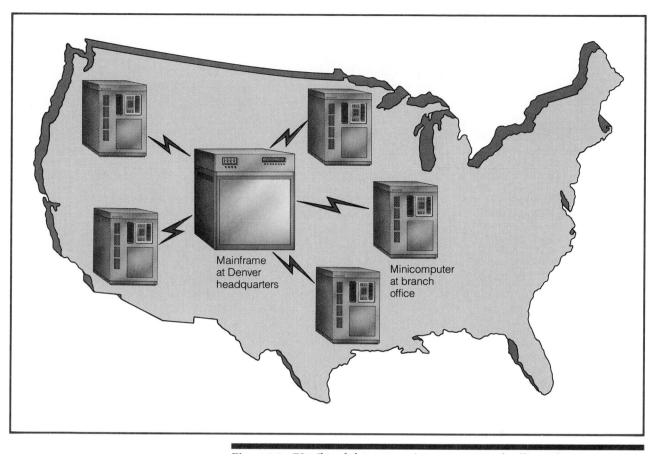

Mainframe
at Denver
headquarters

Minicomputer
at branch
office

**Figure 2-9   Distributed data processing system.** Branch offices of an insurance company have their own computers for local processing, but the branches can tie into the mainframe computer in the headquarters office in Denver.

branches throughout the Midwest might process payments and claims through minicomputers in local offices. However, summary data could be sent regularly by each office for processing by the mainframe in Denver (Figure 2-9).

Many organizations find that their needs are best served by a **network** of microcomputers, that is, microcomputers hooked together so that users can communicate through them. Users can operate their microcomputers independently or in cooperation with other computers—micros, minis, or mainframes—to exchange data and share resources. The concept of connecting microcomputers and mainframe computers is referred to as the **micro-to-mainframe link.** This powerful idea promises to revolutionize the way businesses operate. Users are able to obtain data directly from the mainframe computer and immediately analyze it on their own microcomputers. People have quick access to more information, which leads to better decision making. This important topic will be discussed further in Chapter 7.

## Software: Telling the Machine What to Do

When most people think about computers, they think about machines. The blinking lights on the console, the clacking of the printers, the whirling tape reels, the flashes of color on a computer screen—these are the attention getters. However, it is really the software—the planned, step-by-step instructions required to turn data into information—that makes a computer useful.

### Software for Your Personal Computer

As we have noted, you can buy packaged software that is ready for use. Packaged software for personal computers usually comes in a box that is as colorful as a Monopoly game. Inside the box you will find a diskette (or, in some cases, a tape) that contains the software. There is also an instruction manual, which is sometimes referred to as **documentation.** You insert the diskette in the disk drive, type a specified instruction on the keyboard, and the software begins to run.

Most personal computer software is planned to be user friendly. The term **user friendly** has become a cliche, but it still conveys meaning; it usually means that the software is easy for a novice to use or that it can be used with a minimum of training. Although software can be generalized enough to be mass marketed, it is possible to customize its use by personalizing the data you give it.

Let us consider an example. A software package called Personal Fitness is advertised thus: *"Talk about easy to use! Each day you'll spend less time at the keyboard than you do on a coffee break. With no computer jargon . . . just simple, sensible English."* Well. Sounds easy enough. When you insert the diskette and issue the start-up command, questions appear on the screen. You type responses on the keyboard, and the responses also appear on the screen; the dialogue between you and the computer is recorded in front of you.

If you indicate that this is the first time you have used the software, you will be asked questions about your age, height, weight, and so forth (Figure 2-10). The Personal Fitness program will analyze this data, then make recommendations for a *"new and healthier lifestyle."* As you use the software over time, you will report (that is, key in) items such as caloric intake or pulse rate or miles walked. The software will produce charts and graphs showing weight loss, pulse pattern, and the like to help you monitor your progress. Note the input-process-output here. The *input data* to the program are your own habits (in number form) and personal statistics. The *processing* is the analysis of that data by the software. The *output* is the set of recommendations and the charts and graphs.

It is a short step, conceptually, from packaged software for personal use to packaged software for office use. For example, there are many software packages that help manage accounts payable. These

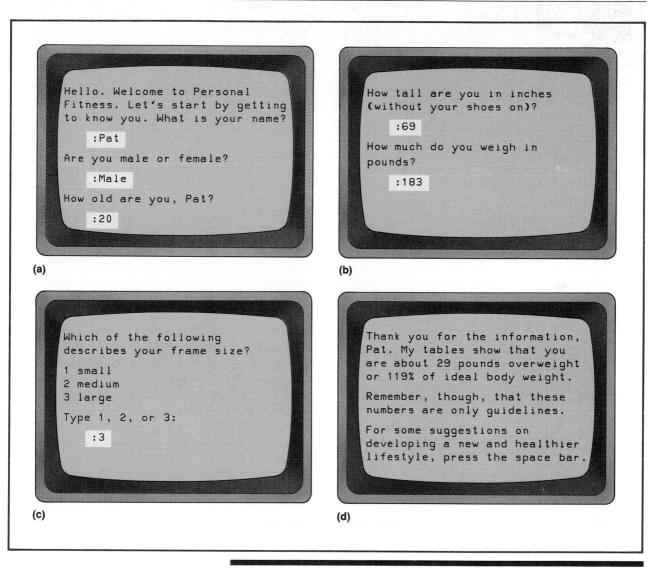

**Figure 2-10 Personal Fitness software screens.** These screens show the dialogue between computer and user.

packages help businesses pay their bills and employ the same principles as home-computer packages. You provide input data such as invoice number, vendor name, and amount owed. The computer processes this data to produce output in the form of computer-generated checks and various reports to help you track expenses.

We have looked at packaged software here, but software can also be written for a specific client. In fact, not so long ago, most businesses had software written exclusively for them. Many organizations still employ a staff of computer professionals for that purpose. Software, whether packaged or not, can be used by a person who has no training whatever in programming. But let us look a bit more closely at what programming entails.

### What Programmers Do

Programs—software—can be written in a variety of programming languages. Most programming languages in common use today are English-like in appearance, and there are very definite rules for using them. Some languages are used specifically for business or scientific applications. BASIC was designed for beginners but has become popular for use on mini- and microcomputers. (BASIC is described in some detail in Appendix A.) Some languages are relatively easy to learn and are used by people whose primary occupation is not programming. We shall discuss these languages in Chapter 10.

Programmers must understand how to use a programming language so that they can convey the logic of a program to the computer in a form it understands. A program is keyed (typed) in line by line on a terminal or microcomputer. The program is then stored in some form of secondary storage, such as disk, from which it can be called into memory for testing and execution. Besides being able to use a programming language, programmers must also understand what the program is supposed to do and design it accordingly, test it to remove errors, and document—write about—what they did.

Because of miniaturization, standardization, and the growing popularity of computers, the cost of hardware is going down. The cost of software, however, depends on whether it is packaged or custom-made. Packaged software prices are going down, partly because of increased competition but mostly because the market is demanding lower prices. The price of custom software, on the other hand, is going up for a variety of reasons. Unlike hardware, producing software depends chiefly on labor, and labor costs keep rising. As the Computer Revolution continues, computers are becoming easier—not harder—for people to use. That is, computers are becoming accessible to more people, and less training is required to use them. But it takes complicated software to give uncomplicated access to the computer—another reason why software costs are going up. For those interested in careers in the computer field, then, we suggest that the future lies in understanding software.

## Processing Operations: College Bound

There are several operations common to the processing of data. With a computer, you can:

- Input
- Store
- Update
- Output
- Summarize
- Inquire
- Sort
- Compute
- Classify
- Retrieve

The best way to explain these is to use an example. Figure 2-11 shows what happens when Karen Burner fills out two forms for college—the application form, which puts her name and personal data on file, and the registration form for classes for a particular semester. The following steps take place in the order of the processing operations we just listed.

①  **Input.** Data is entered into the computer system for processing. In our example Karen's college application form is input by a clerk into the computer system.

②  **Inquire.** A computer user usually inquires about data in a mainframe computer through a computer terminal. Here the registration clerk makes an inquiry to find out if there is room in the classes Karen has said she wants to take, and the computer replies that there is. (And now more input takes place, as Karen's registration data—the classes she signed up for—is entered into the system.)

③  **Store.** Data that has been processed is retained for future reference. Karen's application and registration data are stored in the student file on disk. Her registration data is also stored in the class file; these records are used by the instructors.

④  **Sort.** To sort means to arrange data into a particular sequence. For instance, student names are sorted by the computer into alphabetical order within a class. For DAT 110, "Computer Literacy," Burner, Karen, is second on the class roster.

⑤  **Update.** As new data is obtained, files must be brought up to date. For instance, the preceding steps took place at the start of the school semester. At the end of the semester, when Karen's instructor turns in a grade form, Karen's record is updated with new data: She received an A in DAT 110.

⑥  **Compute.** Addition, subtraction, multiplication, and division are arithmetic operations—computations that the computer can perform. In this example the computer uses these arithmetic operations to calculate Karen's grade-point average: 4.0.

⑦  **Output.** The computer produces the processing result in usable form. Karen's list of grades is printed out and mailed to her home.

⑧  **Classify.** To classify means to categorize data according to characteristics that make it useful. To help college administrators in their planning, the computer program classifies all students enrolled in the college according to age. This report and others mentioned in this example are also output.

⑨  **Summarize.** To summarize means to reduce data to a more concise, usable form. The computer summarizes the total number of students in the various schools and also gives an overall enrollment total—again, to help administrators in their planning.

⑩ **Retrieve.** Data stored in the system can be retrieved later for use. Here, when Karen decides she wants to transfer from this college to another, the computer is able to retrieve an official transcript showing all her grades and courses.

Incidentally, it might seem that there is not much difference between inquiring and retrieving. Normally, making an inquiry involves asking the computer a brief question and getting an answer on the screen; retrieving usually produces a paper printout. There are areas of overlap among many of these processing operations. The important point is to note the flow of data through the computer system.

# People and Computers

We have talked about hardware, software, and data, but the most important element in a computer system is people. Anyone nervous about a takeover by computers will be relieved to know that computers will always need people—both the people who help make the system work and the people for whom the work is done.

## Computers and You, the User

Imagine for a moment that you are the only potential user of computers. That means that makers of computers and software will go to any lengths to please you. They want to convince you that the computer will make you more productive in the workplace and enhance your personal life at home. They use flashy advertisements to court you with promises of power, ease of use, and all kinds of bells and whistles. Salespeople promise you training and ongoing support. Can you be convinced? Probably. They *must* convince you. You are their reason for being. Without you, there is no computer industry.

The story is the same in the real world, although not, of course, for you alone. You, and others like you, are the people being served by the computer industry. As we noted earlier, computer users have come to be called just *users*, a nickname that has persisted for years. But the term did not always mean what it means now. Once users were an elite breed—high-powered Ph.D.s, research-and-development engineers, and government planners; today the population of users has broadened considerably. This expanded user base is due partly to user-friendly software—for both work and personal use—and partly to the availability of small, low-cost computers. There is a strong possibility that all of us will be computer users, but our levels of sophistication may vary.

The novice is the user with no training on computers. From a

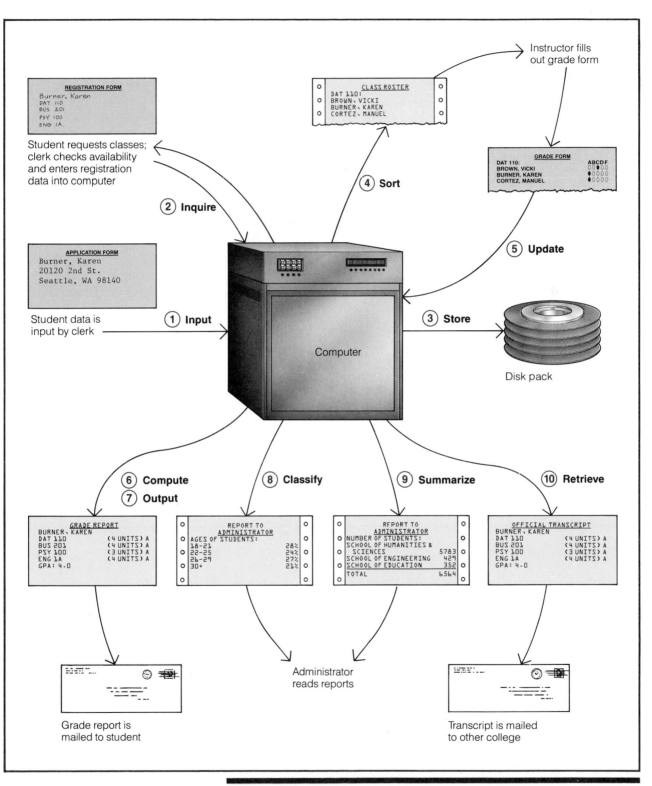

**Figure 2-11  Karen Burner goes to college.** The processing operations illustrated here are described in the text.

child playing computer games to a student experimenting with educational software, the user may be just learning. A more sophisticated user is one who uses a personal computer for home finances or as a hobby.

Above this level users are those who, to varying degrees, use the computer for business or professional reasons, although they are not computer professionals themselves. For instance, a person may be trained well enough to make the inquiries relating to customer service, banking, or airline reservations. At a slightly higher level, a person may know what data is being entered into the computer and what information being produced would be useful in performing the job at hand.

A more sophisticated user is a person who has written some computer programs, understands computer jargon, and is well equipped to communicate with computer professionals.

## Computer People

Another way to think about people and computers is within the context of an organization's **MIS** department. MIS stands for **management information systems.** The MIS department is made up of people responsible for the computer resources of an organization. Whether the MIS department is within a university, a government bureau, or a corporation, this organization may well be the institution's most important asset. Most of the information about that institution is contained in its computer files: research data, engineering drawings, marketing strategy, accounts receivable, accounts payable, sales information, manufacturing specifications, transportation plans, warehousing data—the list goes on and on. The computer professionals are the guardians of this information; they provide service to the users. Let us touch on the essential personnel required to run computer systems.

**Data entry operators** prepare data for processing. **Computer operators** monitor the console, review procedures, and keep peripheral equipment running. **Librarians** catalog the processed disks and tapes and keep them secure.

**Computer programmers,** as we have noted, design, write, test, and implement the programs that process data on the computer system. **Systems analysts** are knowledgeable in the programming area but have broader responsibilities. They plan and design not just individual programs, but entire computer systems. Systems analysts maintain a working relationship with the user organization and work closely with users to plan new systems that will meet the users' needs. The **director of information management** oversees the MIS department and must understand more than just computer technology. The director must understand the goals and operations of the entire organization.

## The End-User Revolution

In this section we have distinguished between *users* and *computer professionals.* In the most general sense, the professionals provide the computer system and the users use it. But these two camps are not so distinct; in fact, there is common ground between them. In addition to buying and using packaged software, a growing number of users are becoming savvy about hardware—especially microcomputers—and many are even using user-oriented languages to write their own software. This phenomenon has been called the **end-user revolution.** The fact that users are beginning to take care of themselves will have a profound effect on the computer industry. We shall return to this theme again in the text, as the story unfolds.

# The End of the Beginning

In this chapter we have painted the computer industry with a broad brush, touching on hardware, software, data, and people. Soon we shall move on to the chapters that explain the information presented in this chapter in more detail. In the next chapter, however, we shall examine our roots, so we can place ourselves on the time line of the Computer Revolution.

## Summary and Key Terms

- The machines in a computer system are called **hardware.** The **programs,** or step-by-step instructions that run the machines, are called **software.** Software sold in stores is usually contained in a box or folder and is called **packaged software. Computer programmers** write programs for **users,** people who purchase and use computer software.

- A **computer** is a machine that processes data (input) into useful information (output). A computer system consists of three main areas of data handling—input, processing, and output—and is backed by a fourth, storage.

- **Input** is data put into the computer. Common **input devices** include a **keyboard;** a **wand reader,** which scans the special letters and numbers on price tags in retail stores; and a **bar code reader,** which scans the zebra-striped **bar codes** on store products.

- A **terminal** includes an input device, such as a keyboard or wand reader; an output device, usually a television-like **screen;** and a connection to the main computer. A screen displays both the input data and the processed information.

- The **processor,** or **central processing unit** (CPU), organizes raw **data** into meaningful, useful **information.** It interprets and executes program instructions and communicates with the input, output, and storage devices. **Memory,** or **primary storage,** is associated with the central processing unit but is separate from it. Memory holds the input data before and after processing until the data is released to the output device. The central processing unit and memory are usually contained in a cabinet that also contains the computer **console,** which allows the computer system to signal the operator when something needs to be done. The operator can communicate with the computer system through the **console terminal.**

- **Output,** raw data processed into usable information, is usually in the form of words, numbers, and graphics. Users can see output displayed on screens and use **printers** to display output on paper.

- The computer's main memory is limited. Therefore, **secondary storage** is needed, most commonly in the form of magnetic disks and magnetic tape. **Magnetic disks** can be diskettes or hard disks. The flexible **diskette,** also called a **floppy disk,** looks like a small phonograph record. The inflexible **hard disk,** usually contained in **disk packs** and read on **disk drives,** holds more data and allows faster access than a floppy disk. **Magnetic tape** comes on reels that are mounted on **tape drives** when the data is to be read by the computer.

- **Peripheral equipment** includes all the input, output, and secondary storage devices attached to a computer.

- Computers can be loosely categorized according to their capacity for processing data. **Mainframes,** the largest computers, are used by such customers as banks, airlines, and large manufacturers to process very large amounts of data quickly. The most powerful and expensive mainframes are called **super-computers. Minicomputers**—which are widely used by colleges, retail businesses, and local government—were originally intended to be small, but their capacity has become increasingly similar to that of mainframes. Therefore, the largest and most expensive minicomputers are now called **super-minis.** The smallest computers, such as desk-top office computers and home computers, are called **microcomputers.**

- In a **decentralized** system the computer itself and some storage devices are in one place, but the devices to access the computer are somewhere else. Such a system requires **data communications**—the exchange of data over communications facilities (the telephone in particular). In a **distributed data processing** system, processing is dispersed to user locations.

- Often organizations use a **network** of microcomputers, which allows users to operate their microcomputers independently or to exchange data and share resources with other computers. Microcomputers connected to a mainframe form a **micro-to-mainframe link,** in which users can obtain data from the mainframe and analyze it on their own microcomputers. The increase in the amount of information that a manager can consider often leads to better decision making.

- Software is accompanied by an instruction manual, which is also called **documentation.** Software that is easy to use is considered **user friendly.** Software may be packaged for general use or specially written for a specific client.

- Processing operations include the capacities to **input** (enter data), **inquire** (ask questions), **store** (retain processed data), **sort** (arrange data in a particular sequence), **update** (bring files up to date), **compute** (perform arithmetic calculations), **output** (produce processing results in usable form), **classify** (categorize data), **summarize** (reduce data to concise form), and **retrieve** (request and receive a paper printout).

- Computer users range from novices with no training to sophisticated users who can communicate with computer professionals.

- People are vital to any computer system. An organization's computer resources department, often called the **management information systems (MIS)** department, includes **data entry operators** (who prepare data for processing), **computer operators** (who monitor and run the equipment), **librarians** (who catalog disks and tapes), **computer programmers** (who design, write, test, and implement programs), **systems analysts** (who plan and design entire systems of programs), and a **director of information management** (who coordinates the MIS department).

- In general, computer professionals who provide computer systems are not the same as the users who use the systems. However, the trend seems to be that users are becoming increasingly knowledgeable about computers and less reliant on computer professionals. This trend is called the **end-user revolution.**

## Review Questions

1. Define *hardware* and *software.*

2. How do a wand reader and bar code reader differ from a keyboard as input devices?

3. Name two functions of the processor, or central processing unit (CPU).

4. Name three common forms of output and two common output devices.

5. Why is secondary storage necessary? Describe the most common forms of secondary storage.

6. Name and describe the three main types of computers.

7. What is distributed data processing?

8. What is documentation?

9. When people call software "user friendly," what do they mean?

10. Name at least three things a computer programmer does.

11. Explain why the cost of custom software is going up.

12. What is the difference between data and information?

13. Name and define ten common processing operations.

14. State what each of the following computer people do:
    a. data entry operator
    b. computer operator
    c. systems analyst
    d. director of information management

## Discussion Questions

1. Of course, input, processing, output, and storage do not relate only to computers. Consider, for instance, the experience of writing a term paper that involves research. What would be the input? The processing? The output? The storage?

2. Why do you think many large companies prefer decentralized computer systems?

3. Since software can be expensive, some people illegally copy packaged software to give to friends. Explain how and why this affects software prices.

## PART 2

# HARDWARE

You will probably come to see software as the main thrust of the computer industry, but first you must understand hardware, the physical equipment that makes up a computer system. We shall begin with the origins of hardware and software—the fascinating history of computers. As you will see, industry experts had no idea that computer power would be as widespread as it is today. And, even as recently as 20 years ago, they could not imagine that computers would be in the hands of everyday people.

In this part we shall consider the hardware components of a computer system, a chapter at a time: the central processing unit and memory, input and output devices, secondary storage devices, and data communications.

# 3

# History and Industry

## The Continuing Story of the Computer Age

The principles are old, but the first computer was born only about four decades ago. Before long, this generation of vacuum-tube computers was replaced by second-generation computers using transistors and then by third-generation machines using integrated circuits. The fourth generation of general-purpose microprocessors may yield to a fifth by the early 1990s. This is not ancient history. It is now, and it moves fast.

As a novice in the computer field, you view the computer industry from a fresh perspective. You may see computers as a bold new thrust, representing the crest of the wave of technological developments. Microcomputers, in particular, may be your main connection to that technology. Microcomputers are always in the forefront of the news, generating endless headlines as they are born and changed and—in some cases—die. But microcomputers did not spring out of thin air. They have, in fact, illustrious ancestors and a noble history. It is important that you be able to place yourself on the computer time line. We shall focus on that time line from its fumbling beginnings to its current sophistication and far-flung scope.

It is appropriate to discuss the history of the computer in this part about hardware because the touchstone of the computer revolution has been its rapidly changing technology—its hardware. However, the history of computers is by no means just a history of machines; it is also a history of software and people.

We could start with the history of methods of representing numbers or quantities—methods such as making piles of stones or marks on wood or employing instruments like the abacus, which was used for 5,000 years in the Orient and is still used in some parts of the world today (Figure 3-1). Or we could start with the idea of numbers being represented by a mechanical gear wheel, as they are on car odometers and old-fashioned adding machines; this idea was first developed in 1642 by Blaise Pascal (Figure 3-2), who built an adding machine based on it. However, it was not until 180 years after Pascal's invention that someone was able to advance the cause of mechanical computation significantly. That someone was Charles Babbage, called the father of the computer. We start with him.

**Figure 3-1 The abacus.** Consisting of beads strung on wires, the abacus is still used in the Orient. Some abacus users have been as nimble at manipulating abacuses as their Western counterparts have been at operating mechanical calculating machines.

**Figure 3-2   Blaise Pascal and his adding machine.** This cigar-box–size mechanical adding machine called the Pascaline involved a set of interlocking cogs and wheels. People dialed the numbers they wanted, and the wheels and cogs inside turned to the appropriate amount; the result was displayed in the little windows above. Fifty Pascalines were built, but they found few buyers for what—in light of today's anxieties about computers—is an interesting reason: Clerks and accountants refused to use them, fearing the machines might do away with their jobs.

## Babbage and the Countess

Born in England in 1791, Charles Babbage was an inventor and mathematician. When solving polynomial equations, he found the hand-compiled mathematical tables he used filled with errors. He decided a machine could be built to solve polynomial equations more easily and accurately by calculating the successive differences between them. He set about making a demonstration model of what he called a **difference engine** (Figure 3-3). The model was so well received that in about 1830 he enthusiastically began to build a full-scale working version, using a grant from the British government.

However, Babbage found that despite tight design specifications and exhortations to workers, the smallest imperfections were enough to throw the tons of brass and pewter rods and gears of the ambitious larger machine out of whack. Babbage was viewed by his own colleagues as a man who was trying to manufacture a machine that was utterly ridiculous. Finally, after spending 17,000 English pounds to no avail, the government withdrew financial support. (A British prime minister later stated that the only use he could see for the difference engine was for calculating the large amount of money spent on it.)

Despite this setback, Babbage was not discouraged. He conceived another machine of cogs and wheels, christened the **analytical engine,** which he hoped would perform many kinds of calculations. Babbage never built the analytical engine (a model was later

**Figure 3-3   Charles Babbage and his difference engine.** This shows a prototype model. Babbage attempted to build a working model, which was to have been several times larger and steam-driven, but he was unsuccessful.

put together by his son), but the design embodied five key characteristics of modern computers:

- An input device

- A storage facility to hold numbers waiting to be processed

- A processor or number calculator

- A control unit to direct the task to be performed and the sequence of calculations

- An output device

Part of Babbage's device was similar to an invention built in 1801 by Frenchman Joseph Jacquard. Jacquard, noting the repetitious nature of the task of weavers, devised a stiff card with a series of holes punched in it; the card blocked certain threads from entering the loom and let other threads go on to complete the weave. Babbage realized that the punched card system could also be used to control the order of calculations in his analytical engine, and he incorporated it into the machine.

**Figure 3-4   The Countess of Lovelace.** Augusta Ada Byron, as she was known before she became a countess, was Charles Babbage's colleague in his work on the analytical engine and has been called the first computer programmer. A programming language sponsored by the Department of Defense has been dubbed Ada in her honor.

---

**NO PRETENSIONS**

In her series of notes entitled "Observations on Mr. Babbage's Analytical Engine," Ada Lovelace wrote: "The Analytical Engine has no pretensions whatever to originate anything. It can do whatever we know how to order it to perform. It can follow analysis; but it has no power of anticipating any analytical relations or truths." In other words, a computer by itself cannot be considered creative. As Christopher Evans writes in *The Micro Millennium*: "It was a very perceptive comment and seems to be the first ever statement of the argument which today crops up unfailingly whenever the intellectual potential of computers is discussed—*a computer can only do what you program it to do.*"

---

If Babbage was the father of the computer, then Ada, the Countess of Lovelace, was the first computer programmer (Figure 3-4). The daughter of English poet Lord Byron and of a mother who was a gifted mathematician, she went to work with Babbage when she was 27 and helped develop the instructions for doing computations on the analytical engine.

Lady Lovelace's contributions cannot be overvalued. She saw that Babbage's theoretical approach was workable and encouraged him to continue. More important, however, she published a series of notes that eventually led others to accomplish what Babbage himself had been unable to do.

## Herman Hollerith: The Census Has Never Been the Same

Since 1790 the U.S. Congress has required that a census of the country's population be taken every ten years. For the 1880 census, tabulation took seven and a half years because all the counting had to be done by hand. Accordingly, there was considerable anxiety in official circles as to whether the tabulation of the next census, to be taken in 1890, could be completed before the turn of the century.

A competition was held to find some way to speed the counting process. The final test involved a count of the population of St. Louis, Missouri, which Herman Hollerith's tabulating machine completed in only five and a half hours. As a result of his system's adoption, an unofficial count of the 1890 population (62,622,250) was announced only six weeks after the census was taken.

Like Babbage, Hollerith had adopted Jacquard's punched cards. In his tabulating machine (Figure 3-5), rods that passed through the holes completed an electrical circuit, which caused a counter to advance one unit. This capability highlights the principal difference between Hollerith's and Babbage's machines: Hollerith was able to use electrical rather than mechanical power to drive his device.

Hollerith, who had been a statistician with the Census Bureau, realized that punched-card processing had considerable commercial potential. He was quite right—punched cards were used extensively into the 1970s and are still used in a few places today. In 1896 he founded the Tabulating Machine Company, which became successful in selling services to railroads and other clients. In 1924 the successor to this company merged with two other companies to form the International Business Machines Corporation—IBM. The original IBM building is shown in Figure 3-6.

(a)                               (b)

(c)                               (d)

**Figure 3-5   Herman Hollerith and his tabulating machine.** (a) Herman Hollerith.
(b) This electrical tabulator and sorter was used to process punched cards.
(c) This operator is entering data on early punched cards. (d) Later punched cards
were a common part of American life at one time ("Do not fold, spindle, or muti-
late"), but few organizations use them today.

Figure 3-6   The original IBM building.

 ## Watson of IBM: Ornery but Rather Successful

For over 30 years from 1924 to 1956, Thomas J. Watson, Sr. ruled IBM with an iron grip. Before becoming its cantankerous, autocratic head, he had worked for the Tabulating Machine Company. There he had carried on a running battle with Hollerith; Watson did not feel Hollerith's business aptitude matched his technical ability. Under supersalesman Watson, IBM became a dominant force in the business machines market, first as a supplier of calculators, then as a developer of computers.

IBM's entry into computers was sparked by a young Harvard professor of mathematics, Howard Aiken. In 1936, after reading Babbage's and Lady Lovelace's notes, Aiken began to think that a modern equivalent of the analytical engine could be constructed. The important difference now would be that it would not be mechanical but electromechanical. Because IBM was already such a power in the business machines market and had ample money and resources,

Aiken worked out a careful proposal and approached Thomas Watson. In one of those autocratic make-or-break decisions for which he was famous, Watson gave him $1 million. As a result, the Harvard Mark I was born.

## The Start of the Modern Era

Nothing like the **Mark I** had ever been built before. It was 8 feet high and 55 feet long, made of streamlined steel and glass (Figure 3-7), and it emitted a sound during processing that one person said was "like listening to a roomful of old ladies knitting away with steel needles." Unveiled in 1944, the awesome sight of the Mark I was accentuated by the presence of uniformed Navy personnel. It was World War II, and Aiken had become a naval lieutenant released to Harvard to help build the computer that was supposed to solve many of the Navy's problems.

Actually, the Mark I was never very efficient, but it had enormous publicity value. When the security wraps came off after the war, it received a great deal of public attention and strengthened IBM's commitment to computer development.

Meanwhile, technology had been proceeding elsewhere on separate tracks.

### WATSON SMART? YOU BET!

Just as computers were getting off the ground, Thomas Watson, Sr. saw the best and brightest called to arms in World War II. But he did not just bid his employees a sad adieu. He paid them. Each and every one received one quarter of his or her annual salary, in 12 monthly installments. The checks continued to arrive throughout the duration of the war. Every month those former employees thought about IBM, and the generosity of their employer.

The result? A very high percentage of those employees returned to IBM after the war. Watson got his brain trust back, virtually intact. The rest is history.

**Figure 3-7 The Mark I.**

**Figure 3-8   Dr. John V. Atanasoff and the ABC.** Atanasoff and his assistant, Clifford Berry, developed the first digital electronic computer, nicknamed the ABC for Atanasoff–Berry Computer.

## As Easy as ABC

During the war American military officials approached Dr. John Mauchly at the University of Pennsylvania and asked him to build a machine that would rapidly calculate trajectories for artillery and missiles. Mauchly and his student J. Presper Eckert, Jr. relied on the work of Dr. John V. Atanasoff (Figure 3-8), a professor of physics at Iowa State University.

During the late 1930s Atanasoff had spent time trying to build an electronic calculating device to help his students solve complicated mathematical problems. One night, the idea came to him for linking the computer memory and the associated logic. Later, he and an assistant, Clifford Berry, succeeded in building the first digital computer that worked electronically; they called it the **ABC,** for **Atanasoff–Berry Computer.** After Mauchly met with Atanasoff and Berry in 1941, he used the ABC as the basis for the next step in computer development. From this association ultimately came a lawsuit, based on a controversy about patents for a commercial version of the machine Mauchly built. The suit was finally decided in 1974, when a federal court determined that Atanasoff had been the true originator of the ideas required to make an electronic digital computer actually work. (Some computer historians dispute this court decision.) But during the war years Mauchly and Eckert were able to use the ABC principles to dramatic effect in creating the next major advance in the computer field.

## The ENIAC

Although Mauchly and Eckert owed much to Atanasoff, they still faced an awesome task. The machine they proposed, which would cut the time needed to calculate artillery and bombing trajectories from 15 minutes to 30 seconds, would employ 18,000 vacuum tubes—and all of them would have to operate simultaneously.

No one had ever had any experience with a project of such magnitude. One critic noted that because "the average life of a vacuum tube is 3,000 hours, a tube failure would occur every 15 minutes. Since it would average more than 15 minutes to find the bad tube, no useful work could ever be done." Even so, at a cost of $400,000, funding was approved to develop the project.

The ENIAC was not built in time to contribute to the war effort (even though the team worked on it 24 hours a day for 30 months). Nevertheless, work continued, and when the world's first general-purpose electronic digital computer was turned on in February 1946, it was impressive. It filled a huge room (Figure 3-9) and drew 140,000 watts, the amount of electricity generated by a small power station. The Electronic Numerical Integrator And Computer—the **ENIAC**—was able to multiply a pair of numbers in about three milliseconds (three-thousandths of a second).

**Figure 3-9    The ENIAC.** Occupying 1,500 square feet, standing two stories high, and weighing 30 tons, the ENIAC could handle 300 numbers per second. The ENIAC cost $486,840 in 1946 dollars; today a $2,000 laptop computer can handle numbers about 20 times faster. The ENIAC was invented by Dr. John Mauchly and J. Presper Eckert, Jr.

## FEEDING TIME

ENIAC scientists had a problem: How could they prevent rodents from nibbling away at the machine and destroying vital parts? The solution was to capture some mice, starve them for a few days, then feed them bits of insulating materials. Any pieces the mice found particularly delicious were removed from ENIAC and replaced with less tasty parts.

However, the heat generated by this enormous system posed serious cooling problems, and the storage capacity was ridiculously small. Worst of all, the system was quite inflexible: Each time a program was changed, the machine had to be rewired. This last obstacle was overcome by the work of world-famous mathematician Dr. John von Neumann.

## The EDVAC and von Neumann

One day in 1945, while waiting for a train in Aberdeen, Maryland, a member of the ENIAC development team ran into von Neumann (Figure 3-10), who was then involved in the top-secret work of designing nuclear weapons. Since both had security clearances, they were able to discuss each other's work, and von Neumann began to realize that the difficulties he was having in the laborious and time-consuming checking of his advanced equations could be solved by the high speeds of ENIAC. As a result of that chance meeting, von Neumann joined the University of Pennsylvania as a special consultant to the ENIAC team.

**Figure 3-10   Dr. John von Neumann.** The Hungarian-born mathematician made many contributions to the development of flowcharting, and he also proposed that computer memories be used to store programs. In addition to being a great mathematician, he held degrees in chemistry and physics, was a great storyteller, and had total recall. "I've met Einstein and Oppenheimer and Teller and a whole bunch of other guys," recalls Professor Leon Harmon of Case Western Reserve, "and von Neumann was the only genius I ever met. The others were supersmart, but von Neumann's mind was all-encompassing."

When the Army asked the university to build a more powerful computer than the ENIAC, von Neumann responded by proposing the Electronic Discrete Variable Automatic Computer, or **EDVAC.** EDVAC utilized what von Neumann called the **stored program concept.** The idea, von Neumann said, was to make the new machine more flexible than ENIAC by allowing it to store all program instructions inside the computer. That is, instead of having people laboriously rewire the machine to go to a different program, the machine would, in less than a second, "read" instructions from computer storage for switching to a new program. The significance of this is noted in *The Micro Millennium* by Christopher Evans:

> *From this moment on, computers were no longer fast but blinkered workhorses, woodenly proceeding down one track, but had become dynamic, flexible information-processing systems capable of performing multitudes of different tasks. In one conceptual jump, the true power of computers moved from the finite to the potentially infinite.*

# The Computer Age Begins

The remarkable thing about the Computer Age is that so much has happened in so short a time. We have leap-frogged through four generations of technology in about 40 years—a span of time whose events are within the memories of many people today. The first three "generations" are pinned to three technological developments: the vacuum tube, the transistor, and the integrated circuit. Each drastically changed the nature of computers. We define the beginning of each generation according to the commercial delivery of the hardware technology. Defining subsequent generations has become more complicated because the entire industry has become more complicated.

## The First Generation, 1951–1958: The Vacuum Tube

The Computer Age began on June 14, 1951. This was the date the first Universal Automatic Computer, or **UNIVAC,** was delivered to a client (the U.S. Bureau of the Census) for use in tabulating the previous year's census. It also marked the first time that a computer had been built for business applications rather than for military, scientific, or engineering use. The UNIVAC (Figure 3-11) was really the ENIAC in disguise and was, in fact, built by Mauchly and Eckert, who in 1947 had formed their own corporation (which was later sold to Remington–Rand).

**Figure 3-11   The UNIVAC.** The younger figure of Walter Cronkite (right) is shown here with J. Presper Eckert, Jr. and an unidentified operator of UNIVAC during vote counting for the 1952 presidential election. UNIVAC surprised CBS executives by predicting—after analyzing about 5% of the vote counted—that Eisenhower would defeat Stevenson. CBS withheld announcement until it could be confirmed by the complete vote. Thus began the use of computers in predicting election outcomes—a practice that evoked criticism in the 1980 Reagan–Carter election, when NBC forecast the winner with only 1% of the vote counted and long before polls had even closed in many western states.

**(a)**

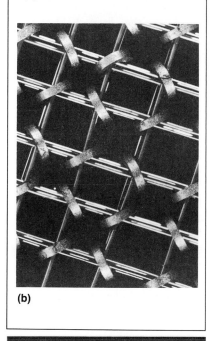

**(b)**

Figure 3-13  **Magnetic cores.** (a) A 6-inch by 11-inch magnetic core memory. (b) Close-up of a magnetic core memory. A few hundredths of an inch in diameter, each magnetic core was mounted on a wire. When electricity was passed through the wire on which a core was strung, the core could be magnetized as either "off" or "on," which could be used to represent a zero (off) or a one (on). Combinations of zeros and ones represented data. Magnetic cores were originally developed by IBM, which adapted pill-making machinery to produce them by the millions.

Figure 3-12  **Vacuum tubes.** Vacuum tubes were used in the first generation of computers. Vacuum tube systems could multiply two ten-digit numbers together in one-fortieth of a second.

In the first generation, **vacuum tubes**—electronic tubes about the size of light bulbs—were used as the internal computer components (Figure 3-12). However, because thousands of vacuum tubes were required, they generated a great deal of heat, which caused many problems in temperature regulation and climate control. All the tubes had to be working simultaneously, and because they were subject to frequent burnout, the people operating the computer often did not know whether the problem was in the programming or in the machine. In addition, input and output tended to be slow, since both operations were usually performed on punched cards.

Another drawback was that the language used in programming was a machine language, which uses numbers. (Present-day higher-level languages are more like English.) Using a language of numbers made programming the computer difficult and time-consuming.

The UNIVAC employed **magnetic core** to provide memory. This consisted of small, doughnut-shaped rings about the size of a pin-head, which were strung like beads on intersecting thin wires (Figure 3-13). Magnetic core was the dominant form of memory technology for two decades. To supplement main memory, first-generation computers stored data on punched cards. In 1957 magnetic tape was introduced as a faster, more compact method of storing data.

The early generation of computers was used primarily for scientific and engineering calculations rather than for business data-processing applications. Because of the enormous size, unreliability, and high cost of these computers, many assumed they would remain very expensive, specialized tools, not destined for general use.

But at Bell Laboratories there had already been a new technological development: the transistor.

## The Second Generation, 1959–1964: The Transistor

Three Bell Lab scientists—J. Bardeen, H. W. Brattain, and W. Shockley—developed the **transistor,** a small device that transfers electric signals across a resistor. (The name *transistor* began as a trademark concocted from *trans*fer plus re*sistor*.) They later received the Nobel prize for their invention. The transistor revolutionized electronics in general and computers in particular. Transistors were much smaller than vacuum tubes, and they also had numerous other advantages: They needed no warm-up time, they consumed less energy, and they were faster and more reliable.

During this generation another important development was the move from machine language to **assembly languages,** which are also called **symbolic languages.** Assembly languages use abbreviations for instructions (for example, *L* for *LOAD*) rather than numbers. This made programming less cumbersome.

After the development of symbolic languages came **higher-level languages.** The first language to receive widespread acceptance was **FORTRAN** (for FORmula TRANslator), which was developed in the mid-1950s as a scientific, mathematical, and engineering language. Then in 1959 **COBOL** (an acronym for COmmon Business-Oriented Language) was introduced for business programming. Both languages, still widely used today, are more English-like than assembly language. Higher-level languages allowed programmers to give more attention to solving problems. They no longer had to cope with all the details of the machines themselves. Also, in 1962 the first removable disk pack was marketed. Disk storage supplemented magnetic tape systems and enabled users to have fast access to data.

All these new developments made the second generation of computers less costly to operate—and thus began a surge of growth in computer systems. In 1960 Bethlehem Steel became the first corporation to use a computer on a real-time basis to handle orders, inventories, and production control. In 1963 the *Daily Oklahoman–Oklahoma City Times* became the first newspaper to use the computer to set type for all its articles as well as for classified advertising. In 1964 American Airlines instituted a real-time reservation system. Throughout this period, however, computers were being used principally by business, university, and government organizations. They had not filtered down to the general public. The real part of the revolution was about to begin.

## The Third Generation: 1965–1970: The Integrated Circuit

One of the most abundant elements in the earth's crust is silicon, a nonmetallic substance found in common beach sand as well as in practically all rocks and clay. The element has given rise

### AN EARLY NONBELIEVER

Many rushed to embrace computer technology, but not everyone. Listen to this voice of hesitation: "Like all other automatic gadgets, computers unfortunately also have a definite numbing influence on the human mind. Just as the car has made walking most unpopular among some members of the new generation, computers have made research people lazy. Such people often prefer to give the calculations to the computer at once rather than to spend a little time and effort in attempting to discover whether human ingenuity can so simplify them as to make a computer unnecessary."

—Mario G. Salvadori
*Mathematics, the Language of Science,* 1960

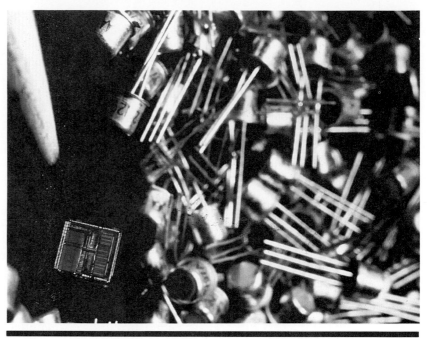

**Figure 3-14   One chip, many transistors.** The equivalent of hundreds of thousands of transistors (right) can now be placed on one tiny chip (left).

to the name *Silicon Valley* for Santa Clara County, which is about 30 miles south of San Francisco. In 1965 Silicon Valley became the principal site where the electronics industry made the so-called silicon chip: the integrated circuit.

An **integrated circuit** (IC) is a complete electronic circuit on a small chip of silicon. The chip may be less than $\frac{1}{8}$ inch square and contain hundreds of electronic components. Beginning in 1965 the integrated circuit began to replace the transistor in machines now called third-generation computers. An integrated circuit could replace an entire circuit board of transistors with one chip of silicon much smaller than one transistor (Figure 3-14).

Integrated circuits are made of silicon because it is a **semiconductor**. That is, it is a crystalline substance that will conduct electric current when it has been "doped" with chemical impurities shot into its latticelike structure. To make integrated circuits, a cylinder of silicon is sliced into wafers, each about 6 inches in diameter, and the wafer is etched repeatedly with a pattern of electrical circuitry. Several layers may be etched on a single wafer. The wafer is then cut up into several hundred small chips, each with a complete circuit so tiny it is half the size of a human fingernail—yet under a microscope the circuit looks as complex as a railroad yard. A chip 1 centimeter square is so powerful it can hold 10,000 words—the length of a daily newspaper. The making of a chip is examined in more detail in Gallery 1.

## THE COMPUTER MUSEUM

The Computer Museum in downtown Boston, Massachusetts, is the world's first and only museum devoted solely to computers and computing. The museum illustrates how computers have affected all aspects of life: science, business, education, art, and entertainment. Over half an acre of hands-on and historical exhibits chronicle the enormous changes in the size, capability, applications, and cost of computers over the past 40 years. Two mini-theaters show computer classics as well as award-winning computer-animated films.

The Computer Museum Store offers a large selection of such unique items as state-of-the-art silicon chip jewelry and chocolate "chips" as well as books, posters, cassettes, and more.

—courtesy of The Computer Museum

Integrated circuits entered the market with the simultaneous announcement in 1959 by Texas Instruments and Fairchild Semiconductor that they had each independently produced chips containing several complete electronic circuits. The chips were hailed as a generational breakthrough because they have four desirable characteristics:

- **Reliability.** They can be used over and over again without failure. Whereas vacuum tubes failed every 15 minutes, chips rarely fail—perhaps once in 33 million hours of operation. This reliability is due not only to the fact that they have no moving parts but also to the fact that semiconductor firms give them a rigid work/no-work test.

- **Compactness.** Circuitry packed into a small space reduces the equipment size. The machine speed is increased because circuits are closer together, thereby reducing the travel time for the electricity.

- **Low cost.** Mass-production techniques have made the manufacture of inexpensive integrated circuits possible. That is, miniaturization has allowed manufacturers to produce many chips inexpensively.

- **Low power use.** Miniaturization of integrated circuits has meant that less power is required for computer use than was required in previous generations. In an energy-conscious time, this is important.

The small-is-beautiful revolution moved from the integrated circuits of 1965 to **large-scale integration (LSI)** in 1970. Thousands of integrated circuits were crammed onto a single ¼-inch square of silicon.

The beginning of the third generation was trumpeted by the IBM 360 series (named for 360°—a full circle of service), first announced April 7, 1964 (Figure 3-15). The System/360 family of computers, designed for both business and scientific use, came in several models and sizes. The equipment housing was blue, and that fact led to IBM's nickname, Big Blue. IBM also offered about 40 different kinds of input, output, and secondary storage devices. All were compatible so customers could put together systems tailor-made to their needs and data-processing budgets.

The 360 series was launched with an all-out, massive marketing effort to make computers a business tool—to get them into medium-size and smaller business and government operations where they had not been used before. The result went beyond IBM's wildest dreams. The reported $5 billion the company invested in the development of the System/360 quickly repaid itself, and the system rendered many existing computer systems obsolete. Big Blue was on its way.

Software became more sophisticated during this third generation. For the first time several programs could run in the same time

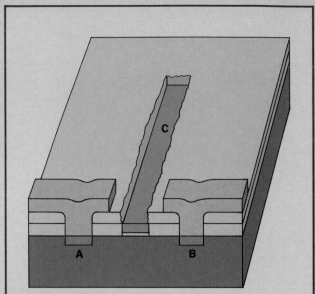

**(a) Transistor off**

**KEY:**

 Positively doped silicon base

Silicon dioxide

Negatively doped silicon

Pathway C

Circuit pathway

→ Direction of electrical charge along pathway C

→ Direction of electrical charge along circuit pathway

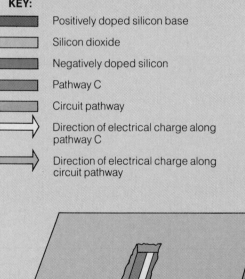

**(b) Transistor on**

**C**omputer power in the hands of the people—we take it for granted now, but not so long ago computers existed only in enormous rooms behind locked doors. The revolution that changed all that was ignited by chips of silicon smaller than your fingernail. Silicon is one of the most common elements found on earth, but there is nothing commonplace about designing, manufacturing, testing, and packaging silicon chips. The collage shown on the opening page includes key elements of the process that we shall explore in this gallery.

## The Idea Behind the Chip

Microchips form the lightning-quick "brain" of a computer. However, these complex devices ultimately work on a very simple principle: they "know" when the electric current is on and when it is off. They process information coded as a series of "on-off" electrical signals. Before the invention of microchips, these electrical signals were controlled by thousands of separate devices laboriously wired together to form an electronic circuit. Then came a revolutionary idea—the various components of a circuit could be created on a single silicon microchip, forming an integrated circuit.

Silicon is a semiconductor—it conducts electricity only "semi"-well. This does not sound like such an admirable trait, but the beauty of silicon is that it can be "doped" with different materials to make it either conduct electricity well or not at all. By doping various areas of a silicon chip differently, pathways can be set up for electricity to follow, surrounded by areas that do not conduct electricity. To create these pathways, layers are added to a silicon chip, grooves are etched in the layers, and the silicon base is doped.

**(1)** This simplified illustration shows the layers and grooves within a transistor, one of thousands of circuit components on a single chip. Pathway C controls the flow of electricity through the circuit. (a) When no electrical charge is added along pathway C, electricity cannot flow along the circuit pathway from area A to area B. Thus, the transistor is "off." (b) An added charge along pathway C temporarily allows electricity to travel from area A to area B. Now the transistor is "on" and electricity can continue to other components of the circuit. The control of electricity here and elsewhere in the chip makes it possible for the computer to process information coded as "on-off" electrical signals.

2

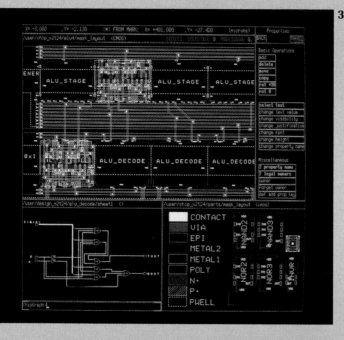

3

4

## Preparing the Design

Try to imagine figuring out a way to place thousands of circuit components next to each other so that all the layers and grooves line up and electricity flows through the whole integrated circuit the way it is supposed to. That is the job of chip designers. Essentially, they are trying to put together a gigantic multi-layered jig-saw puzzle.

The circuit design of a typical chip requires over a year's work by a team of designers. The circuitry is designed one layer at a time. Computers assist in the complex task of mapping out the most efficient electrical pathways for each circuit layer. (2) By drawing with an electronic pen on a digitizing tablet, a designer can arrange and modify circuit patterns and see them displayed on the screen. Superimposing the color-coded circuit layers allows the designer to evaluate the relationships between them. The computer allows the designer to electronically store and retrieve previously designed circuit patterns. (3) Here the designer has requested a close-up view of two small parts of one chip component, in this case the arithmetic/logic unit (abbreviated ALU on the screen display).

(4) The computer system can also provide a printed version of any or all parts of the design. This large-scale printout allows the design team to discuss and modify the entire chip design.

(5) The final design of each circuit layer must be reduced to the size of the chip. Several hundred replicas of the chip pattern are then etched on a chemically coated glass plate called a photomask. Thus, each photomask will be used to transfer the circuit layer pattern to hundreds of chips. One photomask is required for each layer of the chip. A typical chip design requires four to ten photomasks, but more complex chips may require over 15 different photomasks.

5

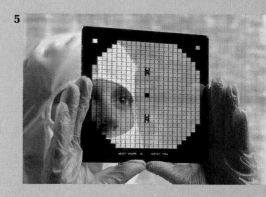

6

## Manufacturing the Chip

The silicon used to make computer chips is extracted from common rocks and sand. It is melted down into a form that is 99.9% pure silicon and then doped with chemicals to make it either electrically positive or negative. (6) The molten silicon is then "grown" into cylindrical ingots in a process similar to candle-dipping. (7) A diamond saw slices each ingot into circular wafers 4 or 6 inches in diameter and $^4/_{1000}$ of an inch thick. The wafers are sterilized and polished to a mirror-like finish. Each wafer will eventually contain hundreds of identical chips. In the photo, an engineer is holding an experimental 8-inch wafer that can produce over 2,000 chips.

Since a single speck of dust can ruin a chip, they are manufactured in special air-filtered laboratories called clean rooms. Workers dress in "bunny suits," and their laboratory is 100 times cleaner than a hospital operating room

(8) Chip manufacturing processes vary, but in one common technique, electrically positive silicon wafers are placed in an open glass tube and inserted in a 1200°C oxidation furnace. Oxygen reacts with the silicon, covering each wafer with a thin layer of silicon dioxide, which does not conduct electricity very well. Each wafer is then coated with a gelatin-like substance called photoresist, and the first photomask pattern is placed over it. Exposure to ultraviolet light hardens the photoresist, except in the areas concealed by the dark circuit pattern on the photomask.

7

8

(9) The wafer is then taken to a washing station in a specially-lit "yellow room" where it is washed in solvent to remove the soft photoresist. Next, the silicon dioxide that is revealed by the washing is etched away by hot gases. The silicon underneath, which forms the circuit pathway, is then doped to make it electrically negative. In this way the circuit pathway is distinguished electrically from the rest of the silicon. This process is repeated for each layer of the wafer, using a different photomask each time. In the final step, aluminum is deposited to connect the circuit components and form the bonding pads to which wires will later be connected.

(10) The result: a wafer with hundreds of chips. This photo shows the natural color of chips.
(11) Photographic lighting enhances this close-up view of a wafer with chips. (12) In this color-enhanced photo of a single chip on a wafer, the square and rectangular bonding pads are visible along the edges of the chip.

9

10

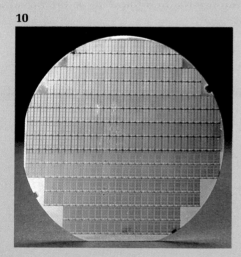

11

12

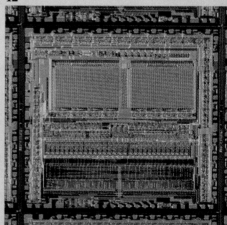

**13**

# Testing the Chip

Although chips on a particular wafer may look identical, they do not perform identically. **(13)** A probe machine must perform millions of tests on each chip, its needle-like probes contacting the bonding pads, applying electricity, measuring the results, and marking ink spots on defective chips. The probe machine determines whether the chip conducts electricity in the precise way it was designed to. **(14)** Rigorous test standards often result in high failure rates—up to 70%. Each dotted chip on this wafer has failed the testing process. **(15)** Yield analyses determine the number of chips that can be expected from each wafer. **(16)** After the initial testing a diamond saw cuts each chip from the wafer, and defective chips are discarded.

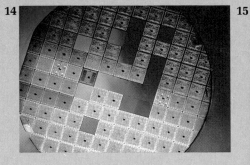

**14**

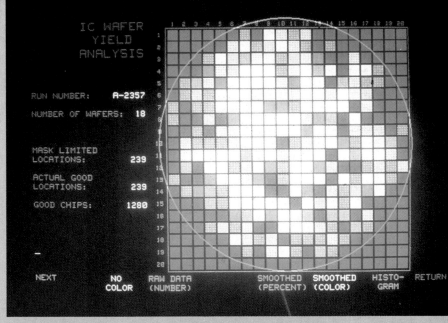

**15**

IC WAFER
YIELD
ANALYSIS

1 2 3 4 5 6 7 8 9 10 11 12 13 14 15 16 17 18 19 20

RUN NUMBER:           A-2357

NUMBER OF WAFERS:     18

MASK LIMITED
LOCATIONS:            239

ACTUAL GOOD
LOCATIONS:            239

GOOD CHIPS:           1280

NEXT        NO        RAW DATA            SMOOTHED    SMOOTHED    HISTO-      RETURN
            COLOR     (NUMBER)            (PERCENT)   (COLOR)     GRAM

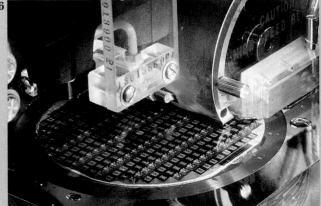

**16**

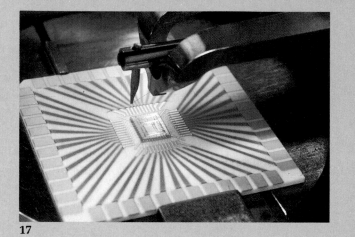

17

18

19

## Packaging the Chip

Each acceptable chip is mounted on a protective package. **(17)** An automated wire-bonding device wires the bonding pads of the chip to the electrical leads on the package, using aluminum or gold wire thinner than a human hair.

A variety of packages are in use today. **(18)** Dual in-line packages, with their double rows of legs, are currently the most common type of packaging. In this photo, the protective cap has been cut away so that we can see the chip. **(19)** Square pin-grid array packages, which are used for chips requiring more electrical leads, look like a bed of nails. Here again the protective cap has been removed, revealing the ultra-fine wires connecting the chip to the package. **(20)** Normally, the legs or pins of a package are inserted into holes in a circuit board. Some manufacturers, however, are experimenting with surface mount packages, which do not have to be inserted in circuit board holes. Instead, a machine drops the package in place on the board, where a laser or infrared beam bonds the package to the board. Another advantage of surface mount packages is that they are smaller than other packages, allowing more computing power in less space. This photo shows two surface mount packages (bottom) compared to a dual in-line package (top).

20

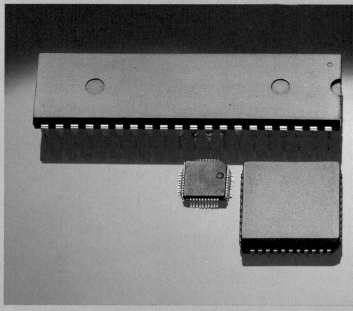

## From Chip to Computer

(21) Dual in-line packages of various sizes have been attached to this circuit board. (22) Metal lines on the board form electrical connections to the legs of the package, as shown in this color-enhanced close-up of some packages on a circuit board. (23) In the final step the board is inserted into one of the many personal computers that owe their existence to the chip. (24) This tiny device has truly brought computers into the hands of the people.

21

22

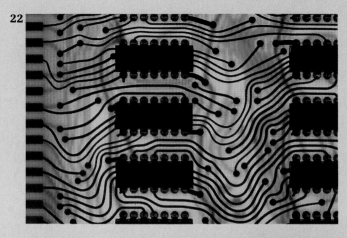

23

24

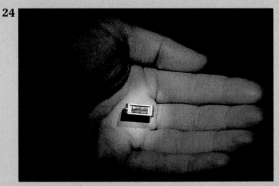

**Figure 3-15  The IBM System/ 360.** This system, which cost $5 billion to develop, marked the beginning of third-generation computer systems.

frame, sharing the computer resources—one program could be processing, another reading from a tape, and a third printing a record. This approach improved the efficiency of the computer system by decreasing CPU idle time. Software systems were developed to support interactive processing, in which the user is in direct contact with the computer through a terminal. This kind of access caused the customer-service industry to flourish, especially in areas such as reservations and credit checks.

Large third-generation computers began to be supplemented by minicomputers, which are functionally equivalent to a full-size system but are somewhat slower, smaller, and less expensive. These computers have become a huge success with medium-size and smaller businesses.

Although the beginning of the third generation can be pinpointed by the introduction of the integrated circuit, there was actually extensive overlapping of the second and third generations. Yet the distinctions between the two seem crystal clear compared with the distinctions between the third and the fourth generations.

## The Fourth Generation, 1971–Present: The Microprocessor

Through the 1970s computers gained dramatically in speed, reliability, and storage capacity, but entry into the fourth generation was evolutionary rather than revolutionary. The fourth generation was, in fact, an extension of third-generation technology.

**Figure 3-16   A microprocessor.** It is common to show a microprocessor chip near a dime or a paper clip to illustrate its small size. We coaxed a bug onto this chip. Yes, that is an ant.

That is, in the early part of the third generation, specialized chips were developed for computer memory and logic. Thus, all the ingredients were in place for the next technological development, the general-purpose processor on a chip, otherwise known as the **microprocessor** (Figure 3-16). First developed by an Intel Corporation design team headed by Ted Hoff in 1969, the microprocessor became commercially available in 1971.

Nowhere is the pervasiveness of computer power more apparent than in the explosive use of the microprocessor. In addition to common applications in digital watches, pocket calculators, and microcomputers, microprocessors can be anticipated in virtually every machine in the home or business—microwave ovens, cars, copy machines, television sets, and so on. In 1975 **very large-scale integration** (**VLSI**) was achieved. As a result computers today are 100 times smaller than those of the first generation, and a single chip is far more powerful than ENIAC.

Computer environments changed, too. Climate-controlled rooms became less necessary to ensure reliability; some recent computer models (especially microcomputers) can be placed almost anywhere.

Countries around the world have been active in the computer industry, but few are as renowned for their technology as Japan, which has announced an entirely new direction.

## The Fifth Generation: Japan's Challenge

An interesting thing happened on the way to the fifth generation: The fourth generation got lost. Experts and books about the industry acknowledged the existence of the first, second, and

## JAPAN'S PERSISTENT SOFTWARE GAP

It is a little discouraging to be told day after day that Japan is running circles around us. The Japanese are, we are told, more productive; they produce quality products that can be priced low enough to be competitive worldwide. In the computer industry they have another broad advantage: government support to the tune of millions of dollars.

But there is a chink in the armor: software. Japanese software is less sophisticated and more expensive than comparable Western software. Although the Japanese shine at computer graphics—they write top-notch programs for video arcades—they have yet to produce sophisticated business software packages. That is the catch: In the computer business, sales are driven more and more by the availability of programs rather than by the price of the hardware. So Japan's efficient computers, although priced competitively, find themselves battling global markets with a crippling disadvantage.

—from an article in *Fortune*

third generations, and all agreed about their characteristics. The beginning and end dates for the first and second generations were well established, but the third generation was rarely given an end date, and some said it was "continuing." In 1980 the Japanese made a startling announcement that signaled a bold move to take the lead in computer technology. The Japanese revealed a ten-year project to develop a so-called "fifth generation," leaving the industry scrambling to define what the fourth generation was—and is. As you have already read, the fourth generation has been tied primarily to the microprocessor.

The term **fifth generation** was coined by Japan to describe its goal of creating powerful, intelligent computers by the mid-1990s. Since then, however, it has become an umbrella term encompassing many research fields in the computer industry. Key areas of ongoing research are artificial intelligence, natural language, and expert systems. These subjects will be discussed more fully in later chapters, but we can offer simple descriptions here. As you will see, these topics are interrelated.

**Artificial intelligence** is a field of study that explores how computers can be used for tasks requiring the human characteristics of intelligence, imagination, and intuition. In other words, we would like to be able to interact with computers in ways that assume that they have more of a human nature and less of a machine nature. To do this the computer would, at the very least, need to have (1) a knowledge base equivalent to that of the average person, and (2) the ability to communicate in natural human language. Both of these are tall orders. **Natural language** refers to an everyday language—in our case, English. That is, we would like to communicate with the computer in plain English. An **expert system** is software that allows the computer to be an expert on some particular subject and be available for consulting. Expert systems already exist in disciplines like geology, chemistry, and medicine. Some expert systems use something close to natural language. Other elements listed as part of the fifth-generation push are robotics, vision systems (whereby a computer takes actions based on what it "sees"), and even new types of hardware that promise greater computer speed and power. We shall be discussing this last topic in detail in the next chapter.

Many view the fifth generation as a horse race between Japan and the United States, with nothing less than world computer supremacy as the prize. Japan's original announcement captivated the computer industry. The Japanese government and private industry have poured what amounts to hundreds of millions of dollars into this project. The real significance is not the money itself, however, but the cooperation among government and Japanese industries. It seems they have written a blank check for computer development.

There has been much speculation about whether Japan, Inc.—the name given to the project—can really succeed. Even if the total aims are never achieved, however, there are at least two results. First, there are significant side effects. Second, the American computer industry is responding to the challenge.

# The Computer Industry Diversifies

As we said, the development of the System/360 cost IBM $5 billion. Clearly, with that kind of astronomical investment, it is extraordinarily difficult for many firms to compete effectively in the mainframe market. Indeed, some big names in American industry have gone into mainframe manufacturing, then changed their minds and pulled out—among them General Electric and RCA. The survivors of the early manufacturers are Burroughs (which purchased Sperry in 1986), NCR, Honeywell, and IBM. IBM's share of the mainframe market is approaching 70%.

In the 1960s and 1970s, however, other companies emerged to give IBM a run for its money. One was Control Data Corporation (CDC). Another was Cray, formed by Seymour Cray, formerly with CDC, who developed the supercomputer called the Cray-1 and, later, the Cray-2.

Hundreds of other manufacturers have entered the computer industry in ventures requiring less capital outlay than the mainframe business. Today a wide range of diverse products and services are offered, including mini- and microcomputers, peripheral equipment, software, and various service industries. Many companies provide specific support for particular aspects of the industry such as data communications or word processing. Digital Equipment Corporation and Hewlett–Packard began the trend to minicomputers in the early 1970s. Microcomputers joined the scene in the late 1970s.

# The Special Story of Microcomputers

Microcomputers are the machines you can "get closest to," whether you are an amateur or a professional. There is nothing quite like having your very own personal computer. Its history is very personal too, full of stories of success and failure, and of individuals with whom we can readily identify.

### I Built It in My Garage

The very first microcomputer was the MITS Altair, produced in 1975. But it was a gee-whiz machine for an obscure technical audience, with lots of switches and dials—and no keyboard or screen! It took two teenagers, Steve Jobs and Steve Wozniak, to capture the imagination of the public with the first Apple computer. They built it in that time-honored place of inventors, a garage, using the $1,300 proceeds from the sale of an old Volkswagen. Designed for home use, the Apple was the first to offer an easy-to-use keyboard

**(a)**

**(b)**

**(c)**

**Figure 3-17   The making of Apple Computer, Inc.** (a) Steve Jobs (left) and Steve Wozniak, cofounders of Apple, examining parts of their home-built Apple I computer. This photograph was taken in early 1976 in Steve Jobs's bedroom, their first business headquarters. (b) Shown here is a collector's item—the very first manual for "operation" of an Apple computer. Unfortunately, the early manuals were a hodgepodge of circuit diagrams, software listings, and handwritten notes. They were hard to read and understand and almost guaranteed to frighten away all but the most hearty souls. (c) The Apple II microcomputer became the foundation of the company.

and screen (Figure 3-17). The company they founded in 1977 was immediately and wildly successful. When its stock was offered to the public in December 1980, it started a stampede among investors anxious to buy in. The Apple II and versions IIe and IIc continue to sell well, as does the Macintosh.

The other major player in those early years was Tandy Incorporated, whose worldwide chain of Radio Shack stores provided a handy sales outlet for the TRS-80 microcomputer. Other manufacturers who enjoyed more than moderate success in the late 1970s were Atari and Commodore. Their number was to grow.

### The Microcomputer Entrepreneurs

Ever thought you would like to run your own show? Make your own product? Be in business for yourself? Entrepreneurs are a special breed. They are achievement-oriented, like to take responsibility for decisions, and dislike repetitive, routine work. They also have high levels of energy and a great deal of imagination. But perhaps the key is that they are willing to take risks. Entrepreneurs often have still another quality—a more elusive quality—that is something close to charisma. This charisma is based on enthusiasm, and it allows them to lead people and to form an organization and give it momentum. Study these entrepreneurs, noting their paths to glory.

#### Ed Roberts

Ed Roberts was a worried man. Like other entrepreneurs before him, he had taken a big risk. He had already been burned once, and now he feared being burned again. The first time, in the early 1970s, he had borrowed heavily to produce microprocessor-based calculators, only to have the chip producers decide to build their own product—and sell them for half the price of Ed's calculator.

But now, this new product, this was different. It was based on a microprocessor too—the Intel 8080—but it was a *computer*. A little computer. The "big boys" at the established computer firms considered their machines to be an industrial product and everyone knew that big business needed big computers. Besides, who would want a small computer? Who, indeed!

Ed was not sure that anyone would want one either, but he found the idea so compelling that he decided to make the computer anyway. Besides, he was so far in debt from the calculator fiasco that it did not seem to matter which project propelled him into bankruptcy. Ed's small computer was given a sharp boost by Les Solomon, who promised to feature the new machine on the cover of *Popular Electronics*. Ed worked frantically to meet the publication deadline, and he even tried to make the machine pretty, so it would look attractive on the cover.

Making a good-looking small computer was not easy. This machine, although named the *Altair* (after a heavenly "Star Trek" destination), looked like a flat box. In fact, it met the definition of a computer in only a minimal way; it had a central processing unit (on the chip), 256 characters

(a paragraph!) of memory, and switches and lights on a front panel for input and output. No screen, no keyboard, and no storage.

But it was done on time for the January 1975 issue and Roberts made plans to fly to New York to demonstrate the machine to Solomon. He sent the computer on ahead by Railway Express. Ed got to New York, but the computer did not—the very first microcomputer was lost! There was no time to build a new computer before the publishing deadline, so Roberts cooked up a phony version for the cover picture: an empty box with switches and lights on the front panel. He also placed an inch-high ad in the back of the magazine: your own Altair kit for $397.

Ed was hoping for perhaps 200 orders. But the machine—that is, the box—fired imaginations across the country. Two thousand customers sent a check for $397 to an unknown company in Albuquerque, New Mexico, for the MITS Altair microcomputer kit. It was an overnight, runaway success.

#### Steve Jobs

Of the two Steves who formed Apple Computer, Steve Jobs was the classic entrepreneur. Although they were both interested in electronics, Steve Wozniak was the technical genius, and he would have been happy to have been left alone to tinker. But Steve Jobs would not let him alone for a minute—he was always pushing and crusading. In

fact, Wozniak had hooked up with an evangelist, and they made quite a pair.

In 1976 when Apple was getting off the ground, Jobs wanted Wozniak to quit his job so he could work full time on the new venture. Wozniak refused. Jobs begged, Jobs cried—Wozniak gave in. While Wozniak built Apple computers, Jobs was out hustling, finding the best marketing man, the best venture capitalist, and the best company president. This entrepreneurial spirit paid off in a spectacular way, as Apple rose to the top of microcomputer companies.

### Bill Gates

When Bill Gates was a teenager, he swore off computers for a year and, in his words, "tried to act normal." His parents, who wanted him to be a lawyer, must have been relieved when Bill gave up the computer foolishness and went off to Harvard in 1974. But Bill started spending weekends with his friend Paul Allen, and they dreamed about microcomputers, which did not exist

yet. When the MITS Altair splashed on the market in January 1975, both Bill and Paul moved to Albuquerque to be near the action at MITS. But they showed a desire even then to chart their own course. Although they wrote software for MITS— and Paul was actually employed there—they kept the rights to their work and formed their own company. Their company was called Microsoft.

When MITS failed, Gates and Allen moved their software company back home to Bellevue, Washington. When IBM came to call in 1980, Microsoft employed 32 people. Gates recognized the big leagues when he saw them and put on a suit. IBM offered a plum: the operating system (a crucial set of software) for IBM's soon-to-be microcomputer. Although he knew he was betting the whole company, Gates never hesitated to take the risk. He and his crew worked feverishly for many months to produce MS-DOS—Microsoft Disk Operating System. It was this product that started Microsoft on its meteoric rise.

### Mitch Kapor

Kapor did not start out on a direct path to computer fame and riches. In fact, he wandered; he was a disk jockey, a piano teacher, and a counselor. Along the way he picked up and then abandoned transcendental meditation. He had done some programming too but did not like it much. But, around 1978, he found he did like fooling around with microcomputers. In fact, he had found his niche.

In 1983 Kapor introduced a software package called Lotus 1-2-3 and there had never been anything like it before. Lotus added the words *integrated package* to the vocabulary: Lotus 1-2-3 was a combination of spreadsheet, graphics, and database programs. Kapor's company catapulted to the top of the list of independent software makers in just two years.

### Champions of Change

Entrepreneurs thrive on change. Jobs and Wozniak left Apple to start new companies. Kapor left Lotus in 1986 to "explore other endeavors." Stay tuned for future breakthroughs from these and other microcomputer entrepreneurs.

# 7 The IBM PC Phenomenon

When IBM announced its first microcomputer in the summer of 1981, Apple placed full-page advertisements in the trade press that said:

**WELCOME, IBM!**

**SERIOUSLY.**

This was a sincere but not entirely altruistic gesture by Apple. Confident about its industry position and head start, Apple felt that IBM's entry into the market would give microcomputers a more serious image, and thus help Apple. Apple's vision was correct, but not complete; IBM captured the top market share in just 18 months, and even more important, became the industry standard (Figure 3-18). This was indeed a phenomenal success.

IBM did a lot of things right, including the possibility of a larger memory, but one key decision made the significant difference: open architecture. That is, IBM provided internal expansion slots so that manufacturers of peripheral equipment could build accessories for the IBM PC. In addition, IBM provided hardware schematics and software listings to companies who wanted to build products in conjunction with the new PC. Many of the new products accelerated demand for the IBM PC.

There is an interesting irony here. Apple pioneered the open architecture concept. IBM had always had closed architecture for its larger machines, but went to open architecture for the PC. Apple, however, having observed success for both themselves and IBM, then turned around and produced its new Macintosh microcom-

**Figure 3-18   The IBM PC.** Launched in 1981, the IBM PC took just 18 months to rise to the top of the best-seller list.

puter as a *closed* architecture machine! This made it difficult for peripheral equipment manufacturers to design add-ons for the Mac. Heavy advertising and fast scrambling saved the Macintosh, but nothing could save Steve Jobs's job. The closed architecture decision was his, and he—a founding father—was removed from all operational responsibilities in 1985. He then left Apple to start a new computer company called Next Inc.

Other microcomputer manufacturers have hurried to emulate IBM, producing PC clones—copycat computers that will run software designed for the IBM PC. Meanwhile, IBM has offered both upscale and downscale versions of its personal computer, carefully marketing all of them with some version of the original name: PC Convertible, PC XT, PC Portable, PC AT, PC RT, and, of course, the ill-fated PCjr. Despite a heavy advertising budget and Charlie Chaplin wheeling the PCjr in a baby carriage, IBM could not recover from the initial design flaws in the PCjr: a flimsy keyboard and insufficient memory. This failure left many surprised customers with orphan computers, but it caused hardly a ripple in IBM's financial picture, which continued to be rosy. Not everyone, however, was so fortunate.

## The Big Shakeout

The personal computer industry grew to about 150 manufacturers in the early 1980s. What is more, an enormous industry developed around the personal computer: manufacturers of peripheral equipment, software producers, computer dealers, and computer magazines. Despite optimistic predictions, sluggish sales and sagging profits brought high-tech industries back to earth. After years of a seemingly unstoppable joyride, the personal computer industry began to experience a period of slowed growth in 1983.

The companies that raised venture capital to jump into the fray now had to scramble to survive in the ensuing bruising competition. Some did not survive. In fact, through the mid-1980s, hundreds of dealers and dozens of manufacturers closed their doors or opened new ones. Companies like Timex, Mattel, and Coleco simply dropped their computer lines, but others, like Gavilan and Beehive, filed for bankruptcy. Meanwhile, the number of computer magazines plummeted from some 150 in 1983 to about 40.

Least affected is the software industry, because almost 20 million personal computers are already in use. This established customer base continues to hunger for more sophisticated software. You could compare this to the home music industry where, even if sales of stereos and tape decks slowed, there would still be customers for more records and tapes.

There is really nothing very wrong with the personal computer industry. The problem is that too many people tried to partake and the market was not bottomless after all. Natural competition, as in other businesses, weeds out the weakest. History shows that many industries go through an exuberant expansion phase followed by a shakeout.

The story of microcomputer history is ongoing, with daily fluctuations reflected in the trade press. The effects of microcomputers are far-reaching, and, as such, they will remain a key topic throughout the book. We shall describe their current status in more detail in Chapter 13.

# Software Comes of Age

It is tempting to talk of computer history in terms of the machines because the changes have been so dramatic and so visually obvious. But hardware is nothing without software, and software has its own history.

## The Early Years: 1950–1964

Few realized the potential of software during its early years. In those days computers were used as fast, stupid clerks. They performed clerical tasks such as keeping track of payrolls and airplane seats. Some people fantasized about a giant "brain," but most people continued to see computers in clerical roles. Computers belonged only to large organizations that could afford their own programmers to produce software. In addition, each program was unique. There was no software industry.

## Growing Pains: 1965–1980

Something really new happened in the world of software: interactive systems. These systems allowed a dialogue to take place between people and computers—users could enter queries or data into the computer and get an immediate response. Interactive systems could respond to input so fast that they could do better work than humans, even though the work was still clerical. Military applications were first: Radar and missiles linked by a computer could aim and fire faster than humans and with greater accuracy. Civilian applications such as air-traffic control and banking followed. By 1980 interactive software was popular on the personal computer. Word processing and computer games enjoyed immense popularity, followed soon by a variety of business programs.

During this period people began to realize that many programs, such as payroll, could be generic. That is, the same program could be used by many different users. This meant that software could be packaged and sold, and the result was a new industry: the software industry (Figure 3-19).

**Figure 3-19   Packaged software.** Early software was developed for the needs of a specific organization. Now most software for microcomputers, and a significant amount for larger computers too, is a standard purchased package.

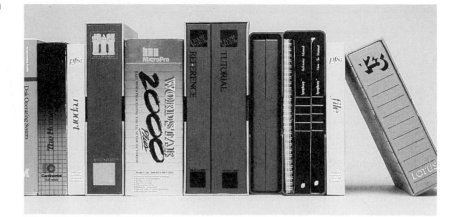

### Adolescence: 1981–1995

Software moved into a new era and now shows the promise of much more versatility. Software is written to mimic human behavior, acting as keeper of a knowledge base. Rather than being limited to interactive, clerical tasks, software—to an increasing degree—can respond to imprecise, unpredictable, human types of problems, acting the way a human would with a certain set of information. Computer-assisted medical diagnosis uses this kind of software, software that brings us close to the field of artificial intelligence. Notice that the dates for this section slip past the present date; we have gone beyond history. Let us take one step further into the future.

### Maturity: 1996 and Beyond

Using computer software we shall be able to do just about anything. We shall be able to point to the computer or speak to it and, with minimum effort on our part, give the computer enough data so it can produce the results we want.

## From the Whole to the Parts

History is still being made in the computer industry, of course, and it is being made incredibly rapidly. A book cannot possibly pretend to describe all the very latest developments. Nevertheless, as we indicated earlier, the four areas of input, processing, output, and storage describe the basic components of a computer system—whatever its date.

In the next three chapters we consider these, beginning with the most fundamental, the processor.

## Summary and Key Terms

- Charles Babbage, a nineteenth-century mathematician, is called the father of the computer. His **difference engine,** which was designed to solve polynomial equations, led to another calculating machine, the **analytical engine,** which embodied the key parts of a computer system—an input device, a processor, a control unit, a storage place, and an output device.

- Babbage used an invention by Frenchman Joseph Jacquard, who devised a punched card for weavers working on looms. Ada Lovelace helped develop instructions for carrying out computations on Babbage's device.

- The first computer to use electrical power instead of mechanical power was Herman Hollerith's tabulating machine, which was used in the 1890 census in the United States. Hollerith founded a company that became the forerunner of International Business Machines Corporation (IBM).

- Thomas J. Watson, Sr., built IBM into a dominant force in the business machines market. He also gave Harvard professor Howard Aiken research funds with which to build the **Mark I** computer, unveiled in 1944.

- John V. Atanasoff with his assistant, Clifford Berry, devised the first digital computer to work by electronic means, the **ABC,** or **Atanasoff–Berry Computer.**

- Dr. John Mauchly at the University of Pennsylvania and his assistant, J. Presper Eckert, Jr., used ABC principles to build the ENIAC. The **ENIAC** (Electronic Numerical Integrator And Computer), first operational in 1946, was the first general-purpose electronic computer.

- John von Neumann devised the **stored program concept,** by which a computer could switch to a new program by reading instructions from computer storage. This principle was successfully used on the **EDVAC** (Electronic Discrete Variable Automatic Computer).

- The Computer Age consists of four generations, which are primarily defined by four technological developments: the vacuum tube (1951 to 1958), the transistor (1959 to 1964), the integrated circuit (1965 to 1970), and the microprocessor (1971 to the present).

- The first generation began on June 14, 1951, with

the delivery of the **UNIVAC** (UNIVersal Automatic Computer) to the U.S. Bureau of the Census. First-generation computers required thousands of **vacuum tubes,** electronic tubes about the size of light bulbs.

- First-generation computers had slow input and output, were programmed only in machine language (rather than English-like higher-level languages), and were unreliable and expensive. The main form of memory was **magnetic core.** Data was also stored on punched cards. Magnetic tape was introduced in 1957 as a faster, more compact storage method.

- The **transistor,** developed at Bell Laboratories, was much smaller than a vacuum tube, needed no warm-up, consumed less energy, and was faster and more reliable. During the second generation, **assembly languages,** or **symbolic languages,** were developed. They used abbreviations for instructions. Later, **higher-level languages,** such as **FORTRAN** (FORmula TRANslator) and **COBOL** (COmmon Business-Oriented Language), which are more English-like than machine language, were also developed. In 1962 the first removable disk pack was marketed.

- The third generation emerged with the introduction of the **integrated circuit** (IC)—a complete electronic circuit on a small chip of silicon. Silicon is a **semiconductor,** a substance that will conduct electric current when it has been "doped" with chemical impurities. A cylinder of silicon is sliced into wafers, which are then etched with a pattern of electrical circuitry and cut up into several hundred individual chips. Integrated circuits were hailed as a generational breakthrough because they have these four desirable characteristics: reliability, compactness, low cost, and low power use.

- The integrated circuits of 1965 progressed by 1970 to **large-scale integration** (LSI), with thousands of integrated circuits on a single chip.

- With the third generation IBM announced the System/360 computers, a family that consisted of several models and sizes.

- During this period more sophisticated software was introduced that allowed several programs to run in the same time frame. Manufacturers also supported interactive processing, in which the user has direct contact with the computer through a terminal.

- The fourth-generation **microprocessor**—a general-purpose processor on a chip—grew out of the specialized memory and logic chips of the third generation. In 1975 **very large-scale integration (VLSI)** was achieved—a single chip was far more powerful than ENIAC. Microprocessors led to the development of microcomputers, which expanded computer markets to smaller businesses and to personal use.

- In 1980 Japanese government and industry began collaborating on a ten-year project to develop a **fifth generation**—radically new forms of computer systems involving artificial intelligence, natural language, and expert systems. **Artificial intelligence** is a field of study that explores computer involvement in tasks requiring intelligence, imagination, and intuition. Research on computer use of **natural language** (everyday human language) would lead to easier interaction between people and computer systems. The development of **expert systems** (software that allows computers to be experts on particular subjects) would enable computers to serve as consultants.

- The first microcomputer, the MITS Altair, was produced in 1975. However, the first microcomputer to offer an easy-to-use keyboard and screen was the Apple computer, developed by Steve Jobs and Steve Wozniak. Their successful company was founded in 1977. Soon other companies, such as Tandy Incorporated and Commodore, entered the microcomputer market.

- IBM entered the market in 1981. The main factor in IBM's success was its policy of open architecture—providing internal expansion slots for accessories.

- From 1950 to 1964 software was used mainly by large organizations to enable computers to perform clerical tasks. The period from 1965 to 1980 saw the development of interactive software, which enabled computers to respond to input data more efficiently than people could. Increased applications of computer software, including word processing and business programs, led to the development of the software industry. Since 1981 software applications have continued to increase, with promise of even greater versatility in the future.

## Review Questions

1. Explain the contributions of the following people to the development of computers in the preelectronic era: Charles Babbage, Joseph Jacquard, Ada Lovelace, Herman Hollerith, Thomas J. Watson, Sr.

2. Explain the contributions of: Howard Aiken; John V. Atanasoff and Clifford Berry; John Mauchly and J. Presper Eckert, Jr.; John von Neumann.

3. Explain the significance of the following computers: Mark I, ABC, ENIAC, EDVAC, UNIVAC.

4. Name and define the main technological development associated with the first generation of computers.

5. Name at least three disadvantages of the first-generation computers.

6. What was the medium for memory in first-generation computers? What replaced this storage medium and why?

7. What main technological development is associated with the second generation of computers? How did this development revolutionize computers?

8. Explain how machine language, assembly language, and higher-level language differ.

9. Name and define the main technological development associated with the third generation of computers.

10. What are the four desirable characteristics of integrated circuits?

11. What do LSI and VLSI mean in relation to a silicon chip?

12. Name and define the main technological development associated with the fourth generation of computers.

13. Name and describe three areas of research associated with the fifth generation.

14. Describe the history of the microcomputer industry.

15. Describe the four stages in the history of software.

## Discussion Questions

1. How would our world be different if the Computer Age had never begun? Give specific examples.

2. How do you feel about the possibility of computers that can "think" and speak? Explain.

3. What do you think will be the future of the personal computer industry? Explain.

# 4

# The Central Processing Unit

## Under the Hood

The problem-solving part of the computer is the central processing unit, made up of the control unit (which directs the computer system) and the arithmetic/logic unit (which controls arithmetic and logical operations). Memory holds data and instructions for processing. Registers, addresses, storage capacity, coding schemes, and types of memory are also explained in this chapter.

Have you ever wondered what is inside a computer? How does a computer work, anyway? In this chapter we shall take a peek inside the computer to look at how it operates. You may be thinking that you do not really need to know how a computer works, but there are rewards for the computer user who chooses to dig a little deeper. For one thing, there is the satisfaction of knowing what is going on inside the "mysterious" machine you use. For another, knowledge of how the computer works can enhance your use of the computer. Finally, familiarity with the subject matter in this chapter could help you make more informed choices about selecting options for a new computer system.

Let us begin by seeing how the central processing unit works to change raw data into information. This is a very complex process, which we have tried to simplify here. Even so, you will find this is one of the more technical chapters, with a number of new terms. Once you get beyond this point, however, the going should be easier.

# The Central Processing Unit

The central processing unit is the part of the computer whose operations we cannot see. The human connection is the data input and the information output, but the controlling center of the computer is in between. The **central processing unit (CPU)** is a highly complex, extensive set of electrical circuitry that executes stored program instructions. As Figure 4-1 shows, it consists of two parts:

- The control unit
- The arithmetic/logic unit

Before we discuss the control unit and the arithmetic/logic unit in detail, we need to briefly consider the kinds of data storage associated with the computer and explain their relationship to the CPU.

Computers actually use two types of storage components: primary storage and secondary storage. The CPU interacts closely with **primary storage,** or **memory,** referring to it for both instructions and data. For this reason memory will be discussed with the CPU in this chapter. Technically, however, memory is not part of the CPU.

Memory holds data only temporarily, at the time the computer is executing your program. **Secondary storage** holds data that is permanent or semipermanent on some external magnetic or optical medium. The diskettes that you have seen with personal computers are an example of secondary storage. Since the physical attributes of secondary storage devices are related to the way data is organized on them, we will discuss secondary storage and data organization together in Chapter 6.

Now, let us consider the components of the central processing unit.

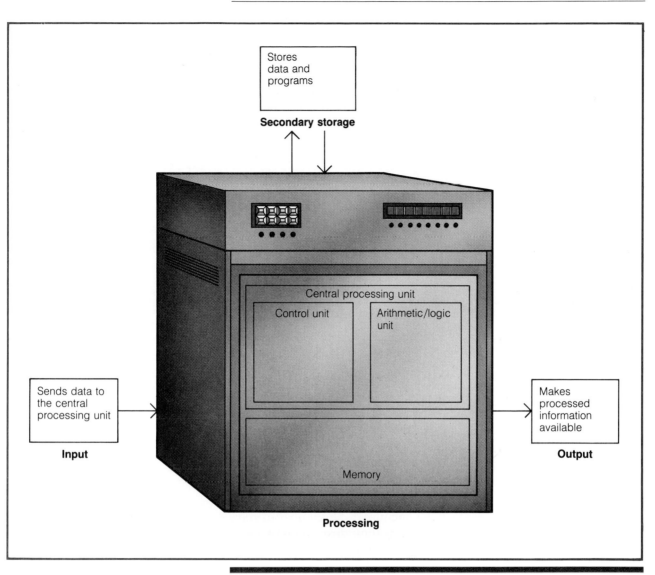

**Figure 4-1   The central processing unit.** The two parts of the CPU are the control unit and the arithmetic/logic unit. Memory holds data and instructions temporarily at the time the program is being executed. The CPU interacts closely with memory, referring to it for both instructions and data.

## The Control Unit

The **control unit** contains circuitry that, with electrical signals, directs and coordinates the entire computer system in carrying out, or executing, stored program instructions. Like an orchestra leader, the control unit does not execute the instructions itself; rather, it directs other parts of the system to do so. The control unit must communicate with both the arithmetic/logic unit and memory.

## The Arithmetic/Logic Unit

The **arithmetic/logic unit** (ALU) contains the electronic circuitry that executes all arithmetic operations and logical operations.

Four kinds of **arithmetic operations,** or mathematical calculations, can be performed on data by this unit:

- Addition
- Subtraction
- Multiplication
- Division

To be strictly accurate, the ALU can only add and multiply; the subtraction and division operations are actually complements of addition and multiplication, respectively. However, for all practical purposes, we can think of the ALU as being capable of these four basic arithmetic operations.

**Logical operations** are usually comparing operations. The arithmetic/logic unit is able to compare numbers, letters, or special characters and take alternative courses of action. This is a very important capability. It is by comparing that a computer is able to tell, for instance, whether there are unfilled seats on airplanes, whether charge-card customers have exceeded their credit limits, and whether one candidate for Congress has more votes than another.

There are three basic comparing operations:

- **Equal to (=) condition:** The arithmetic/logic unit compares two values to determine if they are equal. For example: If the number of tickets sold *equals* the number of seats in the auditorium, then the concert is declared sold out.

- **Less than (<) condition:** In this logical operation the computer compares values to determine if one is less than another. For example: If the number of speeding tickets on this driver's record is *less than* three, then insurance rates are $425; otherwise, the rates are $500.

- **Greater than (>) condition:** A comparison that determines if one value is greater than another. For instance: If the hours this person worked this week are *greater than* 40, then multiply every extra hour by $1\frac{1}{2}$ times the usual hourly wage to compute overtime pay.

These three comparing operations may be combined to form a total of six commonly used operations: equal to, less than, greater than, less than or equal to, greater than or equal to, and less than or greater than. Note that "less than or greater than" is the same as "not equal to." (These comparing operations are used frequently in the decision boxes in flowcharts, as we will show in Chapter 8.)

## Registers: Temporary Storage Areas

**Registers** are temporary storage areas for instructions or data. Registers are associated with the CPU, not memory. They are

## CHIPS GOOD ENOUGH TO EAT

Potato chips, that is. Making a crunchier potato chip is not as easy as you think. It requires the services of structural, electrical, and chemical engineers—and the power of a computer. Potato chips are big business; Americans nibble away over $2 billion worth every year. When front-runner Frito–Lay's marketing research showed that some munchers want a still crunchier chip, they put nearly 200 scientists to work designing and developing it.

The new potato chip was designed by a computer. Engineers started with the Ruffles wavy-form potato chip. They gave the computer varied dimensions for wave height, frequency, and starting point, then had the computer play back the combinations. The optimum chip has a surface that is not too thick and flat (to avoid long frying times) and not too wavy (to avoid breakage).

The final result, christened the O'Grady Chip, is a wavy chip whose upslope is thick to supply crunchiness and whose downslope is thin to supply the fragility. Frito–Lay is very proud of their first computer-generated chip, which they think should satisfy the most macho masticator.

special additional storage locations whose advantage is speed. They can operate very rapidly in accepting, holding, and transferring instructions or data or in performing arithmetic or logical comparisons—all under the direction of the control unit of the CPU. In other words, they are temporary storage areas that assist transfers and arithmetic/logical operations.

Many machines assign special roles to certain registers, including:

- An **accumulator,** which collects the results of computations.

- A **storage register,** which temporarily holds data taken from or about to be sent to memory.

- An **address register,** which tells where each instruction and each piece of data is being stored in memory. Each storage location in memory is identified by an **address,** just as each apartment in an apartment building is identified by an address.

- A **general-purpose register,** which is used for several functions—arithmetic and addressing purposes, for example.

Consider registers in the context of the operation of the entire machine. Registers hold data *immediately* related to the operation being executed. Memory is used to store data that will be used in the *near future.* Secondary storage holds data that may be needed *later* in this same program execution or perhaps at some more remote time in the future. Let us look at a payroll program, for example, as the computer calculates the salary of an employee. As the multiplication of hours worked by rate of pay is about to take place, these two figures are ready in their respective registers. Other data related to the salary calculation—overtime hours, bonuses, deductions, and so forth—is waiting nearby in memory. The data for other employees is available on secondary storage. As the computer continues executing the payroll program, the data for the next employee is brought from secondary storage into memory. Eventually, the data is brought into the registers as the calculations for that employee are ready to begin.

## Memory

Memory is also known as **primary storage, primary memory, main storage, internal storage,** and **main memory**—all these terms are used interchangeably by people in computer circles. Memory is the part of the computer that holds data and instructions for processing. Although closely associated with the CPU, memory is technically separate from it. Memory is used only temporarily—it holds your program and data only as long as your program is in operation. It is not feasible to keep your program and data in memory when your program is not running for three reasons:

- Most types of memory keep data only while the computer is turned on (that is, the data is destroyed when the machine is turned off).

- If your computer is a shared one, other people will be using the computer and will need the memory space.

- There may not be enough room in memory to hold your processed data.

Data and instructions from an input device are put into memory by the control unit. Data is then sent from memory to the arithmetic/logic unit, where an arithmetic operation or logical operation is performed. After being processed the information is sent to memory, where it is held until it is ready to be released to an output unit.

The chief characteristic of memory is that it allows very fast access to data and instructions in any location in it. We shall discuss the physical components of memory—memory chips—in a later section.

## How the CPU Executes Program Instructions

Let us examine the way the central processing unit, in association with memory, executes a computer program. We shall be looking at how just one instruction in the program is executed. In fact, most computers today can execute only one instruction at a time. However, they execute that instruction very quickly. Even microcomputers can execute an instruction in one-thousandth of a second, whereas those speed demons known as supercomputers can execute an instruction in almost one-billionth of a second.

Before an instruction can be executed, program instructions and data must be placed into memory from an input device or a secondary storage device. The control unit then performs the following four steps for each instruction (Figure 4-2):

① The control unit "fetches" (gets) the instruction from memory.

② The control unit decodes the instruction (decides what it means) and gives instructions for necessary data to be moved from memory to the arithmetic/logic unit. These first two steps are called instruction time, or **I-time.**

③ The control unit directs the arithmetic/logic unit to execute

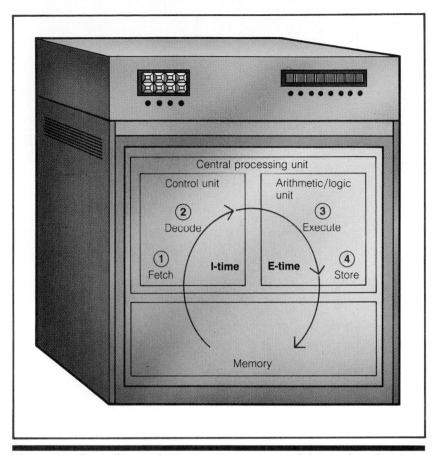

**Figure 4-2   The machine cycle.** Program instructions and data are brought into memory from an external device, either an input device or secondary storage. The machine cycle executes instructions, one at a time, as described in the text. The resulting output is then either delivered directly to an output device or placed in secondary storage.

arithmetic and logic instructions. That is, the ALU is given control and performs the actual operation on the data.

④ The control unit then directs the result of this operation to be stored in memory or a register. Steps 3 and 4 are called execution time, or **E-time.**

After the appropriate instructions are executed, the control unit directs memory to release the results to an output device or a secondary storage device. The combination of I-time and E-time is called the **machine cycle.** Figure 4-3 shows an instruction going through the machine cycle.

Each CPU has an internal **clock,** which produces pulses at a fixed rate to synchronize all computer operations. A single machine-cycle instruction may be made up of a substantial number of subinstructions, each of which must take at least one clock cycle. These

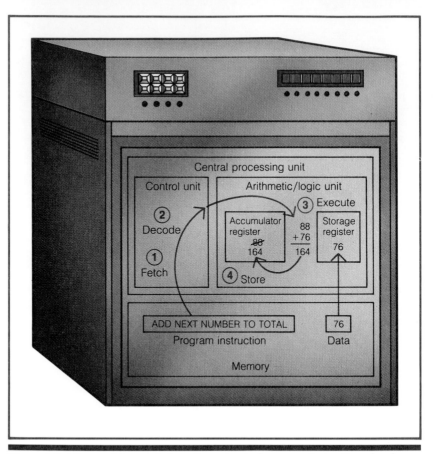

**Figure 4-3   The machine cycle in action.** A set of program instructions has been planned to find the average of five grades. To do this, the five grades must be totaled, then divided by five. One way to proceed is to set the total to zero to begin with and then add each of the five numbers, one at a time, to the total. Suppose the grades are 88, 76, 91, 83, and 87. At this point we have already zeroed the total and added 88 to it. It is time to add the next number, 76, to the total. The instruction to do so would look something like this: ADD NEXT NUMBER TO TOTAL. Now follow the steps in the machine cycle. ① The control unit fetches the instruction from memory. ② The control unit decodes the instruction. It sees that addition must take place and gives instructions for the next number (76) to be placed in a storage register for this purpose. The total so far (88) is already in an accumulator register. ③ The ALU does the addition, increasing the total to 164. ④ In this case the new total is stored in the accumulator register instead of memory since more numbers still need to be added to it. When the new total (164) is placed in the accumulator register, it erases the old total (88).

subinstructions are controlled by the **microcode.** Microcode instructions are executed directly by the computer's electronic circuits. The microcode instructions are permanently set inside the control unit; they cannot be altered. Programmers and users do not need to be concerned with microcode, even though the programmer's instructions actually invoke the microcode instructions. Neither the programmer nor user need be aware of them.

# Storage Locations and Addresses: How the Control Unit Finds Instructions and Data

It is one thing to have instructions and data somewhere in memory and quite another for the control unit to be able to find them. How does it do this?

The location in memory for each instruction and each piece of data is identified by an **address.** That is, each location has an address number, like the mailboxes in front of an apartment house or numbers on bank safe-deposit boxes. And, like the mailbox numbers, the address numbers of the locations remain the same, but the contents (data and instructions) of the locations may change. That is, new data or new instructions may be placed in the locations when the old data or instructions no longer need to be stored in memory.

Figure 4-4 shows how a program manipulates data in memory. When a payroll program is written, for example, it may give instructions to put the rate of pay in location 3 and the number of hours worked in location 6. To compute the employee's salary, then, instructions are given to multiply the data in location 3 by the data in location 6 and move the result to location 8. The choice of locations is arbitrary—any locations that are not already spoken for in the program can be used. Programmers using high-level languages, however, do not have to worry about the actual address numbers—each data address is referred to by a name, called a symbolic address. In this example symbolic address names are *Rate* and *Hours.*

**Figure 4-4 Addresses like mailboxes.** The addresses of memory locations are like the identifying numbers on apartment-house mailboxes. Suppose we want to compute someone's salary as the number of hours multiplied by rate of pay. Rate ($6) goes in memory location 3, hours (40) in location 6, and the computed salary ($6 × 40 hours, or $240) in location 8. Thus, *addresses* are 3, 6, and 8, but *contents* are $6, 40 hours, and $240. Note that the program *instructions* are to multiply the contents of location 3 by the contents of location 6 and move the result to location 8. (A computer language used by a programmer would use some kind of symbolic name for each location, such as R for Rate or Pay-Rate instead of the number 3.) The *data* is the actual contents—what is stored in each location.

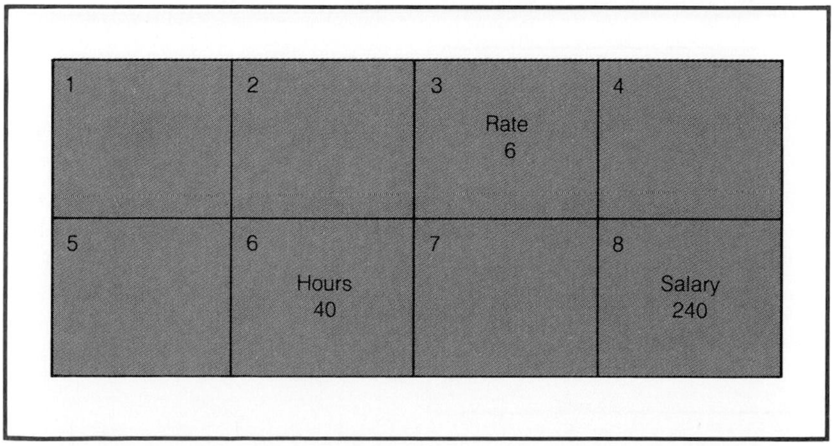

| 1 | 2 | 3 Rate 6 | 4 |
|---|---|---|---|
| 5 | 6 Hours 40 | 7 | 8 Salary 240 |

## BINARY EQUIVALENT OF DECIMAL NUMBERS 0–15

| Decimal | Binary |
|---------|--------|
| 0 | 0000 |
| 1 | 0001 |
| 2 | 0010 |
| 3 | 0011 |
| 4 | 0100 |
| 5 | 0101 |
| 6 | 0110 |
| 7 | 0111 |
| 8 | 1000 |
| 9 | 1001 |
| 10 | 1010 |
| 11 | 1011 |
| 12 | 1100 |
| 13 | 1101 |
| 14 | 1110 |
| 15 | 1111 |

**Figure 4-5  Bit as light bulb.** A light bulb operates as a binary digit, with off representing 0 and on representing 1. Light bulbs, of course, are not used in computers, but vacuum tubes, transistors, silicon chips, or anything else that can conduct an electrical signal can be used. These eight on and off bulbs represent 1 byte.

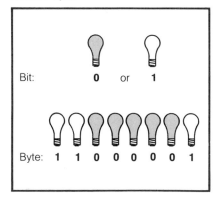

Bit:    **0**  or  **1**

Byte:  **1   1   0   0   0   0   0   1**

# Data Representation: On/Off

We are accustomed to thinking of computers as complex mechanisms, but the fact is that these machines basically know only two things: on and off. This on/off, yes/no, two-state system is called a **binary system.** Using the two states—which can be represented by electricity turned on or off—the computer can construct sophisticated ways of representing data.

Let us look at one way the two states can be used to represent data. Whereas the decimal number system has a base of 10 (with the digits 0, 1, 2, 3, 4, 5, 6, 7, 8, and 9), the binary system has a base of 2. This means it contains only two digits, 0 and 1, which correspond to the two states off and on. Combinations of 0s and 1s are used to represent larger numbers. The binary system is discussed in more detail in Appendix B.

## Bits, Bytes, and Words

Each 0 or 1 in the binary system is called a **bit** (for *b*inary dig*it*). The bit is the basic unit for storing data in computer memory—0 means off, 1 means on.

Since single bits by themselves cannot store all the numbers, letters, and special characters (such as $ and ?) that must be processed by a computer, the bits are put together in a group called a **byte** (pronounced *bite*). There are usually 8 bits in a byte (Figure 4-5). Each byte usually represents one character of data—a letter, digit, or special character.

Computer manufacturers express the capacity of memory in terms of the number of bytes it can hold. The number of bytes is expressed as **kilobytes.** *Kilo,* abbreviated as K, originally represented 2 to the tenth power ($2^{10}$), which is 1024, but the meaning has evolved. Now K stands either for 1024 or is rounded off to 1000. A kilobyte is K bytes—that is, 1024 bytes. Kilobyte is abbreviated **KB.** Thus, the memory of a 2KB computer can store 2 × 1024, or 2048 bytes. Memory capacity may also be expressed in **megabytes** (**MB**), or millions of bytes (*mega* means million). Recently some large computers have expressed memory in terms of **gigabytes**—billions of bytes—abbreviated **GB.**

The memory of a small pocket computer may hold less than 2K (2048) bytes, but memory in microcomputers can hold a minimum of 64K (65,536) bytes on up to 512K and even higher. At the other end of the spectrum, mainframe memories reach 16 megabytes and more.

A computer **word** is defined as the number of bits that constitute a common unit of data, as defined by the computer system. The length of a word varies by computers. Common word lengths are 8 bits (some microcomputers), 16 bits (traditional minicomputers and some microcomputers), 32 bits (full-size mainframe computers, some minicomputers, and even some microcomputers), and 64 bits (supercomputers).

A computer's word size is very important. In general, the larger the word size, the more powerful the computer. A larger word size means:

- The computer can transfer more data at a time, making the computer faster.

- The computer word has room to reference larger address numbers, thus allowing more memory.

- The computer can support a greater number and variety of instructions.

The internal circuitry of a computer must reflect its word size. The parts of a computer are connected by collections of wires called **bus lines** or **data buses.** Each bus line has a certain number of data paths along which bits can travel from one part of the computer to another. Usually, the number of data paths in the bus line is equivalent to the number of bits in the computer's word size. For instance, a 16-bit central processing unit has a 16-bit bus, meaning that data can be sent over the bus lines in groups of 16 bits—that is, a word at a time. Obviously this is more efficient than sending data in groups of 8 bits, which is what an 8-bit central processing unit does.

## Variable-Length versus Fixed-Length Words

Some computers are designed to be character-oriented; that is, they address data as a series of single characters. Computers that process data this way are said to use **variable-length words** and are described as **character addressable.** When an instruction calls for data to be accessed from a memory location, the data is moved a character at a time until the required number of characters has been read. In other words, the length of the data being processed may vary.

Other computers move data a word at a time. These computers are said to use **fixed-length words,** and are said to be **word addressable.** As we mentioned, the size of the word depends on the computer.

There are advantages and disadvantages to each design. Variable-length processors use memory efficiently; they define only the amount of space needed for a given data item. Suppose, for example, that the name DALTON needs to be stored in memory (Figure 4-6). A variable-length processor uses exactly 6 bytes, one for each character in the name. But if the machine uses a fixed-length processor, and the word length is 4 bytes, then DALT fits in one word, but the last

**Figure 4-6  Variable versus fixed-length processors.** A variable-length data item, such as the name DALTON shown here, can be stored in consecutive bytes on a variable-length processor. A fixed-length processor, however, places a fixed number of bytes in a word. In this case a word holds 4 bytes, so DALTON must be split between two words.

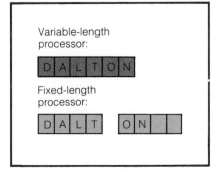

Variable-length processor:

| D | A | L | T | O | N |

Fixed-length processor:

| D | A | L | T | | O | N | |

**Figure 4-7  The EBCDIC and ASCII codes.** Shown are binary representations for letters and numbers. These may be thought of as a series of light bulbs. In the first generation of computers, when vacuum tubes were used, an observer could actually see them light up.

| Character | EBCDIC | ASCII |
|---|---|---|
| A | 1100 0001 | 100 0001 |
| B | 1100 0010 | 100 0010 |
| C | 1100 0011 | 100 0011 |
| D | 1100 0100 | 100 0100 |
| E | 1100 0101 | 100 0101 |
| F | 1100 0110 | 100 0110 |
| G | 1100 0111 | 100 0111 |
| H | 1100 1000 | 100 1000 |
| I | 1100 1001 | 100 1001 |
| J | 1101 0001 | 100 1010 |
| K | 1101 0010 | 100 1011 |
| L | 1101 0011 | 100 1100 |
| M | 1101 0100 | 100 1101 |
| N | 1101 0101 | 100 1110 |
| O | 1101 0110 | 100 1111 |
| P | 1101 0111 | 101 0000 |
| Q | 1101 1000 | 101 0001 |
| R | 1101 1001 | 101 0010 |
| S | 1110 0010 | 101 0011 |
| T | 1110 0011 | 101 0100 |
| U | 1110 0100 | 101 0101 |
| V | 1110 0101 | 101 0110 |
| W | 1110 0110 | 101 0111 |
| X | 1110 0111 | 101 1000 |
| Y | 1110 1000 | 101 1001 |
| Z | 1110 1001 | 101 1010 |
|  |  |  |
| 0 | 1111 0000 | 011 0000 |
| 1 | 1111 0001 | 011 0001 |
| 2 | 1111 0010 | 011 0010 |
| 3 | 1111 0011 | 011 0011 |
| 4 | 1111 0100 | 011 0100 |
| 5 | 1111 0101 | 011 0101 |
| 6 | 1111 0110 | 011 0110 |
| 7 | 1111 0111 | 011 0111 |
| 8 | 1111 1000 | 011 1000 |
| 9 | 1111 1001 | 011 1001 |

part of the name—ON—must be placed in another 4-byte word, and 2 bytes are wasted.

Machines purchased primarily for business data processing usually have variable-length processors. If your main task involves complex calculations, however, a fixed-length processor is more efficient because it calculates much faster. In fact, it can add two words—each containing a number—in a single operation. A variable-length processor must shuffle and align the data before addition can take place. Major scientific research organizations favor a fixed-length processor.

## Coding Schemes: EBCDIC and ASCII

As we said, a byte—a collection of bits—represents a character of data. But just what particular set of bits is equivalent to which character? In theory we could each make up our own definitions, declaring certain bit patterns to represent certain characters. But this would be about as practical as each of us speaking our own special language. Since we need to communicate with the computer and with each other, it is appropriate that we use a common scheme for data representation. That is, we must agree on which groups of bits represent which characters. There are two commonly used coding schemes for representing numbers, letters, and special characters: EBCDIC and ASCII.

**EBCDIC** (usually pronounced *EB-see-dick*) stands for Extended Binary Coded Decimal Interchange Code. Established by IBM and used in IBM mainframe computers, it uses 8 bits to represent a single character. The letter *A*, for instance, is represented by 11000001.

Another code, **ASCII** (pronounced *AS-key*), which stands for American Standard Code for Information Interchange, uses 7 bits for each character. The ASCII representation has been adopted as a standard by the U.S. government and is found in a variety of computers—particularly minicomputers and microcomputers. Figure 4-7 shows the EBCDIC and ASCII codes.

## The Parity Bit: Checking for Errors

Suppose you are transmitting data over a telephone line or even within the computer system itself. How do you know it arrived safely—that is, that nothing was lost or garbled? Sometimes data is lost in transit, owing to timing problems, hardware failure, and the like.

To signal the computer that the bits in a byte have stayed the way they are supposed to, another 0 or 1 bit is added to the byte before transmission as a check. This extra bit is called a **parity bit** or **check bit.** Thus, in an 8-bit EBCDIC byte, the parity bit is the ninth bit.

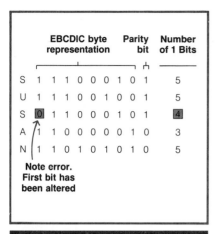

| | EBCDIC byte representation | Parity bit | Number of 1 Bits |
|---|---|---|---|
| S | 1 1 1 0 0 0 1 0 1 | | 5 |
| U | 1 1 1 0 0 1 0 0 1 | | 5 |
| S | 0 1 1 0 0 0 1 0 1 | | 4 |
| A | 1 1 0 0 0 0 0 1 0 | | 3 |
| N | 1 1 0 1 0 1 0 1 0 | | 5 |

Note error.
First bit has
been altered

**Figure 4-8   Example of odd parity.** A 0 or a 1 is added as a parity bit to the EBCDIC byte so that each byte always comes out with an odd number of 1 bits. Thus, with the second S here, the absence of the first 1 produces an even number of bits—which signals the computer that there is an error.

Here is how the system works: In an odd-parity system, a 0 or 1 is added to each EBCDIC byte before transmission so that the total number of 1 bits in each byte is an odd number (Figure 4-8). Then, if a 1 bit is lost in a particular byte during transmission, the total number of 1 bits in that byte is even, not odd. Thus, the computer system is alerted that something is wrong with that byte. Some computers use an odd-parity system and others use an even-parity system. The principle behind the two systems is the same, except that in an even-parity system the total number of 1 bits is even.

As you might suspect, a parity check is not infallible. For instance, for any of the letters in Figure 4-8, if two 1s were dropped, the number of 1 bits would still add up to an odd number—and the computer would not notice that the byte was erroneous. But two bit failures within one byte in one move are not likely to occur.

## Inside Your Personal Computer

It is really pretty easy to have a look inside most personal computers. (Caution: Some manufacturers are *not* interested in having you peer under the hood and doing so will void your warranty. Check your documentation—your instruction manual—first.) You will find an impressive array of electronic gear. Part of what you see before you is related to what we have talked about in this chapter: the central processing unit and memory.

Both the CPU and memory are on silicon chips, which are smaller than thumbtacks. The word *chip* is bandied about a great deal, but it is not always understood. There are two basic kinds of chips; one kind corresponds to a central processing unit and another kind corresponds to memory. (Specific applications such as watches or microwave ovens may combine the CPU and memory on a single chip.) A miniaturized CPU can be etched on a chip, hence the term *computer on a chip*. A central processing unit, or processor, on a chip is a **microprocessor,** also called a **logic chip.** Memory chips are different from microprocessors and come in a number of varieties.

We present the stories of microprocessors and memory chips in separate sections. Incidentally, even though we discuss chips in the context of the personal computer, where they first came to prominence, we want to note that most larger computers also use chips for the CPU and memory.

## Microprocessor: Computer on a Chip

Over the years the architecture of microprocessors has become somewhat standardized. Microprocessors usually contain four key components: the CPU (a control unit and an arithmetic/logic unit), registers, data buses, and a clock. (Clocks are often on a separate chip in personal computers.) These are the items we have discussed in this chapter, all on one tiny chip. (Notably missing is memory, which comes on its own chip or chips.)

How much smaller? How much cheaper? How much faster? Two decades of extraordinary advances in technology have packed increasingly greater power onto increasingly smaller chips. Engineers can now imprint as much circuitry on a single chip as filled room-sized computers in the early days of data processing. But are we approaching the limits of smallness? The next step, according to the experts, is a three-dimensional chip, built in layers. The future does seem limitless now.

*Made in the USA* could be confidently stamped on most microprocessors. American companies have maintained a complete stranglehold on microprocessors, producing over 99% of the microprocessor designs in use worldwide. What is more, our lawmakers want to keep it that way. Congress passed a law in 1985 that states that an original chip design is the property of the chip designer, just as a book or a record is the property of the artist who created it. The law gave chip-makers exclusive rights to make and sell their chip designs for 10 years. See Gallery 1, following page 64, for a look at how chips are designed and manufactured.

## Memory Components

Earlier in the chapter we talked about memory and how it interfaces with the central processing unit. Now we shall examine the memory components. As we saw in Chapter 3, memory components evolved from vacuum tubes to magnetic cores to semiconductors.

### Semiconductor Storage: Let the Chips Fall Where They May

Most modern computers use semiconductor storage because it has several advantages: reliability, compactness (hence increased speed), low cost, and lower power usage. Since semiconductor memory can be mass-produced economically, the cost of memory has been considerably reduced. Chips that once cost $80 to $90 each to build can now be made in volume for less than $1 each. Semiconductor storage has one major disadvantage: It is **volatile.** That is, semiconductor storage requires continuous electric current to represent data. If the current is interrupted, the data is lost.

**Semiconductor storage** is made up of thousands of very small circuits—pathways for electric currents—on a silicon chip. A chip is described as **monolithic** because the circuits on a single chip comprise an inseparable unit of storage. Each circuit etched on a chip

---

### GOOD CHIP, BAD CHIP

Chip defects can be devilishly elusive. They are small enough to make a human hair look thick, but large enough to hobble the whole computer. Searching for a chip defect is—literally—like looking for a needle in a very large haystack. The job becomes increasingly difficult as the chips continue to shrink in size. More amazing than any of these facts, however, is that such errors have traditionally been discovered by the human eye viewing the chip through a powerful microscope.

No more. This intricate task has been turned over to—what else—a computer, which is five times faster than a human inspector. It works like this. A reference image of the chip—what it is supposed to look like—is stored in the computer. Then the new chips are loaded into a peripheral machine that passes them one by one under the lens of a microscope. A camera takes a digitized picture of the chip and sends it to the computer, where it is compared with the stored image. The computer pronounces each chip to be perfect, or it is rejected. The computer does not get tired, and it does not get fooled.

## A LASTING MEMORY: BUBBLE STORAGE

A magnetic bubble memory consists of a chip coated with a thin layer of magnetic film. On this film a microscopic bubble forms when a uniform magnetic field is applied. The presence of a bubble represents a 1 and its absence a 0, the two digits that are the basis of the binary system of representing data.

The advantages of bubble memory are twofold: It has a great deal more capacity than even the most powerful integrated circuit chip now on the market. And it is nonvolatile; it can retain data even when the current is turned off—something present-day chips cannot do.

Bubble memory was introduced by Bell Laboratories in 1966, but the technology never seemed to live up to its expectations. Many companies that followed Bell tried to develop its potential but abandoned the effort. However, not long ago, Intel announced the development of a magnetic bubble-memory chip that could store the equivalent of 240 typewritten pages. Bubble memories are currently being used in specialized applications, such as in portable computers that need to keep data intact until it can be transferred to a larger computer system.

can be in one of two states: either conducting an electrical current or not—on or off. The two states can be used to represent the binary digits 1 and 0. As we noted earlier, these digits can be combined to represent characters, thus making the memory chip a storage bin for data and instructions.

The current-generation memory chip is the 256K chip, which holds 256K bits of data. At present, chip-makers are just beginning to construct 1-megabit memories—chips that hold 1 million data bits at any one time, or the equivalent of about 80 typed pages. The current long-term goal is to create a superchip capable of storing more than 10 million bits (10 megabits) of data, the equivalent of 800 typed pages! Such a superchip would be miniaturized in the extreme, with circuits smaller than half a micron, or approximately seven-thousandths of the diameter of a human hair.

In current vernacular **large-scale integration (LSI)** means a chip has a large number of circuits, and the circuits are integrated—that is, they work together. More recently, the 1-megabit chips are described as **VLSI,** for **very large-scale integration.** In search of ever grander designations, the proposed 10-megabit chip is now referred to as **ULSI,** for **ultra large-scale integration.** Fortunately, no engineer has to speculate on a name to top that one—yet.

In the past decade Japan has been dominant in the production of memory chips. This is due largely to the painful mistakes of American chip manufacturers, who responded to a 1970s slump by slashing payrolls and canceling research. The U.S. Department of Defense worries that computers, weapons, and telecommunications may grow dangerously dependent on foreign memory chips. In recent years the United States has made significant strides in memory chip production.

## RAM, ROM, PROM, and EPROM

The above do not represent some mystical chant. They are acronyms describing different types of memory chips. The two basic types of memory chips in every computer are popularly known as **random-access memory (RAM)** and **read-only memory (ROM).** These terms are actually a little misleading, since every chip, RAM or ROM, provides random-access storage. That is, the computer has access to all locations on each type of chip.

The real difference between RAM and ROM is that the data on ROM chips cannot easily be replaced with new data. ROM contains programs and data that are permanently recorded into the memory at the factory and cannot be changed by the user. The contents of ROM can be read and used, but they cannot be changed by the user. ROMs, often called **firmware,** are used to store programs that will not be altered. For example, a pocket calculator might have a program for calculating square roots in ROM; a microcomputer might have a BASIC interpreting program in ROM. ROM is nonvolatile—its contents do not disappear when the power is turned off.

## THE MICROCOMPUTER CORNER

### Putting on Your High-Tech Sneakers

It had to come: the computerized running shoe. Puma and Adidas both offer running shoes with built-in microprocessors. These chips calculate how far you have run and how many calories you have burned.

Here is how the Puma shoe works. The left shoe has a built-in stopwatch that records the time you spend running and a sensing device that registers each time your foot hits the ground. If you like to make your own music as you run, the shoe can also beep each time it touches down. If you want electronic encouragement, the shoe can beep after you have run a preprogrammed distance.

A chip attached to the heel of the shoe records your running data. When you get home from your run, you simply take off your left shoe and hook it up to your personal computer with a special cable. The data from your run is then input into the computer. The software provided with the shoes estimates the distance you ran and the number of calories you burned. The software can compare this data to previous data, producing graphs that summarize your progress toward your goals.

Adidas, on the other foot, has designed a running shoe that is independent of a personal computer. The shoes display running totals on a tiny four-digit screen that covers the shoelaces. Two buttons allow you to input your weight and the length of your stride. Each running step is sensed and recorded by a sensor under the left big toe. Adidas and Puma will probably continue trying to match each other stride for stride in their development of computerized shoes.

With specialized tools called **ROM burners,** the instructions within some ROM chips can be changed. These chips are known as **PROM** chips, or **programmable read-only memory** chips. A PROM chip that can be erased by exposure to ultraviolet light, then reprogrammed is called **EPROM,** or **erasable PROM.** Other EPROM chips can be **electronically erased** or **electronically altered** and are thus dubbed **EEPROM** and **EAPROM,** respectively. The business of programming and erasing ROM chips is the province of the computer engineer. The rest of us are safe if we just leave ROM alone.

The memory designed for "the rest of us" is RAM, the computer's temporary storage compartments. They hold the instructions and data for whatever programs we happen to be using. In fact, RAM has been described as the computer's scratch pad. RAM chips could accurately be described as read-write chips: A user can read the data stored there as well as write new data to replace what is there. The data can be accessed in an easy and speedy manner. RAM is usually volatile—that is, the data is lost once the power is shut off. This is one of the reasons, you recall, that we need secondary storage.

The more RAM in your computer, the more powerful the programs you can run. In recent years the amount of RAM storage in a personal computer has increased dramatically. An early Apple computer, for example, was advertised as coming with "a full 4K RAM." As the industry turned the corner around 1980, however, most personal computers came with a standard RAM of 64K. Now, since many personal-computer users are in offices, 256K RAM is common, and 512K RAM—or more—is not unusual. You can add to your personal computer's RAM by buying extra memory chips to add to your memory board or by buying an entire memory board full of chips. It is easier—but more expensive—to buy another board since it slips into place more readily than individual chips do. Sophisticated personal-computer software requires significant amounts of memory—a fact we shall discuss more thoroughly in Chapters 14, 15, and 16, which focus on microcomputer software applications.

## Computer Processing Speeds

We have saved the discussion of speed until last. Although speed is basic to computer processing, speed is also an ever changing facet and a good jumping-off point to the future.

The characteristic of speed is universally associated with computers. Certainly all computers are fast, but there is a wide diversity of computer speeds. The execution of an instruction on a very slow computer may be measured in less than a **millisecond,** which is one-thousandth of a second (see Table 4-1). Most computers can execute an instruction measured in **microseconds,** one-millionth of a second. Some modern computers have reached the **nanosecond** range—one-billionth of a second. Still to be broken is the **picosecond** barrier—one-trillionth of a second.

### More Speed? What's the Rush?

Computer speeds are beyond anything that we mortals can physically comprehend. The blink of an eye takes about half a second—2000 times slower than a millisecond, the measuring stick of the *slow* computers. The fastest computers, it would seem, ought to be fast enough for even the most sophisticated computer users. But this is not so. This is not just a greed-for-speed scenario—some people really need still more computer speed.

Just who needs all that speed? A physicist at New York University, for one. He coaxed a big, powerful computer to simulate the

### HOW FAST IS A NANOSECOND?

| If one nano-second is . . . | Then one second is equivalent to . . . |
|---|---|
| one mile | 2000 trips to the moon and back |
| one person | the population of China and the United States |
| one minute | 1900 years |
| one square mile | 17 times the land area of the entire world |

**Table 4-1   Units of Time: How Fast Is *Fast?***

| Unit of Time | Fraction of a Second | Mathematical Notation |
|---|---|---|
| Millisecond | Thousandth: 1/1000 | $10^{-3}$ |
| Microsecond | Millionth: 1/1000000 | $10^{-6}$ |
| Nanosecond | Billionth: 1/1000000000 | $10^{-9}$ |
| Picosecond | Trillionth: 1/1000000000000 | $10^{-12}$ |

behavior of helium atoms at $-459°$ Fahrenheit—that is, near absolute zero. Each time he ran the program, it would grind away all weekend. It took two years to get the first satisfactory results. Scientists often work this way. A scientist has an idea of how something works—atoms or ocean currents or prime numbers—and can describe it in terms of numbers and equations. Then the scientist plays elaborate what-if games by changing the numbers and recalculating the equations. These new calculations, of course, are done on the computer. A lot of data means a lot of computer time—even on supercomputers.

The traditional approach to increased speed has been to decrease the distances that electronic signals must travel. The circuits are packed closer together, making tighter and tighter squeezes into the same physical space. All these electronic devices humming together in close proximity produce an overheating problem, which must be attacked with elaborate cooling systems.

Another frequently mentioned approach has been the use of a material called **gallium arsenide** as a substitute for silicon in chip-making. Currents can pass through gallium arsenide at a tremendous speed. The drawback of this substance, however, is that it is currently too expensive to be of practical use.

Modern approaches to increased computer speeds also include these two categories: RISC technology and parallel processing. These two topics are so important that they deserve sections of their own.

## 7 RISC Technology: Less Is More

It flies in the face of computer tradition: Instead of reaching for more variety, more power, more everything-for-everyone, RISC proponents suggest that we could get by with a little less. In fact, **reduced instruction set computers** (**RISC**) offer only a small subset of instructions, and they claim that the absence of bells and whistles increases speed. So we have a radical back-to-basics movement in computer design.

RISC supporters say that, on conventional computers, a hefty chunk of built-in instructions—the microcode—is rarely used. They believe these instructions are underused, inefficient, and impediments to performance. RISC proponents claim that computers with stripped-down instruction sets zip through programs like racing cars—two or three times faster than conventional models. This is heady stuff for the merchants of speed who want to attract customers by offering more zip for the money.

The idea that less gives more is so compelling that a dozen or so companies are pressing forward with RISC technology. Start-up firms offered the first RISC-based computers in 1983. Now major computing manufacturers are joining the adventure, aiming at the scientific market, where most of the speed demons lurk.

Meanwhile, some people are looking in a different direction altogether. They are actually changing computer architecture to achieve another solution: parallel processing.

## Parallel Processing: The Ultimate Speed Solution

A wave of technological change is poised to sweep over the computer industry. Does that statement shock you? Far-reaching claims such as this are not new in this business, so perhaps we could emphasize this point by saying that this change will be akin to reinventing the computer. Consider the description of computer processing you have seen so far in this chapter: The processor gets an instruction from memory, acts on it, returns processed data to memory, then repeats the process. This is conventional **serial processing.** It is, in fact, the invention of John von Neumann and is called the **von Neumann machine.** But people most often mention the von Neumann machine when they are talking about doing something different, as in "going beyond the von Neumann machine."

The problem with the conventional computer is that the single electronic pathway, the data bus, acts like a bottleneck. The computer has a one-track mind because it is restricted to handling one piece of data at a time. For many applications, such as simulating the air flow around an entire airplane in flight, this is an exceedingly inefficient procedure. A better solution? Many processors, each with its own memory unit, working at the same time: **parallel processing.** Note the comparisons in Figure 4-9.

Even von Neumann saw that parallel processors working in tandem were preferable, but the technology of the day—vacuum tubes!—made parallel processing out of the question. Inventors, rather like composers describing their wonderful new symphonies before they are ever performed, have been tinkering with parallel processors in the lab ever since. Now years of research are starting to pay off: A number of parallel processors are being built, tested, and even sold commercially.

Let us return to the example of the airplane in flight. Using a single conventional processor, the computer could calculate flow between two points on the airplane's surface. Since there are millions of such pairs of points, this calculation method is not very efficient. A serial computer would waste most of its time repeatedly retrieving and storing vast amounts of data, with relatively little time devoted to actual computation. By contrast, a parallel processor could take several pieces of data and perform a series of operations on them in parallel.

The story of computer speeds has been with us since the first stirrings of electronic computers. There is every reason to believe that it will be a continuing story.

**Figure 4-9   Evolution of parallel processing.** (a) The traditional von Neumann machine contains a single processing unit (CPU) and memory. (b) Intermediate computer architectures have a few powerful CPU-memory units under the control of a central computer, pictured here as the control box. Each CPU can work on a job alone or with other CPUs. (c) The third example, the newest architecture, is a latticelike arrangement of many CPU-memory units.

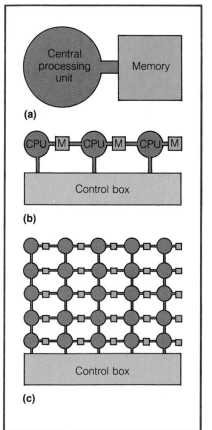

## Next: Future Chip Talk

The future holds some exciting possibilities. As we have indicated, new speed breakthroughs will always be a probability, but we can go further afield than that in our speculations. Would you believe computers that are actually grown as biological cultures? So-called biochips may replace the billions of molecules that make up today's silicon chip with atoms brewed in a test tube. As far-fetched as this sounds, that is precisely the direction of some ongoing research. Tomorrow's processing unit may well be organic.

However, a processor (or processors) cannot be useful without data to process. In the next chapter we shall describe how input data is put into the computer and how it is output after it is processed.

## Summary and Key Terms

- The **central processing unit** (**CPU**) is an extensive, complex set of electrical circuitry that executes program instructions. It consists of two parts: a control unit and an arithmetic/logic unit.

- The CPU interacts closely with **primary storage,** or **memory.** Memory provides temporary storage of data while the computer is executing the program. **Secondary storage** holds the data that is permanent or semipermanent.

- The **control unit** of the CPU coordinates the computer's execution of the program instructions by communicating with the arithmetic/logic unit and memory—the parts of the system that actually execute the program.

- The **arithmetic/logic unit** (**ALU**) contains circuitry that executes the arithmetic and logical operations. The unit can perform four **arithmetic operations:** addition, subtraction, multiplication, and division. Its **logical operations** are usually comparing operations, primarily the **equal to (=) condition,** the **less than (<) condition,** and the **greater than (>) condition.** These operations are commonly combined to form three other operations: less than or equal to, greater than or equal to, and less than or greater than.

- **Registers** are temporary storage areas associated with the CPU that quickly accept, hold, and transfer instructions or data. An **accumulator** is a register that collects the results of computations. A **storage register** temporarily holds data taken from memory or about to be sent to memory. An **ad-**

**dress register** tells where instructions and data are stored in memory. Each storage location in memory is identified by an **address.** A **general-purpose register,** as its name indicates, can be used in several ways, such as arithmetic operations or addressing.

- Registers hold data that will be processed immediately, and memory stores the data that will soon be used in subsequent operations. Secondary storage holds data that may be needed for operations later.

- **Memory** is the part of the computer that temporarily holds data and instructions before and after they are processed by the arithmetic/logic unit. Memory is also known as **primary storage, primary memory, main storage, internal storage,** and **main memory.** Memory allows very fast access to data and instructions within it, but most types of memory keep data only when the computer is turned on. Thus, the data is saved permanently only when it is released to an output unit.

- The control unit follows four main steps when executing an instruction: (1) getting the instruction from memory, (2) decoding the instruction and giving instructions for the transfer of appropriate data from memory to the arithmetic/logic unit, (3) directing the arithmetic/logic unit to perform the actual operation on the data, and (4) directing the result of the operation to be stored in memory or a register. The first two steps are called **I-time** (instruction time), and the last two steps are called **E-time** (execution time).

- A **machine cycle** is the combination of I-time and E-time. The internal **clock** of the CPU produces pulses at a fixed rate to synchronize computer op-

erations. A machine-cycle instruction may include many subinstructions, each of which must take at least one clock cycle period. These subinstructions are controlled by **microcode** instructions permanently set inside the control unit.

- Each location in primary storage is identified by an **address.** Address numbers remain the same, but the contents of the locations may change.

- Since a computer can only recognize whether electricity is on or off, data is represented by an on/off **binary system.** In a binary system two digits, 0 and 1, correspond to the two states off and on. Combinations of 0s and 1s can represent numbers, digits, or special characters.

- Each 0 or 1 in the binary system is called a **bit** (*binary digit*). A group of bits (usually 8 bits) is called a **byte.** Each byte usually represents one character of data, such as a letter, digit, or special character. Memory capacity is expressed in **kilobytes (KB),** which are equal to 1024 bytes; **megabytes (MB),** which are millions of bytes; and sometimes even in **gigabytes (GB),** which are billions of bytes.

- A computer **word** is the number of bits that make up a unit of data, as defined by the computer system. Common word lengths vary from 8 bits to 64 bits. A computer's word length is important because, in general, a larger word length means a more powerful computer. Larger word length means that the computer can transfer more information at a time, can have a larger memory, and can support a greater number and variety of instructions.

- Word length usually determines the capacity of the computer's **bus lines,** or **data buses.** These collections of wires provide data paths for transferring bits from one part of the computer to another.

- **Character-addressable** computers process data one character at a time and are said to use **variable-length words** because the length of the data being processed may vary. **Word-addressable** computers process data one word at a time and are said to use **fixed-length words** because the size of the word depends on the computer's word length. Variable-length computers use memory more efficiently; fixed-length computers provide faster processing.

- Commonly used coding schemes for representing characters are **EBCDIC** (Extended Binary Coded Decimal Interchange Code), which uses 8-bit characters, and **ASCII** (American Standard Code for Information Interchange), which uses 7-bit characters.

- A **parity bit,** or **check bit,** is an extra bit added to each byte as part of a system. The parity bit alerts the computer if a bit is incorrect.

- A CPU on a chip is called a **microprocessor,** or **logic chip.** Microprocessors usually contain a control unit and an arithmetic logic unit, registers, data buses, and a clock. The memory in most modern computers is provided through **semiconductor storage,** thousands of circuits on a silicon chip. The memory chip is **monolithic** because these circuits form an inseparable storage unit. Semiconductor storage is compact and economical, but it is usually also **volatile** because if the computer's power is shut off the data is lost.

- **Large-scale integration (LSI)** means that a chip has a large number of circuits that work together. A 1-megabit chip is described as having **very large-scale integration (VLSI),** and the proposed 10-megabit chip is said to have **ultra large-scale integration (ULSI).**

- There are two basic types of memory chips, **random-access memory (RAM)** and **read-only memory (ROM).** RAM provides volatile temporary storage for data and instructions and can be increased by adding extra memory chips to allow for more powerful programs. Once a program runs, the data in RAM must be saved in secondary storage before the computer is turned off. In contrast, ROM (or **firmware**) is nonvolatile. ROM programs and data, which are recorded into the memory at the factory, remain after the computer power is turned off. However, the data and instructions on some ROM chips, called **programmable read-only memory (PROM)** chips, can be changed with special tools called **ROM burners.** A PROM chip that can be erased by exposure to ultraviolet light, then reprogrammed is called **EPROM,** or **erasable PROM.** EPROM chips that can be **electronically erased** or **electronically altered** are called **EEPROM** and **EAPROM,** respectively.

- Computer speed can be measured in **milliseconds** (one-thousandth of a second), **microseconds** (one-millionth of a second), and even **nanoseconds** (one-billionth of a second). The **picosecond** barrier (one-trillionth of a second) is yet to be broken.

- Research is continuing on various ways of increasing computer speed. One approach is to decrease the distance the electronic signals must travel by packing the circuits closer together. Another possibility is making chips out of **gallium arsenide,** a substance that conducts electricity better than silicon. Research is also continuing on **reduced instruction set computers** (**RISC**), which would increase processing speed by reducing the microcode (built-in instructions). Also promising is increased application of **parallel processing,** the use of many processors working at the same time—a method that could replace the traditional **serial processing,** which was invented by John von Neumann (and often referred to as the **von Neumann machine.**) Unlike serial processing, parallel processing allows the computer to handle more than one piece of data at a time.

## Review Questions

1. Name and describe the functions of the two parts of the central processing unit.

2. How does memory differ from secondary storage?

3. Name and describe the functions of the four types of registers.

4. What is the function of the computer's memory?

5. Describe the steps in the execution of a program instruction.

6. How does the control unit find instructions and data?

7. Explain why the binary system is used to represent data to the computer.

8. Define the following: bit, byte, kilobyte, megabyte, gigabyte, and word.

9. Why is a computer's word size important?

10. What is a bus line?

11. Name and describe the two main coding schemes.

12. Explain how a parity bit identifies errors.

13. What are the advantages of semiconductor storage?

14. Define the following: RAM, ROM, PROM, EPROM, EEPROM, and EAPROM.

15. Define the following: millisecond, microsecond, nanosecond, and picosecond.

16. Describe ways of increasing computer speed.

## Discussion Questions

1. Give an example of a practical application of each of the three basic logical operations.

2. Why is writing instructions for a computer more difficult than writing instructions for a person?

3. Do you think there is a continuing need to increase computer speed? Explain your answer.

# 5

# Input and Output

## Data Given, Information Received

Input is the bridge between data and processing. Input devices include the commonly used keyboard and devices that collect data at its source. Some devices are involved in both input and output. Specialized input and output devices produce computer-generated graphics. Output is the human connection with computing. Output devices include printers, computer output microfilm, and voice output.

**Figure 5-1  An automated teller machine.** By inserting a plastic card and punching in a secret code, a user can perform many banking functions, including deposits, cash withdrawals, and funds transfers.

A Los Angeles woman, Sylvia Webb, approached her local bank's **automated teller machine** (**ATM**), where she inserted her plastic card, keyed in her personal identification number, and instructed the machine to dispense $20 in cash. It did. It also dispensed another $20 bill, and another after that. It continued issuing the bills in an unstoppable flow while the astonished Ms. Webb looked on. The stream of $20 bills spilling from the machine caught the attention of passersby, who eagerly assisted in retrieving the bills from the ground.

Ms. Webb probably did not pause to ponder the amazing fact that this machine could accept her input and, almost instantly, produce output. As we shall see in this chapter, there are many ways of providing input to a computer and still more of getting output from the computer. There are even devices, notably computer screens, that are involved in both input and output. The ATM mentioned above appears to be a single input/output device, but it is actually a complicated machine with a set of input/output devices connected to the bank's computer. Its normal behavior, by the way, is very reliable.

Meanwhile, Ms. Webb received assistance from bank officials, who stemmed the tide of $20 bills. (A bank employee was later able to report that every extra bill had been returned to the bank.) Figure 5-1 shows an ATM, but not the very one that dispensed the bonus cash!

## Input and Output: The People Connection

We have already alluded to the fact that the central processing unit is the unseen part of a computer system. But users are very much aware—and in control—of the input data given to the computer. They submit data to the computer to get processed information, the output. Output is what makes the computer useful to human beings.

Sometimes the output is an instant reaction to the input. Consider these examples:

- Zebra-striped bar codes on supermarket items provide input that permits instant retrieval of outputs such as price and item name right at the checkout counter.

- You use a joy stick—a kind of hand-controlled lever—to input data to guide the little Pac-Man character on the screen, and the output result is that the character moves according to your wishes.

- A bank teller queries the computer through the small terminal at the window by giving a customer's account number as input and immediately receiving the customer's account balance as output on that same screen.

## COMPUTERIZED PARKING LOTS

No, the computer will not park your car, but it will let you into the parking lot if you have a special pass it can recognize. As a monthly customer, you receive a plastic card for entering and exiting the facility. To enter, you insert this card into an optical card reader, which scans the account number. Before the system accepts the card and raises the gate arm, it checks to see that the account is paid up and that no other car in the lot used that account. On exiting, the driver inserts the card again, and the total parking time is recorded for billing purposes.

The system is convenient for regular customers because they do not have to worry about carrying cash for parking. It is lucrative for lot owners, who do not have to pay parking lot attendants. Do you suppose the lower operating costs are passed on to the customers in the form of lower parking rates?

- A forklift operator speaks to a computer directly through a microphone. Words like *left*, *right*, and *lift* are the actual input data. The output is the computer's instant response, which causes the forklift to operate as requested.

- In an innovative restaurant input is your finger touching the listing of the item of your choice on a computer screen. The output is the order that appears immediately on the kitchen screen, where employees get to work on your Chili Hamburger Deluxe.

Some of these input/output examples may seem playful and even frivolous, but all are possible and (usually) practical.

Input and output are sometimes separated by time and/or distance. Some examples:

- Factory workers input data by using their plastic cards to punch in on a time clock as they go from task to task. The outputs, produced biweekly, are their paychecks and management reports that summarize hours per project and other information.

- A college student writes checks whose data is used as input to the computer and eventually processed to prepare a bank statement once a month.

- Charge-card transactions in a retail store provide input data that is processed at month's end to produce customer bills.

- Water-sample data is determined at lake and river sites, keyed in at the environmental agency office, and used to produce reports that show patterns of water quality.

Perhaps you noted in the examples that the same input sometimes can be used for more than one type of output. In fact, the same input data can be used by different people for different purposes, with each of them receiving computer outputs that suit them. Consider, for example, the data input to a mail-order house like Lands' End in Wisconsin, a firm that offers quality preppy and sports clothing. Input is the data related to the customer order—customer name, address, and (possibly) charge-card number—and, for each item, catalog number, quantity, description, and price. If this input data is handwritten on an order form, it is keyed into the system as soon as it arrives in the mail; if the order is received on their toll-free phone line, the Lands' End operator keys the data as the customer speaks the order. This data is placed on customer and order files to be used with files containing inventory data and other related data.

The computer can process this data into a variety of outputs, as shown in Figure 5-2. Some outputs are for individual customers, and some show information combined from several orders: warehouse orders, shipping labels, backorder notices, inventory reports, supply re-order reports, charge card reports, demographic reports (showing which merchandise sells best where), and so forth. And, to keep the whole process going, Lands' End also computer-prints the customer's name and address on a catalog.

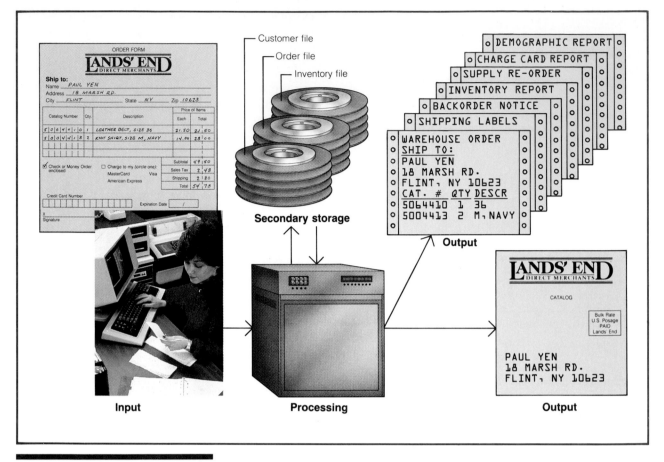

**Figure 5-2   Lands' End.** At this mail-order house, customer order data is input, processed, and used to produce a variety of outputs.

The examples in this section show the diversity of computer applications, but, in all cases, the litany is the same: input-processing-output. We have already had an introduction to processing. Now, in this chapter, we shall examine input and output methods in detail. We begin with a description of forms of input, then consider devices that are used for both input and output, and conclude with devices that are used as output only.

# The Forms of Input

Some input data can go directly to the computer for processing, as in bar codes or speaking or pointing. Some input data, however, goes through a good deal of intermediate handling, such as when it is copied from a **source document** (jargon for the original written data) and keyed to a medium that a machine can read, such as magnetic disk. In either case the task is to gather data to be processed by the computer—sometimes called *raw data*—and convert it into some form the computer can understand. The evolution of input devices is toward equipment that is easy to use, fast, and accurate.

# Keyboard Entry

The most popular input device is the keyboard. A keyboard, which is similar to a typewriter, may be part of a personal computer or part of a terminal that is connected to a computer somewhere else.

## Keyboards and Personal Computer Users

Users of personal computers find that familiarity with a keyboard breeds productivity. Consider the traditional flow of paperwork in an office: A manager writes a memo by hand or dictates it, then a secretary types it. The manager checks the typed memo; if there are changes to be made, the secretary must retype the memo. With a personal computer on the manager's desk, however, the manager can enter the memo through the keyboard, read it on the screen, and make any necessary changes before it is printed (Figure 5-3). This greatly reduces the lag time between writing a memo and getting it in the mail. The bottom line: To succeed in business, learn to type!

## Keyboards and Data Entry Operators

Entering large amounts of data via keyboard calls for the services of data entry operators. **Data entry operators** use computer

**Figure 5-3  Keyboard user.** This executive is working smarter by using a personal computer to increase productivity.

## THE MICROCOMPUTER CORNER

### Finding Your Way Around a Keyboard

The IBM PC, one of the most widely used business machines, has three main parts to its keyboard: the function keys to the left, the main keyboard in the center, and the numeric keys to the right (see drawing below).

The function keys are an easy way to give certain commands to the computer. What each function key does is defined by the particular software you are using. For instance, with WordStar, a popular word processing program, you press function key F4 to set the right margin and F5 to underline text.

The main keyboard includes the familiar keys found on a typewriter keyboard, as well as some special command keys. These keys can have different uses depending upon the software. Some of the common uses are described in this box.

The numeric keys serve one of two purposes depending on the status of the Num Lock key. When the computer is in the Num Lock mode, these keys can be used to enter numeric data; otherwise, they move the cursor, the flashing indicator on the screen that shows where the next character will be inserted.

*Special Keys on Main Keyboard*

 The Escape key allows you to escape to the previous screen of the program.

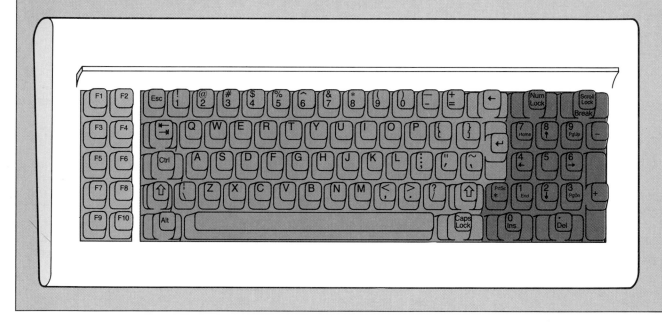

terminals to enter data from some nonautomated form, usually handwriting on paper (see Figure 5-2). Such a system is often used to process large quantities of data that can be handled in groups, or batches, such as engineering drawing data, customer payments, or bank transactions received in the mail.

The data that operators enter into the system is stored on either magnetic tape or magnetic disk. The tapes or disks are then sent to the main computer for processing.

The Tab key allows you to tab across the screen and set tab stops as you would on a typewriter.

 The Control key is used in combination with another key to initiate a command.

 The Alternate key is used along with another key to initiate a command.

 The Back Space key moves the cursor to the left to correct a keying error.

 The Enter or Return key works like a typewriter carriage return.

 The Shift key produces uppercase letters.

 The Caps Lock key controls the entry of lowercase or uppercase letters.

Numeric Keys

 This key returns the cursor to the bottom left-hand corner of the screen.

This key moves the cursor down.

The Page Down key advances one full screen while the cursor remains in the same position.

This key moves the cursor to the left.

This key moves the cursor to the right.

The Home key moves the cursor to the top left-hand corner of the screen.

This key moves the cursor up.

The Page Up key backs up to the previous screen while the cursor remains in the same position.

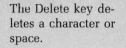 The Insert key can be used to insert additional characters within a line.

 The Delete key deletes a character or space.

 The Scroll Lock key causes lines of text—not the cursor—to move when cursor keys are used.

 The Print Screen key, when pressed with the shift key, causes the current screen display to be printed.

 The Minus key enters a minus sign on the screen.

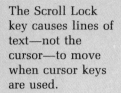 The Plus key enters a plus sign on the screen.

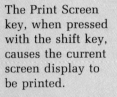

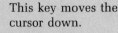

## Source Data Automation: Collecting Data Where It Starts

The challenge to productive data entry is clear: Cut down the number of intermediate steps required between the two words *data* and *processing* so that *data processing* becomes more efficient. This is best accomplished by **source data automation**—the use of special equipment to collect data at the source and

**GAS TERMINAL**

It had to happen. Many gas stations offer limited service; the attendant just takes money—you pump the gas yourself. To take the self-serve concept one step further, let us replace that final vestige of service with a computerized terminal on the pump. A company called Autotank has done just that. Autotank's terminals accept credit cards (Mastercard and Visa) and bills of different denominations. The attendant, of course, is nonexistent, but the station is open 24 hours a day.

Sound good? They think so in Europe, where there are 1200 such installations. But you probably have not yet seen one in the United States. Two American laws are in the way, one that requires a paper receipt for credit charges and another that requires a human on the premises to report fires. The first one is still proving nettlesome, but the second is being solved by designing superpumpers—dozens of pumps with a single attendant, not to take money but to be a trouble-shooter—and a firewatcher.

send it directly to the computer. Source data automation is an enticing alternative to keying input because it eliminates the intermediate keying function and, therefore, reduces both costs and opportunities for human-introduced mistakes. Since data about a transaction is collected when and where the transaction takes place, source data automation also improves the speed of the input operation.

One characteristic of source data automation is that the data entry equipment needs to be fairly easy to use, reliable, and maintenance-free. The people who will use it are data entry personnel who require less training time—meter-readers, shop clerks, and grocery clerks, for example.

For convenience we shall divide this discussion into four areas related to source data automation: magnetic-ink character recognition, optical recognition, data-collection devices, and voice input. Let us consider each of these in turn.

## Magnetic-Ink Character Recognition

Abbreviated **MICR** (pronounced *miker*), **magnetic-ink character recognition** is a method of machine-reading characters made of magnetized particles. The most common example of magnetic characters is the array of futuristic-looking numbers on the bottom of your personal check. Figure 5-4 shows what these numbers and attached symbols represent.

The MICR process is, in fact, used mainly by banks for processing checks. Checks are read by a machine called a **MICR reader/sorter,** which sorts the checks into different compartments and sends electronic signals—read from the magnetic ink on the check—to the computer.

Most magnetic-ink characters are preprinted on your check. If you compare a check you wrote that has been cashed and cleared by the bank with those that are still unused in your checkbook, you will note that the amount of the cashed check has been reproduced in magnetic characters in the lower right-hand corner. These characters were added by a person at the bank using a **MICR inscriber.** (If you find a discrepancy between the amount you wrote on your check and the amount given on your bank statement, look at this lower right-hand number. Maybe someone had trouble reading your handwriting.)

When your check is run through the reader/sorter, it is sorted by account number and put in order so that it can be stored along with all of your other checks and returned to you with your statement at the end of the month. (Some banks, however, keep the checks themselves in the interest of saving handling and postage.) Checks that are torn or otherwise mutilated and cannot be read by the machine are sent to a separate compartment of the machine. The banking transaction is later recorded by a person who handles the check manually.

**Figure 5-4   The symbols on your check.** Magnetic-ink numbers and symbols run along the bottom of a check. The symbols on the left are pre-printed; the MICR characters in the lower right-hand corner of a cashed check are entered by the bank that receives it. Note that the numbers should correspond to the amount of the check.

## SOFTSTRIP

A relatively new entry in the optical-scanner market is the Softstrip System Reader. The reader, shown here, is a slim, page-length machine that can be plugged into your IBM PC or Macintosh computer. The reader passes over a machine-readable strip in the page margin of a book or magazine. Page by page the content of the book or article is placed in computer storage without keying. The obvious benefits are speed and accuracy. The drawback, for the moment, is finding the literature whose publisher has elected to include the strip on each page.

## Optical Recognition

**Optical-recognition** systems read numbers, letters, special characters, and marks. An electronic scanning device converts the data into electrical signals and sends the signals to the computer for processing. Various optical-recognition devices can read these types of input:

- Optical marks
- Optical characters
- Handwritten characters
- Bar codes

### Optical-Mark Recognition

Abbreviated **OMR, optical-mark recognition** is sometimes called mark sensing because a machine senses marks on a piece of paper. As a student, you may immediately recognize this approach as a technique used to score certain tests. Using a pencil, you make a mark in a specified box or space that corresponds to what you think is the answer. The answer sheet is then graded by a

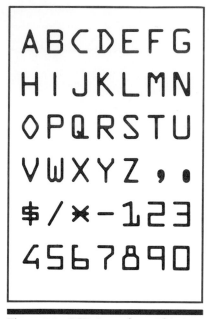

**Figure 5-5  OCR-A typeface.** This is a common standard font for optical-character recognition.

device that uses a light beam to recognize the marks and convert them to electrical signals, which are sent to the computer for processing.

### Optical-Character Recognition

Abbreviated **OCR, optical-character recognition** devices also use a light source to read special characters and convert them into electrical signals to be sent to the CPU. The characters—letters, numbers, and special symbols—can be read by both humans and machines. They are often found on sales tags in department stores or imprinted on credit-card slips in gas stations after the sale has been written up. A standard typeface for optical characters, called **OCR-A,** has been established by the American National Standards Institute (Figure 5-5).

The hand-held **wand reader** is a popular input device for reading OCR-A. There is an increasing use of wands in libraries, hospitals, and factories, as well as in retail stores. In retail stores the wand reader is connected to a **point-of-sale** (**POS**) **terminal** (Figure 5-6). This terminal is like a cash register in many ways, but it performs many more functions. When a clerk passes the wand reader over the price tag, both the price and the merchandise number are entered into the computer system. Given the merchandise number, the computer can retrieve a description of the item from a file. This description is displayed on the screen of the POS terminal along with the price. (Some systems, by the way, input only the merchandise number and retrieve both price and description.) A small printer produces a customer receipt that also shows both the item description and the price. The computer calculates the subtotal, the sales tax, and the total. This information is displayed on the screen and printed on the receipt.

The raw purchase data becomes valuable information when it is

**Figure 5-6  Wand reader.** The photo shows a clerk using a wand reader to scan a price tag printed with OCR-A characters. The price and merchandise number are entered into the computer through the point-of-sale (POS) terminal. The computer retrieves a description of the merchandise from secondary storage and calculates the total price of the purchase. A printer in the POS terminal produces a receipt for the customer. Later, computer reports can be generated for store personnel to use.

summarized by the computer system. This information can be used by the accounting department to keep track of how much money is taken in each day, by buyers to determine what merchandise should be reordered, and by the marketing department to analyze the effectiveness of their ad campaigns. Thus, capturing data at the time of the sale provides many benefits beyond giving the customer a fancy computerized receipt.

By the way, you only need to look as far as the back of this book to see an example of OCR-A type (in the lower right-hand corner). Some bookstores use wand readers to read a book's code number; the computer system then retrieves the price, author, title, and publisher of the book. As in any store, this information helps the bookstore keep track of sales and inventory.

Some OCR readers are less finicky than others. The Postal Service uses scanners that can handle 30,000 letters an hour. The human eye can barely follow individual envelopes as they are sucked out of a feeder, run through the OCR scanner, and dispatched to one of several slots. Eleven people using conventional equipment and their own eyes cannot sort as fast as one machine. There is only a 50-50 chance, however, that a letter dropped in the neighborhood mailbox will end up on the scanner. Handwritten zip codes are sent to human sorters. But if the zip code is typed and in the lower right corner, the machine will probably be able to read it.

### Handwritten Characters

Machines that can read handwritten characters are yet another means of reducing the number of intermediate steps between capturing data and processing it. There are many instances where it is preferable to write the data and immediately have it usable for processing rather than keying it in later by data entry operators. However, not just any kind of handwritten scrawl will do; the rules as to the size, completeness, and legibility of the handwriting are fairly rigid (Figure 5-7). The Internal Revenue Service uses optical scanners to read handwritten numbers on income tax forms. Taxpayers must follow the directions for forming numbers, however.

**Figure 5-7   Handwritten characters.** Legibility is important in making handwritten characters readable by optical recognition, as you can see on the directions—upper right corner—on this IRS tax form.

| | Good | Bad |
|---|---|---|
| 1. Make your letters big | TAPLEY | TAPLEY |
| 2. Use simple shapes | 25370 | 25370 |
| 3. Use block printing | STAN | STAN |
| 4. Connect lines | B5T | I35T |
| 5. Close loops | 9068 | 9068 |
| 6. Do not link characters | LOOP | LOOP |

### Bar Codes

Each product on the grocery shelf has its own unique number, called the **Universal Product Code** (**UPC**). This code number is represented on the product's label by a pattern of vertical marks, or bars, called **bar codes.** These zebra-stripes can be sensed and read by a **bar code reader,** a stationary photoelectric scanner that reads the code by means of reflected light. As with the wand reader in retail stores, the bar code reader in grocery stores is part of a point-of-sale terminal. When you buy a container of, say, chocolate milk mix in a supermarket, the checker moves it past the scanner that reads the bar code (Figure 5-8). The bar code merely identifies the product to the store's computer; the code does not contain the price, which may vary. The price is stored in a file that can be accessed by the computer. (Obviously it is easier to change the price once in the computer than to have to repeatedly restamp the price on each container of chocolate milk mix.) The computer automatically tells the point-of-sale terminal what the price is; a printer prints the item description and price on a paper tape for the customer.

There are a great many benefits of using the UPC system that can help slow the rise of grocery prices:

- Prices determined at the POS terminal by scanning are more accurate than those rung up by human checkers.

- Checkout is faster.

- Checkout training is easier, since the machine does most of the work previously done by people punching keys.

- Cash register tapes are more complete, since they identify not only prices but also the corresponding purchases by name.

- Labor costs are reduced.

- Inventory control is easier. Marketing personnel receive instant data on what shoppers are buying. As goods are moved through the checkout stand, the computer can keep a tally of what is left on the shelves and signal the store manager when restocking and re-ordering are necessary.

Although bar codes were once found primarily in the supermarket, there are a variety of other interesting applications. Bar coding has been described as an inexpensive and remarkably reliable way to get data into a computer. It is no wonder that virtually every industry has found a niche for bar codes. Consider the case of Federal Express, a $1-billion corporation. Their management attributes a large part of their success to the bar-coding system they use to track packages. An 11-digit bar code, printed on all five parts of the Federal Express air bill, uniquely identifies each package. As each package wends its way through the transportation system, the bar-coded tag is read at each point, and the bar-code number is fed to the com-

## CASHLESS SOCIETY? DON'T BET ON IT

You can be cashless and checkless at the supermarket—if you want to. Futurists have been making that prediction for a long time, but it is not happening. The reasons have nothing to do with the technology. It is the people: They do not want to.

Consumers just are not very excited about paying for groceries and other retail products with a credit card that immediately transfers the money owed from their bank account to the store's account. For one thing, lots of people are not all that sure that the money is really in the bank, and they do not want to risk embarrassment at the checkout counter.

Lucky Stores think they have fixed all that. The POS terminals include a credit-card reading system that accepts a variety of bank cards. When the grocery total is rung up, the customer slides the bank card into the slot and punches in a secret code. The customer can avoid the embarrassment of discovering there is not enough money in the bank to cover the purchase by first checking the bank balance on a machine at the front of the store.

There is still a glitch, from the customer's point of view. The customer loses the float time, the time it takes for traditional transaction paperwork like a check to get to the bank and actually cause a transfer of funds. The stores, of course, have gone to all this trouble for exactly this reason. So. As consumers, will we cooperate? Stay tuned.

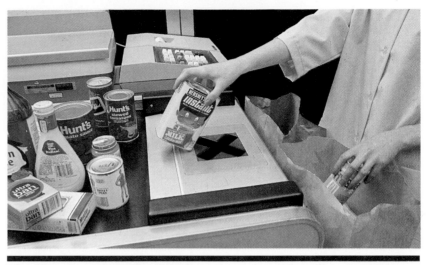

**Figure 5-8 Bar codes.** This photoelectric bar code scanner, often seen at supermarket checkout counters, reads the product's zebra-striped bar code. The code identifies the product to the store's computer, which retrieves price information. The price is then automatically rung up on the point-of-sale terminal.

puter. An employee can use a computer terminal to query the location of a given shipment at any time; the sender can request a status report on a package and receive a response within 30 minutes. The figures are impressive: The company has an accuracy rate in controlling packages of 99.99%.

One of the original uses of bar codes was as identifiers on railroad cars; the scanned data helped the computer system keep track of wayward cars. More recently, the codes have been useful in libraries, keeping track of books checked in and out. Bar codes also have been officially embraced by the promoters of the Boston Marathon: As each runner completes the 26-mile course, he or she hands in a bar-coded tab that helps officials tabulate the final results swiftly. It seems likely that new applications for bar codes will continue to be developed.

## Data Collection Devices

Another direct source of data entry is made through direct **data collection devices,** which may be located in the warehouse or factory or wherever the activity that is generating the data is located (Figure 5-9). This process eliminates intermediate steps and ensures that the data will be more accurate. As we noted earlier in the chapter, factory employees can use a plastic card to punch job data directly into a time clock.

Such devices must be sturdy, trouble-free, and easy to use, since they are often located in dusty, humid, and hot or cold locations.

**Figure 5-9 Data collection device.** Such devices are designed for use in demanding factory environments for collection of data at the source.

They are used by people such as warehouse workers, packers, fork-lift operators, and others whose primary work is not clerical. Examples of remote data collection devices are machines for taking inventory, reading shipping labels, and recording job costs.

## Voice Input

Have you talked to your computer recently? Has it talked to you? Both feats are possible with current technology, even though there are some limitations. We shall examine both "speakers," you and the computer. Since we are presenting input here, we shall begin with you, as you talk to your terminal. What could be more direct than speaking to a computer? Talk about going straight to the source!

**Voice input** is more formally known as **speech recognition,** the process of presenting input data to the computer through the spoken word. Voice input is about twice as fast as keyboard input by a skilled typist. **Speech recognition devices** accept the spoken word through a microphone and convert it into digital code that can be understood by the computer (0s and 1s). There are a great many uses for this process, quite apart from being an aid to status-conscious executives who hate to type. Among current uses are:

- Use in airplane cockpits for such nonflight control jobs as changing radio frequencies

## CAMILLE SPEAKS TO HER COMPUTER

Camille Ohlson was a member of the U.S. Ski Team when she had a skiing accident that left her a quadriplegic. She is now studying broadcast journalism at San Diego State University with the help of a voice recognition system and a personal computer. Camille has limited use of her arms but, with the use of specially designed braces, she is able to hunt and peck—type one letter at a time on a keyboard. Thus, she can input her class assignments on a personal computer using word processing software.

The problem comes when she needs to reformat her work, save files, and so forth. To give such instructions to the computer, most word processing programs require the user to hold down two keys at once—something Camille cannot do. So instead, she speaks commands to the computer through a headset. The system can recognize 50 different words.

As in most speech recognition systems, the computer had to be "trained" to recognize Camille's voice. Initially, she spoke the commands and identified them to the computer. Each spoken word was converted into a digital code and stored by the computer. Now, when she uses the system, each spoken word is converted into a digital code and compared to the library of stored words. By comparing the input code against stored codes until it finds a match, the computer determines what word Camille has spoken, then performs the desired action.

- Asking for stock quotations over the phone
- Sorting packages
- Factory inspections of items coming along an assembly line
- Action commands from physically disabled users
- Controlling your car through voice-activated commands to start the motor, lock the doors, or turn on the windshield wipers.

In each of these cases, the speech recognition system "learns" the voice of the user, who speaks isolated words repeatedly. The voiced words the system "knows" are then recognizable in the future. The package sorter, for instance, could speak digits representing zip codes. The factory inspector could voice the simple words *good* or *bad*, or *yes* or *no*. A biologist can tell a microscope to scan "Up," "Down," "Right," and "Left." Today voice input is even available on personal computers. Video games that anyone can talk to will be here soon, accepting verbal commands like "Bombs away!," "Dive! Dive! Dive!," and other important instructions.

What are the problems of voice recognition? First of all, speech communication is a very subtle process. Computers are not yet discerning enough to cope with all the ambiguities of spoken language. For example, will the computer know the difference between a *pair* of shoes and a *pear* on a plate? (Some systems are indeed this sophisticated, recognizing the true word from its context.) Second, most speech recognition systems are speaker-dependent—that is, they must be separately trained for each individual user. (Speech technologists are still wrestling with the wide range of accents and tonal qualities.) Third, there is the problem of distinguishing voice from background noise and other interfering sounds. Finally, voice input systems usually have a relatively small vocabulary.

Many speech recognition systems, called **discrete word systems,** are limited to isolated words, and speakers must pause between words. Now some systems support sustained speech, so users can speak normally. This type of system is called a **continuous word system,** which can be used, for instance, in the automatic transcription of spoken English into typed text. We can assume that this will eventually lead to word processors that take dictation.

Experts have tagged speech recognition as one of the most difficult things for a computer to do. Some of the world's largest companies—AT&T, IBM, Exxon—have been developing speech technology for years without the hoped-for degree of success. But someday machines that recognize speech will be commonplace. People will routinely talk to their computers, toys, TV sets, refrigerators, ovens, automobiles, and door locks. And no one will stare at them when they do. The research goes on.

# Two for One: Input/Output Devices

The relationship between input and output is an important one. Although some people naively think that the computer wields magical power, the truth is that the output produced is directly related to the input given. Programmers have a slang phrase for this fact: garbage in, garbage out, abbreviated **GIGO.** That is, the quality of the information the computer produces can be no better than the quality and accuracy of the data given to it in the first place. That fact is most obvious when input and output devices are closely related. For instance, computer screens are involved in both input and output: When data is entered, it appears on the screen; the computer response to that data—the output—also appears on the screen. Thus, if a mistake is made in entering data or there is a problem with the computer program, the mistake shows up right away on the screen.

Computer screens come in many different shapes, sizes, and colors. Some screens are **monochrome,** meaning only one color appears on a black background. The most common monochrome screen displays green letters and numbers on a dark background (see Figure 5-3), but amber characters are also available and are thought to be easier on the eyes (Figure 5-10a). Color monitors are available for displaying color graphics (Figure 5-10b). The most common type of screen is the **cathode ray tube,** or **CRT.** Another type of screen is the **liquid crystal display** (**LCD**), a flat display screen found on laptop computers (Figure 5-10c). These screens are much smaller and lighter than CRTs, but the quality suffers. The screens on point-of-sale terminals are even smaller—just large enough to display the item name and price.

## CRT Screen Technology

Most CRT screens use a technology called **raster-scan.** The image to be displayed on the screen is sent electronically from the computer to the cathode ray tube, which directs an electronic beam to the screen. The beam causes the phosphor-coated screen to emit a light, which causes an image on the screen. But the light does not stay lit very long, so the image must be **refreshed** often. If the screen is not refreshed often enough, the fading screen image will appear to flicker. A scan rate—the number of times the screen is refreshed—of 60 times per second is usually adequate to retain a clear screen image.

A computer display screen that can be used for graphics is divided into dots that are called addressable because they can be *addressed* individually by the graphics software. These displays are called **dot-addressable displays** or **bit-mapped displays.** Each dot can be illuminated on the screen. Each dot is potentially a *picture*

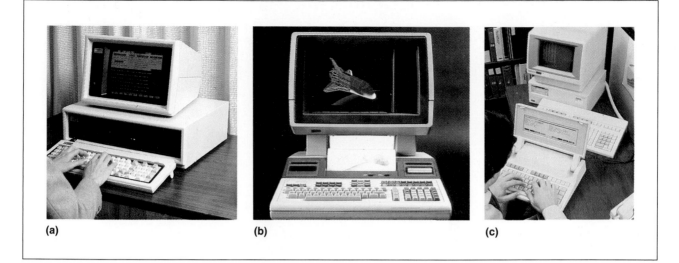

(a)                              (b)                              (c)

**Figure 5-10   A variety of screens.** (a) Studies show that amber screens reduce eyestrain. (b) This high-resolution brilliance is available only on a color graphics display. (c) Laptop computers use liquid crystal display (LCD) technology for their small, lightweight screens. In this picture a sales representative, who carries his laptop computer on trips, is loading data from the laptop model to his office personal computer.

*el*ement, or **pixel.** The **resolution** of the screen—its clarity—is directly related to the number of pixels on the screen: The more pixels, the finer the graphics resolution.

## Terminals

A screen may be the monitor of a self-contained personal computer or it may be part of a terminal that is one of many terminals attached to a larger computer. A **terminal** consists of an input device, an output device, and a communications link to the main computer. Most commonly, a terminal has a keyboard for an input device and a screen for an output device, although there are many variations on this theme. A terminal with a screen is called a **video display terminal** (**VDT**).

There are three kinds of terminals: dumb, smart, and intelligent. A **dumb terminal** does not process data; it is merely a means of entering data into a computer and receiving output from it. A **smart terminal** can do some processing, usually to edit data it receives. In contrast an **intelligent terminal** can be programmed to perform a variety of processing. Most supermarket point-of-sale terminals are smart. They have CPUs in them that can edit data right at the checkout stand.

The keyboard is an important component of a terminal. To communicate with the main computer through a terminal keyboard, you

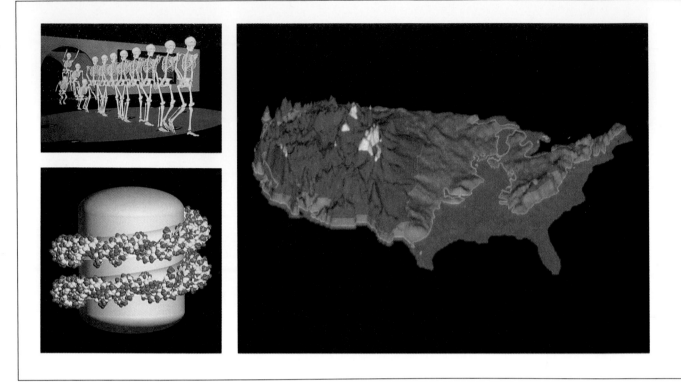

**Figure 5-11  Computer graphics.** This collection of computer graphics shows the combined power of the artist and the computer. The picture on the lower left shows a DNA molecule wrapped around another molecule.

make what is called an **inquiry.** An inquiry is a request for information. The result is usually displayed on the CRT screen very quickly. Sometimes the computer, in turn, will request data of you, the user of the computer. This is known as a **prompt.** Suppose you work in police communications and receive a report that a police officer has sighted a suspicious-looking car with a license plate beginning AXR. You make an inquiry of the computer and ask it to display a list of all stolen cars in your state with licenses beginning AXR. The computer does this, then provides a prompt:

```
DO YOU WISH DETAILS FOR A SPECIFIC
NUMBER FROM THIS LIST?
YES (Y) OR NO (N)
```

You type Y, and the computer provides another prompt:

```
TYPE SPECIFIC LICENSE NUMBER
```

You do so, and you receive details about the make and the year of the car, its owner, address, and so on.

We have lingered over this section to give you the feeling of the give-and-take of input and output, which are sometimes closely related. Now it is time to look at the possibilities in more detail, beginning with everyone's favorite, computer graphics.

## Computer Graphics

Computer output in the form of graphics has come into its own in a major—and sometimes spectacular—way. What reader of this book could possibly be unaware of the form of graphics known as video games? Who has not seen TV commercials or movies that use computer-produced animated graphics? Computer graphics can also be found in education, computer art, science, sports, and more (Figure 5-11). But perhaps their most prevalent use today is in business.

### Business Graphics: Pie Chart Picassos

It might seem wasteful to display in color graphics what could more inexpensively be shown to managers as numbers in standard computer printouts. However, colorful graphics, maps, and charts can help managers compare data more easily, spot trends, and make decisions more quickly. Three pages of confusion can be made into a chart that anyone can pick up and understand. The use of color also has an impact that helps people get the picture—literally. Finally, although color graphs and charts have been used in business

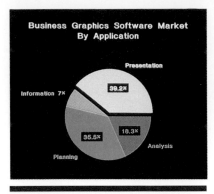

**Figure 5-12   Analytical business graphic.**

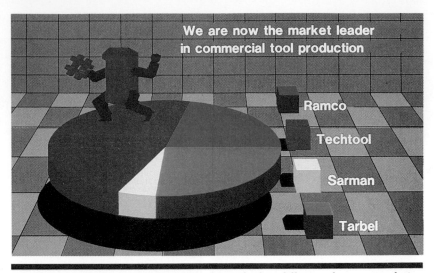

**Figure 5-13   Presentation business graphic.** The key difference between analytical and presentation graphics is quality. Although Figures 5-12 and 5-13 are both pie charts, the quality of the presentation graphics is enhanced by the suggestion of three dimensions, superior labels, and a hint of animation.

for years—usually to make presentations to higher management or outside clients—the computer allows them to be rendered quickly, before information becomes outdated.

The headlines all say about the same thing: THE BOOM IN BUSINESS GRAPHICS or THE BUSINESS GRAPHICS EXPLOSION. The boom is here all right, but the real story is the staggering number of business graphics software packages. The software falls into two categories. The first is called **analytical graphics,** a term referring to the traditional line graphs, bar charts, and pie charts used to illuminate and *analyze* data (Figure 5-12). For example, a stockbroker can view stock price and volume charts of data from the day's sales transactions. One businessperson refers to analytical graphics as "computer-assisted insight."

The second group of business graphics is called **presentation graphics,** the accepted term for an illustration meant for public display; high quality is implied by the definition (Figure 5-13). Getting the quality needed and transferring the graphics to hard copy is a relatively new and complicated story. We shall present this topic and, in fact, the entire spectrum of business graphics, in Chapter 15 on graphics software.

## Video Graphics

Unbound by the fetters of reality, video graphics are as creative as an animated cartoon. Although they operate on the same principle as a moving picture or cartoon—one frame at a time in quick succession—**video graphics** are not made by humans but by

Figure 5-14   *Blowin' in the Wind.* Computer artist William Reeves of Pixar created this computer-animated field of grass. Although it looks like a photograph, each blade is programmed to bend in the "breeze."

computers. Video graphics have made their biggest splash on television, but many people do not realize they are watching the computer at work. The next time you watch television, skip the sandwich, and pay special attention to the commercials. Unless there is a live human in the advertisement, there is a good chance that the moving objects you see, such as floating cars and bobbing electric razors, are computer output. Another fertile ground for video graphics is the network's logo and theme. Accompanied by music and swooshing sounds, the network symbol spins and cavorts and turns itself inside out, all with the finesse that only a computer could supply.

Video graphics do not have to be commercial in nature, of course. Some video artists produce beauty for its own sake, as the image of grass in *Blowin' in the Wind* attests (Figure 5-14). An important scientific use of video graphics is to construct moving models such as a model of DNA molecules whose atoms, represented by gleaming spheres, twist and fold.

## Computer-Aided Design/Computer-Aided Manufacturing

For more than a decade, computer graphics have also been part and parcel of a field known by the abbreviation **CAD/CAM**—short for **computer-aided design/computer- aided manufacturing.** In this area computers are used to create two- and three-dimensional pictures of everything from hand tools to tractors. CAD/CAM provides a bridge between design and manufacturing. As a manager at

### GRAPHICS IN YOUR POCKET

It was just a matter of time. If calculators can be hauled around everywhere, why not add graphics capability? Casio has done it. This model fx-7000G can display numerical equations as graphs on its 2.17-inch by 1.5-inch liquid crystal display screen. The price? Under $100.

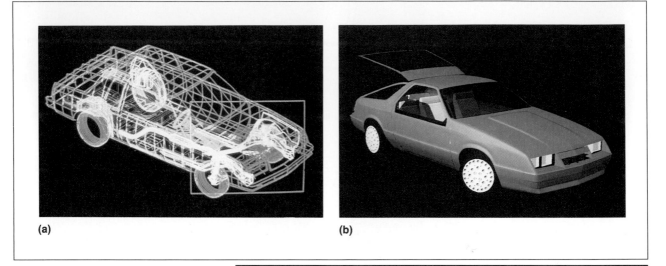

(a)                                              (b)

**Figure 5-15   CAD/CAM.** With computer-aided design and computer-aided manufacturing (CAD/CAM), the computer can keep track of all details, maintain designs of parts in memory, and combine parts electronically as required. (a) A computer-aided design wire frame used to study design possibilities. (b) A polygonal, shaded image used to evaluate the appearance—is it pleasing or not?—of a car's body design.

Chrysler said, "Many companies have design data and manufacturing data and the two are never the same. At Chrysler, we have only one set of data that everyone dips into." For the results of their efforts, see Figure 5-15.

We shall examine CAD/CAM in more detail in Chapter 17, which covers manufacturing systems. In Chapter 15 we shall be looking at the software used to create graphics. For now let us look at the input and output devices that make computer graphics possible.

## Graphics Input Devices

There are many ways to produce and interact with screen graphics. The following are some of the most common. Some of these devices can also be used for input other than graphics.

### Digitizer

An image—whether a drawing or a photo—can be scanned by a device called a **digitizer** (Figure 5-16a), which converts the image into digital data that the computer can accept and represent on the screen. This digital data can also be processed on a computer system. However, a **digitizing tablet** (Figure 5-16b) lets you create your own images. This device has a special stylus that can be used to draw or trace images, which are then converted to digital data that can be processed by the computer.

**Figure 5-16   Digitizers.** (a) This land developer is using a digitizer to input a map of a tract in Alameda County, California. (b) This engineer is using a digitizing tablet and color monitor to verify the design of an integrated circuit.

(a)

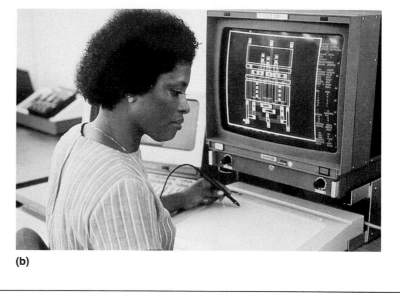
(b)

**Figure 5-17   Light pen.** When a pen with a light- sensitive cell at the end is placed against the screen of this graphics display terminal, it closes a photoelectric circuit, enabling the terminal to identify the point on the screen. This engineer is using a desk-top mainframe computer with a light pen to test a jet aircraft system.

### Light Pen

For direct interaction with your computer screen, few things beat a light pen. It is versatile enough to modify screen graphics or make a menu selection—that is, to choose from a list of activity choices on the screen. A **light pen** (Figure 5-17), has a light-sensitive cell at the end. When the light pen is placed against the screen, it closes a photoelectric circuit that pinpoints the place where pictures or data on the screen are entered or modified.

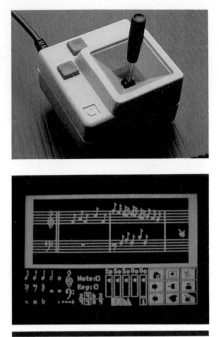

**Figure 5-18   Making a joyful noise.**
You remember the late night movies
that show the composer tinkering at
the piano, with a manuscript-in-prog-
ress on the music holder. A few more
notes—a frown, then a look of success—and our hero pencils in a few
more notes on the scoresheet. This is a
time-consuming, albeit romantic, process, and one that is totally passe. Today's composers use computers and
software such as *Music Construction
Set,* written by high school student
Will Harvey for the Apple II, II+, and
IIe. What's more, the whole process is
controlled by a joy stick. As you can
see on the bottom of the screen pictured here, a composer has a choice of
notes, sharps, clef signs, and other
music symbols, which can be selected
and "picked up" by the joy stick and
placed on the staff above. At any time,
the computer can play the notes so the
user can hear how they sound.

### Joy Stick

Another well-known graphics display device, the **joy stick,** is that gadget dear to the hearts of—indeed, we might say the joy of—video game addicts. It is, of course, a knob that allows finger-tip control of figures on a CRT screen (Figure 5-18).

### Mouse

A **mouse** is a computer input device that actually looks a little bit like a mouse (Figure 5-19a). The mouse wheels are rolled on a flat surface, usually the desk on which your computer sits. The rolling movement that results when you push the mouse causes the related output, a corresponding movement on the screen. Moving the mouse allows you to reposition the **cursor,** a flashing indicator on the screen that shows where the next character will be inserted. (On many computers the cursor can be moved with cursor control keys on the keyboard.)

Mice have figured heavily in the plans of people who write software for personal computers. A typical example is a screen of **icons,** small figures that represent activities, as shown in Figure 5-19b. A picture of a file drawer is a typical representation for saving a file, and a trash can could represent file deletion. If you want to save a file, for example, you roll the mouse on the desk surface, keeping your eye on the screen until the cursor is in the desired place over the file drawer. You then signal the computer that this activity is desired by clicking the mouse button. The file is saved. These actions replace typing word commands such as SAVE FILE on the keyboard.

Some people facetiously suggest that they cannot even keep track of their usual desk tools, much less a rodent. But most users are easy converts, and they often turn to the mouse as a quick substitute for the keyboard. Mice are a hot item for personal computers. Recent mouse models have appeared with rubber-coated control wheels, for smoother, near-silent operation on all surfaces. Variations on the mouse theme turn up regularly in the marketplace. Those who do not want to move their fingers from the keyboard or yield desk space to the rolling mouse, for example, can try a **footmouse,** which is controlled by foot on the floor under the desk.

### Touch Screen

If you disdain pens and sticks and mice, perhaps you would prefer the direct human touch, your finger. **Touch screens** (Figure 5-20) accept input data by letting you point at the screen to select your choice. Sensors on the edges of the screen pinpoint the touch location and cause a corresponding action on the screen.

## Graphics Output Devices

Just as there are many different ways to input graphics to the computer, there are many different ways to output graphics. Es-

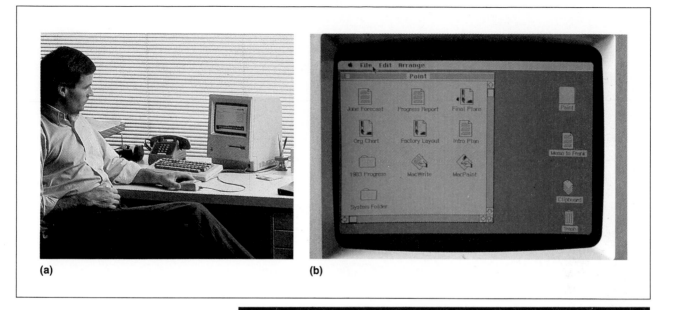

**(a)**                                    **(b)**

Figure 5-19 **Macintosh.** (a) The original Macintosh was so dedicated to using the mouse as an input device that it had no cursor control keys on its keyboard. (The Mac Plus does have cursor control keys.) The rolling mouse moves the cursor to select an option from a list of choices by pressing the button on the mouse. (b) Icons on a screen.

sentially, graphics can be output on a screen, paper, an overhead transparency, or a 35mm slide. We have already discussed screens, so now we shall look at other graphics output devices.

Figure 5-20 **Touch screen.** Light beams from the screen edge detect a pointing finger and note the location of the beams intersecting at the touch point.

### *Plotters*

Plotters draw hard-copy graphics output in the form of maps, bar charts, engineering drawings, and even two- or three-dimensional illustrations. Plotters often come with a set of four pens in four different colors. Most plotters also offer shading features. Plotters are of two types: flatbed and drum.

A **flatbed plotter** looks like a drafting table with a sheet of paper on it and a mechanical pen suspended over it (Figure 5-21a). The pen is at an angle to the table and moves around on the paper under the control of a computer program. The flatbed is commonly used for engineering drawings. Small flatbed plotters are also available for personal computers.

In a **drum plotter,** the paper is rolled on a drum instead of being flat on a table (Figure 5-21b). A pen is poised over the drum. If the pen is placed on the paper while the drum unrolls the paper (to be taken up temporarily on another drum), a straight line will be drawn along its length. On the other hand, if the pen is moved across the paper while the paper remains in place, a line will be drawn across the paper. You can visualize the various diagonal lines and curves that may be drawn with combinations of drum and pen movement.

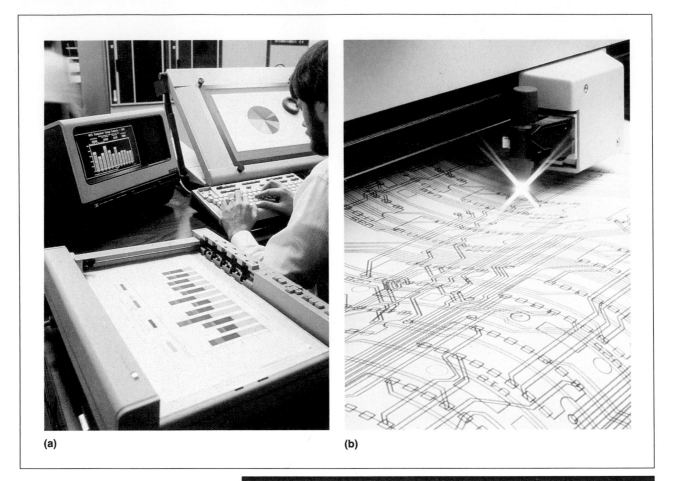

(a)                                              (b)

**Figure 5-21  Plotters.** Designers of circuit boards, street maps, schematic diagrams, and similar applications can work in fine detail on a computer screen, then print the results on a plotter. (a) Flatbed plotter. (b) Drum plotter.

One advantage of a drum plotter is that the sheet of paper can be quite long, which is necessary in certain scientific work.

### Printers

Some printers are capable of producing graphics. Printers are such an important output device that they will be discussed in a separate section.

### Overhead Transparency Makers

When making a presentation to a group, fancy graphics are not much help when they appear only on your computer screen or on paper. Transparencies used on an overhead projector are one way to present information to a group. Some plotters and printers are capable of producing overhead transparencies—just use a sheet of acetate instead of paper. Separate transparency-makers are also available.

### 35mm Slide-Makers

Various devices are available that will produce 35mm slides of computer graphics. The cameras have cones whose narrow end fits over the camera while the wide rectangular end fits exactly over your screen. Click, and you have captured your computer graphic on film. Of course, the film must now be developed. The Polaroid Palette, however, produces instant slides. Also, this system does not photograph your screen; it uses your graphics data to produce an image. You can even create color slides from a black-and-white CRT.

# The Forms of Output

As we have already seen, output can take many forms, such as screen output, paper printouts, transparencies, and 35mm slides. Other forms of output include microfilm and voice. Even within the same organization there can be different kinds of output. You can see this the next time you go to a travel agency that uses a computer system. If you ask for airline flights to Toronto, Calgary, and Vancouver, say, the travel agent will probably make a few queries to the system and receive output on a screen indicating availability on the various flights. After the reservations have been confirmed, the agent can ask for printed output of three kinds: the tickets, the traveler's itinerary, and the invoice. The agency may also keep records of your travel plans, which may be output on microfilm. In addition the agency may periodically receive printed reports and charts, such as monthly summaries of sales figures or pie charts of regional costs, for management purposes.

As you might already suspect, the printer is the principal device used to produce computer output.

# Printers: The Image Makers

A **printer** is a device that produces printed paper output—known in the trade as **hard copy** because it is tangible and permanent (unlike soft copy, which is displayed on a screen). Some printers produce only letters and numbers, whereas others are also able to produce graphics.

Letters and numbers are formed by a printer either as solid characters or as dot-matrix characters. **Dot-matrix printers** create characters in the same way that individual lights in a pattern spell out words on a basketball scoreboard. Dot-matrix printers construct a character by activating a matrix of pins that produce the shape of the

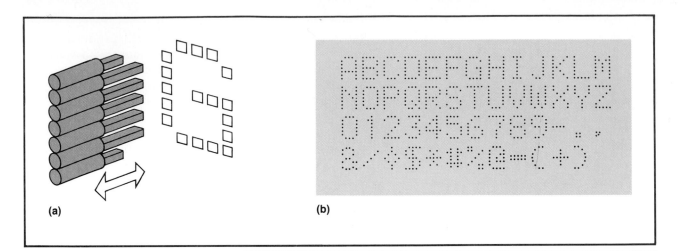

(a)

(b)

**Figure 5-22  Forming dot-matrix characters.** (a) This art shows the letter G being printed as a 5 × 7 dot-matrix character. The moving matrix head has seven vertical pins, which move back and forth as necessary to form each letter. (b) Letters, numbers, and special characters formed as 5 × 7 dot-matrix characters.

character. Figure 5-22 shows how this works. A typical matrix is 5 × 7—that is, five dots wide and seven dots high. Other matrices are 7 × 9 or even larger; the more dots, the better the quality of the letter produced. Printers that form solid characters are being challenged by new dot-matrix printers that place the dots more closely than previous models. Tighter spacing eliminates the polka-dotted look produced by older dot-matrix printers.

Distinguishing printers according to whether they produce dot-matrix or solid characters is one way to distinguish printers. But the two principal ways of classifying printers are

- According to the means of making an image on the paper

- According to the amount of information they print at a time

There are two ways of making an image on paper: the impact method and the nonimpact method. An **impact printer** is much like a typewriter. It forms characters by physically striking paper, ribbon, and print hammer together. A **nonimpact printer** forms characters by using a noncontact process—that is, there is never physical contact between the printer and the paper.

Let us take a closer look at these differences.

## Impact Printers

The term *impact* refers to the fact that impact printers use some sort of physical contact with the paper to produce an image. The impact may be produced by a print hammer character striking a ribbon against the paper or by a print hammer hitting paper and

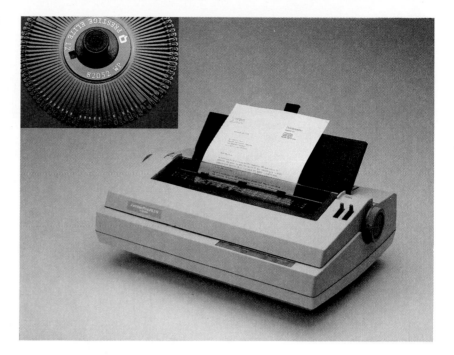

**Figure 5-23   Daisy wheel printer.** The daisy wheel (inset) consists of a set of spokes, and each spoke carries a raised character. A printer can have several interchangeable daisy wheels, each with a different type font. When inserted in the printer, the daisy wheel rotates to the spoke with the appropriate character. A hammer strikes that spoke against the ribbon, which then strikes the paper and leaves an imprint.

ribbon against a character. Impact printers are of two kinds: character and line.

**Character printers** are like typewriters. They print character by character across the page from one margin to the other. A typical character printer is the daisy wheel (Figure 5-23). Noted for high-quality printing, this kind of printer is useful for word processing and professional correspondence. The daisy wheel consists of a removable wheel with a set of spokes, each containing a raised character. The entire wheel rotates to line up the appropriate character, which is then struck by a hammer. The user can change type styles (fonts) by changing wheels.

**Line printers** assemble all characters on a line at one time and print them out practically simultaneously. There are several types of impact line printers:

### Band

The **band printer,** the most popular type of impact printer, uses a horizontally rotating band that contains characters, as shown in Figure 5-24a. The characters on the band are struck by hammers through paper and ribbon. An advantage of band printers is that the bands can be changed to produce different type fonts.

### Chain

The **chain printer** consists of characters on a chain that rotate past all print positions (Figure 5-24b). Hammers are aligned with each position, and when the appropriate character goes by, a hammer strikes paper and ribbon against it. Chain printers are also available with a variety of type fonts.

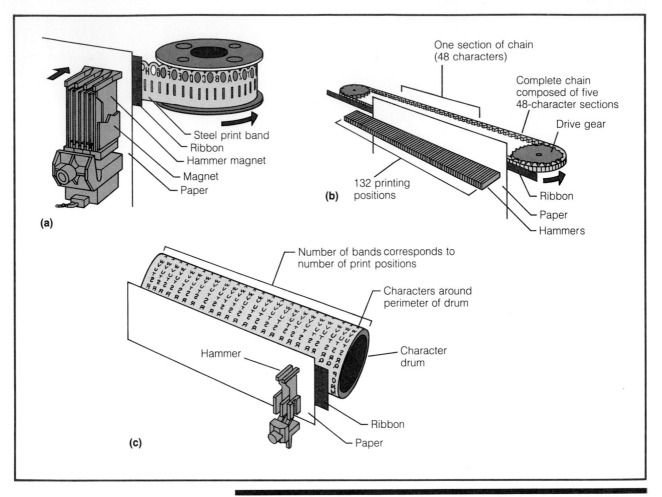

**Figure 5-24   Three kinds of impact line-printer mechanisms.** (a) Band printer mechanism. The band or belt can be easily changed to print different styles of type. Some band printers can print up to 600 lines per minute. (b) Chain printer mechanism. Some print up to 3000 lines per minute. (c) Drum printer mechanism. Some of these also print up to 3000 lines per minute.

### *Drum*

The **drum printer** consists of a cylinder with embossed rows of characters on its surface (Figure 5-24c). Each print position has a complete set of characters (64) around the circumference of the drum. As the drum turns, a hammer strikes paper and ribbon against the drum. A drum printer is considered a dinosaur among printers, but many can still be found hard at work in computer installations.

## Nonimpact Printers

There are many advantages to nonimpact printers, but there are two key reasons for their growing popularity: They are faster and quieter. Speed derives from the fact that nonimpact printers have fewer moving parts; they have no type elements or hammers that move around. The lowering of the noise level results from the absence of the impact—the striking of print hammers against ribbon and paper.

Other advantages of nonimpact printers over conventional mechanical printers are their ability to change typefaces automatically and their graphics capability.

The three major technologies competing in the nonimpact market are thermal, ink-jet, and laser. All of them use the dot-matrix concept to form characters. Let us briefly consider each of these.

### Thermal

**Thermal printers** produce characters using heat in the pins in the print head. The process is essentially one of burning characters into the paper. Early thermal printers needed heat-sensitive paper, which was noted for being slippery to the touch and for turning a dreary brown over time. Newer models can use ordinary paper.

### Ink-jet

Spraying ink from jet nozzles, **ink-jet printers** are up to ten times faster than impact printers. The ink, which is charged, passes through an electric field, which deflects it to produce a dot-matrix character. Ink-jet printers, by using multiple nozzles, can print in several different colors of ink. Color ink-jet printers, as shown in Figure 5-25, produce excellent graphics. However, these printers produce poor-quality text and at relatively slow speeds.

**Figure 5-25   Ink-jet printer.** Ink-jet printers are noted for high-quality graphics output.

*Laser*

A generation of children has watched movies in which space travelers use a laser, a powerful beam of bright light, to cut a hole through a wall or zap a flying target. Lasers have a true home, however, with computers, where **laser printers** use a light beam to help transfer images to paper. A laser beam "writes" the characters onto the surface of a rotating semiconductive metal drum that contains the range of characters. Then inklike toner is deposited on the drum; it adheres where the letters were "written," and is pressed on the paper. The result is extremely high-quality images, printed at record-breaking speeds.

Laser printers have been around for about ten years, but their high cost—hundreds of thousands of dollars—limited their use to companies whose need for speed made them cost effective. Recent technological advancements, however, have significantly reduced costs so that low-end laser printers can be purchased for a few thousand dollars. The Oregon legislature has taken advantage of the new affordability by placing laser printers in key administrative areas. Legislators who used to wait hours for drafts of new legislation to be delivered by courier now have easy access to draft bills from a nearby printer. "It's as quiet as the copy machine," marveled one politician. "All you can hear is the paper moving."

## Which Type of Printer?

A lot has been said about nonimpact printers. Although the trade press and industry consultants have embraced nonimpact technology, in truth the market has not received it well.

Change does not come easily. Experts predict that, by 1990, 75% of printer revenues will still be for impact printers, a technology that was expected to be swept aside by the onrushing wave of nonimpact machines. Why are managers dragging their feet instead of changing to a clearly superior technology?

Part of the reluctance stems from the seeming invincibility of impact printers. They chatter away day after day, year after year, without missing a beat—and rarely need repair. Another reason is pragmatic: multiple-part forms. Companies that print W-2 forms, stock certificates, mass-mailing cards, legal documents—anything requiring copies—will continue to use impact printers.

Choosing a printer does not get any easier for personal computers. Printers made especially for personal computers come in just about all the varieties we have already discussed. People are often surprised to discover that it is as difficult to choose a printer as it is to choose the computer itself. Some people are also startled to find that the printer they want may cost twice as much as the computer. Printers for microcomputers will be examined in Chapter 13.

---

**PRINTER SPEEDS**

This list of printers is not all inclusive, but these speeds are typical. Characters per second is represented by cps, lines per minute by lpm.

Daisy wheel—50 to 80 cps

Dot-matrix character—50 to 500 cps

Dot-matrix line—300 to 900 lpm

Band—400 to 3600 lpm

Thermal—10 to 80 cps

Ink-jet—110 to 400 cps

Laser—10,000 to 20,000 lpm

**Figure 5-26   Continuous form paper.**
Printout paper is continuous form
Z-fold.

## Paper

Now that you know something about printers, you can appreciate the fact that they use a variety of paper. Some printers use ordinary paper; others require special paper.

Computer output may be produced on a variety of different kinds of paper—cheap newsprint, lined-stock tabulating paper (called **stock tab**), shaded-band paper (called **green-bar paper**), or even fancy preprinted forms with institutional logo and address.

Paper may come in a letter-size sheet, but more likely it comes in a roll or in one continuous folded form (Figure 5-26). Continuous folded paper has sprocket holes along the sides, which help feed the paper rapidly through the printer without slippage. A computer operator puts a box of continuous paper on the floor, feeds the paper through the printer, and allows the printer output to accumulate—folded—in another box. The continuous paper must then be separated, a process called **bursting.**

If multiple copies are required, carbon paper for computer printers is available. The process of removing the carbon paper from between the layered copies is called **decollating.** A special paper called **NCR paper** (NCR stands for no carbon required) allows several copies to be made without the need for carbon paper. NCR paper is more convenient but more expensive than carbon-lined paper.

While the intent of data processing is to increase productivity, its misuse has contributed to a scourge of the modern world—paper pollution. The computer may enhance the productivity of direct-mail advertisers, but it may inhibit your own productivity if you find your mailbox clogged with computer-produced junk mail. (Of course, not all of it is the computer's fault; the rise in popularity of the photocopying machine may be even more to blame.) Although we keep hearing about the "paperless office," our complex society still runs on paper.

## Computer Output Microfilm: Small "Fish"

How many warehouses would it take to store all the census data for this country? Or all the FBI records? How many rooms in an insurance company or major bank would be required to hold all the printed customer records?

Computers can produce reams, even miles, of printed output, and although this is the easiest form for people to use, the space required is enormous. To save space, **computer output microfilm** (generally referred to by its abbreviation, **COM**) was developed. Computer output is produced as very small images on sheets or rolls of film. A microfilm record can be preserved on a roll of film (usually

**Figure 5-27   Computer output microfilm (COM).** This COM system can accept data directly from the CPU or from a storage medium such as tape. Sheets of microfiche are produced that store the equivalent of over 200 printed pages.

35mm) or on 4- by 6-inch sheets of film called **microfiche;** users often call them "fish" (Figure 5-27).

COM has many advantages, not the least of which is space savings. At 200 pages per microfiche, this book, for instance, could be stored on four 4- by 6-inch microfiche. A 1-ounce piece of microfiche is equivalent to 10 pounds of computer printout. Space savings also translate into savings in handling, distribution, and—of course—dollars: It costs $6 to print a thousand pages on paper, but it costs only 75¢ to print the same amount on microfilm.

COM does have limitations, however. For one thing, you cannot write on it. For another, it cannot be read without the assistance of a microfilm reader (like those used in libraries to read back issues of newspapers). COM is incompatible with fast-changing data systems such as airline reservations. Finally, COM has what is known as poor file integrity; that is, it is easy to lose one microfiche without the loss or theft being detected. Even so, from the standpoint of paper, it is clear that COM helps to save a lot of trees.

Numbers and pictures are—by far—the most common output forms, but there is a place for other types of output. In situations where it is more convenient to hear the output, voice output is a possibility.

# Voice Output: Your Master's (Digital) Voice

We have already examined voice input in some detail. As you will see in this section, however, computers are frequently like people in the sense that they find it easier to talk than to listen. **Speech synthesis**—the process of enabling machines to talk to people—is much easier than speech recognition.

"The door is ajar," your car says to you in a male voice. Why male? Because male voices have a narrower range than female voices and thus—an interesting, nonsexist reason—require less capacity in the memory of the microprocessor from which the voices originate! These are not, after all, real human voices. They are the product of **voice synthesizers** (also called **voice-output devices** or **audio-response units**), which convert data in main storage to vocalized sounds understandable to humans.

There are two basic approaches to getting a computer to talk. The first is **synthesis by analysis,** in which the device analyzes the input of an actual human voice speaking words, stores and processes the spoken sounds, and reproduces them as needed. The process of storing words is similar to the digitizing process we discussed earlier under voice input. In essence this technique uses the computer as a digital tape recorder.

The second approach to synthesizing speech is **synthesis by rule,** in which the device applies a complex set of linguistic rules to create an artificial spoken language. Synthesis based on the human voice has the advantage of sounding more natural, but it is limited to the number of words stored in the computer. Synthesis by rule has no vocabulary restriction, but the spoken product is often mechanical and sounds like no voice from this planet.

Voice synthesizers can be relatively inexpensive ($200 or so) and connect to almost any computer. Most synthesizers plug into the computer where the printer does and, rather than print the output, they speak it. Speed and pitch can usually be adjusted.

Eager candidates for voice synthesizers are often those who have speech impairments. Several software packages exist that let people communicate on the phone by typing their messages, which are then converted to synthetic speech. For example: "Hello. I am not able to speak, but I am able to hear you, and my computer is doing the talking for me. Would you please tell me if you have tickets for the Beethoven concert on Friday, the 18th?" This message can be keyed before the phone call. After the call is dialed and someone answers, the user pushes the Speak button, and the message goes out over the phone.

In addition, a reading machine has been devised that is of considerable help to the blind. Scanning a page, it recognizes letters and

## MY COMPUTER SINGS, TOO

Many people have heard computers talk in strange synthesized voices. But have you ever heard a computer sing? For a mere $4000 you can purchase DECtalk, a synthetic speech box so versatile that the standard demonstration includes more than half a dozen songs, sung with appropriate vibrato and inflection.

DECtalk can be plugged into almost any computer. Its internal loudspeaker can read out loud any text written on the computer's screen or anything pulled from storage devices.

The box's standard metallic voice will not fool many listeners into thinking it is human. It sounds, in fact, like an alien hurriedly but meticulously pronouncing each syllable. But the machine is surprising because it can talk in seven different voices. You can hear them yourself for the price of a phone call to the Massachusetts headquarters, (617) 493-TALK.

words, applies phonetic rules, and produces spoken sentences. The machine can even put in stresses and accents.

Voice output has become common in such places as airline and bus terminals, banks, and brokerage houses. It is typically used when an inquiry is followed by a short reply (such as a bank balance or flight time). Many businesses have found other creative uses for voice output as it applies to the telephone. Automatic telephone voices ("Hello, this is a computer speaking . . .") take surveys, inform customers that catalog orders are ready to pick up, and remind consumers that they have not paid their bills. (By using voice output one utility company saved the cost of hiring people to call the thousands of customers who do not pay on time.)

One more note. Perhaps it has occurred to you that voice input and voice output systems can go together, and that these topics could have been paired in the section in this chapter called Two for One. This is true. Today's technology permits combined voice input and output—consider the car system that you can talk to and get responses from. But that technology, by today's standards, is really very limited. Applications are few indeed. Keeping voice input and output in separate categories is appropriate, at least for now.

## A Birthday Party for Your Personal Computer

Let us say it is gift-giving time for your personal computer—that is, for you. What kinds of items might you want? There is a dazzling array of possibilities, many of them relating to input and output. Assuming you already have a full keyboard, a classy printer, and a color monitor, you could begin with (eek!) a mouse. A mouse is an inexpensive investment, not counting the software it supports. If graphics are important to you, you could show your creations on a small, quality plotter, and even produce overhead transparencies and 35mm slides.

But perhaps you want even more sophistication. Would you like a talking and hearing personal computer? No problem. All manner of products are available to give your own computer the gift of gab and ears to hear. Adventurous consumers can purchase devices to control their personal computers by voice and can even find speech-activated video games. One young computer buff likes to impress his friends by strolling up to his computer and issuing the command "Talk to me!" It always does.

Most input and output products are available for personal computers. If you want all the bells and whistles (and can afford them), you can have them.

# Yet to Come

Almost weekly, new forms of computer input and output are announced, with an array of benefits for human use. As we shall see in the chapters on personal computers and data communications, they promise to have an enormous impact on our lives. Their effectiveness, however, depends on two components that we have not yet discussed: storage and software. We shall study the first of these in the next chapter.

## Summary and Key Terms

- When bank customers use an **automated teller machine (ATM)**, they are using a complex set of input/output devices connected to a computer.

- Inputting is the procedure of providing data to the computer for processing.

- The keyboard is a common input device used by owners of personal computers, as well as by **data entry operators,** who use computer terminals to enter large amounts of data from **source documents.** The data that operators enter is stored on magnetic tape or magnetic disk before being sent to a main computer for processing.

- **Source data automation,** the use of special equipment to collect data and send it directly to the computer, is a more efficient method of data entry than keyboarding. Four means of source data automation are magnetic-ink character recognition, optical recognition, data collection devices, and voice input.

- **Magnetic-ink character recognition (MICR)** readers read characters made of magnetized particles, such as the preprinted characters on a personal check. The characters are put on documents by **MICR inscribers** and are read by **MICR reader/sorters.**

- **Optical-recognition** systems convert optical marks, optical characters, handwritten characters, and bar codes into electrical signals to be sent to the computer. **Optical-mark recognition (OMR)** devices use a light beam to recognize marks on paper. **Optical-character recognition (OCR)** devices use a light beam to read special characters, such as those on price tags. These characters are often in a standard typeface called **OCR-A.** A commonly used OCR device is the hand-held **wand reader,** which is often connected to a **point-of-sale (POS) termi-**nal in a retail store. Some optical scanners can read precise handwritten characters. A **bar code reader** is a stationary photoelectric scanner used to input a **bar code,** the pattern of vertical marks that represents the **Universal Product Code (UPC)** that identifies a product.

- **Data collection devices** allow direct, accurate data entry in places such as factories and warehouses.

- **Voice input,** or **speech recognition,** is the process of presenting input data to the computer through the spoken word. **Speech recognition devices** convert spoken words into a digital code that a computer can understand. The two main types of devices are **discrete word systems,** which require speakers to pause between words, and **continuous word systems,** which allow a normal rate of speaking.

- **GIGO** stands for garbage in, garbage out, which means that the quality of the output depends on the quality of the input.

- Some computer screens are **monochrome**—the characters appear in one color on a black background. Color screens are also available to display color graphics. The most common type of screen is the **cathode ray tube (CRT).** Another type is the **liquid crystal display (LCD),** a flat screen found on portable computers.

- CRT images are usually created through **raster-scan** technology, in which electronic beams cause the screen to emit light, and the result is the screen image. The screen image is **refreshed,** or kept lit, at a particular **scan rate.**

- **Dot-addressable displays,** or **bit-mapped displays,** are graphics display screens that are divided into dots, each of which can be illuminated as a *picture element,* or **pixel.** The greater the number of pixels, the greater the **resolution,** or clarity of the image.

- A screen may be the monitor of a self-contained personal computer, or it may be part of a **terminal,** an input-output device linked to a main computer. A terminal with a screen is called a **video display terminal (VDT).**

- A **dumb terminal** does not process data; it only enters data and receives output. A **smart terminal** can do some processing (usually data editing), but it cannot be programmed by the user. An **intelligent terminal** can be programmed to perform a variety of processing tasks.

- An **inquiry** is a user's request for information from the computer. A **prompt** is a computer request for data from the user.

- Computer graphics are used in many areas, such as video games, movies, commercials, art, and education, but perhaps are most common in business. The two main types of business graphics are **analytical graphics,** which are the bar charts and pie charts used to analyze data, and **presentation graphics,** which are higher-quality illustrations intended for public display.

- **Video graphics** are computer-produced animated pictures.

- In **computer-aided design/computer-aided manufacturing (CAD/CAM),** computers are used to create two- and three-dimensional pictures of manufactured products such as hand tools and vehicles.

- Common graphics input devices include the **digitizer,** the **digitizing tablet,** the **light pen,** the **joy stick,** the **mouse,** the **footmouse,** and the **touch screen.**

- A **cursor** is a flashing indicator on a screen that shows where the next character will be inserted.

- An **icon** is a small figure that represents a computer activity.

- Graphics output devices include screens, plotters, printers, overhead transparency-makers, and 35mm slide-makers.

- Plotters draw graphics output on paper. **Flatbed plotters** look like drafting tables, but on **drum plotters** the paper is rolled on a drum instead of being flat on a table.

- **Printers** produce **hard copy,** or printed paper output. Some printers produce solid characters; others, **dot-matrix printers,** construct characters by producing closely spaced dots.

- Printers can also be classified as being either **impact printers,** which form characters by physically striking the paper, or **nonimpact printers,** which use a noncontact printing method.

- Impact printers include **character printers** (such as the **daisy wheel**) and **line printers** (a term that includes **band, chain,** and **drum printers.**)

- Nonimpact printers, which include **thermal, ink-jet,** and **laser printers,** are faster and quieter than impact printers.

- The main types of computer paper are lined-stock tabulating paper (**stock tab**) and shaded-band paper (**green-bar paper**). Computer paper is usually continuous folded paper with sprocket holes along the sides. **Bursting** is the process of separating the folded paper after printing. **Decollating** is the process of removing the carbon paper from layered copies. **NCR paper** (no carbon required) is a more convenient but more expensive alternative to carbon paper.

- With **computer output microfilm (COM),** output is stored on 35mm film or 4- by 6-inch sheets called **microfiche.**

- Computer **speech synthesis** has been accomplished through **voice synthesizers** (also called **voice-output devices** or **audio-response units**). One approach to speech synthesis is **synthesis by analysis,** in which the computer analyzes stored tapes of spoken words. In the other approach, called **synthesis by rule,** the computer applies linguistic rules to create artificial speech.

## Review Questions

1. Explain what magnetic-ink character recognition is and how it is used by banks to process checks.

2. Name the types of optical-character recognition devices and explain how each one works.

3. Describe the two types of speech recognition systems and discuss the problems involved in speech recognition.

4. What is the difference between an inquiry and a prompt?

5. Name and describe the two main types of business graphics.

6. Name five graphics input devices and explain how each one works.

7. Name and describe two types of plotters.

8. What is hard copy?

9. How does a dot-matrix printer differ from a solid-character printer?

10. How do character printers differ from line printers?

11. What are the advantages of nonimpact printers? What are the advantages of impact printers?

12. Explain what COM is and why it was developed.

13. Name the two basic approaches to computer speech synthesis and explain how they differ.

## Discussion Questions

1. Do you think that continued research into voice input is worthwhile? In your answer discuss the practicality of current and potential uses.

2. What should a buyer consider when comparing different models of printers?

3. Some people predict that offices of the future will rely on soft copy output rather than hard copy. Explain why you agree or disagree with this prediction.

# 6

# Storage Devices and File Processing

## Facts on File

**Secondary storage allows data to be stored economically, reliably, and conveniently outside the computer itself, using magnetic or optical media. Ways of representing data, organizing it, filing it, retrieving it, and protecting it are described.**

When sixth-grader Kevin Porter wanted a computer for Christmas, his parents were happy to oblige. Even though Betty and George Porter knew nothing about computers themselves, they viewed it as an educational tool. Kevin, however, was primarily interested in a flight simulator game program he had seen at a friend's house.

Betty and George took a little time to investigate personal computers. They wanted a machine that was not just a vehicle for game-playing but one that had growth potential and could be used by the whole family. They decided on a mid-priced model, a 16-bit machine with 256K RAM. They felt that configuration gave them enough power for anything they might want to do and that they could always add more memory later. Since they saw little need for any fancy correspondence, they were content with an inexpensive dot-matrix printer.

They did hesitate about the storage, however. From the start, they considered only disk. Furthermore, a friend convinced them that they would really be glad they had *two* floppy-disk drives; two drives would be more convenient and save time. But salespeople from three different stores extolled the hard disk, making points about speed, convenience, high volume, and security. After thinking it over, Betty and George decided that they were not sophisticated enough to need a hard disk, nor did they want the extra expense. They decided on the two floppy-disk drives.

The choices for storage, whether for a large or small computer, are complicated. Betty and George—and Kevin—did not do too badly. We shall check back with them later in the chapter to see how their choices worked out. We switch now from home storage to the needs of a large corporation or government agency.

# Why Secondary Storage?

Picture, if you can, how many filing-cabinet drawers would be required to hold the millions of files of, say, criminal records held by the U.S. Justice Department or employee records kept by General Motors. The rooms would have to be enormous. Computer storage—the ability to store many records in extremely compressed form and to have quick access to them—is unquestionably one of the computer's most valuable assets.

## The Benefits of Secondary Storage

**Secondary storage,** you will recall, is necessary because memory, or primary storage, can only be used temporarily. Once your program has been run, you must yield memory to someone else; even if you are not sharing your computer with anyone else, your programs and data will disappear from memory when you turn your computer off. However, you probably want to store the data you have used or the information you have derived from processing, and that is why secondary storage, or **auxiliary storage,** is needed. Also, memory is limited in size, whereas secondary storage media can store as much information as is necessary.

The benefits of secondary storage are

- **Economy.** It is less expensive to store data on magnetic tape or disk, the principal means of secondary storage, than in filing cabinets. This is primarily because of the cost savings in storage space and the increased accuracy in filing and retrieving data.

- **Reliability.** Data in secondary storage is basically safe, since the medium is physically reliable and the data is stored in such a way that it is difficult for unauthorized people to tamper with it.

- **Convenience.** Authorized people can locate and access the data quickly with the help of a computer.

These benefits reach across the various secondary storage devices, but—as you will see—some devices are better than others.

## What Are the Choices and Which Is Best?

We shall spend most of the chapter answering these questions. We can take an advance look, however. Magnetic tape is a storage medium that has its place, but almost everyone—small-time and big-time—wants magnetic disk because it offers singular advantages: speed and immediate access to a particular record.

There are other choices too. Shall we stick with traditional magnetic media or consider, instead, the new optical storage technology? As usual, there are advantages and disadvantages both ways.

What about the personal-computer user? We have already hinted that storage decisions in that arena require some thoughtful planning. We shall examine all the possibilities. And, of course, we shall return to the Porters, to see if they are happy with their floppy-disk decision.

First, though, we shall consider how data is organized and how it is processed. These topics are intimately related to our choice of a storage medium.

## Data: Getting Organized

Data cannot be dumped helter-skelter into a computer. The computer is not a magic box that can bring order out of chaos. In fact, submitting data to a computer is not in the least chaotic—it is carefully planned.

To be processed by the computer, raw data must be organized into characters, fields, records, files, and databases (Figure 6-1). We shall start with the smallest element, the character.

- A **character** is a letter, number, or special character (such as $, ?, or *). One or more related characters constitute a field.

- A **field** contains a set of related characters. For example, suppose a health club was making address labels for a mailing. For each person it might have a member-number field, a name field, a street-address field, a city field, a state field, a zip-code field, and a phone-number field (Figure 6-1).

- A **record** is a collection of related fields. Thus, on the health-club list, one person's member-number, name, address, city, state, zip code, and phone number constitute a record.

- A **file** is a collection of related records. All of the member records for the health club compose a file.

- A **database** is a collection of interrelated files stored together with minimum redundancy. Specific data items can be retrieved for various applications. For instance, if the health club is opening a new outlet, it can pull out the names and addresses of all the people with specific zip codes that are near the new club. The club can then send a special announcement about opening day to those people. The concept of a database is complicated; we shall return to it in more detail in Chapter 16.

## Processing Data into Information

There are several methods of processing data in a computer system. The two main methods are batch processing (processing data transactions in groups) and transaction processing (processing the transactions one at a time as they occur). A combination of these two techniques may also be used. We shall now look at these methods and give examples of their use.

### Batch Processing

**Batch processing** is a technique in which transactions are collected into groups, or batches, to be processed. Let us suppose that we are going to update the health-club address-label file. The **master file,** a semipermanent set of records, is, in this case, the list of all members of the health club and their addresses. The **transaction file** contains all changes to be made to the master file: additions (transactions to create new master records for new names added), deletions (transactions with instructions to delete master records of people who have resigned from the health club), and changes or

**Figure 6-1   How data is organized.**
Data is organized into characters, fields, records, and files. A file is a collection of related records.

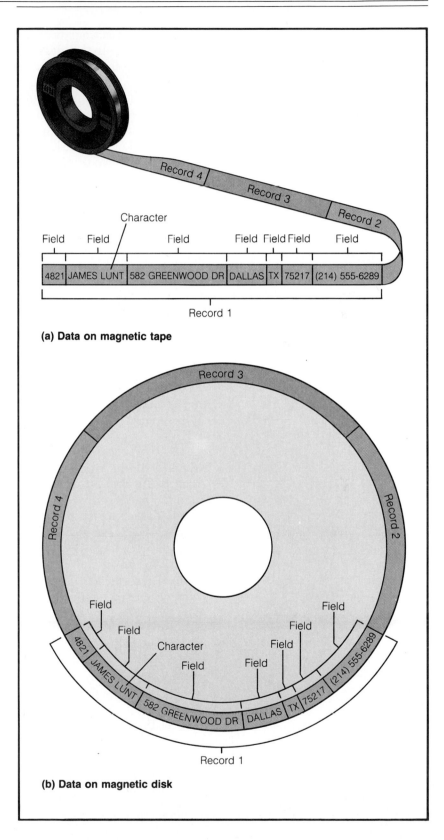

(a) Data on magnetic tape

(b) Data on magnetic disk

revisions (transactions to change fields such as street addresses or phone numbers on the master records). Each month the master file is **updated** with the changes called for on the transaction file. The result is a new, up-to-date master file (Figure 6-2).

In batch processing, before a transaction file is matched against a master file, the transaction file must be **sorted** by computer so that all the transactions are in sequential order according to a field called a key. The **key** is a unique identifier for a record. It is usually a number; since two or more people may have the same name, names are not good keys. Social Security numbers are commonly used as keys. In updating the health-club address-label file, the key is the member number assigned by the health club. The records on the master file are already in order by key. Once the changes on the transaction file are sorted by key, the two files can be matched and the master file updated. Note that keys are also used to locate specific records within a file; that is why you always need to provide your account number when paying a bill or inquiring about a bill. Your record is located by number, not your name.

During processing the computer reads from the master and transaction files and takes action on whichever of the two keys is lower in number. If the keys are the same, the record in the master file should be revised or deleted as specified by the transaction file. If the master file key is higher, the transaction should be added to the master file (if it is not an add, it is some sort of error); if the master file key is lower, there is no change of any sort to that master file record.

As the processing takes place, a new master file is produced; this new file incorporates all the changes from the transaction file. Also, an error report will be printed. The error report calls the user's attention to requests for deletions and revisions of records that do not exist and requests for additions for records that have been added previously.

One advantage of batch processing is that it is usually less expensive than other types of processing because it is more efficient: A group of records is processed at the same time. One disadvantage of batch processing is that you have to wait. It does not matter that you want to know what the gasoline bill for your car is now; you have to wait until the end of the month when all your credit-card gas purchases are added up. Batch processing cannot give you a quick response to your question.

Another disadvantage is that batch processing requires an extensive manual support system. Let us say your department store credit card does not allow you to charge a purchase over $50 without further verification and the new coat you want costs more than that. The sales clerk must call the store's business office, where someone has to leaf through the printout of the results from the most recent batch processing—which was perhaps done the night before—to see if you are creditworthy.

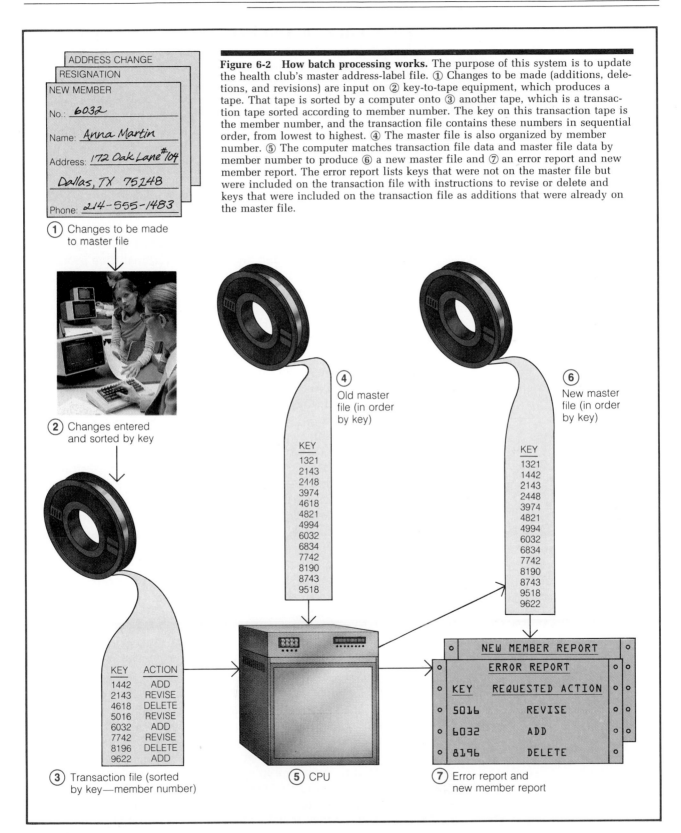

ADDRESS CHANGE

RESIGNATION

NEW MEMBER

No.: 6032

Name: Anna Martin

Address: 172 Oak Lane #104

Dallas, TX 75248

Phone: 214-555-1483

① Changes to be made to master file

② Changes entered and sorted by key

**Figure 6-2   How batch processing works.** The purpose of this system is to update the health club's master address-label file. ① Changes to be made (additions, deletions, and revisions) are input on ② key-to-tape equipment, which produces a tape. That tape is sorted by a computer onto ③ another tape, which is a transaction tape sorted according to member number. The key on this transaction tape is the member number, and the transaction file contains these numbers in sequential order, from lowest to highest. ④ The master file is also organized by member number. ⑤ The computer matches transaction file data and master file data by member number to produce ⑥ a new master file and ⑦ an error report and new member report. The error report lists keys that were not on the master file but were included on the transaction file with instructions to revise or delete and keys that were included on the transaction file as additions that were already on the master file.

④ Old master file (in order by key)

| KEY |
|-----|
| 1321 |
| 2143 |
| 2448 |
| 3974 |
| 4618 |
| 4821 |
| 4994 |
| 6032 |
| 6834 |
| 7742 |
| 8190 |
| 8743 |
| 9518 |

⑥ New master file (in order by key)

| KEY |
|-----|
| 1321 |
| 1442 |
| 2143 |
| 2448 |
| 3974 |
| 4821 |
| 4994 |
| 6032 |
| 6834 |
| 7742 |
| 8190 |
| 8743 |
| 9518 |
| 9622 |

③ Transaction file (sorted by key—member number)

| KEY | ACTION |
|-----|--------|
| 1442 | ADD |
| 2143 | REVISE |
| 4618 | DELETE |
| 5016 | REVISE |
| 6032 | ADD |
| 7742 | REVISE |
| 8196 | DELETE |
| 9622 | ADD |

⑤ CPU

NEW MEMBER REPORT

ERROR REPORT

| KEY | REQUESTED ACTION |
|-----|------------------|
| 5016 | REVISE |
| 6032 | ADD |
| 8196 | DELETE |

⑦ Error report and new member report

# 7 Transaction Processing

**Transaction processing** is a technique of processing transactions in random order—that is, in any order they occur. No presorting of the transactions is required.

Transaction processing is real-time processing. **Real-time** processing can obtain data from the computer system in time to affect the activity at hand. In other words a transaction is processed fast enough that the results can come back and be acted upon right away. For example, a teller at a bank (or you at an automatic teller machine) can find out immediately what your bank balance is. You can then decide right away how much money you can afford to withdraw. For processing to be real-time, it must also be **on-line;** that is, the user's terminals must be directly connected to the computer.

The great leap forward in the technology of real-time processing was made possible by the development of magnetic disk as a means of storing data. With magnetic tape it is not possible to go directly to the particular record you are looking for—the tape might have to be advanced several feet first. However, just as you can move the arm on your stereo directly to the particular song you want on an LP record, with disk you can go directly to one particular piece of data. The invention of magnetic disk meant that data processing is more likely to be **interactive**—the user can communicate directly with the computer, maintaining a dialogue or conversation back and forth. The direct access to data on disk dramatically increases the use of interactive computing.

There are several advantages to transaction processing. The first is that you do not need to wait. For instance, a department store sales clerk using a point-of-sale terminal can key in a customer's charge-card number and a code that asks the computer the question, "Is this charge card acceptable?" and get an immediate reply—immediacy is a distinct plus, since everyone expects fast service these days. Second, the process permits continual updating of a customer's record. Thus, the sales clerk can not only verify your credit but also record the sale in the computer, and you will eventually be billed through the computerized billing process.

Transaction processing systems are usually time-sharing systems. **Time-sharing** is a system in which two or more users can, through individual terminals, share the use (the time) of a central computer and, because of the computer's speed, receive practically simultaneous responses. Thus, an airline can have reservation clerks in far-flung cities interact with the same computer at the same time to keep informed on what flights are scheduled and how many seats are available on each.

Transaction processing does have some drawbacks. One is expense. Unlike batch processing, which uses the computer only for the amount of time needed to get the job done, transaction processing gives you access to the computer at all times. The result is that transaction processing uses more computer resources, so it costs more. However, when weighed against the alternative, such as lack of quick service, the added expense may be a minor matter.

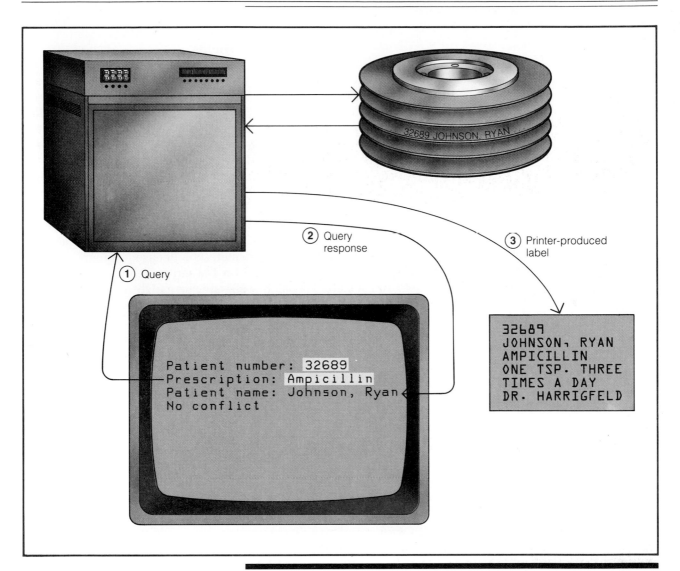

**Figure 6-3   How transaction processing works.** Ryan Johnson, patient number 32689, brings his prescription to the pharmacist. ① The pharmacist queries the computer system through the terminal as to whether the ampicillin prescribed is apt to conflict with other medication the patient might be taking. ② The computer notes that 32689 is Ryan Johnson and displays that information on the screen along with "No conflict," meaning there are apt to be no adverse side effects. The computer then updates Johnson's file so other physicians can see later that ampicillin was prescribed for him. ③ A printer attached to the computer system prints a prescription label that the pharmacist can place on the ampicillin bottle. All this is done while the patient is waiting.

A more serious drawback is the potential for security exposure. If many users have access to the same data, it is more difficult to protect that data from theft, tampering, destruction by disgruntled employees, or unauthorized use. It has become necessary, therefore, for the computer industry to take greater precautions to protect the security of computer files.

An example of transaction processing is given in Figure 6-3, where a patient has submitted a prescription for processing.

## Batch and Transaction Processing: The Best of Both Worlds

Numerous computer systems combine the best features of both of these methods of processing. A bank, for instance, may record your withdrawal transaction during the day at the teller window whenever you demand your cash. However, the deposit that you leave in an envelope in an "instant" deposit drop may be recorded during the night by means of batch processing. Many oil-company credit-card systems also combine both methods: A gas-station employee can instantaneously check the status of your credit by keying your card number on a computer terminal, but for billing purposes all your gasoline purchases may be batched and totaled at one time.

Police license-plate checks for stolen cars work the same way. As cars are sold throughout the state, the license numbers, owners' names, and so on, are updated on the motor vehicle department's master file, usually via batch processing on a nightly basis. But when police officers see a car they suspect may be stolen, they can radio headquarters, where an operator with a terminal checks the master file immediately to see if the car was reported missing.

Both batch and transaction processing can also be used in a store. Using point-of-sale terminals, inventory data is captured as sales are made; this data is processed later in batches to produce inventory reports.

As we have mentioned, two primary media for storing data are magnetic tape and magnetic disk. Since these media have been the staples of the industry for three decades, we shall begin with them.

## Magnetic Tape Storage

**Magnetic tape** looks like the tape used in home tape recorders—plastic Mylar tape, usually $\frac{1}{2}$ inch wide and wound on a $10\frac{1}{2}$-inch-diameter reel (Figure 6-4). The tape has an iron-oxide coating that can be magnetized. Data is stored as extremely small magnetized spots, which can then be read by a tape unit into the computer's main storage. Some tapes (so-called mini-tapes) are only 600 feet in length, but the most common length is 2400 feet.

The amount of data on the tape is expressed in terms of **density**, which is the number of **characters per inch** (**cpi**) or **bytes per inch** (**bpi**) that can be stored on a tape. (A byte is essentially the same as a character.) Although some tapes can store as many as 6250 bpi, a common density is 1600 bpi.

**Figure 6-4   Magnetic tape.** Magnetic tape on $10\frac{1}{2}$-inch-diameter reels has been the workhorse of data processing for years. However, a smaller tape cartridge has been introduced that can hold 20% more data in 75% less space.

## Data Representation

How is data represented on a tape? As Figure 6-5 shows, one character is represented by a cross section of a tape. As the figure also shows, the tape contains **tracks** or **channels** that run the length of the entire tape. On most modern computer tapes, one cross section of the tape, representing one character, contains 9 bits, one on each of the channels. There are nine locations. Each location has either a magnetized spot, which represents the 1 bit, or no magnetization, which represents the 0 bit. A common data representation code is EBCDIC (Extended Binary Coded Decimal Interchange Code), which we discussed in Chapter 4. Eight of the nine bit locations are used to represent a character in EBCDIC; the ninth bit is a parity bit, which we explained in Chapter 4.

Figure 6-5 describes how the tracks are used. In addition you

**Figure 6-5   How data is represented on magnetic tape.** This shows how the numbers 1 through 9 are represented on tape in EBCDIC code, using combinations of 1 bits and 0 bits. For each character there are 8 bits. The ninth bit is a parity bit represented by the letter P. In the odd-parity system illustrated here, each byte is always made up of an odd number of 1 bits. In an odd-parity system, an even number of 1 bits suggests that something is wrong with the data. Note that the parity-bit track appears close to the middle of the tape. The bits are out of order on the tape because the most commonly used bit locations are placed toward the center of the track, as far from dirt and grime as possible.

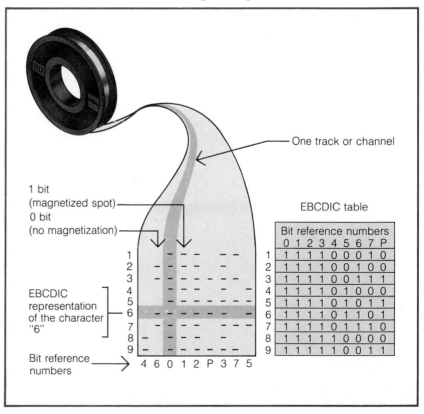

should note that the tracks that have the most magnetized spots are clustered toward the middle of the tape. This is to protect the data from dirt and damage, which are more apt to affect the outer edges of the tape.

## The Magnetic Tape Unit

As Figure 6-6a shows, a **magnetic tape unit** is about the size and shape of a refrigerator and indeed may even have a door that opens in the front. The purpose of the unit is to write and to read—that is, to record data on and retrieve data from—magnetic tape. This is done by a **read/write head** (Figure 6-6b), an electromagnet that reads the magnetized areas on the tape and converts them into electrical impulses, which are sent to the processor. The reverse is called writing. When the machine is writing on the tape, the **erase head** erases any data previously recorded on the tape.

Two reels are used, a **supply reel** and a **take-up reel.** The supply reel, which has the tape with data on it or on which data will be recorded, is the reel that is changed. The take-up reel always stays with the magnetic tape unit. As Figure 6-6b illustrates, the tape is allowed to drop down into vacuum chambers, airless chambers that lessen drag on the tape and prevent it from breaking if there is a sudden burst of speed. When operations are complete, the tape is rewound onto the supply reel.

Several precautions are used in the design of the tape reel and the tape to prevent mix-ups and loss of data:

- **File protection ring.** This plastic ring is also called a **write-enable ring.** The name *file protection ring* seems to imply that the ring is supposed to protect the file. Actually, it is the reverse: The absence of the ring protects the file. That is, you will not be able to record data on a tape unless you have a ring, which prevents you from erasing data already stored by writing over it. Hence the expression: No ring, no write.

- **Leader and load point.** The first 10- to 15-foot portion of a tape has no data and is called the **leader.** The reason no data is recorded here is that the tape may touch the floor or people's fingers, or otherwise be treated in ways that disturb the data. After the leader comes the **load point,** the place where the data starts. At the end of the file is an end-of-file record. There can be more than one file on a reel; if so, there will be one end-of-file record for each file.

- **Labels.** There are two kinds of tape labels: external and internal. The **external label** consists of a sticky piece of paper placed on the side of the tape reel, which identifies the tape (Figure 6-7). **Internal labels** are records on the tape itself and are of two types. The **header label** appears on the tape right after the load point and before the first data record; it contains such identifying information as the file name and date written. The **trailer label** is at the end of the file, before the end-of-file marker, and includes a count

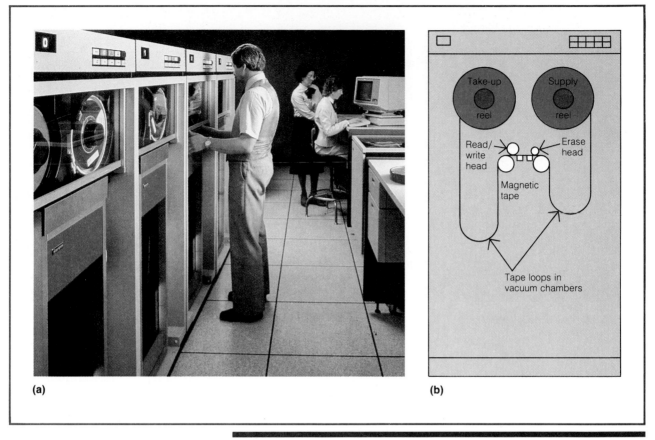

**(a)**

**(b)**

Figure 6-6   **Magnetic tape units.** Tapes are always protected by glass from outside dust and dirt. (a) Magnetic tape on reels is run on these tape drives. (b) This diagram highlights the read/write head and the erase head found in magnetic tape units.

Figure 6-7   **Tape labels.** Tapes have external labels to help prevent mix-ups. Tapes are stored in tape libraries, which are maintained by tape librarians.

of the number of records in the file to be checked against current processing information.

## Fixed-Length Records versus Variable-Length Records

It might be obvious to you that data on tape is stored sequentially: That is, records are written onto the tape one after the other—as the tape travels past the read/write head—in a particular order by key. The key is a field or fields (such as Social Security number) that serves as an identifier.

Records may be either of fixed length or variable length. The term **fixed length** means that all records on a file are of the same length—that is, they have the same number of characters. It is common to have fixed-length records on tape and disk because the program logic to handle fixed-length records is simple and straightforward.

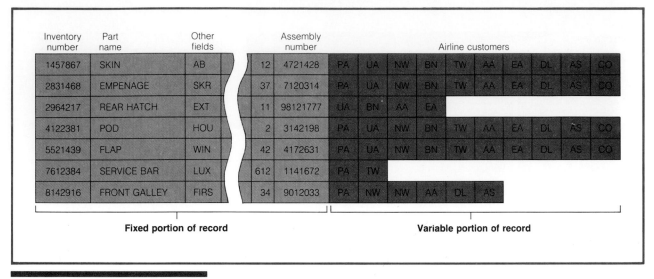

**Figure 6-8  Variable-length records.**
Most of each aircraft part record is of fixed length, but the portion for airline customers varies, depending on the number of customers.

Sometimes the records on a file have different numbers of characters—they are records of **variable length.** While this complicates the programming, variable length is appropriate in some cases. For example, for its airplane parts file, an aircraft manufacturer might plan a fixed number of characters on each record for the part's inventory number, part name, assembly number, and so forth (Figure 6-8). Each record will have at least these fields. However, not every part is used by every customer buying airplanes. The name of each customer using the part—for example, Pan American, United, and Northwest—is added to the fixed number of characters. The variations in the number of customer names added to each record make the records variable in length. As shown, there are differences between the number of customers who order standard parts and those who order an isolated luxury item. Any given file has records that are either of fixed length or variable length. The two types of records cannot be recorded on the same file.

## Blocking

Speed of access to records is important; therefore, magnetic tape units are designed to provide fast access to records processed one after another on tape. However, just as you cannot stop a car on a dime, so you cannot stop a tape instantly. Thus, it is necessary to have some room between records for stopping space. This space is called an **interrecord gap** (**IRG**) or **interblock gap** (**IBG**). Typically, it is blank space on the tape $\frac{3}{5}$ (0.6) inch long.

However, having many IRGs on a tape wastes space and adds to processing time. To avoid this, records are grouped together, using a process called blocking. Figure 6-9a shows how this works. **Blocking**

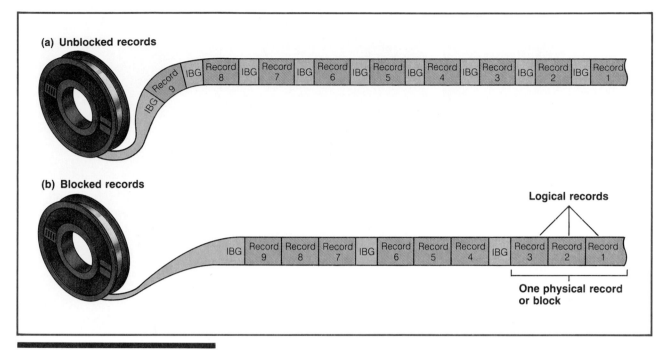

**(a) Unblocked records**

Record 9 | IBG | Record 8 | IBG | Record 7 | IBG | Record 6 | IBG | Record 5 | IBG | Record 4 | IBG | Record 3 | IBG | Record 2 | IBG | Record 1

**(b) Blocked records**

Logical records

IBG | Record 9 | Record 8 | Record 7 | IBG | Record 6 | Record 5 | Record 4 | IBG | Record 3 | Record 2 | Record 1

One physical record
or block

**Figure 6-9   Blocking.** (a) In the un- blocked records each record is a physi- cal record and also a logical record. Each physical record (block) is sepa- rated from the next by an interblock gap (IBG). (b) In the blocked records, three logical records are grouped into one physical record. This saves space, because of fewer IBGs, and increases processing speed.

consists of putting together logical records into one physical record, or block, followed by an interblock gap. By **logical record** here we mean the record written by an application program; it is called logi- cal because it is related to the logic of the program. A **physical rec- ord,** otherwise known as a **block,** is the collection of logical records grouped together on a tape. Programmers use the term **blocking fac- tor** to refer to the number of logical records in one physical record. That is, for the tape shown in Figure 6-9b they would say the block- ing factor is three—there are three logical records in a physical rec- ord. The number of records blocked together—that is, the blocking factor—depends on the amount of memory available to the program, the size of each logical record, and also (if disk is being used) the size of a track on the disk containing the file. With some experience pro- grammers become adept at selecting the blocking factor for a particu- lar file.

Although blocking saves time and space, there are costs in- volved: the time spent to block and deblock as well as the extra memory needed to hold the larger records.

## Magnetic Disk Storage

Magnetic disk storage is another common form of second- ary storage. A **hard magnetic disk** is a metal platter coated with magnetic oxide that looks something like a stereo rec- ord. Hard disks come in a variety of sizes; 14 and $5\frac{1}{4}$ inches are typi- cal diameters. A single disk is contained in a **disk cartridge;** several

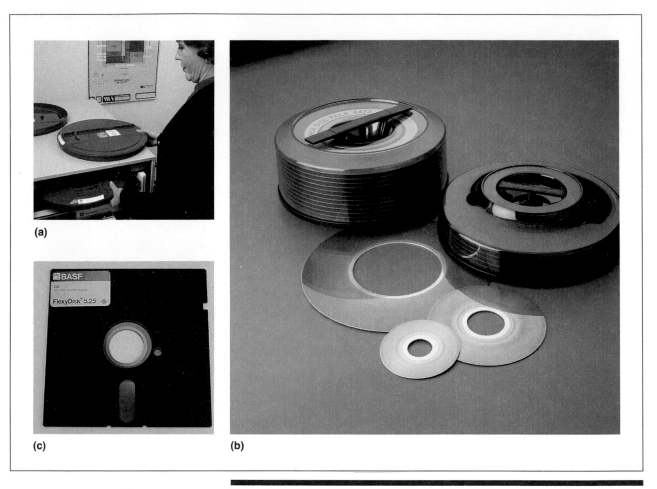

(a)

(c)

(b)

**Figure 6-10   Magnetic disks.** (a) A hard disk cartridge contains a single magnetic disk. The cartridge is shown here being inserted into a cartridge disk drive. (b) Hard magnetic disks come in a variety of sizes, as shown by these three individual disks. Also, disk packs can vary in the number of disks they contain, as illustrated by the two disk packs shown here. (c) This 5¼-inch floppy disk is in a square protective jacket.

disks are assembled together in a **disk pack** (Figure 6-10a and 6-10b). A disk pack looks like a stack of phonograph records, except that daylight can be seen between the disks. There are different types of disk packs, with the number of platters varying by model. Each disk has a top and bottom surface on which to record data. Many disk devices, however, do not record data on the top of the top platter or on the bottom of the bottom platter.

Another form of magnetic disk storage is the **floppy disk,** which is a round piece of flexible plastic coated with magnetic oxide (Figure 6-10c). Floppy disks and small hard disks are used with personal computers. We shall discuss secondary storage for personal computers later in this chapter, but keep in mind that the principles of disk storage discussed here also apply to disk storage for personal computers.

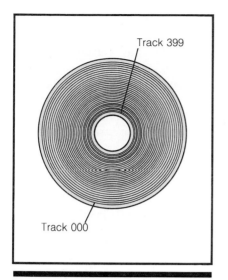

**Figure 6-11   Surface of a disk.** Note that each track is a closed circle, unlike the tracks on a phonograph record. This drawing is only to illustrate the location of the tracks; you cannot actually see the tracks on the disk surface.

## How Data Is Stored on a Disk

As Figure 6-11 shows, the surface of each disk has tracks on it. Data is recorded as magnetic spots on the tracks. The number of tracks per surface varies with the particular type of disk.

But note how a disk differs from a phonograph record: The track on a long-playing record allows the arm of the stereo to move gradually from the outside toward the center; a track on a disk is a closed circle—when the arm is on a particular track, it always stays the same distance from the center. All tracks on one disk are concentric; that is, they are circles with the same center.

The same amount of data is stored on every track, from outermost (track 000) to innermost (track 399 of a 400-track disk), and it takes the same amount of time to read the data on the outer track as on the inner, even though the outer track moves faster. (The disk can be compared to a chain of ice skaters playing crack the whip: The outside skater is racing, but the inside skater is only inching around—but both take the same amount of time to circle.) Disks rotate at a constant speed.

A magnetic disk is a **direct-access storage device (DASD)**. With such a device you can go directly to the record you want. With tape storage, on the other hand, you must read all preceding records on the file until you come to the record you want. Data can be stored either sequentially or randomly on a direct-access storage device.

## The Disk Drive

A **disk drive** is a machine that allows data to be read from a disk or written on a disk. A floppy disk is inserted into a floppy-disk drive that is part of a personal computer. A disk pack, however, is mounted on a disk drive that is a separate unit connected to the main computer (Figure 6-12). Some disks are permanently mounted

**Figure 6-12   Disk drive units.** Looking like cake covers, these disk-pack containers are sitting atop disk drive units. The disk packs themselves sit beneath the top-loading glass doors when the machine is running.

inside a disk drive. Generally, these are used in personal computers or in cases where several users are sharing data. A typical example is a disk with files containing flight information that is used by several airline reservations agents.

In the disk drive the disk or disks rotate at speeds of 300 to 400 revolutions per minute for floppy disks and typically 3600 revolutions per minute for hard disks. In a disk pack all disks rotate at the same time, although only one disk is being read or written on at any one time.

To read or write data on a disk, an **access arm** moves a read/write head into position over a particular track (Figure 6-13). The access arm acts somewhat like the needle arm on a stereo. A disk pack has a series of access arms, which slip in between the disks in the pack. Two read/write heads are on each arm, one facing up for the surface above it, one facing down for the surface below it. However, only one read/write head can operate at any one time.

## Winchester Disks

In some disk drives the access arms can be retracted, then the disk pack can be removed from the drive. In other cases, however, the disks, access arms, and read/write heads are combined in a **sealed module** called a **Winchester disk,** or a **Winnie.** These devices were named by IBM after the Winchester 30-30 rifle because the company planned to produce a dual-disk system with 30 megabytes storage each. (IBM later abandoned the dual-disk idea, but the name *Winchester* remained.) Winchester disk assemblies are put together in clean rooms so even microscopic dust particles do not get on the disk surface. Many Winchester disks are built-in, but some are removable in the sense that the entire module can be lifted from the drive. The removed module, however, remains sealed and contains the disks and access arms.

Winchester disks were originally 14 inches in diameter, but now smaller versions are made. Hard disks on microcomputers—5¼- and even 3½-inch disks always employ Winchester technology. Until 1980 the most common type of high-speed storage consisted of removable disk packs. Since then that technology has been supplanted by Winchester disks; around 85% of all disk storage units sold are of the fixed, Winchester variety. The principal reasons are that Winchester disks cost about half as much but go twice as long between failures compared to removable disk packs. This increased reliability is because operators do not handle the Winchester disk at all and because the sealed module keeps the disks free from contamination.

## How Data Is Organized on a Disk

There is more than one way of physically organizing data on a disk. The methods we shall consider here are the sector method and the cylinder method.

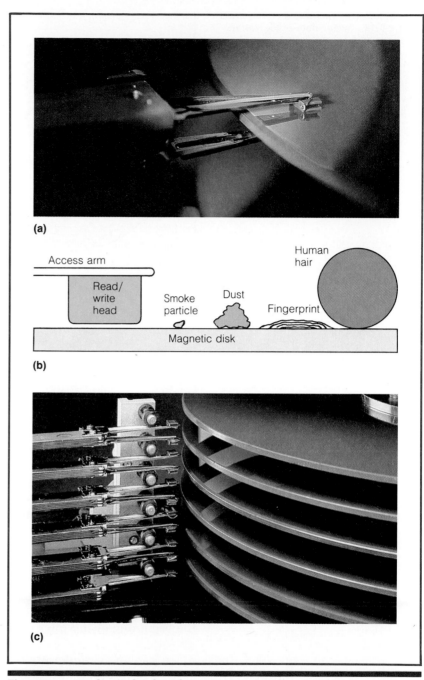

**Figure 6-13   Read/write heads and access arms.** (a) This photo shows a read/write head on the end of an access arm poised over a hard disk. (b) When in operation the read/write head comes very close to the surface of the disk. In fact, particles as small as smoke, dust, fingerprints, and a hair loom large when they are on a disk. If the read/write head crashes into a particle like one of these, data is destroyed and the disk damaged. You can see why it is important to keep disks and disk drives clean. (c) Note that there are two read/write heads on each access arm. Each arm slips between two disks in the pack. The access arms move simultaneously, but only one read/write head operates at any one time.

**Figure 6-14  Sector data organization.**
(a) When data is organized by sector, the address is the surface, track, and sector where the data is stored. (b) A hard-sectored diskette has 16 evenly spaced holes, each indicating where a new sector begins. (c) A soft-sectored diskette has only a single hole because the number of sectors is determined by the software.

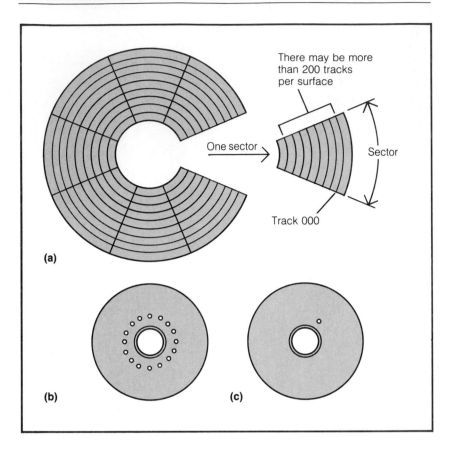

### The Sector Method

In the **sector method** each track is divided into sectors that hold a specific number of characters (Figure 6-14a). Data on the track is accessed by referring to the surface number, track number, and sector number where the data is stored. The sector method is used for single disks as well as disk packs.

A **hard-sectored** disk has a hole in front of each sector, near the center of the diskette (Figure 6-14b). Most personal computers, however, use **soft-sectored** disks, meaning that the disk sectors are determined by the software. A soft-sectored disk has a single hole to mark the beginning of the track (Figure 16-14c).

### The Cylinder Method

Another way to organize data on a disk is the **cylinder method,** shown in Figure 6-15. Most hard disks use the cylinder method. The organization in this case is vertical. The purpose is to minimize seek time, the movement of the access arms. It is clear that once the access arms are in position, they are in the same vertical position on all disk surfaces.

To appreciate this, suppose you had an empty disk pack on which you wished to record data. You might be tempted to record the data horizontally: start with the first surface, fill track 000, then

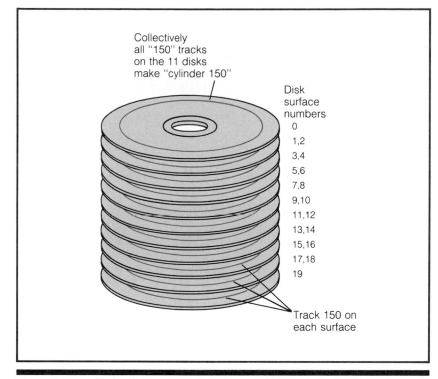

Collectively
all "150" tracks
on the 11 disks
make "cylinder 150"

Disk
surface
numbers
0
1,2
3,4
5,6
7,8
9,10
11,12
13,14
15,16
17,18
19

Track 150 on
each surface

**Figure 6-15  Cylinder data organization.** To visualize the cylinder form of organization, imagine that a cylinder such as a tin can were dropped straight down through all the disks in the disk pack. Within cylinder 150 the tracks are numbered (except for the top and bottom disk) as shown. This is a vertical perspective for track numbering.

track 001, track 002, and so on, then move to the second surface and again fill tracks 000, 001, 002, and so forth. Each new track and new surface, however, would require movement of the access arms, a relatively slow mechanical process. Recording the data vertically, on the other hand, substantially reduces access arm movement: The data is recorded on the tracks that can be accessed by one positioning of the access arms, that is, on one **cylinder.** By using cylinder organization, it is as though you dropped a cylinder (like a tin can) straight down through all disks in the disk pack: The access arms mechanism has equal access to track 000 of all surfaces, and so on. The cylinder method, then, means all tracks of a certain cylinder on a disk pack are lined up one beneath the other, and all the vertical tracks of one cylinder are accessible by the read/write heads with one positioning of the access arms mechanism. Using this vertical perspective, we can now number the tracks vertically within one cylinder: A 20-surface disk pack would number the tracks of a cylinder 0 through 19, top to bottom.

Now that we have seen how data can be written vertically on disk with the cylinder method, we can also see how to establish a disk address for a particular record. The disk address is the cylinder number, surface number, and record number, in that order. For example, the disk address of a record might be cylinder 150, surface 16, record 4. Now consider access to data on disk.

## Disk Access to Data

Four primary factors determine the time needed to access data:

- **Seek time.** This is the time it takes the access arm to get into position over a particular track. (On an IBM 3350 disk drive, for instance, seek time averages about 25 milliseconds.) Keep in mind that all the access arms move as a unit, so actually, they are simultaneously in position over a series of tracks.

- **Head switching.** The access arms on the access mechanism do not move separately; they move together, all at the same time. However, only one read/write head can operate at any one time. Head switching is the activation of a particular read/write head over a particular track on a particular surface. Since head switching takes place at the speed of electricity, the time it takes is negligible.

- **Rotational delay.** With the access arm and read/write head in position, ready to read or write data, the read/write head waits in position for a short period until the record on the track moves under it. (On the IBM 3350 average rotational delay is about 8.4 milliseconds.)

- **Data transfer.** This activity is the transfer of data between memory and the place on the disk track—to the track, if you are writing, from the track to memory if you are reading. The data transfer rate for the IBM 3350 is 1,198,000 bytes per second.

With these four motions users can quickly get at any particular record any place on a disk, provided they have a method of finding where it is.

## File Organization: Three Methods

There are three major methods of storing files of data in secondary storage:

- **Sequential file organization** simply means records are organized in sequential order by key.

- **Direct file organization** means records are organized randomly, not in any special order.

- **Indexed file organization** is a combination of the above two: Records are organized sequentially, but, in addition, indexes are built into the file so that a record can be accessed either sequentially or directly.

We shall study each of these in turn.

## Sequential File Processing

In **sequential file processing,** records are usually in order according to a key field. If it is an inventory file, the key might be the part number. A file describing people might use Social Security number or credit-card number as the key. We have already seen an example of sequential file processing in our discussion of batch processing (see Figure 6-2).

## Direct File Processing

**Direct file processing,** or **direct access,** allows you to go directly to the record you want by using a record key; the computer does not have to read all preceding records in the file as it does if the records are organized sequentially. (Direct access is sometimes called **random access,** because the records can be in random order.) It is this ability to access any given record instantly that has made computer systems so convenient for people in service industries— for travel agents checking a flight for available seats, for example, and bank tellers determining individual bank balances.

Obviously, if we have a completely blank area on the disk and can put records anywhere—in other words, randomly—then there must be some predictable system for placing a record at a disk address and for retrieving the record at a subsequent time. In other words, once the record has been placed on a disk, it must be possible to find it again. This is done by choosing a certain formula to use on the record key, thereby deriving a number to use as the disk address. **Hashing,** or **randomizing,** is the name given to the process of applying a formula to a key to yield a number that represents the address.

There are various formulas, but a simple one is to divide the key by a prime number and use the remainder from the division operation as an address. A prime number is any number that can be divided evenly only by itself or 1; it cannot be divided by any other number. Examples of prime numbers are 7, 11, 13, and 17. Figure 6-16 shows how dividing a key by a prime number produces a remainder that, in this case, indicates the track location. Now the record can be written on the first available location on that track, or, if reading, that track can be read until the desired record is found.

The reason for using remainders is that they produce disk addresses of manageable size. Some keys, such as Social Security numbers, are quite long; indeed, keys may run 20 digits or more. The main reason for using a key is that it is predictable: By applying the same hashing formula to the same key you can obtain the exact same address; therefore, you can always find that record again. For instance, if our hashing formula is to divide the key by prime number 13 and use the remainder as the addresses, then key 54 yields address 2 (54 divided by 13 yields remainder 2). The record for key 54 is then placed on the disk in location 2. (The example is intentionally simple to illustrate this point.) At some later time, this record

**Figure 6-16   A simple hashing scheme.** Dividing the key number 1269 by the prime number 17 yields remainder 11, which can be used to indicate track location on a disk.

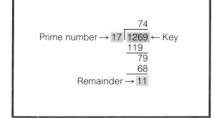

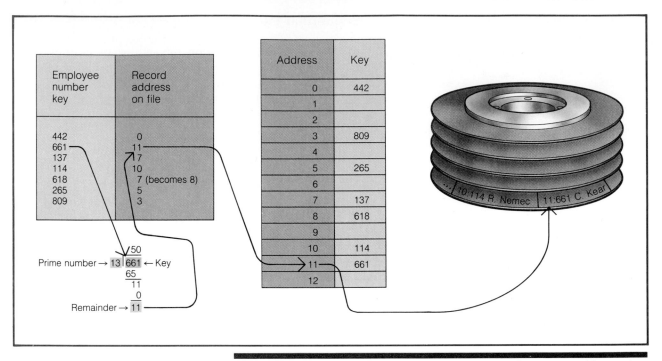

**Figure 6-17   An example of direct processing.** Assume there are 13 addresses (0 through 12) available on the file. Dividing the key number 661, C. Kear's employee number, by the prime number 13 yields remainder 11. Thus, 11 is the address for key 661. However, for the key 618, dividing by the prime 13 yields remainder 7—and this address has already been used (by the key 137); hence, the address becomes the next location, that is, 8. Note, incidentally, that keys (and therefore records) need not appear in any particular order. (The 13 record locations available are, of course, too few to hold a normal file; a small number was used to keep the example simple.)

can be found by applying the same formula to key 54 again; the remainder is still 2, and so we have rediscovered the address.

What happens, you might ask, if two keys divided by the same prime develop the same remainder so that you have duplicate addresses? (For instance, 7 divided by 3 produces remainder 1, but so does 10 divided by 3.) Records with duplicate addresses are called **synonyms.** One approach is to put each synonym in the closest available location—the next address, or, if that one is full, the address after that, and so on.

Figure 6-17 gives a very simplified example of how direct processing works.

## Indexed File Processing

**Indexed file processing** or **indexed processing** is a third method of file organization, and it represents a compromise between sequential and direct methods. It is useful in cases where files need to be in sequential order but where, in addition, you need to be able to go directly to specific records.

An indexed file works as follows: Records are stored in the file in sequential order, but the file also contains an index. The index contains entries consisting of the key to each record stored on the file and the corresponding disk address for that record. The index is like a directory, with the keys to all records listed in order. To access a record directly, the record key must be located in the index; the address associated with the key is then used to locate the record on the disk. Figure 6-18 illustrates how this works.

Records can also be accessed sequentially. The file can be accessed in two different ways. To retrieve the entire file, begin with the first record and proceed through the rest of the records. A second method for sequential retrieval is to begin with the retrieval of a record with a certain key—somewhere in the middle of the file—then proceed through the file as before.

A disadvantage of indexed processing is that the process of looking up the key in the index adds one more operation to the retrieval process. It is therefore not as fast as direct file processing.

**Figure 6-18  An example of indexed processing.** In a credit department a terminal operator can make an inquiry about a customer's account by typing in the customer number on the terminal. The index then directs the computer to the particular disk address, which indicates the customer information.

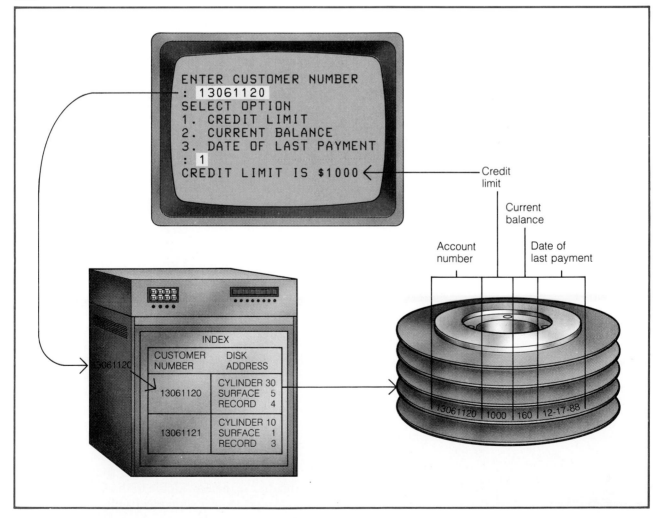

# The Case for Disk Storage

Subtitle: And a few words for tape, too. As we have seen, disk has many advantages over tape. There are those in the industry who wonder why tape is still around at all. Disk does indeed seem the very model of a good storage medium:

- Disk has high data-volume capacity and allows very fast access. Data on disk is very reliable.

- Disk files may be organized directly, which allows immediate access and update of any given record. This is the biggest advantage and is basic to real-time systems that facilitate instant credit checks and airline reservations.

- Using direct access, information may be updated easily. In contrast to a sequentially processed record, a single direct-access record may be read, updated, and returned to the disk without the necessity of rewriting the entire file (this is called being updated in place).

And tape? We have seen that records cannot be processed directly on tape. Even so, tape has certain advantages that make it a viable storage medium. It is portable—a reel of tape can be carried or mailed. It is relatively inexpensive: A reel of 2400-foot tape costs less than $15. (Compare this with a full-size disk pack, which costs $300 and up.)

The chief uses of magnetic tape today are in standard sequential processing (for example, payroll) and as a convenient backup medium for disk files. Backup copies of disk files are made regularly on tape as insurance against disk failure.

# Mass Storage

Mass storage is a third form of secondary, or auxiliary, storage. **Mass storage devices** are able to store enormous volumes of data, such as census records or Internal Revenue Service records, but their drawback is that they are relatively slow—the speed of information retrieval from mass storage devices is measured in seconds rather than milliseconds.

As Figure 6-19 shows, the IBM 3850 Mass Storage System consists of a honeycomblike apparatus. Each cell of the honeycomb contains a cartridge that is 2 inches in diameter and 4 inches long. Each cartridge contains a magnetic tape inside it that is 770 inches long and holds 50 million bytes of data.

Neither the honeycomb nor the cartridges themselves are connected directly to the CPU. When data is needed, a mechanical arm must retrieve the cartridge from the cell, and the data on the cartridge is transferred to a magnetic disk—a process that takes 3 to 8 seconds. The data on the disk is then available to the CPU. Mechanical action of any sort is always slower than electronic action, and in

**Figure 6-19   A mass storage device.** The IBM 3850 Mass Storage System. The cartridges shown inside each honeycomblike cell are about the size of a snack-size fruit-juice can.

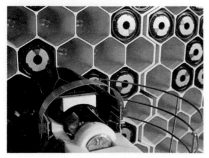

## THE MICROCOMPUTER CORNER

### How to Handle Floppy Disks

Do not lock your disk in the trunk of the car on a hot day, or leave it on the dashboard in the sun, or pin it to the door of your refrigerator with a magnet. Avoid smoking cigarettes around your computer, since particles deposited on the disk will cause the head to scratch the disk surface. Keep disks away from subways and telephones, which have magnetic coils.

These are only a few of the rules for taking care of disks. Others are offered below. The main forces hostile to floppy disks are dust, magnetic fields, liquids, vapors, and temperature extremes.

Disk drives should be cleaned at least once a year with special head-cleaning kits available at computer hardware and software retailers.

this case it can take up to 15 seconds to retrieve the data. This makes the process 600 times slower than the average seek time on IBM 3350 disk storage. Clearly, mass storage devices are most useful in situations where fast access time is not required.

We have mentioned the large volume of data in government files, but many private industries also maintain large files. A large, national insurance company, for example, needs considerable file storage for applications, policies, claims, and related data. It is feasible to use mass storage devices for these files as long as the appropriate files are moved to disk for processing.

# Personal Computer Storage

The market for data storage devices is being profoundly affected by the surge in popularity of personal computers. Storage media are available in three basic forms: cassette tapes, diskettes, and hard disk. Let us consider each of these.

## Cassette Tapes

**Cassette tapes** are the same as the audio tapes you use on a portable tape recorder at home. The advantage of using cassette tapes to store computer data is that there are many cheap tape recorders around, so if you are putting together a home computer system for the first time, this is a way to save money. The disadvantage is the same as that for all tape storage: You cannot access the tape file directly—that is, access any one record. Moreover, tape is slow— very slow.

## Diskettes

**Diskettes** are more popular than cassettes with most microcomputer users. Among computer veterans, a 5¼-inch diskette is known as a **minifloppy,** to distinguish it from the 8-inch model of previous generations. The minifloppy generally holds about 360K bytes of data. A small disk known as a **microfloppy** is also on the market (Figure 6-20).

Apple Computer set the 3½-inch standard size for microfloppy diskettes with its popular Macintosh. As we noted earlier, diskettes have been called floppy disks, but the small 3½-inch disks come in a hard plastic housing and, in fact, do not flop. A better name for these disks is **microdisks.** It is unlikely that the 5¼-inch disk will continue to be the dominant size used in personal computers. The future belongs to smaller disks, which offer some nice advantages. First, the small disk is easier to store, not to mention that it fits into a shirt pocket or purse. It weighs less and consumes less power. Then, of course, its higher capacity allows companies to offer several application programs on a disk, so users do not have to shuffle so many disks around. The long-range advantage of the 3½-inch disk is that manufacturers can make their computers smaller, so they take up

## THE INCREDIBLE EDIBLE DISK

Purveyors of floppy disks have traditionally heaped cautions upon the users of such disks: Do not bend, keep away from heat and dirt and magnets, and above all, do not touch! But Polaroid, a daring diskmaker, placed eye-catching ads in personal-computer magazines showing diskettes covered with such appalling substances as jam, fried eggs, mustard, and melted chocolate. They promised a free data recovery service if such an accident should happen to your disk.

They got more than they bargained for. Users from all over the country took up the challenge, subjecting their disks to such "accidents" as a hot-fudge sundae, cigar ashes, and even canine chewing. Polaroid recovered the data in all these cases. They missed out only on the disk that was maliciously stapled to death.

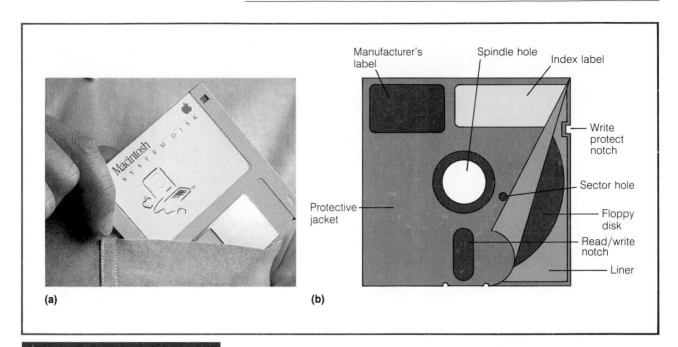

**Figure 6-20   Floppy disks.** (a) This 3½-inch diskette fits in a shirt pocket. (b) Cutaway view of a floppy disk showing the parts of a floppy.

less desk space. Have we reached the ultimate in disk smallness? Apparently not. Maxell Corporation has introduced a 2½-inch 500K byte diskette called the **ultramicro disk.** Perhaps someday we shall carry disks in our wallets.

## Hard Disk

**Hard disks** are 5-inch or 3½-inch Winchester disks in sealed modules (Figure 6-21). They are expensive—over $1000 per unit—but, with a capacity of 10 to 20 and even 30 megabytes of storage, they may be worth the price. Hard disks are extremely reliable, since they are sealed against contamination by outside air or human hands.

But hard disks can save you time as well as space. You do not even have to need all the storage hard disk provides; just the way the hard disk speeds up your computing can make it worthwhile. As one convert noted, "Floppy disks are a pain. The idea of a computer in the first place was to get work done faster, and it seems like juggling floppy disks is a step backward." The promise of speedier processing did far more to win him over than the promise of more disk storage space.

Unlike a floppy disk, however, a hard disk cannot be transported from one computer to another. For that reason any hard-disk system needs one floppy-disk drive to provide users with software portability. Also, hard-disk files should be backed up—copied—to floppy disk or tape regularly as a security measure.

**(a)**     **(b)**

Figure 6-21  **Hard disks.** (a) A bank of hard disks. The police in Sauk County, Wisconsin, use a battery of computers and hard disks to keep track of traffic offenders who cross the county line. (b) Innards of a hard disk. This drive stores about 20 million characters on a pair of 3½-inch disks.

## Hardcard

Imagine your own personal computer with hard disk built-in. Most people, especially in business, are surprised at how fast it fills with data. Now where do you turn? You could buy another hard-disk drive and attach it to your machine. A more attractive option, however, is the **hardcard** (Figure 6-22), which has 10 megabytes of hard disk on a board that fits in a slot inside your computer. The primary advantage of a hardcard is that it is out of sight and not cluttering up your desk.

## RAM Disk: Turning Your Micro into a Hotrod

It is called a **RAM disk,** or an **electronic disk,** or a **phantom disk,** but it is not really a disk at all. A RAM disk is a chip that fools your computer into regarding part of its memory as a third disk drive that can be used to store programs and data. The advantage of a RAM disk is that it works much faster than a standard disk drive.

A RAM disk is particularly helpful if a user is sending data from one computer to another. Instead of delays waiting for the floppy or hard disk to send data, the data can be sent directly from the RAM disk. Another ingenious use of RAM is memory-resident programs.

**Figure 6-22   Hardcard.** (a) This disk drive on a card—a hardcard—is being inserted into a slot inside a microcomputer. (b) Interior of a hardcard showing the disk.

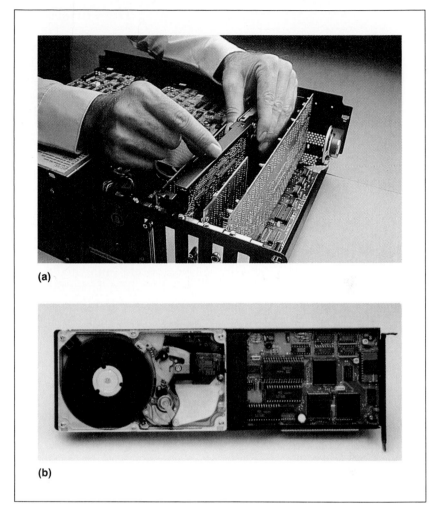

(a)

(b)

For example, as a personal computer is turned on, an "office manager" program is called in from the hard disk to reside temporarily in an unused corner of RAM. Whenever you wish to use this program to make a few notes, or use a calculator, or dial another computer (yes, there are programs that do all these tasks), the instructions are available speedily. If, instead, you had to take the time to slip in a floppy disk, you might as well use a real note pad or calculator or phone directory.

So why not put all files on RAM disk and enjoy the pure speed? RAM disk, alas, is volatile. Its contents are lost if the computer is turned off or there is a power failure. It is acceptable to lose program files in such a way if they are stored permanently on the original disk files. Data files, which are always changing, must be saved on disk before you turn off your computer. In fact, it is a good idea to save your files periodically as you are working on them to avoid data loss due to power surges or power failures. So, in summary, you can load your programs onto RAM disk for the day, but you must save new data on disk files.

## The Porters Revisited

We left Betty and George and Kevin with their personal computer equipped with dual floppy-disk drives. It worked just fine for its original purpose, Kevin's flight simulator game. Betty and George tinkered a bit, each branching out to other software. Betty, a college professor, wanted to learn how to use word processing to prepare tests and other student materials. She took a short seminar at the college and soon found that it was easier to key most everything on a computer file, even her "to do" lists. George, meanwhile, discovered that computer software could help him keep track of his stocks. He gradually diversified to other record keeping and produced a steady stream of output on diskettes. What is more, Betty taught him word processing, and he started using the computer to prepare some of his reports for the office.

You see where this is leading. In less than a year, Betty and George were inundated with floppy disks. They were not too concerned at first, since they kept them handy in plastic disk cases. They flipped the floppies in and out of the drives easily.

But a notable event took place at the college: Betty's department acquired a personal computer. Betty was a natural to be one of the first to put it through its paces. This machine had one significant difference: hard disk. Betty was pleased to see how quickly it could save and retrieve files. At home she was no longer content with her diskettes; they seemed to poke along forever.

This story has an ending, the predictable one. Betty and George bought a hard disk for their own computer and transferred all their files to it. The choice between a 10-megabyte disk and a 20-megabyte disk was an easy one for them, and they did not hesitate. They took the advice that floats freely among personal computer users: Buy twice as much disk space as you think you need.

And Kevin? It was his present, after all. It was another year before he started generating storage files containing his own primitive flight programs. He took hard disk for granted.

## Optical Storage: Superdisk Takes Off

Now that you have a thorough grounding in traditional magnetic media, you can appreciate the technology that is now upon us in the form of **optical disk**, as shown in Figure 6-23. The computer industry is constantly driven to provide storage devices that are higher in capacity, cheaper, more compact, and more versatile. The optical disk is ideal for this demanding shopping list.

## How Optical Disks Work

The technology works like this. A laser hits a layer of metallic material spread over the surface of the disk. When data is

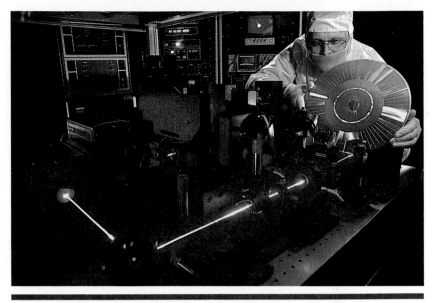

**Figure 6-23   Optical disk.** This 3M optical disk holds 250,000 pages of data.

being entered, heat from the laser produces tiny spots on the disk's surface. To read the data, the laser scans the disk, and a lens picks up different light reflections from the various spots.

Optical storage technology is categorized according to its read/write capability. **Read-only** media are recorded on by the manufacturer and can be read from but not written to by the user. This technology is sometimes referred to as **OROM,** for **optical read-only memory.** Such a disk could not, obviously, be used for your files, but manufacturers could use it to supply software. Current multiple-application packages—word processing, spreadsheets, graphics, database—sometimes take as many as six floppy disks; all these could fit on one OROM disk.    *Write once Read many = WORM*

**Write-once** media may be written to once by the user. Once filled, they become read-only media. Both are nonerasable. For applications demanding secure storage of original versions of valuable documents or data, the primary advantage of nonerasability is clear: Once they are recorded, no one can erase or modify them. Write-once optical media can provide a secure comparison base for auditing changes to original data—an invaluable function to, say, geophysical applications where a difference of a few bits can define the presence of oil. Although optical-disk technology has barely reached the market, it has already opened up a wide range of new capabilities and novel applications.

A variation on the optical technology is the **CD-ROM,** for **compact disk read-only memory.** CD-ROM has a major advantage over

## STORING PAGES IN STORAGE

An ordinary typewritten page, double-spaced, contains about 2K of text—that is, 2048 characters. How many of these pages can be stored in the various secondary storage media? We offer a representative sample here, but note that the capacity of some devices varies considerably from one computer design to another.

| Medium | Bytes | Pages |
|---|---|---|
| Floppy disk | 360KB | 180 |
| Microdisk | 400KB | 200 |
| Hard disk | 10MB | 5,000 |
| 5¼" optical disk | 400MB | 200,000 |

other optical-disk designs: The disk format is identical to *audio* compact disks, so the same dust-free manufacturing plants that are now stamping out digital versions of Bach or Van Halen can easily convert to anything from software to the *Encyclopaedia Britannica*.

## High Capacity, but Watch the Speed

Why is optical disk embraced as "superdisk"? An example will help. To hold the content of the *Encyclopaedia Britannica*, whose 450 million characters reside in 30 volumes, requires 1250 standard floppy disks. But the entire set of volumes can fit quite nicely on a single optical disk (540 megabytes) with room to spare. The optical disk is certainly super in capacity.

Speed is another matter, and it may be the key reason that optical disk will not drive out the competition any time soon. These new disk drives have access times of several hundred milliseconds, compared to only about 15 milliseconds for conventional drives, a significant difference. The reason for this is the lens described above, which, like any mechanical part, moves rather slowly by computer standards.

## The Future Approaches

So the optical disk can hold lots of data—a volume almost beyond the imagining of current users—but you cannot write on it. That is a major limitation. But wait. Here comes—as they say in the trade—the **erasable optical disk.** The 3M Company has developed an optical disk on which data can be stored, moved, changed, and erased, just as on magnetic media. One of 3M's 5¼-inch disks can hold 250,000 pages of text, the equivalent of 25 magnetic hard disks of the same size! These compact disks are designed especially for personal computers.

For the time being there is enough good storage technology on the market that you do not have to wait for the flashy promise of the optical disk. But when it is available, your data storage may have grown to the point where you will need it.

## Onward

What is the future of storage? Whatever the technology, it seems likely that we will be seeing greater storage capabilities in the future. Such capabilities have awesome implications; think of the huge data files for law, medicine, science, education, government, and ultimately . . . you.

To have access to all that data from any location, we need data communications. To which we now turn.

## A CARD WITH SMARTS

You have seen a bank card with the magnetic strip on the back. That strip stores data about your account—probably your account number, last date of use, amount withdrawn from a cash machine, and so forth. The idea behind a new card is the same, but the media and the volume change: New smart cards with microchips in them can store a hundred times as much data as a magnetic strip.

So, who wants to use this card? Just about everyone, it seems. The Army wants to store data for each soldier on a chip instead of a dog tag. Retail stores want to put all your credit data on the card so sales clerks can, by using a special machine that reads the card, approve credit purchases instantly.

The Life Card shown above is used to store your medical history and is updated as you go along with diagnoses, tests, treatments, and other pertinent data. This card uses laser optics technology. Its optical stripe can hold up to 800 typewritten pages. Data can be read, updated, and duplicated with an IBM PC or compatible personal computer equipped with a special read/write unit.

You can see where this will all end. We shall each carry a card that stores all the data about us—credit history, medical data, education, and on and on. Anything on a computer file could potentially be on your own personal smart card.

## Summary and Key Terms

- **Secondary storage,** or **auxiliary storage,** is necessary because memory, or primary storage, can only be used temporarily. The benefits of secondary storage are economy, reliability, and convenience. Two common means of secondary storage are magnetic tape and magnetic disk; optical storage is a newer technology.

- To be processed by a computer, raw data must be organized into characters, fields, files, and databases. A **character** is a letter, number, or special character (such as $). A **field** is a set of related characters; a **record** is a collection of related fields; a **file** is a collection of related records; and a **database** is a collection of interrelated files.

- The two main methods of data processing are **batch processing** (processing data transactions in groups) and **transaction processing** (processing data transactions one at a time).

- Batch processing involves a **master file,** which contains semipermanent data, and a **transaction file,** which contains additions, deletions, and changes to be made to **update** the master file. These new transactions are **sorted** sequentially by a **key,** a field that identifies records. The master file, which is already in order, is then updated by being compared against the transaction file.

- An advantage of batch processing is the cost savings resulting from processing records in groups. Disadvantages include both the delay in receiving the initial output and the additional time needed later to locate a particular record in a group.

- In **transaction processing** the transactions are processed in the order they occur, without any presorting. This is **real-time** processing because the results of the transaction are available quickly enough to affect the activity at hand. Real-time processing requires having the user's terminals **on-line** (directly connected to the computer). The development of magnetic disk made processing faster and more **interactive** by providing users with easier access to data.

- Transaction processing systems are usually **time-sharing** systems, in which users share access to a central computer that can process their transactions almost at the same time.

- Advantages of transaction processing include quick results of individual transactions and continual updating of data. Disadvantages include the expense of providing continuous access to the computer and the difficulty of protecting the security of computer files.

- Many computer systems combine features of batch processing and transaction processing.

- The amount of data on a **magnetic tape** is expressed in terms of **density,** as the number of **characters per inch** (**cpi**) or **bytes per inch** (**bpi**) that can be stored on a tape.

- **Tracks,** or **channels,** run the length of the magnetic tape. On most tapes a cross section representing one character contains 9 bits, one for each channel. A magnetized spot represents a 1 bit, while a location with no magnetization represents a 0 bit.

- A **magnetic tape unit** records and retrieves data by using a **read/write head,** an electromagnet that can convert magnetized areas into electrical impulses (to read) or reverse the process (to write). When the machine is writing, the **erase head** erases any previously recorded data.

- The magnetic tape is inserted into the unit on a **supply reel,** passed through the read/write head, and attached to the **take-up reel.** During processing the tape moves back and forth between the two reels, then is rewound onto the supply reel when the processing is complete.

- The tape reel and the tape are designed to prevent mix-ups and loss of data. A **file protection ring,** or **write-enable ring,** must be on the tape before data can be written. In addition, the **load point,** or place where data begins on the tape, is preceded by a **leader,** 10 to 15 feet of blank tape. An end-of-file record marks the conclusion of a file. Tape identification is provided by an **external label** and by two types of **internal labels.** One type, the **header label,** appears between the load point and the first data record and gives the file name and date. The **trailer label** appears before the end-of-file marker and includes a count of the number of records in the file.

- **Fixed length** means that all records on a file have the same number of characters; **variable length** means that they may have different numbers of characters. The two types of records cannot be recorded on the same file.

- Since the fast-moving magnetic tape cannot stop instantly, some blank stopping space is necessary between records. This space is called an **inter-record gap (IRG),** or **interblock gap (IBG).** To avoid wasting space on a tape, **blocking** is used. That is, **logical records,** the records written by the application program, are blocked, or put together, into **physical records,** or **blocks.** The term **blocking factor** refers to the number of logical records in one physical record.

- A single **hard magnetic disk,** which is a metal platter coated with magnetic oxide, is contained in a **disk cartridge;** several disks are assembled in a **disk pack.** A **floppy disk** is a round piece of flexible plastic coated with magnetic oxide.

- The surface of a magnetic disk has tracks on which data is recorded as magnetic spots. All the tracks are closed circles having the same center, and the same amount of data is stored on each track.

- A disk storage device is a **direct-access storage device (DASD)** because it locates a record directly (unlike magnetic tape, which requires the read/write head to read all the preceding records on the file). With a DASD data can be stored either sequentially or randomly.

- A **disk drive** rapidly rotates a disk or disk pack as an **access arm** moves a read/write head that detects the magnetized data.

- A **Winchester disk,** also called a **Winnie,** combines disks, access arms, and read/write heads in a sealed module. Some disk modules are built-in to the drive; others are removable.

- The two main methods of writing data on a disk are the **sector method** and the **cylinder method.**

- In the sector method each track is divided into sectors, with data identified by surface, track, and sector numbers. Most personal computers use **soft-sectored** disks, in which disk sectors are determined by the software. A **hard-sectored** disk has a hole in front of each sector to physically determine each sector.

- The cylinder method accesses a set of tracks lined up one under the other, one from each surface. Such a set of vertically aligned tracks is called a **cylinder.** The cylinder method means fewer movements of the access arms mechanism and faster processing.

- The time needed to access data is determined by these motions: (1) **seek time**—the time it takes the access arm to get into position over the track, (2) **head switching**—the small amount of time needed

to activate the appropriate read/write head, (3) **rotational delay**—the time necessary for the appropriate record to get into position under the head, and (4) **data transfer**—the time required for data to be transferred between memory and the disk track.

- The three main methods of storing files of data in secondary storage are **sequential file organization, direct file organization,** and **indexed file organization.**

- In sequential file processing, records are usually in order according to a key field.

- Direct file processing, also called **direct access** or **random access,** allows direct access to a record by using a record key; the user does not have to wait for the computer to read preceding records in the file. **Hashing,** or **randomizing,** is the process of applying a formula to a key to yield a number that represents the address. Records with duplicate addresses are called **synonyms.**

- In **indexed file processing,** or **indexed processing,** records are stored in sequential order, but the file also contains an index of record keys so an individual record can be located.

- Disk storage provides high-volume data capacity and allows direct file processing, which enables the user to immediately find and update records. Tape storage does not allow direct file processing, but it is portable and less expensive than disk storage.

- **Mass storage devices** store enormous volumes of data on cylindrical tape cartridges; when needed, the data is transferred to disk.

- Storage media for personal computers are available in three basic forms: cassette tape, diskette, and hard disk. **Cassette tapes** are like the audio tapes on portable tape recorders. **Diskettes** (also called floppy disks) are more popular and include the $5\frac{1}{4}$-inch **minifloppy,** the $3\frac{1}{2}$-inch **microfloppy** (or **microdisk**), and the $2\frac{1}{2}$-inch **ultramicro disk.**

- A **hard disk** is more expensive than a diskette and cannot be moved from computer to computer, but it does provide more storage and faster processing.

- The storage capacity of a personal computer with a built-in hard disk can be increased through the addition of either another hard disk drive or a **hardcard.**

- A **RAM disk,** also called an **electronic disk** or **phantom disk,** is a RAM chip that fools the computer into regarding part of its memory as another disk drive for storing programs and data. A RAM disk works much faster than a standard disk drive and is useful for sending data from computer to computer, but its disadvantage is that it is volatile.

- In **optical disk** technology, a laser beam enters data by producing tiny spots on the optical disk's metallic surface. Data is read by having the laser scan the disk surface while a lens picks up different light reflections from the spots.

- Optical storage technology is categorized according to its read/write capability. **Read-only** media are recorded on by the manufacturer through a technology sometimes called **optical read-only memory** (**OROM**). **Write-once** media can be written to once; then they become read-only media.

- A variation on the optical technology is the **CD-ROM,** which stands for **compact disk read-only memory.** CD-ROM has the same format as audio compact disks.

- An **erasable optical disk** has been developed, which allows data to be stored, moved, changed, and erased—just as on magnetic media.

## / Review Questions

1. Describe the benefits of secondary storage.

2. Define the following: character, field, record, file, and database.

3. Explain how batch processing differs from transaction processing.

4. Discuss the advantages and disadvantages of batch processing.

5. Discuss the advantages and disadvantages of transaction processing.

6. Explain how batch and transaction processing may be combined.

7. Explain how data is represented on magnetic tape.

8. Describe the precautions designed to prevent loss of data on magnetic tape.

9. Explain the function of blocking.

10. Describe how a disk drive works.

11. Explain how the sector method differs from the cylinder method.

12. Describe the three major methods of file organization.

13. How do hard disks differ from diskettes?

14. Describe how optical disks work.

## / Discussion Questions

1. Provide your own example to illustrate how characters of data are organized into fields, records, files, and databases. If you wish, you may choose one of the following examples: department-store data, airline data, or Internal Revenue Service data.

2. Give your own examples to illustrate the use of each of the following types of processing: batch processing, transaction processing, and a combination of batch processing and transaction processing.

3. Imagine that you are buying a personal computer. What would you choose for secondary storage and why?

# 7

# **Communications**

## Reaching Out to Touch a Computer

The world of communications takes on a new meaning when we combine communications technology with computer technology. This chapter describes how data is transmitted and examines the various kinds of communications networks and their uses.

Sally Elliott had a personal computer in her home for about a year before she heard about bulletin boards. They had something to do with sending messages to other computers. She dug around, reading the trade press and talking to colleagues, until she thought she knew enough to give it a try. She knew she needed a modem—a separate piece of equipment—and related software to make a connection to other computers via the phone lines. Modem installed, she went searching for phone numbers of computer bulletin boards to call. That, it turned out, was no problem at all: The first board she called had, among other things, a list of phone numbers of other boards.

As she had heard, the process was simplicity itself. She dialed the phone number of the bulletin board, waited for her modem to establish a link, hit the Return key on her keyboard twice, then read the instructions the bulletin board system delivered to her screen.

A typical board asks if you are a first-time user, in which case it wants your name and state. This was Sally's first indication that some people board-hop all over the country. Most people give their state but use a code name, sort of like a CB handle.

The next screen is usually a menu, giving choices. Here is the one that Sally found:

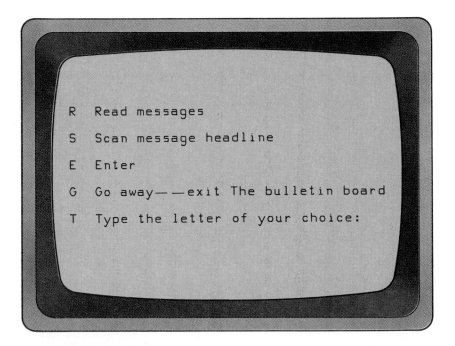

```
R   Read messages

S   Scan message headline

E   Enter

G   Go away——exit The bulletin board

T   Type the letter of your choice:
```

She typed S, then received further instructions for using the message scan.

Sally went from board to board around the country, a pastime that consumed her evenings for several weeks. Eventually, she opened her phone bill and gazed ruefully at the long-distance charges she found there. As she noted to a friend, "I've been drawn into the final trap—giving my computer control of my phone bill!"

Bulletin boards, which we shall examine more closely later in the chapter, have become the grass-roots movement of the computer communications boom. The merger of communications and computers—**telecommunications**—is helping people get full value from each technology. Telecommunications gives people access to on-line information, puts services like banking and shopping into the home, and links professionals together in complex computer networks. These topics and the technology that makes them possible are highlighted in this chapter.

So far we have highlighted bulletin boards, which are often for personal use. The primary telecommunications users are businesspeople, however. To them the use of this technology is an everyday matter. They are just as casual about linking up with a computer in another state or country as they are about being part of a network of computer users in the same office building. Furthermore, businesspeople started it all. We begin at the beginning.

## Data Communications: How It All Began

Mail, telephone, TV and radio, books, and periodicals— these are the principal ways we send and receive information, and they have not changed appreciably in a generation. However, **data communications systems**—computer systems that transmit data over communications lines such as public telephone lines or private network cables—have been gradually evolving through the past two decades. Let us take a look at how they came about.

In the early days large computers were often found in several departments of large companies. There could be, for example, different computers to support engineering, accounting, and manufacturing. However, because department managers generally did not know enough about computers to use them efficiently, expenditures for computers were often wasteful. The response to this problem was to centralize computer operations.

Centralization produced better control, and the consolidation of equipment led to economies of scale; that is, hardware and supplies could be purchased in bulk at cheaper cost. **Centralized data processing** placed everything—all processing, hardware, software, and storage—in one central location. Computer manufacturers responded to this trend by building even larger, general-purpose computers so that all departments within an organization could be serviced efficiently.

Eventually, however, total centralization proved inconvenient. All input data had to be physically transported to the computer, and all processed material had to be picked up and delivered to the users. Insisting on centralized data processing was like insisting that all conversations between people be face-to-face. The next logical step was to connect users via telephone lines and terminals to the central computer. Thus, in the 1960s, the centralized system was made more flexible by the introduction of time-sharing through **tele-processing** systems—terminals connected to the central computer via communications lines. This permitted users to have remote access to the central computer from their terminals in other buildings and even other cities. However, even though access to the computer system was decentralized, all processing was still centralized—that is, performed by one central computer.

In the 1970s businesses began to use minicomputers, which were often at a distance from the central computer. These were clearly decentralized systems because the smaller computers could do some processing on their own, yet some also had access to the central computer. This new setup was labeled **distributed data processing (DDP)**. It is similar to teleprocessing, except that it accommodates not only remote *access* but also remote *processing*. Processing is no longer done exclusively by the central computer. Rather, the processing and files are dispersed among several remote locations and can be handled by computers—usually mini- or microcomputers—all hooked up to the central host computer, and sometimes to each other as well. A typical application of a distributed data processing system is a business or organization with many locations, branch offices, or retail outlets. DDP communications systems are more complex and usually more expensive than exclusively centralized computer systems, but they provide many more benefits to users.

The whole picture of distributed data processing has changed dramatically with the advent of networks of personal computers. By **network,** we mean a computer system that uses communications equipment to connect two or more computers and their resources. DDP systems are networks. Of particular interest in today's business world are **local area networks (LANs)**, which are designed to share data and resources among several individual computers (Figure 7-1). The relatively high cost of quality hard-disk systems and printers makes sharing these resources attractive. A local area network is usually set up within one building or a complex of nearby buildings with cables connecting the various parts of the network. We shall examine networking in more detail in later sections of the chapter.

Another type of connection is the **micro-to-mainframe** link. Although users have a variety of business software available for their personal computer, they often want to use that software to process corporate data that resides in the mainframe files. Giving users access to that data is a hot issue. The connection itself is a problem because the two computers—mainframe and personal—may not be

**Figure 7-1   Local area network.** This photo montage suggests the sharing of resources possible with the hard-wired local area network.

compatible. But a more serious problem is the security and integrity of the data after it has been unleashed. This managerial headache is discussed more fully in Chapter 18.

In the next section we shall preview the components of a communications system to give you an overview of how these components work together.

## The Complete Communications System—And How It All Fits Together

The components are few. The complications are many. The basic configuration—how the components are put together—is pretty straightforward, but the choices for each component are open-ended and the technology ever changing. Assume that you have some data—a message—to transmit from one place to another. The basic components of a data communications system to transmit that message are (1) the sending device, (2) a communications link, and (3) the receiving device. Suppose, for example, that you work at a sports store. You might want to send a message to the warehouse inquiring about a Wilson tennis racquet, an item you need for a customer. In this case the sending device is your terminal at the store, the communications link is the phone line, and the re-

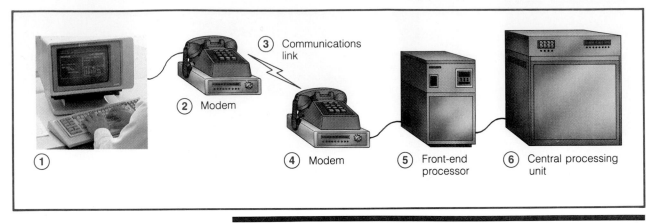

**Figure 7-2   Communications system components.** Data originated from ① a sending device is ② converted by a modem to data that can be carried over ③ a link and ④ reconverted by a modem at the receiving end before ⑤ being processed by a front-end processor and ⑥ sent to the computer.

ceiving machine is the central computer at the warehouse. As you will see, however, there are many other possibilities.

There is another often needed component that must be mentioned in this basic configuration, as you can see in Figure 7-2. This component is a modem, which is sometimes needed to convert computer data to signals that can be carried by the communications link and vice versa.

Large computer systems may have additional components. At the computer end data may travel through a communications control unit called a **front-end processor,** which is actually a computer itself. Its purpose is to relieve the central computer of some of the communications tasks and so free it for processing application programs. In addition a front-end processor usually performs error detection and recovery functions. Small computers, we should note, usually perform communications functions using a special logic board in the computer itself.

Let us see how these components work together, beginning with how data is transmitted.

## Data Transmission

A terminal or computer produces digital signals, which are simply the presence or absence of an electric pulse. The state of being on or off represents the binary number 1 or 0. Some communications lines accept digital transmission directly. However, most telephone lines through which these digital signals are sent were originally built for voice transmission, and voice transmission requires analog signals. We shall look at these two types of transmissions, then study modems, which translate between them.

## Digital and Analog Transmission

**Digital transmission** sends data as distinct pulses, either on or off, in much the same way that data travels through the computer. This means that computer-generated data can be transmitted directly over digital communications media. However, most communications media are not digital. Communications devices such as telephone lines, coaxial cables, and microwave circuits are already in place for voice transmission. The path of least resistance for most users is to piggyback on one of these. These most common communications devices have a common characteristic: They all use analog transmission.

**Analog transmission** uses a continuous electric signal in the form of a wave. The wave form has three characteristics, as shown in Figure 7-3.

- **Amplitude** is the height of the wave, which indicates the strength of the signal.

- **Phase** is the relative position in time of one complete cycle of the wave.

- **Frequency** is the number of times the wave repeats during a specific time interval.

We have already noted that computers produce digital signals but that most communications equipment transmits analog signals. A digital signal, therefore, must be converted to analog before it can be sent over analog lines. It is converted by altering an analog signal, which is called a **carrier wave.** These alterations can be to the amplitude or the phase or the frequency of the wave, as you can see in Figure 7-3.

The height—amplitude—can be changed, for example, to represent a 1 bit, whereas leaving the height alone can represent the 0 bit. This type of change is called **amplitude modulation.** Another alternative is to tamper with the frequency. At the place where the frequency changes, for example, a 1 bit is represented; the resumption of the original frequency is a 0 bit. These types of changes are called **frequency modulation.** You probably know amplitude and frequency modulation by their abbreviations, AM and FM, the methods used for radio transmission.

Conversion from digital to analog signals is called **modulation** and the reverse process—reconstructing the original digital message at the other end of the transmission—is called **demodulation.** So we see that the marriage of computers to communications is not a perfect one. Instead of just "joining hands," a third party is usually needed in between. This extra device is called a modem.

## *USA TODAY:* NEWSPAPER IN SPACE

"Without our satellite system, it would be impossible to produce the newspaper." The speaker is William Hider, who ought to know. He is in charge of telecommunications for *USA Today,* the "nation's newspaper." And around the nation it is, first thing every morning at homes, bus stops, and eateries from Maine to Oregon. This is obviously not a paper delivered in an ordinary way.

*USA Today* is "faxed" via satellite. Four-color graphics for the newspaper are sent in all directions by the world's largest and most sophisticated satellite network. The heart of the system is a dish antenna atop the passageway between two high-rise office buildings at the newspaper's headquarters near Washington, D.C. The dish sends newspaper data to its orbiting satellite which, in turn, relays the data to 31 printing plants scattered across the United States, each equipped with its own receiving dish.

An Asian edition is also published, which is relayed by satellite to Singapore. A European edition is in the works. Perhaps a name change should be considered, too. *World Today?*

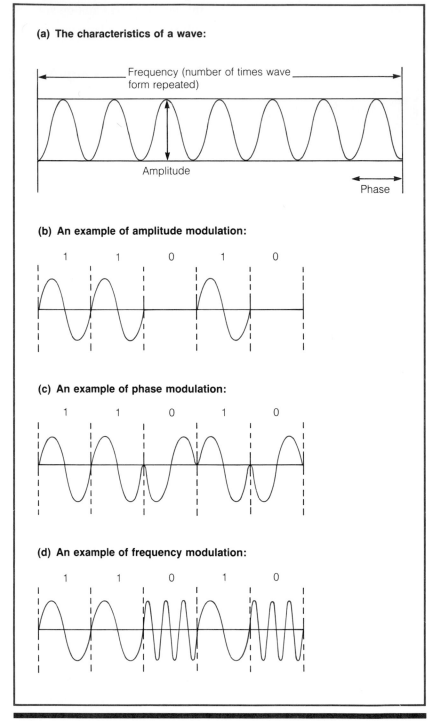

**Figure 7-3   Analog signals.** (a) In this figure a wave is labeled with its characteristics: amplitude, phase, and frequency. The lower figures show how a wave can be changed to accept a message, either through (b) amplitude modulation, (c) phase modulation, or (d) frequency modulation.

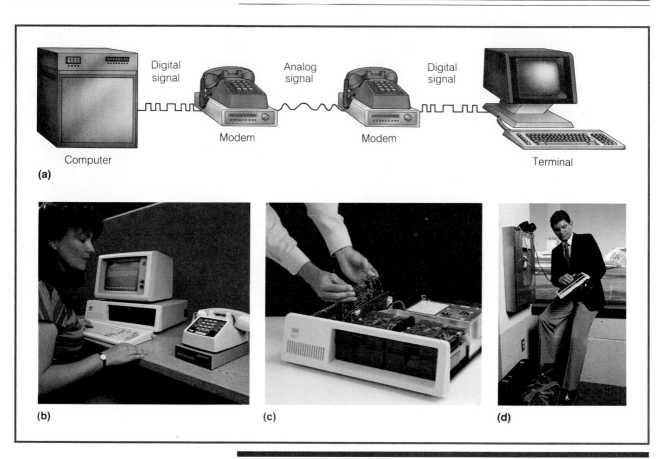

**Figure 7-4   Modems.** (a) Modems convert—modulate—digital data signals to analog signals for traveling over the communications links, then reverse the process—demodulate—at the other end. (b) This external modem rests under the telephone that hooks the computer to the outside world. (c) This internal modem slips into an expansion slot inside the computer. The phone cord plugs into a jack, accessible through the back of the computer. (d) The phone can be cradled by this acoustic coupler, which acts like a modem.

## Modems

A **modem** is a device that converts a digital signal to an analog signal or vice versa (Figure 7-4a). Modem is short for modulate/demodulate. You recall that Sally had to buy a modem before she could computer-communicate over the phone lines to the outside world.

### Types of Modems

Modems vary in the way they connect to the telephone line. There are two main types: direct-connect modems and acoustic coupler modems.

A **direct-connect modem** is directly connected to the telephone line by means of a telephone jack. An **external direct-connect modem** is separate from the computer (Figure 7-4b). Its main advantage is that it can be used with a variety of computers. If you buy a new personal computer, for example, you can probably keep the same modem. Personal-computer users who regard a modem as one more item taking up desk space can buy a modem that is out of sight—literally. All major microcomputer manufacturers now offer **internal modem** boards that can be inserted by users (Figure 7-4c). Some new microcomputers even have an internal modem built-in as part of the standard equipment.

An **acoustic coupler** modem is connected to a telephone receiver rather than directly to a telephone line (Figure 7-4d). Some acoustic couplers are connected to the computer by a cable, but others are built-in. The advantage of acoustic couplers is that they can be connected to any phone, but the quality suffers since they are not connected directly to the telephone line.

### *Modem Features*

Modems now come with features that make communications as automatic and natural as possible. For example, most modems include **auto-answer,** whereby the modem answers all incoming calls from another modem. With **auto-disconnect** a modem disconnects a call automatically whenever the other party hangs up or a disconnect message is received. The **auto-dial** feature allows you to call another modem with a minimum of action on your part. The **automatic redial** feature allows a modem to redial a call that resulted in a busy signal. Finally, a **time-delay** feature allows your computer to call another computer and transfer a file at a future time of your choosing—presumably at night when rates are cheaper. Just a few years ago, when most modems did not have these features, users performed dial and answer functions manually.

### *Modem Data Speeds*

In addition to new features, modems are moving into the fast lane. In general, modem users use normal telephone lines to connect their computers and pay telephone charges based on the time they are connected. Thus there is a strong incentive to transmit as quickly as possible. For years 300 bps (bits per second) was the slow speed and 1200 bps was the high speed for both home and business transmission. Now most manufacturers offer a 2400 bps modem, and even higher speeds are offered for use with some business systems. That is good news for users ever in search of speed and for everyone who wants to save money transmitting data. Note the transmission time comparisons in Figure 7-5.

## Asynchronous and Synchronous Transmission

Sending data off to a far destination works only if the receiving device is ready to accept it. By ready we mean more than just available; the receiving device must be able to keep in step with the sending device. Two techniques commonly used to keep the

**Figure 7-5   Data transfer rates compared.**

| Data transfer rate (bps) | Time to transmit a 20-page single-spaced report |
|---|---|
| 300 | 40 min |
| 1200 | 10 min |
| 2400 | 5 min |
| 4800 | 2.5 min |
| 9600 | 1.25 min |

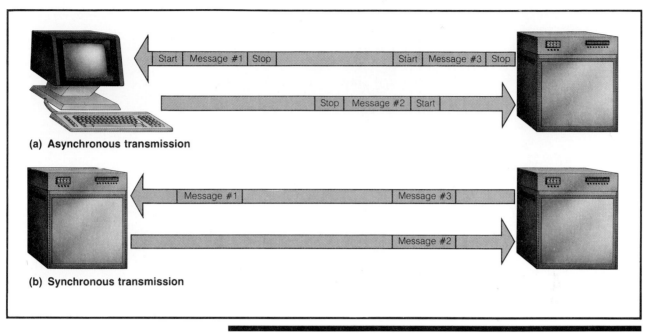

Start | Message #1 | Stop                    Start | Message #3 | Stop

Stop | Message #2 | Start

**(a) Asynchronous transmission**

Message #1                    Message #3

Message #2

**(b) Synchronous transmission**

**Figure 7-6   Asynchronous and synchronous transmission.** (a) Asynchronous
transmission uses start/stop signals surrounding each character. (b) Synchronous
transmission uses a continuous stream of characters.

sending and receiving units dancing to the same tune are asynchronous and synchronous transmission.

When **asynchronous transmission** (also called the **start/stop**
method) is used, a special start signal is transmitted at the beginning
of each group of message bits—a group is usually a character. Likewise, a stop signal is sent at the end of the group of message bits
(Figure 7-6a). When the receiving device gets the start signal, it sets
up a timing mechanism to accept the group of message bits.

**Synchronous transmission** is a little trickier because characters
are transmitted together in a continuous stream (Figure 7-6b). There
are no call-to-action signals for each character. Instead, the sending
and receiving devices are synchronized by having their internal
clocks put in time with each other by a bit pattern transmitted at the
beginning of the message.

Synchronous transmission equipment is more complex and
more expensive than the equipment required for start/stop transmission. The payoff, however, is speedier transmission that is free from
the bonds of the start/stop characters.

## Simplex, Half-Duplex, and Full-Duplex Transmission

As Figure 7-7 shows, data transmission can be characterized as simplex, half-duplex, or full-duplex, depending on permissible directions of traffic flow. **Simplex** transmission sends data in one

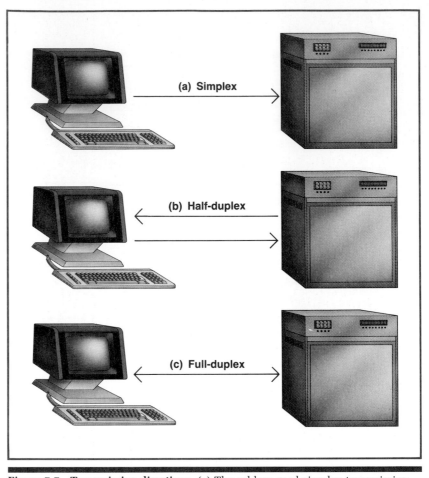

**Figure 7-7   Transmission directions.** (a) The seldom-used simplex transmission sends data in one direction only. (b) Half-duplex transmission can send data in either direction, but only one way at a time. (c) Full-duplex transmission can send data in both directions at once.

direction only. A simplex terminal, for example, can send or receive data, but it cannot do both. It would seem that data collection—say, sending data from a deposit slip to a bank's computer storage—is a good application for simplex transmission. But the operator would want some sort of response, at least a confirmation that the data was received and probably error indications as well. Since simplex transmission will not handle even this limited type of situation, it is rarely used.

**Half-duplex** transmission allows transmission in either direction, but only one way at a time. Using the previous bank deposit example, the operator can send the data and, after it is received, the program in the computer can send a confirmation reply. **Full-duplex** transmission allows transmission in both directions at once. Sys-

## THE MICROCOMPUTER CORNER

### Have Computer, Will Travel

Some people take their work home with them on evenings and weekends. Steve Roberts takes his on the road—every day. Thanks to telecommunications technology, he can work as a free-lance writer while biking across the country, which makes his vocation seem more like a vacation.

His custom bike, which he calls his Winnebiko, is equipped with solar panels that generate power for his CB radio, lights, and one of the two main tools of his trade: a portable computer. The other tool is simply the nearest phone. After each day's writing, he can dial the telecommunications network CompuServe and transmit text from the computer in his mobile "office" to one in his stationary office in Columbus, Ohio. By transmitting the text frequently, he avoids the problem of file storage on the road. His assistant in Columbus then retrieves the text from a CompuServe computer file, edits it on screen, and transmits it to the publisher, either through CompuServe or directly to the publisher's own computer system. Many publishers prefer direct electronic submission of manuscript because there is less chance of human error. And, of course, it is faster than mailing hard copy. In one day text can move from a tent in the Rocky Mountains to

an editor's desk in a New York publishing house.

Telecommunications networks such as CompuServe are not limited to business uses, though. Roberts takes advantage of a number of other applications, such as "discussion" groups for computer owners with similar interests, electronic mail for keeping friends and relatives posted on his adventures, and even a CB network on which he receives messages like "Hey Wordy! Where U B tonight?" Thus, he can have a little social life even when he is practically in the middle of nowhere. Sometimes he probably wishes that

telecommunications technology could also do his writing for him, especially when compelling scenery beckons him away from the computer screen. Indeed, his assistant's duties include prodding him when his CompuServe text file has been empty too long.

However, with computer technology and sufficient self-discipline, Roberts manages to enjoy the scenery and still keep his business moving along, free from the confinement of a traditional office. He credits the "liberating technology" of telecommunications with allowing him to live "unfettered . . . a nomad of the information age."

tems supporting computer-to-computer communications usually are full-duplex to avoid bottlenecks.

We have discussed data transmission at some length. Now it is time to turn to the actual media that transmits the data.

# Communications Links and Channels

As we have seen, computers are no longer islands unto themselves. The cost for linking widely scattered machines can be substantial (as much as one-third of the data processing budget), so it is worthwhile to examine the communications options. Telephone lines are the most convenient communications channel because an extensive system is already in place, but there are many other options.

A communications **link** is the physical medium used for transmission. The communications **channel** is the path over which data travels; some links carry more than one channel. For example, signals could be sent over the same link at different frequencies, each frequency representing a channel.

## Types of Communications Links

There are several kinds of communications links. Some may be familiar to you already.

### Coaxial Cables

Known for contributing to high-quality transmission, **coaxial cables** are bundles of insulated wires within a shield enclosure (Figure 7-8) that can be laid underground or undersea. These cables can transmit data at rates much higher than telephone lines. Coaxial cables are also being used in local area networks, where their high-volume capacity can be put to good use in an office environment.

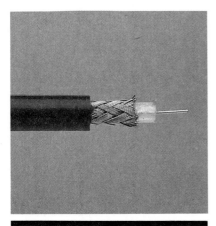

**Figure 7-8   A coaxial cable.** This cable is designed for use with video display terminals.

**Figure 7-9   Microwave transmission.** Microwave signals can follow only a line-of-sight path, so stations must relay this signal at regular intervals to avoid interference from the earth's curvature.

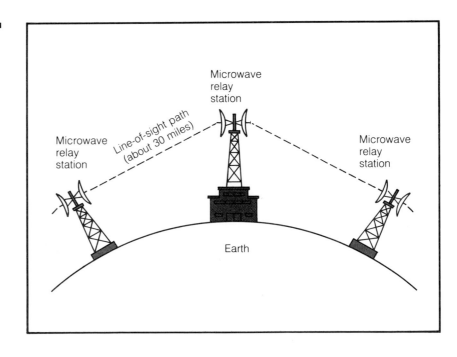

## THE RED PHONE

The phone really is red, but it is more commonly known as the hotline, the direct line between Washington and Moscow. We may never know how the hotline is used, but it is comforting to know that it exists. Technologically, it is not a simple matter.

The present network operates on two independent circuits, each using a completely different satellite system for transmission. These satellite circuits are backed by cable circuits, and all transmissions are secretly coded for security.

The hotline was installed in 1963 after the Cuban missile crisis. The system is being expanded to include facsimile service to permit the exchange of drawings and charts. These documents can be transmitted in less than two minutes per page.

Considering the amount of money both nations spend to electronically snoop on each other, it is nice to know that they are also willing to spend money to upgrade a direct communications system.

### Microwave Transmission

Also popular is **microwave transmission** (see Figure 7-9), which uses what is called line-of-sight transmission of data signals through the atmosphere. Since these signals cannot bend around the curvature of the earth, relay stations—usually antennas in high places such as the tops of mountains, towers, and buildings—are positioned at points approximately 30 miles apart to continue the transmission. Microwave transmission offers speed, cost-effectiveness, and ease of implementation. Unfortunately, there are some real problems with traffic jams in microwave transmission. In major metropolitan areas, for instance, there are difficulties because of electronic interference from intervening tall buildings.

### Satellite Transmission

Communications satellites dangle in space 22,300 miles above the earth. The basic components of **satellite transmission** are the earth stations that send and receive and the satellite component called a transponder. The **transponder** receives the transmission from earth, amplifies the signal, changes the frequency, and retransmits the data to a receiving earth station (Figure 7-10). (The frequency is changed so that the weaker incoming signals will not be impaired by the stronger outgoing signals.)

### Fiber Optics

Most phone lines transmit data electrically over wires made of metal, usually copper. These wires, being metal, must be protected from water and other corrosive substances. **Fiber optics**

**Figure 7-10   Satellite transmission.** A signal is sent from an earth station to the relay satellite in the sky, which changes the signal frequency before transmitting it to the next earth station.

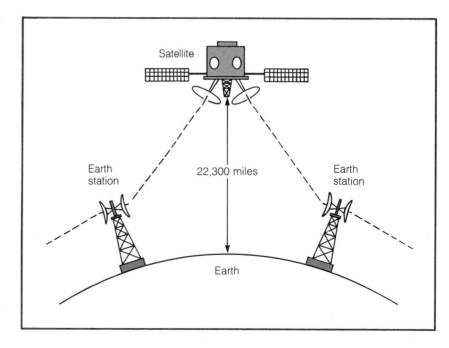

Satellite

Earth station

22,300 miles

Earth station

Earth

technology was developed by Bell Laboratories to solve these problems. Instead of using electricity to send data, fiber optics uses light. The cables are made of glass fibers, thinner than a human hair, that guide light beams for miles. Fiber optics transmits data faster than some technologies, yet the materials are lighter and less expensive than wire cables.

### Bypass Option

A bypass option is not another category of communications media; instead it represents a set of choices. A **bypass** is defined as any communications alternative that does not use the local telephone company. Organizations trying to escape analog constraints and long-distance access fees have turned to digital microwave or satellite links or both. Take a look at the types of organizations doing most of the bypassing today: federal and state governments, *Fortune* 500 companies, banks, universities, utilities, radio stations and newspapers, and office complexes. Obviously, size is their most common characteristic. But this is closely followed by a need for a high volume of data communications.

## 7 Protocol

Can we talk? A line **protocol** is a set of rules for the exchange of data between a terminal and a computer or between two computers.

### Protocol Communications

Two devices must be able to ask each other questions (Are you ready? Did you get my last message? Is there trouble at your end?) and to keep each other informed (I am sending data now). But this must be done in a formal way. For example, ACK may mean that the receipt of a prior message is acknowledged. When communication is desired among machines from different vendors (or even different models from the same vendor), the software development can be a nightmare because different vendors use different protocols. Standards would help.

### Setting Standards

Standards are important in the computer industry; it saves money if we can all coordinate effectively. Nowhere is this more obvious than in data communications systems, where many components must "come together." But it is hard to get people to agree to a standard. Indeed, as the people who serve on standards committees can attest, sometimes it is hard to get people to agree to anything.

Communications standards are, however, on the way. The International Standards Organization (ISO) has defined a set of communication protocols called the **Open Systems Interconnection (OSI)** model. (Yes, that's ISO giving us OSI.) The first commercially available product, however, was IBM's **Systems Network Architecture**

(**SNA**), which differs from the OSI model and has become well entrenched in the United States. (IBM usually sets its own de facto standard.) But wait. There is another player in this cast of characters, a player whose name we would not bother to trip over if it were not so important: the **International Consultative Committee on Telegraphy and Telephony. CCITT,** as it is known, is an agency of the United Nations and has tremendous worldwide clout. In 1984 CCITT endorsed the OSI model. What could IBM do but go along? IBM has announced changes to allow SNA networks to communicate with OSI networks.

## Line Configurations

There are two principal line configurations, or ways of connecting terminals with the computer: point-to-point and multipoint.

The **point-to-point line** is simply a direct connection between each terminal and the computer or computer to computer. The **multipoint line** contains several terminals connected on the same line to the computer, as Figure 7-11 shows. While in many cases a point-to-point line is sufficient, in other cases it is not efficient, convenient, or cost-effective. For instance, if the computer is at the head office in Dallas, but there are several branch offices with terminals in Houston, it does not make sense to connect each terminal individually to the computer in Dallas. It is usually better to run one line between the two cities and hook all the terminals on it in a multipoint arrangement. On a multipoint line only one terminal can transmit at any one time, although more than one terminal can receive messages from the computer simultaneously.

## Line Control

Several terminals sharing one line obviously cannot all use the line simultaneously. They have to take turns. Two common methods of line control are polling and contention.

**Polling** means that the computer asks each terminal if it has a message to send, then allows each in turn to transmit data. This method works well unless no terminal is ready to send a message, in which case the computer's resources have been used unnecessarily.

**Contention** operates from the terminal end. A terminal that is ready to send a message "listens" in to the line to see if any other terminal is in the process of transmitting. If the line is in use, the terminal waits a given period, then tries again; it continues this process until it finally gets on the line. The difficulty with this technique is that, like a long-winded caller telephoning on an old-fashioned party line, one terminal can tie up the communications so that other terminals cannot get their messages through. Thus, polling is probably a better method because a higher authority, in the form of the central computer, is in charge.

**Figure 7-11  Point-to-point and multi-point lines.** (a) In point-to-point lines each terminal is connected directly to the central computer. (b) In multipoint lines several terminals share a single line, although only one terminal can transmit at a time.

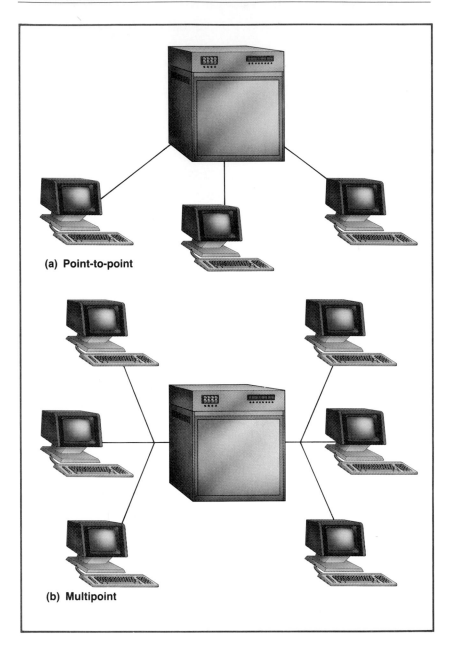

**(a) Point-to-point**

**(b) Multipoint**

## Carriers and Regulation

A company wishing to transmit messages can consider various communications facilities. In the United States these facilities are regulated by an agency of the federal government, the **Federal Communications Commission** (**FCC**), and by state regulatory agencies. Any organization wishing to offer communications services must submit a tariff to the FCC. A **tariff** is a list of services and the rates to be charged for those services. The FCC commissioners' view of the public good determines whether the FCC grants a license to the organization.

An organization that has been approved to offer communications services to the public is called a **common carrier.** The two largest common carriers are American Telephone & Telegraph (AT&T) and Western Union.

Common carriers offer two types of lines: switched and private. **Switched** lines, like those used with your phone service, connect through switching centers to a variety of destinations. You as the user pay only for the services used, but, as with ordinary phone use, you may find the line busy or the connection poor. **Private** (or **leased**) lines offer communication to fixed destinations. A private line is dedicated to one customer. The key advantage of this service is that the line is always available. Another important advantage is security—that is, the private line is indeed private, unshared by others and thus less subject to snooping. Private lines may be conditioned (improved) by the carrier to reduce noise and can accommodate very high transmission rates.

## Ma Bell Changes Everything

In 1968 the FCC handed down the landmark **Carterfone decision,** the first in a series of decisions that have permitted competitors—many from the data processing industry—to enter the formerly regulated domain of AT&T. The gist of the decision is that other companies can interface independent equipment with the public telephone network. These decisions spurred all kinds of independent activity in the communications industry. In 1972 communications companies were even permitted to launch their own satellites.

An outgrowth of this trend is the **value-added network** (**VAN**). In this type of system, a value-added carrier leases communications lines from a common carrier. These lines are then enhanced by adding improvements such as error detection and faster response time.

For many years AT&T and the U.S. government locked horns in an antitrust suit. Finally, in January 1982, the government agreed to drop its charges if the corporation would divest itself of the 22 local operating companies that then made up the Bell System. AT&T got to keep Bell Laboratories, its research arm; Western Electric, which makes equipment; and the long-distance telephone service. Most important, it was allowed to enter areas from which it was formerly barred by federal regulations—namely, data processing, computer communications, and the manufacture of computer equipment. The result is that AT&T emerged as a much leaner entity, free of the local telephone companies (which in turn raised their fees, since they were no longer subsidized by lucrative long-distance rates) and in a position to go head to head with computer giant IBM.

## The Behemoths Lock Horns

But there is not an all-out competitive war. No. It is a cold war. The two superpowers—IBM and AT&T—cautiously move into each other's territory, all the while protecting their own most prized assets. IBM, nicknamed Big Blue for its corporate color, has already obtained 100% control of Rolm, a leading manufacturer of data communications equipment, and taken a stake in MCI, a firm that specializes in long-distance service. IBM-watchers speculate that Big Blue wants to become Ma Blue as well.

But IBM is characteristically buttoned-down about its long-term intentions, except to say that it intends to remain in the communications field. By contrast, AT&T fairly shouts its intentions to be a major computer force in the near future. Watch for the showdown.

## Networking Systems

Networks allow local processing but have the added advantage of access to other hardware and software resources. The advantages of networking are so all-encompassing that the use of networking is increasing at a galloping rate of 35% per year. The list of advantages includes:

- Reduced load on the central computer
- Easier access and better control for users
- Quicker response time
- Better management reporting at the local level

There also may be some drawbacks, such as lack of on-site expertise and software and memory limitations.

Anyone who has been part of the centralized/decentralized decision can tell you about a factor that is far more weighty than any of the advantages or disadvantages listed above. It comes down to an unspoken word: power. If a system is centralized, then political power is concentrated in one place. Can the users in remote locations break that headlock? The politics pervading the organization may have the greatest effect on the decision.

From a people standpoint, networking has some encouraging effects: No longer is the mainframe computer the center of the system and no longer is the individual user a supplicant. Rather, the user—the person—is at the center of the system, powerfully drawing forth on the resources of various networks.

There are a variety of ways to put networks together. We shall begin with a description of network configurations, then pay particular attention to local area networks. This is followed by a separate section on the various uses of networking.

## FAREWELL, MY FLOPPY

The floppy disk will go the way of slide rules and punched cards—to obscurity. This prediction is based on the growing phenomenon called local area networks (LANs), which will be shouldering the storage burden now borne by floppy disks. The LANs will make fast, safe hard-disk storage available to all the microcomputers hooked up to the network. Perhaps, however, we should not consider the floppy a quaint relic just yet—a hard disk does not fit in a briefcase very well.

## Network Configurations

Two common networks are star networks and ring networks.

### Star Network

The classic **star network** consists of one or more smaller computers connected to a central **host** computer. This arrangement is suited to an organization such as a bank, with a headquarters office that houses the central computer and many geographically dispersed branch offices. A variation on the basic star network is the **multistar** network, as shown in Figure 7-12. In this arrangement, several host computers are tied together, but each host has its own star network of computers.

### Ring Network

The **ring network** is as simple as the arrangement shown in Figure 7-13: a circle of point-to-point connections of computers at local sites, with no central host computer. The ring network is frequently used in a decentralized organization where communication is needed between computers but not on a regular basis.

A ring network may be more reliable than a star network since the star has no alternative path between locations if something should happen to interrupt a communications line with the central computer. A ring network, depending on its configuration, may also be less expensive than a star network. Consider, for example, a star network with the host in New York linked to computers in 20 major cities versus a ring network connecting the nearest adjacent cities. The cost of lines for the ring is much lower.

## Local Area Networks

The idea of networking, or connecting several computers, is not new. What is new is local area networks connecting several personal computers—and often larger computers too—that would normally stand alone.

A personal computer, by definition, is a stand-alone, personal device. Even so, personal computers are not exactly isolated since floppy disks are easily shuttled among machines. But, as an organization grows, so does its need to efficiently store, retrieve, update, and correlate the data it collects and uses. As time goes by, users need to share their data with others in the office in a better way, and that way has become the local area network.

A **local area network (LAN)** is a way to share hardware, software, and information. A typical LAN consists of a software package and any of several types of hardware. In simple terms LANs hook microcomputers together through communications media so that

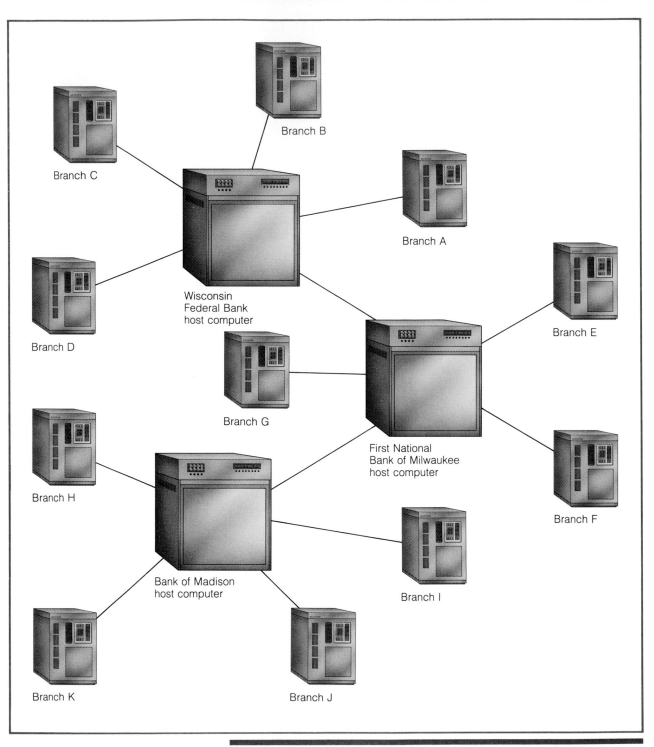

**Figure 7-12   A multistar network.** In this network there are three different bank systems, whose host computers are tied to each other. Each host computer in turn has a series of branch minicomputers. In a system like this, a customer of one bank who wishes to cash a check could go to the teller window of a branch of another bank; the teller would be able to verify that there were sufficient funds in that customer's account to cover the check.

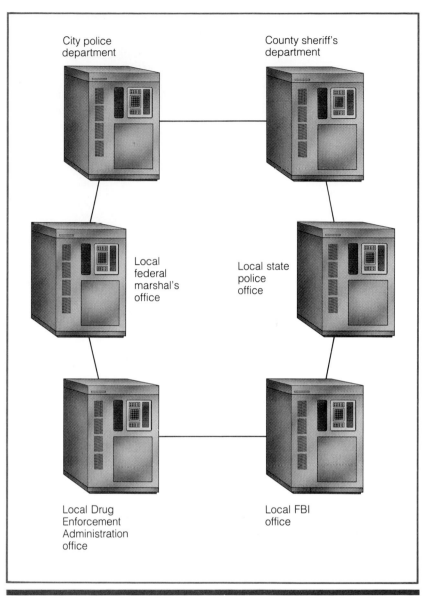

**Figure 7-13  A ring network.** Minicomputers pass messages through each other in this system. The law-enforcement agencies in this hypothetical example may wish to send each other messages on occasion but not constantly.

each micro can share the resources of the others. There are no signals leaping through the air in a LAN; each microcomputer and other piece of equipment must be physically connected by a cable. Each microcomputer in the network is called a **node.** Normally, all nodes will be in proximity, probably in the same building or building complex. LANs can simplify communications among people as well as computers.

Here are some typical tasks for which LANs are especially suited:

- A micro can read data from a hard disk belonging to another micro as if it were its own.

- A micro can print one of its files on the printer of another micro. (Since few people need a letter-quality printer all the time, this more expensive printer could be hooked to only a few computers.)

- A micro can send a message to one or several micros. The message will show up when the user of the receiving micro checks for messages. The name of this arrangement: electronic mail (to be discussed later).

As any or all of these activities are going on, the micro whose resource is being accessed by another can continue doing its own work.

The physical layout of a local area network is called a **topology.** Local area networks come in three basic topologies: star, ring, and bus networks, as you can see in Figure 7-14. A star network, as we have already seen, has a central computer that is responsible for managing the LAN. A **server** is a device that performs specific services for other devices in the network. In a star network the control computer is a server; in this case the shared disks and printers are attached to the central computer. All messages are routed through the server. A ring network links all nodes together in a circular manner without benefit of a server. Disks and printers are scattered throughout the system. A **bus network** allows you to add nodes anywhere in the system, it does not have a circular geometry, and it preserves the system if one component fails. The majority of LANs are bus-structured.

**Figure 7-14   Local area network topologies.** (a) The star topology has a central host computer that runs the LAN. (b) The ring topology connects the computers in a circular fashion. (c) The bus topology assigns a portion of network management to each computer but preserves the system if one computer fails.

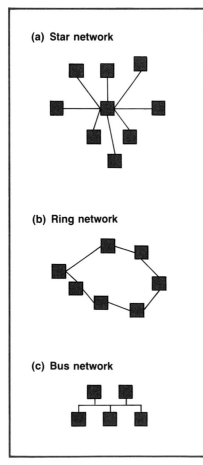

**(a) Star network**

**(b) Ring network**

**(c) Bus network**

## The Work of Networking

Think of it: There are more than 500 million telephones installed throughout the world and, theoretically, you can call any one of them. Further, every one of these phones has the potential to be part of a networking system. Although we have discussed other communications media, it is still the telephone that is the basis for action for the user at home or in the office. Revolutionary changes are in full swing in both places.

Many of the networking examples in this section do begin with the telephone. Others, such as the distribution of government checks directly to banks, may go directly from computer to computer using some kind of bypass system. You have already been introduced to bulletin boards, so let us begin there.

## Bulletin Boards

Person-to-person data communications is one of the more exhilarating ways of using your personal computer, and its popularity is increasing at breakneck speed. You remember Sally's foray into **bulletin board systems** (**BBSs**), telephone-linked personal computers that provide public-access message systems. After she had spent many contented evenings prowling bulletin boards, her friends wanted to know what it was all about. The conversations went something like this:

*Friend:* I don't get it. How can you leave a message on a computer of somebody you don't even know? And why do you call it a bulletin board, anyway?

*Sally:* Well, it's sort of like the bulletin boards you see in Laundromats or student lounges. Somebody leaves a message, but the person who picks it up doesn't have to know the person who left it. As for getting to someone else's computer, all you really have to know is the bulletin board's phone number.

*Friend:* What kind of computer do you need to do all this?

*Sally:* Any kind is OK. But you need a modem so you can communicate over the phone lines.

*Friend:* So who runs all this, the phone company? Or is it IBM?

*Sally:* Well, actually, some big companies do have bulletin boards of their own, but it's mostly just plain folks.

*Friend:* Plain folks?

*Sally:* Sure. Anyone who has a personal computer can set up a bulletin board. It takes a computer, a phone line, a couple of disk drives, and some software that costs around $50. You just tell a few people about your board, and you're in business. But, of course, it isn't really a business. Most boards are free.

*Friend:* Free? You mean you don't have to pay?

*Sally:* Well, of course, there is your own phone bill, but that is a sore subject right now.

In a more serious vein, bulletin boards perform a real service. For example, a message can give advice about a particular vendor's product, post a notice to buy or sell a computer, or even announce a new business venture.

## Electronic Fund Transfers: Instant Banking

You may already be handling some financial transactions electronically instead of using checks. In **electronic fund transfers** (**EFTs**), people pay for goods and services by having funds transferred from various checking and savings accounts electronically, using computer technology. One of the most visible manifestations of EFT is the ATM—the automated teller machine that we described in Chapter 5.

---

### A SAMPLER OF BULLETIN BOARD MESSAGES

These messages are representative of what you might find in a typical bulletin board.

- I would like to know what frequency to use to monitor space-shuttle communication. Leave message for Eddie.

- I would like to take a crack at modifying your program for our mutual benefit. I will call you to set up a convenient time to discuss details. Joe-Whiz.

- Has anyone tried the Computer Diet program from Scarborough Systems? I'd like to know if it works before I spend $80. If you have already lost the weight (!) and want to sell the program, I'll buy it for $40 (Apple IIe version only). Tootie.

- For sale: My version of following the stock market, for only $25. Program will let you track 50 stocks of your choosing. Index and scatter diagram modules included. Write Stock Systems, P O Box 2391, Eugene, OR 97405.

- Want to buy hardcard for the IBM PC. Call Lee Ann, (206) 661-6181 days.

- Has anyone tried PC Paintbrush? Please advise. Egg.

- JAZZ users in the Bay Area. Help! On my own and would like to exchange experiences. Hope to hear from all you Fat Mac users. Sign me . . . Big Mac.

Incidentally, over 650 million Social Security checks have been disbursed by the government directly into the recipients' checking accounts via EFT rather than by mail. Unlike those sent via U.S. mail, no such payment has ever been lost. Moreover, such payments are also traceable—again, unlike the mail.

## The Stock Market

From 1969 to 1970, before computerization, a paper crunch nearly caused Wall Street's stock exchanges to collapse under the pressure of trading 11 million shares a day. Today, with computerization and with terminals throughout the land, 70 million shares make an ordinary trading day. The stock market has handled nearly 170 million shares, and it can be expected to handle more.

## Data Communications Shopping

In recent years there has been a trend toward nonstore retailing in such forms as telephone- and mail-generated orders to department stores, offerings of records and tapes of popular music through television commercials ("Not available in any store!"), and airline in-flight shopping catalogs. One of the newest forms of retailing is interactive, two-way cable **videotex**—data communications merchandising.

Consumers with accounts with the videotex merchandiser shop at home for a variety of products and services. Using an in-home video display catalog, they order products from a participating retailer. When the order is received in the computer, this retailer assembles the goods from a fully automated warehouse. Simultaneously, funds are transferred from the customer's to the retailer's bank account. Customers choose between picking up the order at a nearby distribution point or having it delivered to the door.

## Commercial Communications Services

We have talked about specific services, but some companies offer a wide range of services. Users can connect their personal computers to commercial consumer-oriented communications systems via telephone lines. These services—known as **information utilities**—are widely used by both home and business customers. Two major information utilities are The Source and CompuServe Information Service.

**The Source** offers a broad range of services, including the United Press International news wire, extracts from the New York Times Consumer Data Base, and a Wall Street stock index, as well as electronic games. The Source heavily advertises electronic mail and computer conferencing, services we discuss in the next section.

## COMPUSERVE CRIME WATCH

Perhaps you have thumbed through the "most wanted" list at your local post office. You can look forward to a more intimate look through a new service offered by CompuServe, a commercial communications service. Yes, the ten most wanted are now available electronically. Vital statistics, interesting facts ("considered dangerous"), and even a picture can be beckoned to your waiting screen.

Serious candidates for this service are doctors and dentists who might get a hint about a fugitive's identity from his or her physical condition.

**CompuServe,** far the larger of the two on the basis of subscriptions, offers program packages, text editors, encyclopedia reference, games, a software exchange, and a number of programming languages. CompuServe services include travel reservations, home shopping, banking, weather reports, and even medical and legal advice. Of particular interest to business users are investment information, world news, and professional forums—enough to keep any communications junkie busy.

Other commercial communications facilities offer specialized services, as you can often tell from their names: E. F. Huttonline (stocks), Knowledge Index (general-interest information), NewsNet (news), and Official Airline Guide (travel).

These commercial services usually charge an initiation fee and a monthly fee, neither of which is insignificant. The charges on your phone bill are additional. Some communities, however, have local-line access to information utilities like The Source and CompuServe, so users do not have to pay for long-distance charges.

## Automated Office Technology

Much of the highly touted automated office innovation is based on communications technology. Consider these.

**Electronic mail** permits workers to use terminals or computers at their desks to contact other workers directly via their own desk workstation. **Voice mail** is a little more complicated: A user tries to place a telephone call in the usual way but, the recipient does not answer, so the caller dictates a message into the system. The voice-mail computer system translates the spoken message into digital pulses and stores them for the recipient. Later, when the recipient checks the system, the message will be delivered in reconstructed audio form.

**Facsimile technology** is something like a copy machine connected to a telephone. Facsimile devices can send quality graphics, charts, text, and even signatures to other offices almost anywhere in the world.

**Teleconferencing** is a way to bring people together despite geographic barriers. There are slight variations in the approach. The simplest is called **computer conferencing,** a method of sending, receiving, and storing typed messages as part of a network of users. Add cameras and you have another form of teleconferencing, called **videoconferencing.** The added technology includes cameras and wall-size screens. Although these conferences are not inexpensive, the price pales when compared with the cost of airfare and accommodations to bring scattered participants together in person.

All these office automation features will be discussed further in Chapter 17.

## Computer Commuting

A logical outcome of computer networks is **telecommuting,** the substitution of telecommunications and computers for the commute to work. Many in the work force are information workers; if they do not need face-to-face contact in their work, they are candidates for using telecommuting to work at home.

Although the original idea was that people would work at home all the time, telecommuting has evolved into a mixed activity. That is, most telecommuters stay home two or three days a week and come into the office the other days. Time in the office permits the needed personal communication with fellow workers and also provides a sense of participation and continuity.

Potential benefits of telecommuting include savings in fuel costs and commuting time, an opportunity to work at your own pace, increased productivity, and an opportunity for workers to work in an undisturbed environment.

There are, of course, problems also. One problem associated with telecommuting is the strain on families as a result of a family member working in the home. A more common complaint is that at-home employees miss the interaction with coworkers at the office. At the head of the list, however, is this, from the telecommuters themselves: They work too much!

## Networks and Security

Networks mean that access to information is dispersed; valuable files are in many locations, data is transmitted over different kinds of communications lines, and many people have access to information. Clearly, the question of security arises: If it is so easy for authorized people to get information, what is to stop unauthorized people from tapping it? The safety of data is of paramount importance and deserves a chapter by itself. We shall address this question in Chapter 19.

## Our Crystal Ball

The near future in data communications is not difficult to see. The demand for services is just beginning to swell. Get ready for electronic mail pervading the office, the campus, and the home. Expect instant access to all manner of databases from a variety of convenient locations. Prepare to be blasé about automated services available in your own home and everywhere you go.

What are we waiting for? For easier access. For public education and acceptance. And for the price to come down.

## / Summary and Key Terms

- **Telecommunications** is the merger of communications and computers.

- **Data communications systems** are computer systems that transmit data over communications lines such as public telephone lines or private network cables.

- **Centralized data processing** places all processing, hardware, software, and storage in one central location.

- In **teleprocessing** systems, terminals at various locations are connected by communications lines to the central computer that does the processing.

- Businesses with many locations or offices often use **distributed data processing** (DDP), which allows both remote access and remote processing. Processing can be done by both the central computer and the other computers that are hooked up to it.

- **Networks** are computer systems that use communications equipment to connect two or more computers and their resources. In **local area networks** (LANs), the computers are physically wired together, usually within one building or a complex of nearby buildings. In a network called a **micro-to-mainframe** link, microcomputer users can process data from the files of a mainframe computer.

- The basic components of a data communications system are a sending device, a communications link, and a receiving device. Some large systems also have a **front-end processor,** a computer that functions as a communications control unit, which frees the central computer for processing application programs.

- **Digital transmission** sends data as distinct on or off pulses. **Analog transmission** uses a continuous electronic signal in a wave form having a particular **amplitude, phase,** and **frequency.**

- Computers produce digital signals, but most types of communications equipment use analog signals. Therefore, transmission of computer data involves altering the analog signal, or **carrier wave.** Digital signals are converted to analog signals by **modulation** (change) of the amplitude, frequency, or phase of the carrier wave. **Demodulation** is the reverse process; both processes are performed by a device called a **modem.**

- A **direct-connect modem** is connected directly to the telephone line by means of a telephone jack. An **external direct-connect modem** is not built-in to the computer and can therefore be used with a variety of computers. An **internal modem** is on a board that fits inside a microcomputer. An **acoustic coupler** allows a standard telephone receiver to be coupled to a computer terminal.

- Most modems include **auto-answer, auto-disconnect, auto-dial, automatic redial,** and **time-delay** features.

- Two common methods of coordinating the sending and receiving units are **asynchronous transmission** and **synchronous transmission.** The asynchronous, or **start/stop,** method keeps the units in step by including special signals at the beginning and end of each group of message bits—a group is usually a character. In synchronous transmission, the internal clocks of the units are put in time with each other at the beginning of the transmission, and the characters are transmitted in a continuous stream.

- **Simplex** transmission allows data to move in only one direction (either sending or receiving). **Half-duplex** transmission allows data to move in either direction but only one way at a time. With **full-duplex** transmission, data can be sent and received at the same time.

- A communications **link** is the physical medium used for transmission. A communications **channel** is the path over which the data travels. Common communications links include **coaxial cables, microwave transmission, satellite transmission,** and **fiber optics.** In satellite transmission a **transponder** ensures that the stronger outgoing signals do not interfere with the weaker incoming ones.

- A **bypass** is any communications alternative that does not use the local telephone company.

- A line **protocol** is a set of rules for exchanging information between a terminal and a computer or between two computers. Two standard sets of protocols are the **Open Systems Interconnection** (OSI), developed by the International Standards Organization, and the **Systems Network Architecture** (SNA), developed by IBM. Since the **International Consultative Committee on Telegraphy and Telephony** (CCITT) endorsed the OSI model, IBM has ensured that SNA networks can communicate with OSI networks.

- A **point-to-point line** is a direct connection between a terminal and a computer or between two computers. In a **multipoint line** several terminals are connected on the same line to a computer.

- When several terminals share a line, they must take turns transmitting data. In the **polling** method of line control, the computer asks each terminal in turn if it has a message to send and coordinates the transmission accordingly. With the **contention** method the computer does not provide such invitations; the terminals must detect for themselves when the line is free for transmission.

- Any organization wishing to become a **common carrier,** or supplier of communications services to the public, must apply to the **Federal Communications Commission** (**FCC**) by submitting a **tariff,** or list of services and rates. Common carriers can provide both **switched** lines, which are connected through switching centers, and **private** (or **leased**) lines, which are used exclusively by one customer for communication to a fixed destination.

- The 1968 **Carterfone decision** opened the door for other communications companies to use the public telephone network. This development led to the **value-added network** (**VAN**), in which a communications company leases communications lines from a common carrier and adds improvements.

- A **star network** consists of one or more smaller computers connected to a central **host** computer. A **multistar network** connects several host computers, with a star network connected to each host computer. A **ring network** is a circle of point-to-point connections between computers at local sites and no central host computer.

- A **local area network** (**LAN**) physically connects microcomputers so that each microcomputer can share the hardware, software, and information resources of the others. Each microcomputer in the network is called a **node.** The physical layout of the LAN is called a **topology.** A **server** is a device that performs specific services for other devices in the LAN. The majority of LANs use a **bus network** structure, which allows nodes to be placed anywhere in the network.

- Networking systems can be used in many ways: **bulletin board systems** (**BBSs**), **electronic fund transfers** (**EFTs**), and to shop at home by using **videotex,** a video-display catalog.

- **The Source** and **CompuServe** are two major commercial communications services, or **information utilities.**

- **Electronic mail** and **voice mail** allow workers to transmit messages to the computer files of other workers, while **facsimile technology** can transmit graphics, charts, and signatures. **Teleconferencing** includes **computer conferencing**—in which typed messages are sent, received, and stored—and **videoconferencing**—computer conferencing combined with cameras and wall-size screens.

- **Telecommuting** is the substitution of telecommunications and computers for the commute to work.

- A problem with dispersed information is securing the information against unauthorized persons.

## Review Questions

1. What is telecommunications?

2. Discuss the advantages and disadvantages of centralized data processing.

3. Explain how distributed data processing and teleprocessing differ.

4. What are the functions of a front-end processor?

5. Explain what modems are used for.

6. Why is a high modem speed important?

7. Why is synchronous transmission faster than asynchronous transmission?

8. Define the following types of transmission: simplex, half-duplex, and full-duplex.

9. Describe the advantages of each of the following: coaxial cables, microwave transmission, satellite transmission, and fiber optics.

10. What is protocol, and why are protocol standards important?

11. Describe the two most common methods of line control.

12. What are the advantages of networking systems?

13. How does a star network differ from a ring network?

14. What is a bulletin board system, and how is it useful?

15. Describe how networking systems can be used for banking and shopping.

16. Define telecommuting and discuss its advantages and disadvantages.

## Discussion Questions

1. Describe two situations, one in which a point-to-point line is preferable and one in which a multi-point line is preferable.

2. Discuss the advantages and disadvantages of teleconferencing versus face-to-face business meetings.

3. Discuss your opinion of telecommuting. Do you think you would like to telecommute? Why or why not?

## PART 3

# SOFTWARE

In this section we shall consider what is necessary to produce good software. The five chapters in this section cover beginning programming, structured program design, programming languages, operating systems, and systems analysis and design.

If you are considering a computer career, this section gives you an overview of the software aspect of the industry. Chapter 8 gives you an idea of what programmers do and whether you will like it. The chapters on structure, languages, and operating systems tell you more about programming tools and how to use them. Finally, systems analysis and design tells you how to place software in the larger context of the computer system.

# 8

# Beginning Programming

## Getting Started

We describe how programmers work: They define the problem; plan the solution; and code, test, and document the program. Some basic planning techniques—flowcharting and pseudocode—are also shown. These techniques can be used to represent the first draft of the program solution. The control structures of structured programming are introduced. A problem solution expressed in both a flowchart and pseudocode is developed into a program.

Even when Tom Hollenbeck was a little guy, he had a strong feeling for adventure. As a child he consistently startled his teachers and his dazed parents by reaching out to be in the forefront of the current activity, from the science lab to the baseball diamond. Tom was not some kind of genius, just a kid who wanted to be in on the action. The Computer Revolution was only beginning to stir when Tom was in school, and it was a few more years before personal computers were widely available. By this time Tom was a manager for a publishing house that specialized in how-to books.

Tom perceived the significance of the personal computer earlier than most office workers. New adventures! He purchased a computer with dual floppy-disk drives, a dot-matrix printer, and several software packages. He attended a three-day class sponsored by the store that sold him the software, then settled in to experiment during his evenings at home. By using his training, studying the documentation (booklets that came with the software), and asking a lot of questions, Tom learned to use the software for various business tasks such as preparing reports and planning budgets.

Tom moved the whole operation to his office and gradually convinced others that they too could increase their productivity by using computer software. But Tom did not stop there. He wanted to find out what programming was all about. He returned to the same store, where the salesperson suggested learning BASIC, a programming language often recommended for novices. It was back to the books—BASIC books this time—and more experimenting on his personal computer.

Tom did teach himself to write some elementary programs. But he soon decided that a little formal training was in order, so he signed up for a night class at the local college. He learned to write more complicated programs and also developed good programming habits. Tom felt good about his accomplishments on the computer and made plans to use his new skills in both his business and personal life. More about Tom later.

## Why Programming?

You already may have used software to solve problems. But perhaps now you are ready to learn how to write some software, too. This chapter introduces you to the programming process. When used in conjunction with a guide to a specific language (such as BASIC, which is described in Appendix A), this chapter should help you use the computer for a variety of activities.

There are at least two good reasons for learning programming at this point:

- Programming helps you understand computers. The computer is simply a tool. Learning to write simple programs as you master the machine increases your confidence level.

- Learning programming lets you find out quickly whether you like it and whether you have the analytical turn of mind needed. Even if you decide that programming is not for you, trying your hand at it will certainly increase your computer literacy and give you an appreciation of what programmers do.

An important point before we proceed, however: You will not be a programmer when you finish reading this chapter or even when you finish reading the final chapter. Programming proficiency takes practice and training beyond the scope of this book. But you will have written programs if you put into practice what we are about to describe, and you will have a good idea of what programmers do.

## What Programmers Do

In general, the programmer's job is to convert solutions to the user's problems into instructions for the computer. That is, the programmer prepares the instructions of a computer program and runs, tests, and corrects the program. The programmer also writes a report on the program. These activities are all done for the purpose of helping a user fill a need—to pay employees, bill customers, admit students to college, and so forth. Programmers help the user develop new programs to solve problems, weed out errors in existing programs, or perform changes on programs as a result of new requirements (such as a change in the payroll program to make automatic union dues deductions).

The activities just described could be done, perhaps, as solo activities. But a programmer typically interacts with a variety of people. For example, if a program is part of a system of several programs, the programmer coordinates with other programmers to make sure that the programs fit together well. If you were a programmer, you may also have coordination meetings with users, managers, and with peers who evaluate your work—just as you evaluate theirs.

Let us turn now from programmers to programming.

## The Programming Process

Developing a program requires five steps:

1. Defining the problem
2. Planning the solution
3. Coding the program
4. Testing the program
5. Documenting the program

Let us discuss each of these in turn.

## THE MICROCOMPUTER CORNER

### Home Sweet Home

Maybe programmers should work at home. The idea is not new, but new factors are affecting the decision to work at home or in the office. The first is the freedom derived from the personal computer and the second is the newfound influence of environment on productivity.

First the personal computer. Many programmers still work on dumb terminals that interact with a large mainframe computer. The response time from the mainframe is either uniformly awful or so unpredictable that it becomes difficult to plan work effectively. In contrast, a single-user personal computer provides relatively instant and uniform response times for any programming task.

Now, what about the environment? Recent studies have shown that a programmer's physical work environment influences software productivity more profoundly than managers had suspected. Although programming productivity has long been known to vary dramatically from one individual to another, these variances have usually been attributed to differences in experience and ability. But Tom DeMarco of Atlantic Systems Guild reports that his studies suggest something quite different. When he compared groups of people in different environments, he found that productivity is linked to such environmental factors as desk size, noise levels, and privacy.

The direction to take seems clear. Get a personal computer for home use, place it on a large desk in a quiet room, and lock yourself in. Your productivity should soar. Well, it is hardly that simple, but the findings are worthy of consideration by both programmers and those who manage programmers.

## 1. Defining the Problem

Suppose that, as a programmer, you are contacted because your services are needed. You meet with users from the client organization to analyze the problem or you meet with a systems analyst who outlines the project. Eventually you come to an agreement that, among other things, specifies the kind of input, processing, and output required. This is not a simple process. It is closely related to the process of systems analysis, which is discussed in Chapter 12.

## 2. Planning the Solution

Two common ways of planning the solution to a problem are to draw a flowchart and/or write pseudocode. Essentially, a **flowchart** is a pictorial representation of an orderly step-by-step solution to a problem. It is a map of what your program is going to do and how it is going to do it. **Pseudocode** is an English-like language that you can use to state your solution with more precision than you can in plain English but with less precision than is required when using a formal programming language.

Flowcharts were the primary planning device for many years. They were favored because it is easier to follow logic in a picture than in words. But flowcharts have a key drawback: They are not easy to change. The idea is that a programmer draws a flowchart, then writes a program based on that flowchart; both the flowchart and the program listing are part of the program documentation. As the program changes—and it will—corresponding changes should be made on the flowchart. And therein is the problem: Most programmers simply do not keep flowcharts up-to-date. Pseudocode is much easier to maintain. Since pseudocode is just words, it can be kept on a computer file and changed easily, using text editing or word processing. Although pseudocode is not as clear as a drawing, it is nevertheless a good vehicle for stating and following program logic.

For these reasons, flowcharts have fallen out of favor and pseudocode has become popular. But flowcharts are often used as a teaching device, so we include them here. We shall describe flowcharting and pseudocode in more detail later in this chapter. Most examples in this chapter are illustrated with both a flowchart and pseudocode.

## 3. Coding the Program

As the programmer, your next step is to code the program—that is, to express your solution in a programming language. You will translate the logic from the flowchart or pseudocode—or some other tool—to a programming language. There are many programming languages: BASIC, COBOL, Pascal, FORTRAN, Ada, and C are common examples. You may find yourself working with one or more of these. These languages operate grammatically, somewhat like the English language, but they are much more precise. To get your program to work, you have to follow exactly the rules of the language you are using. Of course, using the language correctly is no guarantee that your program will work, any more than speaking grammatically correct English means you know what you are talking about. The point is that correct use of the language is the required first step. Then your coded program must be keyed, often at a terminal, in a form the computer can understand.

One more note here. An experienced programmer often can write code for simple programs directly at a terminal or microcomputer, skipping the coding-on-paper step. However, we do not recommend that beginners skip any steps.

## 4. Testing the Program

Some experts forcefully support the notion that a well-designed program can be written correctly the first time. In fact, they assert that there are mathematical ways to prove that a program is

---

### A PREDICTION THAT DID NOT COME TRUE

"It may be supposed that, as happened with television and then color television, the enthusiasts and the well-to-do will be the first to install computer consoles in their homes. Eventually, however, everyone will consider them to be essential household equipment. People will soon become discontented with the 'canned' programs available; they will want to write their own. The ability to write a computer program will become as widespread as driving a car."

These immortal words were written by a fellow named John McCarthy and printed in a magazine called *Information* in 1966. That's over 20 years ago, time enough for his prediction to come true. Of course, in 1966, the personal computer was not even invented; Mr. McCarthy thought we would all have individual consoles, a kind of terminal. He did not say so, but he must have imagined all of us hooked up to central computers. Still, his prediction was very bold.

Mr. McCarthy thought programming was pretty easy stuff. He went on to say that programming was not as difficult as learning a foreign language or algebra. He would probably get an argument on that today. At the least, we can say that we have not turned into a nation of programmers. Although making predictions is a risky business, we think we can say with some confidence that this will continue to be the case.

Try your hand at a few programs and see what you think.

correct. However, the imperfections of the world are still with us, so most programmers get used to the idea that there are a few errors in their programs. This is a bit discouraging at first, since programmers tend to be precise, careful, detail-oriented people who take pride in their work. The words *sloppy* and *programmer* seldom go together. Still, there are many opportunities to introduce mistakes into programs, and you, like those who have gone before you, will probably find several of them.

So, after coding and keying the program, you test it to find the mistakes. This step involves these phases:

- **Desk-checking.** This phase, similar to proofreading, is sometimes avoided as a shortcut by the programmer who is eager to run the program on the computer, now that it is written. However, with careful desk-checking, you may discover several errors and possibly save yourself several computer runs. In **desk-checking,** you simply sit down and mentally trace, or check, the logic of the program to ensure that it is error-free and workable. In the process you may also discover keying errors and errors in the use of the language.

- **Translating.** A **translator** is a program that translates your program into language the computer can understand. A by-product of the process is that the translator tells you if you have improperly used the programming language in some way. These types of mistakes are called **syntax** errors. The translator produces descriptive error messages. For instance, if in FORTRAN you mistakenly write, N=2*(I+J))—which has two closing parentheses instead of one—you will get a message that says, ''UNMATCHED PARENTHESES.'' (Different translators provide different error messages.) Programs are most commonly translated by a compiler or an interpreter. A **compiler** translates your entire program at one time, giving you all the error messages—called **diagnostics**—at once. An **interpreter,** often used for the BASIC language, translates your program one line at a time. A BASIC interpreter signals errors as each line is keyed in. This translation process is described in more detail in Chapter 11.

- **Debugging.** A term used extensively in programming, **debugging** is detecting, locating, and correcting ''bugs'' (mistakes) by running the program. These bugs are logic errors such as telling a computer to repeat an operation but not telling it how to stop repeating. In this phase you run the program against test data, which you devise. You must plan the test data carefully to make sure you test every part of the program.

## 5. Documenting the Program

Documenting is an ongoing, necessary process—although like many programmers you may be eager to pursue more exciting

## TELL US ABOUT THE BUGS

Computer-literacy books are bursting with bits and bytes and disks and chips and lessons on writing programs in BASIC. All this is to provide quick enlightenment for the illiterate. But the average newly literate person has not been told about the bugs.

It is a bit of a surprise, then, to find that the software you are using does not always work quite right. Or, perhaps the programmer who is doing some work for you cannot seem to get the program to work correctly. Both problems are ''bugs,'' errors that were introduced unintentionally into a program when it was written. The term *bug* comes from an experience in the early days of computing. One summer day in 1945 the Mark I computer came to a halt. Working to find the problem, computer personnel actually found a moth inside the computer (see photo above). They removed the offending bug, and the computer was fine. From that day forward, any mysterious problem was said to be a bug.

## YOUR CAREER: IS THE COMPUTER FIELD FOR YOU?

There is a shortage of qualified personnel in the computer field but, paradoxically, there is a glut of people at the front end trying to get entry-level jobs. Before you join their ranks, consider the advantages of the computer field and what it takes to succeed in it.

### The Joys of the Field

Although many people make career changes into the computer field, few choose to leave it. In fact, surveys of computer professionals consistently report a high level of job satisfaction. There are several reasons for this contentment. One is the challenge—most jobs in the computer industry are not routine. Another is security, since established computer professionals can usually find work. And that work pays well—you will probably not be rich, but you will always be comfortable. The computer industry has historically been a rewarding place for women and minorities. And, finally, the industry holds endless fascination since it is always changing.

### What It Takes

You need, of course, some credentials, most often a two- or four-year degree in data processing or computer science. The requirements and salaries vary by the organization and the region, so we shall not dwell on these here. Beyond that, the person most likely to land a job and move up the career ladder is the one with excellent communication skills, both oral and written. These are also the qualities that can be observed by potential employers in an interview.

### Open Doors

The outlook for the computer field is promising. In 1980 1.5 million people were in the computer industry, but the U.S. Bureau of Labor Statistics expects 2 million in 1990. Using the Bureau of Labor Statistics as its source, the *Wall Street Journal* reports that in the 1990s the need for programmers will increase 72% and systems analysts 69%. These two professions are predicted to be the number two and number three high-growth jobs. (In case you are curious, the number one high-growth job area is predicted to be the paralegal profession.) The reasons for continued job increase in the computer field are more computers, more applications of computers, and more computer users.

### Career Directions

Traditional career progression in the computer field was a path from programmer to systems analyst to project manager. This is still a popular direction, but it is complicated by the large number of options open to computer professionals. Computer professionals sometimes specialize in some aspect of the industry such as data communications, database management, personal computers, graphics, or equipment. Others may specialize in the computer-related aspects of a particular industry such as banking or insurance. Still others strike out on their own, becoming consultants or entrepreneurs.

### Keeping Up

Your formal education is merely the beginning. In the ever changing computer field, you must take responsibility for your ongoing education. There are a variety of formal and informal ways of keeping up: college or on-the-job classes, workshops, seminars, conventions, exhibitions, trade magazines, books, and professional organizations. Organizations are particularly important; by attending a monthly meeting you can exchange ideas with other professionals, make new contacts, and hear a speaker address some current topic. Some of the principal professional societies are as follows:

- AFIPS. The American Federation of Information Processing Societies is an umbrella federation of organizations relating to information processing.

- ACM. The Association for Computing Machinery is the largest society devoted to developing information processing as a discipline.

- ASM. The Association for Systems Management keeps members current on developments in systems management and information processing.

- AWC. The Association of Women in Computing is open to professionals interested in promoting the advancement of women in data processing.

- DPMA. The Data Processing Management Association, one of the largest of the professional societies in this field, is open to all levels of data processing personnel and encourages a professional attitude toward data processing.

You should also consider pursuing the Certificate in Data Processing (CDP), which is granted on completion of a five-part examination that covers: (1) data processing equipment, (2) computer programming and software, (3) principles of management, (4) quantitative methods (accounting, mathematics, statistics), and (5) systems analysis and design.

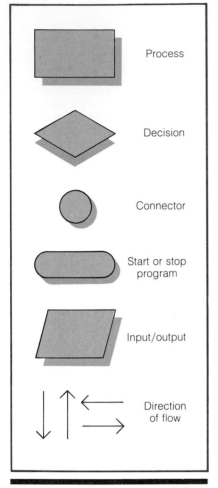

Process

Decision

Connector

Start or stop
program

Input/output

Direction
of flow

**Figure 8-1   ANSI flowchart symbols.**

computer-related activities. **Documentation** is a written detailed description of the programming cycle and specific facts about the program. Typical program documentation materials include the origin and nature of the problem, a brief narrative description of the program, logic tools such as flowcharts and pseudocode, data-record descriptions, program listings, and testing results. Comments in the program itself are also considered an important part of documentation. In a broader sense program documentation could be part of the documentation for an entire system, as described in Chapter 12 on systems analysis and design.

The wise programmer continues to document the program throughout its design, development, and testing. Documentation is needed to supplement human memory, to help organize program planning, and to communicate with others who have an interest in the program. Documentation also is needed so that those who come after you can make any necessary modifications in the program or track down any errors that you missed.

## Planning the Solution: More Detail

We have described the five steps of the programming process in a general way. We noted that the first step, defining the problem, is related to the larger arena of systems analysis and design, a subject we shall examine more closely in Chapter 12. (In fact, in some companies, only a person with the title *programmer/analyst* may participate in the problem-definition phase.) The last three steps of coding, testing, and documenting the program are done in the context of a particular programming language. We offer the BASIC language in Appendix A for this purpose.

We shall study the second step, planning the solution, in this chapter. This discussion will help you understand how to develop

**Figure 8-2   A template containing standard ANSI flowchart symbols.** Templates like this one are used as drawing aids.

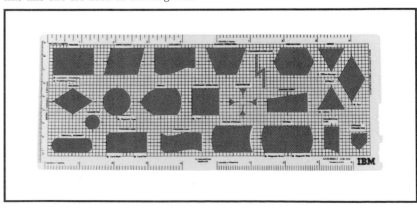

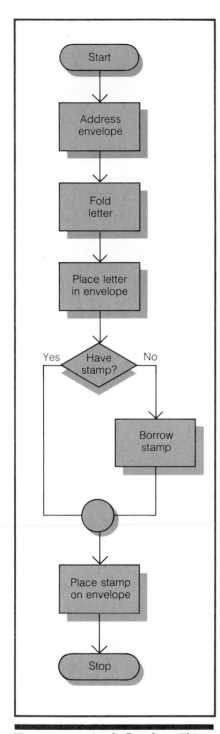

**Figure 8-3   A simple flowchart.** This flowchart shows how to prepare a letter for mailing.

program logic. The following sections in this chapter offer an introduction to flowcharting and pseudocode, then offer examples showing both approaches to the same problem. Note that, normally, only one or the other would be used for a given solution, but it is useful to make a comparison between the two methods.

Another important topic is introduced in these sections: structured programming. Since we begin with flowcharting, we first present the control structures related to structured programming in a flowcharting context. But the control structures are presented again in the pseudocode discussion, where they are even more important. In fact, as you will see, pseudocode is built around the control structures. But we are getting burdened down with technical terms that are easier to understand after some foundation has been laid. So let us begin with the pictures—flowcharts.

 **Planning the Solution with Flowcharts**

As we stated, a flowchart is essentially a picture. The flowchart consists of arrows that represent the direction the program takes and of boxes and other symbols that represent actions. In this discussion we are talking about a **logic flowchart,** a flowchart that represents the flow of logic in a program. A logic flowchart is different from a **systems flowchart,** which shows the flow of data through an entire computer system. We shall examine systems flowcharts in Chapter 12.

**Beginning Flowcharting**

Some standard flowchart symbols have been established and are accepted by most programmers. These symbols, shown in Figure 8-1, are called ANSI symbols. (**ANSI** stands for American National Standards Institute.) Templates of ANSI symbols (Figure 8-2) are available in many office-supply stores and college bookstores and are helpful in drawing neat flowcharts. The most common symbols you will use represent process, decision, connector, start/ stop, input/output, and direction of flow. Let us now look at two examples.

*An Example: Preparing a Letter*

Figure 8-3 shows you how you might diagram the steps of preparing a letter for mailing. There is usually more than one correct way to design a flowchart; this becomes obvious with more complicated examples.

The rectangular **process** boxes indicate actions to be taken— "Address envelope," "Fold letter," "Place letter in envelope."

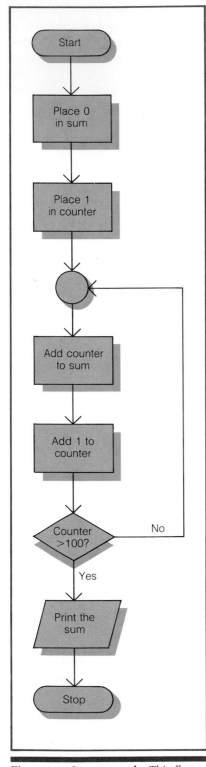

**Figure 8-4    Loop example.** This flowchart uses a loop to find the sum of numbers from 1 through 100.

Sometimes the order in which actions appear is important, sometimes not. In this case the letter must be folded before it can be placed in the envelope.

The diamond-shaped box ("Have stamp?") is a **decision** box. It has two **paths** or **branches**—one path represents the response *yes*, the other, *no*. Note that the decision box is the only box that allows a choice; no other box has more than one exit. The decision box asks a question that requires a yes-or-no answer. Whether you do need a stamp (and therefore have to borrow it) or do not, you take a path that comes back to a circle that puts you on a path to the end. The circle is called a **connector** because it connects the paths. (This symbol can also be used as an on-page connector when transferring to another location on the same sheet of paper.) Notice that the flowchart begins and ends with the oval **start/stop** symbol.

This example of preparing a letter suggests how you can take almost any activity and diagram it in flowchart form—assuming, that is, that you can always express your decisions as choices between yes and no, or something equally specific, such as true or false. Now let us use flowcharting to show just what programming is all about.

### An Example: Summing Numbers from 1 through 100

Figure 8-4 shows how you might flowchart a program to find the sum of all numbers between 1 and 100. There are a number of things to observe about this flowchart.

First, the program uses two places in the computer's memory as storage locations, or places to keep intermediate results. In one location is a counter, which might be like a car odometer: Every time a mile passes, the counter counts it as a 1. In the other location is a sum—that is, a running total of the numbers counted. The sum location will eventually contain the sum of all numbers from 1 through 100: $1 + 2 + 3 + 4 + 5 + \cdots + 100$.

Second, as we start the program, we must initialize the counter and the sum. When you **initialize,** it means you set the starting values of certain storage locations, usually as the program execution begins. We shall initialize the sum at zero and the counter at 1.

Third, note the looping. You add the counter to the sum and a 1 to the counter, then come to the decision diamond, which asks if the counter is greater than 100. If the answer is "No," the computer loops back around and repeats the process. The decision box contains a **compare** operation; the computer compares two numbers and performs alternative operations based on the comparison. If the result of the comparison is "Yes," the computer produces the sum as output, as indicated by the print instruction. Notice that the parallelogram-shaped symbol is used for printing the sum because this is an output process.

A **loop**—also called an **iteration**—is the heart of computer programming. The beauty of the loop, which may be defined as the repetition of instructions under certain conditions, is that you, as the programmer, have to describe certain instructions only once rather than describing them repeatedly. Once the programmer has established the loop pattern and the conditions for concluding (exiting from) the loop, the computer continues looping and exits as it has been instructed to do. The loop is considered a powerful programming tool because the code is reusable; once written, it can be called upon many times. Notice also that the flowchart can be modified easily to sum the numbers from 1 to 1000 or 500 to 700 or some other variation.

## Structured Flowcharting

The techniques of flowcharting have been refined in a method known as **structured flowcharting,** which uses a limited number of control structures to minimize the complexity of the programs and thus cut down on errors. Structured flowcharting is related to **structured programming,** an approach that emphasizes breaking a program into logical sections using certain universal programming standards.

Structured programming makes programs easier to write, check, read, and maintain. The computer industry widely accepts structured programming as the most productive way of programming. We shall examine the rationale and concepts of structured programming more thoroughly in Chapter 9. For now, however, let us introduce some basic concepts of structure in this discussion of flowcharts.

There are three basic **control structures** in structured programming:

- Sequence

- Selection

- Iteration

These three are considered the basic building blocks of all program construction. They are called control structures because they actually control how the program executes. You will see that we have used some of these structures already in Figures 8-3 and 8-4. We present SEQUENCE, IF-THEN-ELSE (selection), and DOWHILE and DOUNTIL (iterations) in this flowchart discussion; the CASE structure appears later, in the pseudocode discussion.

Before we discuss each control structure in detail, it is important to note that each structure has only one *entry point* and one *exit point.* This property makes structured programs easier to read and to debug.

The **sequence control structure** is illustrated in Figure 8-5a. One statement simply follows another in sequence. (As our discussion continues, you may find it helpful to look ahead to Figures 8-8 through 8-12 for actual examples of this and other control structures.)

## A TRUE SOFTWARE TALE

The story takes place several years ago, when teachers were first showing students the ways of computer programming. A student sat, brow furrowed, chewing her pencil as she examined her latest flawed program printout. Suddenly she turned to her instructor, the gleam of discovery on her face, and announced, "I've figured these computers out. They do what you *tell* them to do, not what you *want* them to do!"

Perhaps the essentials of computer wisdom are contained in that one sentence. Nothing has changed in all these years. You still have to make sure that what you tell the computer to do is really what you want it to do.

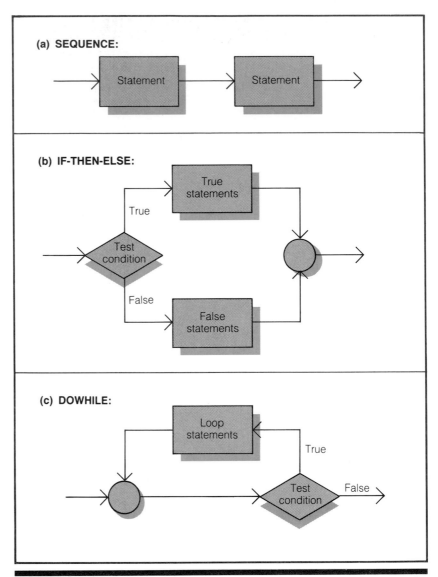

**Figure 8-5 General format of the three basic control structures.** (a) Sequence. (b) Selection (IF-THEN-ELSE). (c) Iteration (DOWHILE).

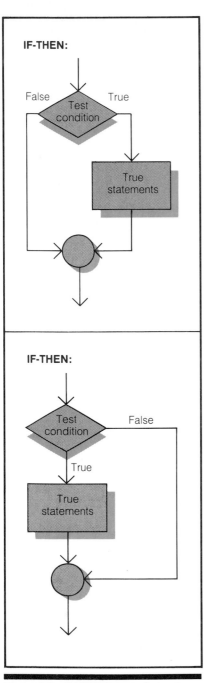

**Figure 8-6 IF-THEN control structure.** The IF-THEN control structure is a subset of the IF-THEN-ELSE (selection) control structure. Two ways of drawing the IF-THEN structure are shown here.

The **selection control structure,** used to make logic decisions, is also shown in Figure 8-5b as IF-THEN-ELSE. The IF-THEN-ELSE control structure works as follows: "IF (a condition is true), THEN (do something), ELSE (do something different)." For instance, "IF the alarm clock goes off and it is a weekend morning, THEN just turn it off and go back to sleep, ELSE get up and go to work." Or, to use a more specific example, "IF a student is full-time, THEN the fee is units times $95, ELSE fee is units times $125."

The IF-THEN variation is shown in Figure 8-6. IF-THEN is a special case of IF-THEN-ELSE. The IF-THEN selection is less complicated: "IF the condition is true, THEN do something—but if it is not true, then do not do it." For example, "IF shift-code is 3, THEN add bonus of $50." Figure 8-6 gives two versions of diagramming the same IF-THEN condition. Note that there will always be some resulting action using IF-THEN-ELSE; in contrast, the IF-THEN may or may not produce action, depending on the condition.

The **iteration control structure** is a looping mechanism. The only necessary iteration structure is the DOWHILE structure ("do . . . while"), as shown in Figure 8-5c. Although DOUNTIL is not one of the three basic control structures, it is convenient to introduce the DOUNTIL structure ("do . . . until") now, as shown in Figure 8-7. We shall describe the difference between DOWHILE and DOUNTIL iterations.

When looping, you must give an instruction to stop the repetition at some point, otherwise you could—theoretically—go on looping forever and never get to the end of the program. There is a basic rule of iteration, which is related to structured programming: *If you have several statements that need to be repeated, a decision about when to stop repeating has to be placed either at the beginning of all the loop statements or at the end of all the loop statements.*

Whether you put the loop-ending decision at the beginning—a **leading decision**—or at the end—a **trailing decision**—constitutes the basic difference between DOWHILE and DOUNTIL. As Figure 8-5 shows, DOWHILE tests at the beginning of the loop—the diamond-shaped decision box is the first action of the loop process. The DOUNTIL loop tests at the end, as you can see in Figure 8-7. The DOUNTIL loop, by the way, guarantees that the loop statements are executed at least once because the loop statements are executed before you make any test about whether to get out. This guarantee is not necessarily desirable, depending on your program logic. Also— an important difference from the DOWHILE loop—note that the test condition must be False to continue the loop.

These basic control structures may seem a bit complex in the beginning, but in the long run they are the most efficient technique for programming, and it is worth taking your time to learn them. Figures 8-8 through 8-12 show examples of the use of the three control structures. (These figures also include pseudocode for comparison purposes. We shall discuss pseudocode shortly.) Let us now consider two extended examples.

### An Example: Counting Salaries

Suppose you have been named manager of a personnel agency that has 50 employees, and you need some salary data about your employees. To take a simple case, let us say you want to know how many people make over $20,000 a year (high salaries), $10,000 to $20,000 (medium salaries), and under $10,000 (low salaries—and presumably, part-time employees!).

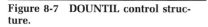

**Figure 8-7   DOUNTIL control structure.**

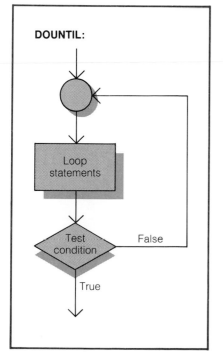

**Figure 8-8 Sequence example: movie extras' salaries.** To compute the total of extras' wages, ① determine one extra's salary for that week's shooting by multiplying the hourly rate times the number of hours worked on the picture that week. ② Add that extra's salary to those of other extras to find the total.

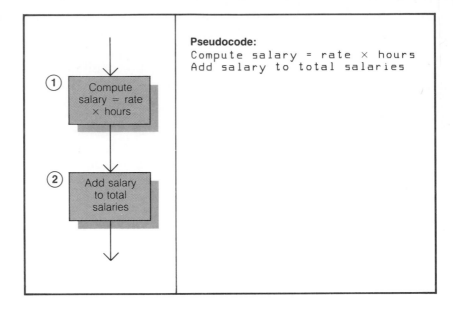

**Pseudocode:**
```
Compute salary = rate × hours
Add salary to total salaries
```

**Figure 8-9 IF-THEN-ELSE selection example: truck tires.** A trucker orders tires at a truck-tire warehouse. IF ① the quantity of tires ordered is greater than the quantity on hand (q.o.h.), THEN ② the computer prints "Incomplete stock" ELSE ③ it prints "Reordered" and subtracts the quantity ordered from the quantity on hand.

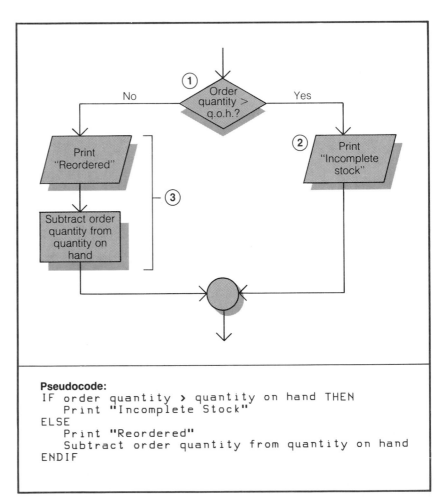

**Pseudocode:**
```
IF order quantity > quantity on hand THEN
    Print "Incomplete Stock"
ELSE
    Print "Reordered"
    Subtract order quantity from quantity on hand
ENDIF
```

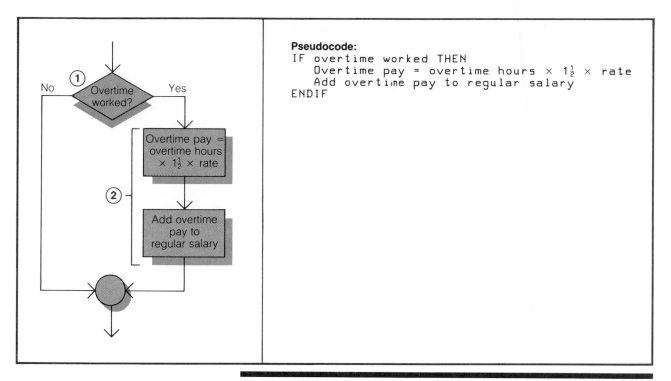

**Pseudocode:**
```
IF overtime worked THEN
    Overtime pay = overtime hours × 1½ × rate
    Add overtime pay to regular salary
ENDIF
```

**Figure 8-10  IF-THEN selection example: Christmas season overtime.** IF ① a department-store employee worked overtime, THEN ② the program computes overtime pay by multiplying the overtime hours by $1\frac{1}{2}$ times the hourly rate; the total is added to the employee's regular salary.

**Figure 8-11  DOWHILE iteration example.** DO ① add counter to total and subtract 1 from counter WHILE ② counter is greater than 0.

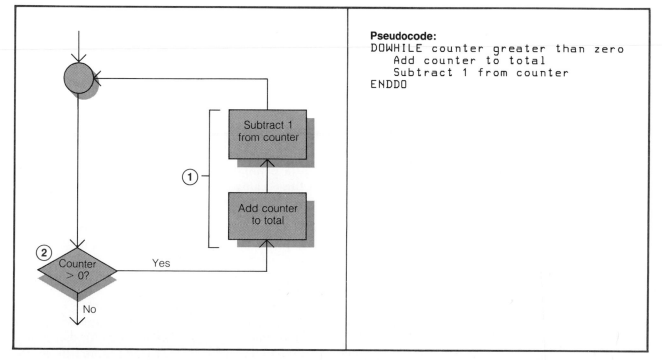

**Pseudocode:**
```
DOWHILE counter greater than zero
    Add counter to total
    Subtract 1 from counter
ENDDO
```

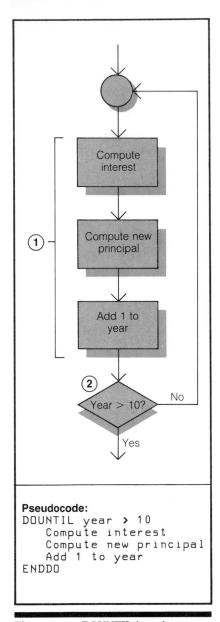

**Pseudocode:**
```
DOUNTIL year > 10
    Compute interest
    Compute new principal
    Add 1 to year
ENDDO
```

**Figure 8-12  DOUNTIL iteration example: computing loan interest and principal.** DO ① compute interest, compute principal, and add the number 1 to the total years UNTIL ② the number of years is greater than 10.

Figure 8-13 shows a solution to your problem. Let us go through the flowchart. The circled numbers below correspond to the circled numbers in the illustration. (Note that, as before, we have included the pseudocode for comparison later.)

We observe the following:

① We initialize four counters to zero. The employee counter will keep track of the total number of employees in the company; the others—the high-salary counter, the medium-salary counter, and the low-salary counter—will count the numbers of employees in the salary categories.

② In the parallelogram-shaped input box, we indicate that the computer reads the salary at this point. **Read** may be defined as bringing something that is outside the computer into memory; to *read*, in other words, means to *get*. The computer will get each employee's yearly salary.

③ The first of the diamond-shaped decision boxes is a test condition that can go either of two ways—"Yes" or "No." Note that if the answer to the question, "Salary > $20,000?" is "Yes," then the computer will process this answer by adding a 1 to the high-salary count. If the answer is "No," the computer will ask, "Salary < $10,000?"—and so on (< means less than and > means greater than).

④ For every decision box, no matter what decision is made, you should come back to a connector. And, as the flowchart shows, each decision box has its own connector. Note that, in this case, each connector is directly below the decision box to which it relates.

⑤ Whatever the kind of salary, the machine adds 1 (for the employee) to the employee counter, and a decision box then asks, "Employee counter = 50?" (the total number of employees in the company).

⑥ If the answer is "No," the computer makes a loop back to the first connector and goes through the process again. Note that this is a DOUNTIL loop because the decision box is at the end rather than at the beginning of the computing process ("DO keep processing UNTIL the employee counter is equal to 50").

⑦ When the answer is finally "Yes," the computer then goes to an output operation (a parallelogram) and prints the salary count for each of the three categories. The computing process then stops.

Review the flowchart and observe that every action is one of the three control structures we have been talking about: sequence, selection, or iteration.

### An Example: Customer Credit Balances

In this example, illustrated in Figure 8-14, let us consider how to flowchart the process of checking a retail customer's credit balance. The file of customer records is kept on some computer-accessible medium, probably tape or disk. This is a more true-to-life

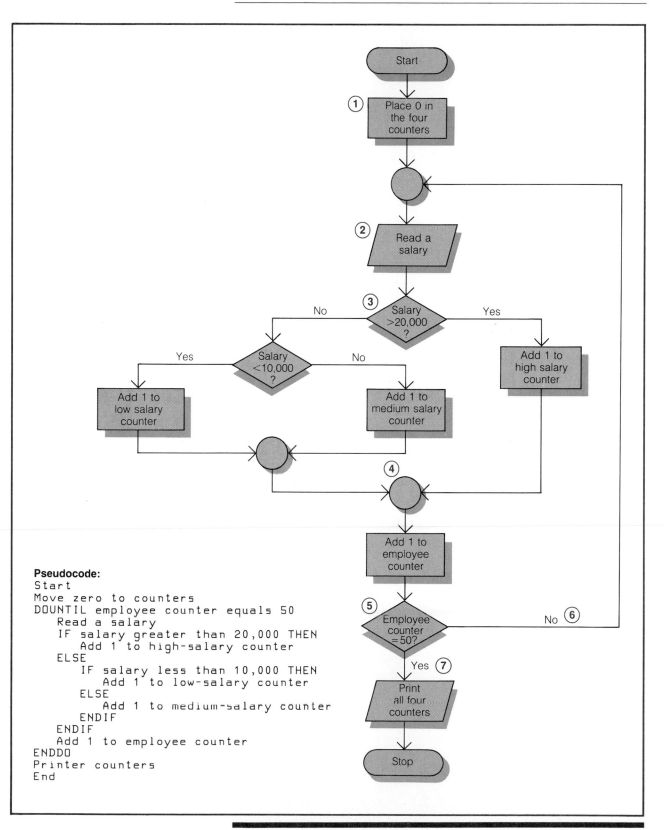

**Pseudocode:**
```
Start
Move zero to counters
DOUNTIL employee counter equals 50
    Read a salary
    IF salary greater than 20,000 THEN
        Add 1 to high-salary counter
    ELSE
        IF salary less than 10,000 THEN
            Add 1 to low-salary counter
        ELSE
            Add 1 to medium-salary counter
        ENDIF
    ENDIF
    Add 1 to employee counter
ENDDO
Printer counters
End
```

Figure 8-13   Counting salaries.

example than the previous salary example because, rather than a file with exactly 50 records, the file here has an unknown number of records. The program has to work correctly no matter how many customers there are.

As store manager, you need to check the customer file and print out the record of any customer whose current balance exceeds the credit limit, so sales clerks will not ring up charge purchases for customers who have gone over their credit limits. (Recall that a record is a collection of related data items; a customer record would likely contain customer name, address, account number, and—as indicated—current balance and credit limit.) The interesting thing about this flowchart is that it contains the same input operation, "Read customer record," twice (see the parallelograms). We shall see why this is necessary. Let us proceed through the flowchart:

① After reading the first customer record and proceeding through the connector, you have a decision box that asks, "Record received?" This is a test to see if you have run out of all customer records (which you probably would not have done the first time through).

② If the answer is "No," you have reached an **end of file**—there are no more records in the file—and the process stops.

③ If the answer is "Yes," the program proceeds to another decision box, which asks a question about the customer whose record you have just received: "Balance > limit?" This is an IF-THEN type of decision. If the answer is "Yes," then the customer is over the limit and, as planned, the computer prints the customer's record and moves on to the connector. If the answer is "No," then the computer moves directly to the connector.

④ Now we come to the second Read statement, "Read customer record." Why are two such statements needed? Couldn't we just forget the second one and loop back to the first Read statement again?

The answer lies in the rules of structure. As we stated, a loop requires a decision either at the beginning or at the end. If we omitted the second Read statement and looped back to the first Read statement, then the decision box to get us out of the loop ("Record received?") would be in the middle, not the beginning or the end of the loop. Why not put the decision box, "Record received?," at the end? You cannot because then you would have done the processing before you were sure you even had a record to process.

In summary: The decision box cannot go at the end, and the rules say it cannot be in the middle; therefore, the decision must go at the beginning of the processing. Thus, the only way to read a second customer record after the computer has read the first one is to have the second Read statement where you see it. The first Read statement is sometimes called the **priming read.** This concept of the double read may seem complicated at first, but it is very important. Rereading the description of this flowchart may help.

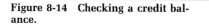

**Figure 8-14   Checking a credit balance.**

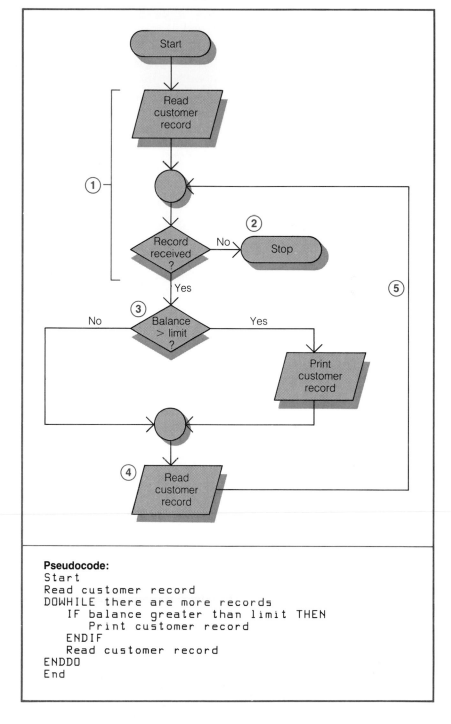

**Pseudocode:**
```
Start
Read customer record
DOWHILE there are more records
    IF balance greater than limit THEN
        Print customer record
    ENDIF
    Read customer record
ENDDO
End
```

⑤ Next, the program loops back to the connector and repeats the process. Incidentally, this is a DOWHILE loop, because the decision box is at the beginning rather than at the end of the computing process ("DO keep processing WHILE records continue to be received").

Note that, as before, each action in the program is either a sequence, a selection, or an iteration. In fact, since you have now seen two totally different examples—counting salaries and checking credit balances—you can begin to see how the control structures can be used universally for different applications. That is, the subject matter of the program may change, but the structured programming principles remain the same. Now let us apply these same principles to pseudocode.

## Planning the Solution with Pseudocode

**Pseudocode** is an English-like way of representing the control structures of structured programming. It is considered a "first draft" because the pseudocode eventually has to be translated into a programming language. Although pseudocode is English-like and has some precision to it, it does not have the very definite precision of a programming language. Pseudocode cannot be executed by a computer. The advantage of pseudocode is that, in using it to plan a program, you can concentrate on the logic and control structures and not worry about the rules of a specific language. It is also easy to change pseudocode if you discover a flaw in your logic, whereas most people find that it is more difficult to change logic once it is coded in a programming language. Another advantage of pseudocode is that it can be translated to a variety of languages, such as Pascal or COBOL.

We have already introduced the three basic structures—sequence, selection (IF-THEN-ELSE), and iteration (DOWHILE)—and a fourth structure, an additional form of iteration called DOUNTIL. DOUNTIL is really just a combination of sequence and DOWHILE.

A fifth structure in common use is CASE. CASE is not considered a basic control structure because it is only a convenient substitute for a series of selections, or IF statements. In languages supporting the CASE statement, the actions that are taken depend on the value of a variable. Study the flowchart form of each of these five control structures in Figure 8-15.

To see how pseudocode works, look at the center column in Figure 8-15. The center column shows the standard pseudocode format for describing the control structures shown in the flowchart. An actual example of pseudocode is given in the right column. (Note that the pseudocode is not as formal as a programming language.) The key control words, such as IF and THEN, are capitalized.

Now consider how these pseudocode statements are used to plan a program solution. (You are already familiar with the examples in Figures 8-13 and 8-14, so it might be helpful to follow the pseudocode for them as you read the discussion that follows.)

| Flowchart format: | Pseudocode format: | Pseudocode example: |
|---|---|---|
|  SEQUENCE | SEQUENCE:<br><br>statement a<br>statement b | Write headings<br>Set counters to zero |
| 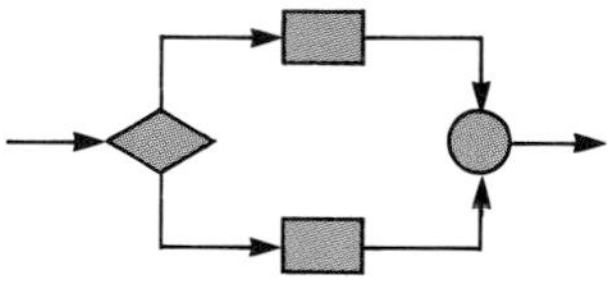 IF-THEN-ELSE | IF-THEN-ELSE:<br><br>IF condition p THEN<br>    statement a<br>ELSE<br>    statement b<br>ENDIF | IF balance > 300 THEN<br>    set service charge to zero<br>ELSE<br>    set service charge to 5.00<br>ENDIF |
| 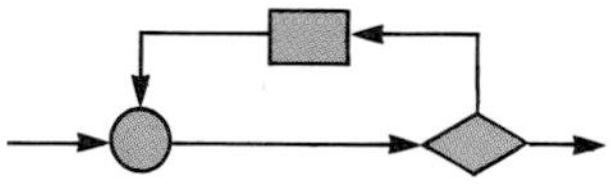 DOWHILE | DOWHILE:<br><br>DOWHILE condition p<br>    statement a<br>ENDDO | DOWHILE there are more records<br>    Write record<br>    Read record<br>ENDDO |
| 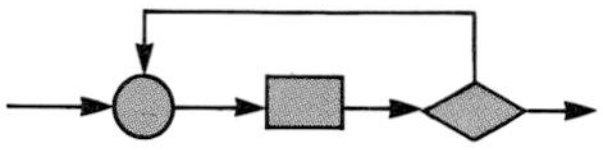 DOUNTIL | DOUNTIL:<br><br>DOUNTIL condition p<br>    statement a<br>ENDDO | DOUNTIL count = 100<br>    Add count to total<br>    Add 1 to count<br>ENDDO |
| 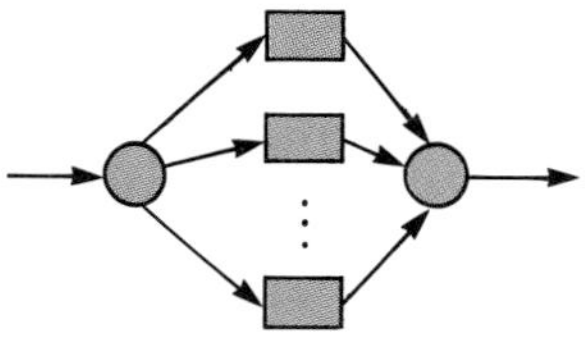 CASE | CASE:<br><br>CASENTRY select value<br>    CASE a<br>        function a<br>    CASE b<br>        function b<br>        :<br>        :<br>    Case n<br>        function n<br>ENDCASE | CASE value is 1, 2, or 3<br>    CASE 1<br>        Add member record<br>    CASE 2<br>        Revise member record<br>    CASE 3<br>        Delete member record<br>ENDCASE |

**Figure 8-15 Control structures.** A flowchart format and the equivalent pseudo-code format.

- Begin each program or program section with a begin, or start, statement and end with an end, or stop, statement.

- Write sequential statements in order, one under the other.

- Use IF-THEN-ELSE for decisions. Begin the decision with an IF and end with ENDIF. THEN goes at the end of the IF line. Use ELSE if needed. IF, ELSE, and ENDIF all begin in the same margin. The statements that go under THEN or ELSE are indented. There may be IFs within IFs, as in Figure 8-13.

- Use DOWHILE or DOUNTIL for iteration (looping). Indent the statements after the DO statement. End each DO with ENDDO, in the same margin as the DO. There may be loops within loops, although none are shown in these examples.

Read this problem description and see if you can write the pseudocode before you study the solution in Figure 8-16. Read a file of records and, if the account type is business, check further. If the order amount is greater than 1000, then set the discount rate to the maximum; otherwise, set the discount rate to the minimum. But if the account type is other than business—an ELSE situation—the discount rate is set to zero. After making these checks compute the discount, compute the amount due, and write the record and the amount due. Note that, as in Figure 8-14, you need a priming read. And remember to start and end the program.

## More Examples Showing Flowcharts and Pseudocode

In this section we offer further flowcharting and pseudocode practice. The first example is not very different from others you have seen in this chapter. The second is an extended problem that includes the program that can be written from the flowchart or the pseudocode.

### Example: Shift Bonus

Here is a description of the problem whose solution is represented in Figure 8-17. This time the pseudocode is first. The problem concerns awarding employees bonuses based on the shift worked. The example is a little more elaborate because it involves

**Figure 8-16   Example of pseudocode.** This shows a DOWHILE loop, with ENDDO signifying the end of the loop. Note that the third line is the beginning of what is called a nested IF; that is, there is an IF within another IF, and each has its own ending, ENDIF.

```
Start
Read a record
DOWHILE there are more records
    IF account-type is business THEN
        IF order amount greater than 1000 THEN
            Set discount-rate to maximum
        ELSE
            Set discount-rate to minimum
        ENDIF
    ELSE
        Set discount-rate to zero
    ENDIF
    Compute discount
    Compute amount due
    Print record and amount due
    Read record
ENDDO
End
```

**Pseudocode:**
```
Start
Move zero to counter
Read employee record
DOWHILE there are more records
    Move employee number and name to report line
    If first shift THEN
        bonus = regular pay × .05
        move bonus to report line
    ELSE
        IF second shift or third shift THEN
            bonus = regular pay × .10
            move bonus to report line
            add 1 to counter
        ELSE
            move error message to report line
        ENDIF
    ENDIF
    Print report line
    Read employee record
ENDDO
Print counter
End
```

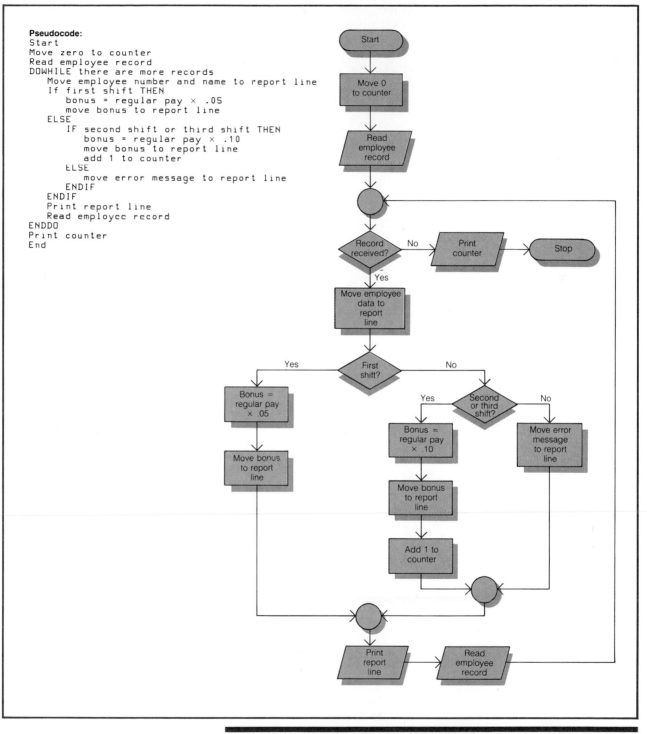

**Figure 8-17   Pseudocode and logic flowchart.** This example describes the logic for awarding employee bonuses. The pseudocode matches the flowchart.

moving data—employee number, name, and bonus—to a report line to set it up before printing. The decisions to be made are these. A first-shift employee gets a bonus of 5% of regular pay, but employees who work the second or third shift get a 10% bonus. Also, a count is needed of employees on the second or third shifts—that is, one count for both shifts. If the shift is not 1, 2, or 3, then an error message is printed instead.

## Example: Student Grades

Now let us translate a flowchart or pseudocode into a program. You could type this program in on a computer terminal connected to a mainframe computer or key it directly into your microcomputer. It would deliver back to you, on a terminal screen or in printout form, the answers you seek. Figure 8-18 shows the flowchart, pseudocode, program, and output.

The program is written in the programming language called BASIC (described in more detail in Appendix A). BASIC is similar to English in many ways, so you can understand the program even with no knowledge of BASIC. There are several "dialects" of the BASIC language, but we have chosen to use simple generic BASIC in this example. Generic BASIC runs on any BASIC version you may have.

In Figure 8-18c, the numbers in the far left column are called statement numbers. REM stands for a remark statement, which simply documents the program—a brief description of what it is supposed to do and a list of all variable names—symbolic names of locations in main storage. The PRINT statement tells the computer what message or data to print out, the READ statement reads the data to be processed, the GOTO (go to) statement tells which statement the computer is to go to, and DATA statements list the data to be read by the computer.

Our problem is, first, to compute the student grades (ranging from 0 to 100) for six students, and, second, to count the number of students who have scored less than 60 points. The grade points are based on student performance on two tests, on a midterm exam, and on a final exam, the scores of which have been weighted in a certain way.

Let us conceive of the problem in terms of input, processing, and output.

### Input

The circled numbers in the text correspond to the circled numbers in the flowchart, but you may choose to follow the pseudocode if you prefer. Corresponding statement numbers from the program follow in parentheses.

① "Print headings" (lines 240 through 300). These are the headings on the report (skip ahead to Figure 8-18d to see what they will look like). The first is the overall heading, "STUDENT GRADE REPORT." Lines that contain only the word PRINT, as line 240 does, cause blank lines to print on the output; this provides better spacing. Next the coding instructs the printer to print the three column headings.

②  "Place 0 in counter" (line 310). This is not a form of input data, but it is an initialization process required here at the outset. This counter will count the number of students who score less than 60 points, as we shall see later.

③  "Read number, name, scores" (line 320). The input data is given in lines 420 through 480.

### Processing

④  "Record received?" (line 330). Note that this is a DOWHILE loop because the decision box is at the beginning of the process. In generic BASIC, DOWHILE is implemented with IF-THEN-ELSE. The decision box asks if the particular student number, name, and scores read are the last ones in the file. How will the computer know this? Because the digits −9999 will tell it "End of file." You will note that the student numbers are four other digits (see lines 420 through 470). The −9999 decision instructs the computer to advance to the statement 390 when the end of the file is reached.

⑤  "Compute total points" (line 340). The scores are weighted 20% for the first test, 20% for the second test, 25% for the midterm, and 35% for the final exam. The total of these weighted scores gives the course grade. In the program these percentages are documented in remark statements (lines 30 through 110). The formula that totals the scores and incorporates the weightings is stated in line 340. Here the expression ".20*S1" means 20% times the first test score. (In BASIC, * is used as the multiplication symbol.)

⑥  "Print number, name, total points" (line 350). (Printing is really an output operation; we include it here for convenience because it is part of the loop.)

⑦  "Total points < 60?" (line 360). This decision box is given as an IF-THEN statement (< means less than). If a student's points are less than 60, 1 is added to COUNT.

⑧  "Read number, name, scores" (line 370). As in our last example, we have here an instance of a double-read statement. A GOTO statement is used to close the loop. That is, we repeat the input instruction given in step 3 above.

We now make the loop back to the first connector and continue to DO this processing WHILE the answer to the question "Record received?" is "Yes."

### Output

⑨  "Print counter" (line 400). When we reach the end of the file, we now also print the total number of students with points less than 60. At this point, then, you should have the printout of results shown in Figure 8-18d.

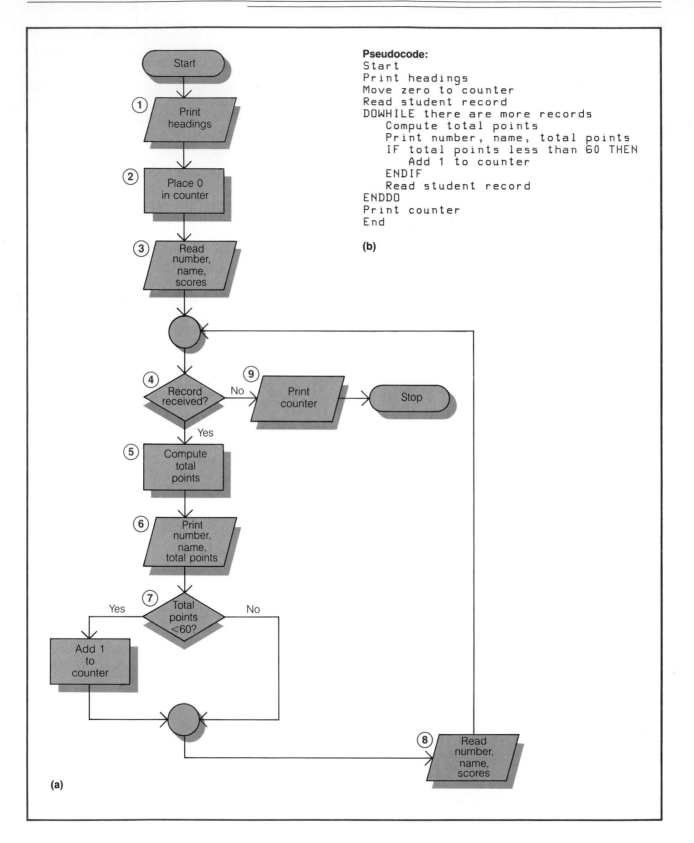

**Pseudocode:**
```
Start
Print headings
Move zero to counter
Read student record
DOWHILE there are more records
    Compute total points
    Print number, name, total points
    IF total points less than 60 THEN
        Add 1 to counter
    ENDIF
    Read student record
ENDDO
Print counter
End
```

(b)

(a)

```
10   REM PROGRAM TO COMPUTE STUDENT POINTS
20   REM
30   REM THIS PROGRAM READS, FOR EACH STUDENT,
40   REM    STUDENT NUMBER, STUDENT NAME, AND
50   REM    4 TEST SCORES. THE SCORES ARE TO
60   REM    BE WEIGHTED AS FOLLOWS:
70   REM
80   REM        TEST 1: 20 PERCENT
90   REM        TEST 2: 20 PERCENT
100  REM        MIDTERM: 25 PERCENT
110  REM        FINAL: 35 PERCENT
120  REM
130  REM VARIABLE NAMES USED:
140  REM
150  REM    COUNT   COUNT OF STUDENTS SCORING LESS THAN 60
160  REM    NUM     STUDENT NUMBER
170  REM    NAM$    STUDENT NAME
180  REM    S1      SCORE FOR TEST 1
190  REM    S2      SCORE FOR TEST 2
200  REM    S3      SCORE FOR MIDTERM
210  REM    S4      SCORE FOR FINAL
220  REM    TOTAL   TOTAL STUDENT POINTS
230  REM
240  PRINT
250  PRINT "    STUDENT GRADE REPORT"
260  PRINT
270  PRINT "STUDENT","STUDENT","TOTAL"
280  PRINT "NUMBER","NAME","POINTS"
290  PRINT
300  PRINT
310  LET COUNT = 0
320  READ NUM,NAM$,S1,S2,S3,S4
330  IF NUM = -9999 THEN 390
340  LET TOTAL = .20*S1+.20*S2+.25*S3+.35*S4
350  PRINT NUM,NAM$,TOTAL
360  IF TOTAL < 60 THEN COUNT = COUNT+1
370  READ NUM,NAM$,S1,S2,S3,S4
380  GOTO 330
390  PRINT
400  PRINT "NUMBER OF STUDENTS WITH POINTS < 60:";COUNT
410  STOP
420  DATA 2164,ALLEN SCHAAB,60,64,73,78
430  DATA 2644,MARTIN CHAN,80,78,85,90
440  DATA 3171,CHRISTY BURNER,91,95,90,88
450  DATA 5725,CRAIG BARNES,61,41,70,53
460  DATA 6994,RAOUL GARCIA,95,96,90,92
470  DATA 7001,KAY MITCHELL,55,60,58,55
480  DATA -9999,XXX,0,0,0,0
490  END
```

(c)

```
      STUDENT GRADE REPORT

STUDENT        STUDENT              TOTAL
NUMBER         NAME                 POINTS


2164           ALLEN SCHAAB          70.4
2644           MARTIN CHAN           84.4
3171           CHRISTY BURNER        90.5
5725           CRAIG BARNES          56.5
6994           RAOUL GARCIA          92.9
7001           KAY MITCHELL          56.8

NUMBER OF STUDENTS WITH POINTS < 60: 2
```

(d)

**Figure 8-18   Student grades.** The (a) flowchart and (b) pseudocode for (c) the program that produces (d) a student grade report.

All this is probably a bit confusing if you are a beginner. Practice helps. Appendix A offers several flowchart-to-program translations for your perusal.

## Is Programming for You?

In this chapter we have glimpsed the habits of mind and carefulness required to write programs. What we have seen is just an overview. The is-this-for-me question can really only be answered after you have given programming a try. The exact process of producing a program from a flowchart is given in Appendix A.

## More How-To Books

There is an epilogue to the Tom Hollenbeck story. Perhaps it is so predictable that we should have seen it coming. From his own struggles with software documentation, Tom perceived that there was a market for simple books to support software users. He promoted a series of such books, which sold very well.

Tom decided to carry this a step further. He was alert to another potential audience for books. Were there not others like himself who wanted to dabble in programming? Although he still considered himself a programming amateur—and he was—Tom knew that his experiments would have been simpler if he had had some easy-to-use guidelines. So, more books came forth on programming topics. The base kept expanding as new specific audiences were identified for different languages or machines or learning approaches.

If you have examined the computer books in your local bookstore, you know that other publishers have had similar ideas. There are, quite literally, thousands of computer how-to books on the market. The selection is gratifying and a comfort to all of us who want to know where to turn.

## Summary and Key Terms

- A programmer converts solutions to the user's problems into instructions for the computer. This process involves defining the problem, planning the solution, coding the program, testing the program, and documenting the program.

- Defining the problem means discussing it with the users to determine the necessary input, processing, and output.

- Planning can be done by using a **flowchart,** which is a pictorial representation of the step-by-step solution, and by using **pseudocode,** which is an English-like language.

- Coding the program means expressing the solution in a progamming language.

- Testing the program consists of desk-checking, translating, and debugging. **Desk-checking** is a mental checking or proofreading of the program before it is run. In translating, a **translator** program -converts the program into language the computer can understand and in the process detects programming errors, which are called **syntax** errors. Two types of translators are **compilers,** which translate the entire program at one time and give all the error messages (**diagnostics**) at once, and **interpreters,** which translate the program one line at a time. **Debugging** is running the program to detect, locate, and correct mistakes ("bugs").

- **Documentation** is a detailed written description of the program and the test results.

- A flowchart consists of arrows representing the direction the program takes and boxes and other symbols representing actions. A **logic flowchart** represents the flow of logic in a program, and a **systems flowchart** represents the flow of data through an entire computer system.

- The standard symbols used in flowcharting are called **ANSI** (American National Standards Institute) symbols. The most common symbols are process, decision, connector, start/stop, input/output, and direction of flow. The rectangular **process** box shows an action to be taken. The diamond-shaped **decision** box, with two **paths** or **branches,** is the only symbol that allows a choice. The **connector** is a circle that connects paths. The oval **start/stop** symbol is used at the beginning and end of a flowchart.

- To **initialize** is to set the starting values of certain storage locations before running a program.

- A **loop,** or **iteration,** is the repetition of instructions under certain conditions. The computer can recognize these conditions by performing a **compare** operation.

- **Structured flowcharting** and **structured programming** use three basic **control structures:** sequence, selection, and iteration.

- In the **sequence control structure,** one statement follows another. The **selection control structure** involves test conditions and has two variations: IF-THEN and IF-THEN-ELSE. The basic **iteration control structure** is DOWHILE, which is used in looping. The three basic control structures are supplemented by a fourth structure, DOUNTIL, which is another form of iteration used in looping. The fifth control structure, CASE, is a convenient substitute for a series of selections (IF statements).

- The basic rule of iteration is: If you have several statements that need to be repeated, a decision about when to stop repeating has to be placed either at the beginning of all the loop statements or at the end of all the loop statements.

- In a DOWHILE loop the loop-ending decision is at the beginning and is called a **leading decision.** The decision in a DOUNTIL loop occurs at the end and is called a **trailing decision.**

- In program instructions, to **read** means to bring something into memory.

- An **end of file** means that there are no more records in the file.

- When a Read statement is repeated, the first Read statement is sometimes called the **priming read.**

- **Pseudocode** must be translated into a programming language before the program can be run. Pseudocode allows a programmer to plan a program without being concerned about the rules of a specific programming language.

## Review Questions

1. Name the five steps in the programming process.

2. Describe the two common ways of planning a program, and discuss their advantages and disadvantages.

3. Describe the phases involved in testing a program.

4. Why is documentation important?

5. Explain what ANSI symbols are used for and name the common ones.

6. Describe the three main control structures in structured programming. Name and describe the specific types of statements.

7. Explain how the three control structures are evident in the flowchart for counting salaries and in the flowchart for checking credit balances.

## Discussion Questions

1. Should students taking a computer-literacy course be required to learn some programming? Why or why not?

2. Do you think you might like to become a computer programmer or other computer professional?

# 9

# Structured Program Design

## Up from Spaghetti Code

Structured programming reduces program testing and maintenance time, increases programmer productivity, and increases clarity and readability. This chapter provides an underlying rationale for the structure concept and describes structured design characteristics such as top-down design and module coupling and cohesion. Egoless programming is also described. Finally, the future of structured programming is considered.

## CONSCIENCE OF THE COMMUNITY

The computer community, that is. He has been hovering over the computer world since the early 1960s. Few people have made such an impact or had such a lasting effect. On the other hand, few have so polarized the industry; no one is neutral about Edsger Dijkstra.

For his outspoken views, Dijkstra has been praised as a visionary by some. Others see him as a dreamer or—worse—a troublemaker. Dijkstra ignores both camps, blissfully going his own way. A prolific writer, Dijkstra turns out articles, essays, and even satires that remind the industry of its faults. In a 1972 address, for example, he denounced some programming languages in typically colorful terms: "The sooner we can forget that FORTRAN ever existed, the better. It wastes our brainpower, and it is too risky and therefore too expensive to use." He did not have kind words for PL/I either, a language he compared to "a plane with 7000 buttons and switches in the cockpit." He continued, "I absolutely fail to see how we can keep our growing programs firmly within our intellectual grip when by its sheer baroqueness the programming language—our basic tool, mind you!—already escapes our intellectual control."

In the 1950s the programmer was hardly noticed, writes the well-known software expert Edsger Dijkstra. For one thing, the computers themselves were so large and so cantankerous to maintain that they attracted most of the attention. For another, Dijkstra (pronounced *DIKE-stra*) said, "The programmer's somewhat invisible work was without any glamour: you could show the machine to visitors and that was several orders of magnitude more spectacular than some sheets of coding." Programmers flourished, nevertheless, as the demand for software grew.

In the 1960s hardware overreached software. The development of hardware and storage capabilities proceeded apace, but software development could not keep up. Projects ran over budget, schedules slipped, and when projects were finally completed they often did not meet the users' needs.

In the 1970s some determined attempts were made to make software development more manageable. Hardware costs had already decreased dramatically, while software costs continued to rise; it was apparent that, if money was to be saved, there would have to be considerable improvements in software. No longer would programmers be allowed to produce programs that were casually tested or that were readable only to them. The use of obscure coding in an attempt to shave a microsecond of computer time was discouraged. It became clear that, first, problem complexity had to be accepted as fact and that, second, tools had to be devised to handle it. The programmer's job was no longer "invisible work."

## The Move to Structured Programming

How did people go about programming in the early '60s? One computer scientist wrote: "Computer programming was so badly understood that hardly anyone even thought about proving programs correct; we just fiddled with a program until we 'knew' it worked." Dijkstra, in fact, has nagged and cajoled programmers to think in advance instead of using a rear-guard action of finding errors *after* the program is written.

Finding program errors after the fact was—and still is in some quarters—an accepted way of programming. That is, a programmer wrote a program that seemed to solve the problem, then the program was put to the test. As soon as an error turned up, that one was fixed. This would continue until eventually the programmer got the program working well enough to use. To Dijkstra, this seemed a shoddy way of doing things. "Program testing," he says, "is a very convincing way of demonstrating program errors but never their absence."

## A Profound Proposal

Enter structured programming. In 1966 C. Bohm and G. Jacopini published a paper in the *Communications of the ACM* (the journal of the Association for Computing Machinery), a paper they had previously published in Italy. In this paper they proved mathematically that any problem solution could be constructed using only three basic control structures. These are the three structures that we have been calling *sequence, selection* (IF-THEN-ELSE), and *iteration*. It is interesting to note that the concept has been unchanged since it was proposed two decades ago.

These three control structures—sequence, selection, and iteration—were, of course, used before 1966. But other control structures were also used, notably the transfer, also known as the GOTO. Since the need for only the three basic control structures was now proven, the time had come to cut down on the number of GOTO statements.

The idea of structured programming was given a boost in March 1968, when Dijkstra published a letter in the *Communications of the ACM* under the heading, "Go To Statements Considered Harmful." In this now famous letter, Dijkstra contended that the GOTO statement was an invitation to making a mess of one's program and that reducing the number of GOTOs reduced the number of programming errors. GOTOs, he said, could be compared to a bowl of spaghetti: If a person took a program and drew a line from each GOTO statement to the statement to which it transferred, the result would be a picture that looked like a bowl of spaghetti. Since then, people have referred to excessive GOTOs in a program as "spaghetti code." Note the comparison of programs with and without GOTOs in Figure 9-1.

## Structured Programming Takes Off

The first major project using structured programming was developed for the *New York Times*. The results were published in 1972. In this large undertaking the newspaper's clipping file was automated in such a way that, using a list of index terms, users could browse through abstracts (summaries) of all the paper's articles, automatically retrieve the text of an article, and display it on a terminal. The project involved 83,000 lines of source code and took 22 calendar months and 11 person-years to produce, yet it was delivered under budget and ahead of schedule. Equally important, there was an amazingly low error rate: Only 21 errors were found during the five weeks of acceptance testing, and only 25 additional errors appeared during the first year of the system's operation.

In December 1973 *Datamation*, one of the principal trade journals of the computer industry, devoted an entire issue to structured programming. This issue brought the subject to the attention of many programmers in the United States. One article hailed structured programming as a programming revolution.

1.   Read in four numbers. Assign
     them to variables A, B, C, D.

2.   If A is greater than B then
     GOTO line 5.

3.   Put the value for B in the
     location called LARGEST.

4.   GOTO line 6.

5.   Put the value for A in
     LARGEST.

6.   If LARGEST is greater than C
     then GOTO line 8.

7.   Put the value for C in the
     variable called LARGEST.

8.   If LARGEST is greater than D
     then GOTO line 10.

9.   Put the value for D in the
     variable called LARGEST.

10.  Print the number stored
     in LARGEST.

**(a)**

1.   Read in four numbers. Assign
     them to variables A, B, C, D.

2.   Put the value for A in
     LARGEST.

3.   If B is greater than largest
     then place the value for B
     in LARGEST.

4.   If C is greater than largest
     then place the value for C
     in LARGEST.

5.   If D is greater than largest
     then place the value for D
     in LARGEST.

6.   Print the number stored
     in LARGEST.

**(b)**

**Figure 9-1   With and without the GOTO statement.** These two programs, written here in plain English, do the same thing: Each finds the largest of four numbers. Such a task could be used, for example, to locate the salesperson with the largest sales for the month. The program in Figure 9-1a, the one with all the arrows, illustrates GOTO programming. Even this small example demonstrates how confusing GOTO programming can be. The program in Figure 9-1b shows the solution for the same problem in GOTOless programming; it does the job in a tidy sequential manner.

And a revolution it has been. The theory—if not total practice—has been universally accepted in the computer industry. One obvious proof of this acceptance is the number of programming language textbooks on the market with the word *structure* in the title. No one would even consider publishing an unstructured text for COBOL, a popular business programming language. So the trainees coming into the industry have "structure" fresh in their heads, and what do they find? For some, the purest of structured shops. Many, however, are shocked to find existing programs—fat, messy programs—dripping with GOTOs. Why is this? These programs were written in the '60s and even the '70s before structured programming had taken hold. Managers would love to have them redone in structured code, but there always seem to be more pressing priorities. Occasionally a trainee is welcomed with open arms as the savior who is going to convert some of the dinosaurs to structured code. This may be the ultimate challenge—structuring a 5000-line program that has been massaged by perhaps 50 different programmers over the last 15 years. The biggest problem may be that no one really understands how it works anymore!

Managers have estimated that structured techniques increase programming productivity by approximately 25%. Here are some of the reasons why this is so. Structured programming:

- Increases the clarity and readability of programs (partly because you can read the program sequentially instead of hopping all over with GOTOs)

- Reduces the time required to test programs

- Decreases the time required to maintain programs (because increased clarity means less time spent in trying to read and understand programs)

So far we have discussed the historical significance and rationale for structured programming and tied it to the three fundamental structures: sequence, selection, and iteration. But the issue of structure cuts deeper.

## Expanding the Structured Programming Concept

When the concept of program structure was first introduced, some people thought their programs would be structured if they simply got rid of GOTOs. There is more to it than that. Structured programming is a method of designing computer system components and their relationships to minimize complexity. So, in addition to limited control structures (again: sequence, selection, and iteration), two important aspects of structured programming are (1) top-down programming design and (2) module independence through coupling and cohesion. Before we describe these concepts, let us pause for a formal definition: **Structured programming** is a set of programming techniques that include a limited number of control structures, top-down design, and module independence.

When a programmer uses **top-down design,** one of the first steps in writing is to identify basic program functions. These functions are further divided into smaller and smaller subfunctions of more manageable size called modules. Top-down design is demonstrated most easily by using structure charts.

## Structure Charts

A **structure chart** graphically illustrates the structure design of a program as hierarchical, independent modules. This high-level picture identifies major functions that are the initial component parts of the structure chart. Each major component is then broken down into subcomponents, which are, in turn, broken down still further until sufficiently detailed components are shown. As we noted, this is considered a top-down approach to program design. Since the components are pictured in hierarchical form, a drawing of this kind is also known as a **hierarchy chart.** A structure chart is easy to draw and easy to change, and it is often used as a supplement to or even a replacement for a logic flowchart.

Consider an example, Figure 9-2. As the illustration shows, the

**Figure 9-2  A structure chart.** The numbers outside the boxes refer to more detailed diagrams of these functions. For instance, module 2.0 is presented in more detail in Figure 9-5.

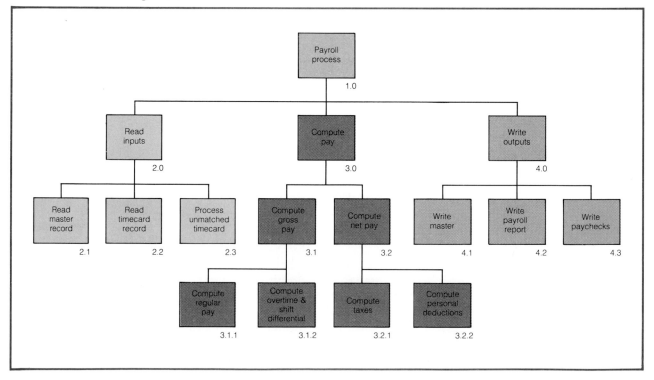

## THE MICROCOMPUTER CORNER

### A CASE of Helpful Software

Professional programmers on large computer systems work within the context of two facts: (1) The system is composed of many small programs, and (2) the system is developed and run by a team. That is, many people are keeping track of many programs, and communication is critical.

A new genre of software has joined the market to help out, and a new acronym comes with it: CASE systems. No, this is not the CASE structure you saw in pseudocode; CASE stands for computer-aided software engineering. CASE systems help in the development stages of a new system in several ways. A typical CASE system is composed of several programs that can help develop flowcharts and data and the relationships among them.

But it is the coordination function that is so crucial. Flowcharts can be drawn on screen, then filled in with data from data dictionaries or databases. If any part of the system changes, related changes can be made readily because the relationships are recorded in the system.

Another point related to communication is that team members can work independently but share information through the system. In fact, CASE software even checks for inconsistencies. It is the inconsistencies that can cause so much trouble further down the development line. It is comforting to know that there is software available to help build more software—in faster and better ways.

top level of the structure chart gives the name of the program, "Payroll process." The next level breaks the program down into its major functions—in Figure 9-2, these are "Read inputs," "Compute pay," and "Write outputs." Each of these major modules is then subdivided further into smaller modules. (We could break them down even further, but space does not permit it.)

Note the relationship of the structure chart in Figure 9-2 to top-down design. The major functions are repeatedly subdivided into smaller modules of manageable size. Each of the modules is also, according to plan, as independent of the others as possible. For example, module 4.1, "Write master," will be executed independently of any activity in module 4.3, "Write paychecks."

Now let us look more closely at the way modules are planned.

### Modularity

Computer professionals recognize that the way to efficient development and maintenance is to break the programs in a system into manageable pieces—modules. The way that a system is divided into various pieces has a significant effect on the structure of the system. We have already noted in our structure chart discussion that structured design involves organizing the pieces of a system in a hierarchical way. High-level components of the structure chart are programs; lower-level components are called modules. Once converted to programmed form, a **module** is a set of logically related statements that performs a specific function.

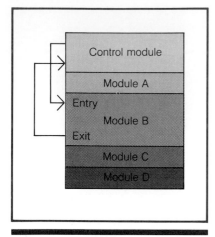

**Figure 9-3  Single entry, single exit.** The program control module executes module B by transferring to its entry point. After the instructions in module B are executed, the module is exited via its exit point. Program control returns, in this case, to the point of departure, the control module.

One relationship between modules is called **coupling.** It is the measure of the strength of the relationship between two modules. Ideally, that relationship should be weak so that the modules are independent; then, later, if a change is made in one module, it will not affect other modules. Another relationship is called **cohesion,** the measure of the inner strength of an individual module. The best relationship here is a strong one; a module should have a single function, although that is not always possible. An example of a single function is the computation of withholding tax. This function would not be included with other functions, such as computing credit-union deductions. Strong cohesion also encourages module independence, which—in turn—makes future changes easier.

In addition, a module should have a **single entry** and a **single exit.** Single entry means that the execution of a program module must begin at the same place, usually at the beginning; the module can be entered at only a single point. Similarly, the module may be exited from only one place, as shown in Figure 9-3. It is easier for us to keep track of what is going on in the program if there is only one way to get in and one way to get out of each module in the program.

A module should also be of manageable size. A single page of coded program instructions is often considered an ideal size.

## HIPO: To Describe the Program Visually

A good program designer uses tools to keep the design process under control. The use of such tools contributes to unity of purpose and clarity of design. More important, good design promotes software reliability. A well-designed program not only helps prevent the introduction of errors, it also makes errors easier to discover. We have already considered the structure chart as a design tool. Pseudocode is also particularly useful in planning program logic using the control structures sequence, selection, and iteration. There are many others. Closely related to the concept of structure, however, is HIPO.

As you will see, HIPO includes a structure chart as a key tool. **HIPO**—pronounced *high po*—stands for Hierarchy plus Input-Process-Output. It consists of a set of diagrams that graphically describes program functions from the general level to the detailed level. Developed as a documentation tool by IBM, HIPO is now used for both design and documentation. As Figure 9-4 indicates, it is a visual tool.

You can see how it supports top-down development. The first of three types of diagrams is a visual table of contents, which presents a structure chart along with a short description of the contents and a legend explaining what the arrows on the other diagrams mean. The second diagram, the overview diagram, shows—from left to right— the inputs, processes, and outputs. This overview diagram (there will likely be more than one) describes the processes of the program

Figure 9-4   A HIPO package.

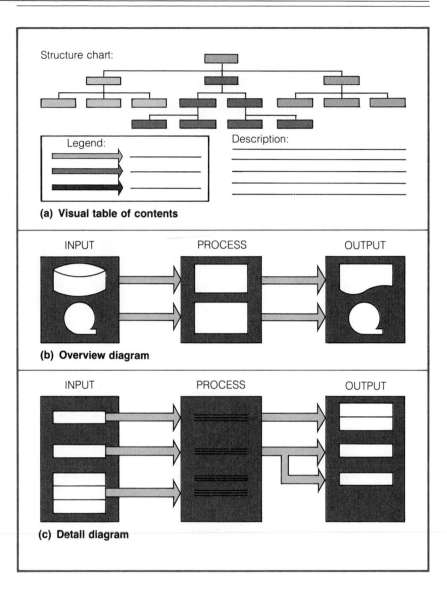

(a) **Visual table of contents**

(b) **Overview diagram**

(c) **Detail diagram**

in general terms. The third diagram, the detail diagram, also describes the inputs, processes, and outputs but in much greater detail.
There can be several detail diagrams for each overview diagram.

The visual HIPO package has developed into a popular tool for
designing programs. To give you a better idea of how the overview
diagram looks, see Figure 9-5, which shows how the "Read inputs"
module of the structure chart in Figure 9-2 (module 2.0) appears at
the input-process-output overview level.

We have considered structured programming and related concepts in a formal way as a technique to foster the goal of programmer
productivity. But other factors are involved in productivity—factors
that are related to social issues.

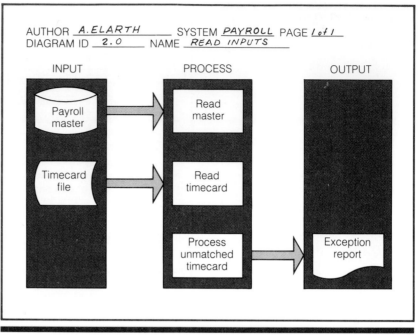

**Figure 9-5   Example of a HIPO overview diagram.** This shows further details of module 2.0 in Figure 9-2.

# The Social Activity of Programming

Programming as a social activity? "What a strange idea," you may say. "As though writing programs were like playing cards."

As it turns out, this concept is a very useful notion. The idea was first popularized in a book by Gerald Weinberg called *The Psychology of Computer Programming*, which was published in 1971. Weinberg pointed out that though many people think of programmers as loners, programming is not really a private activity, and the program itself is not private property: Unless you are totally self-employed, the program belongs to the organization for which you work. Yet many programmers are defensive about letting others look over their work, fearing that they may find mistakes that make the programmer look stupid. Also, some programmers are unenthusiastic about sharing their hard-earned skills and techniques. Their pride, their egos, are bound up with their programs.

## Egoless Programming

The answer to this, Weinberg said, is **egoless programming,** programming with the attitude that one's program is not one's personal property but is open to—indeed, benefits by—inspection by all. The idea of egoless programming sets the stage for mutual

## EGOLESS PROGRAMMING

Bill found Marilyn willing to peruse his code in exchange for his returning the favor. This was nothing unusual in this group; indeed, nobody would have thought of going on the machine without such scrutiny by a second party. Whenever possible an exchange was made, so nobody would feel in the position of being criticized by someone else. But for Bill, who was well schooled in this method, the protection of an exchange was not necessary. His value system, when it came to programming, dictated that secretive, possessive programming was bad and that open, shared programming was good. Errors that might be found in code he had written—not "his" code, for that terminology was not used here—were simply facts to be exposed to investigation with an eye to future improvement, not attacks on his person.

In this particular instance, Bill had been having one of his "bad programming days." As Marilyn worked and worked over the code—as she found one error after another—he became more and more amused, rather than more and more defensive as he might have done had he been trained as so many of our programmers are. Finally, he emerged from their conference announcing to the world the startling fact that Marilyn had been able to find seventeen bugs in only thirteen statements. He insisted on showing everyone who would listen how this had been possible. In fact, since the very exercise had proved to him that this was not his day for coding, he simply spent the rest of the day telling and retelling the episode in all its hilarious details.

As an epilogue to this incident, it should be noted that when this code was finally put on the computer, no further errors were found, in spite of the most diabolical testing possible. In fact, this program was put into use in more than a dozen installations for real-time operations, and over a period of at least nine years no other errors were ever found.

—Gerald Weinberg
*The Psychology of Computer Programming*

assistance. Programmers are not mad coders sitting alone in corners; rather, they should offer each other reinforcement and advice in a nonthreatening environment.

Out of the concept of egoless programming has grown another idea that is becoming standard procedure—namely, the **programming team.** The composition of a programming team varies. Often, the team members are all working on the same programming project, one that requires many programs. Team members review each other's programs both at the design level and at the coding level.

## Early Defect Removal

There is good reason for team members to review each other's work, especially at the design level. Known as **early defect removal,** this approach can save considerable time and money. It has proven far more costly to remove program defects in the later stages of development and testing than in the early stages (Figure 9-6). There are several reasons for this. One is that unresolved errors show up—eventually—in the form of bad output, then the programmer must spend hours tracking the problem to the source. Meanwhile, the error may have infiltrated the files—a possibility that means

**Figure 9-6   Phase versus cost.** Correcting errors late in the development process becomes very expensive and time-consuming. An error discovered during the earliest stage, preliminary design, can be fixed at negligible cost. Errors found in later stages cost progressively more; during the systems testing phase, for example, an error costs 2 to 5 times more to fix and, once in the maintenance phase, 10 to 90 times as much!

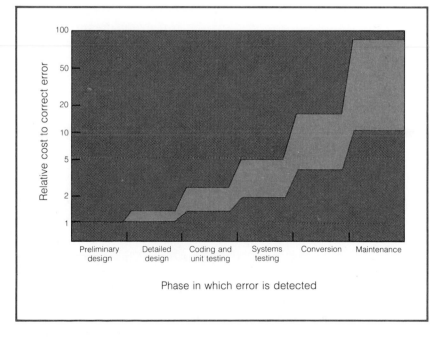

Relative cost to correct error

100
50
20
10
5
2
1

Preliminary design | Detailed design | Coding and unit testing | Systems testing | Conversion | Maintenance

Phase in which error is detected

many more labor hours for cleanup. And, of course, there is the bad output itself, which may cost dearly in terms of bad decisions or lost customers.

To encourage the early removal of defects, many programming teams have turned to the structured walkthrough.

## Structured Walkthroughs

The design review process is called a **structured walkthrough.** This is a formal process among members of a programming team, in which several team members review the design or code of an individual programmer, looking for weaknesses and errors. Managers seldom participate, since it is important that the review of the program not become entangled with notions about evaluating someone's performance. In many installations the structured walkthrough is not for purposes of inviting comparisons. That is, a team member is not allowed to say, "I know a better way of doing this"; he or she is permitted to point out only what is not clear or what will not work and what is outside the organization's standards. There are installations, however, where a suggestion is welcome.

The primary benefit of the structured walkthrough is that since all the programs are going to be reviewed by fellow programmers, the author of the programs tries to make them comprehensible. And that is, of course, one of the main points—to make programs more understandable so they will be easier to maintain. Some managers consider the review as nonproductive time, but studies usually find the effort well spent, with a payoff in reduced testing time and higher-quality programs. And, of course, programmers also learn from each other during these reviews.

Not every organization is using structured walkthroughs, not even a majority. Smaller organizations with fewer than five employees are becoming commonplace; these organizations are less likely to use formal design reviews. There are also many large organizations that have not yet endorsed structured walkthroughs. But the adoption of this practice is clearly on the rise, and we will probably be seeing more of such "social activity" among programmers in the future.

## Structure Forever? A Surprising Answer

This chapter focuses on structure and its acceptance in the computer community. So we have industrywide agreement on this important issue and can consider it settled. No, not quite.

Structured programming only makes sense if you are using what is called a **procedural language**—that is, a language that presents a step-by-step process for solving a problem. It is the steps—program statements—of the procedure that need structuring. Most languages in use today, including the popular COBOL mentioned earlier, are procedural languages.

But nothing stays the same for long in the computer industry. New, easy-to-use languages are being used with increasing frequency. The ease of their use stems from the fact that they do not have procedures. In fact, they are called **nonprocedural languages.** Instead of stating *how* to accomplish a task—the step-by-step way— you just say *what* you want to accomplish. We shall study this development in more detail as we study languages in Chapter 10. For now, just be aware that structured programming may not always be an issue.

## Summary and Key Terms

- During the 1960s development of new hardware outpaced the development of new software, creating the need for more efficient methods of creating software.

- In 1966 C. Bohm and G. Jacopini published a paper on structured programming in which they proved that any problem solution could be constructed using the three basic control structures: **sequence, selection,** and **iteration.** The structured programming concept was further supported by Edsger Dijkstra, who emphasized that programs are less complex if the use of other control structures—especially the GOTO statement—is reduced.

- Structured programming increases programming productivity by increasing the clarity and readability of programs, reducing test time, and decreasing the time required to maintain programs.

- **Structured programming** is a set of programming techniques that includes a limited number of control structures, top-down design, and module independence.

- **Top-down design** identifies basic program functions before dividing them into subfunctions called modules.

- A **structure chart,** or **hierarchy chart,** illustrates the top-down design of a program and is often used to either supplement or replace a logic flowchart.

- When converted to program form, a **module** is a set of logically related statements that performs a specific function.

- **Coupling** is the measure of the strength of the relationship between two modules. Weak coupling is ideal because a change in one module does not affect other modules. **Cohesion** is the measure of the inner strength of a module. Strong cohesion makes modules more independent, a characteristic that facilitates future changes. A module should also have a **single entry** and a **single exit** so that it is easier to keep track of the flow of logic in the program.

- **HIPO** stands for Hierarchy plus Input-Process-Output. It consists of three types of diagrams: a structure chart; one or more overview diagrams showing the input, process, and output in general terms; and one or more detail diagrams showing the input, process, and output in detail.

- **Egoless programming** is programming with the attitude that one's program is not one's personal property and that the program benefits from inspection by other programmers.

- Egoless programming has led to the formation of **programming teams,** or groups of programmers that improve the design and coding of programs written by individuals.

- **Early defect removal** can prevent more costly corrections at the later stages of development and testing.

- The formal design-review process is called a **structured walkthrough,** in which several programming team members look for weaknesses and errors in the design or code of an individual programmer.

- A **procedural language,** such as COBOL, is a language that presents a step-by-step process for solving a problem. **Nonprocedural languages** simply state what task is to be accomplished but do not state the steps that accomplish it.

## Review Questions

1. Explain the contributions that Edsger Dijkstra and the team of C. Bohm and G. Jacopini made to structured programming.

2. How did structured programming differ from the way programming had been done previously?

3. State the benefits of structured programming.

4. Explain how maintaining a limited number of control structures helps to make programming less complex.

5. Describe top-down design.

6. Explain the concept of modularity.

7. Describe HIPO and explain its usefulness.

8. Explain the concept of egoless programming and discuss how it can help programmers and the organizations they serve.

9. Describe the process of the structured walkthrough.

## Discussion Questions

1. Imagine that you are the manager of a large programming organization and that you are weighing the pros and cons of having structured walkthroughs. State the advantages and disadvantages that come to mind, then explain what your decision would be.

2. In your opinion what kind of person makes a good programmer? Discuss specific characteristics and explain why they are important.

1

2

3

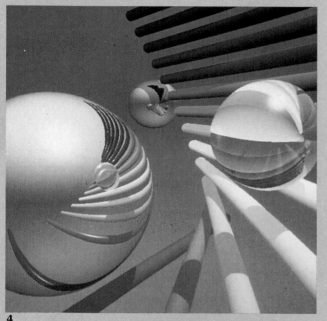

4

In this gallery we shall look at how computers are used in the arts, entertainment, science, health and medicine, education, transportation, agriculture, resource management, and sports. The photo on the opening page shows a computer system that translates sounds into musical notation, bridging the gap between the inspiration that creates new music and the laborious task of writing the notes down.

## The Arts

**(1)** A stunning photo? No, look again. This amazing work, called *Road to Point Reyes*, is a complex computer-generated image produced by a team of programmers at Pixar.

**(2)** This damaged sixteenth century painting has been analyzed by a sophisticated image processing system capable of displaying 32,000 hues. The analysis helps experts at Rome's Central Institute for Restoration select restoration colors.

**(3)** Linda Merk, an art conservator in New York City, uses an IBM PC and Lotus 1-2-3 to track the effectiveness of materials she uses to preserve sculptures.

**(4)** These high-resolution graphics cannot be made with plaything graphics packages; the subtleties of light variation and the brilliant colors require complex hardware and software.

**(5)** An art dealer uses an Apple IIc to track art inventory, customer sales records, and money due the artists.

5

## Entertainment

**(6)** Computers control the braking system on the *Texas Cliffhanger*, a free-fall ride that gives thrill seekers the falling sensation of stepping off a nine-story building. Each people-carrying gondola is monitored by 103 electronic sensors that send messages to the computer during the ride cycle.

**(7)** This is not the old boy-meets-girl, girl-evades-creature, boy-slays-dragon story. *Dragon's Lair* is new because it is an interactive video game whose ending is determined by the skill of the person playing it.

**(8)** To create the stained-glass knight in Steven Spielberg's movie *Young Sherlock Holmes*, an actor set the scene for the camera operators, but other than that it was all up to computers and design engineers. **(9)** A model of a knight was digitized and input into the computer, forming a computerized stick figure. This figure was then programmed for movement and color, including smudges and highlights to make the stained glass look authentic. **(10)** The final scene in the movie lasts 38 seconds—the result of 9 months of painstaking work.

6

7

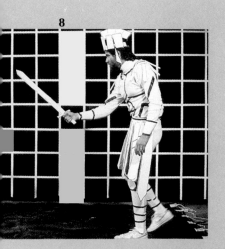

8

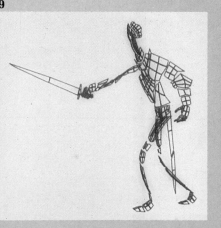

9

10

**(11)** Jim Gardiner's recording studio in Berkeley, California, is built around two microcomputers: an IBM PC and a Macintosh.

**(12)** This Hewlett-Packard television studio uses state-of-the-art computerized video and telecommunications equipment.

**(13)** This "imagineer" is programming a new show for the Country Bear Jamboree at Disneyland and Walt Disney World. After the movements of each figure and the soundtrack are programmed, a computer coordinates the timing of the show.

11

12

13
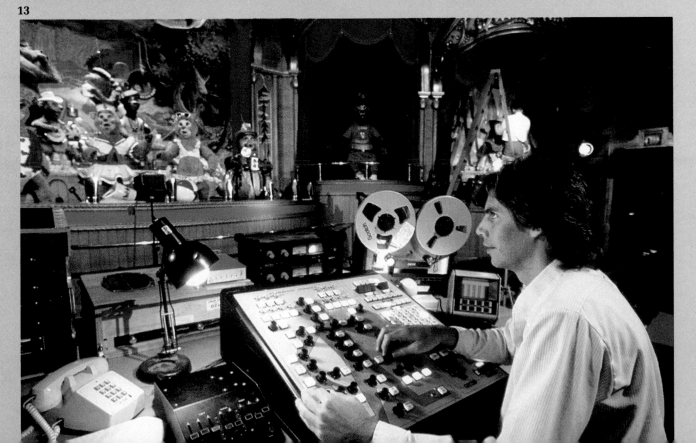

## Science

(14) The San Diego Zoo uses an IBM System/38 computer to maintain a growing database aimed at maintaining healthy animal populations world-wide. (15) The vital statistics of this young orangutan—shown here being examined by a zoo veterinarian—will be added to the database.

(16) The computer is in the background in this picture but it is a critical tool for this researcher, who feeds it endless data and lets the machine discover patterns.

(17) This physicist is using a personal computer to control instruments, collect data, and analyze results.

(18) Three-dimensional computer models of molecules help researchers study the structure of molecules, aiding in drug design, cancer research, and much more. This colorful graphic shows the structure of a virus that causes respiratory infections. (19) Scientists can set this type of model in motion to view it from different angles, zoom in on a certain area, or watch it interact with another molecule. (20) In this simplified representation of a very complex molecule, similar sections of the molecule are given similar shapes. This gives scientists an overview of the molecule's structure.

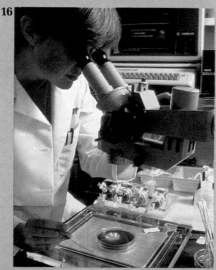

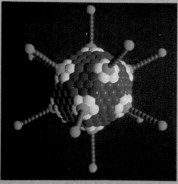

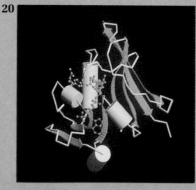

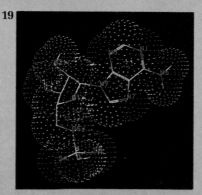

**(21)** When will the storm get here? To improve the science of weather forecasting, researchers program various weather conditions into a computerized global weather model. They can then see what kind of weather develops from those conditions; this photo shows day 42 of a simulation sequence.

**(22)** This computer-enhanced map of Venus, produced with data from Pioneer Venus 1, shows its diverse features, including mountain ranges and volcanic structures.

**(23)** Voyager spacecraft photos are sent to earth in the form of dots; computers then re-assemble and interpret the photos. Here is a color-enhanced image of Saturn. **(24)** This Voyager photo gives us a closer look at Saturn's rings. Color variations indicate different chemical compositions.

21

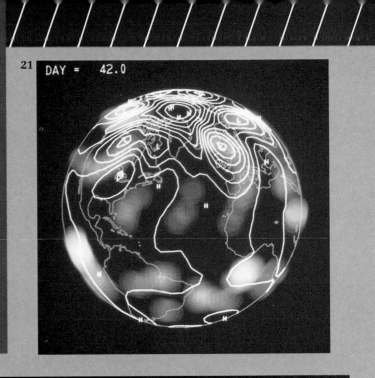

22

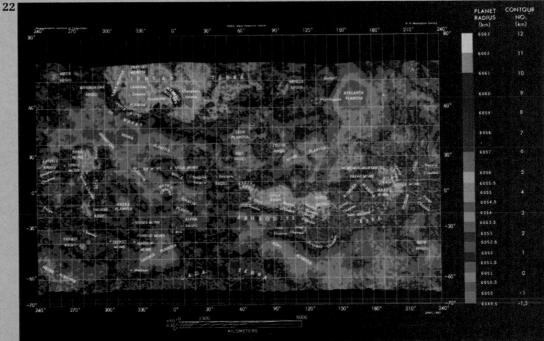

23

24

25

## Health and Medicine

**(25)** This doctor is using special software that aids in making diagnoses.

**(26)** A technician monitors cross-sectional body images on computer screens as the patient passes through the computer-controlled PET (positron-emission tomography) scanner.

**(27)** This PET scan image shows a cross section of the brain of a living person.

**(28)** Hospital nurses monitor patient progress using a computer at the station right on the patient's floor.

**(29)** A deaf and blind man reads configurations formed by a mechanical hand. Each configuration represents a different letter of the American Sign Language. The hand, which can form two letters per second, is directed by a personal computer.

26

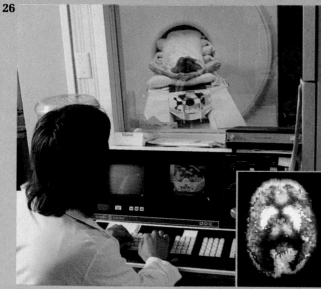

27

28

29

**(30)** This high resolution computer-generated image was produced for a British television series called "The Living Body."

**(31)** This computer-produced image shows a hand (upper left) and a cross section of the hand. The bones, tendons, and so forth are color-coded; for instance, the bones are light blue.

**(32)** This computer-generated image of a knee joint is the beginning of an animation sequence developed at the University of Minnesota. The viewer sees the joint bend on the computer screen. The user can control the movement of the joint and also view it from any angle.

**(33)** A computer-controlled ultrasound machine monitors a baby's progress before it is born.

**(34)** This computer-enhanced image of an ultrasound test shows triplets.

30

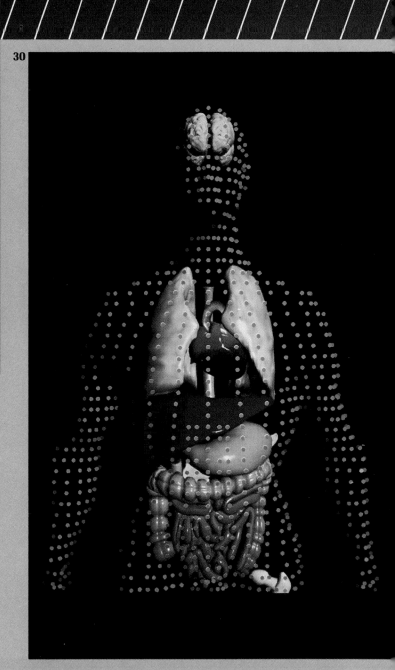

31

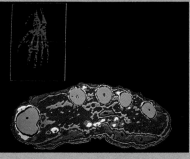

32

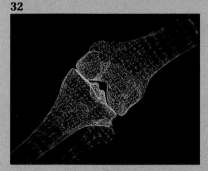

33

34

**35**

**36**

**37**

**38**

**39**

## Education

(35) This giant-sized IBM PC keyboard is used as part of a traveling computer show and exhibit for children in Australia.

(36) Computers in the lab? Yes. This high school chemistry student is using an Apple IIe to analyze results of experiments.

(37) Educators often want students to have fun while learning. It is clear that they do both at the National Computer Camp in Orange, Connecticut.

(38) When a child correctly spells a word by touching the proper letters on the board, the voice synthesizer attached to this computer repeats the word. The computer also corrects the child, if necessary, and provides verbal encouragement.

(39) Students at the Urban League Job Training Center in San Diego, California, prepare for jobs in word processing.

(40) The IBM PC is used in this special education class, where disabled students experience new levels of accomplishment.

(41) Animated graphics programs, used as learning tools in elementary schools, get the attention of small students.

(42) This college student, his Macintosh computer slung over his shoulder in a MacPack, heads home for the day.

40

41

42

43

## Transportation

(43) This interactive training system is used to update train engineers at the General Electric center in Pennsylvania.

(44) This computerized traffic control system in Los Angeles was originally installed for the Olympics. Major thoroughfares around the city are linked to city hall by fiber optics, where traffic flow is controlled by a centralized keyboard. The controller can monitor traffic flow patterns and manipulate signal intervals or even re-route traffic in the case of an accident or emergency.

(45) General Motors and IBM joined forces to produce this computerized automotive maintenance system, designed to diagnose electronic problems in GM vehicles. Note that the technician is using a touch-sensitive screen.

(46) It might be a photo, but, no, a closer look reveals a detailed computer graphics image. This flight simulator is part of a training program for pilots.

(47) When designing shipping routes, a graphics display such as this can be used. Engineers and customers can manipulate the image in a "What if. . ." manner to arrive at a final solution.

(48) Air traffic controllers rely on computers to display and track the positions of aircraft on a large round screen, as shown here. Each controller is responsible for a certain geographical area and "passes" aircraft to another controller as the plane moves into another territory.

(49) Truck stops offer computer terminals that quickly print out state operating permits for truckers who want to change routes.

44

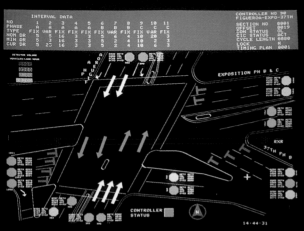

45

46

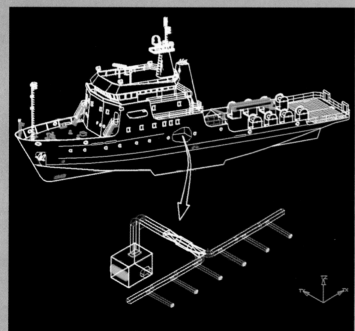

47

48

49

## Agriculture

**(50)** Farmers need every financial edge they can get, and computers often make the critical difference. This Missouri dairy farmer's automated feed system uses input from electric eyes in the feed bins and transistorized sensors around the cow's neck to control the amount of grain consumed.

**(51)** Truckloads of oranges go into this Florida plant, to be processed into frozen juice concentrate. The computerized process is directed from this control panel.

**(52)** A computer system monitors water, fertilizer, and humidity for plants in this Honolulu greenhouse. **(53)** The system is controlled by greenhouse personnel, who also use the computer for tracking plant inventory.

## Resource Management

**(54)** An oil company employee uses a portable computer at the oil refinery.

**(55)** California's Solar One is the world's largest solar electricity-generating station, using computer-controlled solar collectors to catch the sun's rays. In the control room, this technician adjusts the positions of the collectors for maximum exposure to solar rays.

**(56)** Geologists use graphic strata data to study possible sites for oil exploration.

**(57)** This hand-held microcomputer from Norand, with an amazing 512K memory, is used in warehouses, factories, and stores. This photo shows a Pacific Gas and Electric meter reader collecting data on his rounds.

**(58)** Tapping Colorado River water for arid Phoenix and Tucson, the Central Arizona Project is a tangle of aqueducts, pumping stations, siphons, and control gates. The flow is monitored by computers in CAP headquarters in Phoenix, where controllers keep track of the system's operations on a 30-foot-wide map.

54

55
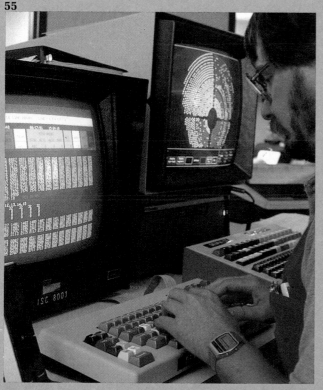

56
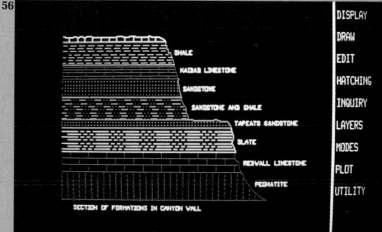

57

58

59

## Sports

**(59)** This computer is integrated with special timing equipment for swimming competitions.

**(60)** At the Olympic Training Center in Colorado Springs, trainers digitize movements of race walkers to produce **(61)** stick figures that are used to analyze performance.

**(62)** This Puma shoe has a built-in chip that calculates how far you have run and how many calories you have burned.

**(63)** Computers at the old ball game? Yes, indeed. Jay Alves, the statistician for the Oakland A's, uses his computer to keep track of the statistics for each game and analyze the team's performance.

60

61

62

63

# 10

# Languages

## A Survey

Five levels of program-
ming language—machine,
assembly, high-level, very
high-level, and natural—
are discussed in their historical context. The seven
most widely used lan-
guages are surveyed: FOR-
TRAN, COBOL, BASIC, Pas-
cal, Ada, C, and RPG.
Special features of each
language are discussed
and sample programs of
the first six languages are
presented. In addition,
other important languages
are described briefly.

Let us suppose that you work for a timber company, and you have an assignment related to manufacturing. You have to configure wood products out of trees and must consider several factors: type of tree, tooling requirements, and foreign and domestic markets. You need to communicate with the computer because you have a task that requires computer power. The easiest way to communicate is to use an existing software package. Using existing software is also the fastest and least expensive way if the software fits your needs.

But this task is too complicated and too company-specific for packaged software. You need a custom program and someone to write it: a programmer. But your decisions are not over yet. What language will the programmer use to communicate with the computer? Surely not the English language, which—like any human language—is loosely configured, ambiguous, full of colloquialisms, slang, variations, and complexities. And, of course, the English language is constantly changing. A programming language is needed. A **programming language**—a set of rules that provides a way of instructing the computer what operations to perform—is anything but loose and ambiguous.

A programming language, the key to communicating with the computer, has certain definite characteristics. It has a limited vocabulary. Each word in it has precise meaning. Even though a programming language is limited in words, it can still be used in step-by-step fashion to solve complex problems. There is not, however, just one programming language; there are many.

## Programming Languages

At present there are over 200 programming languages—and these are the ones that are still being used. We are not counting the hundreds of languages that for one reason or another have fallen by the wayside over the years. Some of the languages have rather colorful names: SNOBOL, INTELLECT, DOCTOR, UFO. Where did all these languages come from? Do we really need to complicate the world further by adding programming languages to the Tower of Babel of human languages?

Initially, programming languages were created by people in universities or in government and were devised for special functions. Some languages have endured because they serve special purposes in science, engineering, and the like. However, it soon became clear that some standardization was needed. It made sense for those working on similar tasks to use the same language.

There are several languages in common use today, and we shall discuss the most popular ones later in the chapter. Before we turn to the hit parade of languages, however, we need to discuss levels of language.

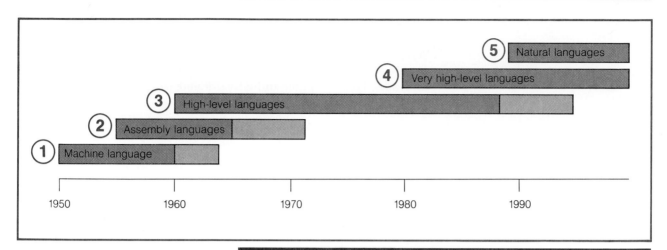

**Figure 10-1  Language generations on a time line.** The darker shading indicates the period of greater use; the lighter shading indicates the time during which a generation faded from use or is expected to fade.

## Levels of Language

Programming languages are said to be lower or higher, depending on whether they are closer to the language the computer itself uses (0s and 1s—low) or to the language people use (more English-like—high). We shall consider five levels of language. They are numbered 1 through 5 to correspond to what is called the generations of languages. Each generation has improved on the ease of use and capabilities of its predecessors. (These generations, we should note, do not quite correspond to the historical computer generations we listed in the history chapter.) The five generations of languages are:

1. Machine language
2. Assembly languages
3. High-level languages
4. Very high-level languages
5. Natural languages

Note the time line for the language generations in Figure 10-1. Let us look at each of these categories.

### Machine Language

Humans do not like to deal in numbers alone—they prefer letters and words. But, strictly speaking, numbers are what **machine language** is. This lowest level of language, machine language, represents information as 1s and 0s—binary digits corresponding to the on and off electrical states in the computer.

An example of machine language is shown in Figure 10-2. This is a language taken from a modern computer. In the early days of

**Figure 10-2  Machine language.** True machine language is all binary—only 0s and 1s—but since an example would take too much space here, we are showing an example of machine language in the hexadecimal (base 16) numbering system. (The letters A through F in hexadecimal represent the numbers 10 through 15 in the decimal system.) The computer commands below, taken from machine language for the IBM 360/370 series computers, are operation codes instructing the computer to divide two numbers, compare the quotient, move the result into the output area of the system, and set the result up so that it can be printed.

```
FD  71  431F  4153
F3  63  4267  4321
96  F0  426D
F9  10  41F3  438A
47  40  40DA
47  F0  4050
```

computing, each computer had its own machine language, and programmers had rudimentary systems for combining numbers to represent instructions such as add and compare. Primitive by today's standards, the programs were not at all convenient for people to read and use. The computer industry moved to develop assembly languages.

## Assembly Languages

Today **assembly languages** are considered fairly low-level—that is, they are not as convenient for people to use as more recent languages. At the time they were developed, however, they were considered a great leap forward. Rather than using simply 1s and 0s, assembly language uses abbreviations or mnemonic codes to replace the numbers: A for Add, C for Compare, MP for Multiply, and so on. Although these codes were not English words, they were still—from the standpoint of human convenience—preferable to numbers alone.

The programmer who uses an assembly language requires a translator to convert his or her assembly-language program into machine language. A translator is needed because machine language is the only language the computer can actually execute. The translator is an **assembler program,** also referred to as an assembler. It takes the programs written in assembly language and turns them into machine language. A programmer need not worry about the translating aspect; he or she need only write programs in assembly language. The translation is taken care of by the computer system.

Assembly language provides almost total flexibility in tapping a computer's capabilities. Although assembly languages represent a step forward, they still have many disadvantages. One is that the assembly language varies according to the type of computer. An assembler for an IBM computer, for instance, will not run on a Sperry or Honeywell, or even on a different type of IBM computer.

Another disadvantage of assembly language is the one-to-one relationship between the assembly language and the machine language—that is, for every command in assembly language there is one command in machine language. Low-level languages require a great deal of technical knowledge and attention to detail. Since assembly language is detailed in the extreme, it makes programming repetitive, tedious, and error prone. This drawback is apparent from Figure 10-3. Assembly language may be easier to read than machine language, but it is by no means crystal clear.

## High-Level Languages

The first widespread use of **high-level languages** in the early 1960s transformed programming into something quite different from what it had been. The harried programmer working on the

```
            PRINT NOGEN
PROG8       START 0
CARDFIL     DTFCD DEVADDR=SYSRDR,RECFORM=FIXUNB,IOAREA1=CARDREC,C
                  TYPEFLE=INPUT,BLKSIZE=80,EOFADDR=FINISH
REPTFIL     DTFPR DEVADDR=SYSLST,IOAREA1=PRNTREC,BLKSIZE=132
BEGIN       BALR  3,0               REGISTER 3 IS BASE REGISTER
            USING *,3
            OPEN  CARDFIL,REPTFIL   OPEN FILES
            MVC   PRNTREC,SPACES    MOVE SPACES TO OUTPUT RECORD
READLOOP    GET   CARDFIL           READ A RECORD
            MVC   OFIRST,IFIRST     MOVE ALL INPUT FIELDS
            MVC   OLAST,ILAST       TO OUTPUT RECORD FIELDS
            MVC   OADDR,IADDR
            MVC   OCITY,ICITY
            MVC   OSTATE,ISTATE
            MVC   OZIP,IZIP
            PUT   REPTFIL           WRITE THE RECORD
            B     READLOOP          BRANCH TO READ AGAIN
FINISH      CLOSE CARDFIL,REPTFIL   CLOSE FILES
            EOJ                     END OF JOB
CARDREC     DS    0CL80             DESCRIPTION OF INPUT RECORD
IFIRST      DS    CL10
ILAST       DS    CL10
IADDR       DS    CL30
ICITY       DS    CL20
ISTATE      DS    CL2
IZIP        DS    CL5
            DS    CL3
PRNTREC     DS    0CL132            DESCRIPTION OF OUTPUT RECORD
            DS    CL10
OLAST       DS    CL10
            DS    CL5
OFIRST      DS    CL10
            DS    CL15
OADDR       DS    CL30
            DS    CL15
OCITY       DS    CL20
            DS    CL5
OSTATE      DS    CL2
            DS    CL5
OZIP        DS    CL5
SPACES      DC    CL132''
            END   BEGIN
```

**Figure 10-3 Assembly language.** This example shows the IBM Assembler Language BAL used in a program for reading a record and writing it out again. The left column contains symbolic addresses of various instructions or data. The second column contains the actual operation codes to describe the kind of activity needed; for instance, MVC stands for "Move characters." The third column describes the data on which the instructions are to act. The far right column contains English-like comments related to the line or lines opposite. This entire page of instructions could be compressed to a few lines in a high-level language.

nitty-gritty details of coding and machines became a programmer who could pay more attention to solving the client's problems. The programs could solve much more complex problems. At the same time they were written in an English-like manner, thus making them more convenient to use. As a result of these changes, the programmer could accomplish more with less effort.

Third-generation languages spurred the great increase in data processing that characterized the '60s and '70s. During that time the number of mainframes in use increased from hundreds to tens of thousands. The impact of third-generation languages on our society has been enormous.

Of course, a translator was needed to translate the symbolic statements of a high-level language into computer-executable machine language; this translator is usually a **compiler.** There are many compilers for each language and one for each type of computer. Since the machine language generated by one computer's COBOL compiler, for instance, is not the machine language of some other computer, it is necessary to have a COBOL compiler for each type of computer on which COBOL programs are to be run.

Some languages are created to serve a specific purpose, such as controlling industrial robots or creating graphics. Many languages, however, are extraordinarily flexible and are considered to be general-purpose. The majority of programming applications have been written in BASIC, FORTRAN, or COBOL, all general-purpose languages. In addition to these three, the most popular high-level languages today are Pascal, Ada, and C.

We noted that high-level languages relieve the programmer of burdensome hardware details. However, with this convenience comes an inevitable loss of flexibility. A few high-level languages such as C and FORTH offer some of the flexibility of assembly language together with the power of high-level languages, but these languages are not well suited to the beginning programmer.

We shall discuss and demonstrate several high-level languages later in the chapter.

## Very High-Level Languages

Languages called **very high-level languages** are often known by their generation number. That is, they are called **fourth-generation languages** or, more simply, **4GLs.** But if understanding the name is easy, the definition is not.

### Definition

Will the real fourth-generation languages please stand up? There is no consensus about what constitutes a fourth-generation language. 4GLs are essentially shorthand programming languages. An operation that requires hundreds of lines in a third-generation language such as COBOL typically requires only five to ten lines in a 4GL. However, beyond the basic criterion of conciseness, 4GLs are difficult to describe.

### Characteristics

Fourth-generation languages share some characteristics. The first is that they are not COBOL; they make a true break with the prior generation. Also, they are basically nonprocedural. A **procedural** language tells the computer *how* a task is done: add this, compare that, do this if something is true, and so forth—a very specific step-by-step process. The first three generations of languages are all procedural. In a **nonprocedural language** the concept changes. Here, users define only *what* they want the computer to do; the user does not detail just how it is to be done. Obviously, it is a lot easier and faster to just say what you want rather than how to get it. This leads us to the issue of productivity, a key characteristic of fourth-generation languages.

### *Productivity*

Folklore has it that fourth-generation languages can improve productivity by a factor of 5 to 50. The folklore is true. Most experts say the average improvement factor is about 10—that is, you can be ten times more productive in a fourth-generation language than in a third-generation language. Consider this request: Produce a report showing the total units sold for each product, by customer, in each month and year, and with a subtotal for each customer. In addition, each new customer must start on a new page. A 4GL request looks something like this:

```
TABLE FILE SALES
SUM UNITS BY MONTH BY CUSTOMER BY PRODUCT
ON CUSTOMER SUBTOTAL PAGE BREAK
END
```

Even though some training is required to do even this much, you can see that it is pretty simple. The third-generation language COBOL, however, requires over 500 statements to fulfill the same request. If we define productivity as producing equivalent results in less time, then fourth-generation languages clearly increase productivity.

### *Some 4GLs*

Introduced about 1970, fourth-generation languages acquired their moniker in 1981 and proceeded to move into the mainstream of data processing about 1983. There are dozens of fourth-generation languages. They were introduced on mainframe computers, and that is where most of them remain, although there is evidence that they may be heading toward the smaller computers. The first significant 4GL was RAMIS. It was invented by Jerry Cohen while he was at Mathematica, Inc., but he left there to form archrival Information Builders, the company that markets the best-selling 4GL called Focus. Although RAMIS showed the way, its glory days seem to be waning. A version of Focus, called PC/Focus, is available for the IBM Personal Computer, and it was recently released on the VAX minicomputer. Thus Focus is the first 4GL to have an equivalent version on a mainframe, a minicomputer, and a microcomputer. See Figure 10-4 for a sample of Focus.

## IF IT'S TOO EASY IT CAN'T BE PROGRAMMING

You have learned to do a job and do it well. You got the training, put in the time, and now you are a respected professional with a salary to match. You are a programmer. But now your hard-earned skills are being eroded in the marketplace: There are new languages that anyone can use. A quiet panic sweeps over you.

This little scene is common across the land. Programmers sometimes are resisting the new tools. Managers complain about underutilization of fourth-generation languages by professional programmers. There is another reason besides the fear of obsolescence: Old habits die hard. When someone has worked in a traditional language for many years, it is hard to make a switch to something new. There is the element of culture shock, and what is more, programmers sometimes think that if a language is easy to use, it must be for someone else. "Real" programmers have to use a language that is difficult.

```
TABLE FILE ENROLL
HEADING CENTER
"FOSTER UNIVERSITY"
"<SEMESTER> <YR>          <CNAME>     <CNUM>"
"</2"
PRINT LNAME AND FNAME
BY CNUM NOPRINT PAGE-BREAK
BY SSN
IF SEMESTER EQ 'FALL'
IF YR EQ 88
END
```

(a)

```
                         FOSTER UNIVERSITY

        FALL 88           DIFFERENTIAL EQUATIONS       MAT482

        SSN               LNAME           FNAME

        ───               ─────           ─────

        101-30-6873       PICKERING       LISA
        124-98-9472       BURTON          MICHAEL
        164-46-3825       ELSLIP          JON
        182-34-0826       OKANO           NOBUKO
        190-89-7463       OFFICER         KEITH
```

(b)

**Figure 10-4   An example of Focus.**  (a) The code here produces (b) the Foster University roster for a differential equations class. To print field names in the heading, you must use brackets (<>) as delimiters. "</2" tells Focus to skip two lines after the heading. The program begins a new page every time the course number (CNUM) changes. The IF clause prints records only if they pertain to the fall semester of 1988.

### The Downside of 4GLs

Fourth-generation languages are not all peaches and cream and productivity. Fourth-generation languages are still evolving, and that which is still evolving cannot be fully defined or standardized. What is more, since many 4GLs are easy to use, they attract a large number of new users, who may then overcrowd the computer system; this use in itself is, of course, good if the computer system can meet the needs of the new users. A common perception of 4GLs is that they do not make efficient use of machine resources; however, the benefits of getting an application finished more quickly far outweigh the extra costs of running it.

### 4GL Benefits

Fourth-generation languages are beneficial because:

- They are results oriented; they emphasize *what* instead of *how*.

- They improve productivity because programs are easy to write and change.

- They can be used by both programmers and nonprogrammers and with a minimum of training.

- They shield users from needing an awareness of hardware and logic.

As recently as the late 1970s, few people believed that 4GLs would ever be able to replace third-generation languages by the 1980s. Now industry gurus believe that the transformation is well under way.

## Natural Languages

The word *natural* has become almost as popular in computing circles as it is in the supermarket. But fifth-generation languages are, as you may guess, even more ill defined than fourth-generation languages. They are most often called **natural languages** because of their resemblance to the *natural* spoken English language. And, to the computerphobic managers to whom these languages are now aimed, *natural* means humanlike. Instead of being forced to key correct commands and data names in correct order, a manager tells the computer what to do by keying in his or her own words.

A manager can say the same thing any number of ways. For example, "Get me tennis racket sales for January" works just as well as "I want January tennis racket revenues." Such a request may contain misspelled words, lack articles and verbs, and even use slang. The natural language translates human instructions—bad grammar, slang, and all—into code the computer understands. If it is not sure what the user has in mind, it politely asks for further explanation.

Natural languages are also referred to as knowledge-based languages, because natural languages are used to interact with a base of knowledge on some subject. The use of a natural language to access a knowledge base is called a **knowledge-based system.** A species of knowledge-based systems is the expert system, although the two terms are often used interchangeably. An **expert system** offers the computer as an expert on some topic. The system's expertise is usually equivalent to that of a human expert and can be queried in a similar way. We shall examine expert systems for business in Chapter 18.

## LANGUAGES AND ARTIFICIAL INTELLIGENCE

**N**atural languages are associated with artificial intelligence (AI), a field of study that explores how computers can be used for tasks that require the human characteristics of intelligence, imagination, and intuition.

But how can a computer understand natural language when there is nothing very predictable about it? For example, Alan sold Judy a book for five dollars. Judy bought a book for five dollars from Alan. Judy gave Alan five dollars in exchange for a book. The book that Judy bought from Alan cost five dollars. It takes a very sophisticated program (not to mention enormous memory) to unravel all these statements and see them as equivalent. Languages today are not up to the task. Progress is being made, but commercial systems available today are not this far along.

But we have already made a start, using natural language to ask the computer expert questions on a variety of subjects. In fact, expert systems promise to be invaluable productivity tools in manufacturing, education, the law, medicine, finance—almost every field requiring human expertise. But expert systems, by definition, are limited to a field of expertise. To imitate the functioning of the human mind, the machine with artificial intelligence would have to be able to examine a variety of facts, not be limited to a single subject, and devise a solution to a problem by comparing those new facts to its vast storehouse of data from many fields. So far, artificial intelligence systems do not do original thinking. Nor can they match the performance of a truly superior intellect, a person who solves problems through original thought instead of using familiar patterns as a guide.

There are many arguments for and against crediting computers with the ability to think. Some say, for example, that computers cannot be considered intelligent because they do not compose like Beethoven or write like Shakespeare; the rejoinder is that neither do we ordinary musicians or writers—you do not have to be superhuman to be intelligent.

Look at it another way. Suppose you beat your brains out on a problem and then—Aha!—the solution comes to you as a jolt. Now, how did you do that? You do not know, and nobody else knows either. A big part of human problem solving seems to be that jolt of recognition, that ability to suddenly see things as a whole. Further experiments have shown that people rarely solve problems using step-by-step logic, the very thing that computers do best. Most modern computers still chug through problems one step at a time. The brain beats computers at "Aha!" problem solving because it has millions of neurons working simultaneously.

So, can a computer think or not? Several years ago, Alan Turing, an English mathematician, proposed a test of thinking machines. In the Turing Test, a person is seated before two terminals that are connected to hidden devices. One terminal is connected to a different terminal run by another person, and the second terminal is connected to a computer. The person is asked to guess, by carrying out conversations through the terminals, which is the human and which is the computer. If the person cannot tell the difference, the computer is said to have passed and is considered, for all practical purposes, a thinking machine.

But perhaps we are asking the wrong question: Will a computer ever *really* think? One possible answer: Who cares? If a machine can perform a task really well, does it matter if it *really* thinks? Still another answer is: Yes, machines will really think, but not as humans do. They lack the sensitivity, appreciation, and passion that mark some of our great human thinkers.

You can see that these ideas sound like the fifth-generation concepts we discussed in Chapter 3 on history. The use of natural language to access a knowledge base is the foundation of **artificial intelligence.** Bill Gates, founder of the Microsoft Corporation, can be credited with a common-sense definition of artificial intelligence as "anything that makes software softer." In other words, the goal is to let the user focus on the task rather than the computer.

Consider this request that could be given in the 4GL Focus: "SUM ORDERS BY DATE BY REGION." If we alter the request and, still in Focus, say something like "Give me the dates and the regions after you've added up the orders," the computer will spit back the user-friendly version of "You've got to be kidding" and give up. But some natural languages could handle such a request. For example, Intellect, a language for mainframes, and Clout, a language for personal computers, have provided tools that approach natural language. Users can relax the structure of their requests and increase the freedom of their interaction with the data.

Here is a typical Intellect request:

```
REPORT THE BASE SALARY, COMMISSIONS AND YEARS OF SERVICE
BROKEN DOWN BY STATE AND CITY FOR SALES CLERKS IN NEW
JERSEY AND MASSACHUSETTS.
```

It would seem that you cannot get much closer to conversational English than that.

But Clout likes to go a step further. For example, advertisements for Clout boast of the software's ability to handle the sample command, "Gimme the average product profit." One trumpeter of Clout's prowess tells the story of the manager who gave this command to Clout: "Are there any sales reps in California who surpassed their quotas?" Literal-minded Clout provided the answer: "YES." Irritated, the manager typed "Prove it!" Not having seen these words before, Clout asked for clarification, and ended up considering *prove it* as the equivalent of *show me,* words it already understood. The report of sales reps was displayed. Interestingly, Clout stands ready to increase its vocabulary at any time; next time it will know what "Prove it!" means. Figure 10-5 shows another natural language sample.

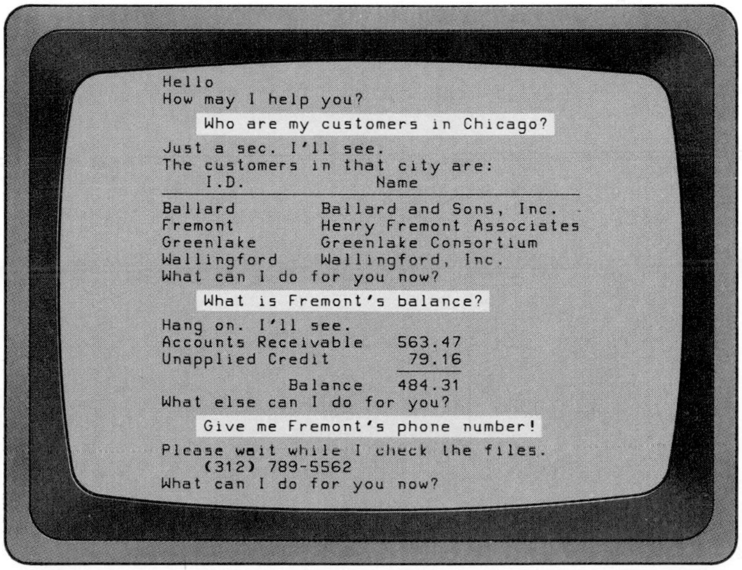

**Figure 10-5  A natural language.** This package, called Cash Management System, uses a language that is so natural that some might think it is a little too cute, as in "Just a sec."

```
Hello
How may I help you?
        Who are my customers in Chicago?
Just a sec. I'll see.
The customers in that city are:
        I.D.            Name
Ballard         Ballard and Sons, Inc.
Fremont         Henry Fremont Associates
Greenlake       Greenlake Consortium
Wallingford     Wallingford, Inc.
What can I do for you now?
        What is Fremont's balance?
Hang on. I'll see.
Accounts Receivable    563.47
Unapplied Credit        79.16
        Balance        484.31
What else can I do for you?
        Give me Fremont's phone number!
Please wait while I check the files.
    (312) 789-5562
What can I do for you now?
```

Natural languages excel at easy data access. Indeed, the most common application for natural languages is interacting with databases. So if we limit our needs to data queries, computer access for the masses seems to be at hand. However, fifth-generation languages are not yet ready to handle complicated logic, so they are not likely to be vehicles for professional programmers in the immediate future.

## Choosing a Language

How do you choose the language in which to write your program? Perhaps you will use a particular language because it is the only one available at your installation. Perhaps your manager has decreed that everyone on your project will use a certain language. Perhaps you know only one language!

A sensible approach is to pick the language that is most suitable for your particular program application. The following sections on individual languages will give you an overview of the languages in common use. We describe these languages: FORTRAN, COBOL, BASIC, Pascal, Ada, C, and RPG—all third-generation languages in common use today. Special features of each language are noted, including the types of applications for which they are often used. The brief discussions of program organization are designed to give you a

**Table 10-1   Features of seven important programming languages**

| Language | Application | Structured features |
|---|---|---|
| FORTRAN—FORmula TRANslator (1954) | Scientific | Limited; FORTRAN 77 has some structured features |
| COBOL—COmmon Business-Oriented Language (1959) | Business | Some structured concepts |
| BASIC—Beginner's All-purpose Symbolic Instruction Code (1965) | Education, business | Limited; some versions are structured |
| Pascal—named after French inventor Blaise Pascal (1971) | Education, systems programming, scientific | Structured |
| Ada—named after Ada, the Countess of Lovelace (1980) | Military, general | Structured |
| C—evolved from the language B at Bell Labs (1972) | Systems programming, general | Structured |
| RPG—Report Program Generator (1964) | Business reports | N/A |

general picture of how a program written in a particular language is organized.

Give special attention to the sections on control structures. Every language has control structures of some kind. We are particularly interested in identifying the languages that have the fundamental control structures mentioned in Chapter 8—sequence, selection (IF-THEN-ELSE), and iteration (DOWHILE and DOUNTIL)—built right into the language. Using a language with structured features does not, unfortunately, guarantee that the programmer will write a structured program. Table 10-1 summarizes the important features of these languages.

To accompany our discussion of FORTRAN, COBOL, BASIC, Pascal, Ada, and C, we shall show a program and its output to give you a sense of what each language looks like. All of these programs are designed to average numbers; in our sample output, we find the average of three numbers. Since we are performing the same task with all six programs, you will see some of the differences and similarities between the languages. We do not expect you to understand each line of these programs; they are here merely to let you see what each language looks like in a program. Figure 10-6 provides a flowchart and pseudocode for the task of averaging numbers. As we discuss each language, we shall provide a program for averaging numbers that follows the logic shown.

## FORTRAN: The First High-Level Language

Developed by IBM and introduced in 1954, **FORTRAN**— for FORmula TRANslator—was the first high-level language. FORTRAN is a scientifically oriented language—in the early days use of the computer was primarily associated with engineering, mathematical, and scientific research tasks. FORTRAN is still the most widely used language in the scientific community.

### Features

FORTRAN is noted for its simplicity and brevity, and those characteristics are part of the reason why it remains popular. This language is very good at serving its primary purpose, which is execution of complex formulas such as those used in economic analysis and engineering. It is not, however, particularly useful for file processing or data processing; its control structures are quite limited, as are its means of describing data. Consequently, it is not very suitable for business applications. Moreover, there is no requirement to define data elements before they are used. This lack contributes to the language's simplicity and brevity but also lends itself to error.

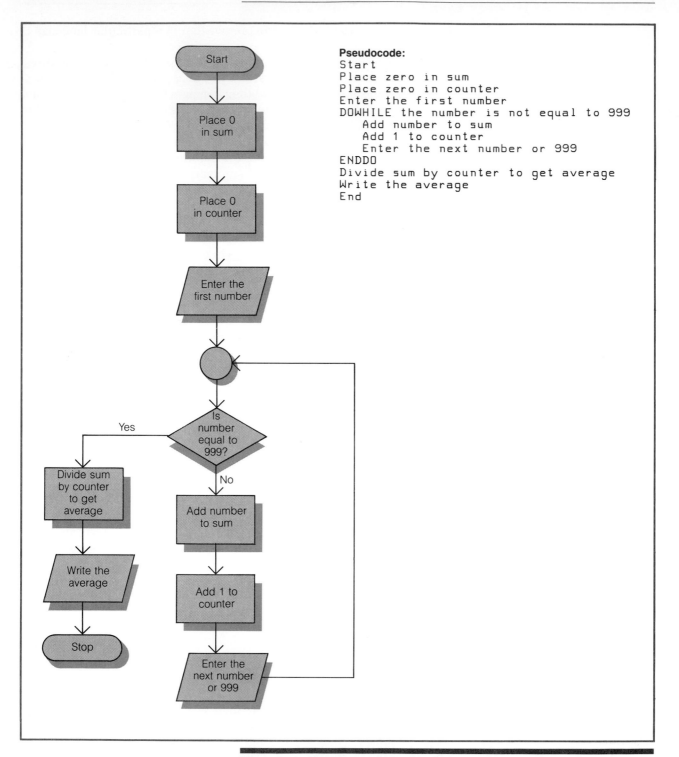

**Pseudocode:**
```
Start
Place zero in sum
Place zero in counter
Enter the first number
DOWHILE the number is not equal to 999
    Add number to sum
    Add 1 to counter
    Enter the next number or 999
ENDDO
Divide sum by counter to get average
Write the average
End
```

**Figure 10-6 Flowchart and pseudocode for averaging numbers.** This figure shows the logic for a program that lets a user enter numbers through the keyboard; the program then averages the numbers. The logic to enter the numbers forms a loop: enter the number, add it to the sum, and add 1 to the counter. When 999 is keyed the loop is exited. The average is then computed and displayed on the screen. This logic is used for the programs in Figures 10-7 through 10-12.

## Program Organization

Not all programs are organized in the same way. They vary depending on the language used. As we shall see, in many languages (such as COBOL), programs are divided into a series of parts. FORTRAN programs are not composed of different parts. A FORTRAN program consists of statements one after the other. Different types of data are identified as the data is used. Descriptions for data records appear in format statements that accompany the READ and WRITE statements.

## Control Structures

As we stated in Chapter 8, the three basic control structures or patterns are sequence, selection, and iteration. FORTRAN was not designed as a structured language. FORTRAN 77, a newer version, contains some added features—the expanded IF (selection) statement in particular—that enhance structured design. Other FORTRAN control structures are the GOTO statement and the DO loop.

The logical IF statement, which is a conditional transfer statement, consists of three parts: the word IF, followed by some condition in parentheses, followed by some other executable statement. For example:

```
IF (SALES.LT.10000) COMM = 500
```

This means "If sales are less than $10,000, then commission earned is $500." In the above statement .LT. is a relational operator that means less than; the computer compares the items on either side of the operator to see if the statement in parentheses is true, and if it is, executes the statement to the right of the parentheses before proceeding to the next statement in the program. If the statement in parentheses is false, the program proceeds directly to the next statement. There are six relational operators.

The GOTO statement, an unconditional transfer statement, simply transfers program control to another statement in the program, one indicated by a line number in the GOTO statement. For example,

```
GOTO 40
```

means transfer to the program statement with line number 40. The DO loop usually is a DOWHILE loop, which means it tests first before going through the loop. For example:

```
    ISUM = 0
    DO 40 I=1,100
    ISUM = ISUM+I
40 CONTINUE
```

We start with the sum ISUM equal to 0 (shown above as ISUM=0). The second line can be translated to mean: "Proceed through all the statements from DO to line 40 and repeat 100 times, taking the sum of all the numbers from 1 to 100."

## SIX FORTRAN RELATIONAL OPERATORS

| Operator | Meaning |
|---|---|
| .EQ. | Equal to |
| .NE. | Not equal to |
| .GT. | Greater than |
| .LT. | Less than |
| .GE. | Greater than or equal to |
| .LE. | Less than or equal to |

```
C         FORTRAN PROGRAM
C         AVERAGING INTEGERS ENTERED THROUGH THE KEYBOARD
          WRITE (6,10)
          SUM = 0
          COUNTER = 0
          WRITE (6,60)
          READ (5,40) NUMBER
    1     IF (NUMBER .EQ. 999) GOTO 2
          SUM = SUM + NUMBER
          COUNTER = COUNTER + 1
          WRITE (6,70)
          READ (5,40) NUMBER
          GO TO 1
    2     AVERAGE = SUM / COUNTER
          WRITE (6,80) AVERAGE
   10     FORMAT (1X, 'THIS PROGRAM WILL FIND THE AVERAGE OF ',
        * 'INTEGERS YOU ENTER ',/1X, 'THROUGH THE ',
        *  'KEYBOARD. TYPE 999 TO INDICATE END OF DATA.',/)
   40     FORMAT (I3)
   60     FORMAT (1X, 'PLEASE ENTER A NUMBER   ')
   70     FORMAT (1X, 'PLEASE ENTER THE NEXT NUMBER   ')
   80     FORMAT (1X, 'THE AVERAGE OF THE NUMBERS IS ',F6.2)
          STOP
          END
```

**(a)**

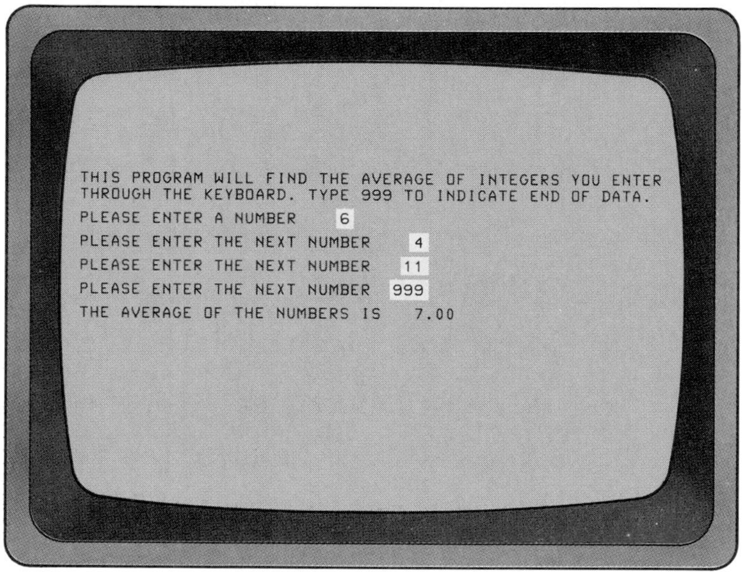

**(b)**

**Figure 10-7   A FORTRAN program and sample output.**  (a) The first two lines are comments indicating that this program averages integers—numbers without decimal places. The WRITE statements send output to the screen; the second number in parentheses indicates the format line to be used for the output. The READ statements accept data from the user and place it in location NUMBER, where it can be added to the accumulated SUM. The IF statement checks for number 999 and, when it is received, diverts the program logic to statement 2, where the average is computed and then written—displayed on the screen.
(b) This screen display shows the interaction between program and user when the program runs. In this example the user wants to find the average of 6, 4, and 11.

**GRACE M. HOPPER: "GRANDMA COBOL"**

Rear Admiral Hopper, a Phi Beta Kappa graduate of Vassar College with an M.A. and Ph.D. from Yale University, joined the U.S. Naval Reserve in 1943. She was assigned to the Bureau of Ordinance Computation Project at Harvard, where she learned to program the first large-scale digital computer, the Mark I.

In 1948 she joined the Eckert–Mauchly Computer Corporation as senior mathematician. She later became senior programmer for the UNIVAC I, the first commercial large-scale electronic computer. There she pioneered in the development of the COBOL compiler and later became one of the prime movers in the development of the COBOL programming language in the 1950s. Hopper remained on active duty in the Navy until August, 1986, when she retired at the age of 79.

Hopper can still rock the boat. In fact, she delights in confounding interviewers. Witness this exchange:

*Interviewer:* What do you think of the IBM PC?

*Hopper:* It's a little bit ahead of the Mark I.

*Interviewer:* Well, what do you see as the next generation of micros?

*Hopper:* I don't know. It hasn't happened yet.

Figure 10-7 shows a FORTRAN program and a sample output from the program.

# COBOL: The Language of Business

In the 1950s FORTRAN had been developed, but there was still no accepted high-level programming language appropriate for business. The U.S. Department of Defense in particular was interested in creating such a standardized language, and so it called together representatives from government and various industries, including the computer industry. These representatives formed **CODASYL**—COnference of DAta SYstem Languages. In 1959 CODASYL introduced **COBOL**—for COmmon Business-Oriented Language. The U.S. government offered encouragement by insisting that anyone attempting to win government contracts for computer-related projects had to use COBOL. The American National Standards Institute (ANSI) first standardized COBOL in 1968 and in 1974 issued standards for another version known as **ANS-COBOL.** And, after more than seven controversial years of vitriolic industry debate, the standard known as COBOL 85 was approved, making COBOL a more usable modern-day software tool. The principal benefit of standardization is that COBOL is relatively machine-independent— that is, a program written for one type of computer can be run with only slight modifications on another for which a COBOL compiler has been developed.

## Features

The principal feature of COBOL is that it is English-like— far more so than FORTRAN or BASIC. The variable names are set up in such a way that even if you know nothing about programming you can still understand the general purpose of a program. For example:

```
IF SALES-AMOUNT IS GREATER THAN SALES-QUOTA
       COMPUTE COMMISSION = MAX-RATE * SALES-AMOUNT
ELSE
       COMPUTE COMMISSION = MIN-RATE * SALES-AMOUNT.
```

Because COBOL is so easy to read, it is also easy for programmers to learn to use; once you understand programming principles, it is not difficult to add COBOL to your repertoire.

COBOL can be used for just about any task related to business programming; indeed, it is especially suited to processing alphanumeric data such as street addresses, purchased items, and dollar amounts—the data of business. However, the feature that makes

COBOL so useful—its English-like appearance and easy readability—is also a weakness because a COBOL program can be incredibly verbose. It is not usual for a programmer to sit down and bat out a quick COBOL program. In fact, there is hardly such a thing as a quick COBOL program; there are just too many program lines to write, even to accomplish a simple task. For speed and simplicity, BASIC, FORTRAN, and Pascal are probably better bets.

## Program Organization

A COBOL program is divided into four parts:

- Identification division
- Environment division
- Data division
- Procedure division

The divisions must appear in this order. Let us see how they work.

### Identification Division

COBOL has certain reserved words—that is, words with exact, special meanings. The programmer may not use these words for variable names. One of these reserved words is PROGRAM-ID, which is required in this first division. It is followed by a period, then by at least one space, then by some sort of name that will uniquely identify the name of the program, which is also followed by a period. For example:

```
PROGRAM-ID. ACCT-REC.
```

Other lines in the identification divisions are optional.

### Environment Division

This division has two sections, which perform specific functions. The CONFIGURATION SECTION describes the computer on which the program will be compiled and executed. The INPUT-OUTPUT SECTION relates each file of the program to the specific physical device, such as tape drive or printer, that will read or write the file. This latter section is the link between the program and the peripheral equipment used.

### Data Division

This division contains all the detailed information about all data processed by the program. It indicates field information such as type of characters (whether numeric or alphanumeric), number of characters, and placement of decimal points. It also indicates data relationships, including hierarchy. Hierarchy refers to levels of data organizations for use within the program. The top of the hierarchy is

**Figure 10-8   A COBOL program and sample output.** (a) The purpose of the program and its results are the same as the FORTRAN program, but the look of a COBOL program is very different. Note the four divisions. In particular, note that the logic in the procedure division uses a series of PERFORM statements, diverting logic flow to other places in the program. After a section has been performed, as indicated by an EXIT statement, logic flow returns to the next PERFORM statement. DISPLAY writes to the screen and ACCEPT takes the user input. (b) This screen display shows the interaction between program and user when the program runs.

```
*****************************************************************
 IDENTIFICATION DIVISION.
*****************************************************************
 PROGRAM-ID.  AVERAGE.
* COBOL PROGRAM
* AVERAGING INTEGERS ENTERED THROUGH THE KEYBOARD.
*****************************************************************
 ENVIRONMENT DIVISION.
*****************************************************************
 CONFIGURATION SECTION.
 SOURCE-COMPUTER.          H-P 3000.
 OBJECT-COMPUTER.          H-P 3000.
*****************************************************************
 DATA DIVISION.
*****************************************************************
 FILE SECTION.
 WORKING-STORAGE SECTION.
 01 AVERAGE        PIC ---9.99.
 01 COUNTER        PIC 9(02)          VALUE ZERO.
 01 NUMBER-ITEM    PIC S9(03).
 01 SUM-ITEM       PIC S9(06)         VALUE ZERO.
 01 BLANK-LINE     PIC X(80)          VALUE SPACES.
*****************************************************************
 PROCEDURE DIVISION.
*****************************************************************
 100-CONTROL-ROUTINE.
     PERFORM 200-DISPLAY-INSTRUCTIONS.
     PERFORM 300-INITIALIZATION-ROUTINE.
     PERFORM 400-ENTER-AND-ADD
             UNTIL NUMBER-ITEM = 999.
     PERFORM 500-CALCULATE-AVERAGE.
     PERFORM 600-DISPLAY-RESULTS.
     STOP RUN.
 200-DISPLAY-INSTRUCTIONS.
     DISPLAY
       "THIS PROGRAM WILL FIND THE AVERAGE OF INTEGERS YOU ENTER".
     DISPLAY
       "THROUGH THE KEYBOARD. TYPE 999 TO INDICATE END OF DATA.".
     DISPLAY BLANK-LINE.
 300-INITIALIZATION-ROUTINE.
     DISPLAY "PLEASE ENTER A NUMBER".
     ACCEPT NUMBER-ITEM.
 400-ENTER-AND-ADD.
     ADD NUMBER-ITEM TO SUM-ITEM.
     ADD 1 TO COUNTER.
     DISPLAY "PLEASE ENTER THE NEXT NUMBER".
     ACCEPT NUMBER-ITEM.
 500-CALCULATE-AVERAGE.
     DIVIDE SUM-ITEM BY COUNTER GIVING AVERAGE.
 600-DISPLAY-RESULTS.
     DISPLAY "THE AVERAGE OF THE NUMBERS IS ",AVERAGE.
```

(a)

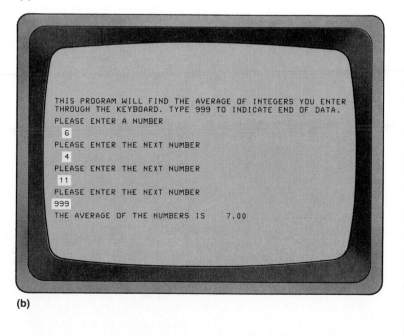

(b)

often a record name, with the next level being data fields; some data fields may be divided into even lower levels.

There are two sections in this division. The FILE SECTION contains general information about each file (information such as record length) and a field-by-field description of each type of record within the file. An FD—file description—statement is required for each file used. The associated record descriptions follow the FD. The WORKING-STORAGE SECTION describes in detail data that is not directly associated with a specific file.

### *Procedure Division*

After the stage has been set in the three preceding divisions, the data can now be acted upon. This last division contains all the statements that give the computer specific instructions to carry out the logic of the program. The instructions use specific verbs from the list of COBOL reserved words, verbs that, in keeping with the English flavor, are often self-explanatory: READ, WRITE, ADD, SUBTRACT, MOVE, DISPLAY, SORT. The procedure division is composed of paragraphs, which are in turn composed of sentences. Each sentence ends with a period. Each paragraph is identified by a paragraph name.

## Control Structures

COBOL was not originally designed as a structured language, but there are structures in it. For instance, there is an IF-ELSE structure, which is really the same as the IF-THEN-ELSE structure we saw in Chapter 8, except that the THEN is missing. There is also a PERFORM/UNTIL structure. This is the same as a DOWHILE loop; a certain set of instructions will be performed repeatedly while a condition is met; otherwise, the program leaves the loop. There is also a GOTO statement, an unconditional transfer to a certain paragraph name.

Figure 10-8 shows a COBOL program and a sample output from the program.

It has been fashionable for some time to criticize COBOL: It is old-fashioned, cumbersome, and inelegant. But this golden oldie is still with us. And all the criticism does not alter the fact that if you are interested in making money as a programmer, COBOL is still your best bet.

## BASIC: For Beginners and Others

We have already touched on **BASIC**—Beginners' All-purpose Symbolic Instruction Code—in Chapter 8 (and we go into it in some detail in Appendix A), but here we will present a quick overview. BASIC is a common language that is easy to learn.

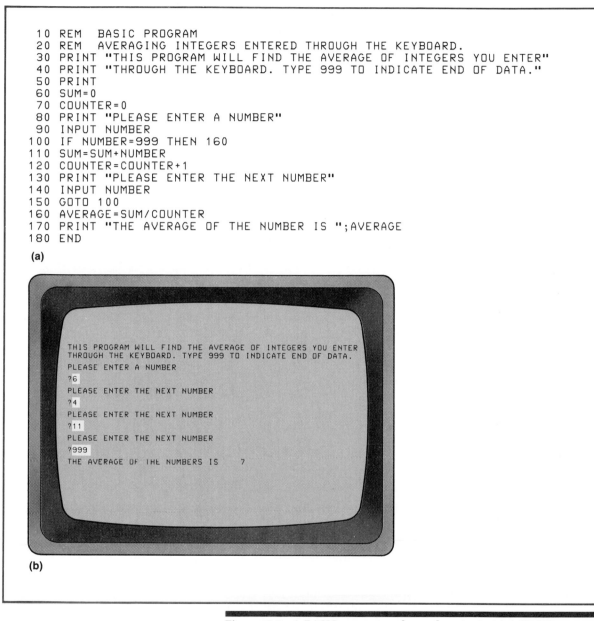

```
 10 REM   BASIC PROGRAM
 20 REM   AVERAGING INTEGERS ENTERED THROUGH THE KEYBOARD.
 30 PRINT "THIS PROGRAM WILL FIND THE AVERAGE OF INTEGERS YOU ENTER"
 40 PRINT "THROUGH THE KEYBOARD. TYPE 999 TO INDICATE END OF DATA."
 50 PRINT
 60 SUM=0
 70 COUNTER=0
 80 PRINT "PLEASE ENTER A NUMBER"
 90 INPUT NUMBER
100 IF NUMBER=999 THEN 160
110 SUM=SUM+NUMBER
120 COUNTER=COUNTER+1
130 PRINT "PLEASE ENTER THE NEXT NUMBER"
140 INPUT NUMBER
150 GOTO 100
160 AVERAGE=SUM/COUNTER
170 PRINT "THE AVERAGE OF THE NUMBER IS ";AVERAGE
180 END
```

(a)

```
THIS PROGRAM WILL FIND THE AVERAGE OF INTEGERS YOU ENTER
THROUGH THE KEYBOARD. TYPE 999 TO INDICATE END OF DATA.
PLEASE ENTER A NUMBER
?6
PLEASE ENTER THE NEXT NUMBER
?4
PLEASE ENTER THE NEXT NUMBER
?11
PLEASE ENTER THE NEXT NUMBER
?999
THE AVERAGE OF THE NUMBERS IS      7
```

(b)

**Figure 10-9   A BASIC program and sample output.** (a) A BASIC program looks very much like a FORTRAN program. The main difference is in the input and output statements. REM stands for remark and is used for placing comments in the program. PRINT displays whatever is between quotation marks on the screen. INPUT accepts data from the user. (b) This screen display shows the interaction between program and user when the program runs.

Developed at Dartmouth College, BASIC was introduced by John Kemeny and Thomas Kurtz in 1965 and was originally intended for use by students in an academic environment. In the late 1960s it became widely used in interactive time-sharing environments in universities and colleges. The use of BASIC has extended to business and personal mini- and microcomputer systems.

### Features

The primary feature of BASIC is one that may be of interest to many readers of this book: BASIC is easy to learn, even for a person who has never programmed before. Thus, the language is used often in training students in the classroom. BASIC is also used by nonprogramming people, such as engineers, who find it useful in problem solving.

### Program Organization

Unlike COBOL, BASIC has no distinct divisions; a program is all one unit. This means also that there are no separate data declarations—that is, data is simply declared as it is used.

### Control Structures

Generic BASIC is an unstructured language, although there are structured versions, notably Dartmouth BASIC, BASIC-PLUS (by Digital Equipment Corporation), TRUE BASIC, and MBASIC—Microsoft BASIC for the IBM PC. Most versions of BASIC have the control structures IF-THEN and a GOTO statement. They also have a FOR/NEXT structure (explained in Appendix A), which allows repetitive execution of instructions. An example of a BASIC program and its output is shown in Figure 10-9.

## Pascal: The Language of Simplicity

Named for Blaise Pascal, the seventeenth-century French mathematician, **Pascal** was developed by a Swiss computer scientist, Niklaus Wirth, and first became available in 1971. Since that time it has become quite popular, first in Europe and now in the United States, particularly in universities and colleges offering computer-science programs.

### Features

The foremost feature of Pascal is that it is simpler than other languages—simpler than PL/I, which has control structures built in but which is a more complicated language to code, and simpler than COBOL, which is wordy and has fewer structured features. One reason for this simplicity is that control structures are built right into the language, and by knowing only a few coding rules you can write some simple programs.

## THE MICROCOMPUTER CORNER

### Languages for Your Microcomputer

Which of these languages will you use on your microcomputer, your own personal computer? Possibly none of them, because many people use software packages exclusively. That is, they buy the software they need and have no need or desire to write any themselves.

But there are two other categories of users: those who write software as part of their jobs and those who want to tinker with writing software as a sideline. Interestingly, they may choose the same language. Most of the languages mentioned in this chapter are available for personal computers. But the language of choice for most people, far and away, is still BASIC. Although the invention of BASIC predates the microcomputer revolution, it took the microcomputer to make BASIC famous. BASIC is still in first place because it is easy to learn and use, and recent versions offer all the power most people need.

Even fourth-generation languages are migrating to microcomputers. Although the microcomputer version may be functionally equivalent to the 4GL on a mainframe, the micro version will have a much richer user interface—more friendly, more helpful—because it is more likely to be used by naive users.

In the early years of small computers, the number of language alternatives was limited. Now, the language you want is probably available for your microcomputer.

Pascal has become very popular in college computer-science departments. Because of its limited input/output capabilities, it is unlikely, in its present form, to have a serious impact on the business community. Pascal is making large strides in the microcomputer market as a simple yet sophisticated alternative to BASIC.

### Program Organization

Program organization is very specific. First, you must write the program name, the name by which you can identify the program. Second, you write data declarations indicating what type a particular kind of data is—that is, integer, real number, string, array, or whatever. Third, you write the functions and procedures. The main part of the program actually appears last and refers back to the various functions and procedures, as needed.

### Control Structures

The beauty of Pascal is that it not only has control structures, including the loop, but that it uses the very words that emphasize how the loop works—IF/THEN/ELSE and WHILE/DO and REPEAT/UNTIL—which helps suggest why the language is easy to learn. There is also a GOTO structure, although the availability of the other control structures limits the necessity of using GOTO.

```
PROGRAM AVERAGE (INPUT, OUTPUT);
(* PASCAL PROGRAM *)
(* AVERAGING INTEGERS ENTERED THROUGH THE KEYBOARD *)
VAR
    COUNTER, NUMBER, SUM : INTEGER;
    AVERAGE : REAL;
BEGIN
WRITELN ('THIS PROGRAM WILL FIND THE AVERAGE OF INTEGERS YOU ENTER');
WRITELN ('THROUGH THE KEYBOARD. TYPE 999 TO INDICATE END OF DATA.');
WRITELN;
SUM := 0;
COUNTER := 0;
WRITELN ('PLEASE ENTER A NUMBER');
READ (NUMBER);
WHILE NUMBER <> 999 DO
    BEGIN
    SUM := SUM + NUMBER;
    COUNTER := COUNTER + 1;
    WRITELN ('PLEASE ENTER THE NEXT NUMBER');
    READ (NUMBER);
    END;
AVERAGE := SUM / COUNTER;
WRITELN ('THE AVERAGE OF THE NUMBERS IS',AVERAGE :6:2);
END.
```

**(a)**

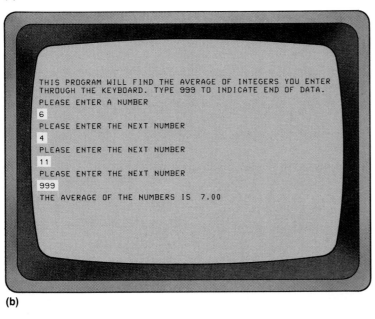

**(b)**

**Figure 10-10   A Pascal program and sample output.** (a) Comments are from * to
*. Each variable name—counter, number, sum, and average—must be declared as
an integer or a real number—a number with decimal places. WRITELN displays
the material between quotation marks on the screen. WRITELN by itself puts a
blank line on the screen. The symbol : = assigns a value to the variable on the
left; the symbol <> means "not equal to." The WHILE statement follows structured concepts. (b) This screen display shows the interaction between program
and user when the program runs.

An example of a Pascal program and a sample output is shown in Figure 10-10.

## Ada: The Language of Standardization?

Is any software worth over $25 billion? Not any more, according to Defense Department experts. In 1974 the U.S. Department of Defense had spent that amount on all kinds of software for a hodgepodge of languages for its needs. The answer to this problem turned out to be a new language called **Ada**—named for Countess Ada Lovelace, "the first programmer" (see Chapter 3). Developed as one of four competitive language designs sponsored by the Pentagon, Ada was originally intended to be a standard language for weapons systems. It has been used not only for military purposes but also for successful commercial applications. The new language, introduced in 1980, has the support not only of the defense establishment but also of such industry heavyweights as IBM and Intel and is even available for some microcomputers. Although some industry experts have said Ada is too complex (futurist Charles Lecht describes it as a klutz), others say that it is easy to learn and that it will increase productivity. Indeed, some experts believe that it is a better commercial language than COBOL and FORTRAN.

### Features

Ada is a structured language. Among its features, Ada encourages modular design because it allows each specialized package or module of a large program to be written and tested separately before the entire program is put together. The modular design encourages the division of various tasks and the use of teamwork to make them compatible. Ada also requires that every data item be defined according to a certain type—an integer, character string, array, or the like—and this permits the compiler to check for errors before the entire program is run. In other words, the language makes it easier for programmers to write error-free programs.

### Program Organization

In its simplest form an Ada program has two parts, a declarative part and a statement part. The declarative section comes first, beginning with the word *procedure*, to give names and types to each data variable that will be used in the statement part. The statement section starts with the word *begin* and finishes with the word *end*; the statements between these two delimiters describe the program logic—that is, actions to be taken on the data.

```
--  ADA PROGRAM
--  AVERAGING INTEGERS ENTERED THROUGH THE KEYBOARD.
with TEXT_IO; use TEXT_IO;
procedure AVERAGE is
    package INT_IO is new INTEGER_IO(INTEGER);
    AVERAGE:                FLOAT                           ;
    COUNTER:                INTEGER             :=       0;
    NUMBER:                 INTEGER                       ;
    SUM:                    INTEGER             :=       0;
begin
    PUT_LINE("THIS PROGRAM WILL FIND THE AVERAGE OF INTEGERS YOU ENTER");
    PUT_LINE("THROUGH THE KEYBOARD. TYPE 999 TO INDICATE END OF DATA.");
    NEW_LINE;
    PUT("PLEASE ENTER A NUMBER");
    INT_IO.GET(NUMBER);
    while NUMBER /= 999 loop
        SUM := SUM + NUMBER;
        COUNTER := COUNTER + 1;
        PUT("PLEASE ENTER THE NEXT NUMBER");
        INT_IO.GET(NUMBER);
    end loop;
    AVERAGE := SUM/COUNTER;
    PUT("THE AVERAGE OF THE NUMBERS IS");
    FLO_IO.PUT(AVERAGE);
end AVERAGE;
```

**(a)**

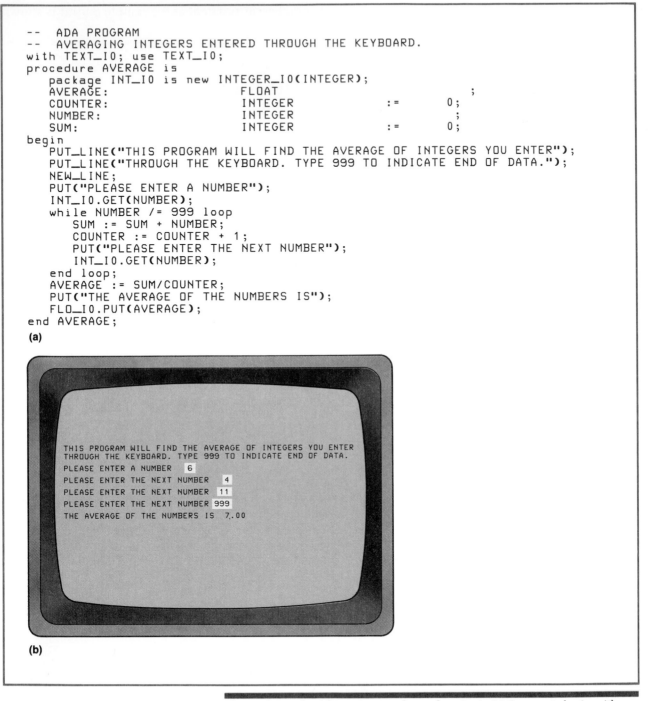

**(b)**

**Figure 10-11   An Ada program and sample output.** (a) Comments begin with a double hyphen. Ada requires that each variable name be declared as an integer or a floating-point number ("float")—a number with decimal places. PUT_LINE displays information on the screen and NEW_LINE displays a blank line. The symbol /= means "is not equal to." The while loop matches structured concepts. (b) This screen display shows the interaction between program and user when the program runs.

### Control Structures

The control structures in Ada closely parallel the basic control structures of sequence, selection, and iteration. The selection statement is IF/THEN, followed by END IF. There are two types of iteration statements, FOR LOOP and WHILE LOOP, each ending with END LOOP.

An example of an Ada program and a sample output is shown in Figure 10-11.

Widespread adoption of Ada is likely to take years, as even its most optimistic advocates admit. Although there are many reasons for this (the military services, for instance, have different levels of enthusiasm for it), probably its size—which may hinder its use on microcomputers—and complexity are the greatest barriers.

## C: A Sophisticated Language

A language that lends itself to systems programming (operating systems and the like) as well as to more mundane programming tasks, C was invented by Dennis Ritchie at Bell Labs in 1972. Its unromantic name evolved from an earlier language named B. C produces code that approaches assembly language in efficiency while still offering high-level language features such as structured programming. C contains some of the best features from other languages, including PL/I, ALGOL, and Pascal. A C compiler is simple and compact. Because C is independent of any particular machine's architecture, it is suitable for writing "portable" programs—that is, programs that can be run on more than one type of computer.

Although C is simple and elegant, it is not simple to learn. It was developed for gifted programmers, and the learning curve is steep indeed. Straightforward tasks may be solved easily in C, but complex problems require mastery of the language.

An interesting sidenote is that the availability of C on personal computers has greatly enhanced the value of PCs for budding entrepreneurs. That is, a software cottage industry can use the same basic tool—the language C—used by established companies like Microsoft.

An example of a C program and a sample output is shown in Figure 10-12.

## RPG: A Language for Business Reports

All the languages discussed so far have been procedure-oriented—that is, designed to allow programmer-users to write logical sequences of instructions. However, RPG—for Report

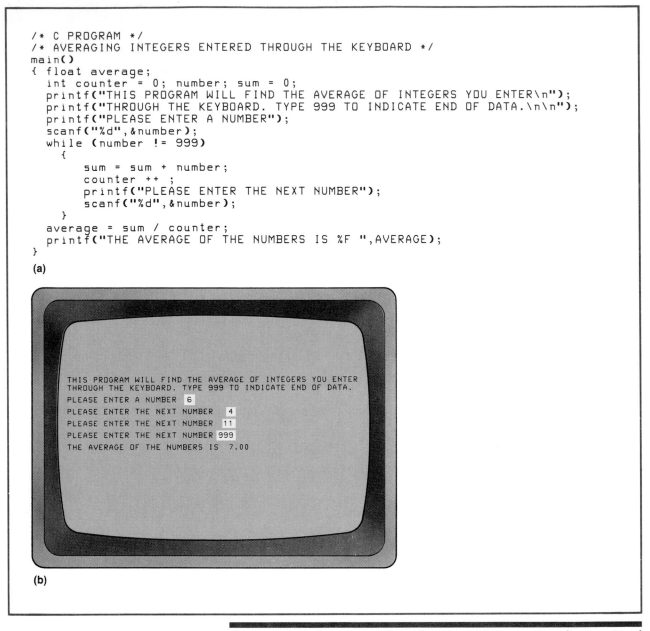

```
/* C PROGRAM */
/* AVERAGING INTEGERS ENTERED THROUGH THE KEYBOARD */
main()
{ float average;
  int counter = 0; number; sum = 0;
  printf("THIS PROGRAM WILL FIND THE AVERAGE OF INTEGERS YOU ENTER\n");
  printf("THROUGH THE KEYBOARD. TYPE 999 TO INDICATE END OF DATA.\n\n");
  printf("PLEASE ENTER A NUMBER");
  scanf("%d",&number);
  while (number != 999)
    {
       sum = sum + number;
       counter ++ ;
       printf("PLEASE ENTER THE NEXT NUMBER");
       scanf("%d",&number);
    }
  average = sum / counter;
  printf("THE AVERAGE OF THE NUMBERS IS %F ",AVERAGE);
}
```
(a)

```
THIS PROGRAM WILL FIND THE AVERAGE OF INTEGERS YOU ENTER
THROUGH THE KEYBOARD. TYPE 999 TO INDICATE END OF DATA.
PLEASE ENTER A NUMBER  6
PLEASE ENTER THE NEXT NUMBER   4
PLEASE ENTER THE NEXT NUMBER  11
PLEASE ENTER THE NEXT NUMBER 999
THE AVERAGE OF THE NUMBERS IS  7.00
```
(b)

**Figure 10-12 A C program and sample output.** (a) Comments are between /* and */. All variable names must be declared as a floating-point number ("float") or an integer ("int"). The command printf sends output to the screen and scanf accepts data from the user. The symbol != means "is not equal to." The while loop reflects structured programming techniques. (b) This screen display shows the interaction between program and user when the program runs.

Program Generator—is a problem-oriented language designed to solve the particular problem of producing business reports. It is also capable of doing some file updating. Developed at IBM, RPG was introduced in 1964 and was intended primarily for small computer systems. An updated version called RPG II was introduced in 1970 and extended the language's original capabilities. A still more recent version, RPG III, is an interactive language that uses menus to give the programmer easy choices to plan programs.

The keys to RPG are special coding forms that the user fills out to describe the report desired. Indeed the forms are labeled in such detail that, with a minimum of training, almost anyone can fill out the forms and produce reports without having to worry about the logic involved in writing the programs.

RPG is so easy to learn that businesspeople believe they get the maximum return on their investment—their investment being the time spent filling out the coding forms. But RPG is necessarily limited and is suitable only for straightforward, relatively uncomplicated data processing problems. It is not used to solve the problems of the world, only to make reports about them.

## Some Other Languages

The languages just described are probably the major ones used today. Many of them occupy their privileged positions for no reason other than they got there first, or they were backed by powerful organizations. But other languages, though not as popular as the most common ones, have still managed to flourish. You are apt to see these mentioned, and it is important to know about them. Notice that many of them are special-purpose languages, a fact that helps to account for their more limited use. Here, in no particular order, are some other noteworthy languages.

### LISP

Developed in 1958 at the Massachusetts Institute of Technology by John McCarthy, **LISP**—short for LISt Processing—is designed to process nonnumeric data—that is, symbols, such as characters or words. LISP can be used interactively at a terminal. It is a popular language for writing programs dealing with artificial intelligence.

### PROLOG

A relatively recent addition to the short list of artificial-intelligence programming languages, **PROLOG** (PROgramming in LOGic) is receiving increasing attention as a tool for natural language programming. It was invented in 1972 by Alan Colmerauer at the University of Marseilles, but it attracted widespread attention only in 1979 when a more efficient version was introduced. PROLOG was selected by the Japanese as the official language of their fifth-generation computer project, and it is rapidly replacing LISP as the darling of the artificial-intelligence crowd.

### ALGOL

Standing for ALGOrithmic Language, **ALGOL** was introduced in 1960. Though popular in Europe, it has never really caught on in the United States. ALGOL was developed primarily for scientific programming and is considered the forerunner of PL/I and Pascal. It has excellent control structures, but, like FORTRAN, it has somewhat limited file processing capabilities.

### PL/I

Introduced in 1964, **PL/I**—for Programming Language One—was sponsored by IBM. It was designed as a compromise for both scientific and business use. PL/I is free-form and quite flexible; in fact, it is easy to learn the rudiments by studying examples. However, being all things to all people, some critics claim, makes the language so loaded down with options that it loses some of its usefulness.

### SNOBOL

Invented in the early 1960s at Bell Labs, **SNOBOL** is considered quite a powerful language. Today it is the most widely used string processing language—that is, a language for manipulating alphanumeric or special characters. Applications for SNOBOL include use by text editors and language processors.

### APL

Short for A Programming Language, **APL** was conceived by Kenneth Iverson and was introduced by IBM in 1968. APL is powerful, interactive, easily learned by programmers, and particularly suited to table handling—that is, to processing groups of related numbers in a table. APL has a score of funny symbols and that is one reason you would have trouble running the language on your home computer—it uses many symbols that are not part of the familiar ASCII character set. Some of these symbols represent very powerful operations. Having a large number of operators means that the APL compiler must be rather large, so it is apt to be available only on systems with large memories.

### Logo

If you overhear a couple of programmers (or even school teachers) using the word *turtle* in conversation, it is a fair guess they are talking about **Logo.** A dialect of LISP developed at the Massachusetts Institute of Technology by Seymour Papert, it is known at this time as a language that children can use. The "turtle" is actually a triangular pointer on the CRT screen that responds to a few simple commands such as FORWARD and LEFT. The language is interactive, which means that a person can learn to use Logo through dialogue sessions with the computer. Figure 10-13 gives an example of a Logo program design.

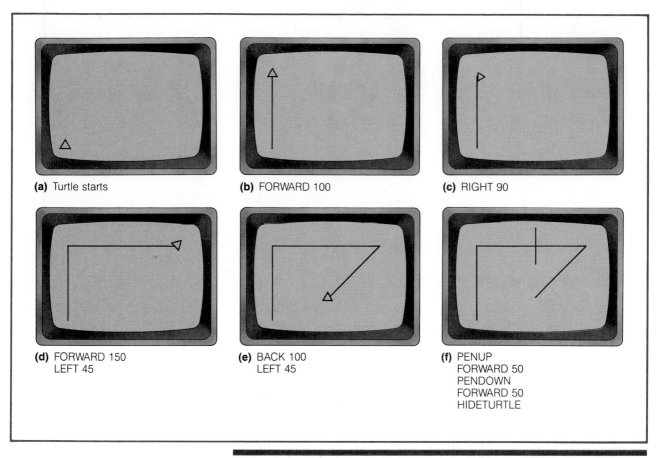

**(a)** Turtle starts

**(b)** FORWARD 100

**(c)** RIGHT 90

**(d)** FORWARD 150
LEFT 45

**(e)** BACK 100
LEFT 45

**(f)** PENUP
FORWARD 50
PENDOWN
FORWARD 50
HIDETURTLE

**Figure 10-13   Logo logic.** The turtle can be moved with a simple sequence of Logo commands. FORWARD moves the turtle in the direction it is facing; BACK moves the turtle backward. The number following one of these commands indicates the length of the line to be drawn. RIGHT and LEFT followed by a number indicates the direction the turtle is to be rotated and the number of degrees it is to be rotated. PENUP and PENDOWN raise and lower the "pen"—the turtle leaves a trace when it moves with the pen down. HIDETURTLE causes the turtle to disappear from the screen.

### PILOT

Invented in 1973, **PILOT** was originally designed to introduce children to computers. PILOT is now most often used to write computer-aided instruction in all subjects. It is especially suited for such instructional tasks as drills and tests. PILOT is not a good choice for complex computational problems.

### Smalltalk

Most interaction with a computer consists of "remembering and typing." With the **Smalltalk** language, however, you "see and print" instead. Here is the way it works: The keyboard is used to enter text into the computer, but all other tasks are accomplished with the use of a mouse, which you move around to direct the movement of a cursor on the CRT screen and on which you press a button to select a command. Invented by Alan Kay at the Palo Alto (California) Research Center, created by Xerox Corporation, Smalltalk represents a watershed of key ideas and concepts that constitute a dramatic departure from traditional computer science because it supports an especially visual computer system. The basis of Smalltalk is that it is an object-oriented language rather than a procedure-oriented language: The interaction is between people and things or classes of objects.

### FORTH

Released by Charles Moore in 1975, **FORTH** was designed for real-time control tasks such as guiding astronomical telescopes, as well as assorted business and graphics programs. But it was also designed to make the best possible use of a computer's memory and speed. Thus FORTH is an excellent language for microcomputers; a typical FORTH program runs much faster and uses much less memory than an equivalent BASIC program. Today, FORTH is available on almost every kind of computer, from micros to mainframes. FORTH requires little computer memory, but only skilled programmers can use it properly.

### Modula-2

Pascal programmers have no trouble recognizing **Modula-2,** because the two languages look almost identical. Perhaps this should not be surprising, since both languages were invented by Niklaus Wirth. Pascal was intended to be a teaching language, a task it performs very well. But Modula-2 shines where Pascal does not— it is specifically designed to write systems software.

## Some Advice

If you are planning to be a programmer, there is a good chance that you will take your first steps in BASIC, then receive more formal training in a business-oriented language— probably COBOL. Perhaps you will be able to add another language like FORTRAN or Pascal. Most newly minted programmers go into the job world with these language tools. But notice something: All of these are third-generation languages.

This chapter has addressed the direction of language use. It seems clear that fourth-generation languages are not just the wave of the future, they are here now. But they are offered at only a few schools. Why is this? There are several reasons. No 4GL has emerged as number one, the way COBOL did for business. Could a school dare to turn out 4GL programmers without a clear signal from the community of local employers? (The schools that have replaced their COBOL courses with a 4GL are almost all in large urban environments where, presumably, some of everything is needed.) Other obstacles—lack of a 4GL compiler or the money for one, a need for

# COMPUTERS AROUND THE WORLD

An International View

**A**lthough the United States is the leading maker and user of computers, other nations are innovators and consumers too. This international photo gallery cannot be comprehensive, but it has sufficient diversity to present a different viewpoint. We will first look at computers being used in a variety of countries and then focus on their use in Japan and France.

## Many Nations, Many Computers

The photo on the opening page shows a young Chinese woman using a Hewlett-Packard laptop computer.

**(1)** In Brisbane, Australia, the Red Cross combines personal computers and laser readers to verify blood type labels.

**(2)** In Heidelberg, Germany, specialists study a planned computer network.

**(3)** Business is brisk in Singapore, as the Chinese embrace computer technology.

**(4)** The Bank of Montreal takes delivery of a new disk drive for its mainframe computer.

**(5)** A special keyboard for the Chinese language lets users enter Chinese characters into the system; a graphics interpretation of the input characters shows on the screen.

**(6)** In Dakar, Senegal, children approach computer literacy using the language Logo. The literacy project is part of a master's thesis by an MIT student who studied the influence of Senegalese culture on the way students learn to use computers.

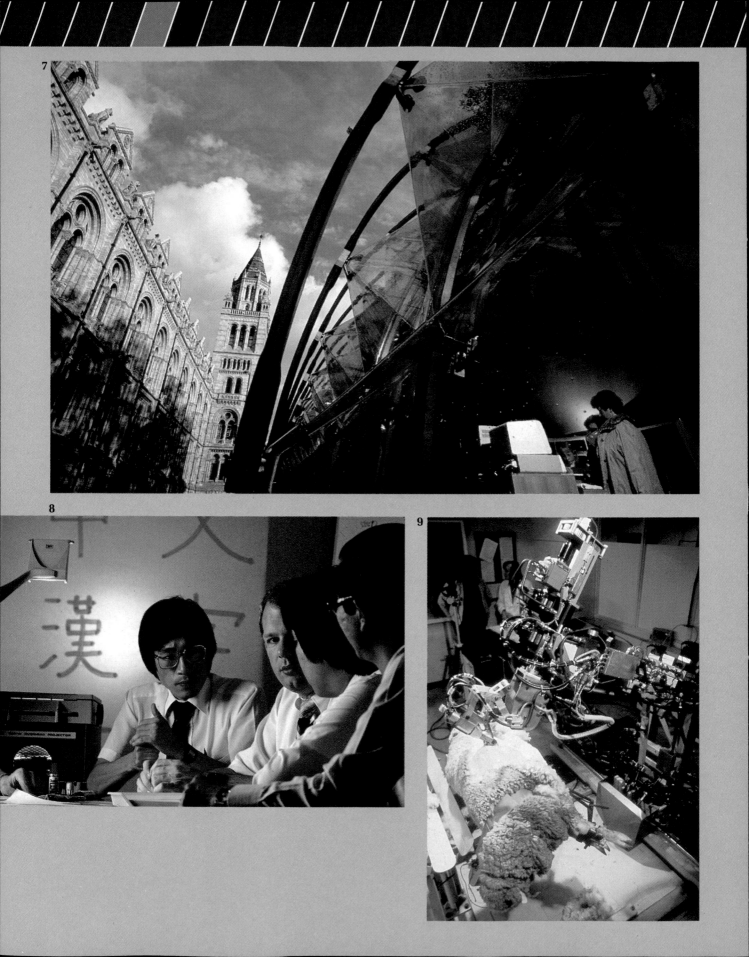

## Many Nations, Many Computers

**(7)** This exhibit of computer products and technology was held in London as part of a 14-nation tour by IBM.

**(8)** Programmers from Korea, China, Japan, and the United States confer on multiple language capabilities.

**(9)** Australia has lots of sheep and shearing them is a labor-intensive process. This experimental robotic shearing device, which was designed at the University of Western Australia, may change all that. The robotic arm follows the contours of each individual sheep.

**(10)** In Jakarta, Indonesia, this technician oversees a computer-driven control panel in a television studio. This studio produces teacher support materials for the Indonesian Ministry of Education.

**(11)** Developed in Boeblingen, Germany, this print head creates camera-ready masters for computer-based printing.

**(12)** Students at a computer fair in Jiddah, Saudi Arabia, view a computer graphics image of Africa and the Red Sea.

**(13)** Italian textile designers view simulated woven cloth patterns on a color display screen. This computer program eliminates the time and cost involved in preparing preproduction samples.

## Japan

**(14)** Engineers in Japan are developing advanced image workstations that will make it easier to create, modify, store, and transmit text, data, and drawings via computer networks.

**(15)** Japan is famous for traffic snarls, but this computer-driven system, which links cameras with traffic lights, has reduced auto accidents and commute time.

**(16)** Parents of these boys at a nursery school in Toyoma, Japan receive daily computer-printed reports on the children's progress, including how much they ate for lunch.

**(17)** Kiioh Ikeda's experimental spider robot is capable of negotiating stairways.

**(18)** A waitress in a Tokyo restaurant uses a nationwide credit verification computer network.

**(19)** This navigation tool from Honda lets drivers drive around cities like Tokyo with the aid of a cursor that traces the route on a dashboard screen map.

20

```
DAR DAR

4 r de Châteaugiron                (99) 50 66 39
35100 RENNES


DEPANNAGE AUTO REMORQUAGE
24H SUR 24H
EN CAS D'ACCIDENT OU PANNE

REMORQUAGE TOUTES DISTANCES AUTO ET MOTO
MISE EN ROUTE - POSE PARE-BRISE
MISE A LA CASSE

DEPANNAGE AUTO RENNAIS

— pour revenir à la liste → RETOUR
```

## France

**(20)** Twenty-four hour tow truck service is as close as your home computer. This commercial message is part of a French videotex network service that reaches a million homes.

**(21)** At the National Institute for Deaf Children in Paris, a child matches his speech to a pattern shown on the computer screen. The feedback on the screen allows the child to adjust his pitch until he makes the correct sound.

**(22), (23)** It is not so bad being the last one in line if you get to carry the computer. Plus, you get to use it first! Apple computers, such as this Apple IIc, are used in education throughout the world.

21

22

23

teacher training, and the difficulty of fitting a 4GL into the existing curriculum—can be overcome once the big question is answered: which 4GL?

Meanwhile, where does this leave you? Your training in third-generation languages is valuable because it teaches you to think analytically and gives you skills in languages that are still in demand. But you must be alert for opportunities on the job to learn a 4GL. Most people who program in 4GLs learned to do so from employer-sponsored classes. Be ready to take the opportunity when it comes your way.

## Summary and Key Terms

- A **programming language** is a set of rules for instructing the computer what operations to perform. A programming language has a limited vocabulary, has a precise meaning for each word, and can be used to solve complex problems in a step-by-step manner.

- Programming languages are described as being "lower" or "higher," depending on whether they are closer to the language the computer itself uses (0s and 1s—low) or to the language people use (more English-like—high). There are five main levels or generations of languages: (1) machine language, (2) assembly language, (3) high-level language, (4) very high-level language, and (5) natural language.

- **Machine language,** the lowest level, represents information as 1s and 0s—binary digits corresponding to the on and off electrical states in the computer.

- **Assembly languages** use letters as abbreviations or mnemonic codes to replace the 0s and 1s of machine language. An **assembler program** is used to translate the assembly language into machine language. Although assembly languages provide great flexibility in tapping a computer's capabilities, they also have disadvantages. For instance, assembly languages vary according to the type of computer and are extremely detailed.

- **High-level languages** are written in an English-like manner. Each high-level language requires a different **compiler,** or translator program, for each type of computer on which it is run.

- **Very high-level languages,** also called fourth-generation languages or **4GLs,** are basically nonprocedural. A **nonprocedural language** only defines *what* the computer should do, without detailing the procedure. A **procedural language** tells the computer specifically *how* to do the task.

- Although fourth-generation languages still require further standardization, they have a number of clear benefits, including primary emphasis on results (*what*) rather than procedure (*how*), improved productivity, and less required training for both programmers and users.

- Fifth-generation languages are often called **natural languages** because they resemble natural human language.

- The use of a natural language to access a knowledge base is called a **knowledge-based system.** One type of knowledge-based system, the **expert system,** offers the computer as an expert on some topic.

- Knowledge-based systems are closely related to **artificial intelligence,** with its emphasis on easier interaction between users and computers. However, natural languages are not yet able to handle complicated logic.

- The first high-level language, **FORTRAN** (FORmula TRANslator), is a scientifically oriented language that was introduced by IBM in 1954. Its simplicity and brevity make it suitable for executing complex formulas but not for describing different types of data. A FORTRAN program is not organized into parts but consists instead of sequential statements. The original FORTRAN was not designed as a structured language, but the newer FORTRAN 77 incorporates some structured features, such as an expanded IF statement.

- **COBOL** (COmmon Business-Oriented Language) was introduced in 1959 by **CODASYL** (COnference of DAta SYstem Languages) as a standard programming language for business. The American National Standards Institute (ANSI) standardized COBOL in 1968, again in 1974 (in a version called **ANS-COBOL**), and more recently in a version known as **COBOL 85.** Since COBOL is English-like, it is useful for processing business data such as street addresses and purchased items, but the wordiness of COBOL programs means a sacrifice of speed and simplicity.

- A COBOL program has four divisions, which appear in the following order: identification, environment, data, and procedure.

- When **BASIC** (Beginners' All-purpose Symbolic Instruction Code) was developed at Dartmouth and introduced in 1965, it was intended for instruction, but its uses now include business and personal computer systems. BASIC has no distinct divisions. In BASIC items of data are identified as they are acted upon. Generic BASIC is unstructured, but structured versions are also available, such as Dartmouth BASIC, BASIC-PLUS, TRUE BASIC, and MBASIC.

- **Pascal,** named for the French mathematician Blaise Pascal, first became available in 1971. Its built-in control structures simplify program coding, making it popular in college computer courses. The language is easy to learn, partly because it uses the very words that emphasize how the control structures work.

- **Ada,** named for Countess Ada Lovelace, was introduced in 1980 as a standard language for weapons systems. Although it also has commercial uses, experts disagree regarding how easy it is to learn. Ada is a structured language that encourages modular program design because each module can be written and tested separately. Control structures closely parallel the basic control structures of sequence, selection, and iteration.

- Invented by Bell Labs in 1974, **C** offers high-level language features such as structured programming while producing code that is almost as efficient as assembly language. C is suitable for writing "portable" programs that can be run on more than one type of computer.

- Originally introduced by IBM in 1964, **RPG** (for Report Program Generator) is a problem-oriented language for producing business reports. RPG allows businesspeople to produce reports by filling out special coding forms.

- Other important languages include: **LISP,** used for nonnumeric data processing and artificial intelligence programs; **PROLOG,** popular for natural language programming; **ALGOL,** developed for scientific programming; **PL/I,** designed for scientific and business uses; **SNOBOL,** used by text editors and language processors; **APL,** used for processing re-

lated numbers in tables; **Logo,** designed as an interactive language that children can use; **PILOT,** used for computer-aided instruction; **Smalltalk,** designed as an object-oriented language; **FORTH,** known for its very efficient use of a computer's memory and speed; and **Modula-2,** a Pascal look-alike designed for writing systems software.

## Review Questions

1. In general, how do programming languages differ from human language?

2. What do *high* and *low* mean in reference to programming languages?

3. Explain how the following types of languages differ: machine language, assembly language, and high-level language.

4. Explain how fourth-generation languages improved the productivity of third-generation languages.

5. Discuss the advantages and limitations of natural languages.

6. How does COBOL differ from FORTRAN and BASIC?

7. How are BASIC and Pascal similar? How do they differ?

8. Discuss the appropriate and inappropriate uses of each of the following languages: FORTRAN, COBOL, and Pascal.

9. Discuss the advantages of each of the following languages: Ada, C, and RPG.

10. Briefly identify the uses of each of the following languages: LISP, PROLOG, ALGOL, PL/I, SNOBOL, APL, Logo, PILOT, Smalltalk, FORTH, and Modula-2.

## Discussion Questions

1. Discuss the advantages of standardizing a programming language.

2. Discuss why a particular language stays in use or goes out of use.

3. Do you think there will be less demand for programmers as languages become easier to use? Explain.

# 11

# Operating Systems

## The Hidden Software

In this chapter we describe an operating system, the set of programs that allows the computer to control resources, execute programs, and manage data. We also consider the special problems related to sharing resources through multiprogramming or time-sharing. After a brief look at translators and service programs, we consider generic operating systems and then give special attention to operating systems for personal computers.

When Larry Black first used his personal computer, he was captivated by the variety of packaged software available for it. He played games, he wrote letters, he balanced budgets, and, in general, he made good use of his machine. In each case Larry only needed to insert the software disk, turn the machine on, and let the software take over from there. This procedure immediately brought easy instructions to the screen, often accompanied by vivid graphics and even music.

But today, Larry wants to use a software package that requires him to participate in the process of getting the software going. Before he can use the software, he must load an operating system into the computer. An **operating system** is a set of programs that allows the computer to control resources, execute programs, and manage data. Once he loads the operating system into the computer, he faces a screen that looks like this:

That is, he sees the letter A followed by the mathematical symbol for greater than, often called *A greater* or the *A prompt* for short. At this point Larry must give some instruction, and the computer is willing to wait all day until he does it. Perhaps all Larry needs to do is insert his packaged software disk, then type certain characters to make the applications software take the lead. But it could be more complicated than that because A> is actually the signal for direct communication between the user and the operating system. Larry is no longer shielded from the operating system, and he must take some responsibility for understanding it.

In two short paragraphs we have taken Larry from novice to sophisticated user—or at least indicated that the possibility exists. As we have indicated before, just about anyone can quickly learn to use certain types of packaged software, the kind that handles the operating system in a way that is transparent—that is, not noticeable—to the user. In other words, using packaged software is like saying, "Tell me what I need to know, but don't confuse me with a lot of technical stuff." But many users want to know more so they can take full advantage of computer resources. Understanding operating systems is an important step in that direction.

An operating system is just more software—but software of a special kind. In this chapter we shall present the rationale for operating systems and give some idea of how they work. Many operating systems concepts apply only to large, multiuser computers, and we shall begin there. But we shall return to a discussion of operating systems for personal computers and, in particular, what to do about A>.

# Operating Systems: Powerful Software in the Background

An operating system is a set of programs that allows the computer system to manage its own resources. Those resources include the CPU, memory, secondary storage devices, and various input/output devices like printers. In a broader sense resources also include data, programs, and people. Figure 11-1 gives a conceptual picture of operating system software as a cushion between the hardware and applications programs such as a word processing program on a personal computer or a payroll program on a

**Figure 11-1   A conceptual diagram of an operating system.** On the outer rim, closest to the user, are applications programs—software that helps a user compute a payroll or play a game or calculate the trajectory of a rocket. The operating system is the set of programs between the applications programs and the hardware.

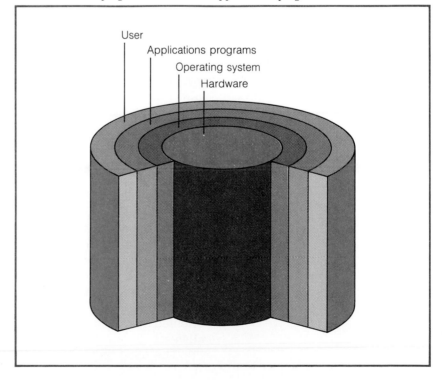

mainframe. In other words, whether or not you are aware of it, using any software application requires that you invoke—call into action—the operating system as well. Whether you are a user of software or a programmer, you will come to appreciate the fact that the operating system takes care of many chores automatically.

Let us pause briefly to trace the beginnings of operating systems and imagine what computer use must have been like without them.

At this point consider the early days of computing, when the primary goal was to get a computer that was bigger and faster. In those days a computer system executed only one program at a time. (This may not seem peculiar in the context of a personal computer, but remember that we now are talking about big, expensive computers.) This meant that all the system's resources—the CPU, all the memory and secondary storage at hand, and all peripheral devices such as printers—were available on demand for that one program. However, it also meant that these components were idle most of the time; while a record was being read from tape, for instance, the CPU and printer were inactive.

Time was also wasted while the system waited for the computer operator to finish tasks: setting up tapes, pushing buttons on the console, and so on. A program came to the end of its run, and the entire system was idle while the operator got the next job ready to run.

All this was inefficient use of an expensive machine. To improve the efficiency of computer operations, operating systems were introduced in the 1960s. An operating system, as we have said, is a set of programs. It handles many chores implicitly, without being told to do so by each individual programmer. An operating system has three main functions: (1) to control the computer system resources, (2) to execute computer programs, and (3) to manage data. The control programs, one part of the operating system, minimize operator intervention so that the computer operations flow smoothly and without interruption. The most important program in the system is the **supervisor program,** most of which remains in memory. It controls the entire operating system and calls in other operating system programs from disk storage as needed (Figure 11-2). These operating system programs stay in memory while they are executing. But they do not remain in memory all the time; that would be an inefficient use of space. To free up space in memory, the supervisor program calls them from disk storage only when they are needed.

The operating system improves efficiency in two ways: (1) It is the medium for cooperation among users, helping them make the best use of computer system resources—such as memory, the CPU, and peripheral devices—so that everyone benefits. (2) It invokes translators and other programs to take care of certain common tasks. This helps free applications programmers from repetitive, machine-oriented details so that they can concentrate on solving problems for clients.

The operating system, in summary, is not hocus-pocus, not a

**Figure 11-2  Retrieving operating system programs from disk.** The operating system supervisor remains in memory and calls in other operating system programs as needed.

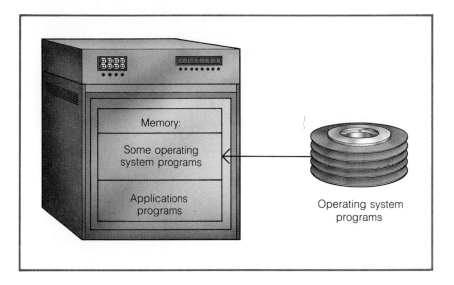

collection of tricks done with mirrors. It is just a set of programs that performs useful functions. Let us now examine some of the various ways operating systems help in sharing resources.

## Sharing Resources

We have noted the inefficiency of running just one program at a time on a big computer and indicated that all that has changed. Indeed it has. Such a computer now can handle many programs at the same time—although we are not saying that the programs run simultaneously. Before we explain that, let us acknowledge some related questions that often come up when computer users first realize that their applications program is "in there" with all those other programs.

*Question:* If there are several other programs in memory at the same time as my program, what keeps the programs from getting mixed up with one another?

*Answer:* The operating system.

*Question:* And if my program and another program both want to use the CPU at the same time, what decides which program gets it?

*Answer:* The operating system.

*Question:* But what if one of the other programs gets in an endless loop and won't give up the CPU? Who is going to step in and set things right?

*Answer:* The operating system.

*Question:* Well, the printer must be a problem. If we all need it, what prevents our output files from coming out in one big jumble?

*Answer:* The operating system!

This litany may be tedious, but it does make a point: The operating system programs anticipate all these problems so that you, as a user or programmer, can share the computer's resources with minimum concern about the details of how it is done.

We begin with the basic process of sharing resources, called multiprogramming, then move to a variation called time-sharing.

## Multiprogramming

**Multiprogramming** means that two or more programs are being executed concurrently on a computer and are sharing the computer's resources. What this really means is that the programs are taking turns; one program runs for a while, then another one. The key word here is *concurrently* as opposed to *simultaneously*. If there is only one CPU, for example (the usual case), it is not physically possible that more than one program use it at the same time—that is, simultaneously. But one program could be using the CPU while another does something else such as writing a record to the printer. Concurrent processing means that two or more programs are using the CPU in the same time frame—during the same hour, for instance—but not at the exact same time. Concurrent, in other words, means that one program uses one resource while another program uses another resource. This gives the illusion of simultaneous processing. As a result, there is less idle time for the computer system's resources. Another way of describing multiprogramming is as **overlapped processing,** which is illustrated in Figure 11-3b. Notice the contrast with **serial processing** in 11-3a, in which one program must finish running before another can begin.

Concurrent processing is effective because CPU speeds are so much faster than input/output speeds. During the time it takes to execute a read instruction for one program, for example, the CPU can execute several calculation instructions for another program. If the first program is in memory by itself, however, the CPU is idle during the read time.

Multiprogramming is **event-driven.** This means that programs share resources based on events that take place in the programs. Normally, a program is allowed to complete a certain activity (event), such as a calculation, before relinquishing the resource (the CPU in this example) to another program that is waiting for it.

The operating system implements multiprogramming through a system of interrupts. An **interrupt** is a condition that causes normal program processing to be suspended temporarily. If, for example, a program instructs the computer to read a record, the program is interrupted and the operating system takes over to pursue this activity. Meanwhile, the program waiting for the record relinquishes control of the CPU to another program; the computer may then proceed to

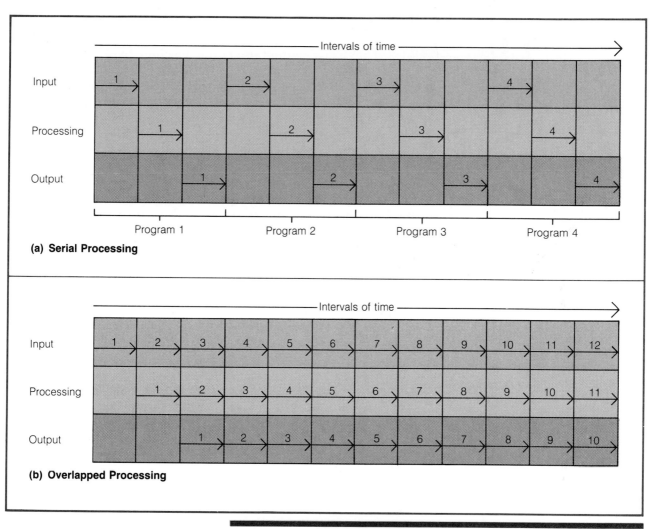

**(a) Serial Processing**

**(b) Overlapped Processing**

**Figure 11-3 Overlapped processing.** (a) Serial processing handles one program at a time. Although the drawing is simplistic, it illustrates that each program has total control of the computer's resources while it is running; all resources not in use are idle. (b) In contrast, overlapped processing shares resources among programs, so that more than one program can be running at once, with each program using a different resource at a given moment.

execute calculations in this second program. When the record for the first program has been read, the interrupt is over, and that program may then continue to execute, subject to the availability of the CPU. Thus, although to the programmer it seems as if the program is executing continuously from start to finish, in fact it is being constantly interrupted as the operating system allocates the computer system resources among different programs.

Programs that run in a multiprogramming environment are usually batch programs. Typical examples are programs for payroll, accounts receivable, sales and marketing analysis, financial planning, quality control, and stock reporting.

### Time-Sharing

The concurrent use of one machine by several people is called **time-sharing.** Time-sharing, a special case of multiprogramming, is usually **time-driven** rather than event-driven. A common approach is to give each user a **time slice,** typically a few milliseconds or even microseconds, during which the computer works on that user's tasks. However, the operating system does not wait for completion of the event; at the end of the time slice, the resources are taken away from the user and given to someone else. This is hardly noticeable to the user: When you are sitting before a terminal in a time-sharing system, the computer's response time will be quite speedy—a matter of a few seconds—and it will seem as if you have the computer to yourself. **Response time** is the time between your typed computer request and the computer's reply. Even if you are working on a calculation and the operating system interrupts it, sending you to the end of the line until other users have had their turns, you may not notice that you have been deprived of service. Not all computer systems give ideal service all the time, however; if a computer system is trying to serve too many users at the same time, response time may deteriorate.

Notice that, generally speaking, you as the user do not have control over the computer system. In a time-sharing environment the operating system has actual control because it controls the users by allocating time slices. Giving the users the processor in turns is called **round-robin** scheduling, as shown in Figure 11-4. However, sometimes a particular user will, for some reason, be entitled to a higher priority than other users. Higher priority translates to faster and better service. A common method of acknowledging higher priority is for the operating system to give that user more turns. Suppose, for example, that there are five users who would normally be given time slices in order: A-B-C-D-E and so forth. If user B is assigned a higher priority, the order could be changed to A-B-C-B-D-B-E-B, giving B every other turn.

Typical time-sharing applications are credit checking, point-of-sale systems, engineering design, airline reservations, and hospital information systems. Each of these systems has several users who need to share the system resources.

## Managing Shared Resources: The Traffic Cop

When several programs share the same computer resources, special problems of control must be considered. Just as a traffic cop controls the flow of vehicles, someone or something must determine which program will be executed next. For example, a given program must be able to access needed devices. Memory space must be available to the program, and that program must

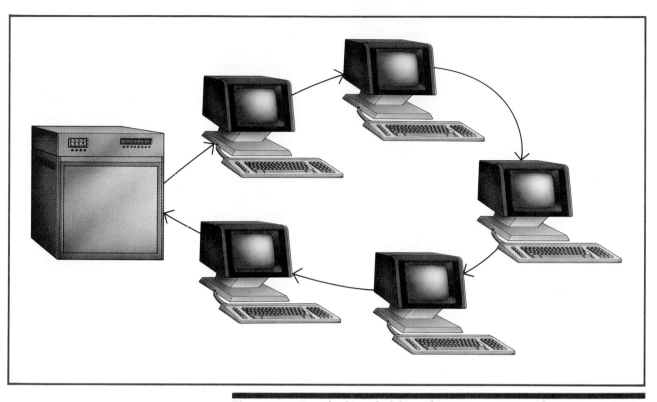

**Figure 11-4   Round-robin scheduling.** The computer gives each user a turn in circular fashion.

be protected from inadvertent interference from other programs. We shall now consider how the operating system handles some of these types of problems.

## Resource Allocation

How does the operating system actually allocate various resources of the computer system to the various programs as they are needed and in a fair manner? **Resource allocation** is the process of assigning resources to certain programs for their use. Those same resources are deallocated—removed—when the program using them is finished, then reallocated elsewhere.

A program waiting to be run by the computer is placed on disk, with other waiting programs. A scheduling program, part of the operating system, selects the next job from the input queue. This decision is based on such factors as memory requirements, priority, and devices needed. In other words, the selection is based to some extent on whether available resources can satisfy the needs of the waiting program.

In the course of the resource allocation, the operating system must consider the input/output devices available and their use. For example, at any given moment, the operating system knows which program is using which particular tape drive and knows which devices are free and can be allocated to a program waiting in the input queue. The scheduling program would not allow a job to begin, for example, if it needed three tape drives and only two were currently available.

It is theoretically possible for two programs to need resources during processing that are unavailable to them; each may want a resource held captive by the other. What is more, neither is willing to give up the resource it is holding until it gets the one the other is holding, a condition known as a **deadlock.** Note the example in Figure 11-5. Most operating systems are able to anticipate and thus prevent deadlocks; others force one of the contenders to back off after the fact.

Memory also needs to be allocated, but this special resource merits its own section.

## Memory Management

What if you have a very large program, for which it might be difficult to find space in memory? Or what if several programs are competing for space in memory? These questions are related to memory management. **Memory management** is the process of allocating memory to programs and of keeping the programs in memory separate from each other.

There are many methods of memory management. Some systems simply divide memory into separate areas, each of which can hold a program. The problem is how to know how big the areas, sometimes called partitions or regions, should be; at least one of them should be large enough to hold the largest program. Some systems use memory areas that are not of a fixed size—that is, the sizes can change to meet the needs of the current assortment of programs. In either case—whether the areas are of a fixed or variable size—there is a problem with slivers of memory between programs. When these slivers are too small to be used, space is wasted.

### Foreground and Background

Large all-purpose computers often divide their memory into foreground and background areas. A **foreground** area is for programs that have higher priority. A typical foreground program is in a time-sharing environment, with the user at a terminal awaiting response. The **background** area, as the name implies, is for programs with less pressing schedules and, thus, lower priorities. Typical background programs are batch programs in a multiprogramming environment. Foreground programs are given privileged status—more turns for the CPU and other resources—and background programs take whatever they need that is not currently in use by another

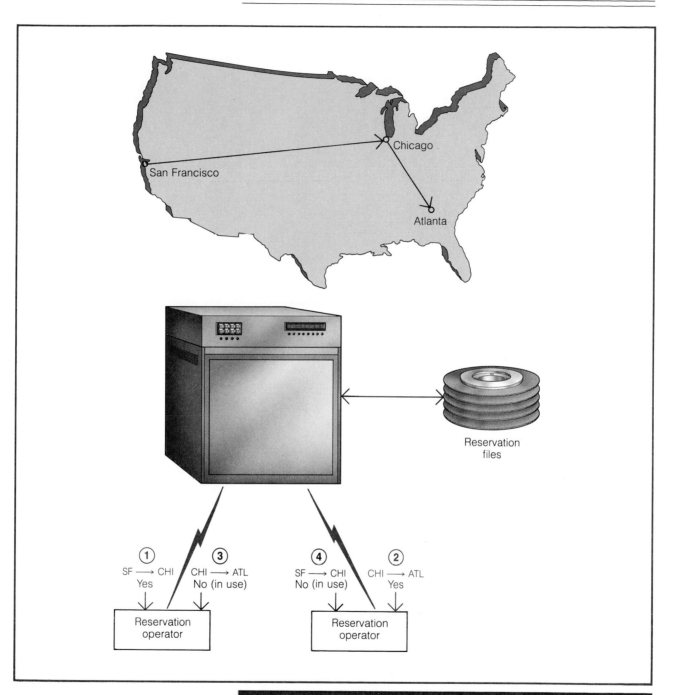

**Figure 11-5   A deadlock.** Each reservation operator, it just so happens, has a customer who wants to fly from San Francisco to Chicago to Atlanta. When an operator wants to make a reservation for a customer, the flight record must be made temporarily unavailable to other operators, lest one operator wipe out another's updates. In this case, let us suppose that ① one operator takes the record for the San Francisco to Chicago flight, while ② the other operator begins with the Chicago to Atlanta flight. ③ When the first operator tries to get the Chicago–Atlanta segment, it is unavailable because the other operator is using it. If the first operator holds onto the San Francisco–Chicago record while waiting for Chicago–Atlanta, ④ he or she might wait forever because the other operator might not give up Chicago–Atlanta until he or she gets San Francisco–Chicago.

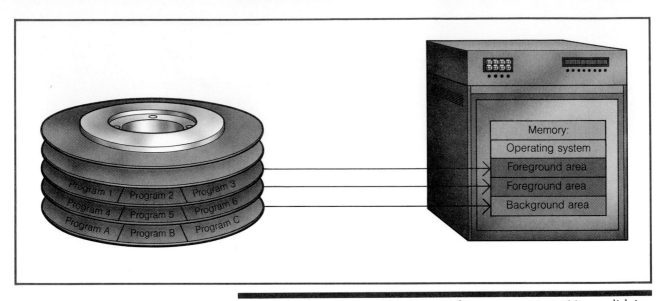

**Figure 11-6   Programs waiting in queues.** These programs are waiting on disk in queues organized by program class. That is, time-sharing programs (1 through 6) wait in their own queue for a foreground area to open up and batch programs (A through C) wait in a queue for a background area to be free.

program. Programs waiting to run are kept on the disk in **queues** suitable to their job class, as you can see in Figure 11-6.

This discussion has been purposely general, but the principles do apply to many large computers. Another technique, however, is virtual storage which, as you will see, expands the memory management possibilities.

### Virtual Storage

Many computer systems manage memory using a technique called **virtual storage** (also called **virtual memory**). Virtual storage means that part of the program is stored on disk and is brought into memory for execution only as needed. (Again, the delay in time may not be noticeable.) The user appears to be using more memory space than is actually the case. Since only part of the program is in memory at any given time, the amount of memory needed for a program is minimized. Memory, in this case, is considered **real storage,** while the secondary storage holding the rest of the program is considered virtual storage.

Virtual storage can be implemented in one of three ways:

- By segmentation
- By paging
- By a combination of segmentation and paging

Again, suppose you have a very large program, which means there will be difficulty finding space for it in the computer's memory. Remember that memory is shared among several programs. If your program is divided into smaller pieces, it will be easier to find places to put those pieces. This is essentially what segmentation does. **Segmentation** is the process of dividing a program into blocks of various sizes and placing these segments in memory in *noncontiguous* locations—that is, locations not necessarily next to each other. These segments are based on the program logic. Logically related program statements, typically a program module (as discussed in Chapter 9), comprise a segment.

Even though the segments are not right next to each other in memory, the operating system is able to keep track of them. It does this through a segment table, which lists the number of segments that are part of the program and the beginning addresses of areas in memory where they are placed.

The problem with segmentation is that it is possible to have many unused fragments of memory. A **fragment** is a portion of real memory that is too small to hold even a segment, and is thus, for the moment, unusable. In response the concept of paging was developed.

Paging is the second method of implementing virtual storage. **Paging** is similar to segmentation, but the program is broken into equal-size pieces called **pages** and stored in equal-size memory spaces called **page frames.** All pages and page frames are the same fixed size—typically, 2K or 4K bytes. Fixed page size means the breaks between pages are not related to the program logic. Fixed page size also means that the pages fit exactly into the page frames in memory—hand in glove, so to speak—thereby eliminating wasted space. This elimination of fragmentation is the key advantage of paging over segmentation.

The third way of implementing virtual storage is a combination of segmentation and paging. With this method the program is first broken into segments, then the segments into pages. For the operating system to keep track of the various pieces, a segment table is needed and, for each segment, a page table. These tables have nothing in them but real memory addresses.

Figure 11-7 shows how this system works. The example shows three segments of 20K, 30K, and 10K bytes, respectively. Each segment is divided into pages of 4K bytes each. Note that the extra 2K in the second and third segments still require full 4K pages, so some memory space is wasted. The pages are then distributed to various locations throughout memory.

### *Memory Protection*

In a multiprogramming environment it is theoretically possible for the computer, while executing one program, to destroy or modify another program by transferring it to the wrong memory locations. That is, without protection, one program might accidentally hop into the middle of another, causing destruction of data and general chaos. To avoid this problem, the operating system confines each program to certain defined limits in memory. If a program inadvertently transfers to some memory area outside those limits, the

**Figure 11-7  Segmentation tables and page tables.** A program is first divided into segments, then each segment is divided into pages, which are distributed throughout memory. In this example the program is divided into segments of 20K, 30K, and 10K bytes. Each page is 4K bytes. Note that the 20K segment fits very nicely into five 4K pages, but we must use eight 4K pages to hold the 30K segment. Since eight 4K pages hold 32K bytes but we are putting in only 30K bytes, 2K bytes of memory space are wasted. Similarly, 2K bytes of memory are unused when the 10K segment is placed in three 4K pages, which hold 12K bytes.

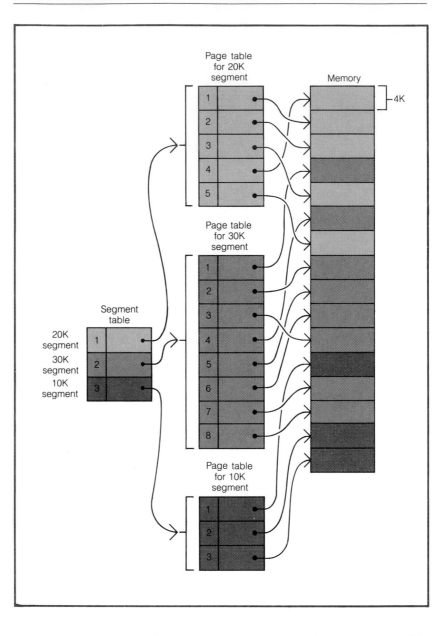

operating system terminates the execution of that program. This process of keeping your program from straying into others' programs and their programs from yours is called **memory protection.**

## Spooling

Suppose you have a half dozen programs active at a given moment, but your system has only one printer. If all programs took turns printing out their output a line or two at a time, interspersed with the output of other programs, the resulting printed report

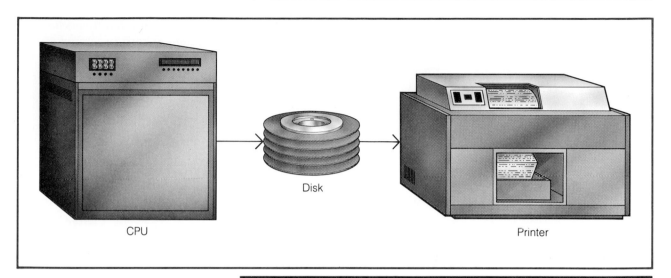

**Figure 11-8   Spooling.** Program output that is destined for the printer is written first to a disk—spooled—and later transferred to a printer.

would be worthless. To get around this problem, a process called **spooling** is used: Each program writes onto a disk each file that is to be printed. When the entire program is on the disk, spooling is complete, and the disk files are printed intact (Figure 11-8).

Spooling also addresses another problem—relatively slow printer speeds. Writing a record on disk is much faster than writing that same record on a printer. A program, therefore, completes execution more quickly if records to be printed are written temporarily on disk instead. The actual printing can be done at some later time when it will not slow the program execution. Some installations use a separate (usually smaller) computer dedicated exclusively to the printing of spooled files.

## Translators and Service Programs

Most of the tasks just described in the section on sharing resources are done by the operating system without applications programmer involvement. Although, as a programmer, you may need to make requests for input and output devices, generally speaking, you do not need to give specific instructions on the use of these operating system features. Activities such as paging and spooling go on without your explicit commands. In the following discussion, however, we will describe situations that do require specific instructions to the operating system. Since the commands vary from computer to computer, we shall make no attempt to include them here. The discussion is general and is applicable to most computer systems.

One more point. Strictly speaking, translators and service programs are not part of the operating system. These programs are invoked by the operating system. We include them in this chapter because, like operating systems, they perform standard services and are not directly related to specific applications programs.

## Translators and the Link/Loader

When you write a program in BASIC, COBOL, or a similar high-level language, you need a **translator,** a program that translates your language into machine language that the computer can understand. There are three types of translators. If you are using a high-level language, the translator program is usually a **compiler,** which translates your program all at once before the program is executed. Sometimes, high-level languages are translated using an **interpreter,** which translates and executes your program one instruction at a time. If you are using an assembly language, you would use a translator called an **assembler.** Compilers, interpreters, and assemblers are programs that use *your* programs as input data, and in this case your program is called the **source module** (or source program).

Compilers and assemblers produce three possible outputs: (1) an object module, (2) diagnostic messages, and (3) a source program listing. The **object module** is a version of your program that is now in machine language. **Diagnostic messages** inform you of **syntax errors.** Syntax errors are not errors in logic but errors in use of the language—errors that could be caused by mistakes in typing or because you did not understand how to use the language. If you have diagnostic messages, your program probably did not compile. (Sometimes, however, the messages are warning messages, which tell you of minor errors that do not prevent compilation.) The **source program listing** is a list of your program as you wrote it. In most cases you will refer to the listing right on the screen, but it is also useful to print the listing at regular intervals. You can use the source program listing to make any corrections necessary to your program.

There are many potential compilers—one for every language and every type of computer on which the language can be used. Thus, for any particular machine, you will have to use a COBOL compiler if you are running a program in COBOL and a FORTRAN compiler if you are running a program in FORTRAN.

Figure 11-9 shows what generally happens during the process of writing and correcting a program. The object module produced is often considered temporary because if you are in the testing phase of program development, you will be correcting errors. Since the program is going to be changed, it will be recompiled. Notice in the figure that after the object module is ready there is a **link/load** phase. The object module of your program may be linked with prewritten, standard programs before it is run on the computer. The link/load program (also called the linkage editor) is used to add such prewritten programs to your program. These other programs are usually

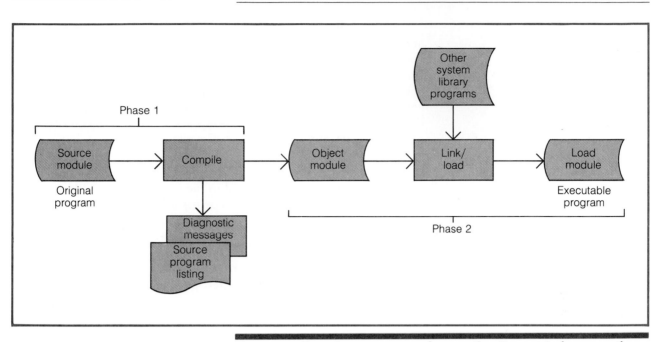

**Figure 11-9   Preparing your program for execution.** Your original program, the source module, is compiled into an object module, which represents the program in machine language. The compiler may produce diagnostic messages, indicating syntax errors. A listing of the source program may also be output from the compiler. After the program successfully compiles, the object module is linked with system library programs, as needed, and the result is an executable load module.

stored on disk in a system library. An example of a standard program is one that computes a square root. By calling in the standard program and adding it to your own, you are spared the tedious process of writing out all the steps of computing the square root. The output from the link/load step is called the **load module.** Stored on disk, the load module is now ready to be read into memory and executed.

Because an interpreter translates and executes your program directly, one instruction at a time, neither an object module nor prior diagnostics are generated. Thus, a disadvantage of using an interpreter is that syntax errors may not be discovered until the program is executed. Interpreters are used, for the most part, with BASIC on microcomputers.

## Utility Service Programs

Why reinvent the wheel? Duplication of effort is what **utility programs** are supposed to avoid. Many repetitive file-handling tasks can be handled easily by prewritten standard programs, once certain information (such as record length) has been specified. Utility programs perform file conversions and sort/merge operations.

File-handling utility programs convert files from one form to another (disk to tape, disk to disk, tape to printer, and so on) and handle the general logic of reading a file from one place and writing it to another. In the course of using these utility programs, you can usually specify certain options. For instance, if the utility program is concerned with printer output, you can elect to do a number of things that will improve the report appearance, such as put in headings, add page numbers, and double space the lines.

To use a sort/merge utility, the programmer specifies the input file name and the file output, then indicates which fields are to be sorted and where they are located in the records. The utility program then performs these operations. For instance, if you wish to sort a file by Social Security number, you indicate in which column the number starts and the length of the field (in this case nine characters) and whether you wish to have records sorted in ascending or descending order. A merging operation combines two sequenced files into one file. For example, two files, each arranged by Social Security number, could be merged into a single file containing all the records from both files in order by Social Security number.

Thus far in this chapter we have examined general properties and services of operating systems. Now we turn to some specific trends in operating systems, especially those related to personal computers.

# The UNIX Phenomenon

Once upon a time when you bought a computer, the operating system came with the hardware. First it was free, later not free, but in the large mainframe world, operating systems still are usually defined by the vendor, with the user silently acquiescing.

But some changes have occurred in recent years. There is a trend toward buying what is known as a **generic operating system,** that is, an operating system with a more general nature that works with more than one manufacturer's computer system. Generic operating systems are frequently created by software companies. There are several generic operating systems, but we shall discuss the one that is particularly influential: UNIX.

## Emerging UNIX

**UNIX** was developed in 1971 by Ken Thompson and Dennis Ritchie at AT&T's Bell Laboratories for use on Bell's DEC minicomputers. The designers were surprised to see UNIX become the dominant operating system of the computer industry during the late 1970s and early 1980s. How did this come about?

Part of the reason may involve a social factor, not the software itself—namely, the "UNIX graduate" phenomenon. In the late 1970s Bell gave away UNIX to many colleges and universities, and students became accustomed to using it. Consequently, when many of these schools' graduates entered the work force, they began agitating for the acceptance of UNIX in industry. Another reason is that in 1981 Bell Labs reduced the price of executable versions of UNIX to as little as $40 a copy, which set in motion a new wave of interest in the operating system.

Some consider UNIX a data processing professional's dream. A multiuser, time-sharing operating system, it was originally implemented for a minicomputer but now also runs on mainframes and even on some microcomputers. However, it is a very sophisticated operating system.

## Pipelining

A notable feature of UNIX is called pipelining, which significantly adds to the speed of processing. **Pipelining,** as illustrated in Figure 11-10, sends the output of one program directly to the next program, where it can immediately be processed as input before the prior program is completed. Having one program's output be the input for another is not new. But having that data processed immediately is a rather sophisticated concept.

**Figure 11-10   Pipelining.** In this example three programs are used to prepare an index for a manuscript. The first program sifts out underlined words and sends them to a second program, which checks their spelling against a file of spelled words. The spelling program then sends the words to a third program, which sorts the words alphabetically and prints the index. The first program sends words directly to the next program, which can begin checking spelling while the first program is still looking for more words. In the same way the checked words can be sent to the next program, where the sorting process can begin while the first two programs are still cranking out words.

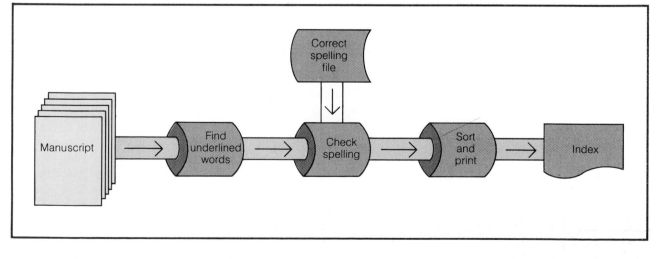

### Drive for a UNIX Standard

Is UNIX a standard? It is struggling mightily to be one. An outgrowth of the UNIX graduate phenomenon is that UNIX is the only operating system that has become user-driven. That is, key UNIX supporters—the scientific community, the federal government, the aerospace industry—often name UNIX in their bid specifications to computer manufacturers. In other words, "If you want our business, you better offer a system that includes UNIX." Vendors, therefore, that cannot offer UNIX-supported hardware are effectively cut out of the bidding process. This is a powerful incentive to offer UNIX with a hardware system. Today UNIX runs on everything from the massive Cray-2 to the IBM Personal Computer.

But UNIX has some drawbacks. It has never been considered very user friendly. Critics point, for example, to capricious use of abbreviations (such as GREP, for global regular expression print—whatever that may mean), and inadequate documentation. However, the unfriendliness has now been successfully replaced by the now traditional menus that look much like those of other systems. Also, UNIX lacks sophisticated security features. Still, UNIX supporters take on a fervor that has been described as cultlike. Said one adherent, "Sure it's got problems—but show me something better." Today nearly all other operating systems are measured against the standard of UNIX.

## Operating Systems for Personal Computers: A> Revisited

We left Larry Black staring at the A> on the screen. We should say at this point that A> is the well-known notation of the IBM Personal Computer's operating system called MS-DOS (for Microsoft Disk Operating System). How did A> get to the screen? Larry, you will recall, loaded the system.

### Booting the Operating System

We have already indicated that some software packages hide the operating system interface, but others want you to use your own copy of the operating system, probably the one that came with the machine. This is called **booting** the system—that is, loading the operating system into memory. The word *booting* is used because the operating system pulls itself up by its bootstraps. A small program (in ROM—read-only memory) "bootstraps" the rest of the operating system in from a floppy disk. (Unlike large computer systems, the entire operating system is now in memory for as long as the computer is being used.) See a description of booting in The Microcomputer Corner. The net observable result of booting MS-DOS is an

A> on the screen. The A refers to the left-hand disk drive. The > is a **prompt,** a signal that the system is *prompting* Larry to do something. The > prompt indicates that the operating system is waiting for a command from the user.

As we said, Larry is using an applications software package that requires him to respond to A>. The common procedure is to first remove the operating system disk from drive A—the operating system will remain in memory until the computer is turned off. Next, the disk for the software package is placed in drive A, and a command is keyed in that causes the operating system to load that software into memory. (This command can be found in the documentation for the software package.)

Besides loading a software package, the interface with the operating system opens up many other possibilities. Table 11-1 shows a sampler of operating system commands and what they do.

But what if Larry wants to use a different computer? Is his knowledge about MS-DOS transferable? Maybe, but probably not. That brings us—yet again—to the issue of standards.

## Standards: Can't We Do Things the Same Way?

Like their forebears, early microcomputer manufacturers took the path already traveled and produced their own unique operating systems: Apple II has DOS (for Disk Operating System), Tandy Incorporated's Radio Shack TRS-80 uses TRS-DOS, and the IBM Personal Computer uses its own version of MS-DOS. What this means is that the terrific piece of software you see somewhere—say, a word

**Table 11-1  Some MS-DOS commands.** Here are some simple operating system commands used on the IBM PC (when you see the A> prompt) and a general description of what they do. Although they are specifically part of MS-DOS, they represent the kinds of things you can do on most personal computers.

| Command | Use |
| --- | --- |
| CHKDSK | Check disk. Display information about the status of a disk, including number of files, number of bytes used in files, and number of bytes available for use. |
| CLS | Clear the screen. |
| COMP | Compare two files to see if they are identical. |
| COPY | Make another copy of a file. |
| DIR | Directory. List all files on a disk. |
| DEL or ERASE | Delete a file. |
| FORMAT | Prepare a disk for use. |
| RENAME | Give a file a new name. |
| TYPE | Display a file on the screen. |

## THE MICROCOMPUTER CORNER

### How to Use MS-DOS

When you learn how to use a computer, you sometimes hear a little voice within you that plants a seed of doubt ("Are you *sure* you want to press *that* key?") and hints that the computer will self-destruct if you make a mistake. Some software saves you from this uncertainty. You simply insert the applications program, turn on the computer, and follow the step-by-step instructions on the screen. However, there are times when the computer waits for *you* to give the instructions. For instance, some tasks require knowing how to use an operating system disk, which prepares the computer for particular applications programs. Below are the directions for loading MS-DOS (an operating system for the IBM PC), followed by directions for two common tasks requiring MS-DOS. The first task is formatting a blank disk, which means preparing it for holding data files and a file directory. The second task is copying files from one disk to another.

### Loading MS-DOS

As you read these steps, follow along on the drawing.

1. Insert the MS-DOS disk in the left-hand disk drive (drive A) and shut the disk-drive door.
2. Turn the PC on. The red light in drive A goes on, and the drive whirs for a few seconds. Then the red light goes off.
3. When the screen requests the date enter the new date (month-day-year; for example, 10-13-88) and press Return.
4. When the screen requests the time enter the new time (military time; for example, 14:30) and press Return.
5. When the A> appears on the screen, MS-DOS is loaded in drive A. (If you are going to insert an applications program in drive A, you may now remove the MS-DOS disk.)

### Formatting a Blank Disk

1. Load MS-DOS in drive A.
2. Insert the blank disk in drive B.
3. After A> type
   FORMAT B:

4. Press Return.
5. Press any key.
6. When the red light in drive B goes off, the disk has been formatted and is ready to use.

### Copying Files

1. Load MS-DOS in drive A.
2. Remove the MS-DOS disk when A> appears.
3. Insert the original disk (the one to be copied) in drive A.
4. Insert a formatted disk (the one to be copied to) in drive B.
5. a) To copy a specific file on the disk in drive A to the disk in drive B, after A> type:
   COPY A:(FILE NAME) B:
   Thus, if the file name is PAYROLL, the screen would read:
   A>COPY A:PAYROLL B:
   b) To copy *all* the files on the disk in drive A to the disk in drive B, after A> type:
   COPY A: *.* B:
6. Press Return.
7. When the light in drive B goes off, the computer has completed the copying.

processing program for sale on a floppy disk at a Radio Shack store—may not work on another manufacturer's microcomputer. The reason: Your computer (say, an Apple or IBM PC) does not have the same operating system. Video game addicts who covet a friend's new acquisition on a different home computer may find this lack of standardization particularly distressing.

The popularity of the personal computer opened the way for software entrepreneurs, who wanted to write programs that would be purchased by the vast personal computer audience. The potential

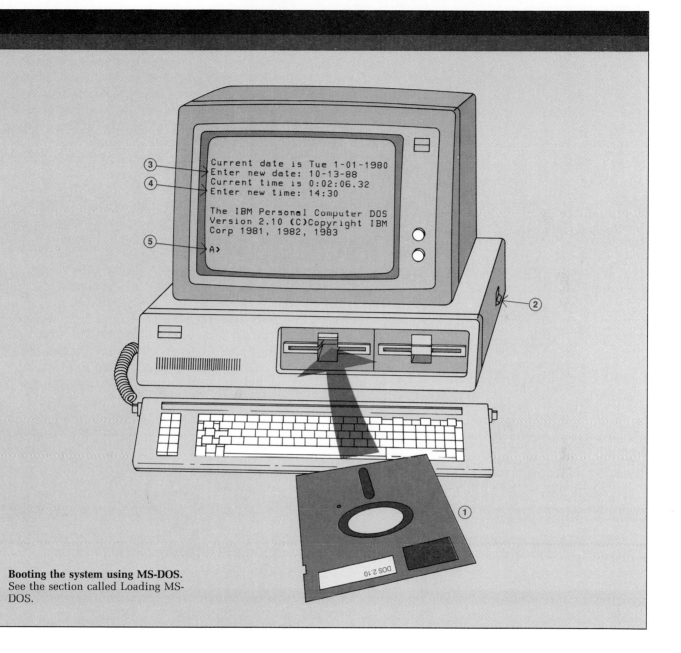

Current date is Tue 1-01-1980
Enter new date: 10-13-88
Current time is 0:02:06.32
Enter new time: 14:30

The IBM Personal Computer DOS
Version 2.10 (C)Copyright IBM
Corp 1981, 1982, 1983

A>

DOS 2.10

**Booting the system using MS-DOS.**
See the section called Loading MS-DOS.

for sales was enormous. Eager as they were, though, they hung back, waiting for a standard operating system to emerge. Since software written to run on one operating system generally will not run on another operating system, nobody wanted to spend a lot of development time on a product only to find that they had guessed wrong about which operating system would become dominant.

For a while CP/M (Control Program for Microcomputers) looked promising because it was an operating system used by a number of manufacturers—but none of them was big enough to gamble on. Then IBM chose MS-DOS from Microsoft. Everybody breathed a sigh of relief that a standard had at last been established. Since that watershed period, IBM has captured a significant market share, and everyone else is fighting for a grip on Big Blue's coattails.

Why IBM? Is it because IBM's operating system has been proven to be the finest or the most efficient? Not necessarily. Quite simply, everyone knows that IBM will sell a lot of personal computers. And where IBM sells hardware, software is sure to follow. Software is written for IBM's operating system because that is the truest path to the greatest software sales. There have been occasional countercurrents—such as the Apple Macintosh—since the IBM wave began to roll, but IBM's influence on the market is enormous.

Even so, new paths are being taken. Now souped-up layered operating systems are being touted in the marketplace. What is a layered system? To find out, we need to explore the concept of the operating environment.

## Operating Environments: The Shell Game

Figure 11-11 tells the story at a glance: Another layer has been added between the operating system and the user. This layer is often called a **shell** because it forms a "coating" around the operating system. More formally, this layer is called an **operating environment** because the user has been moved to a new environment—one more palatable to many users than A>.

**Figure 11-11   Operating environments.** This illustration is identical to Figure 11-1, except that an environment layer has been added to shield the user from having to know commands of the operating system.

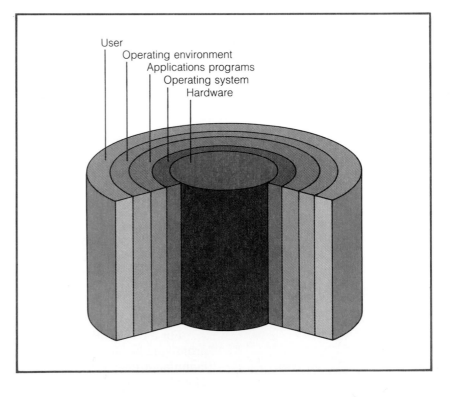

User
Operating environment
Applications programs
Operating system
Hardware

Back to Larry, who is now having his first experience with an operating environment. Instead of the A > , he sees pictures and/or simply worded choices. Instead of having to *know* some command to type, he has only to make a selection from the choices available on the screen. Apple's Macintosh paved the way for simple interfaces between users and the operating system, but new software products are battling over the future operating environment standard for IBM compatibles. Two of the leading contenders are TopView from IBM and Windows from Microsoft. Could one of these become the new standard?

## Do I Really Need to Know All This?

The answer to that question depends on how you expect to use a computer. If your primary use of a computer is as a tool to enhance your other work, then you may have minimum interaction with an operating system. In that case, whether you are using a personal computer or a mainframe, you will learn to access the applications software of choice very quickly.

But there are other options. In fact, there are far more options than we are able to present in this introductory chapter. As a sophisticated user, you can learn your way around the operating system of any computer you might be using. If you plan to be a programmer, then there is no question about whether you need to know everything in this chapter; you will need to know this and much more.

## Summary and Key Terms

- An **operating system** is a set of programs through which the computer manages its own resources such as the CPU, memory, secondary storage devices, and input/output devices. Thus, applications programs do not have to provide all the instructions that the computer requires. This allows programmers to focus on solving problems for clients.

- An operating system has three main functions: (1) to control the computer system resources, (2) to execute computer programs, and (3) to manage data.

- The **supervisor program** controls the entire operating system, ensuring that other programs in the system are called into memory as needed and that memory space is used efficiently.

- The operating system improves efficiency in two ways: (1) by helping users get maximum benefit from the computer system resources, and (2) by invoking translator programs and other programs that take care of certain common tasks.

- **Multiprogramming** is running two or more programs concurrently on the same computer sharing the computer's various resources. Multiprogramming, also called **overlapped processing,** contrasts with **serial processing,** in which one program must finish running before another can begin.

- Multiprogramming is **event-driven,** meaning that one program is allowed to use a particular resource (such as the CPU) to complete a certain activity (event) before relinquishing the resource to another program. In multiprogramming, the operating system uses **interrupts,** which are conditions that temporarily suspend the execution of individual programs.

- **Time-sharing** is a special case of multiprogramming in which several people use one machine at the same time. Each user is usually given a **time slice** (typically a few milliseconds) in which the computer works on that user's tasks before moving on to another user's tasks. **Response time** is the time between the user's typed computer request and the computer's reply. The system of having users take turns is called **round-robin** scheduling.

- Through the **resource allocation** process, the operating system coordinates resource availability with the requirements of the various programs. Most operating systems are able to prevent a **deadlock,** a condition in which two programs come into conflict, with neither one willing to give up the resource it is holding until it gets the resource the other is holding.

- **Memory management** is the process of allocating memory to programs and of keeping the programs in memory separate from each other. Some operating systems divide memory into separate areas of fixed size, while others allow variable sizes. Large all-purpose computers often divide memory into a **foreground** area for programs with higher priority and a **background** area for programs with lower priority. Programs waiting to be run are kept on the disk in **queues.**

- In the **virtual storage** (or **virtual memory**) technique of memory management, part of the applications program is stored on disk and is brought into memory only when needed for execution. Memory is considered **real storage;** the secondary storage holding the rest of the program is considered virtual storage.

- Virtual storage can be implemented in one of three ways: by segmentation, by paging, or by a combination of both.

- **Segmentation** divides a program into groups of logically related program statements, resulting in pieces (segments) of varying size. These segments are then assigned memory locations that are not necessarily next to each other. Segmentation can result in **fragments,** unusable parts of real memory that are too small to hold any segment.

- **Paging** divides a program into equal-size pieces (**pages**) that fit exactly into corresponding memory spaces (**page frames**), thus avoiding fragments.

- When segmentation is combined with paging, a program is first divided into segments, then the segments into pages. The operating system uses segment tables and page tables to locate the pages in memory.

- In multiprogramming, **memory protection** is an operating system process that defines the limits of each program in memory, thus preventing pro-

grams from accidentally destroying or modifying one another.

- **Spooling** avoids printouts that are a combination of the output from concurrently processed programs. Each file to be printed is written temporarily onto a disk instead of being printed immediately. When this spooling process is complete, all the appropriate files from a particular program can be printed intact.

- **Translators** convert programs into machine language. High-level languages usually use a **compiler** (which completes the translation before the program is executed) but sometimes use an **interpreter** (which translates and executes the program one instruction at a time as it executes). A third type of translator program, the **assembler,** is used with assembly languages. All three types of translators use the applications program, or **source module,** as input.

- Compilers and assemblers can generate three types of output: (1) an **object module,** which is the machine-language version of the program; (2) **diagnostic messages,** which indicate **syntax errors** (language errors); and (3) the **source program listing,** which is a list of the program as the programmer wrote it.

- During the **link/load phase,** prewritten programs may be added to the object module by means of a link/loader. The output from the link/load step is called the **load module.**

- **Utility programs** are prewritten standard programs that perform many repetitive file-handling tasks such as file conversions and sort/merge operations.

- A **generic operating system** is one that works with more than one manufacturer's computer system.

- **UNIX,** developed in 1971 by researchers at Bell Labs, has become a dominant generic operating system. One of the notable features of this multiuser, time-sharing operating system is **pipelining,** the immediate sending of one program's output to be processed as another program's input.

- **Booting** the system is the process of loading the operating system into memory. A **prompt** signals the user when this process is complete and the operating system is ready for a command.

- In general, personal computer software written to be run on one operating system will not run on another one. Therefore, most software developers maximize sales by writing programs for the most widely used operating systems, such as IBM's MS-DOS.

■ Some operating systems provide pictures and/or simply worded choices instead of giving a prompt. In effect, these pictures and choices form a user-friendly "coating," or **shell,** around the operating system. They create a comfortable **operating environment** for the user, who does not have to remember or look up the appropriate commands.

## Review Questions

1. What is an operating system?

2. What are the three main functions of an operating system?

3. How does an operating system improve efficiency?

4. Describe how multiprogramming works.

5. Explain how time-sharing works.

6. Describe the process of resource allocation.

7. Why is memory management necessary?

8. Why do some computer systems divide the memory into foreground and background areas?

9. How are segmentation and paging similar? How are they different?

10. In multiprogramming, what prevents one program from destroying or changing another program?

11. Explain how spooling works and why it is useful.

12. Explain what a compiler is, and describe its three possible outputs.

13. How does an interpreter differ from a compiler?

14. What do utility programs do?

15. What is a generic operating system?

## Discussion Questions

1. How would programming be affected if there were no operating systems?

2. Discuss the advantages and disadvantages of having a standard operating system.

# 12

# Systems Analysis and Design

## Change and the Computer

Systems analysis and design are the processes by which a new system supplants an old one. The chapter describes the qualities of a systems analyst's job and the variety of professional skills needed. The systems analyst—the change agent—moves through the five phases of preliminary investigation, systems analysis, systems design, systems development, and implementation to complete a systems project.

People are generally uncomfortable about change, even change in apparently minor matters. If you ponder your own daily activities for a moment, you will probably find a series of routines that vary little from day to day. Check your routine upon arising; chances are that it is the same as it was yesterday and the day before. Also, you probably follow the same route to work or school and even from class to class. Few changes.

Why are we in such a rut? People sense the stress that comes with change and thus tend to avoid change. But sometimes change is someone else's idea, an idea forced upon you. So, not only is the change set in motion externally, but it is accompanied by fear of diminished control. This is often how the stage is set at the first mention of the word *computer*.

## The Systems Analyst

The boss tells you someone is coming to look over the work situation and ask you a few questions, "get a fix on the work flow, maybe see if we can't streamline some things and get them on a computer system."

Your ears perk up. A computer? Suddenly you feel very nervous. They're going to take your job and give it to a computer! Congratulations. You are about to be visited by a systems analyst.

A systems analyst with any experience, however, knows that people are uneasy about having their job situations investigated, that they may be nervous about computers, and that they may react adversely by withholding their cooperation (sometimes subtly, sometimes quite aggressively). Attitudes depend somewhat on prior experience with computer systems.

### The Analyst and the System

What is a systems analyst? Although we shall describe a systems project more formally later in the chapter, let us start by defining what we mean by the words *system*, *analysis*, and *design*. A **system** is an organized set of related components established to accomplish a certain task. There are natural systems, such as the cardiovascular system, but many systems have been planned and deliberately put into place by people. For example, the lines you stand in, stations you go to, and forms you fill out on your college's registration day comprise a system to get qualified students into the right classes. A **computer system** is a system that has a computer as one of its components.

**Systems analysis** is the process of studying an existing system to determine how it works and how it meets user needs. Systems analy-

### THE PERILS OF CHANGE

This true story illustrates the possible effects of change on people in the workplace.

Alice had been the resident sage in the quality-control department for 23 years. No subject was too obscure for Alice—she always knew the answer—so it was natural for all the newer employees to turn to her with their questions. Alice was queen of the realm.

When the new computer system was installed, Alice felt a real loss of status. The tasks she had learned over the years were performed by the computer, which seemed to have all the answers. Other clerks, however, experienced an exhilarating sense of independence. Alice noted their enthusiasm and also their errors, which she documented and presented to her manager with a solemn recommendation that the new system be scratched. The manager recognized Alice's identity crisis and arranged for her to have extra computer training, which she then passed on to the other clerks.

## THE MICROCOMPUTER CORNER

### On the Road

"Rockin' and rollin' with the PC." Ever hear that phrase? Probably not. Big names in rock entertainment do not usually take the stage to talk about the personal computers that hold the whole road-show system together. Yes, the word is *system*, and it takes a computer to keep track of all the system components.

The system components include more than the stars and a few electric guitars. In addition to electronic gear, some components are itinerary, travel, accommodations, and staff.

So new faces, in the form of personal computers, are joining the road crew of rock groups. For music business managers, the personal computer is an indispensable tool that provides information on costs, scheduling, stagehands, contracts, insurance, press releases, mailing lists, and much more.

What about the musicians themselves? Do they appreciate the machine that is keeping them on schedule, balancing their books, and keeping them from going belly up with unplanned expenses? Some musicians have used personal computers to create music, but few are interested in the business end.

sis lays the groundwork for improvements to the system. The analysis involves an investigation, which in turn usually involves establishing a relationship with the client for whom the analysis is being done and with the users of the system. The **client** is the person or organization contracting to have the work done. The **users** are people who will have contact with the system, usually employees and customers. For instance, in the college registration example, the client is the administration, and the users are both the school employees and the students.

**Systems design** is the process of developing a plan for an improved system, based on the results of the systems analysis. For instance, the analysis phase may reveal that students waste time standing in lines when they register in the closing weeks of the fall semester. The new system design might involve plans for a preregistration process.

The **systems analyst** normally performs both analysis and design. (The term *systems designer* is not common, although it is used in some places.) In some computer installations a person who is officially a programmer may also do some systems analysis and may have the title programmer/analyst. Indeed, most persons who get into systems analysis do so by way of programming. Starting out as a programmer helps the analyst appreciate computer-related problems that arise in analysis and design work. As we shall see, programmers depend on systems analysts for specifications from which to design programs.

A systems analysis and design project does not spring out of thin air. There must be an *impetus*—motivation—for change and related *authority* for the change. The impetus for change may be the result of an internal force, such as the organization's management deciding a computer could be useful in warehousing and inventory, or an external force such as government reporting requirements or

**Figure 12-1   Impetus for change.** Internal and external sources can initiate a system change.

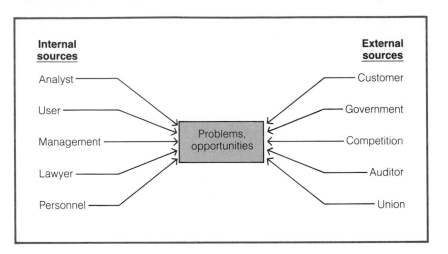

customer complaints about billing (Figure 12-1). Authority for the change, of course, comes from higher management.

## The Systems Analyst as Change Agent

The systems analyst fills the role of **change agent.** That is, the analyst must be the catalyst or persuader who overcomes the natural inertia and reluctance to change within an organization. The key to success is to involve the people of the client organization in the development of the new system. The common industry phrase is **user involvement,** and nothing could be more important to the success of the system. The finest system in the world will not suffice if users do not perceive it as useful. Users must be involved in the process from beginning to end. The systems analyst must monitor the user pulse regularly to make sure that the system being planned is one that will meet user needs.

## What It Takes to Be a Systems Analyst

Not every programmer aspires to the job of systems analyst. Before we can understand what kind of person might make a good systems analyst, we need to look at the kinds of things an analyst does. The systems analyst has three principal functions:

■ **Coordination.** An analyst must coordinate schedules and system-related tasks with a number of people: the analyst's own manager; the programmers working with the system; the system's users, from clerks to top management; the vendors selling the computer equipment; and a host of others, such as postal employees handling mailings and carpenters doing installation.

■ **Communication, both oral and written.** The analyst may be called upon to make oral presentations to clients, users, and others involved with the system. The analyst provides written reports—documentation—on the results of the analysis and the goals and means of the design. These documents may range from a few pages long to a few inches thick.

- **Planning and design.** The systems analyst, with the participation of members of the client organization, plans and designs the new system. This function involves all the activities from the beginning of the project until the final implementation of the system.

With these as principal functions, the kind of personal qualities that are desirable in a systems analyst must be apparent: an *analytical mind* and good *communication skills*. Perhaps not so obvious, however, are qualities such as *self-discipline* and *self-direction*—a systems analyst often works without close supervision. An analyst must have good *organizational skills* to be able to keep track of all the information about the system. An analyst also needs *creativity* to envision the new system. Finally, an analyst needs the *ability to work without tangible results*. There can be long dry spells when the analyst moves numbly from meeting to meeting, and it can seem that little is being accomplished.

Let us suppose that you are blessed with these admirable qualities and that you have become a systems analyst. You are given a job to do. How will you go about it?

## How a Systems Analyst Works: Overview of the Systems Life Cycle

Whether you are investigating how to improve registration procedures at your college or any other task, you will proceed by using the **systems life cycle,** illustrated in Figure 12-2.

**Figure 12-2  Systems life cycle.**

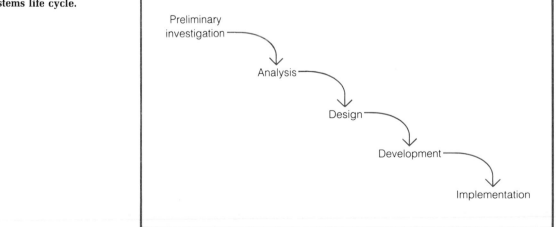

The systems life cycle has five phases:

1.  Preliminary investigation—determining the problem
2.  Analysis—understanding the existing system
3.  Design—planning the new system
4.  Development—doing the work to bring the new system into being
5.  Implementation—converting to the new system

These simple explanations for each phase will be expanded to full-blown discussions in subsequent sections. As you read about the phases of a systems project, follow the Swift Sport Shoes inventory case study in the adjacent boxes. Although space prohibits us from presenting a complete analysis and design project, this case study gives the flavor of the real thing. Let us begin at the beginning.

# Phase 1: Preliminary Investigation

The **preliminary investigation**—often called the **feasibility study** or **system survey**—is the initial investigation, a brief study of the problem. It consists of the groundwork necessary to determine if the systems project should be pursued. You, as the systems analyst, need to determine what the problem is and what to do about it. The net result will be a rough plan for how—and if—to proceed with the project.

Essentially this means you must be able to describe the problem. To do this, you will work with the users. One of your tools will be an **organization chart,** which is a hierarchical drawing showing management by name and title. Figure 12-3 shows an example of an organization chart. Constructing such a chart is not an idle task. If you are to work effectively within the organization, you have to understand what the lines of authority through the formal communication channels are.

## Problem Definition: Nature, Scope, Objectives

Your initial aim is to define the problem. You and the users must come to an agreement on these points: You must agree on the nature of the problem, and then designate a limited scope. In the process you will also determine what the objectives of the project are. Figure 12-4 shows an overview of the problem definition process, and Figure 12-5 gives an example related to the Swift Sport Shoes project.

### Nature of the Problem
Begin by determining the true nature of the problem. Sometimes what appears to be the problem turns out to be, on a

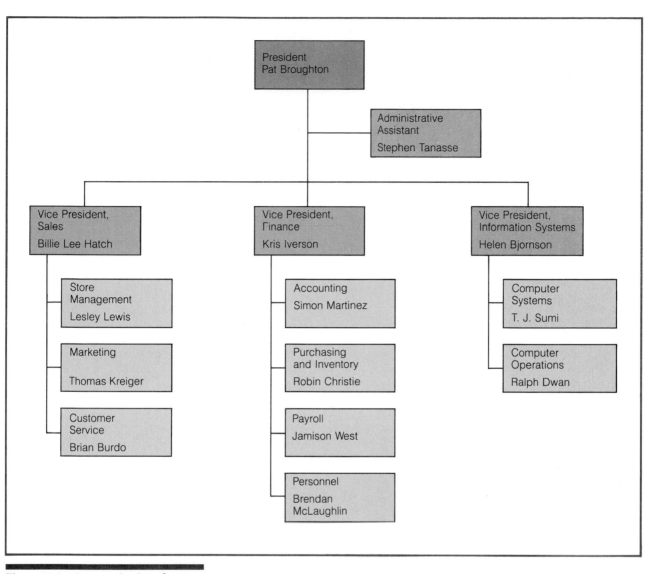

**Figure 12-3   An organization chart.**
The chart shows the lines of authority and formal communication channels. This example shows the organizational setup for Swift Sport Shoes, a chain of stores.

closer look, only a symptom. For example, suppose you are examining customer complaints of late deliveries. Your brief study may reveal that the problem is not in the shipping department, as you first thought, but in the original ordering process.

### Scope

Establishing the scope of the problem is critical because problems tend to expand if no firm boundaries are established. Limitations are also necessary in order to stay within the eventual budget and schedule. So in the beginning the analyst and user must agree on the scope of the project: what the new or revised system is supposed to do—and not do. If the scope is too broad the project will never be finished, but if the scope is too narrow it may not meet user needs.

---

### SWIFT SPORT SHOES: PHASE 1

*Preliminary Investigation*

You are employed as a systems analyst by Software Systems, Inc., a company offering packaged and custom software as well as consulting services. Software Systems has received a request for a systems analyst from Swift Sport Shoes, a chain of stores carrying a huge selection of footwear for every kind of sport. Your boss hands you this assignment, telling you to contact company officer Kris Iverson.

In your initial meeting with Mr. Iverson, who is Vice President of Finance, you learn that the first Swift store opened in San Francisco in 1974. The store has been profitable since the second year. Nine new stores have been added in the city and nearby shopping malls. These stores also show a net profit; Swift has ridden the crest of the fitness boom. But even though sales have been gratifying, Mr. Iverson is convinced that costs are higher than they should be.

In particular, Mr. Iverson is disturbed about inventory problems, which are causing frequent stock shortages and increasing customer dissatisfaction. The company has a superminicomputer at the headquarters office, where management offices are. Although there is a small data processing staff, their experience is mainly in batch financial systems. Mr. Iverson envisions more sophisticated technology for an inventory system and figures that outside expertise is needed to design it. He introduces you to Robin Christie, who is in charge of purchasing and inventory. Mr. Iverson also tells you that he has sent a memo to all company officers and store managers, indicating the purpose of your presence and his support of a study of the current system. Before the end of your visit with Mr. Iverson, the two of you construct the organization chart shown in Figure 12-3.

In subsequent interviews with Ms. Christie and other Swift personnel, you find that deteriorating customer service seems to be due to lack of information about inventory supplies. Together, you and Ms. Christie determine the problem definition, as shown in Figure 12-5. Mr. Iverson accepts your report, in which you outline the problem definition and suggest a full analysis.

### *Objectives*

You will soon come to understand what the user needs—that is, what the user thinks the system should be able to do. You will want to express these needs as objectives. Examine the objectives for the Swift inventory process. The people who run the existing inventory system already know what such a system must do. It remains for you and them to work out how this can be achieved on a computer system. In the next phase, the systems analysis phase, you will produce a more specific list of system requirements, based on these objectives.

### Wrapping Up the Preliminary Investigation

The preliminary investigation, which is necessarily brief, should result in some sort of report, perhaps only a few pages long, telling management what you found and listing your recommendations. At this point management has three choices: They can (1) drop the matter; (2) fix the problem immediately, if it is simple; or (3) authorize you to go on to the next phase for a closer look.

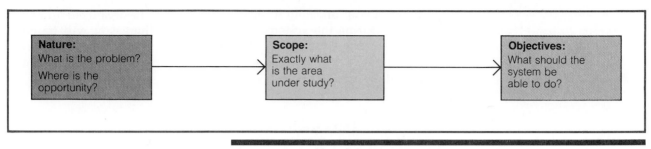

**Nature:**
What is the problem?

Where is the opportunity?

**Scope:**
Exactly what is the area under study?

**Objectives:**
What should the system be able to do?

**Figure 12-4   Problem definition overview.**

```
SWIFT SPORT SHOES: PROBLEM DEFINITION

True Nature of the Problem

The nature of the problem is the existing manual
inventory system. In particular:

-Products are frequently out of stock

-There is little interstore communication about
 stock items

-Store managers have no information about stock
 levels on a day-to-day basis

-Ordering is done haphazardly


Scope

The scope of the project will be limited to the
development of an inventory system using appropriate
computer technology.


Objectives

The new automated inventory system should provide
the following:

-Adequate stock maintained in stores

-Automatic stock reordering

-Stock distribution among stores

-Management access to current inventory information

-Ease of use

-Reduced operating costs of the inventory function
```

**Figure 12-5   Problem definition.** The nature and scope of the problem along with system objectives are shown for the Swift Sport Shoes system.

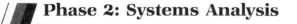

## Phase 2: Systems Analysis

Let us suppose management has decided to continue. Remember that the purpose of **systems analysis** is to understand the existing system. A related goal is to establish the system requirements. The best way to understand a system is to gather all the data you can about it; this data must then be organized and analyzed. During the systems analysis phase, then, you will be concerned with (1) data gathering and (2) data analysis. Keep in mind that the system being analyzed may or may not already be a computerized system.

## Data Gathering

Data gathering is expensive and requires a lot of legwork and time. There is no standard procedure for gathering data because each system is unique. But there are certain sources that are commonly used:

- Written documents
- Interviews
- Questionnaires
- Observation
- Sampling

Sometimes you will use all these sources, but in most cases it will be appropriate to use some and not others. All references to data gathering techniques assume that you have the proper authority and the cooperation of the client organization before proceeding.

### *Written Documents*

These include procedures manuals, reports, forms, and any other kind of material bearing on the problem that you find in the organization. You may find very few documents and no trail to follow. Sometimes the opposite is true: There are so many documents that it is difficult to know how to sift through them. Thus, judgment is required, or you will spend hours reading outdated reports or manuals that no one follows. In particular, take time to get a copy of each form an organization uses. It is especially helpful if you can obtain both clean and used copies, so you can see how the forms are really used. (The user may need to delete confidential information—such as customer names—from filled-in forms before letting you see them.)

### *Interviews*

This method of data gathering has advantages and disadvantages. A key advantage is that interviews are flexible; as the interviewer, you can change the direction of your questions if you perceive a fertile area of investigation. Another bonus is that you can probe with open-ended questions that people would balk at answering on paper. You will find that some respondents yield more information in an interview than they would if they had to commit themselves in writing. You can also observe the respondent's voice inflection and body motions, which may tell you more than words alone. Finally, of course, there is the bonus of getting to know clients better and establishing a rapport with them—an important factor in promoting user involvement in the system from the beginning.

## SOME TIPS FOR SUCCESSFUL INTERVIEWING

- Plan questions in advance—even if you vary from them during the interview.
- Listen carefully to the answers and observe the respondent's voice inflection and body movements for clues to evaluate responses.
- Dress and behave in a business-like manner.
- Avoid technical jargon.
- Respect the respondent's schedule.
- Avoid office gossip and discussion of the respondent's personal problems.

Interviews have certain drawbacks. They are unquestionably time-consuming and therefore expensive. You will not have the time or the money to interview large numbers of people. If you need to find out about procedures from 40 mail clerks, for example, you are better off using a questionnaire. Another disadvantage of interviews is that your client may sit in stony silence or give monosyllabic answers. You may, however, be able to gain trust as you go along.

Interviews are of two types, structured and unstructured. A **structured interview** includes only questions that have been planned and written out in advance. The interviewer sticks to those questions and asks no others. A structured interview is useful when it is desirable—or required by law—to ask identical questions of several people. However, the unstructured interview is often more productive. An **unstructured interview** includes questions prepared in advance, but the interviewer is willing to vary from the line of questioning and pursue other subjects if they seem appropriate. In both cases, however, it is important to plan questions in advance. You should never go into an interview with the idea of just chatting in hope that something useful will turn up.

### Questionnaires

Unlike interviews, questionnaires can be used to get information from large groups. Questionnaires can save the time and expense of interviewing. They allow people to respond anonymously—the respondents just complete forms and turn them in—and, presumably, they respond more truthfully. Questionnaires do have disadvantages, however. A great many questionnaires will simply lie at the bottom of respondents' in-baskets and never be returned. Some people will not return them even if there are strong inducements because they are wary of putting anything on paper, even anonymously. And the questionnaires you do get back may contain biased answers.

Because accurate, complete answers are so difficult to obtain, some people take classes on the subject of questionnaire construction. Although you need not go to such lengths, some reading on the subject is worthwhile. There are many types of questionnaires; the ballot-box type (in which the respondent simply checks off "yes" or "no") and the qualified response (in which one rates agreement or disagreement with the question on a scale from, say, 1 to 5) are two common examples. In general, people prefer a questionnaire that is quick and simple. Analysts also prefer simple questionnaires because they are easier to tabulate. If you have long, open-ended questions, such as "Please describe your job functions," you should probably save them for an interview.

### Observation

As an analyst and observer, you go into the organization and watch how data flows, who interrelates with whom, how paper moves from desk to desk, and how it comes into and leaves the organization. Normally you make arrangements with a group super-visor, who may provide you a desk, and you return on more than one occasion so that the people under observation become used to your presence. The purpose of your visits is known to the members of the organization. One form of observation is **participant observation;** in this form the analyst temporarily joins the activities of the group. This practice may be useful in studying a complicated organization.

### Sampling

You may need to collect data about quantities, costs, time periods, and other factors relevant to the system. How many phone orders can be taken by an order entry clerk in an hour? If you are dealing with a major mail-order organization, such as L. L. Bean in Maine, this type of question may be best answered through a proce-dure called sampling: You need not gather all the data, only a certain representative subset. For example, instead of observing all 75 clerks filling orders for an hour, pick a sample of three or four. Or, in the case of a high volume of paper output, such as customer bills, you could collect a random sample of a few dozen.

Work sampling is particularly appropriate when there is a large volume of data. It would be too expensive to check all the data, but the same information can be obtained by using sampling. How much data is enough? Knowing how much and what data to select is a job for specialists who use statistical techniques. The actual techniques are beyond the scope of this book. Some analysts are trained in sta-tistical sampling; more often the analyst works with a statistician to obtain the needed information.

## Data Analysis

Your data gathering processes will probably produce an alarming amount of paper and a strong need to get organized. It is now time to turn your attention to the second activity of this phase, data analysis. What, indeed, are you going to do with all the data you have gathered? There are a variety of tools—charts and diagrams—used to analyze data, not all of them appropriate for every system. You should become familiar with the techniques, then use the tools that suit you at the time. We shall consider two typical tools: data flow diagrams and decision tables.

The reasons for data analysis are related to the basic functions of the systems analysis phase: to show how the current system works and to determine the system requirements. In addition, data analysis materials will serve as the basis for documentation of the system.

### Data Flow Diagrams

A **data flow diagram (DFD)** is a sort of road map that graphically shows the flow of data through a system. It is a valuable tool for depicting present procedures and data flow. Although data flow diagrams can be used in the design process, they are particu-

---

**CASE STUDY**

## SWIFT SPORT SHOES: PHASE 2

### Systems Analysis

With the assistance of Ms. Christie, you learn more about the current inventory system. She also helps set up interviews with store managers and arranges to have you observe procedures in the stores and at the warehouse. As the number of stores has increased, significant expansion has taken place in all areas related to inventory. These areas include sales, scope of merchandise, and number of vendors.

Out-of-stock situations are common. The stock shortages are not uniform across all ten stores, however; frequently one store will be out of an item that the central warehouse or another store has on hand. The present system is not effective at recognizing this situation and transferring merchandise. There is a tendency for stock to be reordered only when the shelf is empty or nearly so. Inventory-related costs are significant, especially those for special orders of some stock items. Reports to management are minimal and often too late to be useful. Finally, there is no way to correlate order quantities with past sales records, future projections, or inventory situations.

During this period you also analyze the data as it is gathered. You prepare data flow diagrams of the various activities relating to inventory. Figure 12-7 shows the flow of data for purchasing in the existing system. You prepare decision tables, such as the one shown in Figure 12-8b.

Your written report to Mr. Iverson includes the list of system requirements shown in Figure 12-9.

---

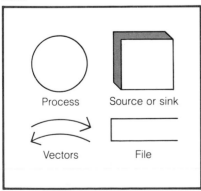

**Figure 12-6   Data flow diagram symbols.**

Process

Source or sink

Vectors

File

larly useful for facilitating communication between you and the users during the analysis phase. Suppose, for example, you spend a couple of hours with a McDonald's franchise manager, talking about the paperwork that keeps the burgers and the customers flowing. You would probably make copious notes on what goes where. But that is only the data gathering function—now you must somehow analyze your findings. You could come back on another day with pages of narrative for the manager to review or, instead, show an easy-to-follow picture. Like everyone else, users prefer pictures.

Data flow diagrams were developed by Gane and Sarson, who wrote a book about them in 1979. DFDs have been promoted heavily by Tom DeMarco, who wrote his own book. The notation used here is DeMarco's, because it is informal and easy to draw and read.

The four elements of a data flow diagram are processes, files, sources and sinks, and labeled vectors, as shown in Figure 12-6. Note also the DFD for Swift Sport Shoes (Figure 12-7) as you follow this discussion.

**Processes** are the actions taken on the data—comparing, checking, stamping, authorizing, filing, and so forth. Processes are represented by circles, often called bubbles. A **file** is a repository of data. You may think of a file as a tape or disk file or even an ordered set of papers in a file cabinet. Any of these is valid, and so are papers on a clipboard, mail in an in-basket, or blank envelopes in a supply bin. In a DFD a file is represented by an open-ended box.

A **source** is a data origin outside the organization. To know what is outside the organization, you must first define the organization. An example is a payment sent to a department store by a charge

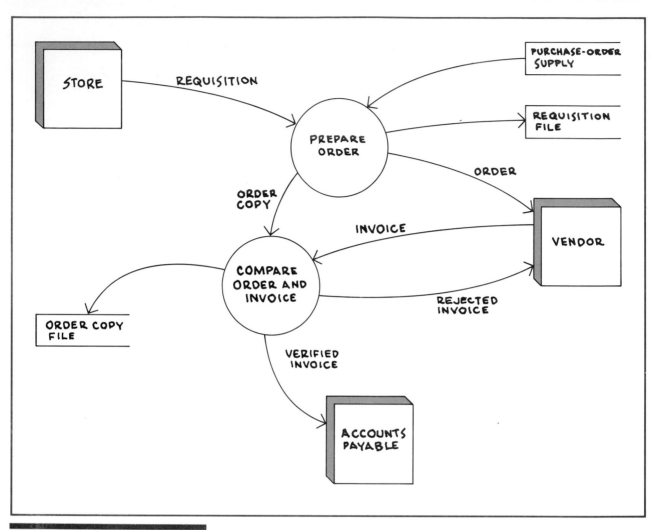

**Figure 12-7  A data flow diagram.**
This "map" shows the current flow of data in the purchasing department at Swift Sport Shoes. The diagram (greatly simplified) includes authorization of purchases for goods, purchase-order preparation, and verification of the vendor's invoice against the purchase order. Note that the stores, vendors, and accounts payable are in square boxes because they are outside the purchasing department.

customer. In this case the customer is not actually part of the department store; since the customer is sending data into the organization, the customer is a source of data. A **sink** is a destination for data going outside the organization; an example is the bank that is sent money from the accounts receivable organization. A source or a sink is represented by a square. **Vectors** are simply arrows, lines with directional notation. A vector must come from or go to a process bubble. An important rule about vectors is that they must be labeled with the data they carry. There is one exception to the labeling rule: Arrows going to or from a file may not need to be labeled because the file is already annotated.

The process of drawing data flow diagrams is a little more complicated than this and beyond the scope of this book. If you take advanced training as an analyst, you will probably learn this technique. One more point: Software packages are available to draw and modify data flow diagrams automatically.

**Figure 12-8  Decision tables.** (a) Format of a decision table. The structure of the table is organized according to the logic that "If this condition exists or is met, then do this." (b) A decision table example. This decision table, which describes the current ordering procedure at Swift Sport Shoes, takes into consideration whether a requisition for goods from a store is valid, ascertains if the wanted goods are available in the warehouse or some other Swift store, checks the order volume to see if it is sufficient to place an inventory order, and checks to see if it is a special order for a customer. Examine rule 4. The requisition is valid, so we proceed. The desired goods are not available in either the warehouse or in another store, so they must be ordered. However, there is not the required volume of customer demand to place a standard inventory order now, so the requisition is put on hold until there is. (In other words, this customer order will be joined with others.) And, finally, since this is a special customer order and the order is on hold, a back-order notice is sent.

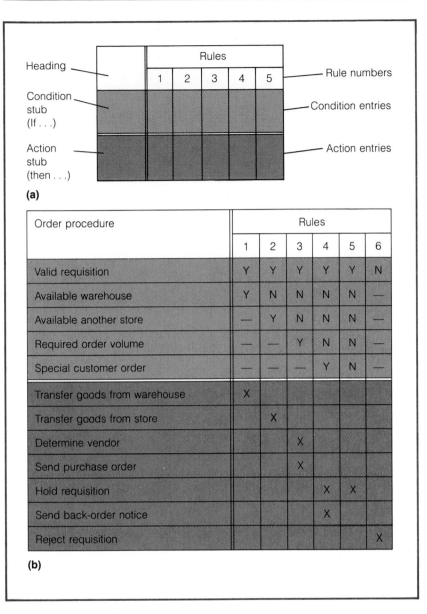

(a)

| Order procedure | Rules | | | | | |
|---|---|---|---|---|---|---|
| | 1 | 2 | 3 | 4 | 5 | 6 |
| Valid requisition | Y | Y | Y | Y | Y | N |
| Available warehouse | Y | N | N | N | N | — |
| Available another store | — | Y | N | N | N | — |
| Required order volume | — | — | Y | N | N | — |
| Special customer order | — | — | — | Y | N | — |
| Transfer goods from warehouse | X | | | | | |
| Transfer goods from store | | X | | | | |
| Determine vendor | | | X | | | |
| Send purchase order | | | X | | | |
| Hold requisition | | | | X | X | |
| Send back-order notice | | | | X | | |
| Reject requisition | | | | | | X |

(b)

### Decision Tables

A **decision table,** also called a **decision logic table,** is a standard table of the logical decisions that must be made regarding potential conditions in a given system. Decision tables are useful in cases that involve a series of interrelated decisions; their use helps to ensure that no alternatives are overlooked. Programmers can code portions of programs right from a decision table. Figure 12-8a shows the format of a decision table; Figure 12-8b gives an example of a decision table that applies to the Swift Sport Shoes system.

The table works as follows: The heading indicates the procedure or problem the table is set up to solve. The numbers across the top are headings for the vertical columns. Each column represents a set of conditions and the corresponding actions; it shows a rule to be followed. The logic of the table is "If these conditions exist, then take these actions." On the left side of the table are the *condition stub*, which describes the different conditions, and the *action stub*, which describes the different actions. The condition entries are listed under the rule numbers and are either Y for *yes* if the condition exists or N for *no* if it does not. (A dash means the condition does not apply.) The action entries indicate which actions to take under a certain set of conditions.

These data analysis vehicles are typical, but the list presented here is by no means exhaustive.

## System Requirements

As we mentioned, the purpose of gathering and analyzing data is twofold: to understand the system and, as a by-product of that understanding, to establish the system requirements. The description of the system was quite broad in the preliminary investigation phase, but now you are ready to list precise system requirements. You need to determine and document specific user needs. A system that a bank teller uses, for example, needs to be able to retrieve a customer record on the CRT screen within five seconds. The importance of accurate requirements cannot be overemphasized because the design of the new system will be based on the system requirements. Note the requirements for the Swift system, in Figure 12-9.

## Report to Management

When you have finished the systems analysis phase, you present a report to management. This comprehensive report, part of the continuing process of documentation, summarizes the problems

**Figure 12-9  System requirements.** These are the requirements for an inventory system for Swift Sport Shoes.

```
SWIFT SPORT SHOES: REQUIREMENTS

The requirements for the Swift Sport Shoes inventory
system are as follows:

-Capture inventory data from sales transactions

-Implement automatic inventory reordering

-Implement a standardized interstore transfer system

-Provide both on-demand and scheduled management reports

-Provide security and accounting controls throughout the
 system

-Provide a user-oriented system whose on-line usage can
 be learned by a new user in one training class

-Reduce operating costs of the inventory function by 20%
```

you found in the system, describes the system requirements, and makes recommendations on what course to take next. If management decides to pursue the project, you move on to phase 3.

# Phase 3: Systems Design

The **systems design** phase is the phase in which you actually plan the new system. This phase is divided into two subphases: **preliminary design,** in which the analyst establishes the new system concept, followed by **detail design,** in which the analyst determines exact design specifications. The reason this phase is divided into two parts is that an analyst wants to make sure management approves the overall plan before spending time on details.

## Preliminary Design

The first task of preliminary design is to review the system requirements, then consider some of the major aspects of a system. Should the system be centralized or distributed? Should the system be on-line? Should packaged software be purchased as opposed to having programmers write new software? Can the system be run on the user's microcomputers? How will input data be captured? What kind of reports will be needed?

The questions can go on and on. Eventually, together with key personnel from the user organization, you determine an overall plan. In fact, it is common to offer alternative plans, called **candidates.** Each candidate meets the user requirements but with variations in features and costs. The chosen candidate is usually the one that best meets the user needs and is flexible enough to meet future needs. The selected plan is expanded and described so that it can be understood by both the user and the analyst.

At this point it is wise to make a formal presentation of the plan or perhaps all of the alternatives. The point is that you do not want to commit time and energy to—nor does the user want to pay for—a detailed design until you and the user agree on the basic design. Such presentations often include a drawing of the system from a user perspective, such as the one shown in Figure 12-10 for the Swift Sport Shoes system. At this point you want to emphasize system benefits also—see the list in Figure 12-11.

## Prototyping

The idea of building a prototype—a sort of guinea-pig model of the system—has taken a sharp upward turn in popularity recently. Considered from a systems viewpoint, a **prototype** is a limited working system—or subset of a system—that is developed quickly, sometimes in just a few days. A prototype is a working

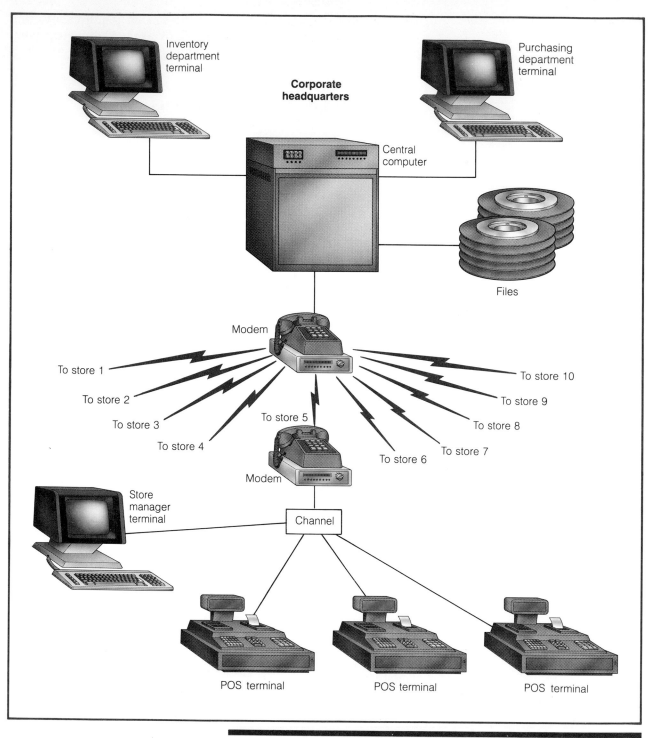

**Figure 12-10   Overview of the system.** This overview shows the Swift Sport Shoes inventory system from a user point of view. *Input* data is from POS terminals. Except for local editing, *processing* takes place on the central computer. All *storage* files are located at the central site. *Output* is in the form of printed reports and screen displays.

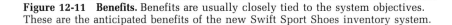

```
SWIFT SPORT SHOES: ANTICIPATED BENEFITS

-Better inventory control

-Improved customer service

-Improved management information

-Reduced inventory costs

-Improved employee morale
```

**Figure 12-11   Benefits.** Benefits are usually closely tied to the system objectives. These are the anticipated benefits of the new Swift Sport Shoes inventory system.

model, one that can be tinkered with and fine tuned. The idea is that users can get an idea of what the system might be like before it is fully developed. If they are not satisfied, they can revise their requirements before a lot has been invested in developing the new system.

Could you adopt this approach to systems development? It seems at odds with this chapter's systems life cycle, which promotes doing steps in the proper order. And yet, some analysts in the computer industry are making good use of prototypes. We need to ask how and why. The "how" begins with prototyping tools.

### Prototyping Tools

The prototype approach exploits advances in computer technology and uses powerful high-level software tools. These software packages allow analysts to build quick systems in response to user needs. In particular recall the fourth-generation languages we discussed in Chapter 10. One of their key advantages was that they could be used to produce something quickly. The systems produced can then be refined and modified as they are used, in a continuous process, until the fit between user and system is acceptable.

### Why Prototyping?

Many organizations use prototyping on a limited basis. For example, prototyping a certain data entry sequence, a particular screen output, or an especially complex or questionable part of a design. That is, prototyping does not necessarily have the scope of the final system. Some organizations use prototyping on a throwaway basis, using it only to get a grip on the requirements; then they begin again and go through the systems life cycle formally. Other organizations start with a prototype and keep massaging it until it becomes the final and accepted version. In either case a prototype forces users to get actively involved.

Prototyping is a possibility if you work in an organization that has quick-build software and management support of this departure from traditional systems procedures.

### *Prototype Results*

What is the net result of a prototype system? What will it produce for users? If the whole system is being prototyped, it initially will look something like this: minimum input data, no editing checks, incomplete files, limited security checks, sketchy reports, and minimum documentation. But actual software uses real data to produce real output. Remember that prototyping is an iterative process; the system is changed again and again.

## 7 Detail Design

Let us say that the users have accepted your design proposal—you are on your way. You must now develop detail design specifications. This is a time-consuming part of the project, but it is relatively straightforward.

In this phase every facet of the system is considered in detail. Here is a list of some detail design activities: designing output forms and screens, planning input data forms and procedures, drawing system flowcharts, planning file access methods and record formats, planning database interfaces, planning data communications interfaces, designing system security controls, and considering human factors. Some analysts choose to plan the overall logic at this stage, preparing program structure charts, pseudocode, and the like.

This list is not comprehensive, nor will all activities on it be used for all systems. These are just some of the possibilities. Normally, in the detail design phase, parts of the systems are considered in this order:

- Output requirements
- Input requirements
- Files and databases
- System processing
- System controls and backup

### *Output Requirements*

Before you can do anything, you must know what the client wants the system to produce—the output. You must also consider the *medium* of the output—paper, CRT screen, microfilm, and so on. In addition, you must determine the *type* of reports needed (summary, exception, and so on) and the *contents* of the output—what data is needed for the reports. What *forms* the output will be printed on is also a consideration; they may need to be custom printed if they go outside the organization to customers or stockholders. You may wish to determine the report format using a **printer spacing chart,** which shows the position of headings, the spacing between columns, and the location of date and page numbers (Figure 12-12). You may also use screen reports, mock-ups on paper of how the CRT will respond to user queries. A sample screen report is shown in Figure 12-13.

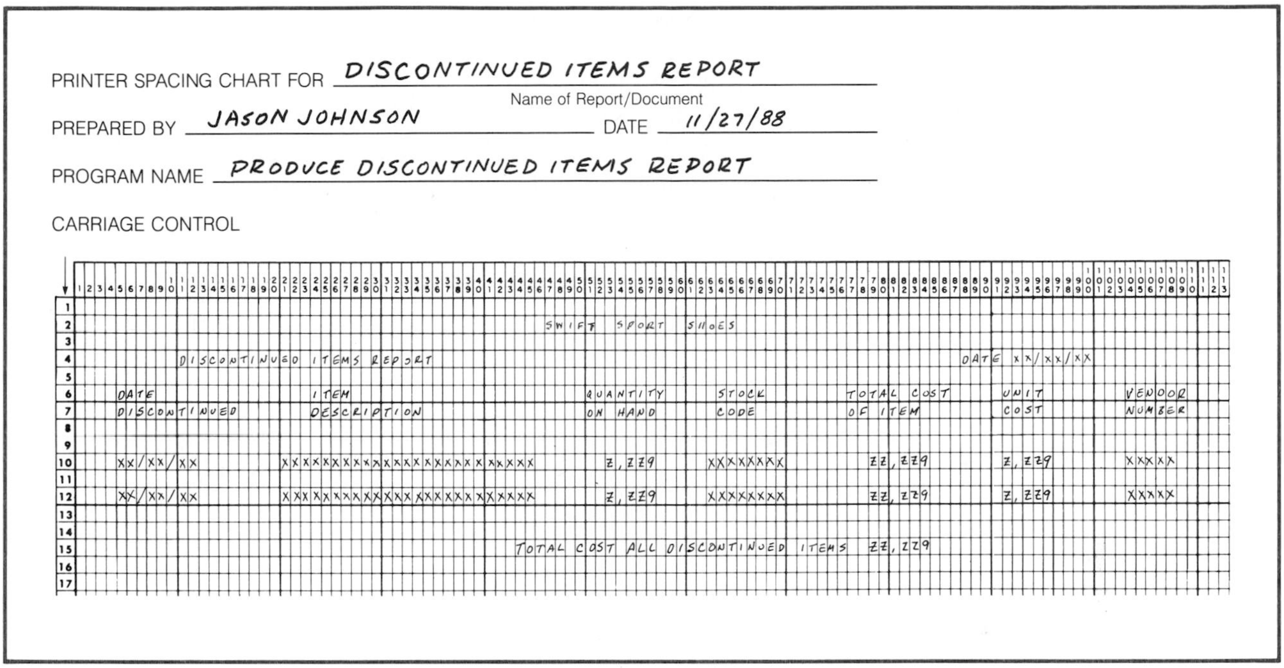

**Figure 12-12   Example of a printer spacing chart.** This chart shows how a systems analyst wishes the report format to look—headings, columns, and so on—when displayed on a printer. This example shows discontinued items, a report that is part of the new Swift Sport Shoes system.

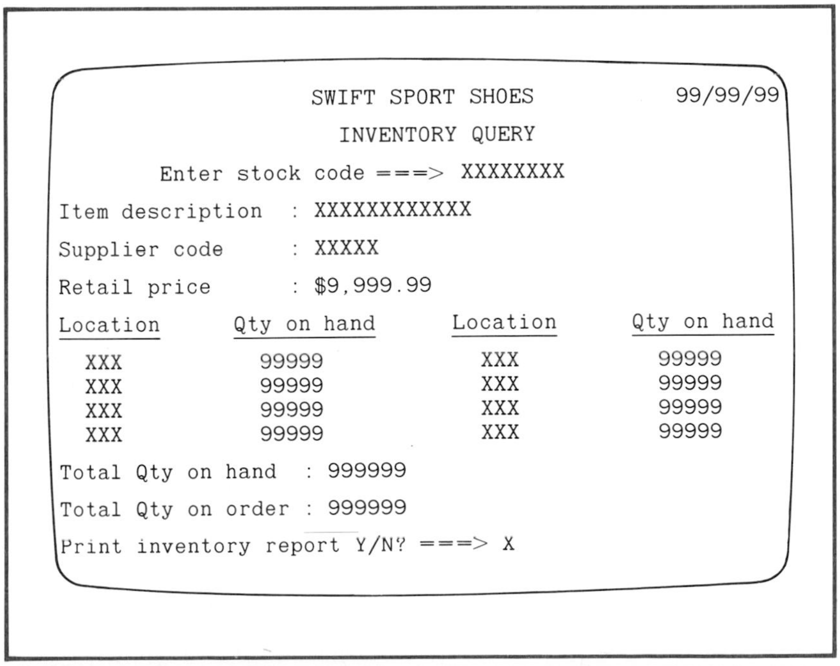

**Figure 12-13   Example of the design for a screen report.** This screen report has been designed as part of the Swift Sport Shoes system to give information about how much of a given stock item is in each store. The report shows an approximation of what the user will see on the CRT after entering a stock code.

### Input Requirements

Perhaps you expected to have to consider input first, before output, but that is not so; you first need to know what you want the system to produce. However, once your desired output is determined, you must consider what kind of input is required to produce it. First you must consider the input *medium:* Will you try to capture data at the source via POS terminals? Will you put it on floppy disks? Next you must consider *content* again—what fields are needed, the order in which they come, and the like. This in turn may involve designing *forms* that will organize data before it is entered. Like questionnaire construction, forms design is a whole subject by itself. For instance, for the sake of brevity, a form may require the person filling it out to use some codes (such as F for *female* or M for *male* or numbers corresponding to one's level of education). You need to plan some kind of input *editing* process, a check as to whether the data is reasonable. Such a check can take many forms. In a scrutiny of salaries, for instance, it would be reasonable for the president to earn a six-figure salary, but a six-figure salary would not be reasonable for someone working in the mail room. Finally, you need to consider input *volume,* particularly the volume at peak periods. Can the system handle it? A mail-order house, for instance, may have to be ready for higher sales of expensive toys at Christmastime than at other times of the year.

### Files and Databases

You need to consider how the files in your computer system will be organized: sequentially, directly, with an index, or by some other method. You also need to decide how the files should be accessed. They might be organized as indexed files but be accessed directly or sequentially, for example. You need to determine the format of records making up the data files. If the system has one or more databases—collections of interrelated data (a subject we shall cover at length in Chapter 16)—then you will have to coordinate your systems design efforts with the database administrator, the person responsible for controlling and updating databases.

### Systems Processing

Just as you drew a flow diagram to describe the old system, now you need to show the flow of data in the new system. One method is to use standard ANSI flowchart symbols (Figure 12-14) to illustrate what will be done and what files will be used. Figure 12-15 shows an example of a resulting **systems flowchart.** Another popular way to describe processing is the structure chart we studied in Chapter 9. Note that a systems flowchart is not the same as a logic flowchart. The systems flowchart describes only the "big picture"; a logic flowchart (which you may have used to write programs) gives detailed program logic.

## SWIFT SPORT SHOES: PHASE 3

### Systems Design

The store managers, who were uneasy at the beginning of the study, are by now enthusiastic participants in the design of the new system they are counting on for better control of their inventory. As part of the preliminary design phase, you offer three alternative system candidates for consideration. The first is a centralized system, with all processing done at the headquarters computer and batch reports generated on a daily basis. The third takes the opposite approach, placing all processing in the stores on their own minicomputers. The second candidate, the one selected, includes processing at the central site; however, data will be edited locally, at the individual stores, before transmission to the central site.

The chosen alternative makes use of point-of-sale terminals at the store checkout counters, where inventory data is captured as a by-product of the sale. There will be continuous two-way data transmission between the stores and the central site. All files will be maintained at the central site.

Output will be in two forms: printed reports and on-demand status reports on terminal screens available to store managers locally and to department managers in the headquarters office. Figure 12-10 shows the overall design from a user viewpoint. The key ingredient of the proposed solution is an automatic reorder procedure: The computer generates orders for any product shown to be below the preset reorder mark.

You make a formal presentation to Mr. Iverson and other members of company management. Slides you prepared on a microcomputer (with special presentation software) accent your points visually. After a brief statement of the problem, you list anticipated benefits to the company; these are listed in Figure 12-11. You explain the design in general terms and describe the expected costs and schedules. With the money saved from the reduced inventory expenses, you project that the system development costs will be repaid in three years. Swift Sport Shoes management accepts your recommendations, and you proceed with the detail design phase.

You design printed reports and screen displays for managers; samples are shown in Figures 12-12 and 12-13. There are many other exacting and time-consuming activities associated with detail design. Although space prohibits discussing them, we list some of these tasks here to give you the flavor of the complexity: You must plan the use of wand readers to read stock codes from merchandise tags, plan to download (send) the price file daily to be stored in the POS terminals, plan all files on disk with regular backups on tape, design the records in each file and the methods to access the files, design the data communications system, draw diagrams to show the flow of the data in the system, and prepare structure charts of program modules. Figure 12-15 shows a skeleton version of a systems flowchart that represents part of the inventory processing. Some of these activities, such as data communications, require special expertise, so you may be coordinating with specialists. Several systems controls are planned, among them a unique numbering system for stock items and editing of all data input at the terminal.

You make yet another presentation on the detail design, but this time the audience has fewer managers and more technical people, including several representatives from the data processing department. Again, you are given the go-ahead to proceed.

### Systems Controls and Backup

To make sure data is input, processed, and output correctly and to prevent fraud and tampering with the computer system, you will need to institute appropriate controls. We begin with the source documents, such as time cards or sales orders. Each document should be serially numbered so the system can keep track of it. Documents are time stamped when received and grouped in batches.

**Figure 12-14   ANSI systems flowchart symbols.** These are the symbols recommended by the American National Standards Institute for systems flowcharts, which show the movement of data through a system.

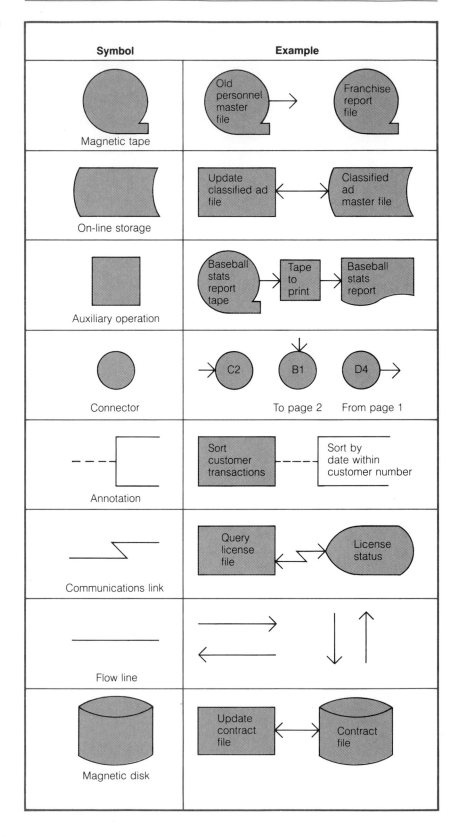

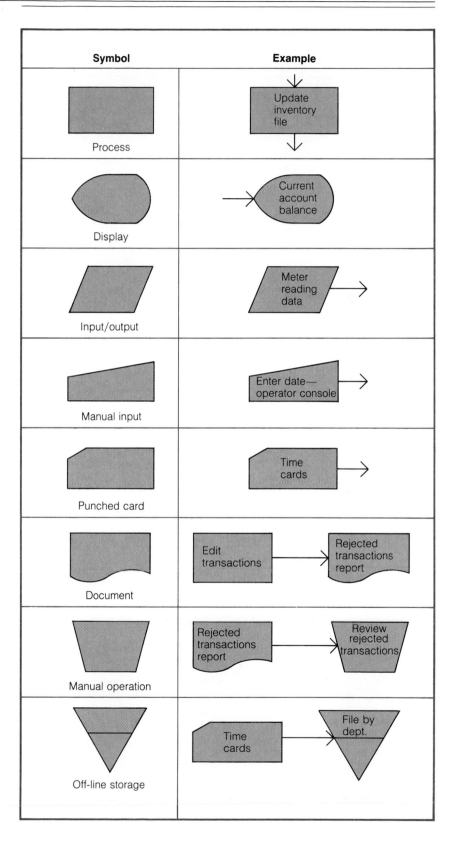

| Symbol | Example |
|---|---|
| Process | Update inventory file |
| Display | Current account balance |
| Input/output | Meter reading data |
| Manual input | Enter date— operator console |
| Punched card | Time cards |
| Document | Edit transactions → Rejected transactions report |
| Manual operation | Rejected transactions report → Review rejected transactions |
| Off-line storage | Time cards → File by dept. |

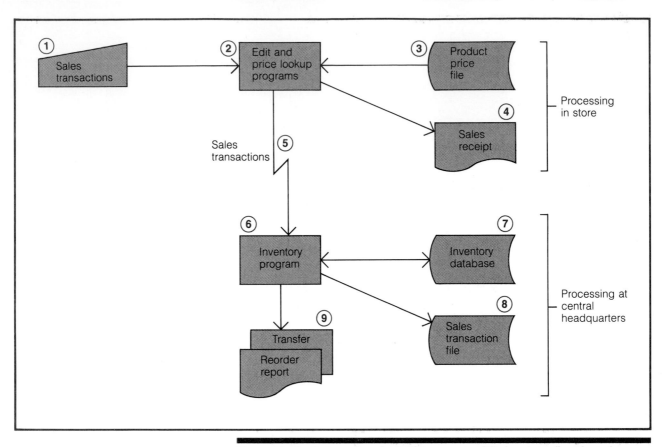

**Figure 12-15   Systems flowchart.** This very simplified systems flowchart shows part of the processing for the new Swift Sport Shoes inventory system. Note that the top half of the drawing shows processing that takes place in the store. The processing uses a sophisticated POS terminal while the customer waits. The bottom part of the drawing shows processing that is done on the computer at the central headquarters site. The clerk ① inputs sales transaction data, which ② is edited by the POS terminal processor. The POS terminal also looks up the item price from the ③ files downloaded earlier in the day from the central site, then ④ prints a sales receipt. That takes care of the customer. Meanwhile, ⑤ the sales transaction data is sent over data communications lines to the central computer, which ⑥ processes it for inventory purposes by updating the ⑦ inventory database, placing the ⑧ sales transaction on its own file for later auditing and producing ⑨ transfer and reorder reports as needed.

Each batch is labeled with the number of documents per batch; these counts are balanced against totals of the processed data. The input is controlled to make sure data is accurately converted from source documents to machine-processable form. Data input to on-line systems is backed up by **system journals,** files whose records represent the transactions made at the terminal, such as an account withdrawal through a bank teller. Processing controls include the data editing procedures we mentioned in the section on input requirements.

It is also important to plan for backup of system files; copies of transaction and master files should be made on a regular basis. These file copies are stored temporarily to back up the originals if they are inadvertently lost or damaged. Often the backup copies are stored off site for added security.

As before, the results of this phase are documented. This large and detailed document, usually referred to as the detail design specifications, is an outgrowth of the preliminary design document. A presentation often accompanies the completion of this stage. Unless something unexpected has happened, it is normal to proceed now with the development of the system.

# Phase 4: Systems Development

Finally, the system is actually going to be developed. As a systems analyst you prepare a schedule to monitor the principal activities in **systems development**—programming and testing.

## Scheduling

Figure 12-16 shows what is known as a **Gantt chart,** a bar chart commonly used to depict schedule deadlines and milestones. In our example the chart shows the work to be accomplished over a given period. It does not, however, show the number of work hours required. If you are the supervisor, it will be common practice for you to ask others on the development team to produce individual Gantt charts of their own activities.

**Figure 12-16   Gantt chart.** This bar chart shows the scheduled tasks and milestones of the Swift Sport Shoes project.

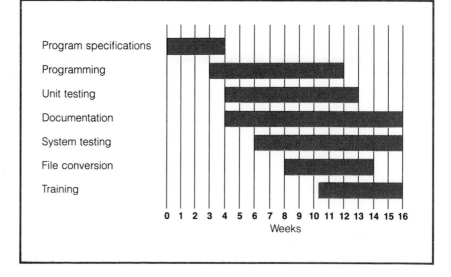

---

**CASE STUDY**

---

**SWIFT SPORT SHOES: PHASE 4**

*Systems Development*

Working closely with Dennis Harrington of data processing, you prepare a Gantt chart, as shown in Figure 12-16. This chart shows the schedule for the inventory project.

Program design specifications are prepared using pseudocode, the design tool Mr. Harrington thinks will be most useful to programmers. The programs will be written in COBOL since that is the primary language of the installation, and it is suitable for this business application. Three programmers are assigned to work with you on the project.

You work with the program-mers to develop a test plan. Some inventory data, both typical and atypical, is prepared to test the new system. You and the programmers continue to build on the documentation base by implementing the pseudocode and by preparing detailed data descriptions, logic narratives, program listings, test data results, and other related material.

---

## Programming

Until this point there has been no programming. (Sometimes people jump the gun and start programming early, but the task often has to be done over if started with incomplete specifications.) Before programming begins, you need to prepare detailed design specifications. Some of this work may already have been done as part of the design phase, but usually programmers participate in refining the design at this point. A program language is selected, although the organization may specify the use of a particular language. Design specifications can be developed through detailed logic flowcharts and pseudocode, among other methods.

## Testing

Would you write a program, then simply turn it over to the client without testing it first? Of course not. Thus, the programmers perform **unit testing,** by which they individually test their own programs, using test data. This is followed by **system testing,** which determines whether all the programs work together satisfactorily. During this process the development team uses test data to test every part of the programs. Finally, **volume testing** uses real data in large amounts. Volume testing sometimes reveals errors that do not show up with test data—errors such as table overflows.

As in every phase of the project, documentation is required. Indeed, documentation is an ongoing activity (as the Gantt chart in Figure 12-16 shows). In this phase, documentation describes the program logic and detailed data formats.

# Phase 5: Implementation

Even though **implementation** is the final phase, the analyst must still consider the following activities.

- Training
- Equipment conversion
- File conversion
- System conversion

- Auditing
- Evaluation
- Maintenance

## Training

Often systems analysts do not give training the attention it deserves because they are so concerned about the computer system itself. But a system can be no better than the people using it. A good time to start training is at some point during the testing, so that people can begin to learn how to use the system even as the development team is checking it out.

An important tool in training is the user manual, a document prepared to aid users not familiar with the computer system. The user manual can be an outgrowth of the other documentation. But user documentation is just the beginning. Any teacher knows that students learn best by doing. Besides, users are as likely to read a thick manual as they are to read a dictionary. The message is clear: Users must receive hands-on training to learn to use the system. The trainer must prepare exercises that simulate the tasks users will be required to do. For example, a hotel clerk learning a new on-line reservation system is given typical requests to fulfill and uses a terminal to practice. The user manual is used as a reference guide. Setting all this up is not a trivial task; the trainer must consider class space, equipment, data, and the users' schedules.

## Equipment Conversion

Equipment considerations vary from almost none to installing a mainframe computer and all its peripheral equipment. If you are implementing a small- or medium-size system on established equipment in a major data processing organization, then perhaps your equipment considerations will involve no more than negotiating scheduled run time and disk space. If you are purchasing a moderate amount of equipment, such as terminals and modems, then you will be concerned primarily with delivery schedules and compatibility. A major equipment purchase, on the other hand, demands a large amount of attention to detail.

For a major equipment purchase you will need site preparation advice from vendors and other equipment experts. You may be considering having walls moved! You will need to know the exact dimensions and weight of the new equipment. There are infamous stories of the new computer being too big to get through the door; one computer, in fact, had to be hoisted by ropes through a window. You will have to consider electrical capacity and wiring hookups. You may need new flooring—probably raised artificial flooring to hide cabling and ease access for repairs to large computers and related equipment. Finally, most medium-to-large machines need air conditioning and humidity control.

Microcomputer systems are far less demanding, but they too require site planning in terms of the availability of space, accessibility, and cleanliness. And, as the analyst, you are probably the one who does the actual installation.

Meanwhile, if you are waiting for equipment, where do you test the new system? There are several possibilities, none of them convenient. You could rent time on a similar computer in another installation. You could buy time on the same configuration from a full-service software house or equipment leasing company. Or you could have your own computer in place before testing begins.

## File Conversion

This activity may be very tricky if the existing files are handled manually. The data must be prepared in such a way that it is accessible to computer systems. All the contents of the file drawers in the personnel department, for instance, must now be keyed to disk or magnetic tape. Clearly, this step requires some time and often the hiring of several temporary employees to do the keying. But there is an even more pressing problem: keeping the files up-to-date while the keying is in progress. Suppose there is a change in a file whose contents have already been keyed to disk. Not only must the change be made to the manual record (which is still in use during file conversion); it must also be keyed as a transaction, so that the automated file is updated once the new system is working.

The good news is that most manual files have already been converted to some machine-accessible form. That is, rather than converting a manual system to an automated system, you will probably convert an old automated system to a better automated system. So it is likely that you will write a program to convert the old files to the format needed for the new system. This is a much speedier process.

## System Conversion

This is the stage in which you actually "pull the plug" on the old system and begin using the new one. There are four ways of handling the conversion.

---

**SWIFT SPORT SHOES: PHASE 5**

*Implementation*

While the system is being developed, you take advantage of this time to write the user and operator manuals. This is done in conjunction with your plans for training store personnel and managers in the use of the system. The training is not a trivial task, but you do not have to do all of it yourself. Training on the new POS cash registers will be done by the vendor. You plan to hold training classes for the people who will use the local micros to run programs and to send data to the computer at headquarters. You will have separate classes to train managers on retrieving data from the system

via terminal commands. In both cases training will be hands on. Company personnel should find the training enjoyable because CRT dialogue procedures are user friendly—that is, the user is instructed clearly every step of the way.

File conversion is painful. One evening after the stores close, the staff works overtime to take inventory in the stores. Temporary personnel are hired to key an inventory master file from this data. Transactions for the master file are accumulated as more purchases are made, up until the time the system is ready for use; then the master will be updated from the transactions generated by the POS terminals. After discussing the relative merits of the various system conversion methods, you and Ms. Christie agree that a pilot conversion would be

ideal. Together you decide to bring up the original store first, then add other stores to the system one or two at a time.

Mr. Iverson puts together a local team consisting of Ms. Christie, a programmer, and an accountant to evaluate the new system. Since your documentation is comprehensive, it is relatively easy for the team to check the system completely to see if it is functioning according to specifications. The evaluation report notes several positive items, including: out-of-stock conditions have almost disappeared (only two instances in one store in one month), inventory transfer among stores is a smooth operation, and store managers feel an increased sense of control. Negative items are relatively minor and can be fixed as the system goes into a maintenance operation.

---

**Direct conversion** means the user simply stops using the old system and starts using the new one—a somewhat risky method since there is no other system to fall back on if anything goes wrong. This procedure is best followed only if the old system is in unusable condition. A **phased conversion** is one in which the organization eases into the new system one step at a time so that all the users are using some of the system. In contrast, in a **pilot conversion** the entire system is used by some of the users and is extended to all users once it has proved successful. In **parallel conversion**—the most prolonged and expensive method—the old and new systems are operated simultaneously for some time, until users are satisfied that the new system performs to their standards.

System conversion is often a time of stress and confusion for all concerned. As the analyst, your credibility is on the line, for you must now come up with a usable system. During this time users are often doing double duty, trying to perform their regular jobs and simultaneously cope with a new computer system. Problems seem to appear in all areas, from input to output. Clearly, this is a period when your patience is needed.

### Auditing

Security violations, whether deliberate or unintentional, can be difficult to detect. Once data is in the system and on media such as disks, it is possible for it to be altered without any trace in the source documents—unless the systems analyst has designed an **audit trail** to trace output back to the source data. In real-time systems security violations can be particularly elusive unless all CRT terminal transactions are recorded on disk or tape for later references by auditors. Modern auditors no longer shuffle mountains of paper; instead, they have computer programs of their own to monitor applications programs and data.

### Evaluation

Is the system working? How well is it meeting the original goals, specifications, budgets, schedules, and so forth? Out of such evaluation will come adjustments that will improve the system. Approaches to evaluation vary. Sometimes the systems analyst and someone from the client organization evaluate the system against preset criteria. Some organizations prefer to bring in an independent evaluating team on the assumption that independent members will be free from bias and expectations.

### Maintenance

Many consider maintenance to be a separate phase, one that begins only when the initial development effort is complete. In any case the maintenance process is an ongoing activity, one that lasts the lifetime of the system. Monitoring and necessary adjustments continue so that the computer produces the expected results. Maintenance tasks also include making revisions and additions to the computer system. As more computer systems are implemented, organizations will obviously have an increased number of systems to maintain. In many computer installations a very high percentage of personnel and effort is dedicated to maintenance. This necessarily limits the number of personnel available for systems development. The net result is often a backlog of development projects.

## Putting It All Together: Is There a Formula?

The preceding discussion may leave the impression that by simply following a recipe a magical system can be developed. In fact, novice analysts sometimes have the impression that there is a formula for developing systems. It would be more correct to say that there are guidelines. Each system is unique, so there can be no one way that fits everyone.

Historically, even analysts who followed the guidelines were not always successful in developing systems. Systems analysts have been embarrassed to find that they were not always good at estimating time, so schedules constantly slipped. (Budget overruns are one of the obvious results of sliding schedules.) Some observers, in fact, think that systems analysis is so ambiguous that analysts do not even know when they are finished. Sometimes it seems that the definition of project completion is the point at which analysts have run out of time on the schedule.

Another frequent problem has been imperfect communication between analysts and users. Poor communication results in poorly defined specifications, which, in turn, result in a supposedly complete system that does not do what the user expects. In addition, by-guess-and-by-gosh methods of analysis and design have often been used instead of formal tools. In the 1960s and 1970s some systems were completed according to plan and schedule, but many others were not.

Out of these experiences, however, have come some solutions. Managers have become more sophisticated—and more realistic—in planning schedules and budgets. Analysts have learned to communicate with users. In addition to the analysis and design approach described here (which is considered the traditional way of creating a system), there are other, newer approaches, which are beyond the scope of this book. If you pursue a career in systems analysis, you will no doubt encounter these approaches and find them useful.

Being a systems analyst can be important work; an analyst is in a position to help institute fundamental changes that alter business operations, work habits, and use of time. As we suggested at the beginning of this chapter, however, a systems analyst must be sensitive to the possible effects of his or her work on people's lives. The real danger, it has been remarked, is not that computers will begin to think like people, but that people will begin to think like computers.

## Getting Closer to Computers

This chapter has addressed a broad spectrum of system change, taking into account its effects on the entire organization. But an organization is composed of individuals, and individuals these days are likely to have their own personal computers. This important topic deserves special consideration, so we devote the next four chapters to personal computers and their applications in business and in the home.

# Summary and Key Terms

- A **system** is an organized set of related components established to accomplish a certain task. A **computer system** has a computer as one of its components. A **client** requests a **systems analysis,** a study of an existing system, to determine both how it works and how well it meets the needs of its **users,** who are usually employees and customers. Systems analysis can lead to **systems design,** the development of a plan for an improved system. A **systems analyst** normally does both the analysis and design. The success of a project requires both *impetus* and *authority* within the client organization to change the current system.

- The systems analyst must be a **change agent** who encourages **user involvement** in the development of a new system.

- The systems analyst has three main functions: (1) coordinating schedules and task assignments, (2) communicating analysis and design information to those involved with the system, and (3) planning and designing the system with the help of the client organization. A systems analyst should have a creative, analytical mind, good communication and organizational skills, self-discipline and self-direction, and the ability to work without tangible results.

- The **systems life cycle** has five phases: (1) preliminary investigation, (2) analysis, (3) design, (4) development, and (5) implementation.

- Phase 1, which is also known as the **feasibility study** or **system survey,** is the **preliminary investigation** of the problem to determine how—and if—an analysis and design project should proceed. Aware of the importance of establishing a smooth working relationship, the analyst refers to an **organization chart** showing the lines of authority within the client organization. After determining the nature and scope of the problem, the analyst expresses the users' needs as objectives.

- In phase 2, **systems analysis,** the analyst gathers and analyzes data from common sources such as written documents, interviews, questionnaires, observation, and sampling.

- The client organization determines what data sources are accessible, but the analyst must then decide which are appropriate. The analyst must evaluate the relevance of **written documents** such as procedure manuals and reports. **Interview** op-

tions include the **structured interview,** in which all questions are planned and written in advance, and the **unstructured interview,** in which the questions can vary from the plan. Although interviews can allow flexible questioning and the establishment of rapport with clients, they can also be time-consuming. **Questionnaires** can save time and expense and allow anonymous answers, but response rates are often low. Another method is simply **observing** how the organization functions, sometimes through **participant observation,** temporary participation in the organization's activities. Statistical **sampling** is also useful, especially when there is a large volume of data.

- The systems analyst may use a variety of charts and diagrams to analyze the data. A **data flow diagram** (**DFD**) provides an easy-to-follow picture of the flow of data through the system. The four elements of a DFD are processes, files, sources and sinks, and labeled vectors. **Processes** are the actions taken on the data. A **file** is a repository of data. A **source** is a data origin outside the organization, while a **sink** is a destination for data going outside the organization. **Vectors** are arrows indicating the direction in which the data travels. Another common tool for data analysis is the **decision table** or **decision logic table,** a standard table indicating alternative actions under particular conditions.

- Upon completion of the systems analysis phase, the analyst submits a report summarizing the system's problems and requirements and making recommendations to the client on what course to take next.

- In phase 3, **systems design,** the analyst submits a general preliminary design for the client's approval before proceeding to the specific detail design.

- **Preliminary design** involves reviewing the system requirements before submitting an overall plan or, perhaps, alternative **candidates.** The analyst presents the plan in a form the users can understand. The analyst may also develop a **prototype,** a limited working system or part of a system that gives users a preview of how the new system will work.

- **Detail design** normally involves considering the parts of the system in the following order: output requirements, input requirements, files and databases, system processing, and system controls and backup. Output requirements include the *medium* of the output, the *type* of reports needed, the *contents* of the output, and the *forms* on which the output will be printed. The analyst might determine the report format by using a **printer spacing chart,** which shows the position of headings, columns, dates, and page numbers. Input requirements include the input *medium,* the *content* of the input, and the design of data entry *forms.* The analyst also plans an input *editing* process for checking whether the data is reasonable and makes sure that the system can handle variations in input *volume.* The organization of files and databases must be specified. The processing must also be described, perhaps by using a **systems flowchart** that illustrates the flow of data through ANSI flowchart symbols or by using the hierarchical organization of a structure chart. The analyst must also spell out system controls and backup. Data input to on-line systems must be backed up by **system journals,** files that record transactions made at the terminal. Processing controls involve data editing procedures. Finally, copies of transaction and master files should be made regularly.

- Phase 4, **systems development,** consists of scheduling, programming, and testing. Schedule deadlines and milestones are often shown on a **Gantt chart.** The programming effort involves selecting the program language and developing the design specifications. Programmers then do **unit testing** (individual testing of their own programs), which is followed by **system testing** (the assessment of how the programs work together). **Volume testing** tests the entire system with real data. Documentation of phase 4 describes the program logic and the detailed data formats.

- Phase 5, **implementation,** includes these activities: training, to prepare users of the new system; equipment conversion, which involves ensuring compatibility and providing enough space and electrical capacity; file conversion, making old files accessible to the new system; system conversion; auditing, the design of an **audit trail** to trace data from output back to the source documents; evaluation, the assessment of the system's performance; and maintenance, the monitoring and adjustment of the system.

- System conversion may be done in one of four ways: **direct conversion,** immediately replacing the old system with the new system; **phased conversion,** easing in the new system a step at a time; **pilot conversion,** testing the entire system with a few users and extending it to the rest when proved successful; and **parallel conversion,** operating the old and new systems concurrently until the new system is proved successful.

## Review Questions

1. What is the distinction between systems analysis and systems design?

2. Describe the main duties of a systems analyst.

3. List some qualities of a good systems analyst, and discuss the importance of each one.

4. Name the five phases of the systems life cycle.

5. Describe the preliminary investigation phase and explain why it is necessary.

6. Discuss the advantages and disadvantages of the most common sources of data about a system.

7. Describe the use of data flow diagrams.

8. Describe the prototyping approach and explain:
   a) how it differs from the traditional systems life cycle, and
   b) why it is useful.

9. Describe the main activities involved in detail design.

10. Discuss what is involved in systems development.

11. Describe the main activities in the implementation phase.

12. Why is documentation of each phase important?

## Discussion Questions

1. Which qualities of a systems analyst do you consider to be the most important? Explain your answer.

2. Does following the traditional guidelines limit the creativity of a systems analyst? Explain your answer.

3. Explain why it is so important that a systems analyst interacts well with others.

4. Should system evaluation be done by the analyst and the client organization or by an independent evaluating team? Explain your answer.

## PART FOUR

# MICROCOMPUTERS AND APPLICATIONS SOFTWARE

Now it is time to give microcomputers space of their
own. This section begins
with a chapter on the computers themselves, followed
by separate chapters on applications software for microcomputers.

After covering the basic
topics from manufacturers to
the marketplace, we present
the burning question: But
what would I use it for? Educators and businesspeople
already have some clear directions, and we suggest
even more possibilities for
home use.

These important types of
applications software are
described in detail: word
processing, spreadsheets,
graphics, database management, and integrated packages. Each is presented with
examples. What would you
use it for?

# 13

# Personal
# Computers

## A Computer of Your Own

Do you really need a personal computer? This chapter will help you answer that question. A description of the components of a personal computer—and the many accessories available—is followed by a discussion of possible uses in the home, school, and business. The rest of the chapter is devoted to the personal computer industry, the marketplace, personal computer care, and associated clubs, fairs, and camps.

A computer of your own. A computer used for personal tasks. Will every home have a computer? Taking this a step further, will each *person* have a *personal* computer? **Personal computers,** or microcomputers, are the fastest-growing sector of the computer industry.

But, people say, do I really need a personal computer? What would I use it for? Before we begin to suggest the numerous possibilities, let us stop to consider what a personal computer—a microcomputer—is.

# The Complete Personal Computer

Just how complete your personal computer will be is a matter of personal taste, interest, and budget. You can scale way down to get by with the bare minimum, or you can go first class from the start with top-of-the-line equipment and all the trimmings. Or, like most people, you can start out with a moderate investment and build on it.

## A Review: The Basic Components

The heart of the personal computer is the microprocessor, the computer-on-a-chip that we discussed in Chapter 4. In addition to the microprocessor, the microcomputer has two kinds of main storage: RAM and ROM. As you also will recall from Chapter 4, RAM stands for random-access memory. This is the computer's "scratch pad," which keeps the intermediate results of calculations. ROM stands for read-only memory. ROM contents are programmed into the hardware by the microcomputer manufacturer. ROM contains systems programs that are not changeable through the keyboard. See Figure 13-1 for a view inside a personal computer, including the RAM and ROM chips.

A keyboard is needed, of course, so you can interact with the computer. A video screen is also needed to display input and output. Some microcomputers combine computer and keyboard and screen in a single unit, but some microcomputers have a separate screen monitor, so you can use a regular television set as a screen—something to keep in mind if you are interested in keeping the initial purchase price down. Most personal computers today also have detached keyboards, so their position can be adjusted for individual comfort.

For secondary storage purposes, a disk drive is needed to read and write on floppy disks. In addition, as we noted in Chapter 6, a hard disk is also available as an option for many personal computers. All in all, however, floppy disks are still the most common storage medium.

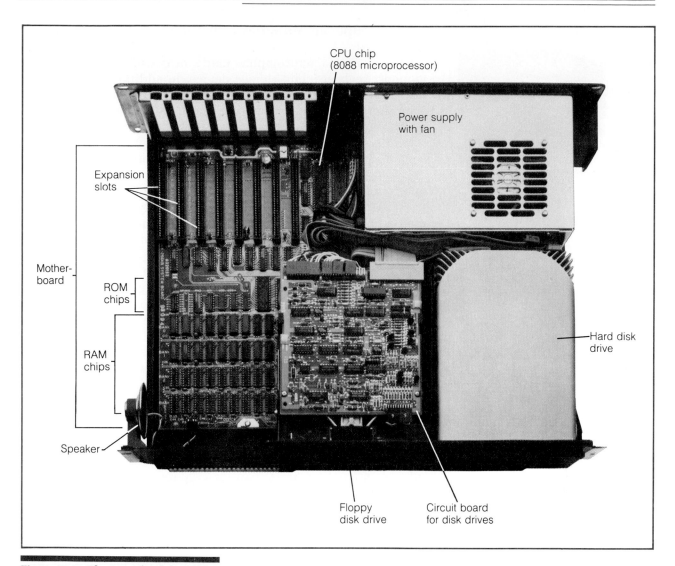

CPU chip
(8088 microprocessor)

Power supply
with fan

Expansion
slots

Motherboard

ROM chips

RAM chips

Speaker

Hard disk
drive

Floppy
disk drive

Circuit board
for disk drives

**Figure 13-1   The innards of the IBM PC XT.**   This photo shows what you would see if you removed the cover from an IBM PC XT. A typical XT probably has some of the expansion slots filled with a memory board and an internal modem.

## Memory: How Much Is Enough?

Early personal computers usually came with a standard 64K RAM—that is, 64K bytes of memory. (Recall that K is 1024.) 64K is not much by today's standards; most of the popular software packages require more. Many machines today come with 256K of memory, but those interested in serious business applications like word processing or spreadsheets, even at home, often buy more. People who have personal computers in business sometimes elect to go even higher, up to 512K, 640K, or even more. Larger memories are particularly appropriate for users of **RAM-resident** programs, programs that the user loads into the computer's memory after turning the power on. A good example of a RAM-resident program is a spelling checker, a program you might want in the background, ready to spring into action when needed.

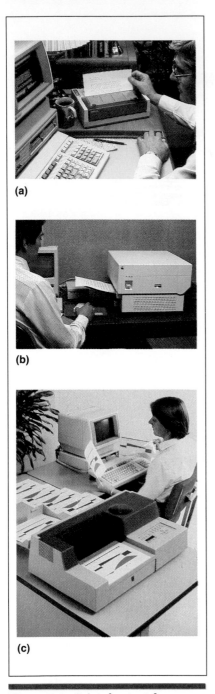

**Figure 13-2   Printed output for personal computers.** (a) Inexpensive dot-matrix printers are the most popular. (b) Laser printers are more expensive but are fast, quiet, and produce high-quality output. (c) Plotters for personal computers produce surprisingly good pictures.

## Special Attention to Printers

Basic microcomputer hardware consists of memory, CPU, monitor, keyboard, and storage device. In addition, many systems have a printer. Personal computer users often want a printer quite soon after they have purchased the basic hardware; paper is a communication medium that is hard to do without. We discussed types of printers in some detail in Chapter 5 on input and output, so you should already be familiar with the basic workings of dot-matrix, daisy wheel, laser, and other kinds of printers. Here we want to focus on printers most often used with personal computers (Figure 13-2).

The choice for a printer has traditionally been between **dot-matrix** printers (which are fast and adequate) and **daisy wheel** character printers (which are slow and very good). Most people with home computers will tolerate neither the high cost nor the sluggish pace of character printers and figure they can manage without the superior **letter-quality** printing that the slower printers produce. The net result has been dot-matrix printers for the masses and character printers for those who need letter-quality printing for formal correspondence and documentation.

But changes are here. **Laser** printers have impressed personal computer users with their speed, their first-rate print quality, and their quiet operation. But while the top-of-the-line laser printer grabs the limelight, that old standby, the dot-matrix printer, has quietly been making some technological leaps of its own. The latest models feature high-quality text, fast printing, and a variety of graphics capabilities. The key to the versatility of the new dot-matrix printers is a 24-pin printhead, which uses many more dots to form a character, thus producing printing known as **near letter quality.**

Picking the best printer from among the hundreds available might seem a herculean task. But once you narrow down your preferences, the choices narrow as well. You can pay as little as a few hundred dollars for a serviceable printer or as much as several thousand for a printer with all the options. But most personal computer users still settle on the versatile dot-matrix printer, somewhere in the $400 range. This type of printer produces standard copy quickly but can print correspondence using the near-letter-quality option.

You may have special considerations for a printer, such as graphics output or color. And, as we noted in Chapter 5, excellent plotters are available for personal computers. Again, there are several choices. We shall examine printer purchases again in the Buyer's Guide.

## The Goodies: Add-ons and Supplies

You have seen people buy every kind of gadget for their boat or car or camper. For computer users, the story is no different. In this discussion *add-ons* refers loosely to any semipermanent device that attaches to the computer so that it can be directly affected

**Figure 13-3  Extra circuitry.** This add-on circuit board is being inserted in an expansion slot of this Apple computer.

by computer processing. An example is an extra disk drive. *Supplies*, on the other hand, are necessary or not-so-necessary accessories such as printer ribbons and dust covers.

Is "the box" open or closed? That is the heart of the architecture—and add-on—discussion. **Open architecture** means that the computer is designed so that users can buy additional circuit boards and insert them in **expansion slots** inside the computer to support add-ons (Figure 13-3). **Closed architecture** means that add-ons are limited to those that can be plugged into the back of the computer. The original Apple Macintosh was offered as a closed machine. It has ports in the back to plug in a mouse, a printer, a modem, and an extra disk drive. But you cannot change its innards to add extra memory or accommodate other peripherals. If you have a machine with open architecture, there is a host of add-ons you might like to consider: more memory, an extra floppy-disk drive, a hard disk, a random-access memory (RAM) disk, a color monitor, a modem, a video camera, and input devices such as a joy stick, light pen, or mouse. See how it grows.

Supplies are readily available and often not dependent on computer brand or model. A dozen catalogs hawk computer supplies, and most items are also sold in computer stores. Supplies for personal computers are many and diverse, from serious to silly. In addition to standard items such as print wheels, printer ribbons, diskettes, and paper, consider these sample goods: locking rolltop diskette trays, disk-drive head cleaning kits, diskette markers, complete microcomputer cleaning kits, keyboard drawers (so you can slide the keyboard under the computer when not in use—see Figure 13-4), CRT stands that swivel and tilt, dust covers, antiglare CRT

**Figure 13-4  Keyboard drawer.** This protective drawer slides under the computer when the keyboard is not in use.

screen shields, hanging CRT racks, wrist supports (to hold your wrists over the keyboard), copyholders, lockup cables, security alarms, surge protectors (to prevent electric surges from hurting your files), printer forms in every conceivable style (letterhead, invoices, paychecks, address labels, Rolodex cards, and so forth), ergonomic footrests, antistatic mats, "sound-barrier" printer covers, and a complete emergency power system. A most appealing item is the portable vacuum cleaner for your printer—it has a shoulder strap for convenient operation. Or perhaps you would prefer the custom waterproof sack ("made from the same material as bulletproof vests") to carry your computer safely. (Monogram optional.) (See Figure 13-5.)

But you need not pick up one item at a time; in fact, you are encouraged to buy the complete computer workcenter, which includes furniture—desk, cabinets, shelves, and adjustable chair—a complete setup with a price to match.

Can computer clothes be far behind? See Figure 13-6.

## And of Course—Software

Would you buy a fine stereo system if there were no records or tapes to play on it? Of course not. Unless you are determined to write all your own software—an unlikely scenario—a computer is only as good as the software available for it. But, of course, software for the personal computer is abundant. And it is more: The range is dazzling, the power dizzying, and the simplicity enticing. In this chapter we shall touch on the variety of packages available. But we shall go further than that—the next three chapters cover the use of software in much greater detail.

## Personal Computers in the Home

But do you really need a computer? There are opposing points of view. Advertisements would have you believe that a personal computer is all but indispensable. Perhaps you remember the dreadful television commercial in which a college-bound young man is bid farewell by his beaming parents—immediate fade to his return, shoulders slouched, parents tearful. *Voice-over:* "He didn't know computers." Until recently, messages in responsible journals have been much the same: Get a computer or be left behind.

But now strident voices can be heard on the other side of the question—voices like this: "Personal computers have been vastly oversold to the public. If you have serious business or education needs, fine. If you want to play games, fine—just buy an inexpensive

**Figure 13-5  Computer sack.** This businessman does not want to hoist his computer onto his back, so he settles for a cloth carrying sack with handles.

computer. But all this talk about recipe files or balancing your check-book: For heaven's sake, use a recipe box or a calculator." Well. Such a speech is persuasive, but let us look further before reaching any firm conclusions.

## Home Sweet Computer

People who use computers now are like the avant-garde types who were always first with new stereo equipment. But the avant-garde is not a sufficient base for an industry—home computers must be useful and easy to use for large numbers of consumers. The big market lies not with those who want to be computer experts but with customers who want machines to do things for them without a lot of fuss. So there it is: Let's have a machine that can do something for plain folks without making them stand on their heads.

But what would make a computer indispensable? That is like asking Thomas Edison what people are going to use electricity for. The personal computer does not yet seem indispensable. That will come. For now, we can say that it can be a convenience in a number of ways.

**Figure 13-6  Computer clothes.** Computer fashions are not limited to hardware and software, as this Macintosh fan can attest.

### Communications

As already noted in Chapter 7 on data communications, home users find many reasons to connect their personal computers to the rest of the world. Some people telecommute—that is, they work at home and use their machines as a link to the office or customers. But most people have more mundane applications. A popular activity is hooking up to information services like CompuServe or The Source. These networks offer, for a fee, an astounding variety of services: stock prices, foreign-language drills, tax assistance, airline and hotel reservation services, consumer guidance, home buying and selling information, daily horoscopes, gourmet recipes, sports news, and much, much more (Figure 13-7). Other people use their networking capabilities to contact friends and colleagues through bulletin boards or use their machines as remote devices to shop or bank or pay bills. Beyond letting "your fingers do the walking," you can let your fingers do the work right at your computer—and in short order, too.

### Education

One mistake that many parents make is thinking that placing a computer in front of a child will automatically create a whiz kid. Another is equating the playing of video games with learning. That might be like saying, "I think my little girl is going to grow up to be a television electronics expert. She watches TV all the time." But, smart remarks aside, a home computer and the right software can create an entertaining environment for learning. Educational software often includes color animation, flashing lights, sounds, and music that can make learning a great deal of fun.

A computer is a patient and consistent tutor for preschool, elementary, and high-school students. One caveat, however: When left to their own devices, most children are more likely to play zap-'em games than to learn grammar or arithmetic. But education is not just for children; adults can learn typing, foreign languages, and even how to play musical instruments. But perhaps you would like something a little more offbeat; there is educational software to help you study Morse code, survival skills, driving safety, stress management, resume writing, or how to predict the eruption of a volcano!

### Word Processing

Other factors being equal, which report will get the higher grade, the typed one covered with smudges and white-out or the neatly presented paper prepared on a word processor? Let's face it: Neatness counts. Children as young as nine or ten are impressing their teachers with word-processed essays and reports prepared at home. And, yes, for the most part, they do it themselves. Word processing really is not much of a trick (we shall look at it in more detail in the next chapter), and the rudiments can be learned easily by all family members able to dress themselves. Many justify a home com-

CHAPTER 13 PERSONAL COMPUTERS **365**

**Figure 13-7 Computer uses through networking.** The electronic gourmet, made possible with a little help from the laptop computer in the background. With a modem or acoustic coupler you can hook your computer up to an information service that provides gourmet recipes and more.

puter for word processing alone. Applications include personal letters, reports, articles, mailing lists, newsletters, announcements, and even books.

### Home Controls

Most of us would welcome a little household help, especially if no salary is expected. But robots have yet to be useful around the house, so why not make the house itself a servant? That is the premise behind a class of products loosely known as **home controls.** Make your dwelling the smartest house on the block by hooking these devices up to your computer.

Rudimentary devices that control lighting, heating and cooling, smoke detectors, burglar alarms, and almost anything else have been available for years. But now there is the possibility of operating all these devices from a single control center: your computer. A person could, for example, arrange sensors to sound an alarm if an infant's breathing stops, or to have a mixer prepare a banana daiquiri at precisely 6 in the evening. The potential uses for computer control in a house are almost unlimited, but there are potential problems too. Software bugs or home electricity glitches could turn on a sprinkler during a garden party or switch the neighbor's lights off.

Home controls work like this: Lamps, air conditioners, or anything else to be controlled are plugged into little boxes that are in turn plugged into wall sockets. The little boxes receive instructions over existing house wiring from a larger box that receives and remembers instructions from a personal computer.

The system can be used to schedule electrical events in a house. You could, for instance, program the heat to be turned down at night or plan a random pattern of lights and radios going on and off during the day to make the house look occupied. Just imagine the sheer luxury of coming home to a house that is lighted and warm and where the plants are watered, the stereo is turned on, and the dinner is bubbling in the oven.

### Entertainment

You have seen the ads: The whole family—even the dog— is gathered merrily around the computer. The message is clear: The computer brings the family together. But family computing does not exist, at least not the way that it is usually portrayed. The home computer is not a shared commodity; it is a device used by individuals to perform specific tasks. Having said all that, however, we can note that entertainment is a possible exception, because family members can take turns keying, or they can use two joy sticks.

Some people scoff at the idea of buying a computer for entertainment. But entertainment is a perfectly valid use. In fact, surveys consistently show that most people use their personal computers for entertainment at least some of the time (Figure 13-8). Games can range from the purely recreational, such as the famous Pac-Man and Donkey Kong, to the more subtle games of knowing trivia or psychoanalyzing your friends. There are several challenging software offerings for chess, backgammon, and bridge. Sophisticated sports-action games provide hands-on versions of pro football, baseball, and basketball. Perusing the dramatic come-ons on the computer store's game rack can keep you amused for some time. For example, "This radical new game of strategy and chance pits you against characters far more cunning than mere trolls, monsters, wizards, gangsters, and aliens: your friends." (If you must know more, its name is Fooblitzky.)

### Cautions about Keyed Input

There is indeed no place like home, but your computer may gather dust there if you buy it to keep track of home records that require a lot of keyed input. Think about it. If you want to use your computer to keep track of your budget or checkbook or business expenses or income taxes, *you must key in every single item*. Not only that, but you probably already wrote the data down once in a checkbook register or someplace else—keying means transferring the record you already have to a computer file. This gets old fast, and only the most dedicated will follow through. Many other uses— recipes, diets, stamp collections—contain the same fatal flaw: They require extensive keying to input data. In short, unless you have the time and energy to support such applications, they are probably insufficient justification for a home computer.

## MY COMPUTER, MY TRAINS

It makes a lot of sense to use your personal computer for word processing if you are a wordsmith by trade. Screenwriter Hal Barwood sings the praises of word processing, which gives him the freedom to experiment and rearrange words easily. But when you work at home, work and play are not so far apart. He uses his computer for his hobby, too—model trains.

Barwood uses his own program— written in BASIC on his Apple II— to draw layouts of railroads, which he saves on disk. Each screen is divided into blocks that can represent a railroad car or a section of track or a bit of scenery. After connecting neighboring blocks he can connect entire screens. In this way Barwood happily plans miles and miles of track without ever leaving his computer. But, of course, he does leave his computer, at least long enough to turn some of his plans into reality. His own creations, shown above, include a 4-foot by 7-foot layout in his home.

**Figure 13-8  Entertainment via computer.** These youngsters are being transported from their home to J.R.R. Tolkien's Middle Earth as they take on the challenges of the software adventure, *The Hobbit*.

### *Miscellaneous*

Many software packages available for personal computers defy categorization, so we shall lump them together here. (And note the box titled But What Would I Use It For? which describes some particular items in more detail.) If you want electronic help managing your life, there are a number of programs standing by to do just that. They will put you on a diet, plot your biorhythms, monitor your daily exercises, schedule a tooth extraction, revise your clothing style, chart your vacation route, and offer relief from rocky relationships. If you are an artist or a dabbler, there are a number of "palette and paintbrush" programs that offer a wondrous array of colors and ways to manipulate them on the screen (Figure 13-9).

There is more. Desktop manager programs offer "pop-up" clocks, calculators, and calendars that momentarily overlay your on-screen work-in-progress at the touch of a key. Want to know about Singapore? Travelogue programs display some facts—location, size, and so forth—accompanied by a graphics screen of local scenes. Musically inclined? Programs can help you do everything from "name that tune" to composing and printing your own musical scores. A new and attractive genre of software lets you participate in writing stories, especially mysteries. And, finally, there is software to nourish a variety of hobbies, from genealogy tracking to stamp collecting. Are all these reasons, collectively, enough to make you rush out to buy your first computer? Possibly not. So what will it take?

**Figure 13-9  The computer as artist.**

## BUT WHAT WOULD I USE IT FOR?

In addition to the general categories we have mentioned in the text, there are some very specific—and idiosyncratic—software packages that find their way into home computers. See if any of the offerings in this sampler appeal to you.

**Mind Prober.** Personality software that "lets you see people as they really are." Answer a series of questions about a given person, then be rewarded with an "in-depth" analysis of his or her rela-tionships, attitudes toward work and fellow workers, personal inter-ests, and methods of coping with stress. (Human Edge Software)

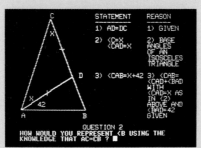

**Mastering the SAT.** The claim is straightforward: This program can dramatically improve your score on the Scholastic Aptitude Test (SAT) to get you into the college or uni-versity of your choice. In addition to teaching and testing, the pro-gram aims at improving test-taking strategies and reducing anxiety. (CBS Software)

**The Visible Computer.** Is the in-side of your computer a mystery? It does not have to be. This pro-gram gives an animated simulation of your computer's microprocessor and makes it easy to understand the basic concepts. (Software Mas-ters)

**Little Black Book.** Why settle for a dog-eared address book full of crossed-out addresses and out-dated phone numbers? With Little Black Book you will have neat, up-to-date listings. The package in-cludes the software to maintain the data easily and a genuine leather book cover to keep the printout in. (Cygnet Technologies)

**The Printing Press.** Design cards, posters, or letterheads using a built-in art library of over 100 ready-made pictures and symbols and a dozen backgrounds and bor-ders. Choose from eight styles of type in various sizes, all with op-tional outline and three-dimen-sional effects. (Power Up! Soft-ware)

## The Real Reason We Will All Buy a Computer

The real reason is becoming clearer each day: money. Cost is certainly the key limiting factor for the mass market today. Would you buy a typewriter that cost $3000? When you look at what the average person buys that costs more than a thousand dollars, you find two things: a house and a car. Those with higher salaries may buy a camper or a boat, but if you are talking about the *masses*, then the price needs to be closer to that of a television set.

## Personal Computers in Schools

During the last few years most of the country's schools, often spurred on by anxious parents, have been trying desperately to work computers into their curriculums. Some have

**Hacker.** Buyer beware! This hot program has no documentation, no company name, no nothing on the package except the instruction to get started. It locks up your computer, and it is then your job to hack your way back—that is, use your computer skills to figure out what is going on. Not for novices.

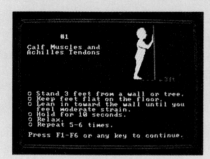

**The Running Program.** Take just a few minutes each day to input your running data so that the program can produce graphs of how you performed over different distances at different paces. It also has screens full of advice, from warm-up exercises—including graphic demonstrations—to remedies for knee pains to what to wear. About the only thing it does not do is get you out of bed in the morning. (MECA Software)

**Seven Cities of Gold.** It's a game, it's an adventure, it's—gulp—education. Like a historical novel, this software weaves a story around actual events. And, in fact, you help create the story, allocating resources such as food, ships, and goods. You join the fifteenth-century conquistadors searching for gold in America. And you better find some gold too—or risk the displeasure of the king! (Electronic Arts)

**HouseCall.** The advertisements for this "computerized home medical advisor," say it was written by physicians. HouseCall offers 400 diagnoses in a program that is touted as fast, easy, and fun to use. (Rocky Mountain Medical Software)

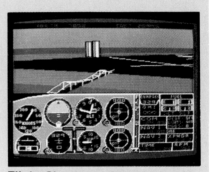

**Flight Simulator.** Climb into the cockpit of a Cessna 182 and get ready for almost anything in a flight simulation so realistic that even licensed pilots have their hands full with it. More than a game, this approaches training and is a real challenge. (Microsoft)

implemented exciting new programs, but, for some, computers have been an expensive distraction.

Not all schools know what they are doing with computers. Some, for instance, have used them exclusively for programming, almost always at the high-school level. Others rely on computers to provide extensive drills and practice exercises. Both high schools and elementary schools need to broaden their approach to computer education. Possible directions are word processing and database accessing, so that early hands-on experiences are more like what the students' parents do at work.

A major problem with using computers in schools is the lack of good software. To help sort through the software maze, the Educational Products Information Exchange of Water Mill, New York, produces a comprehensive listing of software. The listing is arranged by subject and is available in book form or on-line.

The picture is not uniformly bleak. Many schools have resisted introducing computers as substitute teacher devices; they recognize

**Figure 13-10  Computers in education.** Many classrooms include computers in their collection of teaching tools. Once the teacher has helped begin their reinforcing math lessons on the computer, these girls can probably manage on their own for a bit while he helps another student with reading.

that computers are tools, not teachers. Few now expect the classroom of the future to look like a wired cubicle containing student and machine. The classroom, in fact, will look very much as it does today: teacher, students, blackboard, papers, books—and some computers on hand to help out (Figure 13-10).

# Personal Computers in Business

The personal computer market has been enriched by the continuing flood of new uses found in business. Perhaps the most important development is that computers are no longer confined behind the castle walls of the data processing department's computer room. They appear on the desks and even in the briefcases of ordinary businesspeople. Personal computers are used in business for accounting, inventory, business planning, financial analysis, word processing, and many more functions (Figure 13-11).

There is some sentiment in the computer industry that a personal computer is just that: personal, one-on-one, even private. Are personal computers really personal? That notion is being swept aside as businesses press to the outer edges of usefulness. Personal computers are being hooked together in networks, personal computers are accessing mainframes, and personal computers themselves are being used as multiuser devices. So much for sentiment.

The impact of business on computers and vice versa carries major implications; we cannot mention them briefly and toss them aside. They will be examined in more detail in Chapter 17 on the automated office.

**THE BIG GUYS**

Who in private industry has more personal computers than anyone else? Two corporate giants lead the pack: General Motors with 25,000 and General Electric with 23,000. No one else is even close.

# Personal Computer Manufacturers

Nothing we could possibly say here will remain true for long, since the one constant element in the personal computer industry is change.

## The Players: How It All Began and What Is Happening Now

As we noted in Chapter 3, the microcomputer boom began in 1975 when the **MITS Altair** was offered as a kit to computer hobbyists. Building your own computer was an eccentric pastime. But all that has changed. Apple came along to bring a small computer, the Apple II, to the people. Tandy started selling TRS-80 computers to everyday people in Radio Shack stores. Commodore enticed school administrators to let children try their PET computer. These three—Apple, Tandy, and Commodore—led the market from about 1977 to 1982. But there was a significant entry in 1981: IBM announced its own contender, the IBM PC, and nothing has been the same since. In a mere 18 months IBM outdistanced them all.

Along the way there have been other manufacturers of personal computers, up to 200 at one point. Many tried and many failed. We are still in the period referred to as the Big Shakeout. At this point it is difficult to speak with confidence about any firm, but we shall put our money on IBM, Apple, and AT&T. We shall discuss them in the order of their appearance, then give some attention to other key players.

**Figure 13-11  Computers in a business setting.** Applying the phrase "computers in business" to personal computers often suggests an executive image, but these Macintosh computers are used routinely by drafting personnel.

**THE SIGHT AND SOUND OF APPLE**

It's new, it's fun, and it's Apple. Showing commitment to its Apple II line, Apple Computer offers the Apple IIGS. The GS, which stands for graphics and sound, is billed as the computer for the high end of the Apple II market: spectacular color and sound, high-speed processing, and a mouse interface. What is more, Apple guarantees that 10,000 existing Apple II programs run on the new machine.

The GS, designed for home and school enthusiasts, plucks the best features from other Apple computers: the ports and ease of the IIc, the expandability of the IIe, and the user interface of the Macintosh. Apple thinks that whether your screen shows fish or the results of high-speed calculations, you will join in the chorus of cheers for the Apple IIGS.

## Apple: Almost First

Apple Computer was formed in 1977 by Steven Jobs and Stephen Wozniak, who were working in Silicon Valley in California. Apple computers were the first to replace complicated switches-and-lights front panels with easy-to-use typewriter keyboards. They were an immediate success. The popular Apple II, later updated to the IIe (Figure 13-12a), was followed by the bugridden and unsuccessful Apple III, which was discontinued. The IIc spinoff (Figure 13-12b) found a nice niche in the home market, but the innovative Lisa was too pricey ($10,000) for both home and business markets; Lisa was abandoned in 1984, a year after it was introduced.

Apple used Lisa technology—graphics and pull-down menus—to create superb user interfaces for the Macintosh (Figure 13-12c), which it introduced and promoted heavily in 1984. The Macintosh has attracted a devoted following and is particularly attractive to beginners.

## IBM: Front and Center

IBM introduced its personal computer in the summer of 1981 (Figure 13-13). Since then, the computer giant's IBM PC has zoomed to the top in microcomputer sales. In 1983 IBM launched a souped-up version of the PC called the IBM PC XT, which featured more power, more memory, and hard disk. Other models quickly followed, and all are compatible with the original PC, which means they can all use the same software. Examples are the Portable PC, the ill-fated PCjr, the PC AT (Advanced Technology), the PC RT (RISC Technology—a topic we discussed in Chapter 4), and the laptop PC Convertible. IBM dominates. There are reasons.

IBM did not get there first, and many argue that IBM products are not even the best. So why does IBM dominate the personal computer market? It would be easy to say that IBM's preeminence naturally follows from their number one position in the mainframe market, but it is not that simple. There are really two sides to the story.

The first side concerns what the IBM PC provided: a processor that could address a lot of memory, an 80-column screen width, an open architecture, a keyboard with upper- and lowercase and good cursor controls, and function keys for word processing and other software. The second side of the story is the failure of other major companies to provide these same fundamental features early on. The void was there, and IBM stepped in.

The acceptance of this product—and the IBM name—cultivated the ground for others to produce software and peripherals. A standard was established. IBM's standard may not be the last, but it will take a mighty force to overcome its head start.

(a)

(b)

(c)

**Figure 13-12  Three Apples.** (a) The faithful Apple IIe sees service in a bike shop. (b) The Apple IIc is a smaller and sleeker version of the original II. (c) Architect and construction worker discuss plans while the Apple Macintosh stands by, ready to assist. The Macintosh has good graphics capability and is often used to produce drawings.

**Figure 13-13  IBM PC.** From the time of its introduction in August 1981, the IBM PC took only 18 months to lead the competition. The IBM PC XT looks like the original PC except that it has a hard disk on the right side instead of a second floppy disk.

## AT&T: The Phone Company Becomes a Computer Company

This is getting confusing: AT&T makes a PC and IBM makes an AT. Well, no one said divestiture was going to be easy. AT&T's entrance into the computer market was not a total surprise. They had, after all, been a leader in computer technology for years, but they were forbidden by regulation to sell any of it to anyone else. But when AT&T was broken up in January 1984, it gained the right to invade the computer market. Their first personal computer offering, introduced in 1984, was the PC 6300, whose sales exceeded expectations. Buyers chose AT&T over other IBM compatibles because they felt no trepidation over the future of the company.

A series of computers has followed (Figure 13-14). AT&T is too big to be a niche player; it is obvious that they are after the whole market. The company has also been quick to cash in on its communications experience. The new machines can be tied together to swap data easily. AT&T's entry into the personal computer market is probably the most significant event since IBM launched its personal computer in 1981. It is safe to assume that the two behemoths will be major competition for each other.

**Figure 13-14   AT&T PC 6300 PLUS.**
An important business get-together, as shown in this picture, is an appropriate site for this powerful business computer, which can run both UNIX and MS-DOS programs. What is more, users can control both programs through the same easy-to-learn interface—that is, through commands to the computer.

## And Others

We have already noted the fluidity of the personal computer market. But these significant manufacturers must be added to the list.

### Tandy and Radio Shack

Headquartered in Fort Worth, Texas, the Tandy Corporation is better known to the public as the parent company of the Radio Shack electronics stores, of which there are now some 8500 worldwide. Tandy exploited the advantage of having existing sales outlets by offering the TRS-80 through Radio Shacks in 1977. Radio Shack, whose computers were once thought to be no more than fancy toys, now commands respect through a wide range of products (Figure 13-15a).

### Commodore

Based in Norristown, Pennsylvania, Commodore Business Machines entered the personal computer market with the PET (Personal Electronic Transactor). One of the best-selling home computers worldwide is the Commodore 64. Commodore offered the Amiga in 1985. The Amiga has outstanding graphics and sound effects, but users still await significant software.

### Atari

Long involved with video games, Atari offers home computers and a great deal of software. But for the purveyor of Pac-Man, the long joyride may be over. Sales have steadily diminished since 1982 and continue to look bleak as interest in computers for games diminishes.

**COMPAQ'S CHALLENGE**

Compaq® has made imitating IBM its life's work, but now the tables are being turned. Compaq's Deskpro 386, introduced in September 1986, features the powerful Intel 80386 32-bit microprocessor. Compaq offers the machine as the answer for people who need more power and speed but also IBM compatibility. What is more, the Desktop 386 features both the MS-DOS and Xenix—an off-shoot of Unix—operating systems.

Compaq makes no bones about challenging IBM, flatly stating that Big Blue must announce a similar machine soon or be left behind as the market's standard setter.

### *Compaq®*

Compaq plays one game and plays it well: piggybacking on IBM. Founded in Houston in 1982, a few months after IBM's PC went on the market, Compaq bounded onstage with a portable personal computer whose innards were as close to the IBM PC as the law allowed. Even when IBM struck back with its own portable in 1984, Compaq outsold it 5 to 1. Young Compaq continues to do well by hanging on to IBM's coattails (Figure 13-15b). To be "IBM compatible" is everything. Read on.

## The Compatibility Craze

How would you like to invent a new product, then be told that the best way to advertise it is to say that it is just like your competitor's product? In fact, manufacturers of new personal computers often do just that: They proclaim how closely their product resembles the IBM PC family. That kind of imitation is inevitable in light of the phenomenal market acceptance of the IBM PC. Some products are called **compatibles** because, in general, they can run and produce software that will also run on the IBM PC and vice versa. Such compatibility is possible by using microprocessors and operating systems that are the same as or virtually identical to those used by the IBM PC. Some personal computers are called **clones,** because of their deliberate similarity to the IBM PC. Some brand names of clones are Compaq, Panasonic, Corona, Zenith, Epson, and Leading Edge.

**Figure 13-15   Some personal computers.** (a) This businessman is using the Tandy 3000 from Radio Shack. This multiuser system is fully IBM compatible and has optional 20MB hard disk. (b) The Compaq Portable II™ is available with a 20MB hard disk but is small enough to fit under an airline seat.

(a)                                          (b)

Some manufacturers have taken the clone idea one step further; they have produced hybrids. A **hybrid** is a computer with its own unique design that will also simulate another computer, notably IBM. Most companies have accepted the existence of the de facto ("that's the way it is") IBM standard, so they offer IBM compatibility but also find their own way to stand out in a crowd.

## Supermicros: The New Wave

Question: What high-powered personal computer is the model for **supermicros,** the new wave of machines? If you guess IBM you cannot miss: These new machines are all compatible with the IBM PC AT (Figure 13-16a). Like the PC AT, they have a high-speed microprocessor and significantly increased memory and hard-disk storage capacity. In particular, the supermicros are **multiuser** (they can be shared by several users at the same time) and **multitasking** (they can run more than one applications package per user). Currently popular supermicros come from Compaq, Texas Instruments, Kaypro, AT&T, DEC, Hewlett–Packard, Zenith, and Victor (Figure 13-16b). The exact product names are not important here—they will come and go and change. The point is that the high-end market is so potent that brands keep rolling off the assembly line.

**Figure 13-16   Supermicros.** These powerful personal computers are both multiuser and multitasking; these characteristics open up a higher level of personal computing. Pictured are (a) the IBM PC AT and (b) the Hewlett–Packard Vectra.

(a)      (b)

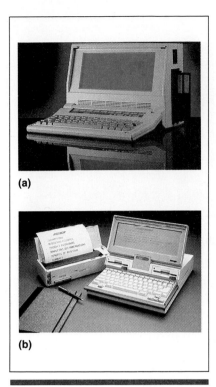

**(a)**

**(b)**

**Figure 13-17 Laptops.** (a) A newsworthy laptop, the Zenith Z-171 won the coveted contract to supply laptops to the Internal Revenue Service. The 15-pound Z-171 has dual 5¼-inch disk drives, 512K memory, and a built-in modem. (b) The IBM PC Convertible broke new laptop ground by using 3½-inch disk drives. It weighs in at 13 pounds with a 256K expandable memory. A modem is optional.

## Laptops: The Incredible Shrinking Micro

A computer that fits in a briefcase? A computer that weighs less than a newborn baby? A computer you do not have to plug in? A computer to use on your lap on an airplane? A computer that is "cute"? Yes, to all questions.

It all began with the first portable computers from Osborne (later in bankruptcy), Kaypro, and Compaq. A **portable computer** looked and carried like a sewing machine. It was portable in that you could take it with you in one piece (the keyboard snapped onto the computer to form a cover), but you would not want to lug its 25 to 40 pounds through an airport. **Laptop computers** are wonderfully portable, sleek, and functional (Figure 13-17). They weigh as little as 9 pounds. Many of them have built-in modems, so a traveling businessperson can send data from the hotel room to the office. Several laptops come with key software packages, such as word processing and spreadsheets, right in the computer—that is, in the ROM chips. And, almost without exception, they are IBM compatible. Many have small screens (16 lines), but some come with full-size screens (25 lines). Some accept floppy disks, so it is especially easy to move data from one machine to another. Laptops are not as inexpensive as their size might suggest; most carry a price tag equivalent to a sophisticated personal computer for business.

The main laptop customers are journalists, who prepare copy on their computers right at the site of the big story. But traveling executives, sales representatives, insurance auditors, and writers also are good candidates. In addition, lawyers frequently use portable computers in courtrooms. Then, of course, there is the Internal Revenue Service, whose agents use 15,000 laptops—the better to monitor their generous customers.

## The Ever Changing Marketplace

The marketplace for personal computers ebbs and flows in a constantly changing scenario. Early forecasts had the general public taking to personal computers as a bear to honey. Indeed, sales rose in a gratifying way through the early 1980s. But then the industry reached a plateau—we have already alluded to the big chill the change in sales growth placed over the manufacturing industry. But other market sectors are affected as well: dealers, the market for secondhand and "orphaned" computers, publicity, and foreign sales. Let us examine each of these.

### Computer Dealers: The Neighborhood Store

The number of retail outlets selling computers is in the thousands, and ComputerLand alone has almost 800 stores (Figure

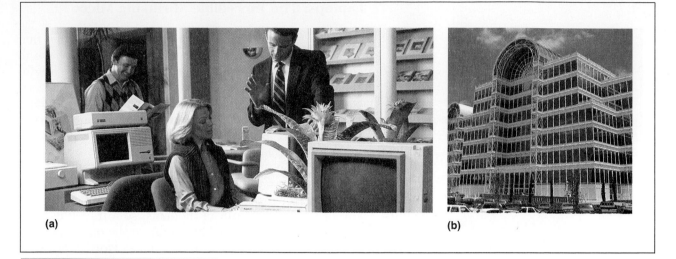

**(a)**  **(b)**

**Figure 13-18  Retail sales.** (a) In a typical retail outlet, customers can "test drive" the hardware and peruse shelves of software. (b) The impressive Dallas Infomart is devoted to computer-related businesses.

## ELECTRONIC PERKS

Standard big-shot perks—short for *perquisites*—have historically been company cars, membership in the country club, and the like. But there is a new perk in town: the opportunity to buy a computer at discount prices. And the perk recipient is not necessarily near the top of the corporate ladder; he or she can be any employee in a computer-conscious company. The most common arrangement is simply for a computer retailer to offer better prices to customers who identify themselves as the favored company's employees; the company makes up the difference.

Companies making such arrangements usually emphasize that employees are not expected to buy a computer to take work home. They feel that if employees simply become more familiar with computers, that will be of sufficient benefit to the company.

13-18a). Whether the outlet is a small independent or part of a large operation such as Sears, Macys, or Radio Shack, it offers you the chance to examine different equipment before you buy. And, speaking of large operations: Some high-tech products are now being hawked in stunning architectural caverns known as **computer marts,** buildings designed to house the dozens of stores that lure customers. The first computer mart, called the Infomart, opened in Dallas in 1985 (Figure 13-18b). Other centers are the World Trade Center in Boston, and the upcoming Techworld in Washington, D.C.

But the retail picture is changing somewhat. It was not so very long ago that consumers marveled at being able to walk right into a store that sold computers. That quaint idea is outmoded in some stores. To put it bluntly, some dealers prefer dealing with business-people.

### Courting Business

For some stores the shift toward professional customers is a matter of survival. Businesspeople do not take up a lot of time with idle questions, and their buying potential for hardware, software, and service is enormous. Oh, there are still home computers for sale, but they are probably upstairs or in a back room. Casual shoppers and confused first-time buyers are not likely to be heavily pursued by these stores. The consumer has not been forgotten altogether, however. At Christmas dealers still hang decorations and stay open late to serve ordinary people, especially if the key manufacturers offer special promotions.

### The Gray Market

Computer stores boomed when IBM introduced the IBM PC in 1981. But the good old days ended in 1984 when IBM authorized hundreds more stores to sell its products and at the same time

## THE MICROCOMPUTER CORNER

### The Shape of Things to Come

Today's sedans came off Detroit's drawing boards more than five years ago. In its brief life the personal computer industry has not yet known the luxury of that kind of advance planning. The future of the industry is not easy to guess, but these people— leading lights all—ought to have a better shot at it than we ordinary folks. Listen to them speak.

*"Two parallel trends are hiking the demand for PCs: The PC is more user-friendly, and users are increasingly PC-friendly."*
—David Wagman, Cochairman
Sofsel

*"Standard applications and hardware will improve dramatically. People will feel that if they don't have a PC, they can't be as productive."*
—Bill Gates, Chairman
Microsoft Corporation

*"Technology will be available in the near future for several exciting new classes of applications: group productivity through networks, intelligent assistance in daily management routines, effective and convenient messaging systems, and idea processors."*
—Mitch Kapor, Founder
Lotus Development Corporation

*"The most important means of opening new horizons is larger data storage. Most people have enough computing power.*

*With more storage, you'll be able to access giant data bases. Online information is the key; it will change how people use their PCs."*
—Philippe Kahn, President
Borland International

*"Novelty and media hype no longer drive the industry. New products can succeed only if they offer true benefit and costs savings to users."*
—Jonathon Rotenberg, President
Boston Computer Society

*"A way to speed growth is by developing simpler products. Most of today's software was built for sophisticated users. Most people not only don't know computers but are afraid of them. That segment will sooner or later constitute the major share of the market."*
—H. Glen Haney, former
President,
Micropro International

*"The PC's great promise is in making information readily available to people so they can search for, retrieve, and display data in ways that are both timely and fun."*
—Gary Kildall, Chairman
Digital Research

*"I would like—and I expect— three things to happen. The first is that PCs will remember their roots and become more personal. The second concerns high-powered machines—that horsepower, combined with local area networks, will draw the PC into what is now the mini and mainframe segment. Third, we will continue to see experiments with natural language and graphics approaches. We'll pull away from character-based applications almost entirely in favor of more understandable picture-based programs.*
—Fred Gibbons, President
Software Publishing
—From an article in *PC World*

slashed prices. Dealers were caught with fewer customers and a narrow profit margin. To compensate, some dealers overstocked, then sold the excess merchandise out the back door to **gray market**— unauthorized—dealers. Price wars raged.

### Vertical Markets

Some dealers saved themselves by turning to **vertical markets,** groups of similar customers such as accountants or doctors. By specializing in complete computer systems for a few vertical markets, dealers are able to give good service for good prices. But serving vertical markets really only works in large urban areas.

## Used Computers: Secondhand Silicon

If you want a personal computer and are willing to settle for less than the latest technology, you can save hundreds of dollars in the fast-growing secondhand market.

### Prices

Just how much of a bargain can you get? It depends. First, the secondhand price is affected by the *current* prices for the same model new, not the original price paid for the computer. Some sellers, in fact, are discouraged to find that prices of new equipment have plunged so far that a buyer can get a new model for less than the offered secondhand price. Still, we can give some ballpark figures. If the computer is still being produced and is still in demand, you can probably find a 25% discount. If the computer's popularity is waning or it is no longer being manufactured, you may be able to get a 50% discount. If the manufacturer has gone out of business, discounts are as high as 70%. Prices for secondhand printers vary less—most are close to 60% of the original price.

### Cautions

All this is very tempting, but bargain hunters beware: Few sellers offer warranties on used equipment, and few retailers will repair them. Even so, demand for used computers far outstrips supply. Few dealers stock them, however, because the profit margin is low, and they do not want the hassle of negotiating prices or of fixing the machines. Occasionally, however, a retailer will accept a used machine as a trade-in. Look for used computers in flea markets, your local want ads, trade journals, and even electronic bulletin boards.

### Test Drive

It is best to buy locally so that you can try out a machine before paying for it. Most used computers are mechanically sound, since there are few movable parts that can easily break. However, some tests are just common sense: Try each of the computer keys, run any diagnostic program that comes with the computer, listen for strange hums from the printer and disk drive, and look for signs of smoke damage. And, most important, bring your own disk files to test. Disk drives can easily be out of alignment and not work, so make sure the machine is capable of processing and displaying your files. But there are less obvious tip-offs. Like the owner whose car is a creampuff, a seller who keeps the original cartons and documentation may also be meticulous in caring for the machine.

## Your Second Computer

Well, it had to happen. If every home has two TVs, can computers be far behind? But how is this "upgrade"—the name it is usually given to justify the strain on the budget—justified? Perhaps you have simply outgrown your old computer; you want a faster, more powerful machine. Besides, you can give the first one to the children. A more compelling reason may be that your first machine was purchased when you meandered into a computer store and succumbed to a sales pitch—that is, your first purchase was not made carefully. But as an experienced user, you are now in much better shape to make an informed decision. And what will it be?

If you simply want to do more of what you are doing already, then you will probably decide on a more powerful version of your current computer. But if, on the other hand, the reason you are considering a second computer is that you want to do different things or run different software than your present system allows, then buying a different brand of computer might make sense. But that means you will almost surely have compatibility problems: The software, data, and peripherals may not match—that is, the files you so carefully constructed for use with the first computer may not work with the second. There are sometimes hardware and software solutions to these problems—conversion problems, in essence—but it is best to know just *how* conversion will be accomplished before you plunge into another purchase.

## Orphans: Where Are They Now?

The shakeout in the personal computer market has left many users with machines that have little support and less software. These white elephants, abandoned by their manufacturers for lack of sales, are nicknamed **orphans.** A partial list: Coleco Adam, Columbia, TI 99/4A, Timex–Sinclair 1000, Franklin Ace, Victor 9000, Osborne, Eagle, Gavilan, Atari 400 and 600, Commodore VIC 20, Mattel Aquarius, Intellivision, Apple III, Apple Lisa, and the IBM PCjr. Some companies simply quit the computer field (Coleco, Mattel, Timex), but others went bankrupt (Franklin, Gavilan, Osborne, Victor). Some companies have continued some form of support. Texas Instruments, for instance, maintains a toll-free hotline to provide help for people who bought its model 99/4A.

But the most common support is from other owners, who band together with a kind of grim camaraderie. Those who cannot afford to scrap their machines turn to fellow users for comfort. Some groups are very active indeed; they publish newsletters, exchange software, and cooperate in finding ever scarcer accessories.

## COMEDY BY COMPUTER

Does the mug in the foreground look familiar? Yes, it is comedian Bob Hope, but it is the fellow at the computer who makes him funny. His name is Gene Perret, and he delivers laugh lines on demand. The three Emmys you see in the picture attest to his reputation among his peers.

But Gene Perret is also a computer convert. He takes his portable Sharp 5000 with him when he travels, always ready to prepare more material for Hope. Perret chose the Sharp because it has a built-in dot-matrix printer, which is adequate for sending letters. Perret envisions all eight of Hope's writers networked via computer.

Meanwhile, the computer itself has become a topic of Hope's (Perret's) humor: "I was going to invest in computers, but I didn't. I don't like to put my money into anything that's smarter than I am. . . . So I put it in government bonds."

## The Publicity Game: Promises, Promises

You know about hardware and you know about software, but now there is vaporware. Coined by the trade press with tongue in cheek, the term **vaporware** describes products, both hardware and software, that are marketed before they exist—that is, the upcoming product is loudly trumpeted, often at a formal press conference, but the product is not available for sale in stores and will not be for some time. What is the point of all this? Why not just announce products when they are available?

A key reason for premature announcements is to head off the competition. In the fall of 1983, for example, IBM announced that its long-awaited (and ill-fated) PCjr would be available in January; they hoped that buyers would not succumb to Christmas promotions for other personal computers. Similarly, Microsoft wanted its buyers to wait for its own operating environment software called Windows, but the four announced (and missed) release dates became embarrassing. Finally, in June 1985, Microsoft stated that the product would be available "before the snow falls," and it was. Another reason for an early announcement is to support an existing product. Apple, for example, was most anxious to have business software for its Macintosh, so—to fill the void—Lotus announced a spreadsheet like Lotus 1-2-3 called Jazz well in advance of the program's release. But Jazz boogied to market nearly two months late.

All this is causing considerable confusion in the marketplace. Sometimes consumers cannot tell what is being sold and what is just being talked about. But consumers are not the only ones who are confused. The delays from announcement to delivery are particularly vexing to venture capitalists, the people who put up the money in the adolescent industry of personal computers. The business is crowded and fast moving and can slam the door on a product that arrives late. The chronic foul-ups have undercut the earnings of dozens of companies. The venture capitalists, stung more than once by high-tech delays, are growing wary about where they invest and whose claims they believe.

## Hands across the Sea: Personal Computers in Europe and Asia

An English accountant casually sips his tea for the 20 minutes it takes his accounting program to load from cassette tape. Some mock the English for their "1980" technology, but they seem not to care about the latest and fastest and flashiest or even about floppy disks. American computer vendors in England are a study in frustration. IBM PCs have not been able to break into the market in a significant way. And the English hardly give the time of day to the oh-so-easy-to-use Macintosh.

It's different across the channel, where France loves *Le Mac*. They love its dash and style, its *joie de vivre*. In fact, if you walk into a computer store in France—charmingly called Informatique—you will see bright graphics and lots of Apple software. France is the third largest market for Apple, right after the United States and Canada.

American vendors are persevering in the European markets. They are not able, however, to plan a single European advertising campaign because the markets in different countries are so different. Also, software translation presents unique problems and so has become an industry in its own right. Translation includes transforming American to English, changing, for example, a baseball reference to soccer or tennis. Particularly irksome are references to dollars, which require manufacturers to devise new graphics to represent different currencies.

And then there is China. Would American computer vendors like to pitch their wares to a land of a billion people? Would a four-year-old like his hand in the cookie jar? The possibilities are palatable indeed as this giant land moves away from an agrarian society. China is carefully planning such a move. Already, a fledgling electronics industry has developed in Shanghai. Before an economic miracle can occur, however, China needs technological help. Competition is fierce as foreign vendors jockey for position. All eyes are on IBM, which is maintaining its characteristic silence.

But what about Japan? Japanese manufacturers have an iron grip on most American markets for consumer electronics but have not yet touched the home computer market. Soon they could be contenders, however, in a rather offbeat way. The concept revolves around the **MSX machine.** MSX stands for **Microsoft Extended Basic,** a computer language that Microsoft has licensed to more than a dozen vendors, many of them in Japan. MSX computers incorporate the first—and so far only—set of technical standards for home computers that has won backing from a number of big manufacturers. The first MSX machines are not big winners: The technology is no more advanced than that of a Commodore 64 or Apple II. What makes this machine different is that the basic computer, no matter where it is made, is always the same. This means that software and peripherals designed for one MSX machine will work on another MSX machine. Even crusaders for the MSX say it is too early to tell whether this idea will really take off in a big way.

For more information on how computers are used in different parts of the world, see Gallery 3.

We have looked at what the machine is and at the people who sell it. Now suppose you have it at home. How will you provide for its care?

## Computer Fitness and Safety

Computers are a hardy lot, primarily because they have so few moving parts. Given proper care, your computer will probably last longer than you want it—that is, you will have your

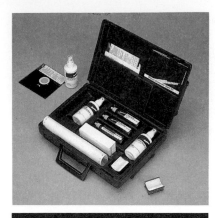

**Figure 13-19   A cleaning kit.** This kit contains mild solutions, a cleaning disk, swabs, and wipes for cleaning disk drives, screens, and keyboards. Follow directions carefully.

eye on the latest new machine long before your current machine wears out. Still, your computer's well-being cannot be taken completely for granted. It needs proper care.

## Proper Care

Here are some tips for keeping your printer, disk, keyboard, and screen in good working order. The printer should be vacuumed periodically and surface areas wiped clean with a light all-purpose cleaner. Do not lubricate the machine because oil will only collect dust, which practically guarantees printer failure. To keep the disk-drive read/write heads clean, use an approved head-cleaning kit occasionally (Figure 13-19). To keep the disk head properly aligned with the disk, avoid sudden jolts to the drive. Diskettes must be properly stored, since dirt is the single most common cause of disk error. A keyboard can be ruined by soda pop, coffee, or anything crumbly; keep them away from your computer. If a spill does occur, immediately take the keyboard to a service center for a good cleaning. The surface area of the keys can be cleaned with any mild cleansing agent, but the place where dirt and grime really love to gather is between and under the keys. A can of compressed air (with a narrow nozzle) effectively blows out all that residue. With the monitor turned off, wipe your screen clean with a mild cleanser occasionally. You may also wish to apply an antistatic solution.

Environmental factors can have a significant influence on computer performance. Your computer should not sit near an open window, in direct sunlight, or near a heater. Computers work best in cool temperatures—below 80° Fahrenheit (27° Celsius). Also, smoking can be hazardous to your computer's health. Smoking adds tar

**Figure 13-20   Service center.** Manufacturers provide outlets where computers and peripherals can be repaired and serviced.

# How to Buy Your Own Personal Computer

**O**wning a personal computer is not like owning a toaster or a television set, nor is buying one like buying a suit off the rack. There is a lot to learn about the new technology and how it might help you.

We cannot pick your new computer system for you any more than we could pick a new car for you. But we can tell you what to look for. We do not mean that we can lead you to a particular brand and model—that would be impossible, since so many new products are introduced into this area every month. If you are just starting out, however, we can help you define your needs and ask the right questions.

## WHERE DO YOU START?

Maybe you have already done some thinking and have decided that a personal computer offers advantages. Now what? You can start by talking to other personal computer owners about how they got started and how to avoid pitfalls. (Plan on a long conversation. Personal computer owners are notoriously talkative on this subject.) Or, you can read some computer magazines, especially ones with evaluations and ratings, to get a feel for what is available. Next, visit several dealers. Don't be afraid to ask questions. You are considering a major purchase, so plan to shop around.

### Analyze Your Needs and Wants

You may want to narrow your computer search by determining what price range you are in. But it might make more sense to begin with a needs/wants analysis. Why do you want a computer? Be realistic: Will it probably wind up being used for games most of the time or for business applications? People use personal computers for a variety of applications, as noted in the box entitled *Who Needs It?* Prioritize your needs; don't plan to do everything at once. At some point you will have to establish a budget ceiling. After you have examined your needs, you can select the best hardware/software combinations for the money. Before we look at hardware and software in detail, pause to consider whether you want to buy now.

**Shopping for software.** There is a wide range of useful software. Many users spend more on software than they did on the original equipment.

### WHO NEEDS IT?

Here are some common home applications for personal computers:

- Education for children
- Filing and retrieving personal records
- Word processing
- Office "homework"
- Entertainment, games
- Running a home business
- Personal finances
- Publishing newsletters
- Access to remote information
- Learning programming
- Shopping and banking from home

gain by waiting. And it is also true that something will no doubt come along in a year or two (or even sooner) that will make present equipment seem inadequate in some way. Improvements may include more power (faster, more memory), easier handling, a wider range of software, or better-designed software. The price may even be lower for a new, improved model.

Yet, clearly, the longer you wait to buy, the longer you miss out on acquiring experience and expertise with personal computers. And, of course, you miss out on the usefulness and fun. Certainly if you want a machine for word processing or for business-related purposes, there is no point in waiting. If you want something that is eas-

### Buy Now or Later?

People who are interested in buying a computer may delay their purchases because the price is too high or because they think more sophisticated computers are coming soon. Prices are certainly variable and it is quite true that you may get a barier to use than the equipment you see now, however, you may be advised to put it off a year or so.

## WHAT TO LOOK FOR IN HARDWARE

The basic microcomputer system consists of a central processing unit (CPU) and memory, video display, keyboard, storage device (floppy disk or hard disk drive), and printer. Unless you know someone who can help you out with technical expertise, you are probably best advised to look for a packaged system, that is, one in which the above components (with the possible exception of the printer) are assembled and packaged by the same manufacturer. This gives you some assurance that the various components will work together.

Let us now take a quick look at the various parts of the system: CPU, memory, video display, keyboard, secondary storage, and printers. Then we shall consider portability and hardware options.

### Central Processing Unit

Personal computers started out with what is known as an 8-bit processor, but now most manufacturers make machines with 16-bit or 32-bit pro-

**Adding memory.** Not just another board, the add-on SixPak series expands memory and includes other features like a clock. The SixPak Premium shown here adds 2 million bytes of memory and multifunction capabilities.

cessors. More bits mean more power and faster processing speed.

### Memory

Memory is measured in bytes. A minimum of 256K bytes (about 256,000 bytes) is suggested for personal computers used for business applications. You may be able to get by with less, however, if you buy a home computer primarily for games or word processing. Most machines have expandable memory, so you can add more later if you need it.

### Video Display

It is possible to use your TV set as a video display for your computer. This may be appropriate if you are trying to keep the price of your new system down. A color TV set may also be a useful adjunct if you are producing color graphics. However, a color video display specifically made for computers will give you higher screen resolution and, therefore, a clearer picture. Let us consider several aspects of video displays.

*Screen Width*   TV sets have several drawbacks, particularly if you plan to use the screen for close work, such as programming or word processing, over a period of time. Take the number of characters on a line. When typing a letter or term paper on a typewriter, you usually get about 70 characters per line. (Characters include letters, numbers, special characters, and spaces.) Some TV sets,

**The complete microcomputer system.** You may not need fine oak furniture right away, but to have a complete microcomputer system you will need a central processing unit and memory, video display, keyboard, storage device, and printer.

however, allow only 40 characters per line. Even inexpensive video displays have 80-column screens with clear characters, making them preferable to most TV sets.

***Screen Readability*** As you shop for your video display screen, be sure to compare readability among screens. First, make sure the screen has minimum flicker. Next, check the shape of the characters. Some screens are difficult to read because they chop off the descenders—the tails that fall below the line—of the lowercase letters g, j, p, q, and y. In addition, you should look to see whether the characters appear crowded on the screen—that is, jammed together to a degree that makes them difficult to read. Glare is another major consideration: nearby harsh lighting can cause glare to bounce off the screen. There are ways to reduce glare—etched glass, chemical coatings, or glare shields—but some of these methods may reduce clarity. The controls that let you adjust the contrast and brightness of screen characters are also important. Try them out on the video display you are considering.

A key factor affecting screen quality is resolution, a measure of the number of dots, or pixels, that can appear on the screen. The higher the resolution—that is, the more dots—the more solid the text characters will appear. For graphics, more pixels mean sharper images. But do not be tempted to pay a higher price for the best resolution unless your applications need it.

***Monochrome versus Color*** Monochrome—single color—screens are the most readable and are particularly recommended for users whose main application is word processing. Monochrome screens usually have a gray or sort of soft black background with green or amber lettering. Amber screens are reputed to be easier on the eyes and are, in fact, standard on European displays. A color screen is desirable for applications like graphics or games; you can use foreground and background colors in a variety of combinations.

***Ergonomic Considerations*** You should look to see whether the video display can swivel and tilt, since this will remove the need to sit in exactly one position for a long period of time. This becomes an important consideration if there are different users for the same computer. Another possibility is to purchase add-on equipment that will perform these functions. Also, there are trade-offs: if you need a portable computer to haul around to different places, the built-in screen contributes to its portability, but not its flexibility.

## Keyboard

Keyboards vary a lot in quality. The best way to know what suits you is to sit down in the store and type for a while. Consider the tactile touch, color, slope, layout, and whether the keyboard is detachable.

**Video displays.** (*Top*) Most video displays made for computers allow 80 characters per line. (*Bottom*) Most TV sets allow only 40 characters per line and the characters are not very clear.

***Keyboard Tactile Touch*** On the inexpensive end are touch-sensitive membrane plastic keyboards, which are just flat surfaces. There is no tactile sensation—no "feel"—as on a keyboard that is similar to an electric typewriter. You could consider a membrane keyboard if you will use the computer only to play games using a joy stick and use of the keyboard is minimal and incidental.

You will find that there also can be real differ-

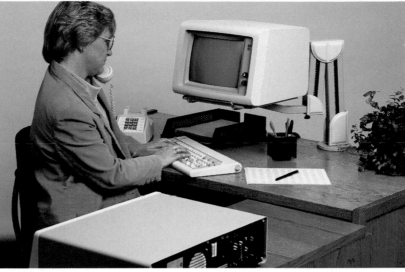

**Ergonomic considerations.** *(Left)* By placing a glare shield over your CRT, you decrease glare and increase the clarity of the characters. *(Right)* This video display stand tilts and swivels so that your neck does not have to.

ences in the feel of keyboards similar to those on office typewriters. Some keyboards do not have a solid touch. It is important that you have a tactile sense with your fingers on the keys, so that you know when you have engaged a key and released it. Make sure the keys are not cramped together, since you will find your typing is error-prone if your fingers are constantly overlapping on some of the keys. This is a special concern if you have large hands, chubby fingers, or long fingernails.

***Keyboard Color*** Ideally, keys should be gray with a matte finish. The dull finish reduces glare.

***Keyboard Slope*** If you plan to use your keyboard for many hours at a time, its slope will be very important to you. A keyboard slope should be a minimum of 7 degrees and a maximum of 15 degrees. Slopes outside this range can cause discomfort in the wrist and, consequently, high error rates. Some personal computer keyboards have adjustable slopes.

***Keyboard Layout*** Besides touch, you should look at the layout of the keyboard itself. Most follow the standard QWERTY layout of typewriter keyboards. However, some also have a separate numeric keypad, located to the right of the keyboard. You may find this useful if you enter a lot of numbers. In addition, some keyboards have separate function keys. The IBM Personal Computer,

for instance, has special keys to the left of the regular keys which are used to set margins, underline, and so on. When using a computer without function keys, on the other hand, you must accomplish these tasks by simultaneously holding down two keys (not labeled as to function). This is more obscure and less convenient.

***Detachable Keyboard*** Although you may be used to typing on a typewriter, where the keyboard is not separate from the rest of the machine, you may find a computer with a detachable keyboard—one that can be held on your lap—a desirable feature. This allows the keyboard to be moved around to suit the comfort of the user. This feature becomes indispensable for a computer that will be used by people of different sizes, adults and small children, for instance.

**Typewriter-style keyboard.** Note the function keys on the left and the numeric keypad on the right.

## Secondary Storage

You will undoubtedly want some secondary storage—that is, some way of keeping whatever you have created on the computer. In fact, you will probably want secondary storage even if all you want to do is play some off-the-shelf computer games. Games and other types of software come on diskettes and you need a disk drive to use them.

***Diskettes*** Although tape cassettes were once an inexpensive option, most personal computer software today comes on diskettes—floppy disks. Minifloppies, used with many personal computers, are 5¼ inches in diameter. Microdisks—

microfloppies—are only 3½ inches across, and were first popularized on the Apple Macintosh. But now they are becoming common on other models. Since microfloppies are smaller, they fit in convenient places, such as a purse or a pocket, and their drives take up less space in the computer. There is little question that microfloppies are the wave of the immediate future.

On most systems, at least one disk drive is built right into the computer console. Although not always necessary, you may find it helpful to have two (dual) disk drives to facilitate copying of disks for safekeeping. If your system has only one built-in drive, you may purchase another drive as a separate component.

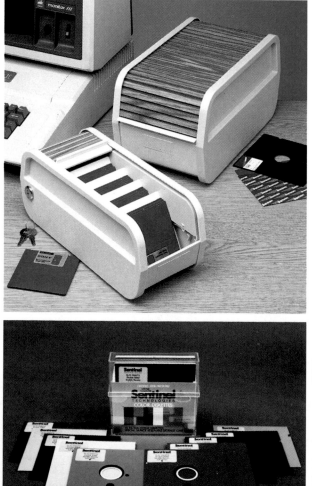

**Secondary storage.** *(Top left)* Microdisks, shown on the left, are 3½ inches across. Minifloppies, shown on the right, measure 5¼ inches across. Diskette cases, which provide safety and convenience, are available in both sizes. *(Bottom left)* Diskettes in a variety of colors provide a quick way to identify different data. *(Top right)* The innards of this hard disk drive shows the access arm hovering over the disk. *(Bottom right)* The Hardcard, which slips into an expansion slot inside the computer, is a convenient way to add another 10 megabytes of hard disk.

***Hard Disks***     Most hard disks are 5-inch or 3½-inch Winchester disks. Although more expensive than floppy disk drives, hard disks are fast and reliable and can hold lots of data. These features have made hard disks an increasingly attractive option for personal computer buyers. Some sophisticated personal computers come with a built-in hard disk drive, with storage capacity of 10 or 20 or even 30 million bytes—characters—of data; greater capacities are available if you can pay for it. But hard disks can be bought separately too, and the price is coming down.

## Printers

A printer is probably the most expensive piece of peripheral equipment you will buy. Although some very inexpensive printers are available, most likely you will find that those $300 and up are the ones most useful to you.

When choosing a printer you will want to consider speed, quality, and cost.

***Dot-Matrix Printers***     For "everyday" printing, a dot-matrix printer, costing $300 or more, will do very nicely. A dot-matrix printer can print as many as 250 characters per second, forming each character out of a grid of pins or dots, much like the lights on a bank temperature sign or stadium scoreboard. The appearance of the characters is not as good as those you would get from an electric typewriter, which is why they are not considered "letter quality"—that is, adequate for office correspondence. Some dot-matrix printers, however, can make a second pass at the characters or use a more dense array of dots to make the letters more fully formed, a result called "near letter quality." Dot-matrix printers can also be used for printing computer-generated graphics.

***Letter-Quality Printers***     A letter-quality printer produces the sharp characters that are a must for business correspondence. Most letter-quality printers use a daisy wheel, which can be removed, like a typewriter element, and replaced with another wheel with a different type font on it. The disadvantage of the daisy wheel printer is that it is relatively slow—often 55 characters per second or less. A letter-quality printer typically costs between $700 and $3000.

**Printers.** *(Top)* A color dot-matrix printer. *(Middle)* A Macintosh computer attached to a laser printer is a popular combination for desktop publishing. *(Bottom)* This man muffles his printer with a cover.

A dot-matrix printer in draft mode can print fast. However, the type is less readable than output from other printers or from a dot-matrix printer in near letter quality mode.

This is an example of near letter quality output. A dot-matrix printer prints each character twice or uses a more dense array of dots for improved quality.

Letter-quality printers with a daisy wheel are relatively slow. However, as shown here, they produce fully-formed characters that rival output from the finest typewriters. This makes them desirable for business correspondence.

Laser printers are fast and they produce high quality output, as shown here. They are useful for desktop publishing, which often combines text and graphics in one document. Generally, laser printers are more expensive than most other printers.

**Examples of output from various printers.**

***Ink-Jet Printers*** Although relatively slow, ink-jet printers can produce text and graphics whose color range and density usually surpass the color graphics of dot-matrix printers. The price spectrum is from $300 to several thousand dollars.

***Laser Printers*** These printers are top-of-the-line in print quality and speed. They also are the most expensive, starting at about $2000. Laser printers are used by desktop publishers to produce text and graphics on the same page.

***Printer Covers*** Both dot-matrix and letter-quality printers are noisy. An unmuffled printer generates about 80 decibels of sound, somewhere between a typewriter (70 decibels) and an outboard motor (90 decibels). If you will be working in an enclosed environment with your printer, the noise may become irritating. First, you should consider inexpensive, sound absorbing pads to go under the printer. If the problem is extreme, plas-

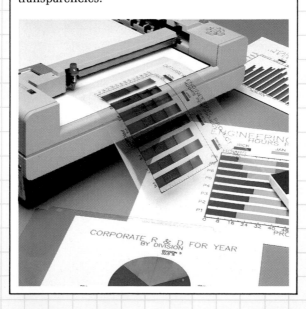

**A plotter.** Plotters for personal computers can produce good-looking charts on paper or transparencies.

tic printer covers are available that will reduce the noise to the level of a quiet conversation.

## Plotters

Plotters draw hard-copy graphics output in the form of maps, bar charts, engineering drawings, and even two-or three-dimensional illustrations. Plotters often come with a set of four pens in four different colors. Plotters for personal computers are becoming more popular as prices drop.

## Portability

Do you plan to let your computer grow roots after you install it, or will you be moving it around? Do you want a large video display or will the smaller versions on portable computers do? Portable computers have found a significant niche in the market. Although not especially lightweight (over 20 pounds), they are packaged to travel easily. The ultimate in portability is the laptop computer, which is lightweight (often under ten pounds) and small enough to fit in a briefcase. There are trade-offs, however, such as screen readability, and you should consider all aspects carefully.

## Other Hardware Options

There are a great many hardware variations; we will mention a few here.

***Communications Connections*** If you wish to connect your computer via telephone lines to electronic bulletin boards or information utilities such as CompuServe or The Source, you will need a modem, a device that converts computer data into data that can be transmitted over telephone lines. The Hayes Smartmodem series has become the industry standard; most new modems claim some degree of Hayes compatibility. A modem can be inside your computer, usually in the form of a plug-in card, or may be a stand-alone unit which plugs into the back of the computer.

***Other Input Devices*** If you are interested in games, you may wish to acquire a joy stick, which looks sort of like the stick shift on a car and allows

**A laptop computer.** These small computers, which often include built-in software, are an attractive option for users who travel.

**Modems.** *(Left)* The advantage of an internal modem, shown being installed in an Apple computer, is that it is out of sight and out of the way. *(Right)* External modems can be moved to another machine.

**An input device.** A mouse is an inexpensive option for controlling the screen cursor.

## Hardware Requirements for Software

When you look at a software package in a store, be sure to read what kind of hardware it requires. For example, you may read: "This package requires two disk drives, an 80-character display screen and printer, 256KB of memory and the MS-DOS operating system." You would hate to get home with your new software package and find you need to spend more for a joy stick or a few hundred dollars for a special circuit board that goes inside the computer. Usually the salesperson can advise you on hardware requirements for any particular software you might want to buy.

## Brand Names

In general, publishers of brand-name software usually offer better support than smaller, less well-known companies. Support may be in the form of tutorials, classes by the vendor or others, and the all-important hotline assistance. In addition, brand-name publishers usually produce superior documentation and offer upgrades to new and better versions of the software.

## Software Demonstrations

Wherever you can, ask to have the software demonstrated. You should not buy anything until you

you to manipulate a cursor on the screen. A more sophisticated device is a mouse, a gadget with wheels on it that you can roll around on a table top and which in turn also moves the cursor on the screen. There are several other input devices available. Ask your dealer about these for the computers you are considering.

*Sound*   Be sure to check out sound effects, particularly if you are interested in games. Make sure there are different tones, that they are not unpleasant, and that you have control over starting and stopping them. Many systems also have packaged software that allows you to produce computer-generated music.

## WHAT TO LOOK FOR IN SOFTWARE

There was a time when standardization on personal computers was nonexistent, because each personal computer had its own operating system. That is, software that ran on one computer did not necessarily run on another. This is still true to some extent, but great strides have been made. In a nutshell, the current standard is MS-DOS, made popular by IBM, and most personal computers today are compatible with the established IBM standard. This fact eases software purchases considerably.

We have noted the main categories of software in the box entitled *Who Needs It?* Now let us consider hardware requirements, brand names, demonstrations, and languages.

**Read the directions.** To make sure your hardware is adequate for the software you are buying, you should read the fine print carefully.

For Personal Computers
from IBM,* COMPAQ™ and
AT&T™ plus 1-2-3
Certified Compatibles.
See System Requirements.

**Release 2**

**System Requirements:**

| Hardware | DOS |
|---|---|
| IBM® PC, XT™, Portable, 3270 PC | 2.0, 2.1, 3.0, 3.1 |
| IBM 3270/G, 3270/GX | 2.0, 2.1 |
| IBM PCjr™ | 2.1 |
| IBM AT™ | 3.0, 3.1 |
| COMPAQ® Portable, PLUS,™ DESKPRO™ | 2.02 or 2.11 |
| AT&T™ PC 6300 | 2.11 |

Note:  IBM 3270 versions supported in stand alone PC mode.
IBM PCjr uses IBM Utility program.
Minimum system configuration is a single 5.25" double-sided, double-density disk drive and 256K bytes of memory.

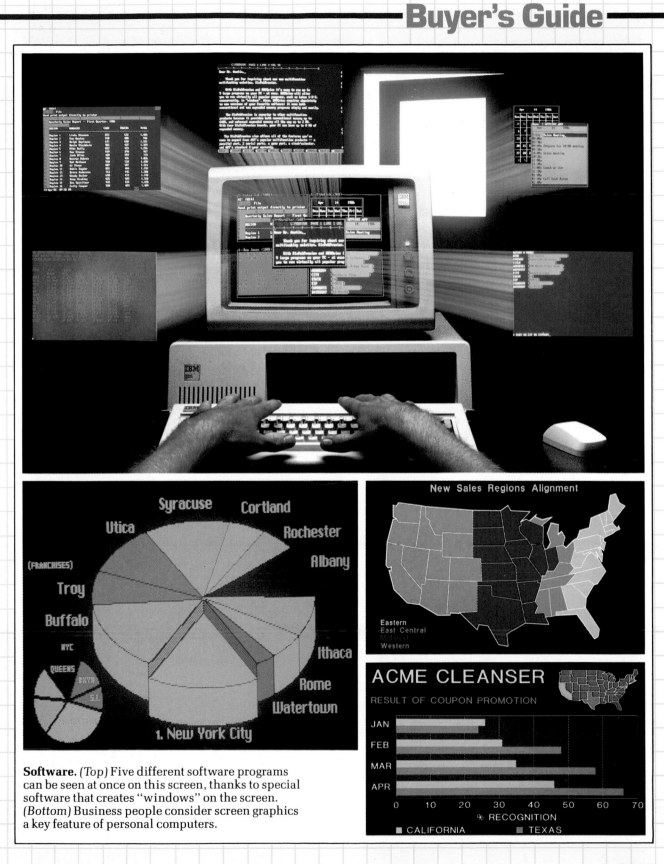

**Software.** *(Top)* Five different software programs can be seen at once on this screen, thanks to special software that creates "windows" on the screen. *(Bottom)* Business people consider screen graphics a key feature of personal computers.

see that it works. Despite this admonition, we must acknowledge that approximately half of the software purchased for personal computers is ordered through the mail from advertisements in computer magazines. In some cases, you may rely on the reputation of the software manufacturer or the recommendation of a friend. Other useful aids are the detailed software reviews found in trade publications such as *InfoWorld*.

### Languages

You may purchase one or more languages if you wish to write your own applications programs. Most microcomputers come with BASIC, the most popular language for personal computers. FORTRAN, Pascal, and other languages are also available for certain microcomputers.

## SHOPPING AROUND: WHERE TO BUY

Where you buy is important, and usually the tradeoff is between price and service—but not necessarily.

### The Dealer

The important point to remember is that you are buying a relationship with a dealer at the same time you are buying your computer. In a sense, you are also paying for your dealer's expertise. Answers to your questions, both now and in the future, may be the single most important part of your purchase. You can buy a personal computer in a computer store such as ComputerLand. You can buy one from a discount house or a department store. You can buy one from the manufacturer's own retail outlet; Tandy-Radio Shack, for example, has their own stores. You can buy one by mail or from an individual; this is not recommended unless you have a lot of experience, because such a sale is usually without dealer support.

> **QUESTIONS TO ASK THE SALESPERSON AT THE COMPUTER STORE**
>
> - How many units of this machine do you sell in a month?
> - Is the machine popular enough to have a user's group in my area?
> - Is there anyone I can call about problems?
> - Does the store offer classes on how to use this computer and software?
> - Do you offer a maintenance contract for this machine?
> - Does someone in your store fix the machines?
> - Can I expand the capabilities of the machine later?

### Financing

One advantage of department stores and some dealers is that the seller can often help you finance the purchase by either carrying the loan or making arrangements with a financial institution.

### Service and Support

Perhaps the biggest single argument for buying at a specialized computer store is service and support. Who is going to help you through the rough spots? Computer-store salespeople may be qualified to demonstrate different equipment and software, make sure everything works before it leaves the store, and help you over the phone with any glitches you later encounter at home. You will have to be your own judge of this, however. There is a great deal of turnover among computer-store personnel; equipment and software change rapidly and you may find, in fact, that the personnel are not as knowledgeable and helpful as you had hoped. However, many stores offer training classes (free or for a price). Many will replace your computer, if there is a warranty to that effect. Some offer a loaner if your computer is being repaired.

### Maintenance Contract

When buying a computer, you may wish to check out getting a maintenance contract, which should cover both parts and labor. Contracts differ in their coverage:

1. The best type of contract offers a repair person to come out and fix your system on-site within a certain number of hours. This option is usually available only for significant business customers.

2. The next best is a courier pick-up and delivery repair service. This usually costs 25 percent

**Repair.** If your computer breaks down you will probably need to take it to a repair center.

less than on-site repair.

3. Carry-in service allows you to bring your machine in for repairs. With courier or carry-in service, the store may provide you with a loaner while they fix it.

4. Another service provides a hotline you can call, and the person at the other end will help you troubleshoot. Clearly, this is just for basic problems of usage, not for getting inside the machine with tools.

5. The least convenient maintenance contract allows you to mail the machine in for repair.

## Used Computers

Used car lots are common enough. Could used computer stores become a staple in society? Probably not, because there is too little profit for dealers, and they do not want to warrant the goods. But it may be possible to pick up a bargain from an individual. Check the ads in your local newspaper.

But be careful. There is no way, for instance, for you to know what kind of workout the second-hand computer has had. Was it merely played with from time to time or was it the office workhorse every day for two years? Try out everything you can, such as each key on the keyboard and the disk drives.

Another angle, and this may be a psychological one, is that the seller may want to charge you a price which is related to the original price paid two years ago. Perhaps the seller paid $5000 for the system and thinks that $3000 is a fair price for the used equipment. But new comparable equipment may now be less than $3000. Always compare the computer system with today's prices. Despite these reservations, there may be some real bargains available in used equipment. Shop carefully.

## PEOPLE CONNECTIONS

"User friendly" is an overused word in the computer industry. It means how easy it is for you, the user, to learn to operate a computer or piece of software.

### Documentation

Nothing is as important as documentation, the written manuals and instructions that accompany hardware and software. Unfortunately, some of it

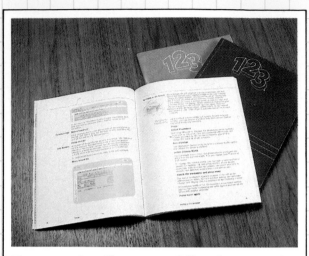

**Documentation.** Clear, easy-to-follow documentation is one of the most important features of a software package.

is inadequate. The weakest link in personal computer systems is the documentation. Ask to see the documentation when you buy. See if you can take something from the documentation and actually try it out on a machine in the store. It should be simple to understand, and have very little jargon in it.

Documentation should include simple instructions that let you actually do something right away. Some documentation goes on and on for many pages for a particular activity. The problem is that they have given you all the variations for all the options for each type of activity, when all you really need to get started is the simplest form of the activity. The frills can come later.

Documentation should also have visual clarity. The instructions should be very easy to follow. Sections in a manual should be separated with durable index tab pages. There should be lots of white space, pictures, demonstrations, and examples so that you have no trouble following what is happening. The documentation should also have attractive packaging (not just be a collection of typewritten sheets), although packaging alone, of course, will not guarantee good documentation.

### Training

Can you teach yourself? Besides the documentation, there are numerous books on the market that can teach you about various software packages

and programming. There are several books on the popular Lotus 1-2-3 package, for example, and possibly hundreds on the BASIC language. Magazines are also available to help you, and several have columns to answer questions from readers.

As mentioned, some computer stores offer classes in the use of computers. Other private parties do, too, although the fees are often substantial. Many local colleges offer courses, although you may want to be sure to get in line early for sign-ups. It also may be possible to get private lessons. Although this may be the most expensive method, it might be very effective.

Some manufacturers provide self-teaching material on diskettes that can teach you, with your "hands-on" participation, right on your own computer. These lessons, called tutorials, may be the most effective teaching method of all.

### THE VERY BEST?

"Best" is a relative term. Some people think that "technologically advanced" is automatically best, but that is of true importance to only a few. For business people, what often matters most is compatibility, that is, assurance that their computers will all run the same software. For the uninitiated, support may be more important than any other single factor: just who is going to be available to answer your questions, once you bring all the boxes home?

**Training.** Hardware and software purchases, especially by businesses, sometimes include classes provided by the dealer.

## A SURVEY FOR THE PROSPECTIVE BUYER

With this background, we hope you are now in a position to answer some questions as to what kind of computer you want. Take this completed survey with you as you shop around.

1. **Price Range.** I can spend
   - ☐ under $500  ☐ up to $1000
   - ☐ up to $2000  ☐ up to $4000  ☐ more

2. **Uses for Computer.** Rank the following in order. I wish to use the computer for:

   _____ Playing video games

   _____ Adult educational purposes (such as foreign language drill, learning programming)

   _____ Children's educational purposes (teaching arithmetic, typing, programming, and so forth)

   _____ Word processing (writing papers, reports, memos, letters)

   _____ Business applications (such as financial spreadsheets, database management, accounting, scheduling)

   _____ Office "homework"

   _____ Mailing lists

   _____ Publishing newsletters

   _____ Personal record keeping (address lists, list of insured possessions, appointment calendar, fitness progress, and so forth)

   _____ Personal finance (taxes, managing expenses, tracking stock market, banking from home)

   _____ Programming

   _____ Information retrieval (from services such as CompuServe, The Source or more specific information sources)

   _____ Shopping from home

   _____ Other: _____

   _____

   _____

**Business software.** A variety of software is available for business users.

3. **Hardware Features Wanted.** I want the following features on my computer:

   _____ 16-bit processor or _____ 32-bit processor

   _____ 128K bytes of memory _____ 256K bytes of memory _____ 512K bytes of memory or _____ 640K bytes of memory

   _____ Expandable memory

   _____ 80-column screen

   _____ Excellent screen readability

   _____ Monochrome screen or _____ color screen

   _____ Screen that can tilt and swivel

   _____ Membrane keyboard

   _____ Keyboard similar to office typewriter

   _____ Numeric keypad

   _____ Function keys

   _____ Detachable keyboard

   _____ Single disk drive or _____ dual disk drive

_____ Hard disk drive

_____ Expandable storage

_____ Dot-matrix printer

_____ Letter-quality printer

_____ Ink-Jet printer

_____ Laser printer

_____ Printer cover

_____ Portability

_____ Modem

_____ Joy stick

_____ Mouse

_____ Sound

_____ Other: _____

_____

_____

**Games.** Software for games often comes in colorful packages.

4. **Software Wanted.** I want the following software:

_____ Games and recreation software

_____ Word processing

_____ Spreadsheets

_____ Database management

_____ Graphics

_____ Information services

_____ Education packages

_____ Personal finances

_____ Home business packages

_____ Home record keeping

_____ BASIC

_____ Pascal

_____ FORTRAN

_____ COBOL

_____ Other: _____

_____

_____

5. **Other Features Wanted.** The following are important to me:

_____ Manufacturer's reputation

_____ Dealer's reputation

_____ Dealer financing

_____ Local service and support

_____ Maintenance contract

_____ Documentation quality

_____ Training

_____ Other: _____

_____

_____

_____

_____

_____

and particle matter to the air, where they then find their way into the computer.

The rewards for your vigilance are largely invisible. Your computer will look a little nicer, of course, but—more important—it will run smoothly for marathon stretches before it needs servicing. When that time comes, however, you will be glad the computer doctor is available.

## The Computer Doctor

The worst has happened. You have just witnessed your computer screen scream, flash, then go dead black. Though increasingly reliable, computers can still fizzle or fry. You need the **computer doctor,** jargon for a repairperson. Some computer doctors make house calls. They remove defective parts and replace them with good ones. Other "doctors" expect you to bring your computer to them (Figure 13-20).

The computer-repair industry is divided among computer manufacturers, retailers, and repair companies. But it is not an easy business. Stocking an inventory of spare parts takes a lot of capital. Also, it is hard to find and train good servicepeople, and, once employed, they are expensive. But so is the service. When computer systems fail, people generally want them fixed as quickly as possible and accept premium charges.

A warning note to the sophisticated buyer who has the skills to shop around and mix and match hardware: Mixed manufacturer systems are the most frustrating to repair because each manufacturer can claim that the problem is in the other guy's equipment.

## Computer Security

When people talk about computer security, they are usually thinking of corporate thieves, government secrets, or teenage hackers. But for you and your personal computer, it becomes more simple: Will the machine still be there when you get home? Burglars pick items that can be easily resold. Stereos and TVs have always been favorites, but now personal computers top the list. In addition to the usual precautions, you may want to consider physical lockups for your computer.

Apple notes that being transportable is one of the Macintosh's advantages, provided it does not go anywhere without you. A specially designed security kit makes sure it doesn't: Metal plates snap into the main unit and keyboard, and a strong cable loops through these and locks to your desk. Many people simply bolt their machines to bulky furniture. Others place their personal computers in specially designed cabinets that open conveniently for use but close and lock.

**ON YOUR NEWSSTAND: COMPUTER MAGAZINES**

If you plan a career as a data processing professional, you will probably want to subscribe to *Computerworld*, a fat weekly newspaper often called the *Wall Street Journal* of the computer industry. There are also classy magazines, such as *Datamation*, that provide general technical information. But most computer magazines focus on the personal computer industry. And—many of them are available in your local supermarket. Here is a representative list.

- *InfoWorld*. This weekly magazine is probably on the must-read list for any serious student of microcomputers. Appeals to both beginners and veterans. Covers new products, conventions, and philosophical issues. Reviews of new hardware and software.

- *Byte*. A serious magazine, pretty heavy on technical issues and bulging with advertising. Of interest primarily to serious computer enthusiasts.

- *Personal Computing*. The best-selling publication in a crowded field, this magazine is aimed at a wide audience. Product reviews tend to be complimentary, but the stated purpose of the magazine is to ignore what it considers inferior products.

- *Compute!* Loaded with programs that you can enter in your own computer if you are so inclined. It also features hardware reviews.

In addition, there are numerous magazines designed for specific users. Some are oriented toward programming and operating systems (*Dr. Dobb's Journal, User's Guide for MS-DOS*); some toward togetherness (*Family Computing*); and some toward software (*Software Digest, Personal Software*). Some are specifically geared to people who own some of the more popular personal computers. Apple users have *InCider* and *Nibble* and *MacWorld*; IBM users have *PC Magazine* and *PC World*. There are still more magazines for TRS-80 and other users.

One more note. Check your household insurance policy—there is a good chance that personal computers are specifically excluded. It is a good idea to buy separate insurance if your investment is substantial. Insurance companies now offer special packages for this purpose for a nominal annual fee.

We shall address the subject of security in detail in Chapter 19.

## Computer Passions: Kits, Clubs, Fairs, and Camps

As we noted earlier, the first computer hobbyist kit came out in 1975; the MITS Altair 8800 was built around the Intel 8080 chip. The kit consisted of all parts needed to construct the computer and included complete, step-by-step instructions. The Altair kit was produced as a last-ditch effort to save the company, but it proved highly successful and has been widely imitated since. Now the best-known kits are made by Heath. But kit-users are definitely a minority; most microcomputer users purchased their machines intact.

Microcomputer users make up their own microcommunity of the computer industry, and in recent years a host of groups of computer enthusiasts has sprung up. The Boston Computer Society, the Chicago Area Computer Hobbyist's Exchange, and the Delaware Valley Computer Society are all examples of computer clubs organized for personal computer owners. Some clubs are organized around particular brands of computers, such as the Orange County (California) TRS-80 Users Group, the Heath Users Group, and such Apple clubs as Apple Core, Apple Pie, and Apple-Holics. There is also a national association called the Personal Computing Society. The presence of a user group gives potential buyers comfort. They know that they can join a group of people with similar problems and interests.

Various manufacturers publish newsletters for users of their equipment, and there are also independently published periodicals, including some catering to a particular professional orientation, such as *The Physicians Microcomputer Report* and *The Computing Teacher*. In addition, many books are published on computing and programming. Finally, for children who are computer fans there are computer summer camps, in which an outdoor program is mixed with instruction in learning how to use microcomputers.

Computer shows and fairs have become extremely popular. In California, for example, there is an annual Computer Swap Meet and also the San Francisco-area West Computer Faire. Conventions such as the National Computer Conference feature exhibits and discussions not only on mainframes and minicomputers, but on micros as well.

# Moving On to the Key Software Packages

In this chapter we have referred to software in a general way, mostly in the context of what you could do with a personal computer. But many people want to know more. Indeed, if you are planning to enter a business environment, you *need* to know more. In the next three chapters we offer descriptions of how key business software packages work. Chapter 14 covers word processing, Chapter 15 covers spreadsheets and graphics, and Chapter 16 covers database management.

We cannot attempt to tell you exactly what key to push for what action because that varies with the brand name of the package. But our look at these important packages will be significant because we can tell you what kinds of things these packages can do for you and, in general, how they work. You may be surprised at how easy it is.

## Summary and Key Terms

- Microcomputers are also called **personal computers.**

- The main components of a personal computer are the microprocessor, random-access memory (RAM), and read-only memory (ROM). A keyboard is used for inputting data, and a video screen displays input and output. A disk drive is used for reading and writing on floppy disks.

- Most of the popular software packages require more than 64K bytes of memory—especially **RAM-resident** programs, which are loaded into memory after the computer is turned on.

- Traditionally, the personal computer user has chosen either the faster **dot-matrix** printer or the slower **daisy wheel** character printers that produce **letter-quality** printing. However, the newer **laser** printers produce fast, letter-quality printing, and the latest models of dot-matrix printers produce **near-letter-quality** printing.

- An add-on is any semipermanent device, such as an extra disk drive, that attaches to a computer and is directly affected by computer processing. Supplies are accessories such as printer ribbons.

- **Open architecture** means that the computer design allows users to insert additional circuit boards in **expansion slots** inside the computer. **Closed architecture** limits add-ons to those that can be plugged into the back of the computer.

- Some personal computer applications include communications, education, word processing, **home controls,** and entertainment.

- In the home personal computers are most conveniently used for tasks that do not require extensive key input.

- A broadly successful integration of computers into elementary and high-school curriculums requires good software and an emphasis on practical applications rather than just drills and exercises.

- Some business applications include accounting, inventory, planning, financial analysis, and word processing. Businesses seek to maximize the use of personal computer portability and networking.

- Personal computer manufacturing, which began in 1975 with the **MITS Altair,** was dominated by three companies—Apple, Tandy, and Commodore—until IBM entered the market in 1981. IBM came to dominate the market with its PC, which offered attractive features such as a processor that could address a lot of memory, open architecture, and function keys. AT&T, which entered the market in 1984, has emphasized convenient communications applications. Other significant manufacturers are Tandy's Radio Shack, Commodore, Atari, and Compaq.

- IBM's dominance led many manufacturers to make **compatibles,** which run the same software that runs on the IBM PC. Some personal computers are **clones** that are deliberately similar to the IBM PC, while others are **hybrids,** which have their unique designs but can simulate another computer, usually the IBM PC.

- **Supermicros** are compatible with the IBM PC AT and are **multiuser, multitasking** personal computers that have a high-speed microprocessor, significantly increased memory, and hard-disk storage capacity.

- The first **portable computers** weighed between 25 and 40 pounds. **Laptop computers,** which can weigh as little as 9 pounds, are especially convenient for journalists and traveling businesspeople.

- **Computer marts** are buildings designed to contain a large number of computer stores.

- Some personal computer dealers see more sales potential in business customers than in home computer customers.

- Some dealers, faced with increased competition and lower profits, compensate by selling excess merchandise to the **gray market** of unauthorized dealers. Some dealers turn to **vertical markets,** groups of customers with similar needs— accountants, for example.

- In the fast-growing secondhand market, a price is affected by the current price for the same model sold new. Still, secondhand prices can offer substantial savings, although buyers should note that secondhand machines are seldom under warranty, and they should test them carefully before buying.

- Software and accessories for discontinued personal computer models are difficult to find. Such models are known as **orphans.**

- **Vaporware** is hardware or software that is marketed before it exists.

- American personal computer vendors are unable to plan a single European advertising campaign because markets vary from country to country. China represents a large potential market. Japan may provide competition in the personal computer market as a result of **MSX machines,** microcomputers that run programs written in **Microsoft Extended Basic.**

- Proper computer care includes such precautions as vacuuming the printer, storing disks properly, keeping food and drink away, cleaning the screen, and keeping the computer away from cigarette smoke and excessive heat. Proper care lessens the chance of needing a **computer doctor,** a repairperson from a manufacturer, retailer, or repair company.

- For personal computer owners computer security may involve specially designed security kits or cabinets and perhaps a separate insurance policy.

- Personal computer hobbyists can buy kits and construct their own computers, join computer clubs, and attend computer shows and fairs.

## / Review Questions

1. What are some factors that affect memory requirements?

2. Why do many personal computer owners buy dot-matrix printers?

3. Distinguish between add-ons and supplies, and give examples of each.

4. Summarize personal computer applications in the following areas: communications, education, word processing, home controls, and entertainment.

5. Why do many consider it impractical to use a personal computer for managing a checking account?

6. How did businesses expand the usefulness of the personal computer?

7. Discuss the impact of the following companies on the personal computer market: Apple, IBM, AT&T, Tandy's Radio Shack, Commodore, Atari, and Compaq.

8. Explain what compatibles, clones, and hybrids are and why they appeared on the market.

9. Explain what the gray market and vertical markets are and why many dealers turned to them.

10. What should a computer buyer know about the secondhand market?

## / Discussion Questions

1. Do you intend to buy a personal computer? Why or why not?

2. If you were to buy a personal computer, what add-ons and supplies would you want and why?

3. Will personal computers eventually become attractive to the average buyer? Explain your answer.

# 14

# Word Processing

## The Most Popular Use of Personal Computers

Word processing programs help people create, edit, format, store, and print text—with wonderful assistance from the computer.

Word processing software packages are the most widely used personal computer application. Many personal computer owners use their machines solely for word processing. Furthermore, there are probably more word processing packages in the marketplace than any other type of software.

When Southwind Community College went on a personal computer binge, they bought ample supplies for classrooms, for the computer lab, and for individual departments. The new personal computer for the social sciences department was set up in the workroom, where it sat unused for several weeks. Instructor Casey Dohse, from the data processing department, offered to teach the social sciences instructors how to use the new machine. She felt that the obvious first application was word processing, so instructors could prepare handouts and tests.

Casey prepared a memo offering one-on-one instruction in word processing. She dropped the memo in the mailboxes of the 23 instructors and six staff members in the department. Several took her up on the offer, but the two notable cases were work-study student Marla Broderick and economics professor Don Chamberlain.

Marla was ecstatic. She could not wait to get her hands on the machine because she thought that added skills would enhance her job possibilities. Don Chamberlain was less enthusiastic. Undeterred, Casey led Don through the step-by-step process. As Don actually produced, revised, and printed a test—touching a computer for the first time—he began to sit up a little straighter. When he realized that, with the help of some printed documentation, he could manage on his own, he felt jubilant. The whole lesson had taken only 25 minutes. It was then that he confessed to Casey that he had been avoiding computers and that the only reason he had learned word processing was that he had been offered private tutoring.

There are two lessons in this true story. One is that there are a variety of people waiting to learn about computers, some fearful, some not. But, in either case, word processing is quite a simple introduction. Although an enthusiast can spend weeks learning all the bells and whistles, the basic process can be learned quite quickly and easily by anyone.

## Word Processing Then and Now

**Word processing** is the creation, editing, formatting, storing, and printing of text. Look at that definition again. Is a computer really needed for all those things? If we consider just putting letters on paper, we could say that word processing existed long before the advent of computers. In addition to handwriting, printing machines and the typewriter have been used in offices for the last century. Journalists, authors, teachers, and students have relied on the typewriter to produce an easy-to-read document. Printed or typed material also has the advantage of being easily reproduced using a copy machine.

But there is a problem with typing. Have you ever left a sentence out of a term paper? And what about the misspelled words or just plain typos? You turn reluctantly to the white-out and reconcile yourself to the smeared and smudged results. You do this because you do not have the time to type it all again.

## WORD PROCESSING AND YOUR POLITICIAN

During a campaign a political speech writer may have to prepare ten or more different speeches for a candidate each day. Sometimes a speech must be modified at the last minute to include comments about late-breaking world or local news or perhaps a juicy scandal in the opponent's campaign.

Political speech writers seem to know a good thing when they see it. The good thing, in this case, is word processing. With word processing programs a speech writer can store the basic political positions of their candidate in separate files on a disk. Then, when a speech is required for a group, the writer combines the comments that are appropriate in one document, then adds a few new paragraphs to customize the speech for the particular group who will hear it. Then the finished product is printed for the candidate.

The writer can even create and pull from a separate file of stories and jokes to be used as "ice-breakers" at the beginning of the speech. In politics not even humor is left to chance, and word processing allows the political writer to access just the right light touch.

## The Need for Perfect Typing

You may be able to hand in a less-than-perfect term paper, but less than perfect is not acceptable in business. The appearance of a document or letter is crucial to the image of a business. But beyond image there may be exacting legal demands. Documents submitted in a court of law, for example, must be originals (not copies), and there may be no corrections on the document. If the same legal document needs to be sent to different persons or offices, one document must be typed perfectly again and again. If an attorney decides to add a sentence or clause, at least one page of all the documents must be retyped.

For you as a student, careful typing is required when you seek employment. A poorly typed resume makes a bad impression. If you pay to have your resume typed, you have to pay again to add courses and experience when the original resume is out of date. A resume that is customized for a particular position might also require partial or complete retyping—even text that does not change (like your high school) may have to be retyped. There is a better way.

## Beginnings: Word Processing in the Computer Age

Many people think that the word processing revolution began with secretaries. Programmers, however, were the first to harness the computer's power for this purpose. In the early 1970s programmers often typed their documentation in the same way that they typed their programs: They entered them from a keyboard into the computer's memory, then stored them on disk. In this way they could modify the documentation as a program was modified. Since the documents were stored electronically, the programmers could make changes quickly, and the computer printed the document with no errors. No one was calling it word processing yet, but the rudiments were there.

Next came the machine that has become a staple in the office: the **dedicated word processor.** It was called dedicated because manufacturers developed computers and software especially for the purpose of word processing. Furthermore, the machines were purchased with the specific intent of dedicating them to the word processing function. Let us examine these machines more closely.

## Dedicated Word Processors in the Office

A secretary using a dedicated word processor can type at a keyboard just as he or she does at a typewriter. However, instead of permanent type on paper, letters and numbers are created electronically in the computer's memory, and the secretary can see them on the screen. Documents are stored on a disk and can be printed now or later. If modifications are necessary, a secretary can keep what is good and delete what is bad. He or she can even include material stored on the disk in new documents. Secretaries like this feature since once a sentence is typed correctly, they never have to retype it. In contrast, a document prepared on a typewriter usually has to be retyped from scratch if there are changes.

Legal secretaries and secretaries in purchasing offices particularly like the ability to store frequently used paragraphs of contractual conditions in separate files on a disk. When these same paragraphs are needed in a new document, secretaries retrieve the paragraphs and insert them in the new document. This means tremendous time savings and relief from monotonous repetitive typing.

## Word Processing for Everyone

Word processing in the office was the opening wedge. Secretaries were the first to appreciate the benefits of word processing, but the phenomenon could not be contained for long. The next natural step was word processing software for personal computers. The leap to personal computers was the signal that word processing was for everyone.

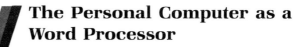

## The Personal Computer as a Word Processor

Word processing on a personal computer is a bargain indeed. A personal computer can do with words almost all that a dedicated word processor can do, although a dedicated word processor is easier to use. On the other hand, a personal computer can perform functions that a dedicated word processor cannot. A dedicated word processor usually can only do word processing. However, with the appropriate software, your personal computer lets you program in a computer language, use spreadsheets, database management packages, and graphics programs. In its spare time the personal computer can even play a mean game of Space Invaders. This ability to perform many functions and to do them all well means that both businesspeople and individuals can often justify the expense of a personal computer.

Schools and colleges have made personal computers and word processing programs available to students to help them write papers. Research shows that students in English composition classes produce superior papers using word processing. Personal computers and word processing software make a winning combination for students. For example, students can insert new sentences or change the

## EQUIPMENT REQUIRED FOR WORD PROCESSING ON A PERSONAL COMPUTER

1. A keyboard that is similar in key layout to a typewriter.
2. A screen that provides a clear, sharp picture and displays 80 characters on a line.
3. A personal computer with at least 128K bytes of memory and one or more floppy-disk drives.
4. A printer that provides clear type.
5. A word processing program on a floppy diskette and extra diskettes for storage.
6. User manuals for the word processing program. You also may find that a book about your word processing program is useful.

order of paragraphs in a paper. Because the printer can quickly "type" a copy of their finished paper, students do not have to spend hours retyping. Some students find uses outside of school for word processing. Let us consider a case in which a student found his knowledge of word processing on a personal computer to be a real time saver.

## Word Processing to the Rescue

Jack Stark knew at the end of his junior year of college that he needed more income or he would have to leave school. He found a job as the assistant manager of an apartment complex. Jack was given a small apartment rent free. That was the good news. The bad news was that most of Jack's work was repetitive and boring. Jack spent a lot of time hunched over his typewriter typing standard letters to tenants. These notices concerned pets, parking regulations, loud parties, and late rent payments. As he listlessly typed messages again and again, he was a victim of both his own poor typing and crushing boredom. He thought that there might be a better way.

## A Little Help from a Friend

Jack's friend Susan had her own personal computer. One day when Jack was complaining about the repetitive letters he had to type, Susan suggested that he consider using word processing. Jack was immediately interested—he had seen a word processing demonstration once before. Susan's word processing package, however, was not the same one that Jack had seen. It seemed to him that it was a lot harder to use. Susan explained that the essential functions performed by word processing packages were the same regardless of which package was used.

## New Skills and the Payoffs

Jack invested some time learning the word processing package. He probably could have typed the first few letters he produced a lot faster on a typewriter. But the advantage of word processing soon became clear. His typing mistakes were easier to correct. But the advantage that saved Jack the most time related to the repetitive nature of the letters. He saved his letters on a diskette. The next time he had to type a similar letter, he loaded the original letter into the computer. Then he just changed some names, places, and dates and printed out the new letter. Jack placed "loud parties," "parking for guests," and "late rent—first notice" form letters on a disk. In only a few minutes he could produce a customized and perfectly "typed" letter for most of the common situations he faced. Word processing freed him from a very time-consuming aspect of his job.

His employer was impressed with Jack's ability to get his work out on time. In the next section we shall describe word processing features and how to use them, and we shall continue to follow Jack's progress.

# The Basics of Word Processing

Word processing programs for a personal computer differ in the exact way in which they let you create text. Their advanced features and price may be different, too. But there are certain essential functions that any word processing package performs. Let us take a look at these functions and see how Jack's word processing program performs some of them.

## Features of Word Processing

A word processing program lets you use the computer's keyboard to enter text into the computer's internal memory. You can see what you are entering on the screen and make modifications to the text. Then the program lets you save the text on a disk and print what you have typed. To do these things, word processing programs have these basic features:

- Material that has already been typed can be updated without retyping material that does not change.

- Left and right margins and tab stops can be set.

- Portions of the text can be copied or moved.

- A permanent copy of the text can be saved on a disk, and a copy of the text can be loaded from a disk back into the computer.

- The text can be printed.

## Getting Started

Suppose that Jack wants to send a letter to a tenant whose rent is late. We shall describe what he must do to create the letter.

He begins by loading the software into the personal computer he has borrowed from Susan. Jack is working with a popular word processing program called WordStar. When he loads WordStar he sees a copyright statement on the screen for several seconds, then he sees the Opening Menu (Figure 14-1a). A **menu** is a list of commands and the keystrokes necessary to execute those commands. A computer user chooses from the various commands on a menu that appears on a screen just as a diner chooses from the offerings on a restaurant menu. Software that uses menus to give choices is referred to as **menu-driven**.

---

## SOME MAXIMS FOR BEGINNERS IN WORD PROCESSING

- **Try before you buy.** In a way word processing programs are like cars. Each one is a little different, and there are some that just seem to "fit" you. Try to "test drive" several packages by entering, saving, and printing a short letter on each one before you decide on the one you want to buy.

- **Now is better than later.** Using a satisfactory program now is better than waiting for that one perfect package to come along later.

- **Keep it simple.** After you have selected a package, learn how to use it to do the essential tasks of word processing: creating, modifying, saving, and printing documents. Practice the commands needed to perform these tasks until you know them well. When you actually use word processing, you will accomplish 95% of your work using only 5% of the available commands. Learn basic commands; worry about the frills later, when you actually need them.

- **Save your documents twice.** Save your document on one disk, then save it again so that you always have a backup copy of your work. Also, if you have a relatively long document to enter, after you type a page or so, save it. That way, if you make a big mistake and lose the document that you have in internal memory before it is completed and saved (or if the electricity goes out!), you still have some of it safely on your disk. Remember, the only permanent copy of your work is what you have saved on your disk.

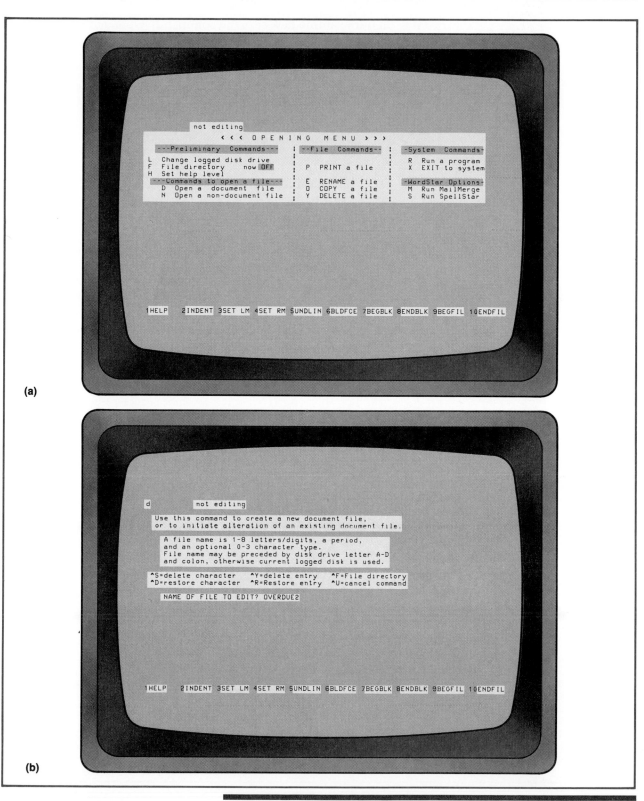

**Figure 14-1  Getting started in WordStar.** (a) The Opening Menu of WordStar. This is the first menu Jack Stark sees. (b) Jack is opening a file called OVERDUE2. He will then type his second-notice letter about overdue rent.

In our example Jack sees the command "Open a document file" next to the letter "D," so he presses D on his keyboard to open a file. A **file** is a document (letter, essay, manuscript, or whatever) created on a computer. Each file must have a name for identification purposes. Jack types in the name OVERDUE2, since this is the second overdue notice he is sending to this tenant (Figure 14-1b). After he presses the Enter, or Return, key on his keyboard, he is ready to start typing his letter.

## A Piece of Electronic Typing Paper

Think of the computer's screen as a page of typing paper. On the screen the word processing program indicates the top of the page and the left and right edges (margins) of the typed material. To show where the next typed character (letter, number, or punctuation) will appear on the screen, the program displays a **cursor** on the screen. The cursor is usually a blinking dash or rectangle that you can see easily. As you type a character, the cursor moves to the next character position; it shows you where your next typed character will appear. You can also move the cursor around on the screen (your electronic typing paper) by using special **cursor control keys** on the keyboard (Figure 14-2). The movable cursor lets you type

**Figure 14-2   The IBM PC keyboard.** The cursor control keys, located on the right side of the keyboard, are used to move the cursor around on the screen. The Enter or Return key is the vertical key with the arrow that is to the left of the cursor control keys. The Enter key is pressed at the end of each paragraph, not at the end of each line as on a typewriter. The function keys, located on the left side of the keyboard, are an easy way to give certain commands to the computer.

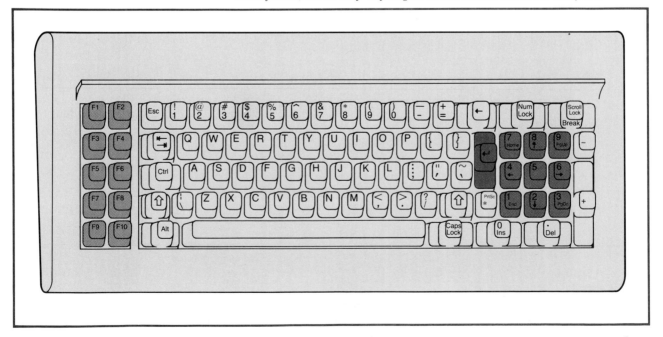

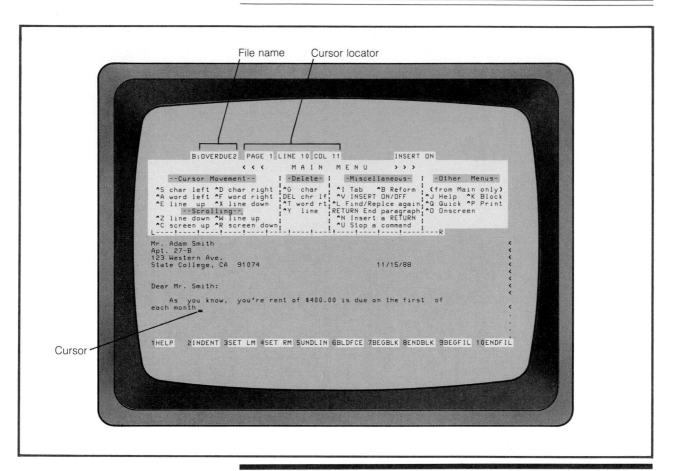

File name    Cursor locator

```
B:OVERDUE2  PAGE 1 LINE 10 COL 11              INSERT ON
             < < <   M A I N   M E N U   > > >
    --Cursor Movement--   : -Delete- :  --Miscellaneous--  : -Other  Menus-
^S char left ^D char right :^G  char  :^I Tab  ^B Reform  :(from Main only)
^A word left ^F word right :DEL chr lf:^V INSERT ON/OFF   :^J Help   ^K Block
^E line  up  ^X line down  :^T word rt:^L Find/Replce again:^Q Quick  ^P Print
     --Scrolling--        :^Y   line :RETURN End paragraph:^O Onscreen
^Z line down ^W line up    :         :   ^N Insert a RETURN
^C screen up ^R screen down:         :   ^U Stop a command
L----!----!----!----!----!---!----!----!----!----!----R
Mr. Adam Smith                                                    <
Apt. 27-B                                                         <
123 Western Ave.                                                  <
State College, CA  91074                  11/15/88                <
                                                                  <
                                                                  <
Dear Mr. Smith:                                                   <
                                                                  <
    As  you know,  you're rent of $400.00 is due on the first  of <
each month_                                                       .
                                                                  .
                                                                  .
1HELP   2INDENT 3SET LM 4SET RM SUNDLIN 6BLDFCE 7BEGBLK 8ENDBLK 9BEGFIL 10ENDFIL
```

Cursor

**Figure 14-3  The beginning of Jack's letter.** Jack has just finished typing the word "month" in his "overdue" letter. The position of the cursor (the dash just to the right of "month") shows where the next character that Jack enters will be placed. The Main Menu at the top of the screen is not entered by Jack—the word processing program displays the menu. The program also displays the dashed line to indicate the top of the page. The text that is under the dashed line was typed by Jack. The < to the right of the right margin is produced by the program and indicates that Jack pressed the Enter key at the end of that line. The < symbols will not show up when the letter is printed. The bottom line indicates functions that can be invoked by the function keys on the left side of the keyboard. Key F1 sets the help level (whether menus are displayed or not), F2 indents, F3 and F4 set the margins, F5 underlines, F6 sets boldface, F7 and F8 mark a block of text, F9 takes you to the beginning of the file (document), and F10 takes you to the end of the file.

where you wish on the screen. The screen displays the line of text you are typing—it looks just like a line of typing on paper. Remember that you are not really typing on the screen; the screen merely displays what you are entering into the computer's memory.

In Figure 14-3 you can see the screen of Jack's computer as he starts to type the letter. Notice that there is a new menu at the top of the screen called the Main Menu. This menu reminds a user of the keystrokes necessary to execute some of the most commonly used commands in WordStar. The right side of the menu refers to additional menus that give keystrokes for other commands. The menus

## TYPES OF WORD PROCESSING PROGRAMS

- **Business.** These programs duplicate the functions of the dedicated word processors used in business offices. Because so many already know how to use the dedicated machines, these packages sometimes cut down on confusion and reduce training costs.

- **Integrated.** These programs combine extensive word processing capability with other functions such as spreadsheets, graphics, and database management. They allow the easy inclusion of tables of numbers and graphs in a text document prepared using the word processing program.

- **Professional.** These programs are designed to be used by people whose job requires a lot of text preparation, especially text that will be published. The functions included go far beyond the essential word processing functions.

- **Scientific.** Used by mathematicians, scientists, and engineers, these programs allow the creation of the symbols (like the letters of the Greek alphabet) that are necessary in mathematics and statistics. These programs also allow the easy entry of algebraic equations.

- **Home.** These streamlined programs include only the essential word processing functions, but they do all the word processing that the average user wants to do. As the name indicates, these programs are meant for home or school work. These packages are less expensive than the professional packages.

can change at the top of the screen, leaving the text below untouched. (Note that since this chapter is a general discussion of word processing, we will not be examining the particular keystrokes for commands—they vary among word processing programs.)

The line above the menu displays the name of the document (OVERDUE2) and the page number, line number, and column number of the cursor. This cursor locator allows you to see where you are in your document. Notice in Figure 14-3 that the cursor is on page 1, line 10, column 11. Notice also the dashed line under the menu and the "L," which indicates the **left margin** of the "page" and the "R," which indicates the **right margin.** The exclamation points on the dashed line mark the **tab settings.**

The line at the very bottom of the screen in Figure 14-3 shows you what the function keys on the keyboard are used for in Word-Star. The **function keys** are ten keys located on the left side of the IBM PC keyboard that are labeled F1, F2, and so on (see Figure 14-2). In WordStar pressing the F1 key sets the help level (whether menus are displayed or not), F2 indents paragraphs, F3 sets the left margin (LM), and so forth.

## No Need to Worry about the Right Margin

When you are typing along with a word processing program, what happens when you reach the right-hand side of the page? The word processing program watches how close you are to the edge of the "paper" (the right margin). If there is not room at the end of a line to complete the word that you are typing, the program automatically starts that word at the left margin of the next line down on the screen. You never have to worry about running out of space on a line. The word processor plans ahead for you. This feature is called **word wrap.** You also do not have to push a Carriage Return key at the end of each line as you would with a typewriter. However, if you wish, the word processing program lets you hyphenate words at the right margin just as you would with a typewriter.

The right margin can be either ragged right or right-justified. **Ragged right** means that the right edge of your document is uneven, just as it would be if it were typed on a typewriter. **Right-justified** means that the right edge is even, as it is in this book.

## Scrolling

A word processing program usually lets you type page after page of material, but a screen can only display about 20 lines of text at any one time. This means that as you continue to type new lines, the lines you typed earlier move up the screen as each new line is added at the bottom. Eventually the first line you typed disappears off the top of the screen. But the line has not disappeared from the computer's memory. To see a line that has disappeared from the top of the screen, use your cursor control keys to move the cursor up to the top of the screen. As you continue to press the cursor control key that moves the cursor up, the line that disappeared drops back down onto the screen. The program treats the text you are typing as if it were all on a long roll of paper like a scroll. You "roll the scroll" up or down on the screen by using the cursor control keys, a process called **scrolling.** This lets you see any part of the document on the screen—but only 20 or so lines at a time.

In Figure 14-4a we see the letter that Jack has typed. We cannot see the top of the letter, but remember that it is still in the computer's memory. Notice that the word wrap and right-justification features have caused the right margin to be even.

## Easy Corrections

If, on the screen, you notice a mistake in what you have typed, you can easily move the cursor to the position of the error and make the correction; word processing programs let you delete characters or whole words or lines that you have already typed. You can also insert new characters in the middle of a line or a word without typing over (and erasing) the characters that are already in the line. The program nudges existing characters to the right of the insertion as you type the new characters. However, if you wish, the word processing program also lets you overtype (replace) characters you typed before.

In Jack's letter shown in Figure 14-4a, he made some typing errors in the third line from the bottom. To correct these, he moves the cursor to the first "a" in "aaction" using his cursor control keys. Then he pushes certain keys to delete the first "a". Next he moves the cursor to the "t" in "againts" and overtypes "st". The corrected line can be seen in Figure 14-4b.

## More Change Options

There are many other ways to make changes with word processing. Perhaps you misspelled some words or used some awkward wording. Or maybe you want to change the order of some paragraphs. Word processing makes it easy.

### Search and Replace

Suppose that you have misspelled a word many times in a word processed document. The word processing program has a function called **search and replace.** When you select this function from the menu, the program asks you to type the misspelled word. Then it asks you to enter the correct spelling. After you have done this, the program *searches* for all the places where the misspelled

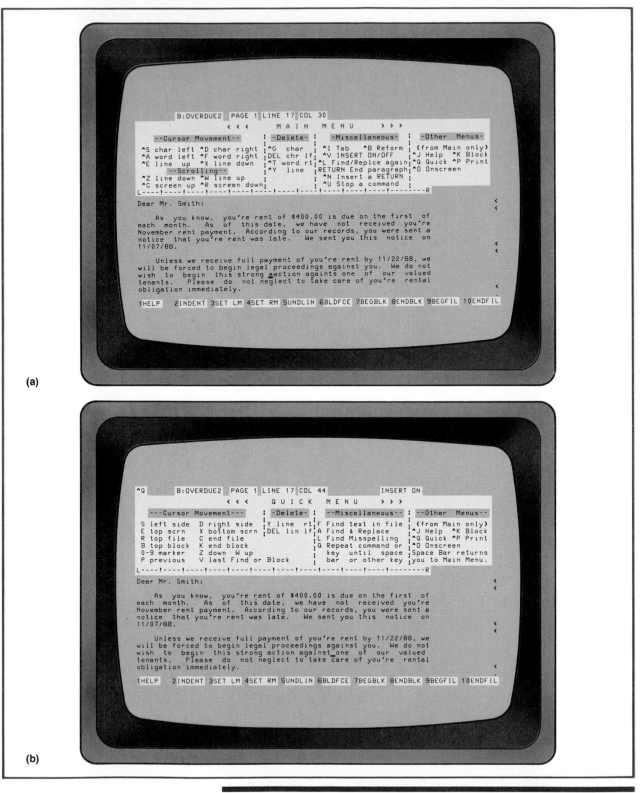

(a)

(b)

**Figure 14-4  Scrolling and correcting errors.** (a) You could see the top of Jack's letter by scrolling with the cursor control keys. (b) As described in the text, Jack has fixed his errors in the third line from the bottom of his letter.

word occurs in your paper and *replaces* each one with the correct spelling. Most word processing programs have a **conditional replace,** which asks you each time the program encounters the misspelled word to verify that you want the misspelled word replaced.

Jack realizes that he has misspelled "your" throughout his letter, so he decides to use WordStar's search-and-replace function to change "you're" to "your." The Quick Menu in Figure 14-4b shows, in the "Miscellaneous" column, the command that Jack can use to "Find & Replace" words in his documents. After giving the proper command, the screen displays "FIND?" and Jack types "you're" (Figure 14-5a). The screen then displays "REPLACE WITH?" and he responds "your"—the correct spelling. The software program searches Jack's letter until it finds "you're." The software then displays "Replace (Y/N):" in the upper right-hand corner of the screen. When Jack types "Y" for *yes,* the word "you're" is automatically replaced with "your," as shown in Figure 14-5b. Jack can then continue to find and replace "you're" by hitting just a few keys.

### Cut and Paste

Most word processing programs also have copy and move commands, generically known as **cut and paste.** These commands are useful for changing the order of sentences or paragraphs. The **copy** command lets a user place a copy of one or more lines in another location in the document. The program moves text apart to allow the insertion of your lines in the new location. The original text is not deleted after it is copied. Now the same text is in two different locations.

When you **move** one or more lines, these lines are copied to the new location, and the lines in the original location are deleted. The text that was moved appears only at its new location in your document. This is similar to cutting a section of typing out of a document and pasting it in a new location on the paper. However, when using the move command the word processing program does not leave a "hole" in your document—the text that surrounded the text before it was moved is adjusted and "closed." Now, by printing the altered text, you have a new document that suits you better. And you did not have to type the whole thing over again!

Jack decides that he would like to rearrange the second paragraph of his letter. He wants to move the last sentence so it becomes the first sentence of the paragraph. To do this, he calls up the Block Menu shown in Figure 14-6a. He marks the sentence to be moved (Figure 14-6a), and with the touch of a few keys it is moved to the new location (Figure 14-6b). Ah, the wonders of word processing!

### Formatting: Making It Look Nice

When you add and delete words and move sentences around, the breaks between lines in your document get messed up— you no longer have an even right edge. To make your document look

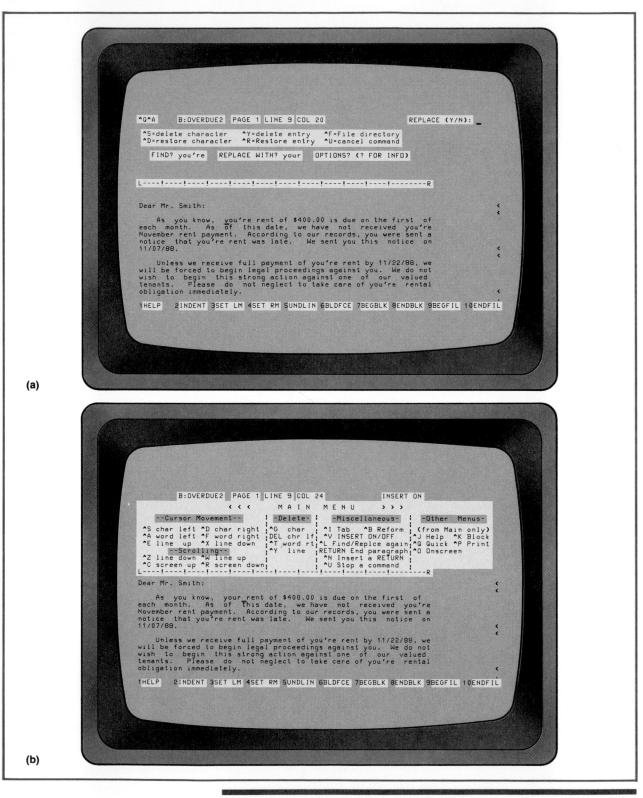

**Figure 14-5   Search and replace.** (a) With this function, Jack can easily search for "you're" and replace it with "your." (b) One "you're" has been fixed automatically, and now Jack can continue searching and replacing by pressing a few keys.

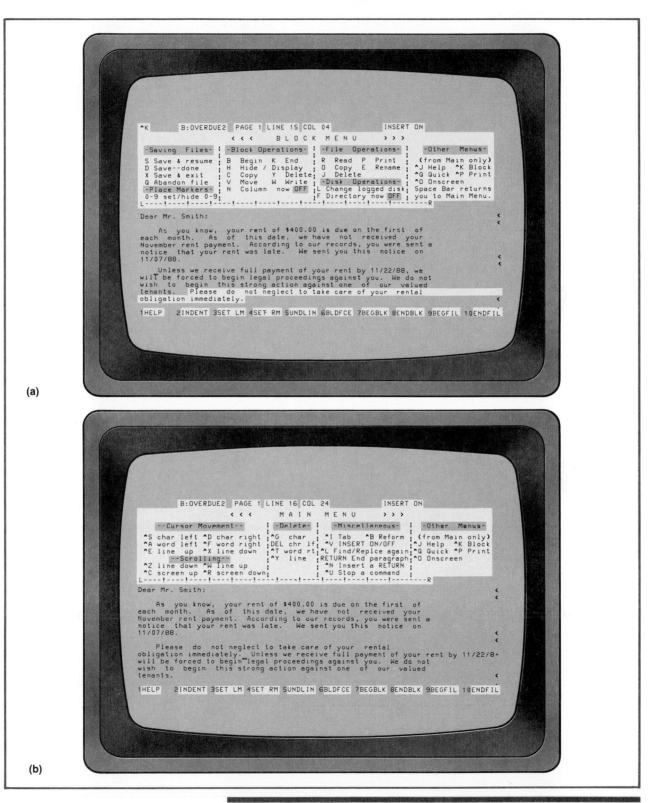

**Figure 14-6 Easy moves.** (a) Jack marks a sentence to be moved, which the computer highlights. Jack then puts the cursor at the new spot where he wants the sentence. (b) The sentence is easily moved but the right margin is no longer even.

nice again, paragraphs that have been altered must be **reformatted.** Some word processing programs do this automatically. In others, including WordStar, you must press certain keys to reformat paragraphs when you are through changing them. You can see in Figure 14-6b that Jack's letter needs to be reformatted after the changes he made. The results of his reformatting are shown in Figure 14-7a.

There are also other ways of changing the format of a document you have entered. You can, for example, change the left and right margins of the "page" shown on the screen. The text that you have typed will be automatically adjusted to the new page width, and your document will be printed with the new margins as you set them. You can also set and use multiple tab stops just as you would use tab stops on a typewriter. Most word processing programs permit single or double line spacing, or even more space between lines. In addition, you can indicate that one character or one or more words should be <u>underlined</u> or printed in **boldface** (darker) type.

In Figure 14-7a you can see the menu that appears on Jack's screen when he wishes to change the format of his documents. These commands allow Jack to set margins and tabs, center text, set line spacing, hyphenate words at the right margin, and more. Jack decides to change the right margin of his letter so that his letter is narrower and longer. By pressing a few keys, he gets the results you see in Figure 14-7b. Here is a helpful trick if you type a letter that runs over onto another page by just a few lines: Set the margins wider, and you may be able to fit the whole letter on one page.

## Screen Oriented versus Character Oriented

Have you seen my WYSIWYG? Well, probably not, because **WYSIWYG** (pronounced *wizzy-wig*) is not a thing. It is an acronym that stands for "what you see is what you get." This desirable feature makes a word processing program **screen oriented,** which means that what you see on the screen—underlined words, boldface words, and the like—is exactly what will print on paper. Some word processing programs, however, are **character oriented,** meaning that they show special characters on the screen that do not show up when the text is printed.

For example, a screen-oriented word processing program will show an underlined word actually underlined on the screen, for example, <u>word</u>. A character-oriented program, however, surrounds a word to be underlined with special characters—SwordS—that are replaced by actual underlining when the word is printed. In general, more recent word processing programs are screen oriented.

## Keeping a Permanent Copy

After you have corrected your document and have formatted it the way you want it, you will want to save it on a disk. You

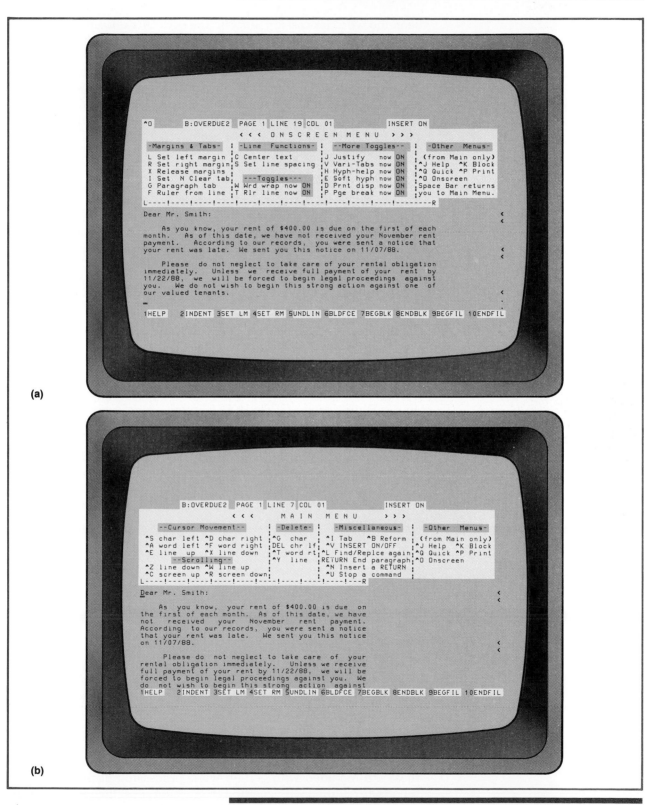

**Figure 14-7 Changing the format.** (a) After Jack made corrections his letter no longer had an even right margin (see Figure 14-6b) so he reformatted it as shown here. (b) Jack has changed the right margin on his letter to make it skinnier.

send the word processing program the save-this-document signal by pressing a certain key or keys. Once your document is saved on the disk, another command from the Opening Menu lets you print the document, assuming you have a printer attached to your computer. When you print the document, the program prints page numbers at either the top or the bottom of the page, or you can turn this option off. You can also command the program to wait after printing each page so you can insert stationery into the printer if desired.

Since the text you want to keep must be stored as a file on a disk, knowing what files are on your disk is very important. Using a felt-tip pen, you should write your file names on a label that you place on your disk. Word processing programs let you see the names of the files you have on your disk. In WordStar a **file directory** appears below the Opening Menu that lists the names of the files saved on your disk. Knowing your file names is necessary because if you want to load a file into the computer so that you can modify it, you must give the computer the correct file name. If you wish to print a file, you must also supply the computer with the file name.

## Taking Time to Learn

Some people take a formal word processing course at a college. After one term of instruction and practice, they are pretty sophisticated users. Others take a more generic course, learning word processing and other skills in the same class. Still others seem to pick up the basics of word processing in a matter of hours from a friend, or a tutorial, or a book. Just how much time does it take?

We have introduced only the basics of word processing here, but for some people the basics are enough. The answer to the question seems to be that the amount of time invested is an individual matter. Many people find that minimal training is adequate for their needs. They pick up some of the fancier features on their own, as needed. Others, especially those who want to do word processing for a living, want and need complete training.

## Extra Added Attractions

The popularity of word processing programs has encouraged the development of some very helpful programs to be used with word processing software. All of these programs analyze the text that has already been entered using a word processing program. We shall discuss programs that can check spelling, write form letters, provide a thesaurus, monitor grammar and style, produce footnotes, and generate tables of contents and indexes. Some of these are included with certain word processing packages. If your reports are riddled with spelling errors and typos, then we are beginning with your favorite, the spelling checker.

## Spelling Checker Programs

First you create a document with your word processing program. Then you instruct your **spelling checker program** to find any errors you may have made in spelling or typing. It compares each word in your document with the words that it has stored in its "dictionary." A dictionary is a list of from 20,000 to 100,000 or more correctly spelled words. If, while looking through your document, the spelling checker program finds a word that is not on its list of correctly spelled words, it assumes that you have misspelled or mistyped that word. Some spelling checker programs place a special mark (like @) next to the offending word. Others highlight the suspect word by making it brighter or a different color. When the checking program is done, you use your word processing program to look through your document for marked words. Then you decide whether the word is actually misspelled. If the word is correct, you delete the mark. If the word is really misspelled, then you correct it easily with your word processing program.

A more sophisticated type of spelling checker program places the cursor next to a word that it believes is misspelled. Then it displays on your screen the correct spellings of some words that it thinks you may have been trying to spell (Figure 14-8). If it has

**Figure 14-8   Spelling checker.** The highlighted word "expences" is misspelled, so the spelling checker offers some alternatives in the boxed area on the screen. In this case pressing A will replace the misspelled word with the correct spelling. The box containing the choices overlaps work in progress and disappears after it has served its purpose.

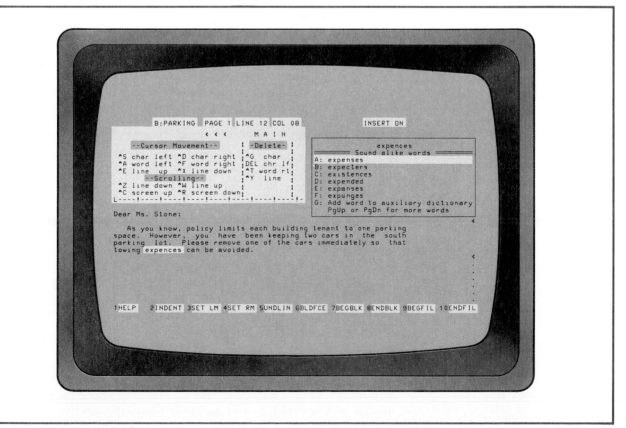

## THE MICROCOMPUTER CORNER

### Choosing a Word Processing Package

If the computer software industry would just sit still for a couple of years, we could make meaningful purchasing recommendations. However, to our delight and confusion, the software industry is an ever-changing kaleidoscope. People looking for "the best" word processing package enter a maze of confusing claims.

There are many word processing packages, and most of them are quite good. But before you invest time and energy in the Big Search, consider using packages already available to you. Many people make their selection based on convenience—they decide on a word processing package offered at school or on the job. This is probably an acceptable solution for most people.

If you plan to do your own buying, then consider the following:

- Check the trade press for ratings. *InfoWorld* offers software reviews as a regular feature. The reviews rate packages on performance, documentation, ease of learning, ease of use, error handling, support, and value. Many computer magazines carry articles comparing brands by name and include prices.

- Examine the features of the package. Most packages can perform standard operations like moving blocks of text, but what else might be appealing and useful? Some extras to consider—and there are many

more—are a mouse, windows, a spelling checker, paragraphing in columns, footnoting, and the capacity to create line drawings. Check the features offered by perusing advertisements in the trade press.

- Check the documentation yourself. Is it straightforward and easy to understand?

- Make sure any package you consider is compatible with your system. Be sure you can use it with the make and model of your computer, your operating system, and your computer's memory capacity.

- Ask around. Comparison shop. And do not forget to look for bargains.

---

guessed right, you select the word you want, and the program uses it to replace the misspelled word. If the word that the spelling checker thought was misspelled is correct, you just leave it unchanged and signal the spelling checker to continue searching through your document. Some spelling checkers even check your spelling as you are typing a document on the word processor. As soon as you type a word that the checker does not recognize, it causes the computer to sound a beep to catch your attention, then it proceeds to offer improvements in the usual way. (Some people do not like machines beeping at them. They prefer to turn this feature off and find their errors later.)

The best spelling checker programs let you create your own special auxiliary dictionaries. If a word in your document is not in its main dictionary, the spelling checker then searches your special dictionaries. This can be very useful. Suppose, for example, that you often write to a client named Mr. *Duffy* and use acronyms such as *CPU* or *CRT* and computerese jargon like *byte* or *mainframe*. An ordinary dictionary would flag the words *Duffy, CPU, CRT, byte,* and *mainframe* as misspelled. If you add these items, which are correct, to your special dictionary, they will be considered correct in the future. So, as you go along, you add to your special dictionary the names of your friends and business associates and words that are related to your job. Some dictionaries include special terms for a particular type of user—typical groups are the medical, legal, and computer professions. You can even buy dictionaries that include words from a foreign language.

## Form Letter Programs

A form letter used to be rather primitive, with your name typed—often in a different font—as an afterthought. No more. Now **form letter programs** can be used to send out masses of "personalized" letters that cannot be distinguished from a letter produced on a fine typewriter. An electronically produced form letter is called a **boilerplate** and the process of producing it is called **boilerplating.** These programs have been a boon to fund-raising and political groups and a bane to the weary public, tired of mounds of junk mail. But, junk or not, these mailings are effective and, therefore, here to stay. In fact, you can join in and use them for your own group or organization. Here is how it works.

- First, you create and store the form letter using your word processing program. Instead of actually typing a person's name, address, profession, or business, you type in some special symbols at the appropriate place in the letter.

- You then store all the individual names, addresses, professions, or businesses in a second file using your word processing program.

- Your last step is to ask the form letter program to print, on your printer, as many form letters as you have names in your second file.

Each time the program prints a letter, it replaces the special symbols in your form letter with a new name and address from the second file. The form letter program automatically adjusts the form letter for differences in the length of each person's name, address, profession, or business. Each one of the letters looks as if it has been typed especially for the addressee. This is the "personal touch" in the electronic age.

## Thesaurus Programs

Have you ever chewed on the end of your pencil trying to think of just the right word—a better word than the bland one that comes to mind? Perhaps you were energetic enough to haul down the thesaurus and look it up. A thesaurus is a book that gives synonyms (words with the same meaning) and antonyms (words with opposite meaning) for common words. But never mind the big

## KEY-ENHANCER PROGRAMS

Word processing programs cut down on the amount of actual typing you have to do to prepare a document. Some users of word processors choose to reduce their typing even more by buying key-enhancer programs for their word processing program. These programs allow you to store a series of keystrokes to be entered in your document and to enter these keystrokes by pressing just one key. The keystrokes saved can include operation commands as well as characters. For example, if you have a heading that must go at the top of all the pages in your 20-page document, store the needed commands using your key-enhancer program. Then when you need the heading, pressing one key inserts it into your document.

Some key-enhancer programs let you type an abbreviation on the keyboard and have the whole words entered in your document. For example, you could type "asap" to make "as soon as possible" appear in your document.

books. Now you can have a great vocabulary at your fingertips—electronically, of course. Your access to the word supply is via a **thesaurus program,** which you can use in conjunction with word processing.

Suppose that you find a word in your document that you have used too frequently or that does not quite seem to fit. Place the cursor on the word. Then press a certain key on the keyboard to alert the thesaurus program. It immediately provides a list of synonyms for the word you want to replace (Figure 14-9). You can then replace the old word in your document with the synonym you prefer. It is easy, and it is even painlessly educational.

## Grammar and Style Programs

A computer program cannot offer creativity, inspiration, class, elegance, or ingenuity. In short, we have no program at present that will make you the next Shakespeare or Hemingway. But there

**Figure 14-9   A thesaurus program.** The box overlaying the word processing program contains synonyms for the highlighted word, "remove." In this context no alternative seems better than the original word.

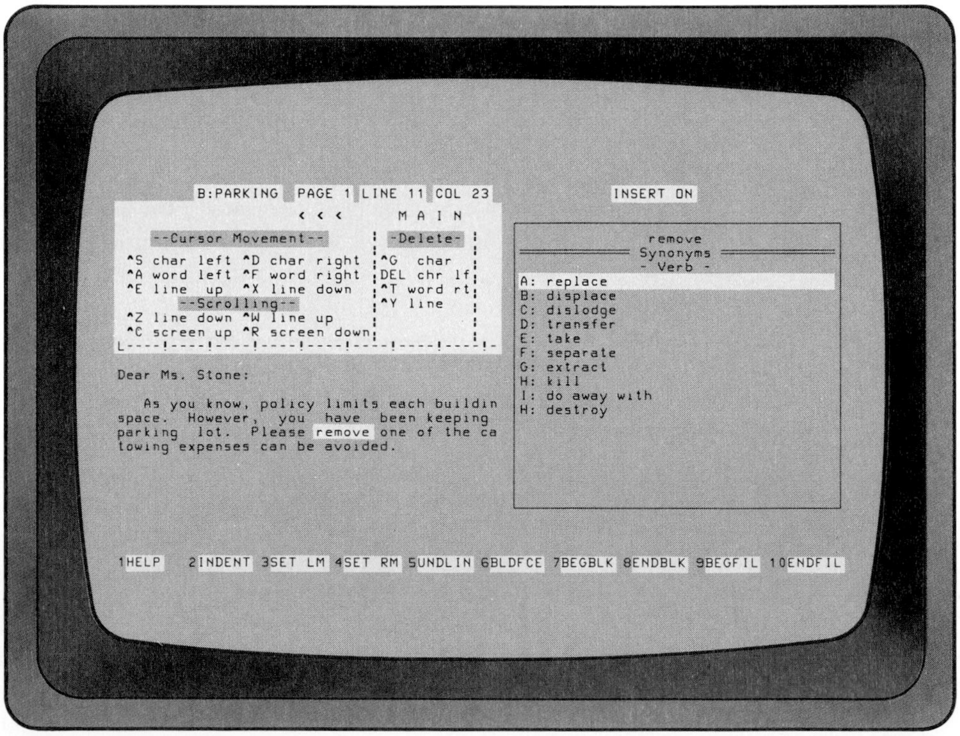

## OUTLINE PROGRAMS

Many believe, and most of us have been taught, that the first step in writing reports, speeches, or essays is to make an outline. Outline programs lack many of the capabilities of a word processing program, but they do allow you to quickly develop outlines and lists. Many people who need only these limited capabilities do not use a word processing program; their outline programs are sufficient.

However, some outline programs that are *memory resident* can run in your computer's internal memory at the same time that you are working with your word processing program. This allows you, at the touch of a key, to have your outline displayed on the screen so that you can see what you need to write about next. If, as you are writing, you think of something that you want to insert in the outline, pressing the same key brings the outline program to the screen so you can add to it. After you have seen or modified your outline, pressing another key brings your word processor and the text you were working on back onto the screen so that you can keep writing.

are programs that can improve your writing: They are called **grammar and style programs.** When you write using a word processing program, these programs can identify some of your grammatical or stylistic flaws. Let us consider some specific features.

A grammar and style program—sometimes called an **editing program**—can identify unnecessary words or wordy phrases that appear in your writing. It can count the number of times particular patterns of words appear again and again. It can check for sentences that seem too long (run-on sentences) and indicate that you should break them up into several short sentences for clearer writing.

Editing programs can also identify spelling errors that a spelling checker program cannot pick up. For example, the word "four" is a correctly spelled word and would not be flagged by a spelling checker. However, "four example" is an incorrect use of the word "four." Editing programs identify this kind of problem. Most spelling checkers also do not notice double-typed words if they are correctly spelled. For example, if you type "on the the table," a spelling checker would pass right over the two occurrences of the word "the." Editing programs spot such errors for you. Most editing programs do not try to correct grammatical errors—they just point them out and let you take it from there. Even if you are not the next great American novelist, you can use these programs to produce correct and clear English.

## Footnoting Programs

Although included in some word processing programs, **footnoting programs** are usually purchased separately. These programs are very useful for people who write scholarly works. The programs number footnotes automatically and place them at the bottom of the appropriate page or save them for a separate page at the end of the document.

## Table of Contents and Index Generator Programs

Now we are talking about lengthy and formal writing, such as books or scholarly tomes. Authors of these works usually benefit from a **table of contents program** used in conjunction with a word processing program. While writing, the author uses a special key on the keyboard to place special marks by chapter headings. When the author is finished with the book, the table of contents generator notes the page numbers on which the marked headings occur and generates a table of contents for the book. The table of contents consists of the headings and the pages on which they occur.

An **index generator program** works in a similar way. The author marks important terms in the text using special keys. When the author is finished, the index generator sorts all the marked terms in alphabetical order. When the index is printed, the terms appear in alphabetical order with the page in the book on which the term is used or explained. As you can imagine, these table of contents and index generators are great labor savers.

## We Hope You Are Convinced

We hope you are convinced that word processing is a great time saver. We hope you are convinced that word processing is easy to learn. We hope you are convinced that word processing is the best software tool—well, one of the best tools—for the personal computer. And, most of all, we hope you are convinced that word processing is essential for your career, no matter what it is.

## Summary and Key Terms

- **Word processing** is the creation, editing, formatting, storing, and printing of text.

- A **dedicated word processor** is a machine specifically designed for word processing. Letters and numbers are created electronically in the computer's memory, allowing the user to store text on disk and modify text easily without repetitive typing.

- A personal computer can do word processing almost as well as a dedicated word processor, and the computer offers additional capabilities such as spreadsheets, database management packages, and graphics.

- With the basic features of word processing programs, users can modify portions of text without having to retype correct material, set left and right margins and tab stops, copy or move portions of text, load text from a disk into the computer while saving a permanent copy on a disk, and print the text.

- A **menu-driven** word processing program presents an on-screen **menu,** a list of commands and the keystrokes necessary to execute those commands. A **file** is a document created on a computer.

- On the screen a word processing program usually indicates the top of the page, the **left margin,** the **right margin,** and the **tab settings.** The **cursor,** usually a blinking dash or rectangle, shows where

the next typed character will appear. **Cursor control keys** on the keyboard allow the user to move the cursor around and type anywhere in the text area on the screen. **Function keys** are used to execute commonly used commands such as commands that indent paragraphs and set margins.

- A feature called **word wrap** automatically starts a word at the left margin of the next line if there is not enough room on the line. The user can also hyphenate a word at the end of a line. The right margin can be either **ragged right** (uneven) or **right-justified** (even).

- The **scrolling** feature allows the user to view any part of the document on the screen, but only about 20 lines at a time.

- Word processing programs allow users to delete characters or whole words, insert characters in the middle of a line or word, and overtype (replace) previously typed characters. The function called **search and replace** finds and corrects each instance of a repeated error, such as a misspelling. Most word processing programs have a **conditional replace;** that is, each time the program finds an instance of a particular error, it asks the user to verify that it should be replaced. Other common functions are **cut and paste** commands, which are used to change the order of sentences or paragraphs. The **copy** command does not delete original text after copying it elsewhere in the document. The **move** command deletes text from its original location and allows the user to place it somewhere else.

- The format, or overall appearance, of a document is influenced by the left and right margins, the tab stops, the line spacing, the number of lines per page, the location (or absence) of page numbers, underlined or italicized words, and **boldface** words (words that appear in darker type). Moving, adding, or deleting words or sentences usually disrupts the format, which means that altered paragraphs must be **reformatted** to make them consistent with the rest of the document. Word processing programs also allow the user to change formats.

- **WYSIWYG,** which stands for "what you see is what you get," describes a **screen-oriented** word processing program. In contrast, a **character-oriented** program shows special characters on the screen that do not appear when the document is printed.

- After the document has been corrected and formatted, the word processing program can be instructed to save the document on a disk and to print the document. A **file directory** lists the names of the files saved on a disk.

- A **spelling checker program** detects spelling errors by comparing each word in a document with the words stored in its dictionary.

- **Form letter programs** can be used to send out many "personalized" letters by automatically adjusting a general form letter to include specific facts about each recipient. An electronically produced form letter is called a **boilerplate,** and the process of producing it is called **boilerplating.**

- A **thesaurus program** can be used to provide a list of synonyms and antonyms for an overused word.

- A **grammar and style program,** also known as an **editing program,** identifies common grammatical and stylistic flaws. Editing programs also detect errors that would elude a spelling checker program, such as double-typed words.

- **Footnoting programs** number footnotes automatically and place them at the bottom of the appropriate page or save footnotes for a separate page at the end of the document.

- With a **table of contents program,** special marks that the author places by a heading tell the program to include the heading in the table of contents. The program also includes the numbers of the pages on which the marked headings appear. An **index generator program** works in a similar way, but it also alphabetizes all marked terms.

## Review Questions

1. What is the significant difference between a dedicated word processor and a personal computer?

2. State five basic features of a word processing program.

3. What is a menu?

4. Discuss the similarities and differences between word processing and typing on paper.

5. State the purpose of each of the following word processing features: scrolling, search and replace, and cut and paste.

6. How does the copy command differ from the move command?

7. What is reformatting, and why is it necessary?

8. Explain how a spelling checker program works.

9. Explain how a form letter program is useful.

10. Describe what the following programs do: thesaurus, grammar and style, footnoting, table of contents, and index generator.

## Discussion Questions

1. Describe two tasks for which word processing would be preferable to using a typewriter. Describe two tasks for which a typewriter would be preferable.

2. Will word processing ever make typewriters obsolete? Explain your answer.

3. What uses could you find for word processing?

# 15

# Spreadsheets and Graphics

## Study and Show

Many people work with numbers: analyzing, summarizing, and then presenting the results to others. In this chapter we discuss three types of programs that make number work easier: electronic spreadsheets, integrated packages, and business graphics. These programs have removed drudgery from the jobs of accountants, marketing managers, stockbrokers, contractors, and others who work with the flow of cash in a business.

We have already seen what word processing has done for people who work with words. In this chapter we shall examine programs that lighten the burden of people who work with numbers. Consider the case of Ray Fleming, who keeps track of the bonus point system for his sales group. The system awards points for sales representatives based on sales volume over certain periods. The system is complicated by many special situations related to sales quotas, salesperson seniority, size of territory, travel time, and the difficulty of the customer. But Ray has it all figured out and can show it to anyone: dozens of columns and rows on an enormous sheet of paper. He can also explain the formulas that hold it all together.

But Ray starts to falter if anything changes. If a customer cancels an order, for example, Ray has to go back and erase the numbers and recalculate all the related totals. After many such changes the paper looks a bit messy, and Ray looks a bit frazzled.

Help is available for Ray in the form of electronic spreadsheets, which we shall discuss in detail in this chapter. In fact, electronic spreadsheets were the first programs used on personal computers for real business applications.

We can take this a step further. Integrated software packages usually combine electronic spreadsheets with word processing, a database management system, graphics, and sometimes data communications functions. Integrated packages are especially useful when numerical data must be included in textual reports or when a graphic representation of numbers can more easily show what the numbers mean.

Integrated packages and electronic spreadsheets help analyze, organize, and summarize numerical data. And if you need to present and explain this information to others in an impressive way, then presentation graphics programs are very useful.

Let us begin with the spreadsheet—as it was a few centuries ago.

# Electronic Spreadsheets

Do you remember Bob Cratchit in Charles Dickens's *A Christmas Carol?* He spent his time shivering in Scrooge's business office copying figures into ledgers. The pages in such books, ruled into rows and columns, are called worksheets or **spreadsheets.** The manually constructed spreadsheet has been used as a business tool for centuries. Spreadsheets can be used to organize and present business data, thus aiding in managerial decision making. But spreadsheets are not limited to businesses. Personal and family budgets, for example, can be organized on spreadsheets.

## The Spreadsheet Concept

The grade sheets used by teachers are a good example of a spreadsheet. A typical grade sheet is shown in Figure 15-1. Each

| Student Name | QUIZ 1 | QUIZ 2 | QUIZ 3 | QUIZ 4 | TOTAL |
|---|---|---|---|---|---|
| ADAMS | 20 | 22 | 19 | 21 | 82 |
| BURKE | 23 | 21 | 25 | 22 | 91 |
| CLEMENT | 17 | 18 | 19 | 18 | 72 |
| DAUTRICOURT | 25 | 23 | 22 | 24 | 94 |
| DUCHAMP | 18 | 17 | 21 | 20 | 76 |
| FRENCH | 24 | 20 | 22 | 21 | 87 |
| IVANCICH | 22 | 23 | 20 | 22 | 87 |
| KEPHART | 17 | 15 | 19 | 18 | 69 |
| MORIARITY | 19 | 20 | 21 | 18 | 78 |
| NIU | 25 | 24 | 25 | 25 | 99 |
| VALLA | 20 | 22 | 21 | 19 | 82 |
| WHITTAKER | 22 | 25 | 22 | 21 | 90 |
| | | | | | |
| | | | | | |
| AVERAGE = | 21 | 20.83 | 21.33 | 20.75 | 83.92 |

**Figure 15-1  A manual spreadsheet.** This grade sheet is a typical spreadsheet of rows and columns. Furthermore, arithmetic operations take place across the rows—totaling—and down the columns—averaging.

student's name appears in a separate row of the grade sheet. The page is ruled into separate vertical columns, and each column is labeled with the name of one of the quizzes, tests, or assignments for that class. The teacher whose grade sheet is illustrated gave four quizzes, each worth 25 points. The number of points that an individual student received for a particular quiz is entered in the space that exists at the intersection of the appropriate row and column.

The right-most column of the grade sheet spreadsheet contains the total points for a given student. The Total column is filled at the end of the grading period: The teacher adds all the points along the row—the four quizzes—for a particular student. This sum is entered in the space at the intersection of the Total column and that student's row. At the bottom of each quiz column, the teacher enters the average number of points for that quiz. The teacher also calculates the average total points and enters the average at the bottom of the Total column. For a teacher who has several classes with many quizzes and assignments for each class, preparing grades is a time-consuming chore. And if the teacher makes an error and assigns the wrong final grade, the affected student will be— to say the least—unhappy.

In business, spreadsheets are used in accounting, budget preparation, planning and forecasting, and numerous other applications. The work involved in doing a large spreadsheet manually is very time-consuming and tedious, even when using a calculator or copying results from a computer printout. Another problem with manual spreadsheets is that it is too easy to make a mistake. You may not discover the mistakes, and this could have serious consequences for the business and possibly your job. If you do discover the mistake after the spreadsheet is finished, you must redo all the calculations that used the wrong number.

## The Dawn of a New Era

In 1977 Daniel Bricklin was a student in the Harvard School of Business. He spent most of his evenings working on case studies for his classes. This work required the preparation of manual spreadsheets to do cash-flow analysis, profit projections, and other types of financial models. In order to make decisions about the way the businesses in his case studies should be run, Bricklin had to prepare separate spreadsheets to analyze each alternative available to him as a manager. He often made errors and had to spend hours redoing his calculations. He, like other students and business managers around the world, were spending too much time doing and redoing arithmetic with a paper, pencil, and calculator. This left them less time to study, understand the results of their calculations, and consider what they meant for their businesses.

## A Better Way

But what was the alternative? Dan toyed with the idea of doing the calculations for each case on the computer. However, each case study was so different that it would require a new computer program to analyze each case. This was just not possible. During the winter of 1978 Bricklin and Robert Frankston, a programmer friend, worked to develop a general-purpose program that could be used to solve any spreadsheet problem. This program evolved into the first **electronic spreadsheet**, called **VisiCalc** for Visible Calculator.

When VisiCalc was modified to run on the inexpensive Apple II personal computer, a combination was formed that was eagerly accepted by students, businesspeople, and professionals who used numbers in their work. In fact, VisiCalc is credited with being a major factor in making the Apple computer a success. For several years VisiCalc was the best-selling software for a personal computer. Since the introduction of VisiCalc, other companies have produced dozens of different spreadsheet programs. Let us see why electronic spreadsheets are so popular.

## Using Electronic Spreadsheets

The electronic spreadsheet eliminates most of the drudgery of setting up the rows and columns of a manual spreadsheet. You enter data, and the computer does all the calculations to produce output in the familiar form of a spreadsheet. Also, you can easily enter additional instructions needed by the program to solve your specific spreadsheet problem. All you need to know is how to get your input into the program and how to tell the program what output you want.

In general it works like this. You enter the headings you want on your spreadsheet, then key in the numbers and formulas. The electronic spreadsheet program automatically does all the calculations. The program does not make any calculation errors, and if you want a printed copy of the spreadsheet, it can be done quickly. Also, you can store your electronic spreadsheet on your disk so that it can be used again. But the greatest labor-saving aspect of an electronic spreadsheet is that when you change one value or formula in your spreadsheet, all the rest of the values on the spreadsheet are recalculated to reflect the change.

## Learning Lotus 1-2-3

Learning to use an electronic spreadsheet program does require time. You must read the manual that comes with the program. You also need to spend some time experimenting with the program. Electronic spreadsheet programs have much greater capabilities than the average user will ever require. To completely explain an electronic spreadsheet program would require an entire book. However, you can understand how such programs work by studying two simple examples. We shall show these examples in Lotus 1-2-3, the most popular electronic spreadsheet program. Lotus has established a standard approach to electronic spreadsheets; most popular spreadsheet programs work in a similar manner.

## A Look at Lotus: The Grade Sheet Problem

Our first example is the grade sheet spreadsheet that we looked at in Figure 15-1. Figure 15-2a shows the grade sheet after it is entered into Lotus 1-2-3. Suppose that the teacher made a mistake in grading Quiz 1 for Adams (the correct score is 22) and Quiz 3 for Kephart (the correct score is 20). If the grade sheet is done manually, then the teacher must recalculate the averages for quizzes 1 and 3, the new totals for the two students, and the new average total points. But the grade sheet is now entered on an electronic spreadsheet. To make the changes, you just type in Adams's new score of 22 over the old score on Quiz 1. The new average for Quiz 1, Adams's new total points, and the average for the total points are recalculated instantly by the spreadsheet program. Now enter Kephart's new grade and, instantly, the average for Quiz 3, Kephart's total points, and the average total points are recalculated and displayed. Figure 15-2b shows the result of typing only the two changed scores. Nothing else had to

## PLANNING YOUR SPREADSHEET

1. Determine the outputs you want to display on your spreadsheet.

2. Determine the data you will have to input to your spreadsheet to calculate the outputs you want.

3. Write down the rules for converting spreadsheet inputs to outputs. These rules will usually be formulas that relate the input values to the output values.

4. Write down the names of the input and output values that you are using in your spreadsheet, then write the equations in the exact form in which you will enter them in your spreadsheet. Double check to make sure that your list is completely correct.

5. Create the electronic spreadsheet by typing in the necessary data. Test your spreadsheet with a range of test values. Check the results produced by the spreadsheet against your own calculations using the test data. If the results differ, go through your spreadsheet to find your mistake.

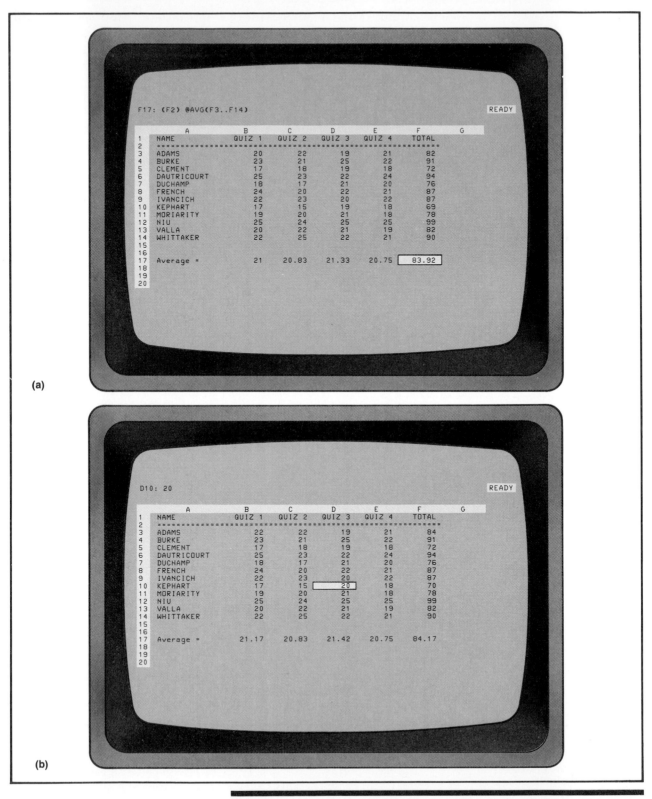

**Figure 15-2    Using Lotus 1-2-3.** (a) The manual grade sheet in Figure 15-1 was entered into Lotus. (b) Only the new grades (Quiz 1 for Adams and Quiz 3 for Kephart) need be entered; totals and averages are calculated automatically.

be changed in the spreadsheet; it automatically adjusted all contents to reflect the changed values.

Automatic recalculation of the whole spreadsheet usually takes only several seconds. This ability to recalculate a spreadsheet at the touch of a button is what has revolutionized the processes of budgeting and financial modeling. Now people who work with numbers can spend their time analyzing their spreadsheets rather than doing arithmetic. Managers are able to explore possibilities, to consider "what if . . ." alternatives that would have required too much time and effort before electronic spreadsheet programs were developed.

Figure 15-3 shows the rows of the spreadsheet that Lotus labels 1 to 20 and the columns that it labels A to G. Notice that column G is empty because we do not need it. The space at the intersection of a row and a column is called a **cell.** The formula used by Lotus to average the total points is stored in cell F17 and shows in the upper left-hand corner when the cursor is placed over cell F17, as it is in

**Figure 15-3   A formula in an electronic spreadsheet.** This spreadsheet is identical to Figure 15-2b, except that the cursor has been moved over cell F17, causing F17's formula to be shown in the upper left-hand corner. The F17 formula is used to calculate the value in F17 (the average of the totals). Note that the cell itself shows the calculated value, the result of the formula.

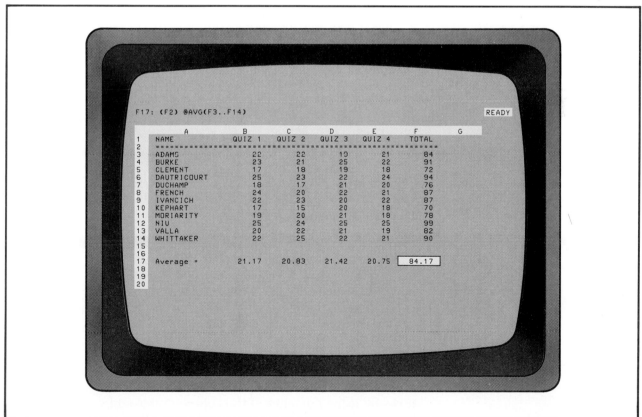

Figure 15-3. The formula @AVG(F3..F14) tells Lotus to average the values currently in rows 3 to 14 of column F and place the result in cell F17. The result of the calculation is what shows on the screen in location F17. As we have seen, when a user enters a new value in a cell that is used in a formula, Lotus automatically recalculates the result of the formula using the new value.

## More Lotus: The Purchasing Problem

Spreadsheets can seem confusing unless you see how they are set up, so we shall begin our second example from scratch. Consider this situation. Purchasing manager Grace Seto must prepare spreadsheets on alternative purchases of personal computers for the marketing department. Her manager has indicated that he wants a cost breakdown for four possible alternatives:

1. twenty personal computers with a graphics printer for each machine

2. twenty personal computers with only five of the computers having graphics printers

3. fifteen personal computers with a graphics printer for each machine

4. fifteen personal computers with only five of the computers having graphics printers

To start her work, Grace loads Lotus 1-2-3 from a disk into her computer's memory. When it is loaded, she sees the display in Figure 15-4, indicating that Lotus has prepared an electronic spreadsheet in the computer's memory. Each row of the spreadsheet is numbered down the left-hand side of the screen. Each column is identified by a letter at the top of the screen. Because a personal computer's screen can display only about 24 lines on a screen with 80 characters per line, we can see on the display only a part of all the rows and columns that are available to us in the computer's memory. Figure 15-4 shows only rows 1 to 20 and columns A to H. This is just the "upper left-hand corner" of the electronic spreadsheet. If your personal computer has enough memory, Lotus 1-2-3 (release 2) makes 8192 rows and 256 columns available in the computer's memory (Figure 15-5). In our example columns A to F and rows 1 to 20 will give Grace enough room for all her work. An electronic spreadsheet is like a piece of paper; you only use as much as you need.

We can move around to any area of the spreadsheet that we want to view simply by using the cursor control keys or entering a special command. In spreadsheet programs the cursor is a highlighted rectangle on the screen; in Figure 15-4 it is located in the first row of column A. Lotus identifies any cell—a row and column intersection—by using the letter of the column followed by the number of the row. For example, A1 represents the intersection of column A and row 1. When you move the cursor, it will move from one cell to

### TRY LYING ON YOUR SIDE

When you are displaying your spreadsheet on your computer's screen, you can move along a row to see all the columns of data in that row. Even if your screen will display only 80 characters on a line, you can still scroll sideways along a line by moving the cursor. However, when a wide spreadsheet is printed, the columns that will not fit across the page appear on a separate page. This means that you will have to cut and paste—literally—your printed copy of the spreadsheet.

Most printers can print 80 characters per line or 132 characters per line when printing in compressed mode. If this is insufficient to print all of the columns in your spreadsheet, you can purchase software that will turn your spreadsheet sideways and print it along the length of the printer paper. With the output from your spreadsheet in this form, you will have all the columns of each row running continuously on the same piece of paper. This makes the printed spreadsheet much easier to read.

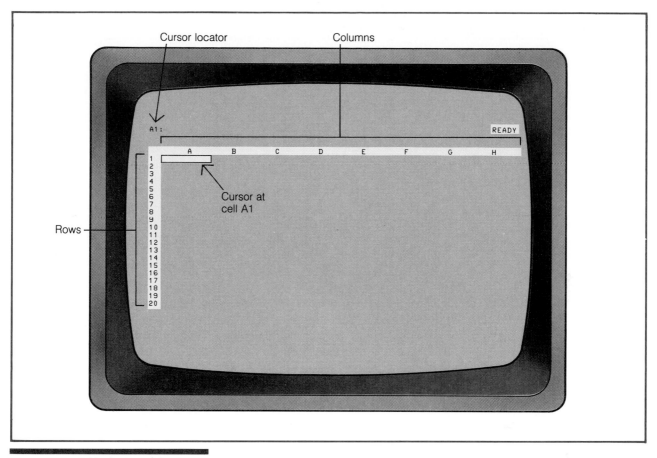

**Figure 15-4  A blank spreadsheet.**
The blank display indicates that Lotus has prepared an electronic spreadsheet in the computer's memory. It shows 20 rows numbered down the side and eight columns labeled A through H.

another cell. The cursor location is identified in the upper left-hand corner of the screen (see Figure 15-4).

Grace has already sketched out on paper what she wants her spreadsheet to look like. Lotus always starts with each of its columns nine characters wide. This means that a cell can display up to nine letters or digits. Sometimes this is just what a user wants. However, Grace can see from her sketch that some of the columns will need to be wider than nine characters, and some can be smaller. To set the column widths, she first presses the / key on her keyboard to signal to Lotus that she wants to use one of Lotus's special commands. The **command menu** that Lotus then displays is shown in Figure 15-6.

- **Menus.** The menu in Figure 15-6 shows the command selections. The top row of the menu lists the major commands. The second row shows subcommands that are available through the major command on which the **menu cursor** is currently placed. For example, in Figure 15-6, the second menu row shows subcommands—Global, Insert, Delete, Column-Width, and so forth—for the major command Worksheet, on which the menu cursor now rests. Moving the menu cursor to another major command on the top row causes a different set of subcommands to appear in the second row.

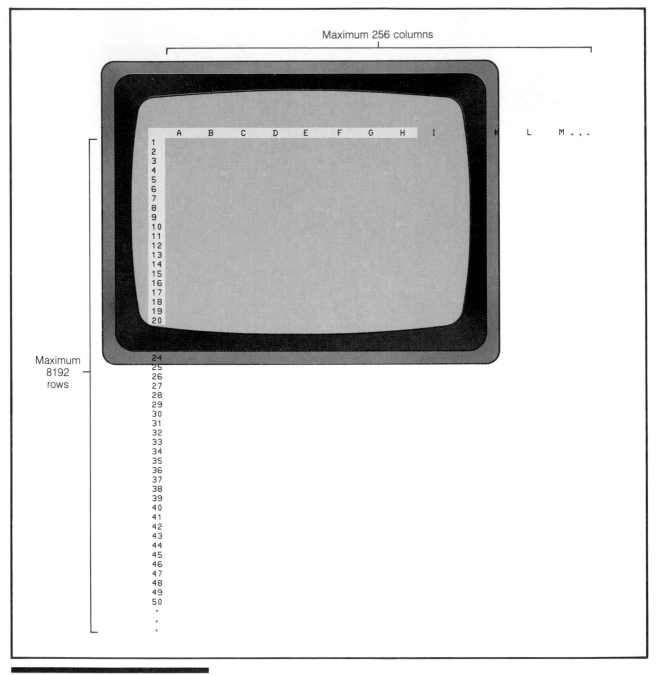

**Figure 15-5   There's more to it than meets the eye.** When you first load Lotus 1-2-3, you see only rows 1 to 20 and columns A to H on the screen. However, the spreadsheet actually extends far beyond what will fit on a screen. If your microcomputer has enough memory, you can use up to 256 columns and 8192 rows. By pressing certain keys you can view any part of the spreadsheet you wish to see.

- **Formatting the worksheet.** Since Grace wants to use the Column-Width subcommand to format her spreadsheet, she places the menu cursor on the major command Worksheet and presses the Enter key (also called the Return key). She then places the menu cursor on the Column-Width subcommand and presses the Enter key again. Lotus (release 2) permits setting the width of any column at 2 to 240 characters. Grace sets the width of column A to 7

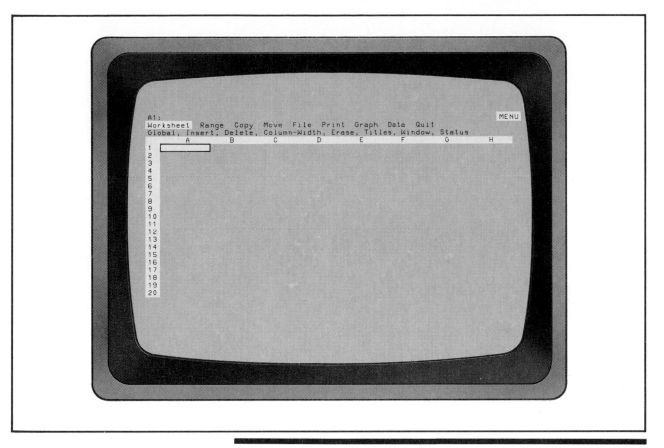

**Figure 15-6  The Lotus menu.** As indicated in the upper right-hand corner, the top two rows are menu choices. A command can be selected by moving the cursor over it and depressing the Enter key. The second line of commands is related to the first. In this case, since the cursor is over Worksheet, the commands Global, and so forth, belong to it. The commands on the second row change when the cursor is moved to another command on the top line.

characters, B to 9, C to 25, D to 9, E to 10, and F to 12 to reflect the desired number of characters. Now she is ready to actually enter data in her spreadsheet.

- **Cell data.** Lotus lets a user enter three types of data in a spreadsheet cell:

    1. **Labels.** Words, special symbols, or numbers (such as part numbers) that will not be used in calculations.

    2. **Numbers.** Digits (such as those indicating unit cost) that will be used in calculations.

    3. **Formulas.** Spreadsheet calculations (such as total cost = unit cost*quantity). (In Lotus * means to multiply.)

- **Labels and numbers.** To enter a label, number, or formula in the spreadsheet, Grace simply moves the cursor to the appropriate cell and types what is to be entered. Then she either presses the Enter

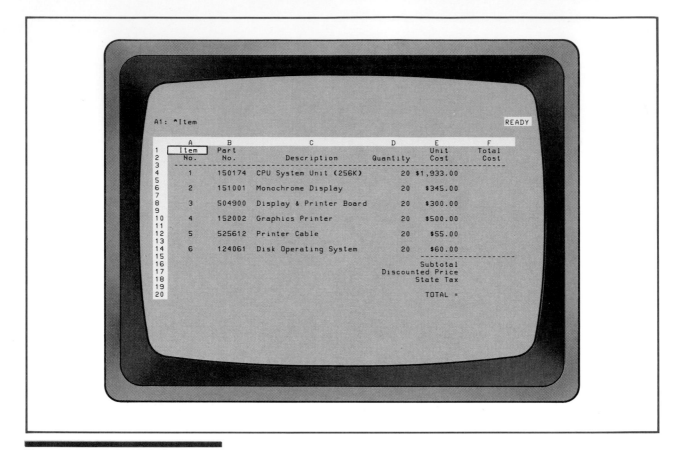

```
A1: ^Item                                                                    READY

        A       B              C              D          E          F
1     Item    Part                                     Unit       Total
2     No.     No.        Description        Quantity    Cost       Cost
3     -------------------------------------------------------------------
4       1     150174  CPU System Unit (256K)     20  $1,933.00
5
6       2     151001  Monochrome Display         20    $345.00
7
8       3     504900  Display & Printer Board    20    $300.00
9
10      4     152002  Graphics Printer           20    $500.00
11
12      5     525612  Printer Cable              20     $55.00
13
14      6     124061  Disk Operating System      20     $60.00
15                                              ---------------------
16                                                   Subtotal
17                                          Discounted Price
18                                                  State Tax
19
20                                                  TOTAL =
```

**Figure 15-7   Entering data for the purchasing problem.** Notice that the column widths were adjusted before the data was entered.

key or moves the cursor to another cell. Lotus will store the data in the computer's memory and display it on the screen. Figure 15-7 shows Grace's spreadsheet with all the labels and numbers entered in their cells.

■ **Formulas.** As the next step, Grace must enter the formulas that will calculate the total costs. She will need formulas in rows 4, 6, 8, 10, 12, and 14 of column F. The general formula is to multiply the contents of the Quantity cell in column D by the contents of the corresponding Unit Cost cell in column E. The formula is written this way for row 10: (D10*E10). This formula means "Multiply the contents of cell D10 by the contents of cell E10." You can see this formula in the upper left-hand corner of Figure 15-8. Let us explain how this works. Figure 15-8 shows the spreadsheet after the appropriate formulas have been entered in rows 4, 6, 8, and 10 of column F. Notice that the cells in column F do not show the actual formulas—instead they show the *results* of the formulas. So, in cell F10 we see "$10,000.00," the result of multiplying the contents of cell D10 (20) by the contents of cell E10 ("$500.00"). To actually see the formula, the user moves the cursor to the cell that contains the result of the formula. Then the formula appears in the upper left-hand corner of the screen. Notice how formulas

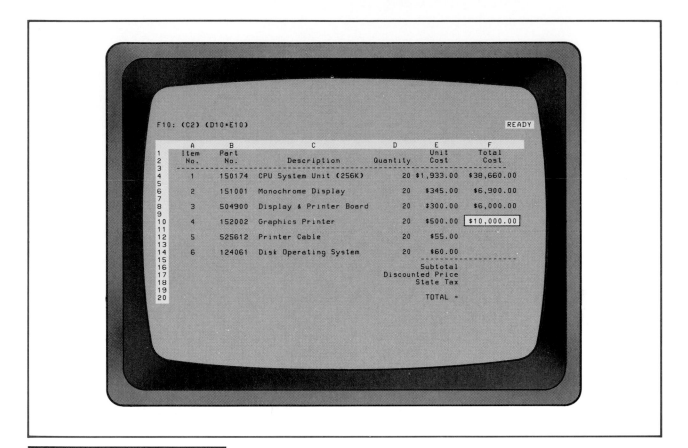

F10: (C2) (D10*E10)                                                    READY

|   | A | B | C | D | E | F |
|---|---|---|---|---|---|---|
| 1 | Item | Part | | | Unit | Total |
| 2 | No. | No. | Description | Quantity | Cost | Cost |
| 3 | --- | --- | --- | --- | --- | --- |
| 4 | 1 | 150174 | CPU System Unit (256K) | 20 | $1,933.00 | $38,660.00 |
| 6 | 2 | 151001 | Monochrome Display | 20 | $345.00 | $6,900.00 |
| 8 | 3 | 504900 | Display & Printer Board | 20 | $300.00 | $6,000.00 |
| 10 | 4 | 152002 | Graphics Printer | 20 | $500.00 | $10,000.00 |
| 12 | 5 | 525612 | Printer Cable | 20 | $55.00 | |
| 14 | 6 | 124061 | Disk Operating System | 20 | $60.00 | |
| 15 | | | | | --------- | |
| 16 | | | | | Subtotal | |
| 17 | | | | | Discounted Price | |
| 18 | | | | | State Tax | |
| 20 | | | | | TOTAL = | |

**Figure 15-8 Calculation formulas for the purchasing problem.** The cursor is on cell F10, so the formula to calculate the F10 value is shown in the upper left: Multiply the contents of cell D10 by the contents of cell E10.

are expressed. To place in cell F10 the result of multiplying the contents of cell D10 by the contents of cell E10, you store the formula (D10*E10) in cell F10. One more thing: The (C2) in the upper left-hand corner of Figure 15-8 means that the result is to be expressed in currency (dollars and cents) with two decimal places.

■ **Subtotals.** Figure 15-9 shows the completed spreadsheet for the company's first alternative—purchasing 20 personal computers with a graphics printer for each machine. Grace can calculate the subtotal by placing the formula (F4+F6+F8+F10+F12+F14) in cell F16. However, Lotus provides a simpler way of summing columns or across rows by using the @SUM function. For example, instead of the extended addition, Grace can place the formula @SUM(F4..F14) in cell F16. This formula instructs Lotus to add up the contents of cells F4 through F14. You may have noticed, by the way, a similar activity in Figure 15-3, which has the formula @AVG(F3..F14) in the top left-hand corner of the screen. This formula tells Lotus to calculate the average of the values in cells F3 through F14.

■ **Discounts, taxes, and the bottom line.** Grace's company gets a 30% discount when it buys ten or more computers. Therefore the for-

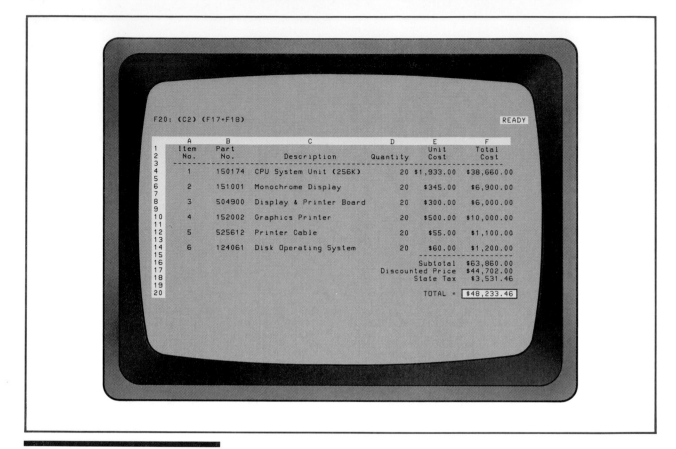

```
F20: (C2) (F17+F18)                                                  READY

          A       B              C              D         E         F
     1  Item    Part                                    Unit      Total
     2  No.     No.          Description      Quantity   Cost      Cost
     3  ----------------------------------------------------------------
     4    1     150174   CPU System Unit (256K)    20  $1,933.00  $38,660.00
     5
     6    2     151001   Monochrome Display        20    $345.00   $6,900.00
     7
     8    3     504900   Display & Printer Board   20    $300.00   $6,000.00
     9
    10    4     152002   Graphics Printer          20    $500.00  $10,000.00
    11
    12    5     525612   Printer Cable             20     $55.00   $1,100.00
    13
    14    6     124061   Disk Operating System     20     $60.00   $1,200.00
    15                                               --------------------
    16                                        Subtotal           $63,860.00
    17                               Discounted Price            $44,702.00
    18                                       State Tax            $3,531.46
    19
    20                                          TOTAL =          $48,233.46
```

**Figure 15-9   The complete spreadsheet for the purchasing problem.** The cursor is over cell F20, the final total, which was computed by adding the contents of cells F17 and F18.

mula (F16 − (F16*0.30)) is placed in cell F17. The state in which the company is located requires a 7.9% sales tax. This is computed by entering the formula (F17*0.079) in cell F18. The results of these calculations can be seen in Figure 15-9. The cursor in Figure 15-9 is on cell F20—as you can see, the bottom line is calculated using the formula (F17+F18), which yields $48,233.46.

- **Filing and printing.** The spreadsheet is now complete. It can be saved by using the File command and can be printed by using the Print command. You can see these major commands in the command menu in Figure 15-6.

- **The other three alternatives.** Grace went to a bit of trouble to produce that first spreadsheet, the one that represents the first of the four alternatives her boss wants her to consider. But now, as she gears up for the other three choices, the spreadsheet technology really pays off. To obtain the spreadsheet for the second alternative (20 computers with only five printers), Grace simply enters the number 5 in cells D10 and D12. The result is shown in Figure 15-10. Notice that recalculation of all the formulas is automatic. This spreadsheet is then saved. Grace produces the third and fourth alternatives with similar ease and in a matter of minutes. As

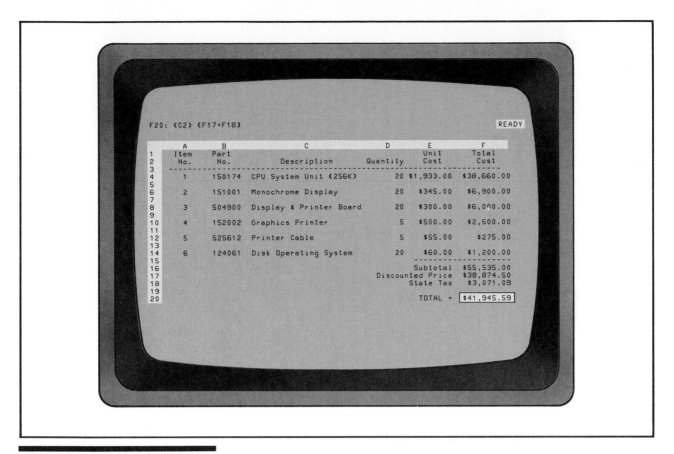

```
F20: (C2) (F17+F18)                                              READY

        A       B           C           D       E           F
   1   Item    Part                            Unit        Total
   2   No.     No.        Description   Quantity Cost       Cost
   3  ---------------------------------------------------------------
   4    1     150174   CPU System Unit (256K)   20  $1,933.00  $38,660.00
   5
   6    2     151001   Monochrome Display       20    $345.00   $6,900.00
   7
   8    3     504900   Display & Printer Board  20    $300.00   $6,000.00
   9
  10    4     152002   Graphics Printer          5    $500.00   $2,500.00
  11
  12    5     525612   Printer Cable             5     $55.00     $275.00
  13
  14    6     124061   Disk Operating System    20     $60.00   $1,200.00
  15                                   -------------------------
  16                                   Subtotal   $55,535.00
  17                            Discounted Price  $38,874.50
  18                                   State Tax   $3,071.09
  19
  20                                   TOTAL =    $41,945.59
```

**Figure 15-10 Alternative for the purchasing problem.** The number of printers has been changed from "20" to "5," with a corresponding change in the bottom line, cell F20.

you can see, once the initial spreadsheet is set up, changes and recalculations are made easily and quickly. Grace then prints all four spreadsheets and presents them to her boss.

### The Selection

Which of the four alternatives did Grace's company select? None of them. Her boss said, "What if we try to get the most computers with at least three printers for under $35,000? Show us the best possible computer and printer combination." Managers are very fond of such "What if . . ." questions. However, Grace is armed and ready. New questions mean another trip to the computer but not a lot of mind-numbing calculations. You can see why thousands of people have purchased electronic spreadsheet programs for personal computers and will *never* give them up.

## Prewritten Electronic Spreadsheet Templates

Because electronic spreadsheet programs have become so popular, many spreadsheet experts have constructed hundreds of different templates to use with your spreadsheet program. **Templates**

Excel from Microsoft Corporation is an integrated package consisting of an extremely powerful spreadsheet, graphics, and database management system. The spreadsheet is by far the largest available on a personal computer: 246 columns by 16,384 rows for a total of 4,194,304 cells. In order to create spreadsheets this large, a user will have to purchase internal memory for the Mac beyond the 512K required to run Excel.

An Excel user creates a database by defining an area of the spreadsheet as a database. Rows in the spreadsheet that are in the database area can be searched to identify entities that match certain selection criteria. This means, for example, that you can find all customers who have owed you more than $1000 for more than 60 days.

The graphics function in Excel can produce five styles of area charts, seven kinds of bar charts, eight types of column charts, seven styles of line charts, six varieties of pie charts, and five kinds of scatter graphs. What is more, you can combine more than one style on the same screen. All types of graphs are produced from data that you have entered in the spreadsheet.

Jazz from Lotus Development Corporation (the creators of Lotus 1-2-3) is a fully integrated package that offers strong spreadsheet, word processing, graphics, database, and communications capabilities. Data is easily transferred among the five separate functions by an interface program called HotView. Jazz requires a 512K Macintosh with an external disk drive.

The spreadsheet measures 8192 rows by 256 columns. The user can create pie charts, line, bar, area, scatter, and percent graphs, and a special stock-market chart from data in the spreadsheet or the database. When using the word processing program in Jazz, you can import any data that you have stored using one of the four other programs in the package. Thus, it is convenient to insert graphs and spreadsheet tables of numbers into a document.

are spreadsheets with all the commands, labels, and formulas already entered. All you have to do is to enter your numbers to get your results. Templates are available for most of the standard applications of spreadsheets. These templates are available on disks, ready for you to load into your spreadsheet program and use. Books are also available that contain a listing of all the labels, commands, and formulas for common uses of spreadsheet programs. Personal computing magazines also carry articles describing particularly useful spreadsheet templates that you can enter from your keyboard and store on disk.

Some templates are for personal applications, such as home budgeting, mortgage amortization, checkbook balancing, and stock portfolio analysis. Other templates have business applications such as balance sheets, depreciation calculations, break-even analysis, monthly sales reports, quality-control analysis, payrolls, inventories, and accounts-receivable ledgers. One advantage of templates is that you can enter and use them without understanding all the details of their construction. Another advantage is that they are usually well tested before they are offered to the public. Finally, if you have a unique application for a spreadsheet program, you can probably find an existing template that, with a few modifications, will suit your purpose.

## Integrated Packages

The concept of an **integrated,** all-in-one package of programs is very appealing: Join word processing, spreadsheet, database, and graphics programs into one package. With an integrated package you do not need to learn four completely different programs that use different commands. Perhaps the most difficult steps you have to take when you learn to use a new program are the first few. After that, you have oriented yourself to the "feel" of the program and can start being productive with it. Programs in an integrated package share a common methodology and command structure so that you do not have to begin anew to use a particular program in the package. There is a familiar flavor in each of the other programs in the package.

A second advantage is the fast, easy transfer of data among the programs in the package. For example, it is easy to move a table of spreadsheet numbers into a word processing report. Graphs can be prepared using the graphics program, then easily inserted into text prepared using the word processing program. However, if you are using a separate word processing program and separate spreadsheet and graphics programs, you will find that moving data from one program to another program is not simple. And even though there are certain standard file types, they cannot always store exactly what you want to pass to the second program. Ease of information transfer among programs and a common command structure has created a user demand for integrated packages.

## Lotus at Yosemite

Never mind the image of Lotus in a three-piece suit, reaching the remotest corners of corporate America. Park ranger Jim Sano knows that Lotus fits right in with the bears and wildflowers at Yosemite National Park. His organization uses Lotus 1-2-3 for an array of administrative tasks. Some of these tasks, such as budgeting and staffing, are familiar. But Yosemite has additional concerns: people and—yes—bears.

Using the spreadsheet and database capabilities of Lotus 1-2-3, Sano tracks the 2.5 million annual visitors. He wants to know the kind of visitors and their needs, so he can plan effectively for the future. If, for example, most of the visitors arrived in campers but only a few visitors planned to pitch tents, Yosemite administrators could allocate space accordingly.

None of this happened overnight. In fact, there was little planning. Jim Sano pioneered the endeavor by bringing his own personal computer to work. Now there are 13 personal computers at Yosemite.

About the bears. Jim uses the computer to track incidents, sightings, and related parameters.

The parameters include damage and food storage. Jim notes that the problems rarely originate with the bears; he says that problems usually arise because a visitor has done something stupid.

## The First Integrated Package: Lotus 1-2-3

Lotus 1-2-3 integrates a very powerful spreadsheet program with a business graphics program and a limited database program (Figure 15-11). All three functions in the package are based on storing data in a spreadsheet. After you enter the data in the spreadsheet, you can view the data graphically using the graphics program. You can also use commands available through the database program to sort the data in your spreadsheet or to find rows in the spreadsheet that match certain conditions.

**Figure 15-11   Lotus 1-2-3.** This popular software package includes spreadsheet, graphics, and database functions.

**Figure 15-12   Comparison spreadsheet.** This spreadsheet shows expenses and sales for salesman Ian James.

Each of the programs has a menu that lets you choose what task you want to perform. You also can move instantly from one program to another by making a selection from a menu. Furthermore, once your graphs and database are set up, you can stay in the spreadsheet program and see graphs of your data or select records from your database by simply pressing one key. Lotus also stores the graphs and database with the spreadsheet file on which they are based.

To see how this is done in Lotus, consider this situation. Mark Chan manages a small business. He wants to compare two sets of numbers. Mark wants to analyze the relationship between the dollars that salesman Ian James spent entertaining clients with the dollar amount of sales that Ian generated. Mark has data for each month of the first half of the year. Figure 15-12 shows the data as it has been entered using Lotus's spreadsheet.

Mark does not need to use a separate command in order to see a graph of the relationship. He simply selects the Graph option from Lotus's command menu, which automatically lets him set up a line graph, bar graph, or pie chart by selecting options from the graph program menu. In Figure 15-13, you can see a line graph and a bar graph of the data as it would appear on Mark's screen. If Mark wants a hard copy of the data and a graphics printer or a plotter is attached to his computer, Lotus can print the same graphs.

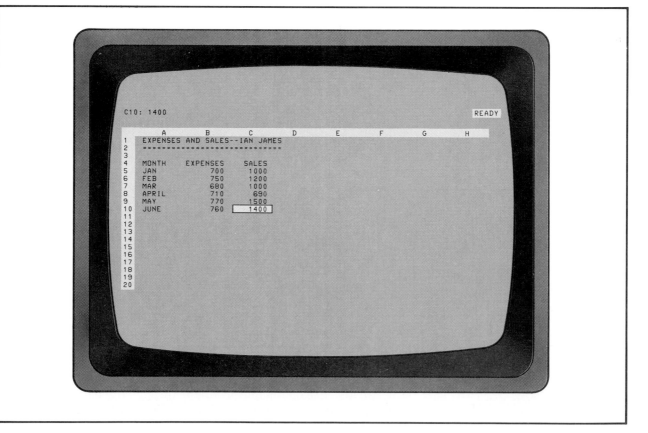

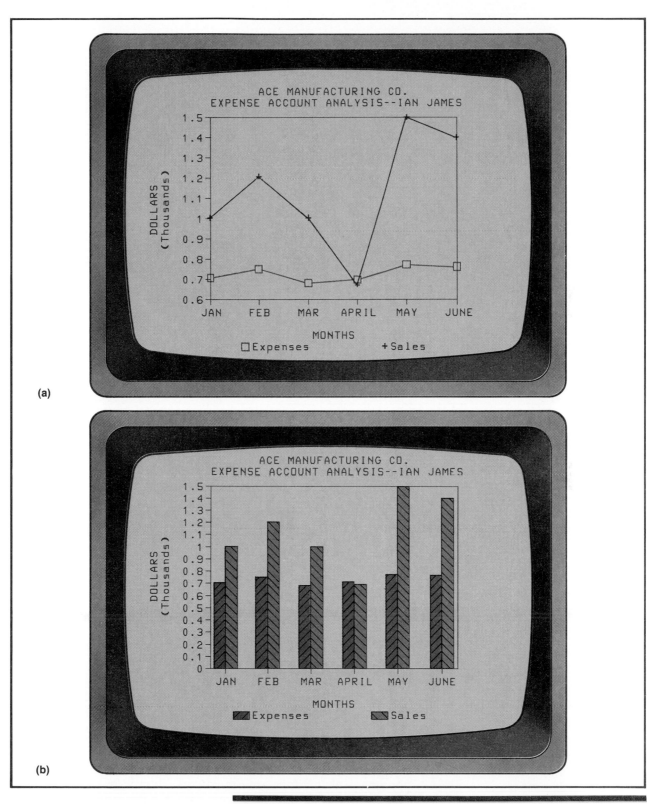

**Figure 15-13  Comparison graphs.** (a) Lotus 1-2-3 presents a line graph of the sales and expense figures shown in the spreadsheet in Figure 15-12. (b) Lotus can also render a bar graph of the same data.

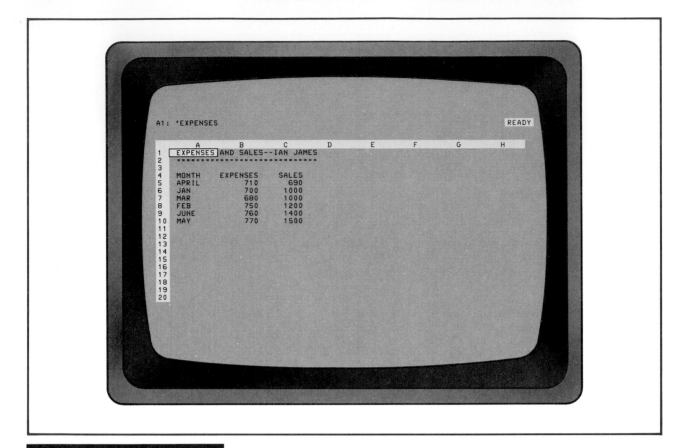

**Figure 15-14   Sorting data.** Here the sales figures for Ian James have been put in ascending order automatically using the Lotus 1-2-3 database function.

Mark can use the database program to sort the sales figures in ascending order by selecting Data (for database program functions) from Lotus's command menu. Instantly, the program begins executing. Then he can select the Sort option from the database program's menu, enter the letter of the column containing the sales figures, and indicate ascending order. Figure 15-14 shows the screen results. If Mark wants to find any month where entertainment expenses exceeded income from sales, he can use the Find option from the database program's menu. (Database functions like Sort and Find are really needed only if the user must work with large volumes of data.)

## To Integrate or Not?

The popularity of Lotus has led to the development of a number of different packages that integrate program functions. Two different approaches have been taken by software developers:

1. Including word processing, spreadsheet, graphics, and database capabilities in one program package. Some of the more popular programs of this type are Framework, Symphony, and ENABLE for the IBM PC, and Excel and Jazz for the Apple Macintosh.

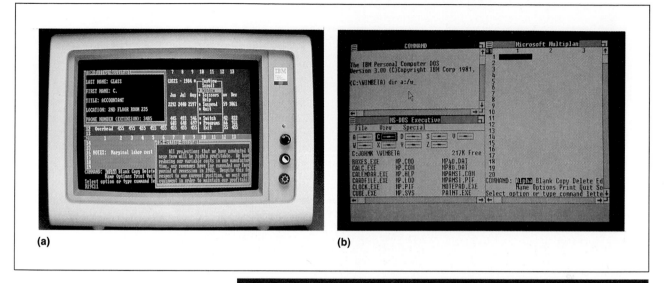

(a)  (b)

**Figure 15-15 IBM's TopView and Microsoft's Windows.** These IBM PC operating environments can run several programs concurrently and let users follow their progress on a screen divided into windows. Both TopView and Windows offer easy-to-use menu systems, the ability to transfer data among different types of files as well as user-friendly access to the operating system. (a) TopView uses overlapping windows, but (b) Windows uses an approach called tilting, which arranges windows to fit the screen completely to make the best use of the screen display area.

2. Allowing a user to purchase the individual word processing, spreadsheet, graphics, and database programs that are most appealing for that user. These **stand-alone** programs are then integrated by a **universal manager program** that coordinates the separate programs. The manager program also presents a common interface to the user and handles data transfer among the programs. Examples of this approach are Microsoft's Windows and IBM's TopView for the IBM PC and software already built into Apple's Macintosh (Figure 15-15).

Despite their many advantages, sales of integrated packages have not skyrocketed. There are several reasons for this. First, the individual functions—like word processing or graphics—within an all-in-one integrated package are not usually as strong as those in stand-alone packages. If you need state-of-the-art word processing and state-of-the-art database management, you would probably be better served by buying two stand-alone programs. Second, integrated packages are rather expensive, and you pay for all the functions in the package even if you really need only two or three. Third, integrated packages require more computer memory than one stand-alone program does. You may have to purchase additional memory for your computer to run the integrated package.

The universal manager program approach avoids, to some extent, the three objections. You can buy just the stand-alone programs that you need. The manager programs generally cost less than $200,

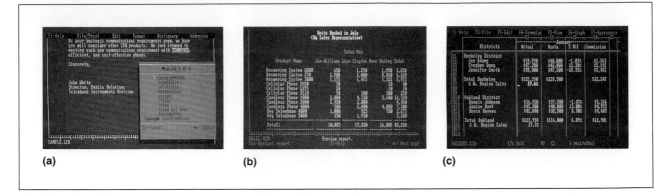

(a)                    (b)                    (c)

**Figure 15-16   The PFS Professional Series.** The PFS family of programs includes (a) PFS:Professional Write (word processing), (b) PFS:Professional File (data management), and (c) PFS:Professional Plan (spreadsheet). Not shown is PFS:Professional Network, which allows five users to simultaneously access a program on a local area network.

and they are not overly hungry for memory. However, the manager programs can integrate only some of the many word processing, spreadsheet, graphics, and database programs that are available. Furthermore, the level of integration does not reach that of the all-in-one package.

Finally, the competition has improved. Some software developers have responded to integrated packages by developing families of separate programs that have similar commands. These family programs also provide a means to move data between the separate programs. An example is the PFS Professional series from Software Publishing (Figure 15-16). Such programs let you select the fairly integrated stand-alone programs you need without the extra cost of an all-in-one package or a universal manager program.

Today, integrated packages are well entrenched, but that could change.

## Graphics

The graphics programs that are available for personal computers fall into two general categories: analytical graphics and presentation graphics.

**Analytical graphics** let you construct and view line, bar, and pie-chart graphs (Figure 15-17a-c). They accept their input from the spreadsheet or database program you used to enter the data you want to graph. The purpose of analytical graphics is to let you see patterns in the data that numbers alone do not show. If you want a hard copy of a graph that the program is displaying on your screen, your graphics program can send a copy of the graph to a graphics printer or a plotter.

These programs do a good job of producing simple graphs. They are very useful if you want to visualize your own data. However,

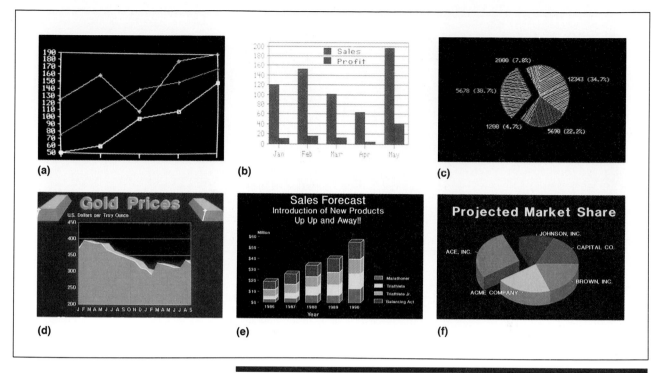

(a)   (b)   (c)

(d)   (e)   (f)

**Figure 15-17   Analytical graphics compared to presentation graphics.** Analytical graphics (a, b, and c) are certainly serviceable, but they lack the clarity and appeal of presentation graphics (d, e, and f). Compare the line graphs (a and d), bar graphs (b and e), and pie charts (c and f).

such programs are generally too limited and inflexible if you need to communicate information to others in a professional manner. Analytical graphics such as those in Lotus 1-2-3 are restricted to only a few types of graphs and offer the user little control over the size of a graph or the types of lettering.

**Presentation graphics** are designed to let the user share information with others. They are especially useful when you must prepare presentations for your managers or your clients. You can prepare brilliantly colored charts, graphs, and other visual aids that look as if they were prepared by a professional graphic artist (Figure 15-17d-f). However, you have more control over the way the final product looks when you do it yourself using a presentation graphics package. Generally, you can produce graphs with greater speed than traditional graphics production allows, and you have the ability to make last-minute changes if necessary.

Using a presentation graphics package to make visual aids is less expensive than paying a graphic artist. Presentation graphics programs can produce output on a screen, on printers or plotters, on overhead transparencies, or on slides for projection.

Some presentation graphics programs let you store your pictures, text slides, graphs, and charts on a disk. This lets you use your

Here are sales figures for hot dogs and hamburgers at Farley's Famous Food Faire. In January 13,000 hot dogs were sold and 45,000 hamburgers were sold. In February hot dog sales dropped slightly to 10,000, while hamburger sales increased slightly to 47,000. In March hot dog sales increased greatly to 23,000, while hamburger sales continued to increase slightly to 50,000. In April hot dog sales increased

SALES OF HAMBURGERS AND HOT DOGS AT FARLEY'S FAMOUS FOOD FAIRE

J F M A M J J A S O N D
☐ HAMBURGERS    ☐ HOT DOGS

**Figure 15-18   Words and pictures.** Compare the time it takes to read and understand the paragraph with the time it takes to understand the graph. With graphics, information can be conveyed more quickly and in less space.

computer to present a series of screens of text or graphic images one after the other on your display. When you deliver your presentation, you can either run it manually or have it timed automatically by a computer. A few programs even let you animate your images. For example, graph bars might grow as product sales increase.

In addition, these presentation graphics programs have been successfully used to develop training materials for classes in schools and industry. Some computer companies use presentation graphics packages to teach you how to use their computers—computers teaching you about computers.

## Why Use Graphics?

Graphics generate and sustain the interest of your audience by brightening up any dull lesson, report, or business document. In addition, graphics can help you get your point across to your boss, to your client, or to a large audience by distilling thousands of dull data values into one simple and clear graph (Figure 15-18). What is more, that simple graph can reveal a trend that could be lost if buried in long columns of numbers.

Presentation graphics increase the impact of your message. They make the information you are presenting visually appealing, meaningful, and comprehensible. Finally, graphics have been shown to increase both the amount that a listener learns in a presentation and the length of time that the information is retained by the listener. Let us look at some presentation graphics programs that will give you the ability to create graphics.

## Presentation Graphics

Most presentation graphics programs help a user to do three kinds of tasks:

1. They edit and enhance charts created by other programs, such as the analytical graphs produced by Lotus 1-2-3. A user can combine one or more separate Lotus graphs on one page or overhead transparency, or insert graphs in a text document.

2. They create charts, diagrams, drawings, and text slides from scratch.

3. They use a library of symbols and pictures that comes with the graphics program. This capability lets even a nonartist create professional-looking illustrations by combining some of the thousands of shapes and symbols that are stored in the library. The shapes and symbols can also be inserted in graphs or charts (Figure 15-19).

In addition, some presentation graphics programs have advanced features that let the personal computer give presentations on its own.

Although a large number of excellent presentation graphics programs are available, we will consider only three packages, all for the IBM PC: The Grafix Partner, Chart-Master, and PC Storyboard.

The Grafix Partner from Brightbill–Roberts and Co. enhances graphic images produced on the IBM PC screen by other programs. Enhancement possibilities include more colors, a variety of text fonts (lettering styles), and improved labeling. When used with a

**Figure 15-19   Enhancing graphics with symbols.** Presentation graphics programs provide a library of symbols which users can choose from. As shown here on the left, such symbols can add interest to columns of numbers.

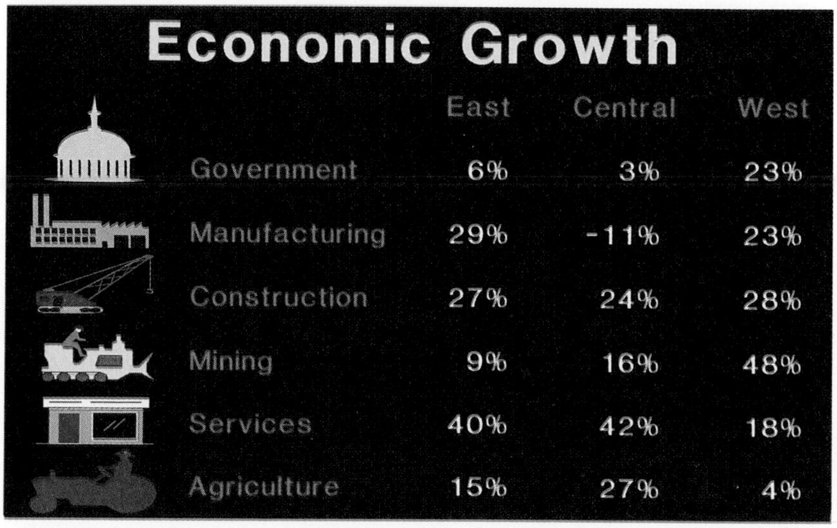

## Economic Growth

|               | East | Central | West |
|---------------|------|---------|------|
| Government    | 6%   | 3%      | 23%  |
| Manufacturing | 29%  | -11%    | 23%  |
| Construction  | 27%  | 24%     | 28%  |
| Mining        | 9%   | 16%     | 48%  |
| Services      | 40%  | 42%     | 18%  |
| Agriculture   | 15%  | 27%     | 4%   |

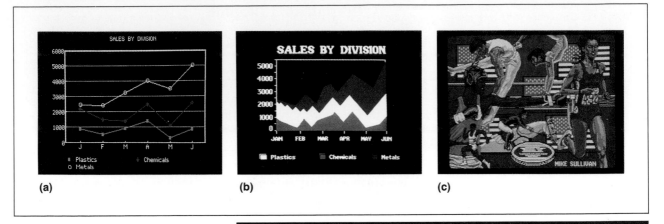

**Figure 15-20  Examples from The Grafix Partner.** (a) This analytical line graph created with another program can be enhanced by The Grafix Partner into (b) a presentation graph. (c) Free-form graphics can also be created with this software.

program like Lotus 1-2-3, The Grafix Partner "sits in the background" of your computer's memory as you develop graphs and charts with Lotus. Then by pressing several keys, you can call on The Grafix Partner to spruce up your Lotus graph (Figure 15-20a-b). The result can be stored on a disk to be used to produce a "slide show" on the computer's display screen. The result can also be produced on paper or on overhead transparencies using a graphics printer or a plotter. By using a device called the Polaroid Palette, you can reproduce the image on Polaroid color prints or on special rapidly developing 35mm color slides. The Polaroid Palette will be discussed in a later section of the chapter.

The Grafix Partner can also be used as a stand-alone drawing program (Figure 15-20c). You can use it to draw your own shapes like boxes or circles and to include symbols from a library of commonly used symbols that is included with the program. The Grafix Partner also gives you access to 20 different fonts to use for labeling pictures created in the program or charts and graphs from other programs.

Chart-Master from Decision Resources is a highly rated business graphics program. It is a member of a family of programs that includes Sign-Master, Diagram-Master, and Map-Master (Figure 15-21). Chart-Master translates data from the popular spreadsheet programs into line, bar, area, and scatter graphs and pie charts. You have over 40 options to use in improving the impact of these graphs. The program lets you size and draw a graph or chart anywhere on a display screen, graphics printer, or plotter. This is especially useful when you want to reserve the top or bottom of a chart for text created with a word processing program. A large library of standard symbols is also available to include in graphs or charts. The images produced by Chart-Master can be reproduced on screens, graphics printers, plotters, slides, or color prints.

PC Storyboard, from IBM, has rapidly become a standard for

Figure 15-21   **Map Master.** This versatile package can produce just about any map in a variety of colors.

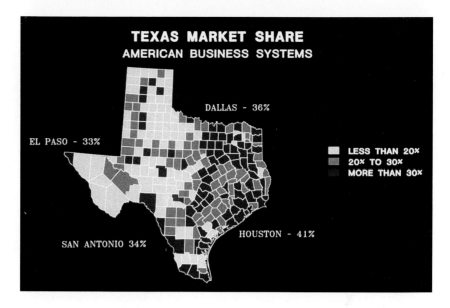

Figure 15-22   **PC Storyboard.** PC Storyboard offers a variety of (a) letter fonts and (b) icons to produce finished presentation graphics such as (c).

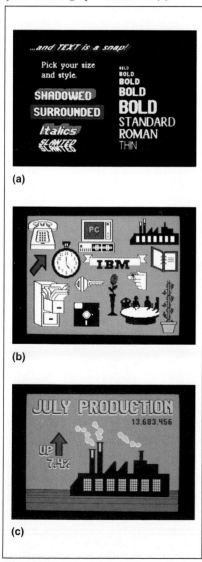

business presentation graphics. Storyboard is a system of four programs (or modules) that prepare and give color presentations using an IBM PC with a color graphics monitor. The four programs are:

1. Picture Taker. Accepts text and graphics screen images from other packages (like Lotus 1-2-3) for inclusion in a presentation. Digitized photographs can also be stored for use in a presentation.

2. Picture Maker. Creates screen displays of text, figures, and graphs. It also contains a library of symbols to use in creating pictures.

3. Story Editor. Organizes the pictures (captured or created in the previous two programs) into stories that can be presented with a variety of special effects and timings.

4. Story Teller. Presents the finished version of the presentation created by the story editor.

PC Storyboard, like The Grafix Partner and Chart-Master, lets you improve graphs and charts created in other packages. It lets you create charts, graphs, and freehand drawings from scratch or by using symbols from its library (Figure 15-22). PC Storyboard really shines when it gives the completed presentation. It has very sophisticated capabilities for moving from one screen to the next. You can even animate your presentation. The PC Storyboard demonstration disk, for example, generates images of a bird flying, a ship sailing, and flags waving.

A PC Storyboard presentation can be stored on a disk. One disk can contain 45 pictures, enough to build a 20-minute presentation. Story Teller can be loaded on a disk and used for presentations in homes or offices. A disk could be sent through the mail from corporate headquarters, for example, to present a self-running management report to employees.

## Special Hardware for Presentation Graphics

If you wish to display graphics on your screen, you will need a graphics adapter board for your personal computer. To produce presentation graphics, you may wish to add a special color monitor to your system. To produce hard copy of your graphics on paper or an overhead transparency, you will need a graphics printer or a plotter. To create color prints or slides of screen images, you will need to use special peripherals from Kodak or Polaroid. Now we shall take a look at some of this special hardware.

## Graphics Adapter Boards

Personal computers like the IBM PC display text on their screens when you use them to do word processing or spreadsheets. In order to display pictures or graphs instead of text, an IBM PC must have a **graphics adapter board** (also called a **graphics card**). To use color graphics, you will need both a color monitor and a color graphics card. Before you purchase a graphics card, you should verify that the graphics software you plan to purchase is compatible with the card. Most software producers write their programs so that they can be used with the most commonly used graphics cards—those from IBM, Hercules Computer Technology, AST, and Quadram.

You should also check the graphics card to see whether it allows text programs (word processing, spreadsheets, and databases) to display text characters on your monitor. Again, this is usually possible with cards from the major manufacturers.

To create most business graphics, a standard graphics card and color monitor usually provide all the features a user requires. However, if you have a special use for very clear, precise images or need to produce very fancy or detailed graphics, then you might want to purchase special high-resolution monitors and graphics cards.

Images on a computer's display screen are made up of dots called **pixels.** The more pixels that a monitor and graphics card can display on a screen, the more clearly defined the image. Levels of **resolution,** or image sharpness, are described in terms of the number of pixels displayed horizontally by the number of pixels displayed vertically. There are three common levels of resolution for graphics:

1. Medium—capable of displaying 320 by 200 pixels.
2. High—capable of displaying 640 by 200 pixels.
3. Super-high—capable of displaying 1024 by 1024 pixels.

Currently, the standard for high resolution is IBM's Enhanced Graphics Adapter (EGA). This card can display 16 colors at 640 by 200 resolution on a standard color monitor. With optional added memory and IBM's Enhanced Color Display monitor, the EGA can display 16 colors at a resolution of 640 by 350.

## Graphics Printers and Plotters

Letter-quality printers cannot print graphic output, but there are many types of printers that can. Some can print only on paper, and some can print on both paper and transparency sheets for overhead projection. These printers are referred to as **graphics printers.** Graphics printers are usually dot-matrix, ink-jet, or laser printers. If you wish to have color in your graphics, then you will probably need an ink-jet printer, or you can use a plotter. These output devices are described in detail in Chapter 5.

## Color Photographs from Your Screen

Projected 35mm color slides produce a very clear image and are convenient to use in presentations. Kodak's Instagraphic CRT Slide Imager lets you photograph your computer's display screen. The Polaroid Palette transfers the input from your computer's signals to the Polaroid Palette's own high-resolution display screen. You can then photograph this display and produce Polaroid color prints or special Polaroid color slides that develop in 15 minutes (Figure 15-23).

## A New Day

If you are just beginning to explore personal computer software, then you must be impressed with the power of the tools described in this chapter. But perhaps more impressive

**Figure 15-23  Photos of your graphics.** Data from the computer screen is transferred to the Polaroid Palette's own screen, where it can be photographed and developed quickly into color prints, slides, or overheads.

than their power is their ease and elegance in action. It is easy to look good using this software. It is hard to make a mistake.

This software heralded a new day for businesspeople—a day when they threw off the chains of drudgery and gave themselves time to think. We hope you have the opportunity to learn more about these types of packages, either in school or on the job. We hope you can join the new day.

## Summary and Key Terms

- Pages that are used to organize data into rows and columns are called worksheets or **spreadsheets.** At the intersection of each row and column is a space called a **cell,** in which data can be entered. Creating and correcting manual spreadsheets is time-consuming.

- In 1978 Daniel Bricklin and Robert Frankston developed **VisiCalc,** the first **electronic spreadsheet.**

- The user of an electronic spreadsheet enters the data, the appropriate mathematical formulas, and any other instructions needed by the computer to solve the problem. The electronic spreadsheet program quickly and automatically performs the calculations to reflect changes in the data or formulas.

- The user can only see a part of the electronic spreadsheet on the screen at any one time. The user can see any part of the spreadsheet by using the cursor control keys on the keyboard or entering a special command. The cursor, which is usually a highlighted rectangle on the screen in electronic spreadsheets, can be moved to any cell. Lotus 1-2-3 identifies cursor location in the upper left-hand corner of the screen.

- Most popular spreadsheets follow the standard approach established by Lotus 1-2-3. The user moves the **menu cursor** to a major command in the **command menu,** then to the appropriate subcommand. After formatting the spreadsheet, the user can create a label, number, or formula in a cell. When the data in any cell is changed, the electronic spreadsheet quickly recalculates values that are affected.

- **Templates**—spreadsheets with all the commands, labels, and formulas already entered—are available for most personal and business spreadsheet applications.

- Word processing, spreadsheet, database, and graphics programs are often combined into an **integrated** package. With an integrated package a user does not have to learn four completely different programs that use different commands. Data can be moved quickly and easily from one program to another within the package.

- An alternative to using an integrated package is to buy separate **stand-alone** programs that can then be coordinated by a **universal manager program.**

- Individual program functions are usually stronger in stand-alone packages, which also are less expensive and require less memory than integrated packages. However, integrated packages are more effective at coordinating different programs.

- **Analytical graphics** programs allow a personal computer user to construct and print simple graphs.

- **Presentation graphics** programs produce more sophisticated graphics that are appropriate for formal presentations.

- With most presentation graphics programs, a user can: (1) edit and enhance charts created by other programs, (2) create new charts, diagrams, drawings, and text slides, and (3) create professional-looking illustrations by using a library of symbols and pictures that comes with the program. Presentation graphics programs enhance charts through such means as adding more color, providing a variety of text fonts, and improving graph labels.

- A **graphics adapter board,** or **graphics card,** enables an IBM PC to display pictures or graphs. A color monitor and a color graphics card are required to produce color graphics.

- The **resolution,** or image sharpness, of a computer display screen is described in terms of **pixels,** the small dots that make up the images on the screen. The more dots that a monitor and graphics card can display on the screen, the clearer the image.

- Dot-matrix, ink-jet, and laser printers are commonly used as **graphics printers.** Color graphics are done with ink-jet printers and with plotters.

- Special equipment from Kodak or Polaroid allows users to convert graphics screen images to 35mm color slides for use in presentations.

## Review Questions

1. How are electronic spreadsheets useful?

2. Describe how a Lotus 1-2-3 user would format a spreadsheet and enter spreadsheet data.

3. Explain what templates are, and state three advantages of using them.

4. What are the advantages of using an integrated package?

5. How do stand-alone packages differ from integrated packages?

6. How do analytical graphics and presentation graphics differ?

7. What are the three main capabilities of presentation graphics programs?

8. Describe how the PC Storyboard system works.

9. What is the purpose of a graphics card? What should a user do before buying one?

10. What is resolution and how is it measured?

## Discussion Questions

1. Set up a spreadsheet for your own personal budget. Use an electronic spreadsheet if you have access to software and a personal computer; otherwise, write out your spreadsheet on paper. Put labels for months of the year in the columns across the top. Put labels for income and expenses in the rows along the left side. Expenses may include tuition, books, supplies, rent, food, telephone, entertainment, and clothing. Write formulas to calculate total expenses per month and monthly balance (the difference between income and expenses). Also, write formulas to calculate the total of each row for the year.

Now use your budget spreadsheet to answer the following "What if . . ." questions:

a) What if you bought a new car with monthly payments of $150 and moved home for the summer to reduce expenses? Would your yearly balance be positive or negative? Could you afford the car?

b) What if you got a part-time job during the school year that paid $240 per month and became a full-time job in the summer months that paid $650 per month? What would your new yearly balance be?

2. Suppose you are the manager of a fast-food restaurant. What could you use an electronic spreadsheet for?

# 16

# Database Management Systems

## Getting Data Together

The most important non-human asset of a company is data. Typical data pertains to customers, suppliers, employees, and sales. But this data is only useful if it is easily accessible. In this chapter we shall discuss why data is sometimes not accessible and how a database system can solve that problem. We also present the theory behind database management and discuss related management activities.

What if—right now—you had your own business. You parlay your special expertise and your business savvy into a lucrative enterprise. You even get a computer to help keep track of everything. Your success breeds more success, and the business grows.

But things begin to unravel—first in small ways, then in frightening larger ways. Your data is in segregated computer files, and you cannot put information together the way you need it. You have bits and pieces of information about your business but not the big picture. You worry about what you do not know and what you cannot get. And, most of all, you worry that you lack control.

How could this have happened? The computer is the very tool to help businesses! This, of course, is true. But any tool can be used in ways that turn out to be counterproductive, especially when a business has growing pains.

In this chapter we shall travel a similar road with Gerry Russell, whose business fell into the same trap: I know the data is in there somewhere, if I could just get it! Along the way we shall explain in detail how it happened, exactly what the problems were, and what she did about it.

This chapter is about database management, so you can guess that a database is the solution to Gerry's problem. For now we can say that a **database** is a collection of data that is accessible in a variety of ways. The software to control the database and make it accessible to users is called a **database management system** (**DBMS**). A database management system is a set of programs that creates, manages, protects, and provides access to the database. Databases are widely used in many businesses, large and small. We shall consider the rationale for databases and examine the theory behind them. Along the way we shall look at some database packages for personal computers.

Now let us look at Gerry's problem and how it grew.

## A Case of Insufficient Information

Gerry Russell's business was suffering growing pains. From a small office-supplies business that she ran herself, Russell Supply Company had really grown in the last ten years. Now she had over 150 customers in three states and a staff of 11 full-time employees. But growth led to control problems—Gerry felt she was losing her sure touch with her company's daily operation. This worried her because she felt that it was her attention to detail and her understanding of her customers that had shaped her success. She was no longer able to monitor details and provide special customer services. She also worried about finding more time to contact new customers. She was beginning to feel that she could not find out exactly what was happening in her own company.

## THE MICROCOMPUTER CORNER

### Computers Play Ball

Baseball statistics have traditionally been kept by hand or in someone's head. How is it that a business with $600 million in revenues can ignore computers?

Baseball managers are among the most hide-bound traditionalists around. However, some of them are actually entering the Computer Age and crediting the computer with some wins. That last fact is the attention getter.

The secret, you see, lies in those years of accumulated records, now stored in a database and quickly accessible by a computer that is right in the ball park. The manager matches the player to the situation at hand—park, pitcher, inning, and score—based on the player's past performance. Even the weather is factored in, so the manager can know how the current conditions will affect curveball or fastball pitchers.

Consider this example of computer coaching. A particular left-handed batter was usually replaced with a pinch hitter in the lineup against left-handed pitchers. When the computer revealed that he actually hit lefty pitchers better than righties, he was no longer automatically benched.

## Scattered Data

When Gerry was the lone employee of her fledgling company, she kept the information she needed to run her business in her head or in card files. As her business grew, she bought a personal computer and accounting software. A consultant wrote inventory management and sales tracking programs for Gerry to run on her personal computer. Later Gerry purchased a second personal computer—a different brand from the first but at a bargain price—and word processing and spreadsheet software to run on it. The second computer turned out to be a mixed blessing, since it could not exchange disks with the original machine. Gerry and several staff people used the new computer often and stored vital information on its diskettes. Gerry recently hired a computer service bureau so that she could do on-line order entry for her high-volume customers. Much important information was now stored on the third computer at the service bureau.

Gerry continued to receive regular reports on her company's performance from three computers. But a nagging doubt was forming in Gerry's mind. The data about her company and her customers—her most valuable asset—was scattered in fragments. One piece was stored on one computer, another piece on another. There was no way to lump everything together and get an overview. The reports she received were good in their own areas, but Gerry needed something more for decision making: She needed reports based on information extracted from different files that were on different computers. She had been told by her staff that this could not be done without a lot of extra work.

## And Other Data Problems

Furthermore, her staff told her that some kinds of information were not available. But Gerry knew that it was. She knew that the data she needed had been put into the computers using the various programs she had purchased. Gerry tried to extract the mix of information she needed from the computer files and reports, but she could not do it. A staff member explained that the data could be brought together by writing special computer programs, but Gerry recognized that this would mean further delays and also that the programming effort would have to be made again for other types of reports. There was no easy way to merge the necessary data together to give her the information she needed.

Data inaccessibility was not the only problem. One day a vital customer file was accidentally deleted. There was no backup copy of the data; it was just gone. Other information was abundant, however: It was being entered every day in two separate files by two different employees, neither of whom recognized the duplicate effort. Perhaps more disconcerting to Gerry, however, was that the data on the two files did not even match. The last straw, however, was the discovery that an employee had "borrowed" some customer data for a political mailing.

## A Better Way to Manage Information

Gerry phoned Alan Shaw, a friend from her business-school days. Alan worked for a large shipping company. Gerry explained that her company's information system was experiencing growing pains. She wondered how the shipping company managed its information.

Alan described the problems his company had had with its information processing system and how they had solved their problems. It turned out that although Gerry's and Alan's situations were different, their problems were actually quite similar.

At Alan's company in the past, information stored on their mainframe computer was not accessible in the ways people needed it. Corporate data could not be shared among departments, and reports were sometimes inconsistent. Data entry costs were inflated because the same information was stored on the computer in different files by different departments. This had increased the amount of duplicate information occupying storage space on the computer's disks and tapes. No one person knew everything that was being stored on the computer, although some people mistakenly thought that they did. Also, a top-level manager who asked for some specific information was told by the data processing department that it would require several months and many hours of programming effort to extract the information from the computer's files. This same manager was even less pleased when a key data file was accidentally deleted. Furthermore, in some cases information was being stored and accessed by individuals who had no authorization to do so.

Let us pause here a moment to note the similarities between the problems in Gerry's and Alan's systems. Although Gerry's data is spread over three computers and Alan's was spread over several mainframe files, the problems are much the same:

- Segregated files, making data inaccessible and unshareable

- Inability to get the "big picture"

- Duplication of effort and data

- Inconsistent reports

- Delays in extracting data

- Unauthorized data access

- Inadequate backup of data

To resolve their information management problems, Alan's company found a better way: They purchased a database management system. They used it to consolidate their many files into a few large databases managed by the DBMS software. The conversion to the database management system had been costly and a lot of work, but it had solved most of the company's information problems. Alan suggested that Gerry consider buying a powerful personal computer and a DBMS to run on it. There are, he noted, many advantages to that approach.

## Asking Questions about the Data

But Gerry was not convinced. She already had most of the information she needed stored on computer files. She could see the benefits of storing all her information in one place, to be processed by one computer. But how could buying one more program—the DBMS—benefit her? Alan explained that even with her files stored on the same computer, the data in each file is still segregated from data in other files. That is, it still would be troublesome to relate data across files. Gerry wanted to be able to retrieve related information from several different files. Consider some typical requests that Gerry wants to make and the process required to fulfill those requests using the current system.

- Last year, how much commission did our sales representative to Fiorini Stationers make from the Fiorini account? (Look up Fiorini in the customer file; the Fiorini record says the sales rep is Thompson. Look up Thompson in the sales rep file to find commission on the Fiorini account.)

- List vendor name and address for vendors who provided spiral notebooks for orders of more than 1000 notebooks. (Look in the order file to extract the vendor number for all records of spiral

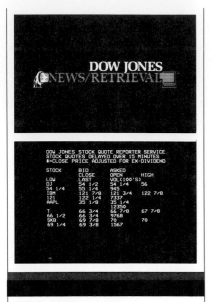

## DOW JONES NEWS/ RETRIEVAL

A personal computer and a modem let you access on-line database services. Hundreds of these are available, and they offer information on everything from airline reservations to medical diagnoses to zodiac profiles.

People in business find financial and business news services like the Dow Jones News/Retrieval to be very useful. This service uses database technology to provide electronic access to *The Wall Street Journal*. It also provides constantly updated world, government, industry, and company news. Interest and exchange rates are updated constantly. Stock-market quotations are available in real time. The fact that this information is stored in databases permits rapid and accurate updating of the information. It also lets you access vast quantities of information quickly and easily.

notebooks with a quantity greater than 1000. Use those vendor numbers to look up vendor name and address on the vendor file.)

- List quantity on hand for all products on order 71286. (Find order 71286 in the order file. For each product number in the order, look in the product inventory file to find the available quantity of that product.

As you can see, each of these requests calls for some sort of cross-referencing between files. These requests are fairly simple, yet filling them calls for more than one file. This situation underscores Gerry's need for integrated files, as opposed to her current system of segregated files. Keep the nature of these examples in mind; we shall refer to them again. One more point: All of these requests can be fulfilled by writing custom programs that follow steps similar to those of a human file clerk. But Gerry—and businesspeople like her— cannot spend the money or take the time to have special programs written; they need speedy access to data and answers. A database system can provide it.

## Superprogram

Gerry does indeed need a superprogram to organize and integrate her files so that data in one file can be joined to related data in other files. That superprogram is a database management system. Here are some of the things Gerry and her employees can do with a DBMS:

- All the data can be stored in files in the same database so that the files can be combined.

- Data can be entered into a file, then easily accessed, modified, or deleted without the data entry operator having to know all the details about how the DBMS does its job.

- Data in the files can be shared among employees. Separate files for each department or function are unnecessary. Data is stored once and accessed by everyone who has reason and authorization to access it.

- A report can be produced from one or more files with just a few simple instructions.

- Files can be backed up quickly so that no information is lost.

These functions describe what can be done with a database; now also consider the benefits. A DBMS has benefits that are the flip side of the problems we described earlier.

- **Integrated files.** An overview of the business is possible because data from separate files can be joined together. This improves data accessibility. Questions that "cross" files can be answered easily without the delay of separate programming efforts.

- **Reduced redundancy.** If data is stored in just one place, then duplicate data can be reduced. Although redundancy cannot usually be eliminated completely, it can be minimized. In any case, with a database the same data is not scattered among numerous files.

- **Shared data.** With pooled resources, data can be used relatively easily for many applications. The data does not need to be described differently for each user; rather, the user defines the subset of the database that is needed, and the database system provides the data as requested.

- **Consistent reports.** With data centralized in one place, the correct updated data appears on all—not just some—related reports extracted from the database.

- **Centralized security.** If data is all in one place, we have better control over access to it. Scattered files, on the other hand, are more difficult to protect. Security is particularly important for personnel files, restricted product information, customer credit ratings, marketing plans, and similar sensitive information.

The story about Gerry Russell's business is not finished yet. So far we have laid out a typical problem scenario and described the benefits of choosing a database as the solution to the problem. We also want to describe the system Gerry chose and how she used it to solve her problems. That discussion will center around using a database on a personal computer. But we need to pause first and consider databases in general and the theory behind their use.

 ## The Theory behind a Database Management System

Many companies have several databases. A manufacturing company, for example, may have one database for the manufacturing process (engineering design, assembly process, quality control), another for financial applications (general ledger, accounts payable, accounts receivable), and still another for records about people (personnel, payroll). The relationships among the data stored in a database are often complex because data relationships in the real world are themselves complex. But, as we noted earlier with Gerry's sample questions, users often need information in a way that relies on complex relationships. This is the main reason for having a database.

People cannot access a database directly. A database management system is a set of programs that lets users access the database for a particular application. In other words, the DBMS shields the user from the technical details of managing the physical database. The logical organization of the data in the database is called the

**schema.** The schema describes the data elements in the database and the relationships among them. The logical organization of the data for a particular user application is called a **subschema,** that is, a subset of the whole database.

## Representing Real-World Data Relationships in a Database

In a file system, data is stored in segregated files. A file system cannot store information about how data in one file is related to data in another file. A database, however, has integrated files. To make those files integrated, a database management system uses a modeling concept. A **model** is an image of something that actually exists. **Database models** represent data relationships found in the real world. We can store more than just data on records in our database; we can also store the actual relationships or associations among the data. This is a very important point to grasp. To respond to cross-file requests, such as those that Gerry made, a DBMS stores both data and the relationships that occur in the real world between the data items.

Gerry, for example, may need data from both the sales representative file and the customer file. The database stores information on the relationship between sales representative data and customer data. Thus, related data from both files can be pulled together as needed by the database management system to respond to questions posed by the users.

A database management system uses modeling to mimic real-world relationships. The three basic database models are hierarchical, network, and relational. Simple overview diagrams of these three models are shown in Figure 16-1. We begin with a discussion of the model that is easiest to understand, the hierarchical model.

## Hierarchical Model

In a **hierarchical model,** records in a file in a database are always associated in a one-to-many, or parent-child, relationship. A child record "belongs to" one and only one parent record. Hierarchical relationships are common in real life: One department in a company has many employees, a salesperson makes many sales, a landlord has many tenants, a doctor has many patients. An individual record in a hierarchical database can never have more than one parent. Data stored in records at lower levels of the hierarchy can be accessed only through their parent record. This is illustrated in Figure 16-2.

This model is somewhat confining, however, because relationships in the real world are not necessarily hierarchical. This limitation encouraged the development of the network model.

**Figure 16-1    Skeleton drawings of database models.**

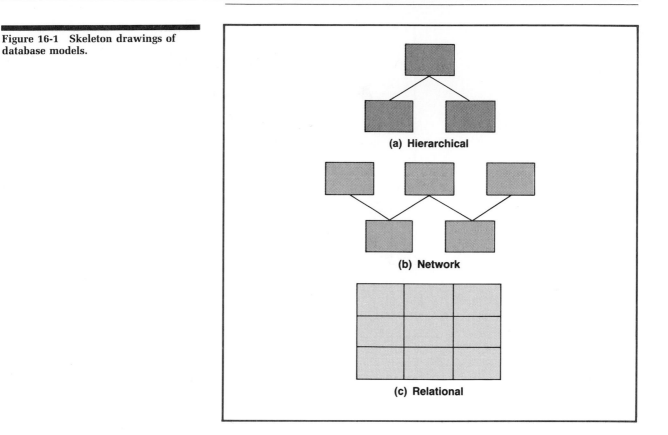

(a) Hierarchical

(b) Network

(c) Relational

## Network Model

A **network model** is similar to a hierarchical model, except that a child record can be associated with more than one parent record. For example, consider the hierarchical relationships advisor-student and major-student. In a college each student's record is associated with both an advisor record and with a major record. This means that a given student record is associated with parent records of both advisor and major record types. Although this situation cannot be modeled directly in the hierarchical model, the network model can model such relationships. An example of a network model is shown in Figure 16-3.

## Relational Model

This is the newest of the database models. It was proposed by E. F. Codd of IBM in 1970. It was designed to be simpler and easier to use than the two previous database models. The **relational model** organizes data logically in tables, using a fixed number of columns and a variable number of rows. A table is called a **relation.** Each column of the relation is called an **attribute,** and each row is called a **tuple.** Each attribute of each tuple contains a **data value.**

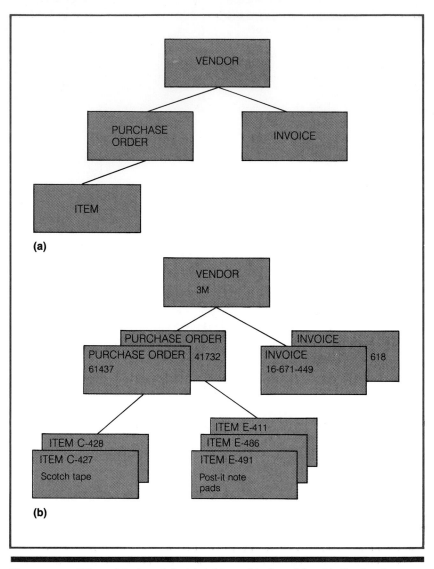

**Figure 16-2   Hierarchical models.** (a) A hierarchical model, with Vendor the parent of Purchase order and Invoice, and Purchase order the parent of Item. (b) The example shows the same hierarchical relationship as the model but with the possibility of many children for one parent. For example, Purchase order 61437 has two Items, and Purchase order 41732 has three Items.

As you can see from Figure 16-4, relations are like files. The rows of a relation are records and each record consists of a fixed number of fields.

We have noted that a database model can handle relationships between files. How is this done in the relational model? The answer is in the data manipulation capabilities of the relational model and in the use of link fields. **Link fields** are common data items included in the relations that are to be related. For example, if you had several relations (or files) in a relational database about company employees, the Social Security number could be used in each relation. The

**Figure 16-3  Network model.** (a) The model shows that a child—Purchase order—can have more than one parent, in this case Department and Vendor. (b) In the example these Purchase orders have the same Department and Vendor.

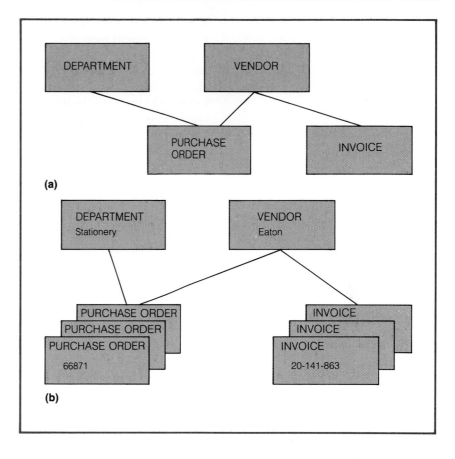

(a)

(b)

Social Security number is thus the common field—the link field—in those relations. This causes some redundancy in our database, but the payoff is that we no longer have segregated files. Now the relational DBMS can be used to extract related data from separate files through the link field that is common among them.

Let us consider how this is done. Relations can be reduced or combined in various ways to answer questions about the data. The processes that manipulate relations are called **relational operations.**

**Figure 16-4  A relational example.** In this example there are five tuples—rows—and five attributes—columns. Each attribute of each tuple contains a data value; the 30,000 highlighted is the data value for attribute Salary of the first tuple.

| Number | Name | Phone | Salary | Quota |
|--------|------|-------|--------|-------|
| 011-34-3626 | Akers, Todd | 789-4400 | 30,000 | 100,000 |
| 545-18-2682 | Brown, Ann | 789-4436 | 30,000 | 100,000 |
| 288-00-5289 | Chandler, Jay | 789-4405 | 41,000 | 150,000 |
| 376-12-0851 | James, Susan | 789-4421 | 30,000 | 100,000 |
| 194-63-8491 | Mead, Ken | 789-4430 | 50,000 | 210,000 |

An attribute

A data value

A tuple

The three basic relational operations are select, project, and join. A **select relational operation** forms a new relation by selecting certain tuples from a given relation (Figure 16-5a). A **project relational operation** selects certain attributes (fields) from a relation (Figure 16-5b). Any duplicate tuples that may then exist in the new projected relation are eliminated. A **join relational operation** is used to combine two relations based on common attributes into a new relation (Figure 16-5c). The common attributes are what we have been calling link fields. The ability to join two or more relations is a crucial quality. Otherwise, the data would be segregated in separate relations just as, in the past, data was segregated in separate files. A true relational DBMS must be able to join two or more relations.

Although early relational database management systems did not perform as efficiently with a high volume of data as hierarchical or network database management systems, this is no longer true. The processing efficiency of most relational database management systems is good. Users have found relational databases much easier to learn and to use than database management systems based on the other two models. The most popular database management systems for personal computers are all based on the relational model. R:base 5000 and dBASE III are both relational database management systems because they use the relational data model.

Database management systems have become workhorses on mainframe computers. Virtually every large company uses a DBMS and employs a highly trained staff of database experts to oversee the use of the database and to write programs to access it.

## PC/FOCUS

Focus, a fourth-generation language and information management software tool from Information Builders, has long been a popular package on mainframe computers. Now a version for personal computers is also becoming popular.

PC/Focus, as it is called, gives you the ability to query and report from files, build systems, and manipulate data. It incorporates the capabilities of a relational database, graphics, financial modeling, and statistical analysis.

One of the features that makes it so popular is its natural language, TableTalk, that lets a user interface with the program using simple English statements.

Another feature that is much appreciated by users is PC/Focus's ability to download data extracted from mainframe files and databases.

## Applications Programs and Query Languages

With a database management system in place, there are basically two ways to access the database: through applications programs and through query languages.

Applications programs can call up special access programs that are part of the database management system. Instructions to access the database can be embedded in a program that is written in a language such as COBOL. Instead of the standard COBOL instruction READ, for example, an applications program uses special instructions to call on the DBMS to retrieve the data from the database.

Most database management systems also provide a **query language,** a high-level nonprocedural language that people with no formal programming training can use to specify their requirements. A user can be taught to use a query language with minimal instruction. By using English-like requests for information, the user can interactively access the database (Figure 16-6). In response to queries the DBMS searches the database for the information and returns it to the user.

An important tool that is often part of a DBMS package is a data dictionary. The **data dictionary** contains an on-line description of

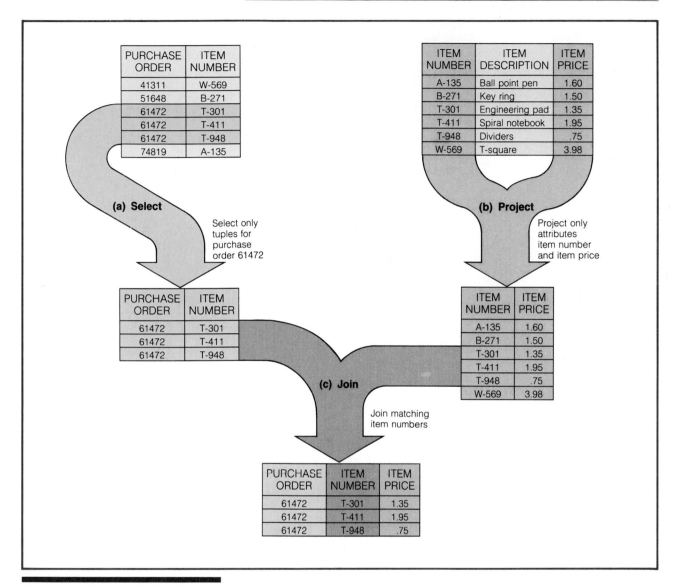

**Figure 16-5  Relational operations.** In this example all three relational operations are used to create a new relation that supplies information to the query, ''Display all item numbers and prices for purchase order 61472.''

all the items of data contained in the database. A database management system may include software to help you develop the data dictionary. Some DBMS data dictionary software displays a screen template to guide you in entering data about each dictionary element—its name, size, usage, and so forth. The data dictionary enables users to find out what data is contained in the organization's databases and what the characteristics of that data are.

Although databases began in large organizations and are extensively used by their programmers and users, they have become widely known to home users and users in small business through database systems for personal computers. The same advantages of pooling data and integrating files by storing relationships with the data are available on personal computers.

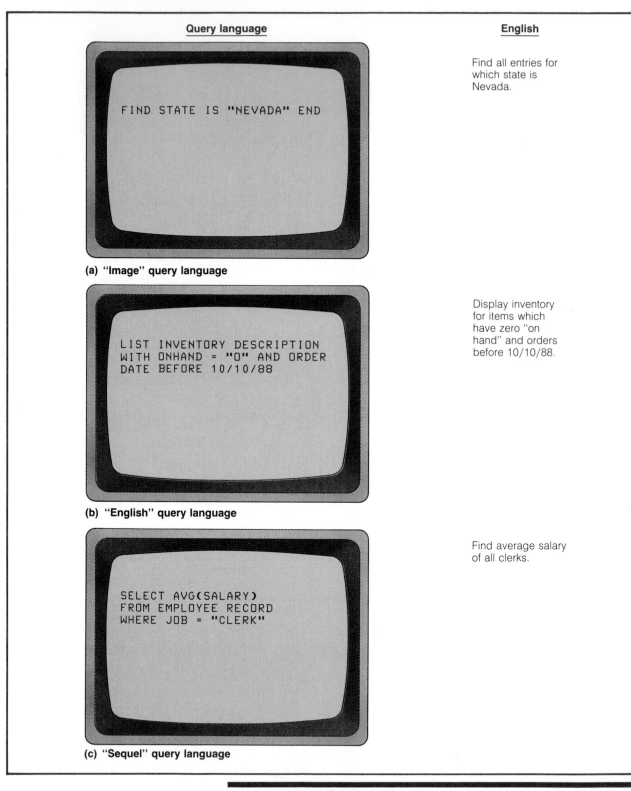

**Figure 16-6 Query languages.** Three samples of query languages are shown here. A query language permits a user to retrieve data instantly from a database.

## The Personal Computer Factor

The first database management systems were designed to run on large mainframe computers. As personal computers became popular in the early 1980s, however, database management systems were developed to run on personal computers. Database management systems for personal computers are usually user friendly. Early database management systems were concerned primarily with getting the data on file and giving it back. For microcomputers, however, it has been estimated that 80% of the DBMS software is devoted to offering a smooth user interface. Because of this attention, users are able to learn to use a personal computer DBMS rather quickly; they are soon able to establish the data in the database and to use it for business purposes.

Some of the popular information management programs for personal computers are PFS:Professional File, dBASE II and III, and R:base 5000. These programs are much simpler than the database management systems used on mainframes. Versions of dBASE (dBASE III PLUS) and R:base (R:base 5000 Multi-User) are also available that allow multiple users in networks to access the same data at the same time. Even though the packages are easy to use, they are sophisticated and powerful.

Not all database management systems for personal computers work exactly the same way, nor do they all provide the same functions. In fact, a range of products that manage information is available for personal computers. For those who have minimal needs for information management, a relatively inexpensive file management program suffices. For use in a business like Gerry's, however, a full-capacity personal computer DBMS is needed. But before we describe her new system, we want to explain how a simpler version works. To be sure that we understand exactly what a true DBMS is, let us contrast it with what is called a low-end DBMS: a file management program.

## File Management Programs for Personal Computers

A **file management program** is not a true DBMS because it cannot join information from separate files. However, many personal computer users have found file management programs very helpful. For example, Dan Holtz, a college drama instructor, wanted to use his new microcomputer to store information about plays that could be used in his classes. He needed to know how many acts and scenes each play had. Dan also needed to know how many male and female roles were available in each play. This information would let him match a play to each class.

Dan asked computer science instructor Max Erbach to help him hook up his new computer. Once the machine was out of its box, plugged in, and turned on, Dan turned to Max expectantly. "OK," he said, "Now how do I start typing in information about these plays?" He was stunned to find out that the computer alone was not able to accept the information he typed at the keyboard. That was certainly not what he had seen on television!

However, it is a fact that the operating system on his computer could not store and retrieve data in the way he wanted. To let him identify files, define what fields are in a record, then display the records, Dan needs additional software. He may choose either a file management system or a database management system. His choice will be determined by his needs and perhaps by his budget.

## A Typical File Management Program in Action

Max recommended that Dan buy a file management program. Although it is not a true DBMS, it did let Dan do exactly what he wanted. Learning the program was relatively easy. First, he selected the "Design File" function from the main menu, shown in Figure 16-7. This let him create a **form.** It was easy to do because the software let him visualize each record in a file as an index card. The form is similar to an index card printed with the names of the data fields for each record.

Whenever Dan indicates that he wants to add records to his file of plays, the software displays a blank form on the computer's screen. The names of the data fields in the record are displayed on the screen, as shown in Figure 16-8a. Then Dan can simply fill in the blanks in the form on the screen (Figure 16-8b). When he is finished filling in the form, he presses a key to store the completed record. The software stores his blank form on the disk with the file so that he only needs to set up the data collection form once. Then he can use it whenever he wishes to add more records.

## Storing Data

After Dan creates the form, he can store information about more plays in his file. To do this he selects the "Add forms" function from the main menu. The software then displays the blank data collection form (see Figure 16-8a) that he had previously created. He then fills in the form, as before. After he enters the last item of information (the number of women in the play), he pushes a key that causes the software to actually store the information in a file on his disk.

As soon as one play record has been stored in the file, the program again displays the blank form on the computer's screen. When

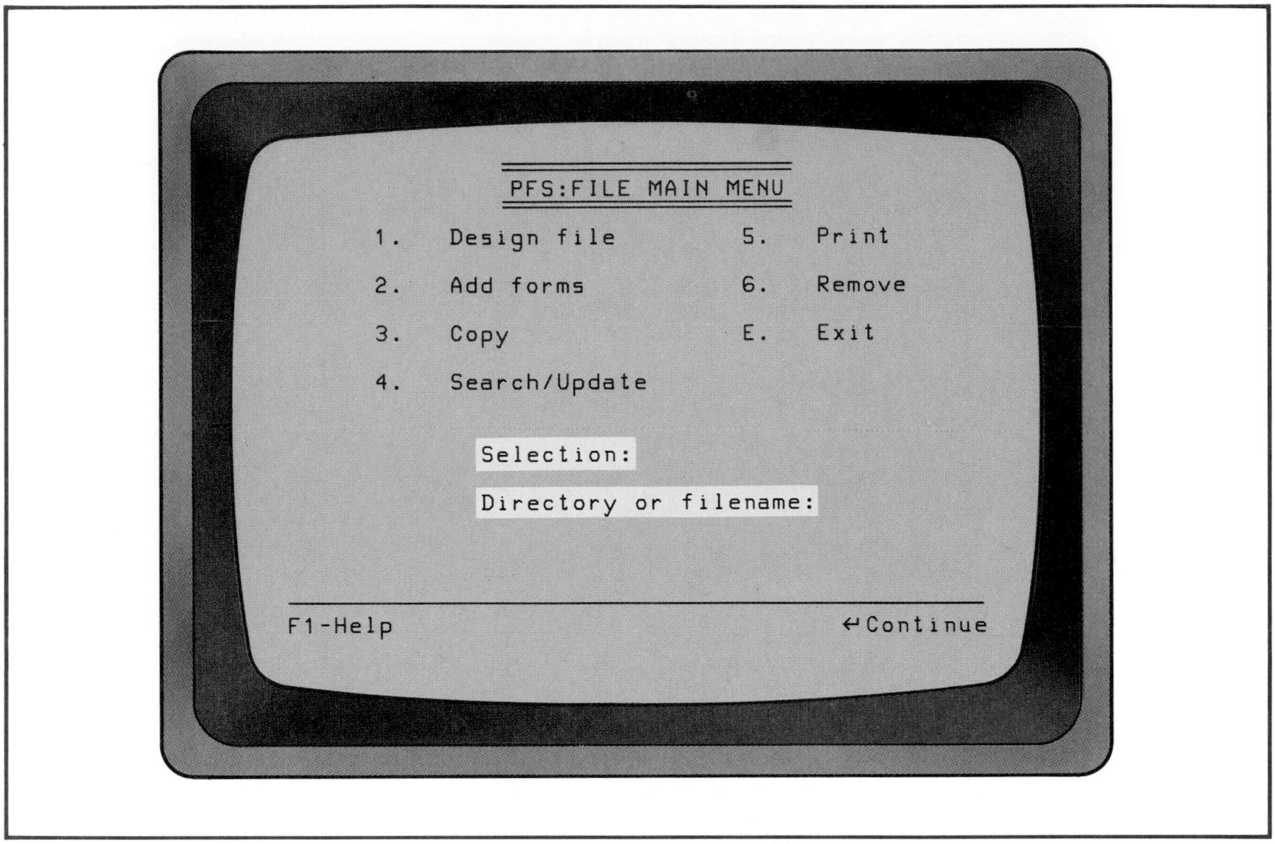

```
            PFS:FILE MAIN MENU

     1.    Design file      5.    Print

     2.    Add forms        6.    Remove

     3.    Copy             E.    Exit

     4.    Search/Update


           Selection:

           Directory or filename:


     F1-Help                            ↵ Continue
```

**Figure 16-7   File management main menu.** By entering a number from 1 to 6 or E, you can select the corresponding function.

all plays are entered, Dan presses the key the software designates to indicate that there is not any more data to enter. The program saves the completed forms on the disk, then displays the main menu once more on the screen.

## Other Options

Now Dan has all his information stored in a file on disk. We have taken the trouble to show you how to enter data in the file so that you can see how easy it is. Although we cannot go through all the other functions here, you can see from the menu that Dan can add plays or remove plays from his file and update—change—the data on an existing record. But the most powerful operation is the search function: Dan can ask the software to display all the plays with one act or all the plays that require three male characters and five females. And, of course, Dan can print the contents of his records. Since these capabilities allow Dan to do precisely the tasks he wants, the file management program suits him perfectly.

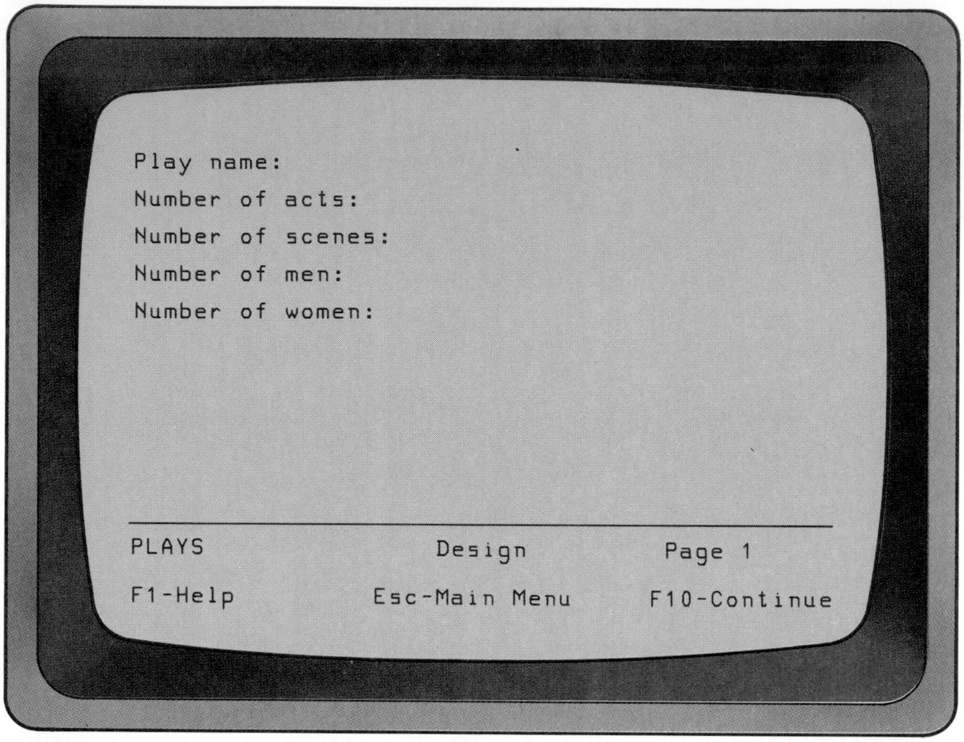

```
Play name:
Number of acts:
Number of scenes:
Number of men:
Number of women:




PLAYS                    Design              Page 1

F1-Help             Esc-Main Menu        F10-Continue
```

(a)

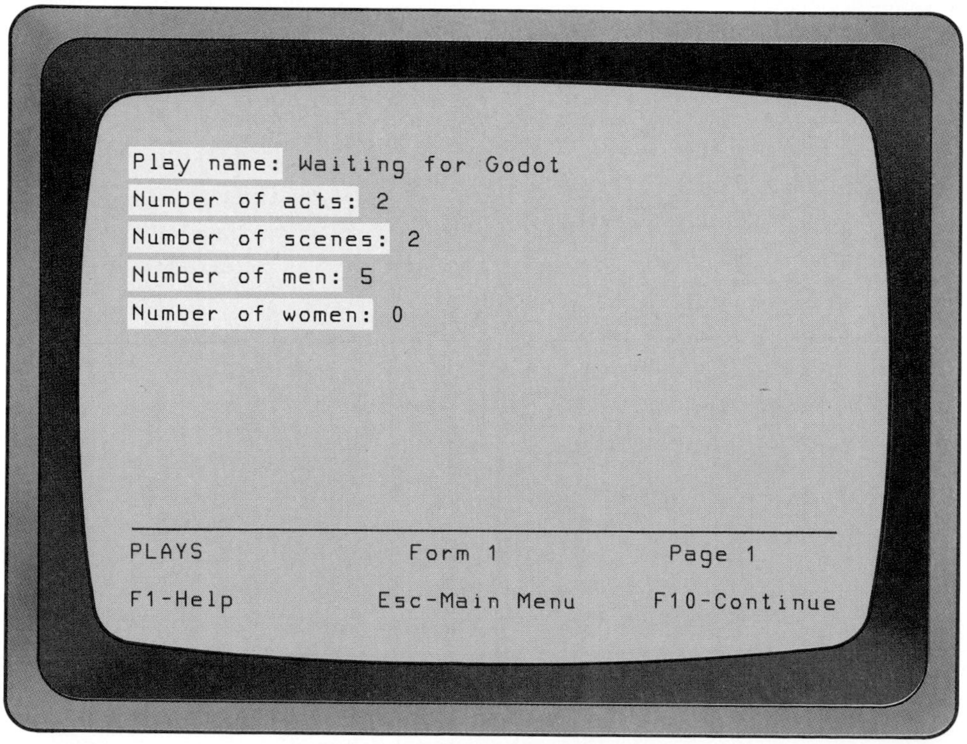

```
Play name: Waiting for Godot
Number of acts: 2
Number of scenes: 2
Number of men: 5
Number of women: 0




PLAYS                    Form 1              Page 1

F1-Help             Esc-Main Menu        F10-Continue
```

(b)

**Figure 16-8   Filling in a form.** (a) A form for a record looks like an index card. It lists the data names for the record. (b) The data names can be filled in with data, as shown in this example for the play *Waiting for Godot*.

A file management program is not a true DBMS because it does not have the ability to relate and present to the user information from two or more files. To return to the example of Gerry Russell, this means that a file management program would not be sufficient for her needs.

In Chapter 15 we mentioned that some integrated packages like Lotus 1-2-3 contain a database component. In fact, the database in the majority of integrated programs is really not a true DBMS. Most of the "databases" in these packages, although they are very useful, can only handle one file at a time. Most integrated packages cannot truly relate information in multiple files. For this reason, such a package would not meet Gerry's needs either.

# Database Management Systems for Personal Computers

Gerry, as we have noted, needs to be able to extract related information from multiple files. Two programs that can relate and extract associated information from more than one file at a time are dBASE III PLUS and R:base 5000. These programs are both true database management systems for personal computers. As we shall see, Gerry Russell chose dBASE III PLUS for her business.

## dBASE III PLUS—The Choice for Russell Supplies

Gerry hired computer consultant Ken Koffman, who studied Gerry's business and recommended dBASE III PLUS, a relational multiuser database management system. Russell Supplies bought a powerful personal computer with a 20-megabyte hard disk to run dBASE III PLUS. Ken worked with Gerry and her staff to ensure that their database files were designed properly. Gerry's business is complex and needed eight separate database files for customers, vendors, sales representatives, customer orders, supplies, back orders, products, and payroll. Ken explained that unless Gerry's database was properly designed, it would perform poorly. Ken also used the DBMS high-level programming language to set up a system for producing several complex reports that Gerry needed on a regular basis.

Ken trained Gerry and her staff to add data to the database and to update or delete existing data. And they learned to query the database to find answers that were not answered in the regular reports. They also discovered that the dBASE III PLUS query language was relatively easy to learn. They learned to make queries in a simple English-like way. They did not need to learn a programming language. They also learned how to use the system to produce simple reports.

## A LEMON BY ANY OTHER NAME MIGHT STILL BE A LEMON

The French government may have come up with an antidote for getting stuck with a lemon. The nationally supported electronic information service now offers a database of used cars.

The French government has a new law that requires a used car to pass a government inspection before being sold. Those cars that pass the inspection can be entered in the national used-car database. The listing is available 24 hours a day via the network. By entering any of six criteria—make, model, year, mileage, region where available, and price range—shoppers can search the database for the car they want. The seller's name and address appears automatically with the listing.

Now that we have a general idea of what Gerry and her employees can do with this system, let us take a closer look at dBASE III PLUS. Other personal computer relational database management systems share its general features.

## dBASE III PLUS—A DBMS in Action

Like a relational DBMS on a large system, dBASE III PLUS provides a systematic way to organize, integrate, manage, and retrieve a large collection of related information. It does not have all the functions of some relational systems on mainframes. In particular, it does not implement any real security restrictions. It is, however, very capable of meeting the data storage and retrieval needs of personal computer users and businesses that use personal computers for data processing.

As all relational DBMSs do, dBASE III PLUS organizes a database as a two-dimensional table (a relation) consisting of rows (tuples) and columns (attributes) (see Figure 16-4). Each row in a table is a record that contains data that belongs to a given entry in the database (for example, a customer). The DBMS can store up to 128 data fields (attributes) per record. It can store up to one billion records in one relation. dBASE III PLUS calls the relations *database files*. It uses the *join* relational operator to extract related information from different relations—database files—in the database. This means that queries or reports can extract data from more than one file. dBASE III PLUS can extract related information from up to ten database files.

## dBASE III PLUS—Storing Data

dBASE III PLUS is quite easy to use. Just as with the file management software that we discussed earlier, you must first create a file before you can store data. This is done by using the *create* command. The DBMS asks you to give a name to the database file (relation). Then it prompts you for the names, types, and widths of the data fields in a row (record) in the file. When you are finished you press a key, and the description of the file that was entered is stored in the database. This description is called a **relational schema.** This schema is used by dBASE III PLUS when it needs to access a file or to relate files. The schema is also used to generate the form that is displayed on your screen when you want to add records to the database. The blank form is displayed on the screen, then the user fills in the blank next to a data field name with the value to be stored in that field. When the data for one record (tuple) has been entered, the user presses the Enter key to store the record. Commands are available to delete database files or records in a particular file. You can follow the process of creating files, storing data, and extracting information from them in Figure 16-9.

## dBASE III PLUS—Using Indexes

You may wish to maintain the records in a database file in several different orders. For example, Gerry may need sales representative records sorted by salesperson name for a certain report but sorted by annual total sales amount for another report. To do this, the DBMS lets the user define **index files.** Indexes let the same data be presented in up to seven different sequential orders. However, the data records are only stored once in the database. The indexes are used to present the same data records in different ways.

A key advantage of a DBMS is its ability to search a file for certain records. Index files let you search for a record in a database file very rapidly. If an index file has been created for a particular field on a record, then dBASE III PLUS can quickly find any record with a given value in that field. For example, you might want to find all customer records in which MAINE appeared as the value in the STATE field. Even with hundreds of thousands of records in a database file, records can be found by dBASE III PLUS in a few seconds.

## dBASE III PLUS—The Report Generator

A **report generator** is available in dBASE III PLUS and many other relational database management systems. The report generator lets you prepare common types of business reports without using a programming language. The user creates a **report form** by responding to prompts from the DBMS. The process is similar to the way file forms for data entry are created. The DBMS asks you for the name of the report form, the report headings, data fields to appear on the report, number of lines per page, and data field totals required on the report. This form can be stored and used whenever a particular report is needed. dBASE III PLUS retrieves data from a database file and prints the data in the format expressed in the report form.

## dBASE III PLUS—The Programming Language

A powerful high-level programming language is available with dBASE III PLUS. It is only necessary to use this language for certain special purposes. Many users of dBASE III PLUS never need or use it. However, if a complex report is needed, the report generator may not be able to produce it. Then it would be necessary to write a program to create the report. If complicated calculations must be performed on the data, it may be necessary to write a program to do the calculations. Programs can be saved in the database and used when needed. Programs can also be written to make complex database operations appear simple to an untrained user.

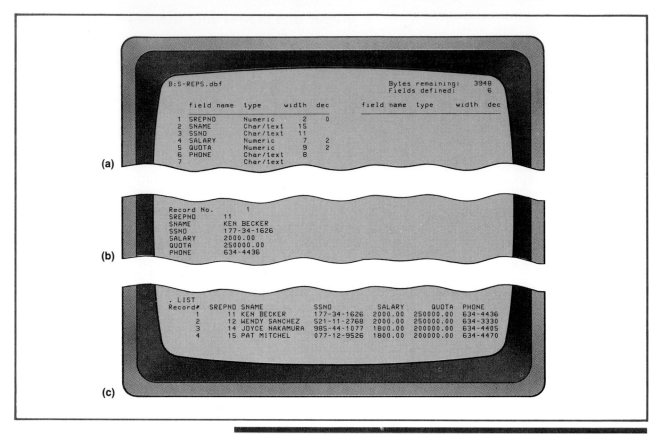

**Figure 16-9   A dBASE III PLUS example.** This example shows the construction of two files and the actions taken to join them—that is, to combine some of their data. (a) Using the create command, the record format for a file called S-REPS (for sales representatives) is established. Each field—SREPNO, SNAME, SSNO, and so forth—is named, followed by the type of field (Numeric or Character/text), its maximum width, and the number of decimal places (if applicable). (b) Shown next is the process to enter data, using the record format established. In this case data is being entered for sales representative Ken Becker. (c) After all data records have been entered (four in this example), they are listed. The process is repeated for another file called CUSTOMERS: (d) The user establishes the record format, (e) enters data records, and (f) lists them. Now we can combine the two files to answer a request that needs data from both of them. The request is to list the customers serviced by each sales representative. We can join the records based on their link field sales representative number (for example, 11 for Ken Becker). (g) The commands shown select S-REPS as the primary file and CUSTOMERS as the secondary file. (h) The next command joins the files on the sales representative number field, asking that the resulting new file contain the SNAME field from the primary file S-REPS and the NAME field from the secondary file CUSTOMERS. (i) The list of the new file shows names of sales representatives on the right.

## dBASE III PLUS—Multiuser Capability

Although some relational database management systems for personal computers are designed for just one user at a time, Gerry's DBMS, dBASE III PLUS, is a multiuser system. This means that

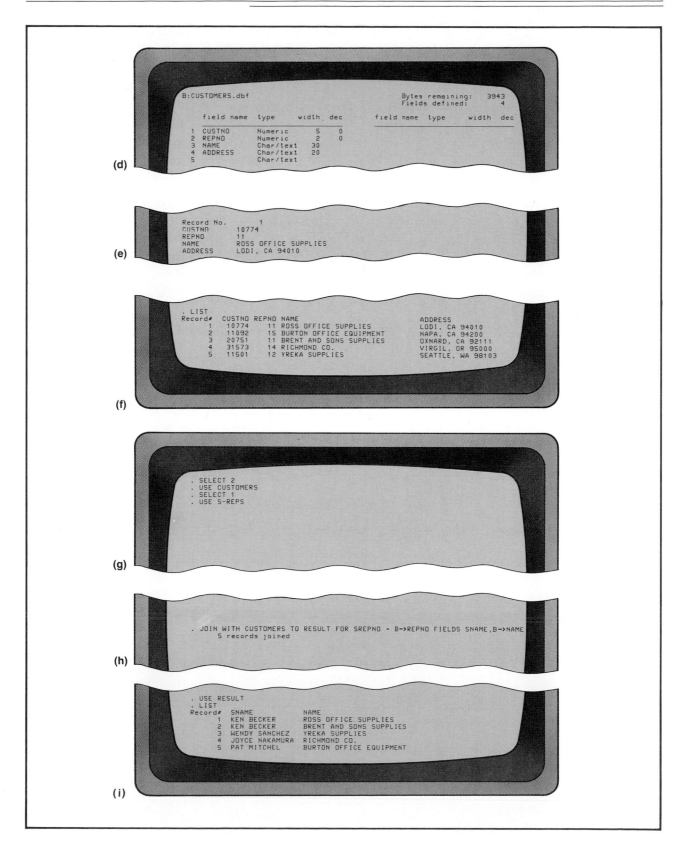

```
B:CUSTOMERS.dbf                                  Bytes remaining:   3943
                                                 Fields defined:       4

       field name   type      width  dec    field name   type      width  dec

     1 CUSTNO        Numeric       5    0
     2 REPNO         Numeric       2    0
     3 NAME          Char/text    30
     4 ADDRESS       Char/text    20
     5               Char/text
```
(d)

```
Record No.         1
CUSTNO      10774
REPNO       11
NAME        ROSS OFFICE SUPPLIES
ADDRESS     LODI, CA 94010
```
(e)

```
. LIST
Record#   CUSTNO REPNO NAME                          ADDRESS
      1   10774    11  ROSS OFFICE SUPPLIES          LODI, CA 94010
      2   11092    15  BURTON OFFICE EQUIPMENT       NAPA, CA 94200
      3   20751    11  BRENT AND SONS SUPPLIES       OXNARD, CA 92111
      4   31573    14  RICHMOND CO.                  VIRGIL, OR 95000
      5   11501    12  YREKA SUPPLIES                SEATTLE, WA 98103
```
(f)

```
. SELECT 2
. USE CUSTOMERS
. SELECT 1
. USE S-REPS
```
(g)

```
. JOIN WITH CUSTOMERS TO RESULT FOR SREPNO = B→REPNO FIELDS SNAME,B→NAME
     5 records joined
```
(h)

```
. USE RESULT
. LIST
Record#   SNAME            NAME
      1   KEN BECKER       ROSS OFFICE SUPPLIES
      2   KEN BECKER       BRENT AND SONS SUPPLIES
      3   WENDY SANCHEZ    YREKA SUPPLIES
      4   JOYCE NAKAMURA   RICHMOND CO.
      5   PAT MITCHEL      BURTON OFFICE EQUIPMENT
```
(i)

Gerry's data can be stored on the hard disk and used by all her staff at the same time via a network. The DBMS ensures that the users do not interfere with each other's data activities.

## Back in Control Again

Gerry has found that managing her company's data using dBASE III PLUS is the solution to her problem. She knows that she is once again in control. She can obtain information on any aspect of her business easily and quickly.

The primary benefit of Gerry's DBMS is that the business is operating from a single set of integrated files, files that can be related to each other. The DBMS does away with the "walls" between files and as the walls come tumbling down, data becomes more accessible and, therefore, more useful.

## The Database Administrator

We have talked at length about the database management system and how it takes care of data. But who is going to take care of the database management system? Whenever information is shared, someone must be responsible for managing the access of users to the information. The **database administrator,** or **DBA,** is the person or group of persons responsible for monitoring and coordinating all activities related to the database. The DBA has several major functions:

- **To coordinate users.** The DBA helps users define data requirements and helps resolve conflicts regarding data, usually through regularly scheduled meetings. Obviously, user involvement is critical to the success of the database since they use it.

- **To enforce standards.** The DBA makes sure the data standards of the organization are disseminated and enforced and maintains any documentation associated with them. Sample candidates for standardization are data names, data formats, record names, and access techniques.

- **To monitor database system performance.** To keep the database and the DBMS operating efficiently, the person or persons in charge must be alert for changes that might lower efficiency. The DBA would certainly be concerned, for example, if access time steadily deteriorated. Monitoring involves keeping statistics, correlating information, and publishing results.

- **To plan recovery procedures.** If the database system fails, the DBA must be prepared. This person develops contingency plans and recovery procedures so that the system can continue to operate with minimal inconvenience or disruption.

- **To monitor the security system.** As we mentioned, data is wealth, and a database contains an organization's most important material asset—its data. Consequently, the DBA must exercise considerable care to keep the system secure. The DBA ensures that the DBMS monitors system security. For instance, whenever someone wishes to gain access to the database and gives a password, identification number, budget number, or the like, the DBMS checks to see if that person is actually authorized to use the data. Data security is discussed in more detail in Chapter 19.

In large organizations with many and diverse users, the DBA's tasks are defined as a separate job. But even in a small company that keeps its database on a personal computer, someone needs to be designated as the person in charge of the database.

# Databases in the Overall Scheme of Things

The database concept is the most difficult one in this book. Advanced students usually take an entire course on the subject, studying its theory and inner workings in some detail. The important concept for you to take with you from this chapter is the idea that a database is needed to share information among files in a timely manner.

You may someday be one of many users sharing a mainframe database in a large organization. But the most likely place for you to discover a database is on a personal computer in an office. Database management is one of many tools used in today's modern office. Collectively, these tools create the automated office, the subject of the next chapter.

## Summary and Key Terms

- A **database** is a collection of data that is accessible in a variety of ways. A **database management system (DBMS)** is a set of programs that creates, manages, protects, and provides access to the database.

- A database management system can solve information management problems, such as inaccessible data due to segregated files, inability to get the "big picture," duplication of effort and data, inconsistent reports, delays in extracting data, unauthorized data access, and inadequate backup of data.

- Typical requests for data involve finding related data from several different files. If these files are segregated, the user must separately request data from each file. A database management system is more efficient because it integrates files so that data in one file can be easily joined to related data in other files.

- The functions of a database management system provide a number of benefits. Integrated files allow an overview of the user's business and improve access to data. Also, the amount of data stored in separate files can be reduced because users have access to the centralized database files. The data can easily be shared and used for many applications, and reports extracted from the database will be consistent. Having the data centralized in one place also allows better security.

- A **schema** describes what types of data are in the database and how the data is related within the database. The logical organization of the data for a particular application is called a **subschema.**

- A **model** is an image of something that actually exists. **Database models** represent data relationships found in the real world. Thus, a DBMS stores both the data itself and the relationships among the data. The three basic database models are the hierarchical, network, and relational models.

- In a **hierarchical model,** records in a file in a database are always associated in a one-to-many, or parent-child, relationship. To access a child record, a user must first know the one parent record to which it belongs.

- A **network model** is similar to a hierarchical model, except that a child record can be associated with more than one parent record. The network model was developed because relationships in the real world are not necessarily hierarchical.

- The **relational model** organizes data logically in tables, using a fixed number of columns and a variable number of rows. A table is called a **relation.** Each column of the relation is called an **attribute,** and each row is called a **tuple.** Each attribute of each tuple contains a **data value.** The relations are like files. The rows of a relation are records, and each record contains a fixed number of fields.

- **Link fields** are common data items included in the relations that are to be related. A link field makes it possible to get related data from all the different relations (files) in which it appears.

- **Relational operations** are processes that manipulate relations. A **select relational operation** forms a new relation by selecting certain tuples (records) from a given relation. A **project relational operation** selects certain attributes (fields) from a relation. A **join relational operation** is used to combine two relations based on common attributes into a new relation.

- With a database management system there are two basic ways of getting access to the database: through custom-made applications programs and through query languages. Applications programs can be used to call up special access programs that are part of the database management system. Most database management systems also provide an easily learned **query language,** which allows users to make English-like requests for information.

- An on-line **data dictionary** enables users to find out what data is contained in the organization's database and what the characteristics of that data are.

- Database management systems for personal computers, such as dBASE II and III and R:base 5000, are much simpler than those used on mainframes. dBASE III PLUS and R:base 5000 Multi-User allow multiple users in networks to access the same data at the same time. Personal computer users who have minimal needs for information management can use a **file management program** such as PFS:FILE, which allows the user to enter data on **forms** (on-screen "index cards") and make requests for particular types of data items.

- With dBASE III PLUS, a relational DBMS, a user first provides a **relational schema,** or description of the types of data that a file will contain. This schema is stored and used by the program to access a file, relate files, and generate the form displayed on the screen.

- dBASE III PLUS lets the user define **index files** that allow the same data to be presented in different sequential orders. Index files also allow the user to quickly search for a record in a database.

- dBASE III PLUS, like many other relational DBMSs, has a **report generator,** which allows the user to create common types of business **report forms** by responding to prompts. Report forms can be stored and used whenever a particular report is needed.

- The **database administrator,** or **DBA,** is the person or group of persons that monitors and coordinates database activities. The DBA is responsible for coordinating users, enforcing data standards, monitoring database system performance, planning recovery procedures if the database system fails, and monitoring the security of the database.

## Review Questions

1. What is a database management system?

2. Describe the typical problems that can indicate the need for a database management system.

3. Explain how a database management system benefits users.

4. Define the following terms: schema, subschema, and database model.

5. Explain how the hierarchical model differs from the network model.

6. Explain how a relational DBMS organizes data.

7. How is a relational DBMS able to relate data from two or more files?

8. Describe the three basic relational operations.

9. Describe the two methods of accessing a database.

10. What are the duties of a database administrator?

## Discussion Questions

1. Discuss the pros and cons of a nationwide database that would connect data from the IRS, FBI, Department of Motor Vehicles, and so forth.

2. Suppose you are the database administrator for your college. What data do you need to store about students and faculty? Who should have access to what data?

## PART 5

# COMPUTERS IN THE WORKPLACE

Most of us know that computers are found in offices and factories, but computers are also found in stores, repair shops, restaurants, and anywhere else that people work. Most of these machines use some subset of the office automation topics we shall discuss in Chapter 17. In particular, most workplaces have personal computers and the business software that runs on them. Also included in Chapter 17 are the significant new trends in factory automation.

Someone must manage all these computer resources, and that is the subject of Chapter 18.

And, finally, company resources must be applied to keep computers and their data secure and private—the subject of Chapter 19.

# 17

# Computers in Business

## From the Office to the Factory Floor

If you don't have one yet, you will soon. A workstation, that is. In the office there will be an electronic desktop device for each worker from the secretary to the top executive. All office workers will use computer technology to help them do their work faster and better.

But why stop there? Computers are also moving into the factory in ways that will greatly alter existing automation.

A rancher or a boat builder or a restaurant owner does not spend much time behind a desk. Still, each of them has to have a place in which to pay bills, make plans, read, write, and communicate—in short, a space that could be called an office, no matter what it looks like. But you will probably be in a more conventional office, recognizable as such by desks and chairs and filing cabinets. And by its electronic gadgetry. Consider Wendy Earl's office.

Wendy's office is at Benson/Coolidge Publishing, where she coordinates book production. When Wendy comes to work in the morning, she turns on her personal computer, which is part of a network of office computers. The screen lists a menu of options. She selects the item "Today's Calendar," and the screen displays "10:30 AM—Morgan book, photo research meeting." This reminds her that she needs to ask editor Pat Burner to bring a certain set of slides to the meeting. She uses word processing to compose a quick list, then sends it to Pat's computer via electronic mail.

Wendy returns to her menu and chooses "Read Mail." The screen now displays a list of three memos, two letters, and a report that have been sent to her electronically. Wendy scans the mail list on her screen. She decides that the memo from Tony Andrea about a particular photo session needs immediate attention and displays it on her screen. She uses her voice mail system to contact Tony; when Tony does not answer, Wendy dictates a response that will be waiting for him—as a voice message—when he calls in.

Less than half an hour has passed, but Wendy has already done work that might have required half a morning if done manually. She uses this electronic wizardry as casually as she does the phone or the copy machine.

## The Dream Office versus the Reality Office

Can you expect to find an array of electronic devices when you go to work in an office? Possibly, but not necessarily. For we are talking about office automation, and its use is as variable as the offices themselves. In general, **office automation** is the use of technology to help achieve the goals of the office. This definition, however, has a wide range of interpretations. It was only a few years ago that office automation was synonymous with word processing. But word processing was only the seed of technological change in the office. Now office automation conjures up much more elaborate visions: networks, workstations that process words one minute and numbers the next, facsimile machines that act as copiers and computer printers, electronic publishing systems that create documents with text and graphics, teleconferencing rooms tied together by satellite, and even office furniture with built-in cabling for electronic devices. For some office workers software that was stunning several years ago—word processing, graphics, spreadsheets,

**STEPS FOR SUCCESSFUL OFFICE AUTOMATION**

- Obtain the backing of higher management.
- Recognize and understand the political issues in your organization.
- Identify a need and meet it; do not wait until all needs are known.
- "Sell" the concept of office automation to key office personnel.
- Develop applications that will help key personnel.
- Select a pilot group of enthusiasts.

database access, executive calendars, and the like—is becoming commonplace. Few offices have all the automated options, but most have some.

Some people think of office technology as a foregone conclusion. But it is not that simple. There are a number of problems associated with introducing office automation, from reluctant workers to incompatible machines. Despite the miles of columns computer magazines have devoted to this subject, office automation remains elusive for many organizations. We will first examine the trends in office automation, then tackle some of these related complexities.

## Personal Computing: Who Needs It and Why

Just which worker does office automation serve? The secretary? Clerical workers? Professionals? Managers? Executives? Yes, all of these people. Office automation may begin with the secretary, but it is a game that everyone can—and will—play:

Secretaries and anyone else who produces text documents need word processing.

- Clerical employees need database access to capture, store, retrieve, and update records.
- Professionals need spreadsheets and graphics to help them analyze, process, and present information.
- Executives need spreadsheets and other software tools to help them in the decision-making process.
- All employees need networking support to communicate more effectively.
- Any employee who needs to prepare attractive documents with both text and graphics can use electronic publishing.

Personal computing is *the* dominating force in office automation. After one taste of the joys of personal computing, everyone wants—and needs—his or her own machine. And that is exactly where office automation is heading: one person, one machine.

We have discussed word processing, spreadsheets, graphics, and databases in their own separate chapters. But let us say a few words here about electronic publishing.

## Electronic Publishing

Would you like to be able to produce really slick-looking pages that combine elaborate charts and graphics with text and headlines in a variety of typefaces? Let us take that one step

**Figure 17-1  Desktop publishing.** This sample output shows how electronic publishing can combine text, charts, graphics, and varied type fonts in one document.

further: Would you like to be able to do all this at your desk, but without ruler, pen, or paste? The technology is here today, and it is called **electronic publishing,** or **desktop publishing** (Figure 17-1). The "publisher," of course, is your personal computer, which, using special software, can generate very high-quality material on a laser printer. Do not confuse this with typewriterlike letter-quality printer output; desktop publishing has filled the gap between typewriters and typesetting.

Because of their speed, flexibility, and output quality, desktop publishing systems can rapidly produce forms, newsletters, and technical documents as well as business cards with company logos and manuals with magazinelike layouts. And although the time and money savings are important, what users value most is control—the ability to decide exactly what a change or layout will look like and see the results immediately on the computer screen. No more amateur company newsletters full of typos and pathetic drawings—most offices will be moving to greener publishing pastures.

We have noted the many uses for a personal computer in the office, from word processing to electronic publishing. But if it is easy to buy a personal computer for an individual, it is not so easy to incorporate the machines into the automated office. This chapter addresses some of the issues involved.

# Getting Computers to Talk to Each Other

Personal computers are most valuable to an office when they increase productivity without upsetting the office's budget. One way to minimize the costs of computer operation is to share computer resources among two or more computers. We discussed local area networks (LANs) in Chapter 7 on data communications. LANs are a key factor in sharing resources such as storage, printers, and data files.

Networking can be carried several steps further. Although managers may start out using personal computers for spreadsheet and other data-massaging purposes, they soon want to communicate by computer, too. The natural next step is electronic mail.

## Electronic Mail

You know all about telephone tag. From your office you call Ms. Jones. She is not in, so you leave a message. You leave your office for a meeting, and when you return you find a message from Ms. Jones; she returned your call while you were out . . . and so it goes. Few of us, it seems, are sitting around waiting for the phone to ring. It is not unusual to make dozens of calls to set up a meeting

**W**hen computers first emerged from the labs and universities, they were quickly put to use by business and government. In fact, today the biggest computer customer is still the federal government. This gallery captures some of the many applications for computers in workaday transactions.

## Retail

The photo on the opening page shows a Wrangler traveling salesperson, who uses her Sharp laptop computer to retrieve up-to-date information about inventory availability and also transmit orders from retailers instantly.

**(1)** The Metropolitan Museum of Art in New York uses this NCR point-of-sale terminal in its store.

**(2)** Small businesses use personal computers to keep track of orders and inventory and to perform other accounting functions.

**(3)** The unusual aspect of this design store system is that it accepts voice input data about textile goods.

**(4)** Lumber dealers may be retailers or wholesalers; in either case they need computers to track stock in order to be competitive.

## Architecture

**(5)** This is just one view of a house design, drawn from specifications in the computer's database.

**(6)** An architect can consider changes to a building design, make them quickly and easily on the computer, and then use a plotter to produce a new printed version of the design.

**(7)** A digitizer is used to input drawing data to the computer.

**(8)** On site, this construction foreman keeps track of schedules and costs with the help of a computer.

7

5

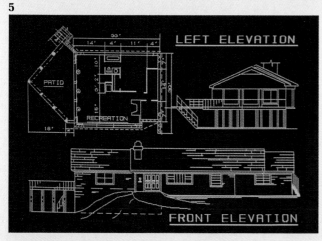

6

8

9

## Post Office

(9) Endless sacks of mail are emptied by hand, but the next moves are all automated.

(10) The envelopes being fed into this Burroughs optical character reader will be sorted by zip code. Envelopes are sorted by their first three digits at the first main post office they arrive at; this gets them started to the correct geographical location. At regional sorting centers envelopes are resorted by the fourth and fifth digits and sent on to local post offices for delivery.

(11) Postage-paid envelopes are read by a bar code reader to facilitate mass mailing charges.

(12) This shows the exit points for sorted envelopes. As each chute fills up, it is unloaded, and the envelopes are sent on to their next destination.

(13) In a large postal facility, automated operations are monitored at a central location. Overloaded areas of the system can be spotted quickly so steps can be taken to prevent any backups.

(14) Special status mail, such as next day Express Mail, is tracked through computer systems, making possible inquiries from any location.

10

11

12

14

13

## Manufacturing

**(15)** This touch terminal provides an effective interface in factory process control operations. Such terminals are especially useful in harsh environments, allowing operators to control dangerous equipment from a safe distance.

**(16)** Spray-painting robots are directed from the control room of this General Motors auto plant.

**(17)** Factory workers record their attendance and the time they spend on each task on this NCR system. The data is used for billing, planning, and scheduling.

**(18)** Inspecting new refrigerators, this technician uses voice input to record quality control test results.

**(19)** At Apple Computer's automated Macintosh factory in Fremont, California, it takes only 26 minutes to build a brand-new Macintosh computer. Before a Mac emerges from its computers-built-by-computers factory, however, it must run for 24 hours in the "burn-in" tower shown here. It is subjected to temperature changes and software tests so that any defects will show up. Once the computer passes these tests an automated packing machine places it in a box for shipping. A new Mac is ready to go every 27 seconds.

15

16

17

18

19

**20**

# Banking

**(20)** An automated teller machine gives bank customers a direct connection to the bank's computer, so that withdrawals, deposits, and transfers can be made at any time.

**(21)** Everyone at the bank uses a computer terminal, from the loan officer who calculates payment schedules to the branch manager who monitors cash flow.

**(22)** Tellers use terminals connected to the computer to check account balances and record customer transactions.

**(23)** At Connecticut Bank and Trust, 60 proof stations handle almost 300,000 checks per day. The proofer keys in the dollar amount on the check, causing the machine to print it at the bottom of the check, where it can later be input to the computer system by optical character readers.

**21**

**23**

**22**

## Services

**(24)** Some of the nation's finest restaurants keep computers in the kitchen to store and retrieve recipes, and keep tabs on stock on hand. Restaurant software, of particular use for catering, also calculates ingredient quantities for large groups.

**(25)** Even our pets need services. Ever-growing veterinarian businesses increasingly use computers to keep the records of their furry customers.

**(26)** When something breaks down you want service fast. These service coordinators use a computer-based dispatch system to assign service representatives to customers in need of repairs.

**(27)** Can the computer fix my car? Not yet, but it comes in handy as a diagnostic tool, reporting likely problem areas in response to a set of symptomatic input data.

**(28)** A telephone company repairman consults a computer-produced repair order. AT&T uses computers to conduct a nightly analysis of a region's telephone cable system.

24

25

26

27

28

## Law Enforcement

**(29)** Joe Salvadore, a police officer in Lakeland, Florida, uses his own personal computer, a Commodore 64, in his patrol car. He has programmed the computer to keep track of needed daily information, such as recently stolen cars to be on the lookout for.

**(30)** With the Vancouver, British Columbia, skyline in the background, a policeman uses his in-car terminal to query a database in Ottawa. He can input names or license plate numbers and receive information about fugitives or stolen vehicles within seven seconds.

**(31)** The Automated Fingerprint Identification System (AFIS) matches crime-scene fingerprints with fingerprints on computer files; its success lies in the speed—a matter of minutes instead of the days it takes humans. In one second the system can check a fingerprint against 650 file prints. The system cracked 34 unsolved crimes in its first four days of operation in San Francisco. The numbers shown on this print represent locations where a line stops or splits. These identifying characteristics are used to classify fingerprints.

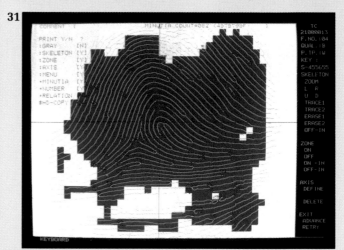

**(32)** As this Chicago court reporter records the trial, the transcript is immediately available on three IBM PC XT screens—one for each of the opposing attorneys and one for Judge Marshall.

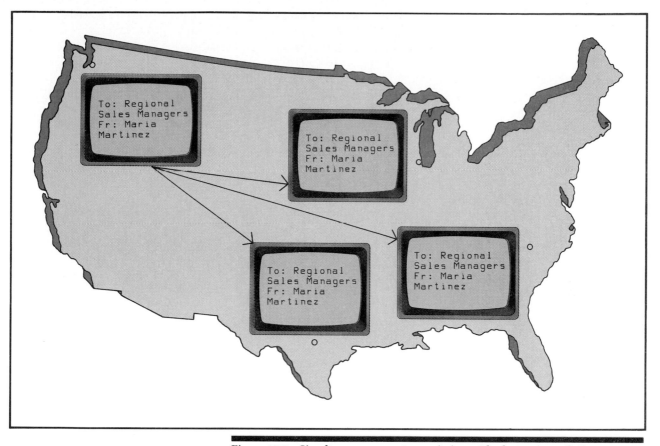

**Figure 17-2   Simultaneous memo transmission with electronic mail.** From company headquarters in Seattle, Maria Martinez is able to send a memo simultaneously to sales managers in Chicago, Raleigh, and San Antonio. This is made possible by an electronic mail system linking the computers in the home office and the regional offices.

with even a few people. **Electronic mail** is the process of sending messages directly from one terminal or computer to another. Electronic mail releases workers from the tyranny of the telephone.

Perhaps a company has employees who find communication difficult because they are geographically dispersed or are too active to be reached easily. Yet these employees may need to work together frequently, so communication among them is valuable and important. This company is an ideal candidate for electronic mail.

A user can send messages to his or her supervisor downstairs or a query across town to that person who is never available for phone calls. The user can even send memos simultaneously to regional sales managers in Chicago, Raleigh, and San Antonio (Figure 17-2). The beauty of electronic mail, or e-mail, is that a user can send a message to someone and know that the person will receive it.

Electronic mail works, of course, only if the intended receiver has the electronic mail facility to which the sender is connected.

## THE MICROCOMPUTER CORNER

### We Are Users Too

You may be using your own personal computer in an office—sooner than you think. That makes you a statistic, contributing to the trend toward office automation. It is comforting to know that proponents of office automation are doing the same thing. Consider IBM.

While preaching the office automation gospel elsewhere, IBM is taking its own advice at home. The IBM headquarters office has a staff of 4400, and every one of them has a personal computer. The screen here shows the main menu for a system that offers typical office automation functions. The menu also includes a calendar for the month and a clock. The numbers on the left of the screen—PF1, PF2, and so forth—refer to the function keys on the IBM PC keyboard. Function key 2, for example, lets a user "open the mail"—that is, show a screen listing of messages identified by

```
                    CHQ's OFFICE SYSTEM

Press one of the following PF keys.              Time:  12:16 PM
PF1  Process schedules
PF2  Open the mail                          1988     APRIL     1988
PF3  Search for documents                   S   M   T   W   T   F   S
PF4  Process notes and messages                             1   2
PF5  Prepare documents                      3   4   5   6   7   8   9
PF6  Telephone Directory                   10  11  12  13  14  15  16
PF7  Process the mail log                  17  18  19  20  21  22  23
PF8  Check the outgoing mail               24  25  26  27  28  29  30
                                                       Day of Year: 096
PF10 Add an automatic reminder
PF11 Look at main menu number 2
                                                    PF9 Help   PF12 End
For ASSISTANCE type AID and press Enter - Highest Level - IBM Confidential


===>                                       MAIL WAITING
```

sender, time received, and topic. Messages that have not yet been "read"—displayed on the screen—are highlighted in boldface. Messages can be viewed, forwarded, and answered.

As you can see, the menu includes other routine office automation tasks.

There are several electronic mail options. A user can enlist a third-party service bureau that provides electronic mail service for its customers. Another popular option is to use a public data network such as CompuServe. Or a user may purchase an electronic mail software package for a microcomputer or large computer system.

If a company decides to use a third party, the service bureau creates as many electronic mailboxes—space allotments on its computer's disk storage—as needed for each user company. Users get their mail by giving proper identification from their own computers.

Public data services offer their own version of electronic mail. CompuServe users, for example, can send e-mail messages to any other CompuServe subscriber. Users get flashing messages when they turn on their machines if mail awaits them.

If a company decides to install an e-mail package, it will find a growing number to choose from. Major hardware manufacturers are becoming more communications oriented and are offering software or office systems packages that support e-mail. A key advantage of such packages is that the purchaser pays for them just once; third-party services must be paid on a continuing basis.

Electronic mail users shower it with praise. It crosses time zones, it can send the same message to many people, it reduces the paper flood, and it does not interrupt meetings the way a ringing phone does. Electronic mail has its limitations, however. The current problem is similar to the problem faced by telephone users a hundred years ago: It is not of much use if you have the only one. As usage of electronic mail escalates, so will its usefulness.

### Voice Mail

Here is how a typical **voice mail** system works. A user dials a special number to get on the voice mail system, then tries to complete a call by dialing the desired number in the normal way. If the recipient does not answer, the caller can then dictate a message into the system. The voice mail computer system translates the words into digital impulses and stores them in the recipient's "voice mailbox." Later, when the recipient dials the mailbox, the system delivers the message in audio form (Figure 17-3).

**Figure 17-3   A voice mail system.** The caller's message is stored in the recipient's voice mailbox on disk. Later, the recipient can check the mailbox to get the message.

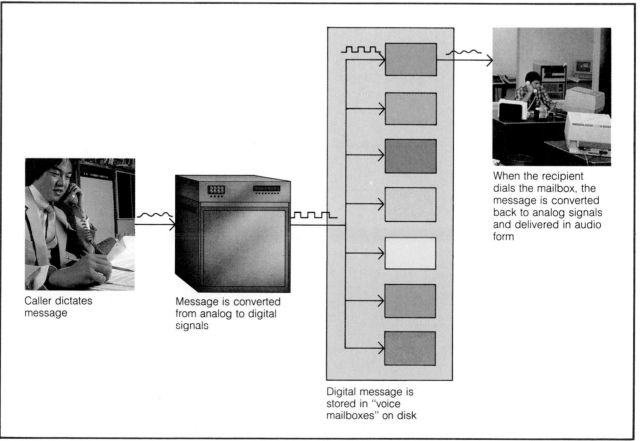

Caller dictates message

Message is converted from analog to digital signals

When the recipient dials the mailbox, the message is converted back to analog signals and delivered in audio form

Digital message is stored in "voice mailboxes" on disk

This may sound like a spoken version of electronic mail. There is one big difference between electronic mail and voice mail, however. To use an electronic mail system, you and the mail recipient must have compatible devices with keyboards. In contrast, telephones are everywhere and everyone knows how to use them.

Senders can instruct some voice mail systems to redial specific numbers at regular intervals to deliver urgent messages, or they can simply set one delivery time and date. Another useful feature allows users to circulate messages among associates for comment. This method is far more efficient than circulating the traditional paper intraoffice memo.

There are some problems, however—not with the technology, but with user acceptance of the technology. Some people do not like talking to a machine. Others will not tell a machine anything important. A more serious problem is the lack of editing capability—most users simply cannot organize their thoughts as well when they speak as they do when they write.

But electronic "meetings" are more spontaneous and less demanding of perfection. That brings us to teleconferencing.

## Teleconferencing

An office automation development with great promise is **teleconferencing,** a method of using technology to bring people and ideas "together" despite geographic barriers. The technology has been available for years, but the acceptance of it is quite recent. The purpose of teleconferencing is to let people conduct meetings with others in different locations.

There are several varieties of teleconferencing. The simplest, **computer conferencing,** is a method of sending, receiving, and storing typed messages within a network of users. Computer conferences can be used to coordinate complex projects over great distances and for extended periods. Participants can communicate at the same time or in different time frames, at the users' convenience. Conferences can be set up for a limited time to discuss a particular problem, as is a traditional office gathering. Or computer conferences can be networks that operate for weeks or months or even years.

A computer conferencing system is a single software package designed to organize communication. The conferencing software runs on a network's host computer, either a mini or a mainframe. In addition to the host computer and the conferencing software, each participant needs a personal computer or word processor, a telephone, a modem, and data communications network software.

Computer conferencing is a many-to-many arrangement; everyone is able to "talk" to everyone else. Messages may be sent to a specified individual or set of individuals or broadcast to all receivers. Recipients are automatically notified of incoming messages.

Figure 17-4   **Videoconferencing.** These businesspeople have rented a teleconferencing room which has the necessary equipment in place—including a large wall screen to see their colleagues in another city.

Would you like your picture broadcast live across the miles for meetings? Add cameras to computer conferencing, and you have another form of teleconferencing called **videoconferencing** (Figure 17-4). The technology varies, but the pieces normally put in place are a large screen (possibly a wall-size one), three-dimensional cameras, and an on-line computer system to record communication among participants.

Although this setup is expensive to rent and even more expensive to own, the costs seem small when compared to travel expenses for in-person meetings. Airfare, lodging, and meals for a group of employees are very expensive.

But there are drawbacks to videoconferencing. Consider that picture of you. Most people do not like the way they look on camera. We tend to be uncomfortable about our appearance, and balk when we envision slouching posture, crooked tie, or fidgeting fingers. There is also fear that the loss of personal contact will detract from some business functions, especially those related to sales. But employees are overcoming their reluctance. Videoconferencing may be an idea whose time has come.

## Facsimile Technology

An alternative to meetings is to use computers and data communications technology to send documents from one location to another. Perhaps you remember the television commercial featuring the desperate office worker who resorted to hand-shadow cartoons on the wall screen to make his presentation for the brass. This unhappy scene was the result of misdirected charts that should have been received in time for the presentation. The closing line was something like "I should have faxed it." Sent a facsimile, that is. **Facsimile technology** operates something like a copy machine con-

**Figure 17-5   Faxing it.** Facsimile technology can send important documents requiring fast attention to remote locations within seconds. This AT&T machine transmits superb images, text, and graphics. The paper shown here being withdrawn from the machine was input to a different machine in another location just moments before.

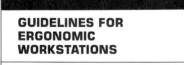

## GUIDELINES FOR ERGONOMIC WORKSTATIONS

- **Hardware.** Provide detachable keyboards, tilting and swiveling screens, and adjustable document holders.

- **Lighting.** Avoid glare from windows. Use matte-finished keyboards to reduce glare. Control direct lighting.

- **Noise.** Supply acoustic covers for printers. Place other noisy peripherals in an enclosed area.

- **Seating.** Provide ergonomically designed chairs with a five-legged star base (to avoid tipping) and an adjustable back and seat. Leave plenty of legroom under the desk.

nected to a telephone; it uses computer technology to send quality graphics, charts, text, and even signatures almost anywhere in the world. The drawing—or whatever—is placed in the facsimile machine at one end, where it is digitized. Those digits are transmitted across the miles, then reassembled at the other end into the original picture (Figure 17-5). All this takes a matter of minutes or less.

# Ergonomics: The Person-Computer Connection

**Ergonomics** is the study of human factors related to computing. Ergonomics is an aspect of a great many subjects related to both hardware and software. A discussion of ergonomics applies particularly to office automation, however, because the automated office contains so many workstations, and the workstation has become one of the focal points for ergonomics experts. From an ergonomic standpoint, a workstation should have a high-resolution screen that is easy to read, it should have minimal glare, and it

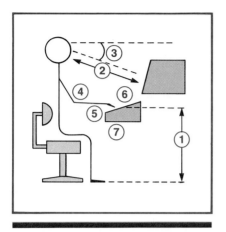

**Figure 17-6 Workstation design.** ① The European recommendation for the height of the home-row keys is $28\frac{1}{4}$ to $29\frac{1}{2}$ inches. The U.S. military standard is $29\frac{1}{4}$ to 31 inches. ② The viewing distance should be between $17\frac{1}{4}$ and $19\frac{3}{4}$ inches, with a maximum of $27\frac{1}{2}$ inches. ③ Generally, the center of the screen should be at a position between 10 and 20 degrees below the horizontal plane at the operator's eye height. One researcher recommends that the top of the screen be below eye height, another that the top line of the display be 10 to 15 degrees below the horizontal, with no portion of the screen at an angle greater than 40 degrees below the horizontal. ④ One researcher recommends that the angle between the upper and lower arms be between 80 and 120 degrees. ⑤ The angle of the wrist should be no greater than 10 degrees. ⑥ The keyboard should be at or below elbow height. ⑦ Do not forget to provide enough room for your legs. (From *Potential Health Hazards of Video Display Terminals*)

should be built in such a way that it can be tilted, swiveled, and adjusted for height (Figure 17-6). If a workstation is designed to address such ergonomic concerns, job satisfaction and productivity should increase and fatigue and errors should decrease. Managers are very interested in ergonomically designed terminals, and many manufacturers of terminals are careful to use the word *ergonomic* in their ads because it is in vogue.

# Joys and Woes of the Automated Office

The automated office is not without growing pains. Now that the excitement has subsided, it is possible to view the automation process objectively. Although problems do exist, it is clear that the good outweighs the bad. First we shall examine the problems.

## Problems with the Automated Office

Implementing an office automation system is not like plugging in an appliance. The hardware and software employed can shape the organization that uses it in fundamental ways. Automating an office is a tough job and a lot of work.

### Hidden Costs

Automating an office may incur hidden costs. In addition to the obvious costs of the hardware, software, and supplies, connection to a local area network, shared long-distance communications, shared database management systems, or shared mainframe access may generate expenses. There also may be a need for changes in the office environment, such as improving lighting, rewiring the site for additional electric power, increasing the amount of air conditioning, and providing improved acoustics to reduce the noise generated by the new equipment. Start-up costs for training are obvious, but hidden start-up costs may include inefficiencies in serving customers by new and unfamiliar means, time spent converting existing files to computer-readable form, job interruptions due to unfamiliar procedures, and time spent in meetings to negotiate changes in handling the work.

### Personnel Problems

Fear tops the list: fear of looking stupid, fear of diminished power, fear of job loss. All of these fears have some basis; or at least all are possibilities. But a manager should anticipate these problems and alleviate them with thorough training. There is also

## TONE UP AT THE TERMINALS

Office exercises? Yes, indeed. And it is no joke: *Tone Up at the Terminals* is the name of a program developed by Verbatim Corporation in response to a survey of office workers' views about technology in the workplace. The survey showed that the respondents had health concerns about the computer equipment they used, especially regarding eyestrain and backstrain.

So, here we go. Music. Stand beside your desk. One, two, one, two. Stretch, move, limber up. Volunteers lead the exercises for five minutes twice a day. Stress and tension drain away. Is everyone happy? Yes, even the managers, who report a 5% increase in productivity.

some worry about health problems. Anxiety has centered on radiation from terminals, but studies thus far are not conclusive. There is also a concern about eyestrain and backstrain.

### Mixing and Matching

Electronic gear for the automated office is rarely acquired in one gigantic purchase. While this has some advantages for cash flow, it produces an Excedrin headache in terms of compatibility—separately purchased machines often cannot communicate or exchange data. This is particularly true among personal computers, which often cannot communicate with the mainframe, either. We shall address this issue again in Chapter 18.

### Security

Office automation is presenting a new variety of security problems. Office systems and home systems have much in common, and both well-intentioned users and system abusers find that this compatibility leads to migration of software to home computer systems. Another costly problem is that office workers are finding it easy to steal keyboards, modems, software, diskettes, and supplies. Creative fixes are coming to the market. One, for example, sounds a piercing alarm if a component is disconnected. This does not do much, however, about the software-laden floppy disks going out the door in briefcases.

Office systems are particularly vulnerable to security lapses because they use data that is in more "finished" form. Rather than the masses of detail data being manipulated on mainframes, office systems accumulate correspondence and summary information. Clearly, there is a need for security measures in office automation systems. We shall discuss security in more detail in Chapter 19.

## Why the Automated Office Will Triumph Anyway

Perhaps the main reason for the inevitability of the automated office is that the technology, whatever its imperfections, is *here*. Few organizations are willing to simply ignore it. A second persuasive reason is that the automated office does not come as whole cloth; organizations can take a piecemeal approach, picking and choosing technologies. And they can suit their budgets as they go along.

Now consider these general benefits of office automation:

- Reduced work
- Competitive edge
- Improved decision making
- Improved quality of work life
- Improved services

Examples abound. Work is eliminated when a secretary makes a small change to a document without retyping an entire page. Accountants can improve decision making by using "what if . . ." sce-

## SMART BUT NOT SMART ENOUGH

*Smart* does not always mean better. In one computerized—smart—building, for example, lights flick on automatically as soon as they sense motion and flick off 12 minutes after all motion stops. But the arrangement backfired for some employees who wanted to set up a slide show: The only way to turn out the lights was to sit absolutely still for 12 minutes. One person finally climbed atop a table and unscrewed the bulbs. In another building, a sprawling engineering complex, a computer monitors the facility hourly at night, turning off all lights. Overtime workers left in the dark must navigate to the override panels once an hour to turn them back on. And there is the building complex where the computerized lawn-sprinkling system doggedly waters the lawn during every rainstorm.

But still, it had to come—the building whose functions are controlled by computers. About a dozen exist now, and another 200 or so are under construction. These buildings may have the sleek high-rise, glass-and-marble look of other buildings, but inside they are different. In fact, they are changing the way that people do business. Enter your office and the lights turn on. At your desk, check your electronic mailbox. Send data to an associate over the same phone line that you use for talking. To order lunch, call up menus of the building's restaurants on your own desktop screen.

And, while it takes care of you, the building is also quietly taking care of itself. Automated systems control lights, heating, air conditioning, security, electricity, and elevators. For example, sensors record heat changes and make adjustments when the sun comes out or a cloud rolls by or even when the number of bodies in a room raises the temperature. If a sensor feels fire, that information is relayed by computer to firefighters. Some buildings take the smart function a bit further, doing everything from turning on atrium fountains to adjusting window shades.

narios on a spreadsheet. Customers can get better service when the local area network is used to check stock in the warehouse. The competitive edge can be sharpened when data accessed from the database can be displayed graphically at a sales presentation. Quality of work life can be improved for workers who know how to use the computer to reduce or eliminate tedious tasks.

A hidden bonus of office automation is that sharp people are often attracted to leading-edge technology. They see these new skills as the ticket to advancement, so they make full use of computer resources. And, of course, there is the bottom line: productivity. In most offices improved productivity is not a luxury—it is a necessity. Office technology is more than just a collection of machines—it represents a change that digs right into the heart of the organization. People do their own work in a new way and also interact with others in a new way. Both those ways are better and faster.

## Computers in the Factory

Most people think that American factories are already automated. This is true but not true. That is, they are automated in fits and starts, here and there, but there is no overall automated picture. This must be changed if U.S. factories want to compete effectively with foreign producers. As we shall see, the process is painfully slow, but we are on our way.

### The Beginnings: Manufacturing Resource Planning

There are a lot of acronyms floating around the automated factory concept, but first and foremost is **MRP,** for **manufacturing resource planning** software. MRP blossomed in the 1960s as a method for ordering and scheduling materials. MRP's main function is to maintain the needed inventory levels, but it also tracks billing for materials and keeps track of parts needed for a given production schedule. Because of the number of items tracked and the constant changes in production needs, the computer is a natural tool for this purpose. MRP programs are now available for mainframes, minicomputers, and microcomputers. Basically, MRP keeps track of what is going on and helps plan it. That is a far cry, however, from actually doing the work. When we talk about automating the work itself, we are talking about the factory of the future.

### The Factory of the Future

Exhibition halls at conferences are brimming with robots and flashy computerized equipment designed to save America's creaking factories from being swallowed whole by foreign competition. But a walk through most U.S. plants would quickly show that the ballyhooed "factory of the future" is just that—somewhere in the future. Even though factories have been "automated" for years, the automation is piecemeal and largely ineffective. A master stroke is needed here in the form of *integration*, the key concept of **computer-integrated manufacturing** (**CIM**). To state the case plainly, the goal of CIM is for all the automated machines and computers in the factory and elsewhere in the company to talk to each other and to work together. This is not simple and it will not happen soon. But progress is being made.

## CAD/CAE/CAM

CAD, CAE, and CAM represent three strides toward the factory of the future. Ideally, computer-integrated manufacturing would work something like this: Products conceived at the headquarters office are devised and drawn through **computer-aided design** (**CAD**), allowing designers to use interactive graphic displays to optimize their ideas. CADs can be done on computer screens faster, and errors can be corrected more easily than on paper. Another plus is that the results are in a form ready to be used by others. The CAD data is passed electronically to a **computer-aided engineering** (**CAE**) system, where engineers use special software to verify that the design will work and can be made economically. The data needed to make the product can then be sent—electronically again—to a **computer-aided manufacturing** (**CAM**) system, which transmits instructions for making the product to computer-controlled machine tools, robots, and other automated factory equipment. These acronyms for getting the job done are often strung together as **CAD/CAE/CAM.** Ideally, the designer who conceives the part, the engineer who analyzes it, and the factory operator who handles the machines all use the same computer-based description (Figure 17-7). But this is not always so.

We used the word *ideal* to describe the factory of the future because there are a number of obstacles: workstation power limitations that do not permit CAD users to model three-dimensional parts, slow data transfer rates between workstations and other machines, and—most important—lack of standards for data communications among machines.

## General Motors Sets the Standard

We have spoken forcefully about the issue of standards in other places in this book. To repeat: Life will be easier—and certainly more economical—for all of us if we can just agree on a few

**Figure 17-7  Computer-aided design and engineering.** (a) Engineers establish computer-based information as they design. (b) This information can be retrieved in a variety of ways, including these car specifications. (c) Engineers can draw from the same set of information when they test new models.

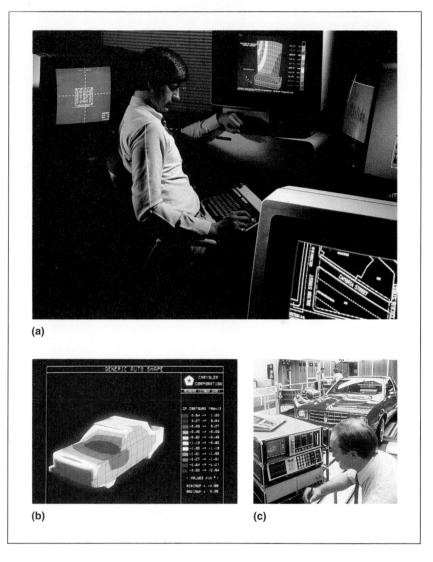

(a)

(b)

(c)

basic things. Sometimes committees forge standards, but often an entire industry rallies around a powerful leader. In the case of computer-integrated manufacturing, General Motors—although not part of the computer industry—has used its clout to take the lead.

Let us look at the problem more closely. In addition to the design and engineering workstations already mentioned, the factory itself is teeming with high-tech gadgets: drives for managing electric motors, controllers to turn on machines and robots and tell them what to do, sensors and cameras to monitor the work, and—of course—computers and software. But these are only little islands of automation in the factory; those islands can rarely communicate with each other. Enter General Motors. The new GM standard is **Manufacturing Automation Protocol,** more commonly called **MAP.** First introduced in 1984, MAP is an evolving technology. MAP is a

**THE MUSIC MAN**

What next! Can a robot really play the piano? No. Although the picture is an exaggeration, the idea is not completely farfetched.

Early robots worked like the dumb drones they were, standing in one place and repeating the same motions over and over. The next wave of robots also stood in place, but they had some ability to sense their surroundings and react to them. Then robots were equipped with humanlike sensors so they could move around and react to their environment. The next goal is to give robots agile hand and arms, so they can accomplish tasks with the same finesse as humans.

The hands are still a problem for robotic engineers. In the past hands have been activated by bulky, noisy electric motors to clench and un-clench the fingers. A new approach is embedded wires that heat up and shrink when an electric current is passed through them. Switching the current on closes the fingers; turn-ing it off makes the fingers open. Although the open and close mo-tions are smooth, they are not speedy. In fact, the hand move-ments are still too sluggish to be practical.

As for piano playing, Wabot-2's brain can read sheet music, but con-cert pianists need not worry about mechanical competition just yet.

protocol for a local area network that provides communications be-tween the equipment of all of the factory automation vendors that support it.

And just who are those vendors? Well, IBM is the biggest vendor lined up behind General Motors. Some others are Digital Equipment Corporation, Hewlett–Packard, Honeywell, AT&T, and NCR. In fact, representatives from these companies sat next to each other on stage at an AutoFact conference, proudly extolling the virtues of MAP. GM, by the way, has a compelling reason to address the communica-tions issue: The company has 40,000 computer-aided devices from a dozen vendors but only 15% of them can communicate with each other!

The MAP standard makes widespread use of local area networks to connect the corporate mainframe with personal computers and all the machines used in manufacturing. Since the key ingredient of computer-integrated manufacturing is a communications standard, the value of MAP cannot be overestimated.

## Your Not-So-Friendly Robot

Many people smile at the thought of robots, perhaps re-membering the endearing C-3PO of *Star Wars* fame and its "per-sonal" relationships with humans. But vendors have not made even a small dent in the personal-robot market—the much heralded do-mestic robots never materialized. So, where are the robots? In the factory, spray-painting and welding and taking away jobs. The Cen-sus Bureau, after two centuries of counting people, has now branched out to robots. About 15,000 existed in 1985, and 5,000 more were sold that year. In 1990, the bureau expects 10,000 more to be sold. That number will double again, to 20,000, by 1995. These numbers make job predictions even more bleak. What do robots do that merits all this attention?

A loose definition of a robot is a type of automation that replaces human presence. But a **robot** is more completely defined as a com-puter-controlled device that can physically manipulate its surround-ings. There are a wide variety of sizes and shapes of robots, each designed with a particular use or function in mind. Often these are functions that would be dangerous or tedious for humans to perform. The most common industrial robots sold today are mechanical de-vices with five or six axes of motion, so they can rotate into place to perform their tasks (Figure 17-8).

We mentioned spray-painting and welding applications, but a more intelligent robot can adapt to changing circumstances. For ex-ample, with the help of a TV camera eye, a robot can see the compo-nents it is meant to assemble. It is able to pick them up, rearrange them in the right order, or place them in the right position before assembling them. Another key use of robots is in security work. The robot patrols the factory and can spot if anything has been moved.

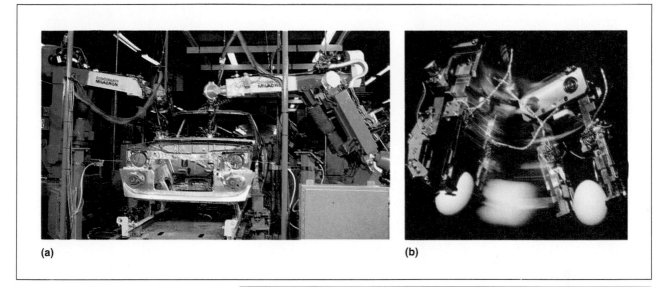

(a)

(b)

**Figure 17-8  Industrial robots.** (a) These standard robots are used in the auto industry to spray-paint new cars. (b) This robot is not making breakfast. Hitachi uses the delicate egg, however, to demonstrate that its visual-tactile robot can handle fragile objects. Its sensors detect size, shape, and required pressure, attaining sensitivity almost equal to that of a human hand.

Sensors are used to detect intruders and—if necessary—summon help by radio. Such a robot is certainly less expensive than a human guard or even a guard dog.

## Vision Systems

We mentioned that the most intelligent robots can "see"—that is, they are able to use some sort of vision system to locate the items they are manipulating. A **vision system** is a set of computer-controlled machines that can take automatic action based on what is seen. Most machine vision systems work something like this: Light shines on an object, and a digital camera picks up the reflected light. Microprocessors in the camera convert the light images to electronic signals. A microcomputer then interprets the signals, comparing them to patterns it has been programmed to recognize. After deciding what it is looking at, the computer issues appropriate commands. The recipient of the commands may be a robot, which will then go on about its assembly work.

The vision system may also be used for simple inspection, however, in which case the microcomputer issues a terse "accept" or "reject" command. For example, a vision system could count the number of holes in a part or inspect surfaces for flaws (Figure 17-9).

Some vision systems use more than one camera in order to "see" in three dimensions. In fact, anything that can be done with the human eye is something that can potentially be done with vision systems to replace humans who now inspect or assemble parts.

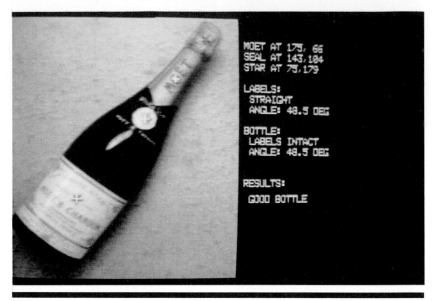

**Figure 17-9   Vision system.** This screen is part of a vision system that inspects label position and fill levels of Moet champagne. As you can see, the final computer-produced message is "Good bottle."

## FOLLOW THAT CAR

U.S. customs agents at the borders read car license plates and manually enter each number into a computer terminal to search a national computer data bank. They are looking for stolen vehicles, fugitives, or drug traffickers. The looking and keying time become significant if there is a long line of cars at the border. Vision systems to the rescue!

Reading a license plate sounds easy enough, but it is surprisingly complicated. To begin with, a vision system has to find the plate—which can be in a number of different places—and, in addition, not confuse it with a bumper sticker or a rectangular taillight. Then the system must differentiate the 200 North American license plate types, which show different layouts and type styles. To add another layer of difficulty, many states have superimposed designs such as mountains or sunsets over the plate numbers.

But Battelle Laboratories is up to the challenge. The Battelle system's closed-circuit camera views license plates and checks against templates of plate types stored in the computer system. The vision system can identify a plate even if only half of it is visible.

The system may have other commercial uses, including manufacturing inspection, materials sorting, and as a security system to spot intruders in a controlled area.

## Just in Time

We have all known about mass production since we studied the Industrial Revolution in the sixth grade: Buy raw materials in high volume, then propel identical products down an assembly line to get efficient labor, maximum control, low cost, and a massive product supply to be distributed to buyers. In fact, this describes factories in the United States, which run on the style known as **production-push:** We run our machines at their full potential, building up parts for more advanced production steps and, finally, stock for our customers. The opposite approach is **demand-pull,** meaning that parts are not made until there is a request for them downstream in the factory process—that is, until they are needed. Another name for demand-pull is **just-in-time** (**JIT**), meaning that there is just enough inventory for the job, and just in time. Just-in-time manufacturing means that an item is not built if it would have to go into warehouse inventory and wait for other parts; it is built only when it is needed immediately (Figure 17-10). The difference between these two approaches, in the most general sense, is that production-push has stacks of parts sitting around while demand-pull (just-in-time) does not. As a result, just-in-time costs less.

The just-in-time concept, long familiar in Japan, is sweeping through factories in America. It has picked up some trimmings along the way. Just-in-time has just one goal—reducing inventory—and the approach achieves this by striving for zero defects and breakdowns and reduced handling time and lead time. Although all these are ideals, they do point the way to more efficient factories.

**Figure 17-10   Just in time.** When parts are delivered to the factory just in time to be used, inventory can be reduced; therefore, money can be saved.

## Microcomputers in the Factory

Would you move your personal computer from its desk home to the harsh environment of the factory floor? Somehow, a personal computer does not seem so personal in the factory. Actually, factory-bound microcomputers are made to be a bit more hearty and robust (Figure 17-11). Some computer manufacturers are introducing so-called "ruggedized" microcomputers especially for industrial use. But there are other considerations for microcomputers in the factory. They have to be serviced very quickly, since the factory

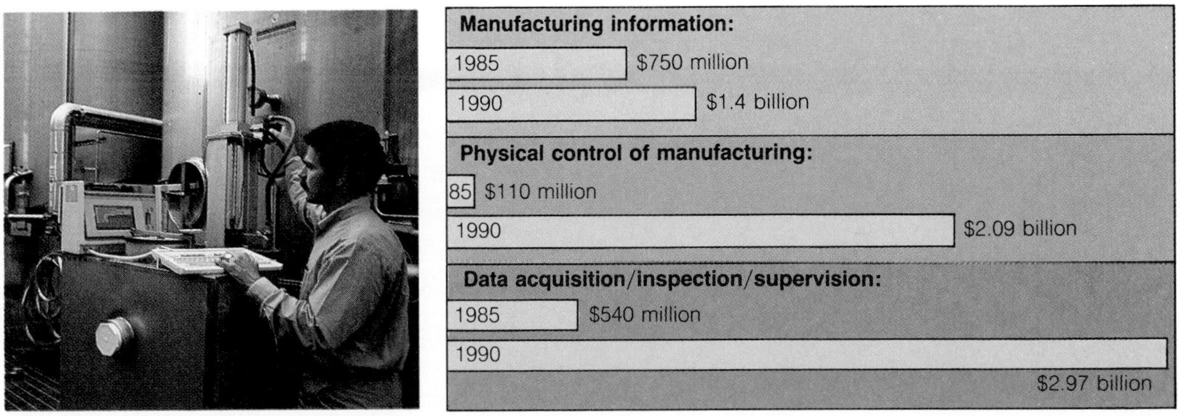

**Figure 17-11   Micros move into the factory.** (a) This Hewlett–Packard personal computer is involved in measuring the chemical content of wines in the Krug Winery. (b) By 1990 the use of microcomputers in manufacturing applications is expected to increase dramatically.

**Manufacturing information:**

| 1985 | $750 million |
| 1990 | $1.4 billion |

**Physical control of manufacturing:**

| 85 | $110 million |
| 1990 | $2.09 billion |

**Data acquisition/inspection/supervision:**

| 1985 | $540 million |
| 1990 | $2.97 billion |

(a)                              (b)

schedule depends on them. In addition, shop personnel must be able to understand and use them easily—no computer jocks here. Once these concerns are handled, microcomputers will be a key factor in the local area networks in the factory.

## Bye-Bye Blue Collar?

And what about the workers? Is it true that they will lose their jobs? Will they be replaced by robots? The answer is "Yes," but not right away. American industry has gone through economic cycles in the past where workers are laid off, then hired back again. But layoffs in the past decade reflect something more than an economic downturn—they signal a permanent reduction in the blue-collar work force. These jobs, of course, are being replaced by automation.

However, long before factory *workers* become an endangered species, automation could make most factory *management* jobs extinct. First in line for departure is the factory foreman. Factory computers can do a better job of collecting and analyzing the information now handled by foremen. Computers on the shop floor can display easily understood screen reports about scheduling, parts, and so forth, enabling workers to seize direct control of production without foremen. General Motors, for example, now operates an engine assembly plant with roughly 100 workers and two salaried coordinators. Before it was automated, the line needed twice as many workers and a dozen foremen. The downward trend in factory jobs is another sign that we are moving from an industrial age to an information age.

## Made in the U.S.A.

Can automation save the day for America's factories? The task rests squarely on the shoulders of the nation's computer and communications equipment makers. They have the tools and the expertise to do the job. And they have a strong desire to do the job. But confusion is the dominant theme in the rush toward computer-integrated manufacturing. So we need to pause for a moment to realize that MAP is not a miracle and CIM is not a certainty. Automation may be inevitable, but it is still in its infancy. In the 1990s we shall see it grow and mature and reach its full potential (Figure 17-12).

## And Now a Word from Our Management

We have discussed current and evolving technologies in the business arena, from the office to the factory. Although the array of offerings is glittering, technologies can be integrated into a business only if they meet the needs of that business.

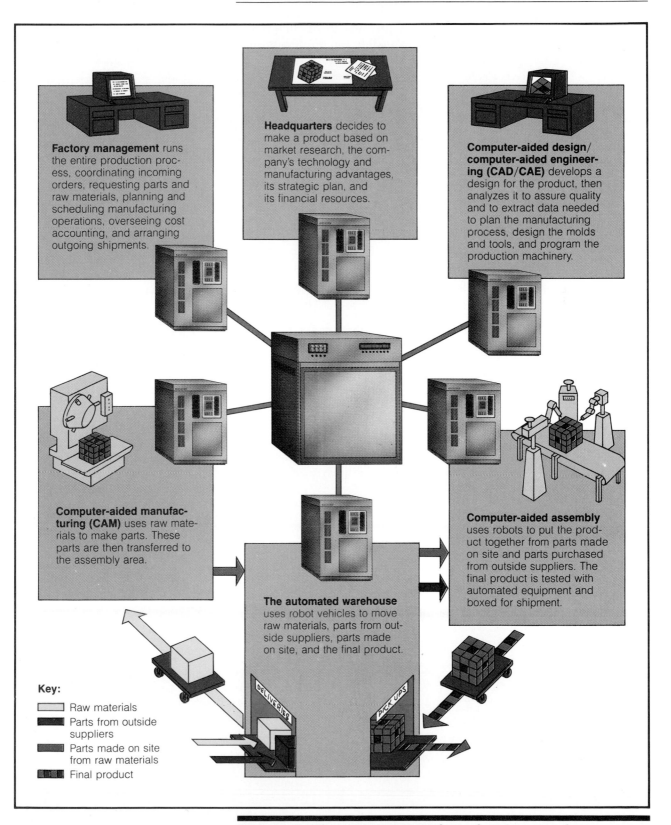

**Headquarters** decides to make a product based on market research, the company's technology and manufacturing advantages, its strategic plan, and its financial resources.

**Factory management** runs the entire production process, coordinating incoming orders, requesting parts and raw materials, planning and scheduling manufacturing operations, overseeing cost accounting, and arranging outgoing shipments.

**Computer-aided design/ computer-aided engineering (CAD/CAE)** develops a design for the product, then analyzes it to assure quality and to extract data needed to plan the manufacturing process, design the molds and tools, and program the production machinery.

**Computer-aided manufacturing (CAM)** uses raw materials to make parts. These parts are then transferred to the assembly area.

**Computer-aided assembly** uses robots to put the product together from parts made on site and parts purchased from outside suppliers. The final product is tested with automated equipment and boxed for shipment.

**The automated warehouse** uses robot vehicles to move raw materials, parts from outside suppliers, parts made on site, and the final product.

Key:
- Raw materials
- Parts from outside suppliers
- Parts made on site from raw materials
- Final product

Figure 17-12 **When computer-integrated manufacturing comes of age.**

And just who is in charge of making this kind of decision? Who is responsible for implementing the new technologies? Management, of course. The following chapter deals with managers in a computing environment.

## Summary and Key Terms

- **Office automation** is the use of technology to help achieve office goals. It can be used by a variety of businesspeople—secretaries, clerical employees, professionals, and executives—for a variety of purposes: word processing, database access, spreadsheets, graphics, networking, and electronic publishing.

- **Electronic publishing,** or **desktop publishing,** is the use of a personal computer and a printer to generate high-quality publications such as newsletters, technical documents, and manuals.

- Local area networks (LANs), which share resources such as storage, printers, and data files, help businesses control the costs of a computer operation.

- **Electronic mail,** or e-mail, is the process of sending messages directly from one terminal or computer to another, ensuring that people receive each other's messages.

- A **voice mail** system translates phone messages into digital impulses and stores them for later delivery in audio form.

- There are several varieties of **teleconferencing,** which is the combination of computer and telephone technology to bring people and ideas together despite geographic barriers. **Computer conferencing** is a method of sending, receiving, and storing typed messages within a network of users. Computer conferencing allows coordination of projects over great distances and, if necessary, over extended periods. **Videoconferencing** normally involves three-dimensional cameras, large video screens, and an on-line computer system to record communication among participants.

- **Facsimile technology** uses computer technology to send quality graphics, charts, text, and even signatures almost anywhere in the world.

- **Ergonomics,** the study of human factors related to computing, is especially relevant to the design of comfortable, efficient working environments for computer users.

- Office automation can involve a number of problems: hidden costs, the negative reaction of personnel, equipment incompatibility, and the theft of hardware and software.

- Office automation provides a number of important benefits, including reduced work, improved decision making, improved services, a competitive edge, and improved quality of work life. All of these benefits lead to improved productivity.

- The progress toward extensive automation in American factories has been slow but steady. A key element is **manufacturing resource planning (MRP)** software, which plans appropriate inventory, tracks billing, and keeps track of parts needed for a given production schedule. However, MRP software only aids in planning the work; automating the work itself is the goal of computer-integrated manufacturing (**CIM**). The purpose of CIM is to ensure that all the computers and automated machines in a factory work together.

- In an ideal CIM situation, product designs are developed and refined on screen in a process known as **computer-aided design** (**CAD**). Design data passes electronically to a **computer-aided engineering** (**CAE**) system, where engineers use software to determine whether the design is workable and economical. A **computer-aided manufacturing** (**CAM**) system then transmits instructions for making the product to computer-controlled manufacturing equipment. The entire process is often called **CAD/CAE/CAM.** Progress toward such an automated factory is hindered, however, by a number of obstacles: including workstation power limitations, slow data transfer, and the lack of standards for data communications among machines.

- In 1984 General Motors introduced a communications standard called **Manufacturing Automation Protocol** (**MAP**), which was soon supported by a number of major factory automation vendors, including IBM.

- A **robot** is a computer-controlled device that can physically manipulate its surroundings. The most common industrial robots have five or six axes of motion, allowing them to rotate into place to perform tasks.

- A **vision system** is a set of computer-controlled machines that can take automatic action based on what they "see." Vision systems can be used in both assembly and inspection of factory products.

- Two basic approaches to factory production are **production-push,** in which parts are produced in volume and kept in stock for later production steps, and **demand-pull** or **just-in-time** (**JIT**), in which parts are produced only as they are needed.

- Microcomputers used in factories should be durable ("ruggedized"), easy to service, and easy to use.

- Automation will eventually replace some factory jobs, probably beginning with the foreman's job of controlling production schedules and inventory. However, computer-integrated manufacturing is still in the early stages of development.

## / Review Questions

1. How has the meaning of *office automation* changed?

2. Describe electronic publishing.

3. Discuss the advantages of each of the following: electronic mail, voice mail, teleconferencing, and facsimile technology.

4. What is ergonomics, and how does it relate to office automation?

5. Define MRP and describe its functions.

6. What is the purpose of computer-integrated manufacturing?

7. Name and describe the three main systems involved in computer-integrated manufacturing.

8. Define MAP and explain its significance.

9. Define the two main approaches to factory production and explain how they differ.

10. Explain how automation may replace factory jobs.

## / Discussion Questions

1. What do you consider to be the most significant advantages and disadvantages of office automation? Explain your answer.

2. What do you think will be the positive and negative effects of factory automation? What is your overall opinion of factory automation? Explain your answer.

# 18

# Management Information Systems

## Managing Computer Resources

Who is going to manage the computer sprawl—the corporate mainframes, the automated office, the computer-controlled factory, and all the networks that tie them together? In this chapter we shall discuss how management is aided by information systems and look at the Management Information Systems (MIS) department, which has the responsibility for computer systems. We shall also consider how managers themselves benefit from personal computers.

The view from the top—say, from a company president's office on the fortieth floor—is a lot different from the view from below. And the viewpoint from the top is also different: A top-level manager must have a different outlook than a middle-level or lower-level manager. But whether managing an airline, or a bank, or an assembly line, the challenge is the same: to use available resources to get the job done on time, within budget, and to the satisfaction of all concerned. Let us begin with a discussion of how managers do this, then see how computer systems can help them.

## Classic Management Functions

Managers have five main functions:

- **Planning.** Managers devise both short-range and long-range plans for the organization and set goals to help achieve the plans.

- **Organizing.** Managers decide how to use resources such as people and materials.

- **Staffing.** Managers hire and train workers.

- **Directing.** Managers guide employees to perform their work in a way that supports the organization's goals.

- **Controlling.** Managers monitor the organization's progress toward reaching its goals.

All managers perform these functions as part of their jobs. The level of responsibility associated with these functions, however, varies with the level of the manager.

Whether they are the head of General Electric or an electrical appliance store or of a large company or a small one, top-level managers have to be concerned with the long-range view—with **planning** (Figure 18-1a). Are American families watching fewer standard television series but going more for televised movies and miniseries? To the president of a company making videotape recorders, this may suggest real opportunities for expansion since, presumably, people will want to preserve some of these movies for later viewing.

Middle-level managers must be able to take a somewhat different view because their main concern is **organizing** (Figure 18-1b). The middle manager will prepare to carry out the visions of the top-level managers, assembling the material and personnel resources to do the job. Note that these tasks include the **staffing** function. So the public is suddenly finding videotape recorders desirable if they are affordable? To a production vice-president, this may mean organizing production lines using people with the right skills at the right wage and perhaps farming out portions of the assembly that can be done by cheaper, less-skilled labor.

Lower-level managers, usually known as first-line supervisors, are primarily concerned with **directing** and **controlling** (Figure

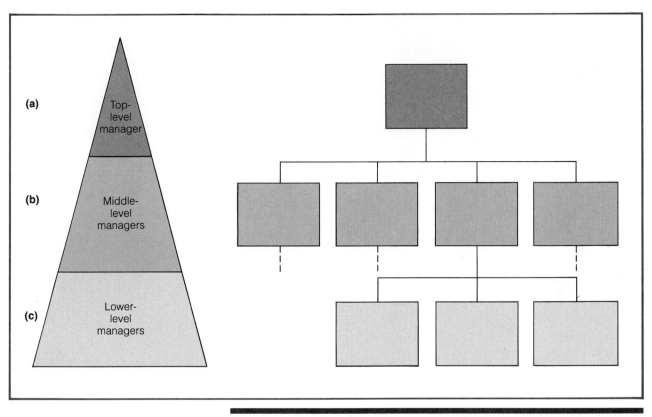

**Figure 18-1 The three levels of management.** (a) Top managers handle long-range planning, while (b) middle managers are more concerned with the organizational and personnel issues involved in carrying out such plans. (c) Lower-level managers direct and control day-to-day operations.

18-1c). Personnel must be directed to perform the planned activities. These managers must also monitor progress closely. In the process the supervisor—an assembly-line supervisor in our video recorder example—will be involved in a number of issues: making sure that workers have the parts needed when they need them, checking employee attendance, maintaining quality control, handling complaints, keeping a close watch on the schedule, tracking costs, and much more.

To make decisions about planning, organizing, staffing, directing, and controlling, managers need data that is organized into information that is right for them. An effective management information system can provide it.

## MIS for Managers

A **management information system** (MIS) may be defined as a set of formal business systems designed to provide information for an organization. (Incidentally, you may hear the

## THE MICROCOMPUTER CORNER

### Trying Out Your Management Skills

So you want to be a manager. One of the jobs of a manager is juggling resources—such as people and materials—for a project. If the project is large, this process can become complicated whether the goal is construction, manufacturing, or a new computer system. We turn, of course, to the computer for help in keeping track of everything. The special kind of software for this purpose is called project management software, and it can run on your personal computer.

A popular project management package for the personal computer is Microsoft Project, which helps managers oversee complex projects effectively in three ways. The first is by dividing the overall project into manageable tasks. The second is by assigning resources (people, machines, materials) to each task. The third is by reassigning resources to tasks as a situation changes—if, for example, a temporary service was able

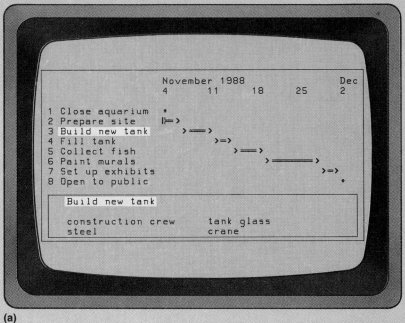

(a)

to supply only half the people originally promised for an office move. Microsoft Project lets a manager quickly and easily enter

data. The manager can then see when various portions of the job will be completed and which resources are being used on differ-

term *MIS system*, even though the S itself stands for *system*; this is an accepted redundancy.) Whether or not such a system is called an MIS, every company has one. Even managers who make hunch-based decisions are operating with some sort of information system—one based on their experience. The kind of MIS we are concerned with here includes a computer as one of its components. Information serves no purpose until it gets to its users. Timeliness is important, and the computer can act quickly to produce information.

The extent of a computerized MIS varies from company to company, but the most effective kinds are those that are integrated. An integrated MIS incorporates all five managerial functions—planning, organizing, staffing, directing, and controlling—throughout the company, from the most mundane typing to top-executive forecasting. An integrated management computer system uses the computer to solve problems for an entire organization, instead of attacking them piecemeal. Although in many companies the com-

**Microsoft Project.** These screens show a schedule and budget for preparing a new exhibit at an aquarium. (a) When you enter a list of activities, the time required for each activity, and a starting date, Microsoft Project will draw a schedule for you. If any of these parameters change, or if you want to see what would happen if they did change, a new schedule can be generated automatically. At the bottom of the screen you can view the resources assigned to each activity. (b) When you enter the unit cost for each resource, Microsoft Project will calculate the total cost of each resource, the total cost of the project, and the cost to complete the project from the current day onward. If the schedule or unit costs change, the budget can be automatically recalculated. Thus, you can quickly see the effect on the bottom line.

| Resource | Unit Cost | Per | Cost to Complete |
|---|---|---|---|
| 1 artists | 25.00 | Hour | 9600.00 |
| 2 divers | 32.00 | Hour | 2560.00 |
| 3 boat | 310.00 | Day | 1550.00 |
| 4 bulldozers | 413.00 | Day | 3717.00 |
| 5 crane | 700.00 | Day | 3500.00 |
| 6 water pump | 134.99 | Day | 404.97 |
| 7 constr. crew | 9315.00 | Week | 26856.73 |
| 8 aquarist | 3200.00 | Month | 1765.00 |
| 9 explosives | 310.00 | Use | 930.00 |
| 10 tank glass | 9750.00 | Fixed | 9750.00 |
| 11 steel | 5321.89 | Fixed | 5321.89 |

Cost to complete: 26400.00          Total: 65954.70

**(b)**

ent tasks. These outputs can be seen in graphs or in tables.

A successful project is usually the result of good planning based on good information. With Microsoft Project, you can increase the quality, quantity, and timeliness of the information you use.

plete integrated system is still only an idea, the scope of MIS is expanding rapidly in many organizations.

The **MIS manager** runs the MIS department. This position has been called Information Resource Manager, Director of Information Services, Chief Information Officer, and a variety of other monikers. In any case, the person who serves in this capacity will be comfortable with both computer technology and the organization's business.

## MIS Reports for Managers

A computer system can produce different kinds of reports, which can be described as summary, exception, or detail reports. Reports can also be categorized as periodic or on-demand. **Periodic reports** are produced on a regular schedule, such as daily or monthly, and are preplanned to produce detail, summary, or exception data. **On-demand reports** reflect their name, giving information

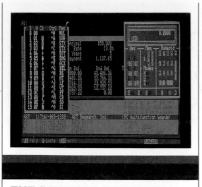

## THE DESKTOP METAPHOR

Office software, says the metaphor, should resemble a desktop in two ways: It should contain office tools for different tasks, and the user should be able to set aside one tool temporarily while another tool is in use. Work is often interrupted. A user gets started on one project, then has to spend five minutes on another project. When interrupted, a user may jump from one tool to another, from typewriter to calculator to notebook.

The type of software package that specializes in an interrupt feature is usually billed under the generic heading *desktop organizer.* A typical package offers a calculator, notepad, desk calendar, and telephone dialer. In true desktop fashion any of these tools can be used at any time and in the middle of another project that involves other software. At the stroke of a key, you can, for example, interrupt a word processing project to use a calculator; another keystroke "puts away" the calculator and returns you to where you were on your document. The desktop organizer software is always there, "underneath" whatever other software you are using. When you return to the other software, you can continue as if nothing had happened.

in response to an unscheduled demand—a request—from a user. Let us look more closely at these reports in the context of their value to managers.

- **Top-level managers.** For strategic planning, high-level managers need to be able to see historical information—an analysis of data trends—not for just some parts of their business but for the total business. Moreover, such managers must be able to make decisions about things that happen unpredictably. The MIS, therefore, must be able to produce on-demand reports that integrate information and show how factors affecting various departments are related to each other. An on-demand report might show the impact of strikes or energy shortages on all parts of the company.

- **Middle-level managers.** To do their tactical planning and organizing functions, middle-level managers need to be aware of trends; they need to know what the business is doing and where it is going. Thus, these managers are most in need of summary reports and exception reports. **Summary reports** are limited to totals or trends. Examples of summary reports showing trends are those showing past and present interest rates or sales data (Figure 18-2a). **Exception reports** show only data that reflects unusual circumstances. Examples of exception reports are those showing depleted budgets, payments being made to temporary employees, and books temporarily out of stock or not yet published (Figure 18-2b).

- **Low-level managers.** Concerned mainly with day-to-day operations, low-level managers need **detail reports,** which give complete, specific information on routine operations that will help them keep offices and plants running. Examples are overtime information from this week's payroll, spare parts that need to be ordered, quality-control results of yesterday's inspections at Dock B, and books to be shipped (Figure 18-2c). Many computer-based MISs are self-determining—that is, they can take some preplanned actions on their own. An MIS can, for example, automatically reorder depleted stock as directed by an inventory management program or automatically issue bonuses for salespeople when incoming orders reach a certain level.

It should be clear that an MIS must be capable of delivering both detailed and general information not only on a regular schedule but also to fill unpredictable requests.

## The Scope of Responsibility: Turf Wars

Is the MIS manager responsible for the whole company? Not really, but sometimes it seems that way. If computers are everywhere—and they are—can the MIS department be far behind? Think about it. For a long time—through the 1960s and 1970s—anyone

**(a) Summary report:**

```
FOUR-YEAR SALES TITLE REPORT AS OF 1/31/88
MATHEMATICS-AUTHOR & TITLE

50239 LYON TRIGONOMETRY
1987 QTY        1986 QTY        1985 QTY        1984 QTY
 15,813          16,239          20,871          23,918

50240 SMITH LINEAR MATH
1987 QTY        1986 QTY        1985 QTY        1984 QTY
 25,031          25,502          29,193          22,108

50241 ANDREWS COLLEGE MATH
1987 QTY        1986 QTY        1985 QTY        1984 QTY
 20,013          18,925          19,931          23,206
```

**(b) Exception report:**

```
AVAILABILITY DATE LISTING-
TITLES TEMP OUT OF STOCK OR NOT YET PUBLISHED 1/31/88

CODE AUTHOR & TITLE                      AVAILABLE

00089 BYRNE ELEM STATISTICS              APR  2, 88
00093 BLUESTONE ANTHROPOLOGY             MAR  3, 88
00156 ALBRIGHT INFECTIOUS DISEASES       APR 28, 88
```

**(c) Detail report:**

```
DAILY SALES REGISTER BY TYPE OF SALE   1/31/88   PAGE 1

SHIP-TO ADDRESS        CODE AUTHOR&  LIST   QTY  TOTAL
                            TITLE    PRICE       AMOUNT

THE SOUTH MAIN         36980 WILSON  22.95  100  2295.00
BOOKSTORE              ANATOMY &
209 SOUTH MAIN         PHYSIOLOGY
CHICAGO, IL 60625

UNIVERSITY BOOKSTORE   50239 LYON    17.95  300  5385.00
OLD STATE COLLEGE      TRIGONOMETRY
800 W VICTORIA ST
STAMFORD, CT 06903

EASTERN ARCATA UNIV    34102 SPENCE  17.95  400  7180.00
BOOKSTORE              GENETICS
PO BOX 8769
ARCATA, CA 95521
```

**Figure 18-2   Three kinds of reports.** These are examples of the kinds of reports a book publisher might use. (a) This report summarizes the sales of math books over the previous four years. (b) This exception report lists titles temporarily out of stock or not yet published. (c) This report provides the details on books to be shipped.

who needed computer services made a formal request to the computer professionals. That is, employees had to present their needs to the official keepers of automated power, where information was dispensed. A great deal of power, both computer and political, was concentrated in one place. Distribution of power has come in a variety of ways. As we noted in Chapter 7, for example, placing smaller computers in remote locations, such as branch offices, gave computer users better access and, consequently, more control. But the biggest change was made by placing personal computers directly in the hands of users.

In many ways, however, this distribution of power is an illusion. Users are constrained by their needs for the corporate data, and the data is still firmly in the hands of the MIS department. Many personal computers are plugged in to networks that the MIS department must control and monitor. Users also rely heavily on MIS-run information centers, which help them with computer-related problems. It certainly seems that a lot of power still rests with the MIS manager.

And recently a new Goliath—manufacturing—has appeared on the horizon for the MIS department to slay. The demand from top management to increase productivity in the manufacturing arena is escalating, and computer technology is looked to as the answer. So, there is one more set of technologies for the MIS manager to contend with. What this will probably mean, however, is a battle over territory. Manufacturing managers would prefer to keep the MIS department out of the production process but, as more technologies are introduced, they have no choice but to include MIS—that is, if they want to meet their end goal of increasing productivity.

The MIS manager is gaining authority over an empire that is getting more and more unruly, with computers and computer users spread all over the company. The role of the MIS department is changing from the caretaker of large computers to the supporter of computers and their networks right in the user's environment. And there is a more subtle change: MIS managers can no longer hide behind the protective cloak of technical mystery because their users have become more sophisticated. In effect, even the interpersonal style of the MIS manager is changing.

There are two issues here: control of power and the nature of the MIS manager's job. Although it is clear that the MIS department dominates the company's use of computers, ultimate control lies with the users themselves, who pay the bills for computer services. As for the MIS manager, that job will be in flux for the foreseeable future. As technology changes, so will the focus and scope of the job.

## Managing Microcomputers

Microcomputers—personal computers—burst on the business scene in the early 1980s with little warning and

**NOW WE KNOW
ALL ABOUT IT**

It has not always been a smooth transition. In fact, the change from classroom to office sometimes has been frightening for students and frustrating for employers. The classic statement from employers is that trainees do not graduate with enough day-to-day business knowledge and thus do not pull their own weight for perhaps six months. But in jobs related to computer technology, this is changing.

Part of the problem has been that schools could not afford up-to-date equipment. The microcomputer has made the difference. For the first time, schools can afford to provide their students with leading-edge technology, the same technology currently revolutionizing businesses. So the business world derives even more benefit—in computer-literate new-hires—from microcomputers.

less planning. The experience of the Rayer International Paper Company is typical. One day a personal computer appeared on the desk of engineer Tim Griffin—he had brought his in from home. Then accountants Sandy Dean and Mike Molyneaux got a pair of machines—they had squeezed the money for them out of the overhead budget. Keith Wong, the personnel manager, got personal computers for himself and his three assistants in the company's far-flung branch offices. And so it went, with personal computers popping up all over the company. Managers realized that the reason for runaway purchases was that personal computers were so affordable: Most departments could pay for them out of existing budgets, so the purchasers did not have to ask anyone's permission.

Managers, at first, were tolerant. There were no provisions for managing the purchase or use of personal computers, and there certainly was no rule *against* them. And it was soon apparent that these were more than toys. Pioneer users had no trouble justifying their purchases with increased productivity. In addition to mastering software for word processing, spreadsheets, and database access, they declared their independence from the MIS department.

Managers, however, soon were faced with several problems. The first was incompatibility—the new computers came in an assortment of brands and models and did not mesh well. Software that worked on one machine did not necessarily work on another. Secondly, users were not as independent of the MIS department as they had thought—they needed assistance in a variety of ways. And, finally, no one person was in charge of the headlong plunge into personal computers. Many organizations solved these management problems in these ways:

- They addressed the compatibility problem by establishing acquisition policies.

- They solved the assistance problem by creating information centers.

- They corrected the management problem by creating a new position called the microcomputer manager.

Let us examine each of these solutions.

## Microcomputer Acquisition

In an office environment managers know they must control the acquisition and use of micros, but they are not always sure how to do it. As we noted, workers initially purchased personal computers before any companywide or even officewide policies had been set. The resulting compatibility problems meant that they could not easily communicate or share data. Consider this example: A user's budget process may call for certain data that resides in the files of another worker's micro or perhaps output incorporating the figures produced by still a third person. If the software and machines these people use do not mesh, compatibility becomes a major problem.

In many companies MIS departments have now taken control of microcomputer acquisition. The methods vary, but often include the following:

- **Standards.** Most companies now have established standards for personal computers, for the software that will run on them, and for data communications. Users can still buy what they want, but they must stick to the standards if they want to tie into corporate resources. For example, if IBM PC architecture is the standard, then any IBM-compatible machine is acceptable.

- **Limited vendors.** Some companies limit the number of vendors—sellers of hardware and software—from whom they allow purchases. MIS managers have discovered they can prevent most user complaints about incompatibility by allowing products from just a handful of vendors.

- **Limited support.** MIS departments generally control a company's purchases by specifying which hardware and software products will be supported by the MIS department.

As you can see, these methods overlap. But all of them, in one form or another, give the MIS department control. In other words, users are being told, "If you want to do it some other way, then you're on your own."

## The Information Center

If personal computer users compared notes, they would probably find that their experiences are similar. Budget analyst Gwen Price is typical. She convinced her boss to let her have her own personal computer so she could analyze financial data. She purchased a popular spreadsheet program and, with some help from her colleagues, learned to use it. She soon thought about branching out in other areas. She wanted a statistics software package, but was not sure which one was appropriate. She thought it would be useful to have a modem but did not feel she was equipped to make a hardware decision. And, most of all, she felt her productivity would increase significantly if she could get her hands on the data in the corporate data files.

The company information center is the MIS solution to these kinds of needs. Although no two are alike, a typical information center gives users support for the user's own equipment. The information center is devoted exclusively to giving users service. And, best of all, user assistance is immediate, with little or no red tape.

Information center services often include the following:

- **Software selection.** Information center staff helps users determine which software packages suit their needs.

**Figure 18-3  The information center.** Classes are held at the information center to teach managers and other employees how to use the company's computers.

- **Data access.** If appropriate, the staff helps users get data from the large corporate computer systems for use on the users' own computers.

- **Training.** Education is a principal reason for an information center's existence. Classes are usually small, frequent, and on a variety of topics (Figure 18-3).

- **Technical assistance.** Information center staff members stand ready to assist in any way possible, short of actually doing the users' work for them. That help includes advising on hardware purchases, aiding in the selection and use of software, finding errors, helping submit formal requests to the MIS department, and so forth.

To be successful, the information center must be placed in an easily accessible location. The center should be equipped with microcomputers and terminals, a stockpile of software packages, and perhaps a library. It should be staffed with people who have a technical background but whose explanations feature plain English. Their mandate is "The user comes first."

## The Microcomputer Manager

And who is going to manage the revolution? The users-get-computers revolution, that is. The benefits of personal computers for the individual user have been clear almost from the beginning: increased productivity, worker enthusiasm, and easier access to information. But once personal computers move beyond maverick status, standard corporate accountability becomes a factor; large companies are spending millions of dollars on personal computers and top-level managers want to know where all this money is going. Company auditors begin worrying about data security. The company legal department begins to worry about workers illegally copying software. Before long, everyone is involved, and it is clear that someone must be placed in charge of personal computer use. That person is the **microcomputer manager.**

There are four key areas that need the attention of the micro manager:

- **Technology overload.** The micro manager must maintain a clear vision of company goals so that users are not overwhelmed by the massive and conflicting claims of aggressive vendors plying their wares. Users engulfed by phrases like *network topologies* or *file gateways* or a jumble of acronyms can turn to the micro manager for guidance with their purchases.

- **Cost control.** Many people who work with personal computers believe the initial costs are paid back rapidly, and they think that should satisfy managers who hound them about expenses. But the real costs entail training, support, hardware and software extras, and communications networks—much more than just the CPU, CRT, and keyboard. The micro manager's role includes monitoring *all* the expenses.

- **Data security and integrity.** Access to corporate data is a touchy issue. Many personal computer users find they want to **download** data from the corporate mainframe to their own machines, and this presents an array of problems. Are they entitled to it? Will they manipulate the data in new ways, then present it as the official version? Will they expect MIS to take the data back after they have done who-knows-what with it? The answers to these perplexing questions are not always clear-cut, but at least the micro manager will be tuned in to the issues.

- **Computer junkies.** And what about the employee feverish with the new power and freedom of the computer? When they are in school, these user-abusers are called hackers, but on the job they are often called junkies because their fascination with the computer seems like an addiction. Unable to resist the allure of the machine, they overuse it and neglect their other work. Micro managers usually respond to this problem by setting down guidelines for computer use.

The person selected to be the micro manager is usually from the MIS area. This person ideally has a broad technical background, understands both the potential and limitations of personal computers, and is well known to a diverse group of users.

One way that the micro manager can keep the support of top-level managers is to make sure those managers have their own computers.

## When the Boss Gets a Computer

All over this land business executives, frustrated by the backlog of unfinished work in their corporate MIS departments, have opted for do-it-yourself, buying their own personal computers and packaged software. Sometimes these executives are even the heads of companies.

One chief executive officer of a pharmaceutical company, for instance, felt he could not be sure of the information he was getting from his accounting, finance, and data processing people, so he purchased a personal computer and experimented with it at home for a few months. After discovering the benefits of word processing, he ordered 20 microcomputers for his office and asked employees to learn to use the machines for memos and report writing. In addition, he discovered the advantages of working with spreadsheet software, which enabled him to examine issues of business strategy such as the level of sales discounts and advertising support needed to reach

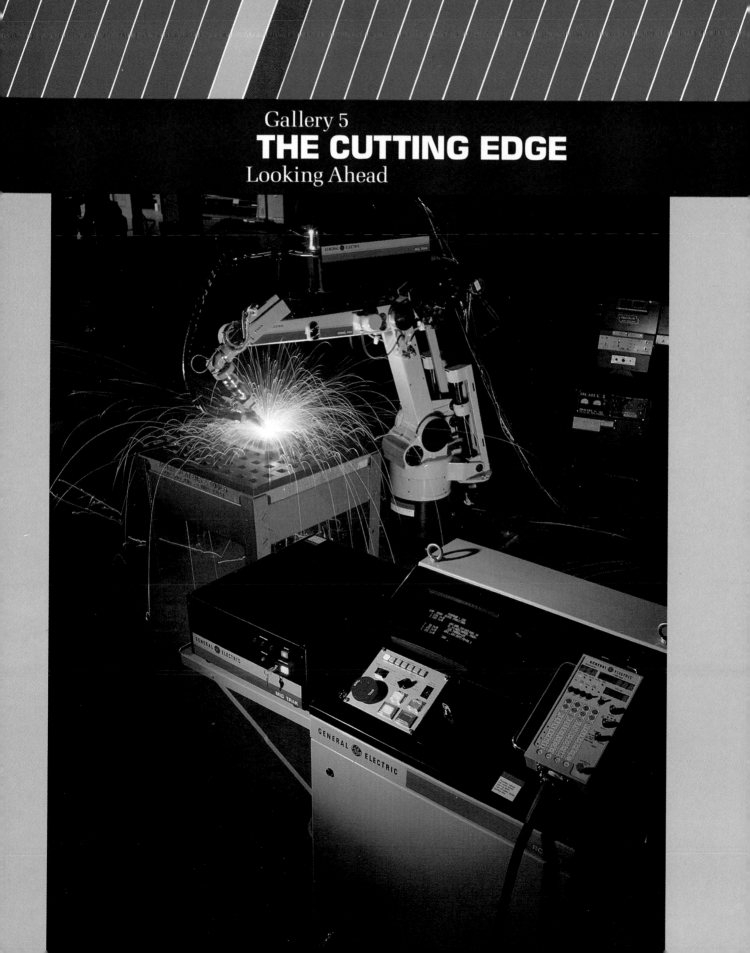

Gallery 5
# THE CUTTING EDGE
Looking Ahead

**1**

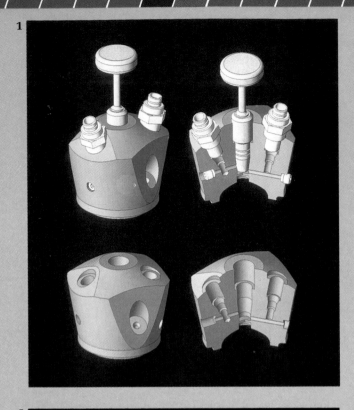

**2**

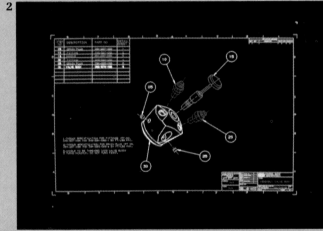

The galleries have used pictures to show the uses of computers in business and government, where you expect them, and in everyday life, where you may not expect them. But now it is time to be a little more bold and glimpse the future, or at least the cutting edge of technology as we look to the future.

The photo on the opening page shows a sophisticated six-axis robot from General Electric. It uses a laser tracking system and a welding torch to simultaneously track and weld along irregular surfaces.

## CAD/CAE/CAM

This string of letters represents the ideal factory of the future: New products are devised and drawn on a computer-aided design (CAD) system. The CAD data is then transmitted electronically to a computer-aided engineering (CAE) system, where an engineer tests and finalizes the design. The modified data is then sent electronically to a computer-aided manufacturing (CAM) system, which uses the data to direct machine tools, robots, and other automated factory equipment. The final product then enters an automated warehouse. Computers coordinate every step of the process, making them the ultimate factory tool.

The photos on these two pages show the computer-aided design, engineering, and manufacturing of a plexiglass valve housing for an aircraft fuel system. The entire process uses Control Data's Integrated Computer-Aided Engineering and Manufacturing (ICEM) system. All graphic data and documentation remain on the computer system throughout the project, eliminating time-consuming drawings and reports.

**3**

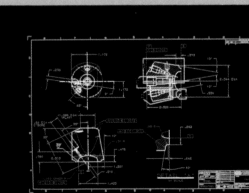

**4**

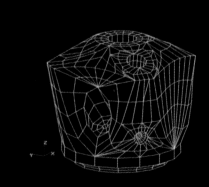

(1) The engineer-designer begins by creating a solid geometric model, which is then "exploded" into component parts. (2) The engineer then creates a wire frame model that produces data for (3) conventional 3-D drafting and 2-D drawings. (4) A mesh model, generated from the original solid model, can be subjected to stress analysis; (5) a cross section shows the internal stresses generated by fuel pressures—the color scale on the right indicates the stresses. Depending on the testing results, the design may be revised until performance is satisfactory. (6) The setup data for the specific machine tool to produce the valve is produced automatically. (7) The two views here show the valve housing (yellow) displayed as it would appear when being machined from a solid plexiglass rod held in a fixture (solid white lines). (8) Finally, the valve housing is produced automatically on a machine tool.

5

6

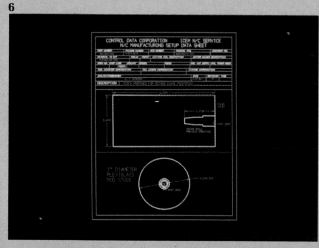

7

8

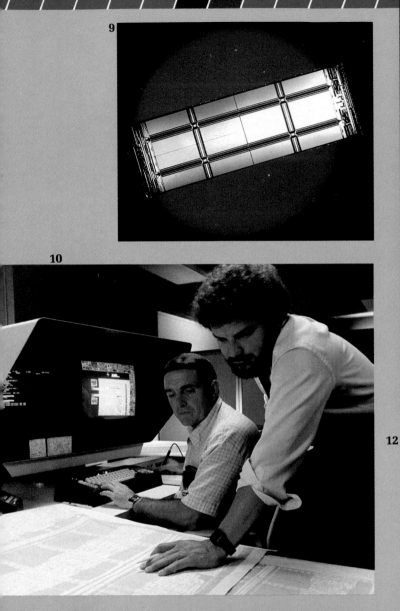

9

# New Developments in Hardware

Hardware developers are breaking through old boundaries almost daily as computers continue to become faster and easier to use. As always, once hardware breakthroughs take place, software developers must catch up quickly to make full use of the new technologies.

**(9)** AT&T's new megabit memory chip stores over a million bits of data.

**(10)** Designers at Rockwell International's research center use a computer-aided design system to develop complex gallium arsenide chips. Gallium arsenide is of particular interest because electricity moves through it at extraordinary speeds.

**(11)** With its phenomenal storage capacity, optical disk technology is leading the way to new uses of computers. **(12)** In one application, an optical disk contains a database of images of Aspen, Colorado. These images can be assembled into a movie-like presentation of a drive through Aspen under the control of the viewer.

10

11

12

**(13)** Designer Daniel Hillis sits in front of his Connection Machine which, with its pulsing red lights, looks—and is—different from other mainframe computers. The secret is the machine's extraordinary speed, derived from its 65,536 processors, each with its own small memory bank. Says Hillis: "The conventional machine is to the Connection Machine what the bicycle is to a supersonic jet."

**(14)**, **(15)**, **(16)** These exceptionally clear Conrac Corporation screens show leading edge 3D display technology, with 1280 by 1024 resolution.

14

13

15

16

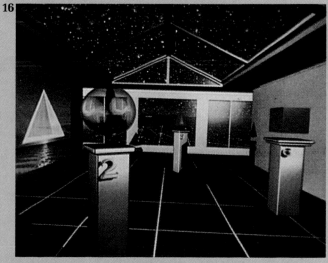

# Artificial Intelligence/ Expert Systems

Artificial intelligence (AI) is a fascinating field that explores how computers can be used to perform tasks that require the human characteristics of intelligence, imagination, and intuition. Although in its infancy, the field of artificial intelligence holds implications beyond what we can even imagine. At the moment, one of the most practical uses of artificial intelligence principles is in expert systems, which are also called knowledge-based systems. Each expert system program is "intelligent" about only one particular topic, however. A user provides the computer with data about a particular problem and the expert system responds with an answer and an explanation. To make its analysis, the expert system uses facts and rules derived from human experts.

**(17)** PROSPECTOR is an expert system developed by SRI International that predicts the potential for finding mineral deposits in a certain area. PROSPECTOR was developed by interviewing expert prospectors—geologists who are experts in locating underground mineral deposits. In the photo, geologist Dennis Cox *(left)*, an authority on copper deposits, is being interviewed by an SRI knowledge engineer, who will convert Cox's knowledge about geology into thousands of rules a computer can use. By formalizing the rules that expert geologists follow and putting them into a computer system, the expert's knowledge is available for more people to use. **(18)** Geologic maps, such as the one shown here, are digitized and input as data for PROSPECTOR. **(19)**, **(20)**, **(21)** The system produces screen images of PROSPECTOR's analysis.

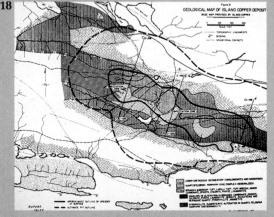

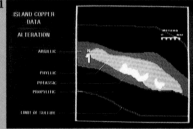

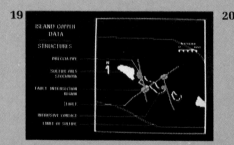

**(22)** The Ford Motor Company uses a knowledge-based system called Maintenance Assistant to help maintenance technicians diagnose problems with factory robots.

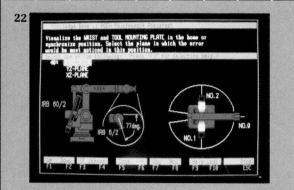

**(23), (24)** These colorful screens show the structures of two proteins. The structures were deduced by PROTEAN, a knowledge-based system developed at Stanford University. To figure out the structures of molecules, PROTEAN analyzes experimental results using some of the knowledge that a biochemist would apply to such problems.

**(25)** Golden Common LISP, an artificial intelligence programming language for personal computers, was used to develop an emergency monitoring system for power plants. The system alerts the operator to any changes in emergency status and provides an explanation. The system also provides a model of how the power plant works so that an operator can test the consequences of changes to plant operation before the change is actually made.

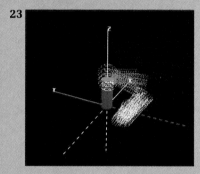

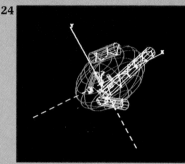

## Communications

The importance of communications cannot be underestimated—when computers are linked to each other they become even more powerful tools. We are just beginning to see the effects of the new information age made possible by improved communications systems.

**(26)** The satellite dish—in designer colors!—is becoming a common sight as organizations and even individuals expand their communications horizons.

**(27)** An IBM instructor in New York City provides technical training via satellite network to customers in Minneapolis, Houston, and other cities.

**(28)**, **(29)**, **(30)** These menus provide a representative sample of sales options on your home computer, available from the Viewdata Corporation.

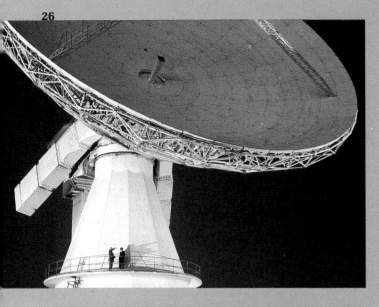

26

27

28

Exotic Gardens
FLORISTS SINCE 1914
1 Express Ordering
2 Roses
3 FTD - Flowers by Wire
4 Catalog Ordering

Send flowers on-line and on time, coast to coast, any time day or night.

* INDEX

29

CITIBANK⊕
IT PAYS TO USE OUR CARDS
▷1 All About Our Cards
▷2 Apply for a MasterCard
▷3 Apply for a Visa Card
▷4 Apply for a Preferred Visa Card
▷5 CitiDollar$ Discount Shopping
▷6 CitiDining (R) Information

If you already have a Citibank credit card, you can options 5 and 6.

* INDEX

30

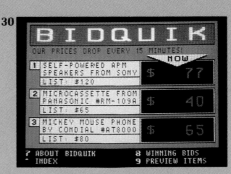

BIDQUIK
OUR PRICES DROP EVERY 15 MINUTES!
                                      NOW
1 SELF-POWERED APM SPEAKERS FROM SONY    $  77
  LIST: $120
2 MICROCASSETTE FROM PANASONIC #RM-109A  $  40
  LIST: $65
3 MICKEY MOUSE PHONE BY CONDIAL #AT8000  $  65
  LIST: $80
7 ABOUT BIDQUIK      8 WINNING BIDS
* INDEX               9 PREVIEW ITEMS

his company's sales targets. Earlier strategic planning was fairly informal: "We just eyeballed the numbers and made our best guesses." Now all that has changed. In fact, computers make a very significant difference in how managers do their jobs.

## How Computers Change the Way Managers Work

People who dismiss the impact of the personal computer sometimes say, "It's just another tool." Some tool. The personal computer is making profound changes in the work lives of businesspeople who use it, though some seem unaware of what is going on.

Regional business manager Martha Miller, for example, stoutly insists, "The computer hasn't changed *my* life." But listen to the changes. When asked how she uses her machine, she begins by describing her early microcomputer projects. One was drawing up a budget and the other was designing a compensation package for the 180 people under her supervision. Later, she added hardware and software to send electronic messages to people in the office, dispatch electronic mail to other parts of the country, and call up articles from the business press. She also uses her computer to write memos and reports—"a piece of cake," she says.

Martha eventually succumbed to a second personal computer at home, which she uses to do office work in the evening. She finds it easier to carry diskettes to and fro than to lug a briefcase full of paper. Most mornings, in fact, Martha tosses her diskettes into her out-box, knowing the secretary will take it from there. Finally, Martha reflects on all this activity. "Everything I do on the computer," she says, "I do ten times faster than I used to do it."

For many managers, the machine that is "just a tool" speeds analysis to a breakneck pace, answers all sorts of "What if . . ." questions, sends and receives mail, and lets executives stay home more. In earlier chapters we discussed some of the key software packages—word processing, spreadsheets, graphics, and database access—that help make these things possible. Now we want to take a closer look at software of special significance to managers: decision support systems and expert systems.

## Decision Support Systems

Imagine yourself as a top-level manager trying to deal with a constantly changing environment, having to consider changes in competition, in technology, in consumer habits, in government regulations, in union demands, and so on. How are you going to make decisions about those matters for which there are no precedents? In fact, making one-of-a-kind decisions—decisions that no

---

### DO AS I SAY

A major computer trade journal interviewed a major player from the corporate computer division of a major oil company. All these *majors* are inserted to underline the weight we shall give this interview. Mr. Smith waxed euphoric about the importance of workstations on the desk of every employee. He portrayed himself as an early believer, a pioneer of sorts. He described how the machines have started changing relationships and the way people work: "The secretary is no longer the font of all knowledge. Documents get prepared without the secretary even seeing them in many cases. A lot of our people are now beginning to use their computers in lieu of yellow pads. They just don't write anymore. They are creating on their computers. We are seeing things done much more effectively."

So far, so good. But now the interview turns to Mr. Smith himself. It is safe to assume that he is leading the way, right? Wrong. In his own words, "I do everything verbally. I dictate. I don't type. I don't like to type. I can, but I won't." In other words, do as I say, not as I do.

one has had to make before—are the real test of a manager's mettle. In such a situation, you would probably wish you could turn to someone and ask a few "What if . . ." questions.

"What if . . . ?" That is the question businesspeople want answered, at least for those important decisions that have no precedent. A **decision support system** (**DSS**) is a computer system that supports managers in nonroutine decision-making tasks. The key ingredient of a decision support system is a modeling process. A **model** is a mathematical representation of a real-life system. A mathematical model can be computerized. Like any computer program, the model can use inputs to produce outputs. The inputs to a model are called **independent variables** because they can change—and the outputs are called **dependent variables** because they depend on the inputs.

Consider this example. Suppose, as a manager, you have the task of deciding which property to purchase for one of your manufacturing processes. You have many factors to consider: the asking price, interest rate, down payment required, and so on. These are all independent variables—the data that will be fed into the computer model of the purchase. The dependent variables, computed on the basis of the inputs, are the effect on your cash resources, long-term debt, and ability to make other investments. To increase complexity, we could add that the availability of workers and nearness to markets are also input factors. Increasing the complexity factor, in fact, is appropriate because decision support systems often work with problems that are more complex than any individual can handle.

Using a computer model to reach a decision about a real-life situation is called **simulation.** It is a game of "let's pretend." You plan the independent variables—the inputs—and you examine how the model behaves based on the dependent variables—the outputs—it produces. If you wish you may change the inputs and continue experimenting. This is a relatively inexpensive way to simulate life situations, and it is considerably faster than the real thing.

A decision support system does not replace MIS; instead DSS supplements MIS. There are distinct differences between them. MIS emphasizes planned reports on a variety of subjects; DSS focuses on decision making. MIS is standard, scheduled, structured, routine; DSS is quite unstructured and available on request. MIS is constrained by the organizational system; DSS is immediate and friendly.

The decision-making process must be fast, so the DSS is interactive: The user is in direct communication with the computer system and can affect its activities. In addition, most DSSs cross departmental lines so that information can be pulled from the databases of a variety of sources such as marketing and sales, accounting and finance, production, and research and development. A manager trying to make a decision about developing a new product needs information from all these sources.

## GROWN-UP GAMES

Want to make it big in business? Test your mettle with this software game. You have to be tough to play—it's not for kids. Written by people from the prestigious Wharton School of Business at the University of Pennsylvania, the game teaches you to be a survivor in the world of business. The name of the game is—take a deep breath—the Individual Learning Edition of The Strategic Management Game.

The point of the game is to run a profitable business while the computer changes economic and political conditions. The program is set up to provide increasing levels of difficulty as you prove that you can cope with increasingly complicated conditions.

The game originally was designed to train managers at some of America's largest corporations—AT&T, IBM, and General Foods. Perhaps, when you have successfully navigated level five, you could compete with the managers of these firms. Interested? Call SMG Inc. at (215) 387-4000. Oh, and the price is $350.

Several commercial software packages are available for specific modeling purposes. The purpose might be marketing, sales, or advertising. There are also more general packages available that provide rudimentary modeling but let you customize the model for different purposes such as budgeting, planning, or risk analysis.

There is another possibility. Suppose that a full-scale decision support system is not needed. In fact, let us say that the key decisions that need support involve exploring a number of alternatives by varying assumptions about market size, market share, selling prices, manufacturing costs, and expenses. Sound familiar? Right, we are talking about a perfect application for a spreadsheet program. Today's most widely used decision support system, with buyers one million strong, is the financial modeling program from Lotus Development Corporation called 1-2-3. So although a DSS can be very formal and complicated and suited to the needs of a sophisticated user, there are several common high-quality packages that serve the needs of everyday people who make decisions.

## Expert Systems in Business

An **expert system** is a software package used with an extensive set of organized data that presents the computer as an expert on some topic. The user is the knowledge seeker, usually asking questions in a natural—English-like—language format. An expert system can respond to an inquiry about a problem—"What will happen if the bill of particulars is not received before the adjourned deadline?"—with both an answer and an explanation of the answer. (This is a legal question using a lawyer's "natural language," and the answer is probably: "Prepare a motion to dismiss the case.") The expert system works by figuring out what the question means, then matching it against the facts and rules that it "knows." These facts and rules, which reside on disk, originally come from a human expert.

For years, expert systems were no more than a bold experiment, the exclusive property of the medical and scientific community. Special programs could offer medical diagnoses or search for mineral deposits or examine chemical compounds. But in the early 1980s, they began to make their way into commercial applications. Expert systems are slowly finding a place in big business.

The cost of an expert system can usually be justified in situations where there are few experts but great demand for knowledge. It is also worthwhile to have a system that is not subject to human failings such as fatigue. Some organizations choose to build their own expert systems to perform well-focused tasks that can easily be crystallized into rules. A simple example is a set of rules for a banker to use when making decisions about whether to extend credit. But very few organizations are capable of building an expert system from scratch. The sensible alternative is to buy an **expert shell,** which consists of the basic structure to find answers to questions. It is up to the buyer to fill in the actual knowledge on the chosen subject. You could think of the expert shell as an empty cup which becomes a new entity once it is filled—a cup of coffee or a cup of apple juice.

We noted that expert systems are often in a natural-language format. Some industry analysts feel that expert systems are beginning to mimic the analytic processes of humans and that, as a result, these programs border on artificial intelligence. To make a computer have **artificial intelligence,** a program must be able to understand the facts it knows, come up with new thoughts, and engage in a wide-ranging coherent conversation. By these standards, expert systems today are rather dim-witted. In particular, they have intelligence on only a given topic. The subject of artificial intelligence is a fascinating one and the source of many debates. Gallery 5 and the box in Chapter 10 examine this topic in more detail.

Expert systems will infiltrate companies department by department, much as personal computers did before them. Some expert systems are now available on personal computers. The main limitation of an expert system on a personal computer is that it requires a substantial amount of internal memory. A large amount of data in terms of rules, facts, and source code must be stored, dictating the use of hard disk. Even so, it seems likely that more expert systems for personal computers will appear in the near future.

## Hire a Computer Person for the Top Job?

Someone once remarked, somewhat facetiously, that all top management—presidents, chief executive officers (CEOs), and so forth—should be drawn from the MIS ranks. After all, the argument goes, computers pervade the entire company, and people who work with computer systems can bring broad experience to the job. Today, most presidents and CEOs still come from legal, financial, or marketing backgrounds. But as the computer industry and its professionals mature, that pattern could change.

## Summary and Key Terms

- All managers have five main functions: planning, organizing, staffing, directing, and controlling. Top-level managers primarily do long-range **planning;** middle-level managers focus more on the **organizing** and **staffing** required to implement plans; and lower-level managers are mainly concerned with **controlling** schedules, costs, and quality, as well as **directing** the personnel.

- A **management information system** (MIS) is a set of business systems designed to provide information for decision making. A computerized MIS is most effective if it is integrated.

- The **MIS manager,** a person familiar with both computer technology and the organization's business, runs the MIS department.

- An MIS can produce detail, summary, and exception reports, either on a regular schedule (**periodic reports**) or in response to unscheduled requests from users (**on-demand reports**). **Detail reports** provide complete, specific information, while **summary reports** are limited to totals or trends. **Exception reports** show only data that reflects unusual circumstances.

- Top-level managers frequently require information that aids strategic planning. They often request on-demand reports on the impact of unpredictable occurrences. Middle-level managers usually need summary reports showing expenses and sales trends and exception reports on unexpected expenses and projects behind schedule. Low-level managers typically require detail reports on factors affecting routine operations.

- When microcomputers first became popular in the business world, most businesses did not have general policies regarding them, which led to several problems. Many businesses developed acquisition policies to solve the compatibility problem, established information centers to provide assistance to users, and created the position of microcomputer manager to ensure coordination of microcomputer use.

- Microcomputer acquisition policies may include establishing standards for hardware and software, limiting the number of vendors, and limiting the hardware and software that the MIS department will support.

- An **information center** typically offers employees classes on a variety of computer topics, advice on selecting software, help in getting data from corporate computer systems, and technical assistance on such matters as hardware purchases and requests to the MIS department.

- The main concerns of a **microcomputer manager** are (1) avoiding technology overload, (2) monitoring all the expenses connected with microcomputers, (3) being aware of potential data security problems when users **download** data from the corporate mainframe to their own microcomputers, and (4) setting guidelines for microcomputer use to combat user-abusers.

- An increasing number of business executives use their own microcomputers to assist them in strategic planning (mainly through spreadsheets, database access, and graphics) and communication (mainly through electronic mail and word processing).

- A **decision support system** (**DSS**) is a computer system that supports managers in nonroutine decision-making tasks. A DSS involves a **model,** a

mathematical representation of a real-life situation. A computerized model allows a manager to try various "what if . . ." options by varying the inputs (**independent variables**) to see how they affect the outputs (**dependent variables**). The use of a computer model to reach a decision about a real-life situation is called **simulation.** Since the decision-making process must be fast, the DSS is interactive, allowing the user to communicate directly with the computer system and affect its activities.

- An **expert system** is a software package, used with an extensive set of organized data, that presents the computer as an expert on some topic. A user can ask questions, often in a natural-language (English-like) format, and the system can respond with an answer and an explanation of the answer. An organization that wants an expert system can purchase an existing one, develop its own, or add the appropriate knowledge to an **expert shell** that already contains the basic structure to find answers to questions.

- One debate among computer industry analysts concerns whether expert systems are approaching **artificial intelligence,** the ability of a program to understand facts, come up with new thoughts, and engage in coherent conversation.

## Review Questions

1. Describe the five main functions of managers, explaining how the emphasis varies with the level of management.

2. What is an MIS? Why is an integrated MIS the most effective type?

3. Define the following terms: detail report, summary report, exception report, periodic report, and on-demand report.

4. Explain how the various types of MIS reports are related to the different management levels and functions.

5. Explain why the MIS manager can be regarded as a powerful person within a company.

6. Name the three main microcomputer management problems and explain how they arose.

7. Describe three common methods through which MIS departments control microcomputer acquisition.

8. Describe the functions of an information center.

9. Describe four ways in which a microcomputer manager can help a company.

10. Discuss why an executive might buy a microcomputer.

## / Discussion Questions

1. Describe a problem situation that could be simulated through a decision support system. Specify the input factors and the types of output.

2. If you were seeking information on a complex topic, which source would you prefer—an expert system or a human expert? Explain your answer.

# 19

# Security, Privacy, and Ethics

## Protecting Hardware, Software, and Data

Computer security has not kept up with the rapid growth of the computer industry. With more people and more computers, the security problem becomes complex. In this chapter we shall examine the most manifest security breach—computer crime. Then we shall explore security needs for hardware, software, and data. We shall also consider privacy and the safeguarding of personal information and the issue of computer ethics.

Todd Meredith was fourteen when he stood outside the gates of Allied Chemical one fine spring afternoon. Todd had a winning way about him, and he bestowed his best aw-shucks smile on Allied employees as they streamed out of the building after work. He waylaid as many of them as he could. Would they mind—he stumbled over the words—just filling out a little survey for a school project? He handed each one a form to fill out. Sure. No problem. The questions were simple; they asked about their job descriptions, what kinds of equipment they were trained to use (including computers), and their hobbies, type of car, children's names, pets, and so forth.

These agreeable people did not know it, but they had walked right into a trap because Todd is a **hacker.** A hacker is a person who gains access to computer systems illegally, usually from his or her own personal computer. Todd has used his home computer to access Allied computers, but he needs passwords to actually trespass into employee files. Passwords, as Todd well knows, are usually assigned by the employees themselves. What is more, people often choose passwords that have personal meanings, such as their children's names, because they are easy to remember. And therein lies Todd's devious scheme: Ask the employees themselves!

Farfetched? Not at all. This story—except for the names—is true. It could happen again tomorrow because few employees choose passwords with care and because hackers are endlessly creative. Hacker stories make fascinating reading, but hackers are only a blip on the security problem. The security of computers and computer-related information is a large, critical issue. Let us begin by examining the most fascinating of security breaches: computer crime.

# Computer Crime

Although teenage hackers are a real annoyance, the most serious losses are caused by electronic pickpockets who are a good deal older and not half so harmless. Consider these examples.

- A Denver brokerage clerk sat at his terminal and, with a few taps of the keys, transformed 1700 shares of his own stock worth $1.50 each to the same number of shares in another company worth ten times that much.

- A Seattle bank employee used her electronic fund transfer code to move money to the account held by her boyfriend as a "joke"; both the money and the boyfriend disappeared.

- In an Oakland department store, a keyboard operator changed some delivery addresses to divert several thousand dollars worth of store goods into the hands of accomplices.

- A ticket clerk at the Arizona Veteran's Memorial Coliseum issued full-price basketball tickets, then used her computer to record the

## DIAMONDS ARE A BANK'S BEST FRIEND

Stanley Mark Rifkin had been a computer consultant for a Los Angeles bank, so his face was familiar to the guards. That is how he was able to slip by one day—with a friendly wave—into the bank's wire transfer room, where he obtained the electronic fund transfer code for the day. Later, posing as a bank manager, he called and used the code to transfer over $10 million to his own account in a New York bank. Stanley was on the next plane to New York, where he removed the funds and flew to Switzerland to deposit them in a Swiss bank account. He then drew from that account to invest in diamonds.

This story has an interesting twist. Stanley flew back to the United States and stopped off in New York to visit an old friend. He could not resist bragging about his feat. The friend was horrified and immediately notified the authorities. Stanley was arrested and convicted. The bank, ironically, came out ahead: The recovered diamonds were worth more than the original stolen funds.

sales as half-price tickets and pocketed the difference.

These stories point out that computer crime is not necessarily a romantic activity done by geniuses and involving millions of dollars.

Stories about computer crime continue to fascinate the general public. They are "clean" white-collar crimes; no one gets physically hurt. They often feature people beating the system—that is, beating an anonymous, faceless, presumably wealthy organization. Sometimes the perpetrators even fancy themselves as modern-day Robin Hoods, taking from the rich to give to the poor—themselves and their friends. One electronic thief, in fact, described himself as a "one-man welfare agency."

Computer crime is serious business, however, and deserves to be taken seriously by everyone. After all, if computer criminals can steal money from major banks, can they not steal from you? If unauthorized persons can get at your money, can they not also get at your medical records or private family history? It is not a long step between a thief violating your bank account and an unseen "investigator" spying on your private life.

The problems of computer crime have been aggravated in recent years by increased access to computers. More employees now have access to computers on their jobs. A great many more people are using home computers. And more students are taking computer training (Figure 19-1).

## The Computer Criminal: Who and Why?

Here is what a computer criminal is apt to be like. He (we shall use *he* here, but of course *he* could be *she*) is usually someone occupying a position of trust in an organization. Indeed, he is likely to be regarded as the ideal employee. He has had no previous law-breaking experience and, in fact, will not see himself as a thief but as a "borrower." He is apt to be young and to be fascinated with the challenge of beating the system. Contrary to expectations, he is not necessarily a loner; he may well operate in conjunction with other employees to take advantage of the system's weaknesses.

What motivates the computer criminal? The causes are as varied as the offenders. However, a few frequent motives have been identified. A computer criminal is often the disgruntled employee, possibly a long-time loyal worker out for revenge after being passed over for a raise or promotion. In another scenario an otherwise model employee may commit a crime while suffering from personal or family problems. Not all motives are emotionally based. Some people simply are attracted to the challenge of the crime. In contrast, it is the ease of the crime that tempts others.

In many cases the criminal activity is unobtrusive; it fits right in with regular job duties. One offender noted that his colleagues would never ask what he was doing; instead they would make comments like, "That turkey, that technician, all he ever does is talk his

## THE GAME THAT NEVER WAS

Jan Kegal and Ted Williams decided to pull their prank on national television at the biggest college game of them all—the Rose Bowl. Jan and Ted, students at CalTech, tampered with the software that runs the scoreboard, and rigged it to flash

CALTECH 38, MIT 9

at half time. Jan and Ted were just amusing themselves since no Cal-Tech–MIT game is played. Pasadena city officials were *not* amused, since their little caper caused $4200 worth of damage to the sign. Jan and Ted were put on probation and obligated to hours of community service.

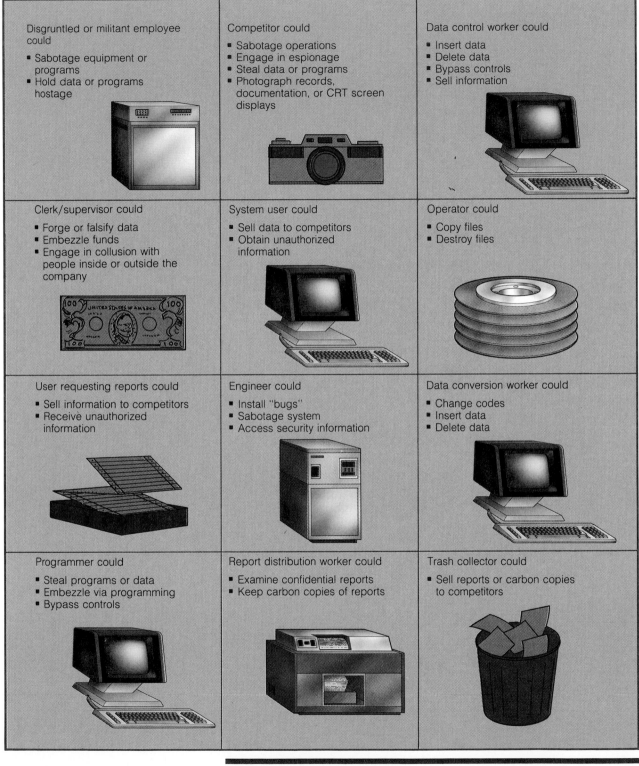

**Figure 19-1   The perils of increased access.** By letting your imagination run wild, you can visualize numerous ways in which people can compromise computer security. Computer-related crime would be far more rampant if all of the people in these positions took advantage of their access to computers.

## A GLOSSARY FOR COMPUTER CROOKS

Although the emphasis in this chapter is on preventing rather than committing crime, it is worthwhile being familiar with computer criminal terms and methods. Many of these words or phrases have made their way into the general vocabulary.

**Data diddling:** Changing data before or as it enters the system.

**Data leakage:** Removing copies of data from the system without a trace.

**Logic bomb:** Sabotaging a program to trigger damage based on certain conditions and usually set for a later date—perhaps after the perpetrator has left the company.

**Piggybacking:** Using another person's identification code or using that person's files before he or she has logged off.

**Salami technique:** Using a large financial system to squirrel away small "slices" of money that may never be missed.

**Scavenging:** Searching trash cans for printouts and carbons containing not-for-distribution information.

**Trapdoor:** Leaving an illicit program within a completed program that allows unauthorized—and unknown—entry.

**Trojan horse:** Placing covert illegal instructions in the middle of a legitimate program.

**Zapping:** Bypassing all security systems with an illicitly acquired software package.

buzzwords, can't talk to him," and walk away. So the risk of detection is often quite low. Computer criminals think they can get away with it. And they do—some of the time.

## Computer Crime Types and Methods

Computer crime falls into three basic categories:

- Theft of computer time for development of software, either for personal use or with the intention of selling it.

- Theft, destruction, or manipulation of programs or data.

- Alteration of data stored in a computer file.

While it is not our purpose to be a how-to book on computer crime, the margin note called "A Glossary for Computer Crooks" mentions some criminal methods as examples.

## Discovery and Prosecution

Prosecuting the computer criminal is difficult because discovery is often difficult. Many times the crime simply goes undetected. In addition, crimes that are detected are—an estimated 85% of the time—never reported to the authorities. By law, banks have to make a report when their computer systems have been compromised, but other businesses do not. Often they choose not to report because they are worried about their reputations and credibility in the community.

Most discoveries of computer crimes, unfortunately, happen by accident. For example, a bank employee changed a program to add 10¢ to every customer service charge under $10 and one dollar to every charge over $10. He then placed this overage into the last account, a bank account he opened himself in the name of Zzwicke. The system worked fairly well, generating several hundred dollars each month, until the bank initiated a new marketing campaign in which they singled out for special honors the very first depositor—and the very last. In another instance some employees of a city welfare department created a fictitious work force, complete with Social Security numbers, and programmed the computer to issue paychecks, which the employees would then intercept and cash. They were discovered when a police officer found an illegally parked overdue rental car—and found 7100 fraudulent checks inside.

Even if a computer crime is detected, a prosecution is by no means assured. There are a number of reasons for this. First, some law enforcement agencies do not fully understand the complexities of computer-related fraud. Second, few attorneys are qualified to handle computer crime cases. Third, judges and juries are not educated in the ways of computers and may not consider data valuable.

In short, the chances of committing computer crimes and having them go undetected are, unfortunately, good. And the chances that,

## ACTUAL PROOF THAT CRIME DOES NOT PAY

District attorney Nolan Brown of Jefferson County, Colorado, was worried about his insurance premiums. He asked a motor vehicle bureau employee to delete a pair of speeding tickets from the department's computer system. They don't fool around in Colorado: Mr. Brown was convicted of computer crime, forgery, and abuse of public records. What is more, he was sentenced to five days in jail, fined $2000, placed on probation for four years, and ordered to perform 200 hours of community service. He also resigned. All this to save a few dollars on insurance premiums.

if detected, there will be no ramifications are also good: A computer criminal may not go to jail, may not be found guilty if prosecuted, and may not even be prosecuted.

But this situation is changing. In 1984 Congress passed the **Computer Fraud and Abuse Act,** which covered crimes involving United States government computers. In 1986 the Act was expanded to include interstate computer crimes in the private sector. The law makes it a federal misdemeanor to traffic in stolen passwords or trespass in a computer to observe or obtain data; it is a felony to steal by computer or alter or destroy computer data. In 1986 the Electronic Communications Privacy Act was also passed, which outlaws the interception of data communications, such as electronic mail and electronic funds transfers. These federal laws are supplemented by state statutes. As of this writing, 45 of the 50 states have passed some form of computer crime law. The number of safe places for computer desperados is dwindling fast.

# Security: Keeping Everything Safe

As you can see from the previous section, the computer industry has been extremely vulnerable in the matter of security. Until fairly recently, computer security meant the physical security of the computer itself—guarded and locked doors. But locking up the computer by no means prevents access, as we have seen. Since the mid-1970s, management interest in security has been heightened, and MIS managers are now rushing to purchase more sophisticated security products.

What is security? We may define it as follows: **Security** is a system of safeguards designed to protect a computer system and data from deliberate or accidental damage or access by unauthorized persons. That means safeguarding the system against such threats as burglary, vandalism, fire, natural disasters, theft of data for ransom, industrial espionage, and various forms of white-collar crime.

## Who Goes There? Identification and Access

How does a computer system detect whether you are the person who should be allowed access to it? Various means have been devised to give access to authorized people without compromising the system. They fall into four broad categories: what you have, what you know, what you do, and what you are.

- **What you have.** You may have a key or a badge or a plastic card to give you physical access to the computer room or a locked up terminal. A card with a magnetized strip, for example, can give you access to your bank account via a remote cash machine.

- **What you know.** Standard what-you-know items are a system password or an identification number for your bank cash machine.

Cipher locks on doors require that you know the correct combination of numbers.

- **What you do.** Your signature is difficult but not impossible to copy. Signatures lend themselves to human interaction better than machine interaction.

- **What you are.** Now it gets interesting. Some security systems use **biometrics,** the science of measuring individual body characteristics. Fingerprinting is old news, but voice recognition is relatively new. Both of these techniques are now in use along with other procedures. They enable a machine to recognize a properly authorized human.

Some systems use a combination of the preceding four categories. For example, access to an automated teller machine requires both something you have—a plastic card—and something you know—a personal identification number.

## When Disaster Strikes: What Do You Have to Lose?

In Italy armed terrorists singled out corporate and state computer centers as targets for attack, and during a ten-month period bombed ten such centers throughout the country. In the United States industrial espionage has been on the rise. In a famous case IBM security staff helped the FBI arrest employees of two leading Japanese electronics firms, who were charged with conspiring to transport stolen IBM property out of the United States. Computer installations of any kind can be struck by natural or man-made disasters that can lead to security violations. What kinds of problems might this cause an organization?

Your first thoughts might be of the hardware, the computer and its related equipment. But loss of hardware is not a major problem in itself; the loss will be covered by insurance, and hardware can be replaced. The true problem with hardware loss is the diminished processing ability that exists while managers find a substitute facility and return the installation to its former state. The ability to continue processing data is critical. Some information industries, such as banking, could literally go out of business in a matter of days if their data processing operations were suspended.

Loss of software should not be a problem if the organization has heeded industry warnings—and used common sense—to make backup copies.

A more important problem is the loss of data. Imagine trying to reassemble lost or destroyed master files of customer records, accounts receivable, or design data for a new airplane. The costs would be staggering. We shall consider software and data security in more detail later in this chapter. First, however, let us present an overview of disaster recovery, the steps to restoring processing ability.

## Disaster Recovery Plan

A **disaster recovery plan** is a method of restoring data processing operations if those operations are halted by major damage or destruction. There are various approaches. Some organizations revert temporarily to manual services, but life without the computer can be difficult indeed. Others arrange to buy time at a service bureau, but this is inconvenient for companies in remote or rural areas. If a single act, such as a fire, destroys your computing facility, it is possible that a mutual aid pact will help you get back on your feet. In such a plan, two or more companies agree to lend each other computing power if one of them has a problem. This would be of little help, however, if there were a regional disaster and many companies needed assistance.

Banks and other organizations with survival dependence on computers sometimes form a **consortium,** a joint venture to support a complete computer facility. Such a facility is completely available and routinely tested but used only in the event of a disaster. Among these facilities, a **hot site** is a fully equipped computer center, with hardware, environmental controls, security, and communications facilities. A **cold site** is an environmentally suitable empty shell in which a company can install its own computer system.

The use of such a facility or any type of recovery at all depends on advance planning—specifically, the disaster recovery plan. The idea of such a plan is that everything except the hardware has been stored in a safe place somewhere else. The storage location should be several miles away, so it will not be affected by local physical forces such as a hurricane. Typical items stored there are program and data files, program listings, program and operating systems documentation, hardware inventory list, output forms, and a copy of the disaster plan manual.

The disaster recovery plan should include these items:

- **Priorities.** This list identifies the programs that must be up and running first. A bank, for example, would give greater weight to account inquiries than to employee vacation planning.

- **Personnel requirements.** Procedures must be established to notify employees of changes in locations and procedures.

- **Equipment requirements.** Planners list needed equipment and where it can be obtained.

- **Facilities.** Most organizations cannot afford consortiums, so an alternative computing facility must be located.

- **Capture and distribution.** This part of the plan outlines how input and output data will be handled in a different environment.

Remember the fire drills when you were in grammar school? They may have been a bit of a lark for you and your friends, but the school officials knew how important they were. A little practice can make all the difference if a true emergency strikes. The same is true for computer installations. They actually practice emergency drills. At some unexpected moment a notice is given that "disaster has struck," and the computer professionals must run the critical systems at some other site.

## Software Security

Software security has been an industry concern for years. It was first posed as a question: Who owns a program? Is the owner the person who writes a program or the company for whom the author wrote the program? What is to prevent a programmer from taking listings of programs from one job to another? Or, even simpler, what is to prevent any user from copying microcomputer software onto a floppy disk or cassette?

These perplexing questions do, however, have answers. If a programmer is in the employ of the organization, the program belongs to the organization, not the programmer. If the programmer is a consultant, however, the ownership of the software produced should be spelled out specifically in the contract—otherwise, the parties enter extremely murky legal waters.

According to a U.S. Supreme Court decision, software can be patented. Our last questions, unfortunately, also have easy answers: Very little can be done to prevent the stealing of microcomputer software. Although it is specifically prohibited by law, software continues to be copied as blatantly as music from tape to tape. We shall examine this issue more closely when we consider ethics later in the chapter.

## Data Security

We have discussed the security of hardware and software. Now let us consider the security of data, which, as we said, is one of an organization's most important assets. Here too there must be planning for security. Usually, this is done by security officers who are part of top management. There are five critical planning areas for data security:

- Determination of appropriate policies and standards. A typical statement of policy might read: "All computer data and related information will be protected against unauthorized disclosure and against alteration or destruction."

- Development and implementation of security safeguards such as passwords.

- Inclusion of new security precautions at the development stage of new automated systems, rather than after the fact.

### THE PARTY SEASON: SECURITY ON THE BRINK

'Tis the season to lose output, divulge passwords, and, especially, allow unauthorized persons into the computer room. Although these and other computer-related breaches do not occur exclusively during the holiday season, well-intentioned security tends to sag as spirits soar. Lax security and parties sometimes mix in such a way that a computer organization becomes vulnerable. Security managers must strike a balance between acting like Scrooge and Santa Claus to maintain a secure shop during the festive season. Although it is not usually necessary to install extra measures, it probably is necessary to be particularly alert to mistakes.

- Review of state and federal laws related to security. This is particularly significant in banking.

- Maintenance of historical records associated with computer abuse.

What steps can be taken to prevent theft or alteration of data? There are several data protection techniques; these will not individually (or even collectively) guarantee security, but at least they make a good start.

### Secured Waste

Discarded printouts, printer ribbons, and the like can be sources of information to unauthorized persons. This kind of waste can be made secure by the use of shredders or locked trash barrels.

### Passwords

As we mentioned earlier, passwords are the secret words or numbers that must be typed on the keyboard to gain access to the system. In some installations, however, the passwords are changed so seldom that they become known to many people. And some groups even tape a password right on the terminal. (In a case prosecuted by the federal government, the defendant admitted that he got a secret code by strolling into the programmer area and yelling, to no one in particular, "Hey, what's the password today?" He got an answer.) Good data protection systems change passwords often and also compartmentalize information by passwords, so that only authorized persons can have access to certain data.

### Internal Controls

Internal controls are controls that are planned as part of the computer system. One example is a transaction log. This is a file of all accesses or attempted accesses to certain data.

### Auditor Checks

Most companies have auditors go over the financial books. In the course of their duties, auditors frequently review computer programs and data. From a data security standpoint, auditors might also check to see who has accessed data during periods when that data is not usually used and who has received unusually high overtime payments. They can also be on the lookout for unusual numbers of correction entries of data, usually a trouble sign. What is more, the availability of off-the-shelf audit software—programs that assess the validity and accuracy of the system's operations and output—promotes tighter security because it allows auditors to work independently of the programming staff.

### Cryptography

Data being sent over communications lines may be protected by scrambling the messages—that is, putting them in code that can be broken only by the person receiving the message. The

---

## BULLETIN BOARDS UNDER ATTACK

Bulletin boards provide wonderful advantages to users calling in from across town or across the country. Participants give software hints, exchange news, sell wares, and share a variety of information. But there is one bit of sharing that authorities think goes beyond mischief: sharing the phone numbers and passwords—that is, access—to computer systems. Some bulletin boards carry such information as casually as they post the time of the next club meeting. Information that is supposed to be a closely guarded secret is on view for the bulletin board public. One government official noted that you might as well have a billboard on the street that says "Here is the combination to the bank vault in case you want to use it." In some states legislation has been introduced to curb such practices.

## SOME GENTLE ADVICE ON SECURITY

Security experts often are consultants who move from company to company. They often write books and articles in which they usually include long and detailed checklists. Do this, do that, and you will be OK. We cannot attempt such a set of lists, but here is a small subset that includes some of the most effective approaches.

- **Beware of disgruntled employees.** Ed Street was angry. Seething. How could they pass over him for a promotion again? Well, if they were not going to give him what he deserved, he would take it himself. . . . Ah, the tale is too common. Be forewarned.

- **Sensitize employees to security issues.** Most people are eager to help others. They must be taught that some kinds of help, such as assisting unauthorized users with passwords, are inappropriate. Most security breaches are possible because people are ignorant, careless, or too helpful.

- **Call back all remote-access terminals.** Don't call us, we'll call you. If you arrange a computer-kept list of valid phone numbers for access to your system, you eliminate most hackers. With such a system the computer has to call the caller back for the user to gain remote access, and it will do so only if the user's number is valid. The fact that the hacker has the computer's phone number is irrelevant. What matters is: Does the computer have the hacker's?

- **Keep personnel privileges up to date.** And, we might add, make sure they are enforced properly. "Hi, Bill, how ya doin'?" "Pretty good, Frank, good to see you." Bill, the guard, has just swept unauthorized Frank into the computer area. Some of the biggest heists have been pulled by people who *formerly* had legitimate access to secured areas. They can often still get in because the guard has known them by sight for years.

process of scrambling messages is called **encryption.** The American National Standards Institute has endorsed a process called **Data Encryption Standard** (**DES**), a standardized public key by which senders and receivers can scramble and unscramble their messages. Although the DES has been broken, companies still use it because the method makes it quite expensive to intercept coded messages, forcing interlopers to use other methods of gathering data that carry greater risk of detection. Encryption software is available for personal computers. Borland's SuperKey, for example, offers (among other things) a variety of security features: file encryption, keyboard lock, and password protection.

### Applicant Screening

The weakest link in any computer security system is the people in it. At the very least, employers should verify the facts that job applicants list on their resumes to help weed out dishonest applicants before they are hired.

### Separation of Employee Functions

Should a programmer also be a computer operator? That would put him or her in the position of being able not only to write unauthorized programs but also to run them. By limiting employee functions so that crossovers are not permitted, a computer organization can restrict the amount of unauthorized access. Unfortunately, separation of functions is not practical in a small shop; usually one or more employees perform multiple functions.

### Built-in Software Protection

Software can be built into operating systems in ways that restrict access to the computer system. One form of software protection system matches a user number against a number assigned to the data being accessed. If a person does not get access, it is recorded that he or she tried to tap into some area to which they were not authorized. Another form of software protection is a user profile: Information is stored about each user, including the files to which the user has legitimate access. The profile contains each person's job function, budget number, skills, areas of knowledge, access privileges, supervisor, and loss-causing potential. These profiles are available for checking by managers if there is any problem, but they may in some ways violate a person's privacy, a subject we shall discuss shortly.

## Security Considerations for Personal Computers

One summer evening two men in coveralls with company logos backed a truck up to the building that housed a university computer lab. They showed the lab assistant, a part-time student, authorization to move 23 personal computers to another lab on campus. The assistant was surprised but not shocked, since lab use was light in the summer quarter. The computers were moved, all right, but not to another lab. There is an active market for stolen personal computers and their internal components. As this unfortunate tale indicates, personal computer security breaches can be pretty basic. One simple, though not foolproof, remedy is to lock micro hardware in place.

In addition to theft personal computer users need to be concerned about the computer's environment. Personal computers in business are not coddled the way bigger computers are. They are designed, in fact, to withstand the wear and tear of the office environment, including temperatures set for the comfort of people. Most manufacturers discourage eating and smoking near computers and recommend some specific cleaning techniques, such as vacuuming the keyboard and cleaning the disk drive heads with a mild solution. The enforcement of these rules is directly related to the awareness level of the users.

Most personal computer data is stored on diskettes, which are vulnerable to sunlight, heaters, cigarettes, scratching, magnets, theft, and dirty fingers. The data, consequently, is vulnerable as well. Hard disk used with personal computers is subject to special problems too. If a computer with a hard disk is used by more than one person, your files on the hard disk are available for anyone to browse through.

There are several precautions that can be taken to protect disk data. One is to use a **surge protector,** a device that prevents electrical problems from affecting data files. The computer is plugged into the surge protector, which is plugged into the outlet. Another precaution is to back up all files. Hard disk files should be backed up on diskettes or tape. Diskettes should be under lock and key.

Awareness of personal computer security needs is gradually rising. However, security measures and the money to implement them are directly related to the amount of the expected loss. Since the dollar value of personal computer losses is often relatively low, personal computer security may be less than vigorous.

# Privacy: Keeping Personal Information Personal

Think about the forms you have willingly filled out: paperwork for loans or charge accounts, orders for merchandise through the mail, magazine subscription orders, applications for schools and jobs and clubs, and on and on. There may be some forms you filled out with less delight—for taxes, military draft registration, court petitions, insurance claims, or a stay in the hospital. And remember all the people who got your name and address from

## THE MICROCOMPUTER CORNER

### Your Own Security Checklist

With the subject of security fresh on your mind, now is a good time to consider a checklist for your own personal computer and its software. We shall confine this list to a computer presumed to be in the home.

- No eating, drinking, or smoking near the computer.

- Do not place the computer near open windows or doors.
- Do not subject the computer to extreme temperatures.
- Clean equipment regularly.
- Place a cable lock on the computer.
- Use a surge protector.

- Store disks properly in a locked container.
- Maintain backup copies of all files.
- Store copies of critical files off site.

your check—fund-raisers, advertisers, and petitioners. We have only skimmed over the possibilities, but we can say with certainty where all of this information went: straight to a computer file.

Where is that data now? Is it passed around? Who sees it? Will it ever be expunged? In some cases we can only guess at the answers. It is difficult to say where the data is now, and bureaucracies often are not anxious to enlighten us. It may have been moved to other files without our knowledge. In fact, much of the data is most definitely passed around, as anyone with a mail box can attest. (A gentleman in Colorado deliberately put his name on every list he could find and received enough junk mail to heat his house—with a wood stove—for the winter.) As for who sees your personal data, the answers are not comforting. Government agencies, for example, regularly share data that was originally filed for some other purpose. IRS records, for example, are compared with draft registration records to catch dodgers and also with student loan records to intercept refunds to former students who defaulted on their loans. More recently, the IRS created a storm of controversy by announcing a plan to use commercial direct-mail lists to locate tax evaders. Many people are worried about the consequences of this kind of sharing (Figure 19-2). And finally, few of us can be certain that data about us, good or bad, is deleted when it has served its legitimate purpose.

There are matters you want to keep private. You have the right to do so. Let us see what kind of protection is available to preserve privacy.

Significant legislation relating to privacy began with the **Fair Credit Reporting Act** in 1970. This law allows you to have access to and gives you the right to challenge your credit records. In fact, this access must be given to you free of charge if you have been denied credit.

Businesses usually contribute financial information about their customers to a community credit bureau, which gives them the right to review a person's prior credit record with other companies. Before

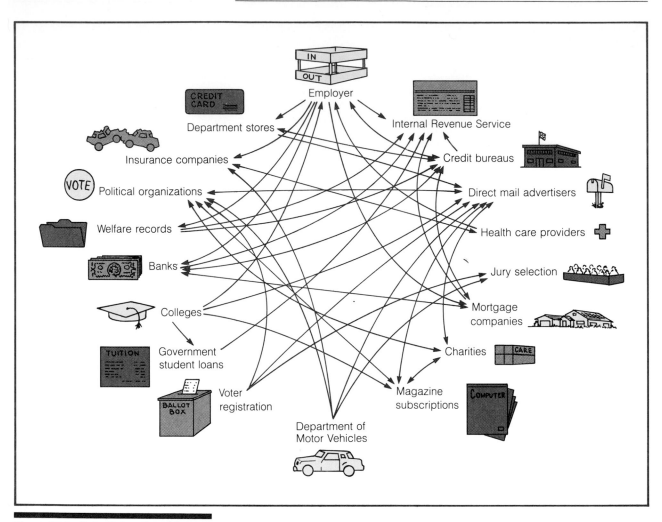

**Figure 19-2   Potential paths of data.**
When an organization acquires information about you, it is often shared with—or sold to—other organizations.

the Fair Credit Reporting Act, many people were turned down for credit without explanation because of inaccurate financial records about them. Under the act people may now check their records (usually for a nominal fee, if they have not been turned down for credit) to make sure they are accurate. The **Freedom of Information Act** was also passed in 1970. This landmark legislation allows ordinary citizens to have access to data about them that was gathered by federal agencies (although sometimes a lawsuit has been necessary to pry data loose).

The most significant legislation in the privacy area was the **Federal Privacy Act** of 1974. Born out of post-Watergate fears, the Federal Privacy Act stipulates that there can be no secret personal files, that individuals must be allowed to know what is stored in files about them and how it is used, and that the law applies not only to government agencies but also to private contractors dealing with government agencies. These organizations cannot obtain data willy-nilly, for no specific purpose; they must justify obtaining it.

This act applies to the government and its contractors, but it

## ACRES OF COMPUTERS

It is true—literally. Acres of computers, $5\frac{1}{2}$ acres. And many of them underground, too. They could belong to none other than the federal government, specifically the National Security Agency, which keeps a low profile with much behind-the-scenes activity. Experts say it has the largest computer complex in the world.

This profusion of crime-fighting and spying computers, some of them secret, has privacy advocates worried. These critics say that the incredible power of today's computer systems offers an immense potential for abuse.

does not apply to the private sector. However, the last sentence of the act reads: "A commission will be formed to study privacy in the private sector." The resulting Privacy Commission published a thick document, the heart of which consisted of some basic principles on which to build a privacy act for the private sector.

The Privacy Commission also recommended that Social Security numbers be restricted to authorized use, that no new system should rely on these numbers for unique identification purposes, and that a separate group be established to monitor the use of Social Security numbers. It further recommended that the federal government not foster the development of a unique identification.

The Privacy Act is not as effective as originally planned. Critics note that it still permits agencies to exchange information, virtually without restriction. The act is ineffective mainly because no single person or agency is in charge of enforcement. No watchdog, nothing watched.

What are the side effects of privacy legislation? Does it hamper customer service, give corporations yet another set of regulations to complain about, and add to the cost of doing business? Cost may indeed be the decisive factor in this matter. We all want privacy, but you can be sure private enterprise will pass the costs of ensuring it along to us. Are we prepared to pay the price?

## A Matter of Ethics

There has always been the problem of professional computer personnel having access to files. In theory, they could do something as simple as snooping into a friend's salary on a payroll file or as complex as selling military secrets to foreign countries. But the problem has become more tangled as everyday people—not just computer professionals—have daily contact with computers. They have access to files, too. Many of those files are on floppy disks and may be handled in a careless manner. As we noted earlier, data is the resource most difficult to replace, so increased access is the subject of much nail biting among security officers.

Where do you come in? As a student you could easily face ethical problems involving access and much more. Try some of these. A nonstudent friend wants to borrow your password to get access to the school computer. Or you know of a student who has bypassed computer security and changed grades for himself and some friends. Perhaps a "computer freak" pal collects software and wants you to copy a commercial disk used in one of your classes. And so on.

The problems are not so different in the business world. You will recognize that, whether you are a computer professional or a user, you have a clear responsibility to your own organization and its customers to protect the security and privacy of their information. Any compromise of data, in particular, is considered a serious

### THE DATA PROCESSING MANAGEMENT ASSOCIATION'S CODE OF ETHICS

In recognition of my obligation to my employer, I shall: make every effort to ensure that I have the most current knowledge and that the proper expertise is available when needed; avoid conflicts of interest and ensure that my employer is aware of any potential conflicts; protect the privacy and confidentiality of all information entrusted to me.

breach of ethics. Many corporations have formal statements saying as much and present them to employees individually for their signatures.

If you plan to be a computer professional, you will be bombarded by articles on ethics in the trade press. Professional ethics for the computer industry is also a key topic at conferences and a lament in the halls of lawmakers. Any theme that gets this much attention usually results in action.

Most experts talk of self-regulation via the professional computer organizations. Several organizations, such as the Data Processing Management Association (DPMA) and the Association for Computing Machinery (ACM), already have a code of ethics. Handling this "among ourselves" is considered preferable to regulation imposed by a federal agency.

Let us move from general principles of ethics into the thorny issue of software copying, also known as **software piracy.** Consider this incident. Bill Huston got his data processing degree at a local community college. One of his courses taught him how to use software on microcomputers. He had access to a great variety of software in the college computer lab. After graduating, he got a job at a local museum, where he used database software on a microcomputer to help them catalogue museum wares. He also had his own computer at home.

One day Bill stopped back at the college and ran into a former instructor. After greetings were exchanged, she asked him why he happened to drop by. "Oh," he said, "I just came by to pick up some free software." He wasn't kidding. Neither was the instructor who, after she caught her breath, replied, "You can't do that. It's illegal." Bill was miffed, saying "But I can't afford it" and, finally, "I'm sorry I mentioned it!" But the instructor was not sorry at all. She immediately alerted the computer lab. As a result of this encounter, the staff strengthened policies on software use and increased the vigilance of lab personnel. In effect, schools must protect themselves from people who lack ethics or are unaware of the law.

There are many people like Bill. He did not think in terms of stealing anything; he just wanted to make copies for himself. But, as the software industry is quick to point out, it *is* stealing because the software makers do not get the revenues to which they are entitled. Unfortunately, some corporations also have buccaneer ethics, and their attitude magnifies the software protection problem many times. Software piracy is met head-on by copy protection, the subject of the following section.

## The Copy Protection Mess

Have you ever copied a friend's record or tape onto your own blank tape? Many people do so without much thought. It is also possible to photocopy a book. Both are clearly illegal, but there is much more fuss over copying software than over copying music or books. Why is this? Well, to begin with, few of us are likely to undertake the laborious task of reproducing *War and Peace* on a copy machine. The other part of the issue is money. A pirated copy of a top-20 tape will set the recording company—and the artist—back about $10. But a pirated program may be valued at hundreds of dollars. The problem of stolen software has grown right along with the microcomputer industry.

## Why Those Extra Copies?

Copying software is not always a dirty trick—there are lots of legitimate reasons for copying. To begin with, after paying several hundred dollars for a piece of software, you will definitely want to make a backup copy in case of disk failure or accident. You might want to copy the program onto a hard disk and use it—more conveniently—from there. Or you might want to have one copy at the office and another to use at home. Software publishers have no trouble with any of these types of copying. But thousands of computer users copy software for another reason: to get the program without paying for it. And therein lies the problem. Software publishers place **copy protection** on their software—a software or hardware roadblock to make it difficult or impossible to make pirated copies. In effect, they punish the innocent with the guilty.

Those opposed to copy protection—and there are many—argue that it is unfair to restrict paying customers just to outsmart a few thieves. In addition to the legitimate reasons for making a copy just mentioned, some people insist that software makers cause the problem by pricing software too high. This kind of statement makes otherwise mild-mannered software people agitated. "Just because a Cadillac is expensive," said one, "doesn't mean you have the right to steal it." But piracy is rampant. Some have estimated bootlegged software at 40% of the market.

Some software manufacturers have decided to get tough. In 1984 Lotus Development Corporation, a leading purveyor of software, brought a suit against the Rixon Corporation for $10 million, charging them with making illegal copies of Lotus 1-2-3. The suit was settled out of court, but it served notice to the corporate community, which began pressing for permission to copy *legally*. Thus comes, carrying heavy baggage, site licensing. Can it solve the problem?

## Site Licensing

Although there is no clear definition industrywide, in general a **site license** permits a customer to make multiple copies of a given piece of software. The customer needing all these copies is usually a corporation, which can probably obtain a significant price discount for volume buying. The exact nature of the arrangement between the user and the software maker can vary considerably. Typically, however, a customer obtains the right to make an unlimited number of copies of a product, agrees to keep track of who uses it, and takes responsibility for copying and distributing manuals to its own personnel.

The advantages seem to be all on the user's side:

- A big price break, sometimes as high as 50%.

- The availability of as many copies as needed.

- Freedom from potential lawsuits from the software vendor.

The software maker, on the other hand, stands to lose money and is unenthusiastic about giving anyone a license to copy its work. So why would any software manufacturer subscribe to this? The main reason is sales. The "little guys" are accepting licensing because they can get large sales that would normally go to the more established software vendors. Another reason is that corporate customers with enormous clout are bringing pressure to bear. Who can ignore General Electric or Exxon? Even the microcomputer software industry's largest publishers are aggressively planning discount programs.

## Paying Attention Because We Must

The issues raised in this chapter are often the ones we think of after the fact—that is, when it is too late. The security and privacy factors are somewhat like insurance that we wish we did not have to buy. But we do buy insurance for our homes and cars and lives because we know we cannot risk being without it. The computer industry also knows that it cannot risk being without safeguards for security and privacy. As a computer professional, you will share responsibility for addressing these issues. As a computer user, in whatever capacity, you can take comfort in the fact that the computer industry recognizes their importance.

## Summary and Key Terms

- A **hacker** is a person who gains access to computer systems illegally.

- Computer criminals are likely to be trusted employees with no previous law-breaking experience. Many are motivated by resentment toward an employer, by personal or family problems, by the challenge of beating the system, or the tempting ease with which the crime can be committed.

- Three basic categories of computer crime are: (1) theft of computer time for development of software; (2) theft, destruction, or manipulation of programs or data; and (3) alteration of data stored in a computer file.

- Prosecution of computer crime is often difficult because law enforcement officers, attorneys, and judges are usually unfamiliar with the issues involved. However, in 1984 Congress passed the **Computer Fraud and Abuse Act,** which is supplemented by local laws in most of the states.

- **Security** is a system of safeguards designed to protect a computer system and data from deliberate or accidental damage or access by unauthorized persons. Common threats include burglary, vandalism, fire, natural disasters, theft of data for ransom, industrial espionage, and various forms of white-collar crime.

- The means of giving access to authorized people are divided into four general categories: (1) what you have (a key, badge, or plastic card), (2) what you know (a system password or identification number), (3) what you do (by signing your name), and (4) what you are (by making use of **biometrics,** the science of measuring individual body characteristics such as fingerprints or voice).

- Loss of hardware and software is generally less of a problem than loss of data. Loss of hardware should not be a major problem, provided that the equipment is insured and a substitute processing facility is found quickly. Loss of software should not be critical, provided that the owner has taken the practical step of making backup copies. However, replacing lost data can be quite expensive.

- A **disaster recovery plan** is a method of restoring data processing operations if they are halted by major damage or destruction. Common approaches to disaster recovery include relying temporarily on manual services, buying time at a computer service bureau, making mutual assistance agreements with other companies, or forming a **consortium,** a joint venture with other organizations to support a complete computer facility.

- A **hot site** is a fully equipped computer facility with hardware, environmental controls, security, and communications equipment. A **cold site** is an environmentally suitable empty shell in which a company can install its own computer system.

- A disaster recovery plan should include: (1) priorities indicating which programs must be running first, (2) personnel requirements specifying where employees should be and what they should do, (3) equipment requirements, (4) an alternative computing facility, and (5) specifications for how input and output data will be handled in a different environment.

- Software can be patented. If a programmer is employed by an organization, any program written for the organization belongs to the employer. If the programmer is a consultant, however, the contract must clearly state whether it is the organization or the programmer that owns the software.

- There are five critical planning areas for data security: (1) determination of appropriate policies and standards, (2) development and implementation of security safeguards, (3) inclusion of security precautions during development of new automated systems, (4) review of state and federal laws related to security, and (5) maintenance of historical records associated with computer abuse.

- Common means of protecting data are securing waste, separating employee functions, and implementing passwords, internal controls, auditor checks, cryptography, applicant screening, and built-in software protection.

- Data sent over communications lines can be protected by **encryption,** the process of scrambling messages. The National Standards Institute has endorsed a process called **Data Encryption Standard** (**DES**).

- Personal computer security includes such measures as locking hardware in place, providing an appropriate physical environment, and using a **surge protector,** a device that prevents electrical problems from affecting data files.

- The security issue also extends to the use of information about individuals that is stored in the computer files of credit bureaus and government agencies. The **Fair Credit Reporting Act** allows individuals to check the accuracy of credit information about them. The **Freedom of Information Act** allows people access to data that federal agencies have gathered about them. The **Federal Privacy Act** allows individuals access to information about them that is held not only by government agencies but also by private contractors working for the government. Individuals are also entitled to know how that information is being used.

- An important issue relating to computer ethics is illegal software copying, also called **software piracy.** Software purchasers are allowed to make a backup copy, but copying software to avoid paying for it is illegal.

- Software publishers frequently put **copy protection** on their software, which makes copying difficult or impossible. Critics of this policy argue that in the process of preventing theft it unfairly restricts paying customers.

- In response to pressure from corporate customers, many software publishers offer a **site license,** which permits a customer to make multiple copies of a given piece of software.

## Review Questions

1. What are some common motivations for computer crime?

2. What are the three main categories of computer crime?

3. Why is it often difficult to find and prosecute a computer criminal?

4. Name and describe the four general techniques for identifying authorized users.

5. Why is loss of data a more serious problem than loss of software or hardware?

6. What should a disaster recovery plan include and why?

7. Name five critical planning areas for data security.

8. Describe the security considerations for personal computers.

9. Name three privacy laws and explain why each one was enacted.

10. What is site licensing?

## Discussion Questions

1. Before accepting a particular patient, a doctor might like access to a computer file listing patients who have been involved in malpractice suits. Before accepting a tenant, the owner of an apartment building might want to check a file that lists people who have previously sued landlords. Should computer files be available for such purposes? Explain your answer.

2. Discuss your reaction to the following statement: "Some software is just too expensive for the average personal computer owner to buy. Besides, I am only copying my friend's disk for personal use."

# Appendix A
## A Course of Programming in BASIC

This appendix explains how to design and run some simple programs in BASIC, the computer language whose name is an acronym for Beginners' All-purpose Symbolic Instruction Code. To make sure this discussion is meaningful to you, you should first read Chapter 8, "Beginning Programming," which explains how program logic is developed and the rules of flowcharting.

BASIC was invented in 1965 by John Kemeny and Thomas Kurtz for use at Dartmouth College as a simple language for beginners in programming. With the explosive growth of microcomputers, the language has become widely popular, and—gradually—more sophisticated BASIC versions have emerged. As a result, there is no one standard version of BASIC. Thus, you may find different versions at different computer installations. This diversity means we cannot be comprehensive here in describing BASIC. However, we shall present the common features, and where there are known variations, we shall mention them.

## Getting Started

Following is a simple BASIC program that will be used to illustrate some elementary BASIC concepts. At this point you will not completely understand how the program works, but if you read through it you will see that even without a knowledge of the language, you can understand much of what the program is instructing the computer to do.

A brief word of explanation is needed. The lines numbered from 100 to 999 represent the listing of the BASIC program. The word RUN is an instruction to the computer; RUN tells it to execute the program. The program is followed by the output generated by the program as it executes.

*Example 1*

```
100 REM THIS PROGRAM PRODUCES A CHART OF MONTHS
110 REM AND THE NUMBER OF DAYS FOR EACH MONTH.
120 REM
130 REM          MONTH$ = MONTH NAME
140 REM          DAYS = NUMBER OF DAYS PER MONTH
150 REM          COUNTER = LOOP COUNTER
160 REM
170 PRINT "MONTH", "NAME", "DAYS"
180 PRINT
190 FOR COUNTER = 1 TO 12
200     READ MONTH$, DAYS
210     PRINT COUNTER, MONTH$, DAYS
220 NEXT COUNTER
230 REM          DATA
240 DATA JANUARY,31,FEBRUARY,28,MARCH,31,APRIL,30
250 DATA MAY,31,JUNE,30,JULY,31,AUGUST,31
260 DATA SEPTEMBER,30,OCTOBER,31,NOVEMBER,30,DECEMBER,31
999 END

RUN
```

| MONTH | NAME | DAYS |
|---|---|---|
| 1 | JANUARY | 31 |
| 2 | FEBRUARY | 28 |
| 3 | MARCH | 31 |
| 4 | APRIL | 30 |
| 5 | MAY | 31 |
| 6 | JUNE | 30 |
| 7 | JULY | 31 |
| 8 | AUGUST | 31 |
| 9 | SEPTEMBER | 30 |
| 10 | OCTOBER | 31 |
| 11 | NOVEMBER | 30 |
| 12 | DECEMBER | 31 |

The program begins with comments, lines that explain the program but are not executed. Lines 170 and 180 print the headings and a blank line, respectively. Lines 190 through 220 form a loop—that is, they are executed repeatedly, 12 times in this case. Line 200 picks up data from line 240, JANUARY for MONTH$ and 31 for DAYS, and line 210 prints that information. This process is repeated until the last month is read and printed, at which time the program stops. This minimal explanation is just to give you a handle; these BASIC statements and all the others will be explained in detail in the sections that follow.

A program is a series of instructions telling the computer how to solve a problem. In BASIC programming each statement is composed of a line number, a BASIC command or instruction, and various **parameters,** which are elements that complete the skeleton structure whose functions are to change a general format into a specific format. Example 2 shows the format for a BASIC statement.

*Example 2*

**Statement Format:**
Line number INSTRUCTION Parameters

**Sample Statement:**
```
200     READ MONTH$, DAYS
```

## Line Numbers

Every BASIC statement appears on a separate line and has its own **line number.** The line number can be any whole number between 1 and 9999. Although programmers can number the statements 1, 2, 3, . . . , it is common programming practice to number the lines by tens rather than by ones. This numbering system allows the programmer to insert a statement between two existing statements without having to renumber the entire program. The computer will perform statements in numerical order unless specifically instructed otherwise. Each line number can be used only once. If the programmer uses a number that has been used previously, the last statement with that number will replace any previous one. This is a technique that programmers often use to correct lines containing errors. Example 3 illustrates what takes place.

*Example 3*

```
190 FOR COUNTRE = 1 TO 12
```
This statement contains an error.

```
190 FOR COUNTER = 1 TO 12
```
This correct statement replaces the previous statement.

Likewise, if you want to delete a line from a program, enter the number of the line to be deleted and press the Return key. The line will be deleted from the program.

Sometimes programmers use one line number for more than one instruction by separating each instruction with a colon. For example:

```
170 PRINT "MONTH", "NAME", "DAYS": PRINT
```

Although this saves time by reducing keying, it produces a program listing that is not as easy to read and understand. Therefore, we will not use this technique.

## The REM Statement

A BASIC instruction called a **REMARK** instruction, abbreviated **REM,** allows the programmer to include lines in the program listing that the computer will not execute. There are many instances when the programmer wants to include **documentation,** or information concerning the program, to make it easier for a future reader to understand. The REM statement provides the capability to document internally.

If a REM statement requires more than one line, each line must have a unique line number and a REM instruction. Because the REM statements are helpful to future readers, they should be used throughout the program. Since the computer will ignore all REM statements during translation, the program will execute the same way whether or not there are any REM statements in it.

Suggested uses for the REM statement include:

1. Explaining the program or segments of the program
2. Defining variable names—that is, programmer-assigned names of locations in memory
3. Adding blank lines within the program to increase readability

The statements in Example 4 tell the reader what the program is about, but BASIC will ignore these statements. Therefore, they will not be executed.

*Example 4*

```
100 REM THIS PROGRAM PRODUCES A CHART OF MONTHS
110 REM AND THE NUMBER OF DAYS FOR EACH MONTH.
```

## The END Statement

The **END** statement tells the computer that the last program statement in the program has been reached. The END statement also terminates execution. There is only one END statement, and it has the highest line number in the program. Frequently, programmers assign line number 9999 to the END statement to make certain that it will be the last one. See Example 5.

*Example 5*

**Statement Format:**
Line number END

**Sample Statement:**
9999 END

## The STOP Statement

The **STOP** statement terminates program execution. In fact, a program can contain more than one STOP statement, thus creating the possibility of stopping the program in different places. Where the program stops depends on the circumstances of a particular program run. For example, it is possible that certain input data may cause the program to stop, but another program run using different data may run to a normal completion stop. Both the END statement and the STOP statement, when encountered, cause program execution to terminate. The difference between the two statements is that there is only one END statement, and it must be the last program statement.

*Example 6*

**Statement Format:**
Line number STOP

**Sample Statement:**
320 STOP

## Variables

The purpose of writing programs is to process data to produce a predetermined, desired output such as a phone bill or an inventory report. The data that will be processed must be placed into memory locations during the execution of the program, and the values of the data in these storage locations may change as the processing occurs. With BASIC we do not know which memory locations are used to store the data, but we must have a method for identifying each of our elements of data so that the computer can store and retrieve them as needed. We accomplish this by naming each of our data elements, then referring to them by this assigned name. The programmer-assigned name for the memory location where the data is kept is called a **variable.** The computer finds locations in memory and associates them with the given variable names, then it is able to reference the desired data. Example 7 illustrates this:

*Example 7*

| Data | Memory location |
|------|----------------|
| JANUARY | Variable name is MONTH$ |

When the programmer uses the variable name MONTH$, the computer retrieves the data JANUARY from its memory location.

The variables that we use consist of:

1. Numeric characters **(numeric fields)**
2. Alphabetical characters or a combination of alphabetical and numeric characters **(alphanumeric fields)**

These two types of variables are handled slightly differently.

### Numeric Variables

A **numeric variable** is a name for a memory location that is to contain only numbers as data. The method of naming variables differs among systems. All variable names must start with a letter, but the number of characters in the name depends on the system. Throughout this appendix we shall assume the capability of using up to 40 characters. Sample numeric variable names are COST, T1, and A.

### Alphanumeric Variables

An **alphanumeric variable,** also called a **string variable,** is the name for a memory location for data that is composed of either alphabetical characters or a combination of alphabetical, numeric, and/or special characters. To name these variables, use the same naming rules that apply to the numeric variables but follow the name with $. Sample variable names are NAMES$, ADDRESS$, and DESCRIPTION$.

It is the programmer's responsibility to name the variables. It is good programming practice to assign names that make sense or coincide with the type of data being identified. For example, if we were naming a storage location that is to contain the names of employees, we might name it NAMES$. An appropriate name for a field to contain the number of books read might be BOOKS or NUMBER. This method of assigning the variable a name that reflects the contents of the storage location helps the programmer remember the variable name used and also makes it easier for someone else to read and understand the program.

We have already discussed the use of a REM statement for documenting the name given to a particular variable. Example 8 illustrates this use.

*Example 8*

```
130 REM          MONTH$ = MONTH NAME
150 REM          COUNTER = LOOP COUNTER
```

## Constants

A **constant** is a fixed value. Much of the processing we do involves manipulation of constants. We are able to put constants into the computer in several ways, and we receive constants as output. (The methods of input and output will be described later.) There are two types of constants: (1) **numeric constants** and (2) **alphanumeric constants.**

### Numeric Constants

There are three types of numeric constants allowed in BASIC:

1. Integers
2. Decimals
3. Exponential forms of numbers

When expressing any numeric constant, do not include commas or dollar signs because these symbols are reserved for other purposes.

**Integers** are numbers without decimal points. Integers can be either positive or negative, including zero. If you input a number without a decimal point, the system assumes the decimal point belongs to the right of all given digits. If the number is a negative number, it should be preceded by a minus sign. If there is no minus sign, the system will assume it is a positive number.

The following are examples of integers:

```
12    -3    0
```

**Decimals** are numbers that include a decimal point. These decimal numbers can be either positive or negative. Examples of decimals are

```
18.    -15.03    21.8    0.0506
```

The **exponential form of numbers** is used to express either very large or very small numbers. This form is also called **scientific notation,** and the numbers are sometimes referred to as floating-point constants. Scientific notation involves raising a number to a power. The following are examples of the exponential form of numbers:

```
2.53E-04    54.23E02
```

These numbers are in a shorthand style. The number 2.53E-04 means that 2.53 is multiplied by 10 to the power—the exponent—of minus 4, or .0001. Multiplying 2.53 by .0001 gives .000253, the equivalent of 2.53E-04. Similarly, 54.23E02 means that 54.23 is multiplied by 10 to the power of 2, or 100, so 54.23E02 is the same as 5423.

### Alphanumeric Constants

BASIC programming allows for alphanumeric constants as well as numeric constants. These alphanumeric data are referred to as **character strings,** or **literals.** A character string is one or more letters, numbers, or special characters and must be enclosed within quotation marks. The only character that cannot be included in a character string is a quotation mark. If you need a quotation mark within the string, use the single quotation (apostrophe). When character strings are used within the program, they are enclosed within quotation marks, but when they are output, the quotation marks are not displayed. Example 9 illustrates this concept.

*Example 9*

```
100 REM THIS PROGRAM ILLUSTRATES THE USE OF QUOTATION
110 REM MARKS WITH ALPHANUMERIC CHARACTER STRINGS
120 PRINT "THIS IS A CHARACTER STRING"
999 END

RUN

THIS IS A CHARACTER STRING
```

Alphanumeric data cannot be used for calculations. This is because alphanumeric data can include alphabetical, numeric, and special characters, and you cannot calculate with a letter of the alphabet or with a special character, such as &.

The following are examples of character strings:

```
"C"    "DATA"    "PROGRAMMING IN BASIC"    "CALCULUS 205"    "#$%%"
```

## System Commands

Up to this point you have been learning some BASIC programming commands or instructions such as REM and END. While you are entering a program into the computer, or after you have completed entering it, you need to communicate with the operating system of your computer to tell it what to do with the program. These instructions to the operating system are called **system commands.**

There are a number of different system commands. These instruct the computer to perform activities such as displaying a program on the screen or printer, executing a program, or starting a new program. Only the most common commands will be presented here, and it is important to keep in mind that the commands may differ from one system to another. All systems can perform these functions, but you may have to refer to your instruction manual for the exact system commands for your particular computer.

A very simple BASIC program is presented here to let you try some of the system commands and see what results from each. At this point you may not understand all of the program statements. If you make an error as you enter a statement of the program, the computer displays an error message, or **diagnostic,** on the screen. If that happens, reenter the complete, correct statement.

```
100 REM THIS PROGRAM WILL BE USED TO TRY
110 REM SOME SYSTEM COMMANDS.
120 LET X = 2 + 2
130 PRINT X
999 END
```

Now you are ready to try a system command. When you first logged onto the computer and told the operating system that you were going to work with a BASIC program, the operating system allocated an area in memory for you to use, an area called **work space.** When you keyed in your program, it was placed in this work space. Any intermediate or final results of program execution will also be placed there.

## LIST and LLIST

The first command to try is **LIST.** LIST instructs the computer to display on the screen each line of the program that is in the work space.

Simply key in, on a line by itself (without a line number), the word LIST, press the Return key, and see what happens. You should see the five lines you keyed in previously appear on the screen. Always use LIST to see your program, then verify that it is correct before executing it.

**LLIST** instructs the computer to print the contents of the work space on the printer rather than on the screen.

Let us manipulate the program a little to demonstrate some of the programming concepts already presented. Do you remember that we numbered our lines by increments of ten so we could add lines without retyping the complete program? Try it. Key in:

```
125 LET Y = 4 + 4
135 PRINT Y
```

These lines are added to the existing program. Now use LIST to see your program. Your program should look like Example 10.

*Example 10*

```
100 REM THIS PROGRAM WILL BE USED TO TRY
110 REM SOME SYSTEM COMMANDS.
120 LET X = 2 + 2
125 LET Y = 4 + 4
130 PRINT X
135 PRINT Y
999 END
```

Notice that the new lines have been added into the program according to numerical order. Placing them in order helps you read and understand the program, but even if you had not used LIST to see the program, the computer would have performed the instructions in numerical order.

Now key in LLIST. The program listing should be directed to your printer to produce a hard copy of the program.

## RUN

Shall we see if the program works? When you have finished your program or a portion of your program and you want the computer to execute your instructions, key in the system command **RUN** and press the Return key. RUN instructs the operating system to actually perform the statements of the program that are located in the work space. Try it. Based on our preceding program, what you should see on the screen is shown in Example 11. Be sure to note that system commands are *not* preceded by line numbers.

*Example 11*

```
4
8
```

If you did not get the correct output, you probably made an error as you entered the program. In that case your computer may have given you a message such as: "SYNTAX ERROR IN LINE 120."

Each system has unique methods for correcting errors; you will need to refer to your instruction manual to learn how to perform such editing functions as inserting characters, deleting characters, and replacing characters. One method you can use at this point to correct an error, however, is to retype the line number, then type the correct instruction and parameters. Recall that you can use this procedure to replace the previous incorrect line with a new line that has the same number. Try it. Key in:

```
120 LET X = 5 + 5
```

Notice that, by using line number 120, the original line numbered 120 is replaced. LIST your program to verify that this is true. Now use RUN to execute the program. Your output should look like Example 12.

*Example 12*
```
10
8
```

A line can be deleted by keying only the line number of the line to be removed. Let us delete two lines from the program. Key in:

```
120
130
```

Now LIST the program again, and you can see that lines 120 and 130 are indeed gone. If you RUN the program again, the result is a single 8 on the screen.

## NEW

If you want to start your program over or begin another program, key in the system command **NEW.** This command erases the work space and your program. Key in NEW and press the Return key. Now use LIST to see your program. Nothing! The program is gone.

If you neglect to key in the word NEW before starting another program, the first program will remain in the work space; as you enter the second program, it will become part of the first program. When you key in line 100 of the second program, for example, it will replace line 100 of the first program. If there are line numbers in the first program that are not used in the second program—that is, the lines are not replaced—those old lines will show up in a listing of your combined first and second program.

## SAVE

There will be numerous occasions when you will write a program and want to keep it to use at some future time. Because the size of your memory is limited and because memory is volatile (that is, what is not saved on a secondary storage medium will disappear when the computer is turned off), you will want to store the program on whatever secondary storage medium your system uses—probably magnetic disk. This requires a system command that will vary depending on your system, but the command will probably be **SAVE.** If you want to call your program PROGX, for example, a typical command is SAVE "PROGX", which places PROGX on the disk for future use. Refer to your instruction manual.

## LOAD

You saved your file on your secondary storage medium to have it available for use at a future time. When you are ready to use the file, you will need to copy it back into memory. Although the system command to copy the file from secondary storage to the work space in primary storage varies among systems, LOAD is frequently used. Notice that the file is *copied* to primary storage; therefore, it also remains on your secondary storage medium. The command, typically, is LOAD "PROGX". Now PROGX is in memory and on the disk.

## Additional System Commands

Some of the other system commands that you will probably need to use will enable you to perform the following:

1. Delete programs that you no longer need from secondary storage.
2. Display a list of the names of all programs (files) you have stored on your secondary storage medium.

Because the system commands for these and many other activities differ substantially among computers, you must refer to your instruction manual for specific system commands.

## Exercises

Key in the following program:

```
100 REM THIS PROGRAM WILL PROVIDE ADDITIONAL PRACTICE.
110 LET A = 5
120 LET B = 8
130 LET C = 13
140 PRINT A + B + C
999 END
```

1. Use LIST to see the program. What is displayed?

2. Use RUN to execute the program. What are the results?

3. Key the following lines:

```
150 LET D = (A + B + C) / 2
160 PRINT D
```

Use LIST to see the program. What is displayed?

4. Use RUN to execute the program. What are the results?

5. Delete line number 140. Use RUN to execute the program. What are the results?

6. Remove one of the parentheses in line number 150. Use RUN to execute the program. What happens?

/ **Answers to Exercises**

1. The original program should be displayed.

2. 26

3. 
```
100 REM THIS PROGRAM WILL PROVIDE ADDITIONAL PRACTICE
110 LET A = 5
120 LET B = 8
130 LET C = 13
140 PRINT A + B + C
150 LET D = (A + B + C) / 2
160 PRINT D
999 END
```

4. 26
   13

5. 13

6. A message will indicate a syntax error in line 150.

## //▌ Output

Data processing applications involve some form of input, processing, and output. Building on the concepts just presented, various methods for inputting information from the computer will be explained later. At this point we shall focus on output.

Providing information in an appropriate format is one of the primary goals of programming. Output, then, is of tremendous importance, and techniques that provide it need to be thoroughly understood.

### The PRINT Statement

The BASIC instruction used to output information from the computer onto the terminal is **PRINT.** This is illustrated in Example 13. Notice that the statement format has the instruction name—PRINT, in this case—in capital letters.

*Example 13*          **Statement Format:**
Line number PRINT Parameters

**Sample Statement:**
280 PRINT "CUSTOMER NO", NUMBER

The PRINT instruction is used to print parameters that are numeric constants, character strings, or the value of variables at the time the PRINT statement is executed. We shall examine each of these in the next three sections. Output using the PRINT statement might be a heading in a report, a detail data line, or a total line, incorporating the variables and constants as needed. Let us take a closer look at how printing works.

### Printing Numeric Constants

To print a numeric constant, simply follow the instruction PRINT with the desired numeric constant, as shown in Example 14.

*Example 14*

**Sample Statement:**
```
160 PRINT -13
```

**Output:**
```
-13
```

We are now able to write a simple program. Notice the output when we use RUN to execute the program in Example 15.

*Example 15*
```
100 REM THIS PROGRAM ILLUSTRATES PRINTING NUMERIC CONSTANTS.
110 PRINT 1
120 PRINT 2
130 PRINT 3
999 END

RUN

  1
  2
  3
```

Since the REM statement was only for internal documentation, it did not result in any output. The three PRINT statements instructed the computer to print the numeric constants 1, 2, 3 on separate lines.

### Printing Character Strings

To print a character string, follow the PRINT instruction with the desired literal output. Do not forget to enclose the character string in quotation marks. Whatever is within the quotes is printed. Example 16 illustrates this procedure.

*Example 16*

**Sample Statement:**
```
130 PRINT "YEARLY SALES REPORT"
```

**Output:**
```
YEARLY SALES REPORT
```

Example 17 illustrates the use of the PRINT command to output character strings.

*Example 17*
```
100 REM THIS PROGRAM USES CHARACTER STRINGS AS OUTPUT
110 REM TO PROVIDE INSTRUCTIONS TO THE USER.
120 PRINT "ENTER YOUR NAME, SOCIAL SECURITY NUMBER AND"
130 PRINT "ADDRESS."
140 PRINT "SEPARATE EACH BY COMMAS."
999 END
```

*Example 17 continues*

*Example 17, continued*   RUN

```
ENTER YOUR NAME, SOCIAL SECURITY NUMBER AND
ADDRESS.
SEPARATE EACH BY COMMAS.
```

Again, the REM statements did not result in any output. The three PRINT statements instructed the computer to output the three character strings on separate lines, one line per PRINT statement.

### Printing Variables
A variable value can also be part of the output. To incorporate a variable value, follow the PRINT instruction with an appropriate variable name. Upon execution the computer will print the current value of the variable on the screen. See Example 18, in which STEPHEN RYAN has been assigned to the variable NAMES$. That is, STEPHEN RYAN is the actual data in the memory location called NAMES$.

*Example 18*   **Sample Statement:**

```
280 PRINT NAMES$
```

**Output:**

```
STEPHEN RYAN
```

The program in Example 19 uses the PRINT command for character strings, numeric constants, and variables. At this point we must assume that the computer has established the value of the variable. (Caution: This program is incomplete. If you key and RUN it, it will not give the output shown here. This is because we have *assumed* that there is already a data value in the variable NAMES$.)

*Example 19*
```
100 REM THIS PROGRAM USES THE PRINT COMMAND TO OUTPUT
110 REM CHARACTER STRINGS, NUMERIC CONSTANTS, AND
120 REM VARIABLES.
130 PRINT NAMES$;" WILL BE YOUR INSTRUCTOR."
140 PRINT "THERE WILL BE";30;"STUDENTS IN THAT CLASS."
150 PRINT "PLEASE BE ON TIME TO YOUR CLASS."
999 END

RUN

ANN ROGER WILL BE YOUR INSTRUCTOR.
THERE WILL BE 30 STUDENTS IN THAT CLASS.
PLEASE BE ON TIME TO YOUR CLASS.
```

The first PRINT statement instructs the computer to print a variable value—ANN ROGER—followed by a character string. The second PRINT statement instructs it to print character strings and a numeric constant—30. The third PRINT statement instructs the computer to print a character string. The spacing of the output lines will be discussed in the next section.

### Formatting Output

When the computer executes a PRINT instruction, the output is displayed at the left side of the screen. This placement is usually appropriate if there is only one item in the output. Frequently, however, you want the output to include multiple variable values, constants, or combinations of both. In that case you may follow the PRINT instruction with a list of parameters, each separated by a comma or semicolon, as in Example 20. The following sections describe the differences in using commas and semicolons.

*Example 20*

**Sample Statement:**
```
360 PRINT "CUSTOMER NAME",NAMES$
```

**Sample Statement:**
```
360 PRINT "CUSTOMER NAME";NAMES$
```

With BASIC programming the computer divides the output area (for example, the terminal screen) into **zones.** While the size of these zones may vary by computer, a common output area contains zones of 14 spaces each. A sample layout for a screen is shown in Example 21. (Microsoft BASIC uses five zones of 16 spaces each.)

*Example 21*

| Columns 1-14 Zone 1 | Columns 15-28 Zone 2 | Columns 29-42 Zone 3 | Columns 43-56 Zone 4 | Columns 57-70 Zone 5 | Columns 71-80 Zone 6 |
|---|---|---|---|---|---|

The placement of the output on the screen depends on whether you use a comma or a semicolon to separate the output parameters.

### Formatting Output with Commas

Separating the parameters in a PRINT statement with commas causes the information contained in each parameter to print out beginning at the next available zone. In Example 22 you can see the column number directly above each character string. The column numbers are used here as examples; they do not show on the screen.

*Example 22*

**Sample Statement:**
```
100 PRINT "SALESMAN","AMOUNT","DEPARTMENT"
```

**Output:**
```
1               15              29 ←─────────── Column number
SALESMAN        AMOUNT          DEPARTMENT
```

Notice that the commas between the character strings have placed SALESMAN beginning at column 1, AMOUNT beginning at column 15, and DEPARTMENT beginning at column 29. Each of these columns is the beginning of the next print zone.

The commas between parameters will have the same result if they are placed between two variables or between a character string and a variable. Assuming that WENDY DOUGLAS is in variable NAMES$, notice the output in Example 23.

*Example 23*

**Sample Statement:**
```
560 PRINT "WELCOME",NAMES$
```

**Output:**
```
1               15 ←─────────── Column number
WELCOME         WENDY DOUGLAS
```

If an output parameter is longer than the zone size, the output will continue into the next zone, and the following parameter will start at the beginning of the next available zone. This is illustrated in Example 24.

*Example 24*

**Sample Statement:**

```
180 PRINT "SALESPERSON OF THE YEAR",NAMES$
```

**Output:**

```
1               15          29 ←——————Column number
SALESPERSON OF THE YEAR      ERIN
```

The ability to use commas to separate parameters in PRINT statements is important when producing tabular reports—that is, reports with columns of data. The zones function like tab stops on a typewriter, and the columns can be positioned easily.

### *Formatting Output with Semicolons*

There will be many applications where you will not want the output results to be spaced so far apart. Look at the output in Example 25. Variable COST has been assigned the value 4000, and variable ITEM$ has been assigned the value "TERMINAL". The commas caused each item to print out beginning at the next print zone, leaving unattractive gaps. This is not the way we would want the sentence to appear. (On the output, the column numbers are correct, although this page width prohibits accurate placement.)

*Example 25*

**Sample Statement:**

```
180 PRINT "THE COST WOULD BE",COST,"FOR A NEW",ITEM$
```

**Output:**

```
1             15     29      43            57 ←——————Column number
THE COST WOULD BE    4000    FOR A NEW     TERMINAL
```

Placing semicolons between parameters in a PRINT statement instructs the computer to print out the information in the parameters so they are immediately next to each other, as shown in Example 26.

*Example 26*

**Sample Statement:**

```
150 PRINT "THE COST WOULD BE";COST;"FOR A NEW";ITEM$
```

**Output:**

```
THE COST WOULD BE 4000 FOR A NEWTERMINAL
```

But there is still a problem. Notice that in this example the semicolons between parameters did exactly what they were supposed to do—they caused the information in the parameters to print right next to each other. Although we did not want our line spread out the way it was when we used commas to separate parameters, we also do not want it to be printed with no spaces between words.

To correct this situation, it will be necessary to force desired spacing by enclosing spaces within the quotation marks. Remember the computer is going to print character strings exactly as they are contained within the quotation marks, and this includes any spaces. To correct the output in Example 26, we need to insert a space at the end of the character string, "FOR A NEW". For example:

**Sample Statement:**
```
150 PRINT "THE COST WOULD BE";COST;"FOR A NEW ";ITEM$
```

**Output:**
```
THE COST WOULD BE 4000 FOR A NEW TERMINAL
```

You might have noticed that we did not force a space before or after the numeric variable in Example 26. When a numeric value is printed, a space is reserved for the sign preceding the value. If the value is a positive value, no sign is printed, and a space is printed out. A space will automatically be printed following a numeric value. In Example 27, you can see illustrations of this concept.

*Example 27*     **Sample Statement:**
**Positive Value**
```
420 PRINT "TOTAL DUE";AMOUNT
```

**Output:**
```
TOTAL DUE 546
```

**Sample Statement:**
**Negative Value**
```
PRINT "TOTAL DUE";AMOUNT
```

**Output:**
```
TOTAL DUE -592
```

Of course, you can combine the spacing of output using both commas and semicolons as illustrated in Example 28.

*Example 28*     **Sample Statement:**
```
160 PRINT "MEGAN IS";AGE1,"BRIAN IS";AGE2,"RAYMOND IS";AGE3
```

**Output:**
```
MEGAN IS 9       BRIAN IS 12    RAYMOND IS 44
```

If you end a PRINT statement with a semicolon or a comma, it instructs the computer to print the information from the next PRINT statement on the same line, as illustrated in Example 29.

*Example 29*     **Sample Statement:**
```
280 PRINT "THREE BLIND MICE,"
290 PRINT "THREE BLIND MICE"
```

**Output:**
```
THREE BLIND MICE,
THREE BLIND MICE
```

**Sample Statement:**
```
280 PRINT "THREE BLIND MICE, ";
290 PRINT "THREE BLIND MICE"
```

**Output:**
```
THREE BLIND MICE, THREE BLIND MICE
```

At this point you should recognize that there are various methods for controlling the spacing in a PRINT statement. One very common use of the PRINT statement is to print headings on a report.

*Example 30*

```
100 PRINT "              MONTHLY REPORT"
110 PRINT
120 PRINT "SALES","PROFIT","LOSS"
130 PRINT
```

**Output:**
```
              MONTHLY REPORT

SALES              PROFIT              LOSS
```

In Example 30 spaces inserted in the character string in line 100 move the first heading line over to the right. Line 110 causes a blank line to be placed between the first and second heading lines. Commas between character strings in line 120 cause each to print starting at the next print zone. Line 130 causes a blank line to be printed after the second heading line.

### TAB Function

There will be times when formatting your output by using commas or semicolons to separate the parameters does not provide enough flexibility. For these instances BASIC provides a **TAB function,** which is used with the PRINT statement to improve control over the spacing in output. The TAB function operates like a tab on a typewriter and is very convenient for formatting columnar reports.

*Example 31*

**Statement Format:**
Line number PRINT TAB (N) Parameters      N is a column number

**Sample Statement:**
```
150 PRINT TAB(20) COST;TAB(40) ITEM$
```

The sample statement in Example 31 instructs the computer to have the value of COST printed out beginning at column 20 and the value of ITEM$ printed out beginning at column 40. The value of N in the statement format expresses the distance in columns from the left margin that the value should be printed and *not* how many columns from the previous printing position. The value of N must be a positive number that can be expressed with a numeric constant, a numeric variable, or an arithmetic expression.

Numeric variables, alphanumeric variables, and character strings can all be included in PRINT statements using the TAB function. See Example 32.

*Example 32*

**Sample Statement:**
```
230 PRINT TAB(2) "CITY";TAB(19) CITY$;TAB(29) DIST
```

**Output:**
```
2                19        29
CITY             SAN ANTONIO  456
```

Notice that the TAB function can be used more than once in a statement. Each use of the TAB function may be separated from the rest of the statement by semicolons.

## PRINT USING

Although the PRINT statement with the TAB function permits increased flexibility for formatting output, there will still be times when your formatting ability is limited. Most versions of BASIC provide a means for programmers to designate an exact picture of the desired output format. This feature uses the **PRINT USING** statement. The use of the PRINT USING statement will differ on most machines, but understanding the concepts here should enable you to adjust easily to your system's PRINT USING method.

Some of the things you may want to do with a PRINT USING statement are

1. Placing a dollar sign to the left of a value
2. Inserting commas in a long number
3. Controlling the placement of a decimal point
4. Lining up numbers in columns
5. Inserting plus or minus signs before or after numbers
6. Placing asterisks in unused positions to the left of numbers

Example 33 provides the statement format and a sample statement for the PRINT USING statement.

*Example 33*

**Statement Format:**
Line number PRINT USING "Literals and/or format";Variables and/or literals

**Sample Statement:**
130 PRINT USING "$##.##";TOTAL

The sample statement in Example 33 instructs the computer to output the current value of TOTAL according to the format provided between the quotation marks.

The PRINT USING statement can be used to format lines consisting of constants and/or variables. The constants and the variables may be either alphanumeric or numeric.

### *Numeric Formats*

The examples that follow illustrate some of the format notations used to produce specified numeric output.

Sample Format: ###
The number sign reserves space for one numeric character. Any digit 0 through 9 may be output for each number sign. Any unused positions to the left of the first significant digit will be filled with spaces.

Sample Format: $$###
Two dollar signs placed at the left of a format produce a floating dollar sign. The floating dollar sign causes a dollar sign to print out in the position immediately to the left of the first significant digit. One of the two dollar signs also reserves a space for a digit.

Sample Format: ###.##
A decimal point inserted within a format causes a decimal point to print out in that position.

Sample Format: ##,###

A comma inserted within a format causes a comma to print out in that position when the number is large enough to warrant it.

Example 34 illustrates output that will result from the use of various format notations.

*Example 34*

| Data in Memory | Format | Output |
|---|---|---|
| 684.23 | #,###.## | 684.23 |
| 57.23 | $$###.## | $57.23 |
| 2634.53 | $$##,###.# | $2,634.5 |

### String Formats

The PRINT USING statement can be used to output a line that includes string data—either constants or variables. The following examples illustrate the use of the PRINT USING statement to output string data.

*Example 35*

**Sample Format:**

```
\    \
```

**Sample Statement:**

```
400 PRINT USING "\          \";NAMES$
```

Backslashes reserve spaces for string data. The number of positions reserved is equal to the number of spaces between the two backslashes plus one for each of the backslashes. If the value of NAMES$ is "PEARL LEE", when the sample statement in Example 35 is executed, the output will be as shown below.

```
PEARL LEE
```

If the number of characters in the string is greater than the number of positions reserved by the backslashes, the rightmost characters will be truncated. If the number of characters in the string is less than the number of spaces reserved by the backslashes, spaces will be printed in the rightmost positions.

*Example 36*

**Sample Format:**

```
!
```

**Sample Statement:**

```
440 PRINT USING "!";LAST$
```

An exclamation mark instructs the computer to print the first character of a string. The sample statement in Example 36 instructs the computer to print the first character in the string LAST$. If the value of LAST$ is JEFFRIES, the output for this statement would be

```
J
```

The various numeric and string formats can be combined in one PRINT USING statement by inserting appropriate horizontal spacing as illustrated in Example 37.

*Example 37*

```
300 PRINT USING "\                \        ###.##";CUSTOMER$,DUE
```
**Output:**
```
ROGER STEWART    543.33
```

```
350 PRINT USING "!       !       !        ##";A$,B$,C$,V
```
**Output:**
```
J            A            T              45
```

```
350 PRINT USING "THE TOTAL IS $$###.## FOR \                \";T,I$
```
**Output:**
```
THE TOTAL IS $13.98 FOR ENVELOPES
```

```
450 PRINT USING "\        \       $$#.##";"TOTAL",3.99
```
**Output:**
```
TOTAL               $3.99
```

# INPUT

One technique for inputting data into the computer uses an INPUT statement; the other technique uses READ/DATA statements. The INPUT statement is used to input data into the computer as the program is executing, but the READ/DATA statements are used to provide data for the program prior to processing. Let us look at each in detail.

## The INPUT Statement

The **INPUT** statement is used when the program needs data supplied by a user in an interactive mode. This means that the user and computer are communicating as the program is executing; there is input from the user and output from the computer.

*Example 38*

**Sample Format:**
Line number INPUT Parameters

**Sample Statement:**
150 INPUT NAMES$

The INPUT command instructs the computer to obtain data that has just been keyed in and to place this data into memory locations. The sample statement in Example 38 tells the computer to obtain the data keyed in at the terminal, place it in memory, and assign the variable name NAMES$ to that memory location. From this point on, when the programmer uses the variable name NAMES$, whatever data is in that storage location will be retrieved.

An INPUT statement may have more than one alphanumeric or numeric variable as parameters. When there are more than one, separate each with commas. For example:

```
260 INPUT NAMES$,ADDRESS$,CITY$,STATE$
```

When the computer executes an INPUT statement, a question mark appears on the screen to inform the user that the computer is waiting for a response. The user must key in a response and press the Return key to make the data available to the computer. To help the user supply the desired data, the programmer uses a PRINT statement to **prompt** the user for data. For example, if the program needs the name and address of a person to process a credit application, the programmer may prompt for the correct data with the PRINT statement shown in Example 39. The highlighted rectangle indicates the information entered by the user. Notice that the INPUT statement caused a question mark to appear on the screen.

*Example 39*

```
280 PRINT "ENTER THE APPLICANT'S NAME AND ADDRESS"
290 PRINT "SEPARATED BY A COMMA."
300 INPUT NAMES$,ADDRESS$
999 END

RUN

ENTER THE APPLICANT'S NAME AND ADDRESS
SEPARATED BY A COMMA.
?RHONDA TRAINOR, 2008 DEER COVE LANE
```

If the variable named in the parameter is a numeric variable, the computer will not accept a user response that is not strictly numeric. If nonnumeric data is entered, the user receives a prompt from the computer to resubmit the data. Frequently, the prompt is the statement ?REDO FROM START. The computer will not execute the next statement until the INPUT statement has been satisfied, so the programmer needs to anticipate user responses when designing PRINT statements to be used as prompts.

## The READ and DATA Statements

When data is available before the program executes and when there is a large amount of data to input, the programmer may enter it into the computer through the use of **READ** and **DATA** statements. The READ statement instructs the computer to find values within the DATA statements and assign these values to the variables in the READ statement. See Example 40.

*Example 40*

**Statement Formats:**
Line number READ Parameters
Line number DATA Parameters

**Sample Statements:**
```
140 READ PRICE,DESCRIPTION$
350 DATA 250,END TABLES
```

The DATA statement provides the values to be assigned to the variables listed in the READ statement. In Example 40 value 250 is placed in the memory location whose variable name is PRICE. Similarly, END TABLES goes to the memory location whose variable name is DESCRIPTION$. A DATA statement may contain multiple constants (numeric or string) as parameters. If more than one constant is used, separate each with commas. Enclose string constants that include commas or semicolons with quotation marks. Some systems require quotation marks around all string constants.

If you indicate a numeric variable in a READ statement, be sure the corresponding DATA element is a numeric constant. If you have a numeric variable in the READ statement that is paired with an alphanumeric constant, a syntax error will occur. That is, the DATA statement cannot offer nonnumeric data when numeric data is expected.

A program may contain multiple DATA statements, and, although it is permissible to place the DATA statements anywhere within the program, it is common practice to place them in a group just preceding the END statement. The programmer may place READ statements throughout the program, wherever logic dictates.

The computer will access the data elements in the order in which they are found in the statements. It is not necessary to pair each READ statement with a DATA statement having the same number of elements. The only requirement is that the total number of elements within all DATA statements be sufficient to supply a data element for every parameter in all READ statements.

Each READ statement may contain multiple numeric or alphanumeric variables, each separated by a comma as shown in Example 41.

*Example 41*

```
160 READ POINTS,AVERAGE,TEAM$
300 DATA 89,76,SPARTANS
```

Upon executing statement 160, the computer establishes memory locations for the variables POINTS, AVERAGE, and TEAM$ and places the values 89, 76, and SPARTANS, respectively, into those locations. Any future reference to those three variables will enable the computer to retrieve or use the values now associated with them.

## / Exercises

1. Give an appropriate PRINT statement to produce the following output. (The underlined words are values of variables.)
   a. YOUR CHANGE WILL BE 2.53
   b. YOUR DATSUN 280ZX WILL GET 28 MILES PER GALLON.
   c. YOUR NEW BOSS WILL BE CLAYTON LONG.

2. Write a PRINT USING statement to produce the following output. (The items underlined are variable values.)
   GROSS SALARY $1,215.26          NET SALARY $1,042.99

3. Write a simple program that asks a person to key in his or her name at the terminal. The program places that name in memory, then displays it on the screen within a message.

4. Use the following statements to determine what values the listed variables have.

```
100 READ A,B,C,D$
160 READ T,Y$,S

300 DATA 152,-13,43.6,WILLIAM
310 DATA-10,TRIBUNE,194
```

a. B
b. D$
c. Y$
d. S

5. Give appropriate DATA statements to accompany the following READ statements.
   a. `230 READ N$,P,T`
   b. `240 READ I$,A`

## Answers to Exercises

1. a. `200 PRINT "YOUR CHANGE WILL BE";CHANGE`
   b. `200 PRINT "YOUR ";AUTO$;" WILL GET";GALLON;" MILES PER GALLON."`
   c. `200 PRINT "YOUR NEW BOSS WILL BE ";BOSS$;"."`

2. a. `200 PRINT USING "GROSS SALARY $$#,###.##";GROSS,`
      `210 PRINT USING "NET SALARY $$#,###.##";NET`

3. `100 REM THIS IS A SIMPLE PROGRAM TO USE THE PRINT AND INPUT`
   `110 REM STATEMENTS.`
   `120 PRINT "WHAT IS YOUR NAME?"`
   `130 INPUT NAMES$`
   `140 PRINT "HELLO, "NAMES$;" IT'S NICE TO MEET YOU."`

4. a. `-13`
   b. `WILLIAM`
   c. `TRIBUNE`
   d. `194`

5. The following are only a sample of the many possibilities. Just be sure that you show alphanumeric data for an alphanumeric field and numeric data for a numeric field.

   `550 DATA BILL,100,123`
   `560 DATA TRICYCLE,38.99`

## Calculations

We have examined ways to get data in and out of the computer. Now it is time to consider how to use data for calculations. We begin with the LET statement, which has several uses.

### The LET Statement

The INPUT and READ/DATA statements provide a means to enter data into your program. The LET statement provides a third method; the **LET** statement enables you to assign a value to a variable.

*Example 42*      **Statement Format:**
Line number `LET` Variable name = Arithmetic expression or constant

*Example 42 continues*

*Example 42, continued*

**Sample Statement:**
```
200 LET NET = GROSS - DEDUCTIONS
```

The LET statement is called an **assignment statement** because the variable to the left of the equal sign is assigned the value of the expression or constant to the right of the equal sign. In Example 42 numeric variable NET is assigned the value of the difference between the values GROSS and DEDUCTIONS. The value of NET is placed in memory to be used later, and it remains there until it is changed. The word LET is optional on most systems.

## Arithmetic Operations

There are five common arithmetic operations: (1) exponentiation, (2) addition, (3) subtraction, (4) multiplication, and (5) division. These are illustrated in Example 43.

*Example 43*

```
Addition          200 LET A = B + C
Subtraction       200 LET A = B - C
Multiplication    200 LET A = B * C
Division          200 LET A = B / C
Exponentiation    200 LET A = B ^ C
```

Notice the symbols used for exponentiation, multiplication, and division.

## Hierarchy of Operations

Combinations of mathematical operators and numeric variables and constants make up arithmetic expressions. The computer performs the mathematical operations according to a hierarchy. **Hierarchy** means the order from the top down; as applied to computer math, it means the order in which operations are performed. Since the computer works according to a hierarchy, so must you. Operations are performed in the following order: exponentiation, division and multiplication, then addition and subtraction. The computer evaluates an arithmetic expression moving from left to right performing mathematical operations according to the hierarchy. First, all exponentiation; then moving again from left to right, all multiplication and division; then, moving again from left to right, all addition and subtraction. Example 44 illustrates this concept. The circled numbers indicate the order of operation.

*Example 44*

```
              ①   ③   ②
240 LET B = 5 * 4 + 2 / 2
            20  + 2 / 2
            20  + 1
                 21
```

Example 44 demonstrates the order in which the computer solves the problem. Realize, of course, that the programmer enters only the LET statement, and the computer does not print intermediate results. The value of B that is calculated can be printed by using a PRINT statement, or it can be used in subsequent calculations.

## Using Parentheses

Often a programmer wants the computer to perform addition or subtraction *before* multiplication or division. Correct placement of parentheses within the arithmetic expression allows the programmer to do this.

The parentheses override the rules of the hierarchy. The computer performs the operations within parentheses first, then reverts to the rules of the hierarchy—division and multiplication first, followed by addition and subtraction. See Example 45.

*Example 45*

```
                    ①      ③      ②
    150 LET E = (2 + 5) * (6 - 4)
                   7       *     2
                           14
```

In statement 150 the computer performs the calculations of 2 + 5 and 6 − 4 first because each is within parentheses. After evaluating the expressions within the parentheses, the computer calculates the remainder of the expression which, in this case, is the multiplication of the interim values 7 and 2.

## Assigning a Value to a Variable Using LET

You can assign a value to a variable using a LET statement. This assignment is illustrated in Example 46.

*Example 46*

```
150 LET TOTAL = 0
160 LET COURSE$ = "BEGINNING BASIC"
```

Notice the quotation marks around the character string. These quotation marks are required by most systems.

## Writing Programs Using LET

Using the READ/DATA, INPUT, END, and PRINT statements, a programmer can incorporate the LET statement. The following programs illustrate principles covered to this point. The REM statements in each program tell which principle the program applies.

In the program in Example 47, the values for variables A, B, and C are assigned using the LET statement, then the values are used to calculate the value of variable D. (Note that multiplication is done before addition.)

*Example 47*

```
100 REM PRINTING A CALCULATION OF NUMERIC VARIABLES
110 LET A = 39
120 LET B = 20
130 LET C = 2
140 LET D = A + B * C
150 PRINT D
999 END

RUN

79
```

The PRINT statement is used in Example 48 to print a character string and the sum of two numbers.

*Example 48*

```
100 REM PRINTING A CHARACTER STRING AND THE RESULT OF A
110 REM CALCULATION
120 LET A = 5 + 4
130 PRINT "THE SUM OF 5 + 4 =";A
999 END

RUN

THE SUM OF 5 + 4 = 9
```

READ/DATA statements are used in Example 49 to supply variable values for the calculations to be performed in the program.

*Example 49*

```
100 REM PRINT A CHARACTER STRING AND THE RESULT OF A
110 REM CALCULATION USING READ/DATA STATEMENTS
120 PRINT "CALCULATION OF NUMERIC VARIABLES"
130 READ B,C
140 LET A = B * C
150 PRINT A
160 READ D,E
170 LET F = D + E
180 PRINT F
190 READ X,Y
200 LET Z = X / Y
210 PRINT Z
220 DATA 3,3
230 DATA 5,3
240 DATA 4,4
999 END

RUN

CALCULATION OF NUMERIC VARIABLES
 9
 8
 1
```

The program in Example 50 illustrates the use of the INPUT statement to supply the numeric values for the calculation in the LET statement. The highlighted rectangle indicates the numbers input by the user.

*Example 50*

```
100 REM CALCULATIONS USING THE INPUT STATEMENT
110 PRINT "ENTER 2 NUMBERS SEPARATED BY COMMAS"
120 INPUT X,Y
130 LET Z = X + Y
140 PRINT "THE SUM OF";X;"AND";Y;"IS";Z
999 END

RUN

ENTER 2 NUMBERS SEPARATED BY COMMAS
?4,10
THE SUM OF 4 AND 10 IS 14
```

Example 51 illustrates the use of the LET statement to set constant values and the use of the PRINT statement to print the values.

***Example 51***

```
100 REM PRINTING NUMERIC CONSTANTS
110 LET D = 10
120 LET A = 30
130 LET C = 50
140 PRINT D,A,C
999 END

RUN

    10              30              50
```

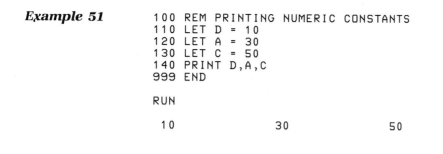

## Exercises

1. Determine the values for the variables in the following LET statements.

    a. LET D = 10 / 2 * 3 + 5
    b. LET A = 4 + 5 * 3 / 3
    c. LET T = 5 * 8 * (8 - 2) * (4 - 1)
    d. LET N = 6 / 2 + (4 + 4)

2. Correct any errors in the following statements:

    a. LET N = 3 - 2 X 1
    b. LET Z = TOTAL AMOUNT
    c. LET 4 = A
    d. LET A AND B = 0

3. What is the value of N in the following program?

```
100 LET A = 4
110 LET C = 10
120 LET T = A * C
130 LET N = C + T
140 PRINT N
999 END
```

4. Write a program to calculate the product of 6 and 4 and print the following output:

```
6 MULTIPLIED BY 4 = 24
```

## Answers to Exercises

1. a. 20
   b. 9
   c. 720
   d. 11

2. a. LET N = 3 - 2 * 1
   b. LET Z$ = "TOTAL AMOUNT"
   c. LET A = 4
   d. LET A = 0:LET B = 0

3. 50

```
4. 100 REM THIS PROGRAM CALCULATES THE VALUE OF 6
   110 REM MULTIPLIED BY 4.
   120 LET M = 6 * 4
   130 PRINT "6 MULTIPLIED BY 4 =";M
   999 END
```

## Sample Program: Floor Covering

The sample program in Example 53 on page 568 illustrates concepts that have been presented thus far. The flowchart used to design the logic of the problem is shown in Example 52b. Pseudocode for the problem is also included in Example 52a to give you the opportunity to compare the two design tools. Refer to Chapter 8 for an in-depth discussion of pseudocode as a program design tool. The flowchart in Example 52b includes circled numbers that correspond to the text discussion below. Statement numbers are included to the right of the flowchart symbols so that you can see how the flowchart symbols directly relate to the program. This program calculates the cost of floor covering. Data used in the calculations is input by the user.

*Example 52a*
*(Pseudocode for Example 53)*

**Pseudocode:**

```
Begin floor covering program
    Output general instructions
    Prompt for length and width
    Obtain length and width
    Prompt for price per square yard
    Obtain price per square yard
    Calculate area = length X width / 9
    Calculate cost = area X price per square yard
    Output area, price per square yard, and cost
End floor covering program
```

① Referring to the flowchart in Example 52b, step 1 indicates that general instructions to the user describe what the program does. The flowchart symbol used is the input/output symbol because we are writing information to the user on the screen.

② Step 2 in the flowchart involves prompting for and obtaining (inputting) the room dimensions from the user. (The user inputs the data.) The input/output symbols are used again.

③ Step 3 instructs the computer to prompt for and obtain the price per square yard from the user. Once again the input/output symbols are used. Notice that the notes within the symbols are *not* BASIC syntax. Rather than writing PRINT and INPUT, *prompt for* and *obtain* are used to indicate the processes that should occur. This technique of not using BASIC commands within notes allows the programmers to fully concentrate on the logical development of the program rather than to concern themselves at this point with BASIC syntax.

④ Step 4 initiates the processing that takes place, so a processing symbol is used. Two calculations must take place, as shown by the two separate processing symbols.

⑤ Step 5 writes a message to the user including the information calculated in the program: the number of square yards needed, the price per square yard, and the total cost based on this information.

***Example 52b***
*(Flowchart for
Example 53)*

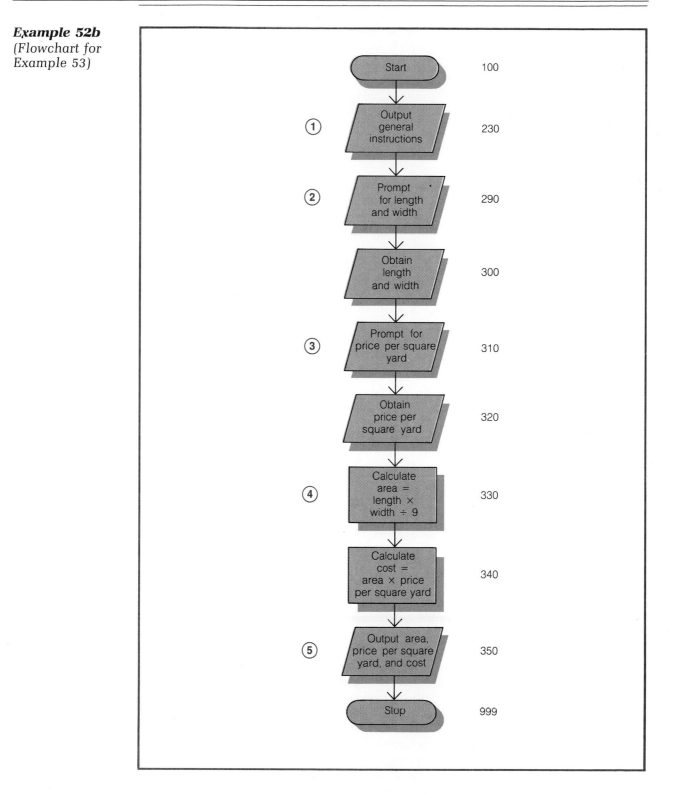

*Example 53*

```
100 REM COST OF FLOOR COVERING PROGRAM
110 REM
120 REM THIS PROGRAM CALCULATES COST OF FLOOR COVERING BASED
130 REM ON THE INPUT OF LENGTH AND WIDTH OF THE AREA TO
140 REM BE COVERED AND THE PRICE PER YARD ENTERED.
150 REM
160 REM     VARIABLE NAMES:
170 REM     LENGTH = LENGTH OF AREA
180 REM     WIDTH = WIDTH OF AREA
190 REM     YARD = PRICE PER YARD
200 REM     COST = TOTAL COST
210 REM     AREA = AREA TO BE COVERED
220 REM
230 PRINT "THIS PROGRAM CALCULATES THE COST OF FLOOR COVERING,"
240 PRINT "GIVING YOU AT THE END THE TOTAL SQUARE YARDS YOU NEED"
250 PRINT "AND THE TOTAL COST. YOU WILL BE ASKED TO ENTER THE"
260 PRINT "LENGTH AND WIDTH OF YOUR ROOM, SEPARATED BY A COMMA,"
270 PRINT "AND ALSO THE COST PER SQUARE YARD."
280 PRINT
290 PRINT "ENTER ROOM DIMENSIONS: LENGTH, WIDTH"
300 INPUT LENGTH, WIDTH
310 PRINT "ENTER PRICE PER SQUARE YARD"
320 INPUT YARD
330 LET AREA = LENGTH * WIDTH / 9
340 LET COST = AREA * YARD
350 PRINT USING "YOU NEED ##.## SQUARE YARDS AT $$##.##";AREA,YARD
360 PRINT USING "PER YARD FOR A TOTAL OF $$#,###.##";COST
999 END

RUN

THIS PROGRAM CALCULATES THE COST OF FLOOR COVERING,
GIVING YOU AT THE END THE TOTAL SQUARE YARDS YOU NEED
AND THE TOTAL COST. YOU WILL BE ASKED TO ENTER THE
LENGTH AND WIDTH OF YOUR ROOM, SEPARATED BY A COMMA,
AND ALSO THE COST PER SQUARE YARD.

ENTER ROOM DIMENSIONS: LENGTH, WIDTH
?20,40
ENTER PRICE PER SQUARE YARD
?5.99
YOU NEED 88.88 SQUARE YARDS AT $5.99
PER YARD FOR A TOTAL OF $532.39
```

The sample program in Example 53 begins with line 100. The lines between 100 and 220 are REM statements that serve as internal documentation. Notice that this documentation consists of an explanation of the program and a definition of variables used in the program.

Lines 230 through 270 are the PRINT statements that provide general instructions to the user. These lines correspond to the sample flowchart symbol ①. Although it may seem repetitious to state the purpose of the program again (we already did in the REM statements), remember that only the PRINT statements, those in lines 230 through 270, are actually displayed on the terminal. Notice how the PRINT statements are written. The literals are enclosed in quotation marks, and the absence of any punctuation at the end of the lines ensures that each line will be printed on separate lines as shown in the output of the program. The single PRINT statement on line 280 leaves a blank line between the general instructions and the first prompt for data. This increases the readability of the program.

Lines 290 and 310 issue the input instructions using the PRINT statement. Lines 300 and 320 cause question marks to appear on the screen, prompting the user to key in length and width and price per square yard. The values keyed in by the user are then placed in memory locations. The PRINT and INPUT statements code the logic depicted in the sample flowchart at the points ② and ③.

Calculations occur in lines 330 and 340, which code the logic represented by the calculation symbols after ④ in the sample flowchart. Data given by the user is used in the calculations to determine the area and the total cost.

Lines 350 and 360 code the output of the program using PRINT USING statements. This is a message to the user giving the number of square yards needed, the price per square yard, and the total cost. Notice the $$ used in the formats to float the dollar sign to the left of the first significant digit. These statements represent the logic labeled ⑤ in the sample flowchart.

The program ends with line number 999, which signals the end of the program using the END statement.

## Control Structures

**Control structures** allow the programmer to exercise control in the program by changing the sequence in which program statements are executed. All of the programs we have written thus far have been executed line by line beginning with the lowest line number and ending with the highest number. A programmer often wants to reroute the logic to statements other than the line of code immediately following the one the computer is currently executing. We shall now use the GOTO, the IF-THEN, and the IF-THEN-ELSE statements to control the logic of the program and allow the programmer much greater programming versatility.

### The GOTO Statement

The **GOTO** statement is called an **unconditional transfer** statement. If you consider the meaning of the word *unconditional*, you may be able to understand more easily the use of this statement. An unconditional situation is one in which the action is taken regardless of the conditions. This is in sharp contrast to the IF-THEN statement, for which a specific condition must be met before the statement is executed. Look at the unconditional nature of the GOTO statement in Example 54.

*Example 54*

**Statement Format:**
Line number GOTO Line number

**Sample Statement:**
200 GOTO 180

The unconditional nature of the transfer, or branch, occurs in the sample statement in line 200. When the computer executes line 200, it will go automatically back to line 180 rather than on to the next line of code following line 200.

Example 55 uses this sample statement in a program to further illustrate the use of the GOTO statement.

*Example 55*

```
170 LET A = 0
180 LET A = A + 1
190 PRINT A
200 GOTO 180
999 END
```

The computer will move through the program statements in Example 55 in this order: 170, 180, 190, 200; 180, 190, 200; and so on. In the sequencing of program statements, the repetition of statements is called a **loop.** The loop involves the repetition of lines 180, 190, and 200 over and over again. When will the program end? You may conclude that the program will end when the computer reads statement 999, which is the END statement. However, the computer will never get to line 999 because every time it gets to line 200, it is unconditionally directed to line 180. This is an **endless loop,** or **infinite loop;** the computer repeats the same statements over and over again, never coming to an END statement. Make certain that you always provide a means to exit a loop. We shall discuss this in more detail in the section about IF-THEN.

## Using the READ/DATA Statements with the GOTO Statement

Used in conjunction with the READ/DATA statements, the GOTO statement is a valuable addition to your programming knowledge. Example 56 illustrates a program written without the GOTO statement. Example 57 shows the same program written with the GOTO statement. Look closely and compare the two programs.

*Example 56*

```
100 REM THIS PROGRAM CALCULATES THE VALUE OF VARIABLE A.
110 READ B,C
120 LET A = B * C
130 PRINT A
140 READ B,C
150 LET A = B * C
160 PRINT A
170 READ B,C
180 LET A = B * C
190 PRINT A
200 DATA 5,3,3,3,4,4
999 END

RUN

 15
 9
 16
```

*Example 57*

```
100 REM THIS PROGRAM CALCULATES THE VALUE OF VARIABLE A.
110 READ B,C
120 LET A = B * C
130 PRINT A
140 GOTO 110
150 DATA 5,3,3,3,4,4
999 END

RUN

 15
 9
 16
OUT OF DATA IN LINE 110
```

In comparing Examples 56 and 57, did you notice that there are more program statements in Example 56 than in Example 57? The GOTO statement in Example 57 creates a loop in lines 110 through 140, causing the computer to repeat certain statements within the program. Referring to the definition of a control statement, the GOTO statement in this program lets the programmer change the order of the sequence of program instructions being executed. Notice the message "OUT OF DATA IN LINE 110" in Example 57. The message appears because, after completing the third loop, there was no more data in the DATA statement for the next READ statement, which is at line 110. You will learn how this message can be eliminated from a program in the section about checking the end-of-file condition.

Example 58 uses READ/DATA statements with the GOTO statement to count the number of records that are processed in a program. The loop has no stopping mechanism, so it potentially goes on forever. Although useful for illustration purposes, this would never be used deliberately in a program, as indicated by the X over the flowchart.

*Flowchart for Example 58*

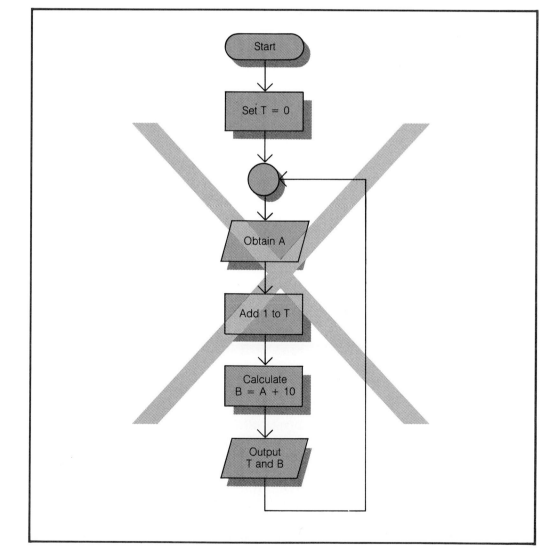

*Example 58*

```
100 REM THIS PROGRAM COUNTS THE RECORDS AS THEY ARE PROCESSED
110 REM AND PRINTS THE TOTAL NUMBER OF RECORDS PROCESSED.
120 REM THE VALUE OF VARIABLE B IS CALCULATED BY ADDING 10 TO
130 REM EACH VALUE READ FROM THE DATA STATEMENT.
140 LET T = 0
150 READ A
160 LET T = T + 1
170 LET B = A + 10
180 PRINT T,B
190 GOTO 150
200 DATA 10,15,20,25,30
999 END

RUN

1               20
2               25
3               30
4               35
5               40
OUT OF DATA IN LINE 150
```

In Example 58, variable T, which serves as the record counter, is initialized to 0 in line 140. The value 1 is added to T each time a loop is performed. The value of variable B, which is printed as output, is calculated in line 170. The GOTO statement in line 190 directs the flow of logic back to line 150, thus establishing the loop. The message "OUT OF DATA" is given after all the data has been processed because the computer is directed to read a value for A in the READ statement in line 150, but no more data is available in the DATA statement.

## The IF-THEN Statement

The IF-THEN statement is called a **conditional transfer** because a particular condition must exist before the computer will transfer to the line number or statement specified, instead of automatically executing the line immediately following the IF-THEN statement. Example 59 provides the statement format and sample statements.

*Example 59*

**Statement Format:**
Line number IF Condition exists THEN Line number or statement

**Sample Statements:**
```
310 IF NAMES$="END OF FILE" THEN 440

420 IF C > B THEN PRINT "OVER"
```

In the first sample statement, if the alphanumeric variable, NAMES$, equals the alphanumeric constant, "END OF FILE", then the computer is directed to immediately execute line 440. If NAMES$ does not equal "END OF FILE", the computer executes the next line of code following the IF-THEN statement.

In the second sample statement, if variable C is greater than variable B, the computer prints OVER. After performing the PRINT statement, the computer executes the line immediately following the line that contains the IF-THEN statement.

The = and > conditions are tested in the sample statements. Altogether, there are six conditions, called **relational operators,** which can be tested using the IF-THEN statement.

### Relational Operators within the IF-THEN Statement

The relational operators that make comparisons possible within an IF-THEN statement are shown in Example 60.

*Example 60*

| | Operator Symbol | Meaning | Example |
|---|---|---|---|
| 1. | = | equal to | 220 IF A = 6 THEN 410 |
| 2. | < | less than | 220 IF A < B THEN 410 |
| 3. | > | greater than | 220 IF A$ > B$ THEN PRINT "LATE" |
| 4. | <= | less than or equal to | 220 IF A <= (B + C) THEN 410 |
| 5. | >= | greater than or equal to | 220 IF A >= B THEN 410 |
| 6. | <> | not equal to | 220 IF A$ <> "DATE" THEN 410 |

Within the IF-THEN statement format in Example 59, the "condition exists" portion is made up of comparisons of numeric and alphanumeric variables and numeric and alphanumeric constants made possible by the relational operators in Example 60. Notice the variety of comparisons that can be made. ① uses the relational operator = to compare numeric variable A with numeric constant 6. ③ compares the alphanumeric variable A$ with the alphanumeric variable B$ using > (greater than). ④ compares the numeric variable A with the arithmetic expression (B + C) using the ≤ (less than or equal to). ⑥ uses < > (not equal to) to compare the alphanumeric variable A$ with the alphanumeric constant "DATE".

A partial program in Example 61 illustrates the use of relational operators.

*Example 61*

```
100 REM THIS PARTIAL PROGRAM PRINTS THE EMPLOYEE'S NAME IF THE
110 REM EMPLOYEE IS FEMALE AND UNDER 40 YEARS OLD WITH AT LEAST 4
120 REM YEARS OF EMPLOYMENT.
130 REM
140 READ EMPLOYEE$,SEX$,AGE,YEARS
150 IF SEX$ = "M" GOTO 999
160 IF AGE => 40 GOTO 999
170 IF YEARS < 4 GOTO 999
180 PRINT EMPLOYEE$
190 DATA MARION SCHORR,F,29,6
999 END

RUN

MARION SCHORR
```

### Checking the End-of-File Condition

The flowchart in Example 62 on page 574 depicts the logic for the program in Example 63.

In the program in Example 63, there are READ statements in lines 170 and 200. The first READ statement, called the **priming read,** makes the data to be processed the first time through the IF-THEN loop available. (Review the discussion of the double read in Chapter 8.) The IF-THEN statement in the program on line 180 directs the computer to check for the end-of-file indicator, "END OF FILE". The END OF FILE on line 230 is called a **trailer record** because it trails, or is the last record, following the data records that are to be processed by the program. It is frequently referred to as a **dummy record.** If a record is received that is not END OF FILE, the

*Example 62*
(Flowchart for
Example 63)

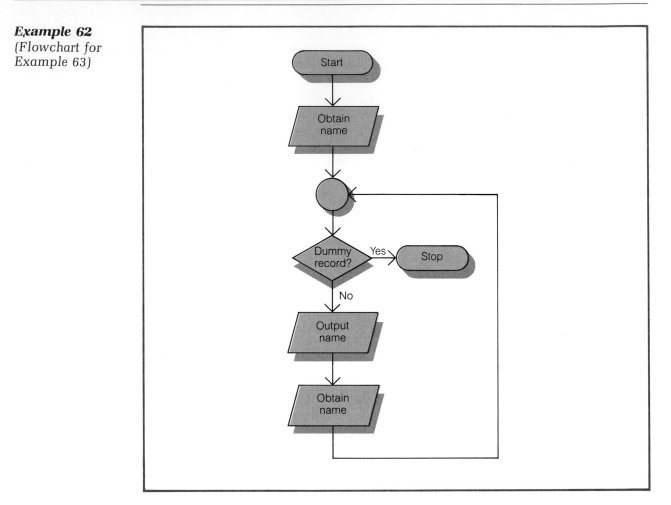

processing of the loop continues. The instructions within the loop will be executed until the condition of the end-of-file indicator is checked and found to be true. When true, the computer executes the line number following the THEN portion of the statement format, or line 999, which ends the program.

The end-of-file indicator is particularly useful when the number of data values to be read varies from one program execution to the next. The logic is not planned to loop a certain number of times; instead, it loops through whatever data values are present until it reaches a trailer value—that is, some end-of-file indicator. As we shall see in subsequent examples, however, some loops are controlled by counters instead, meaning that the loops will execute a predetermined number of times.

*Example 63*

```
100 REM THIS PROGRAM COMPARES AN ALPHANUMERIC VARIABLE TO AN
110 REM ALPHANUMERIC CONSTANT TO CHECK FOR THE END-OF-FILE
120 REM CONDITION IN THE DATA STATEMENT.
130 REM
140 REM     VARIABLE NAMES:
150 REM        NAMES$ = NAMES OF EMPLOYEES
160 REM
170 READ NAMES$
180 IF NAMES$ = "END OF FILE" THEN 999
```

*Example 63 continues*

*Example 63, continued*

```
190      PRINT NAMES$
200      READ NAMES$
210 GOTO 180
220 DATA MEREDYTH CHAMP,TOM MYERS,RICHARD ALLAN,DAVID BYARD
230 DATA END OF FILE
999 END

RUN

MEREDYTH CHAMP
TOM MYERS
RICHARD ALLAN
DAVID BYARD
```

Example 63 includes two important programming techniques: (1) internal documentation using REM statements and (2) indentation of statements with the loop. Both these techniques make the source program easier to read.

Note that the output from Example 63 does not include the OUT OF DATA line that was present in Examples 57 and 58. Example 63 eliminates that problem by checking for an end-of-file condition.

A numeric value could also be used as an end-of-file indicator. When choosing the value, whether alphanumeric or numeric, be sure to use a value that would not occur in the actual data elements. Remember, each READ instruction must be fulfilled. If your READ statement contains more than one variable, your trailer record must contain sufficient data elements. Be sure to match string variables with string data and numeric variables with numeric data. Example 64 illustrates these concepts. Assume that there are other data statements, although only the trailer record, line 500, is shown here. Notice that there are exactly two trailer values, which match the two variables in the READ statement. Also note that the type of trailer values matches the type of variable: XXX for NAMES$ (both alphanumeric) and 00 for AGE (both numeric).

*Example 64*

```
200 READ NAMES$,AGE
500 DATA XXX,00
```

Example 65 uses the LET statement to count the number of records being processed and prints an item count and item list as output.

*Example 65*

```
100 REM THIS PROGRAM PRINTS AN INVENTORY LISTING INCLUDING AN
110 REM ITEM COUNT.
120 REM
130 REM      VARIABLE NAMES:
140 REM         ITEM$ = INVENTORY ITEMS
150 REM         C = COUNTER
160 REM
170 LET C = 0
180 READ ITEM$
190 IF ITEM$ = "END OF FILE" THEN 999
200      LET C = C + 1
210      PRINT C,ITEM$
220      READ ITEM$
230 GOTO 190
240 REM      DATA
250 DATA SHOES,TIES,SOCKS,SLACKS,SHIRTS
260 DATA END OF FILE
999 END
```

*Example 65 continues*

*Example 65, continued*   RUN

```
1                SHOES
2                TIES
3                SOCKS
4                SLACKS
5                SHIRTS
```

The counter (C) in line 170 was initialized to 0 prior to accumulating. Numeric variables are automatically initialized to 0 at the beginning of a program, but this step was taken for the purpose of internal documentation.

The program in Example 66 also uses a counter, but rather than an item counter as in Example 65 the next program prints a single total for all items processed.

**Example 66**

```
100 REM THIS PROGRAM PRINTS THE TOTAL NUMBER OF ITEMS IN AN
110 REM INVENTORY LISTING.
120 REM
130 REM    VARIABLE LIST:
140 REM
150 REM       NUMBER = NUMBER OF ITEMS SOLD
160 REM       ITEM$ = NAME OF ITEM
170 REM       PRICE = PRICE OF ITEM
180 REM       TOTAL = TOTAL NUMBER OF ITEMS PROCESSED
190 REM
200 LET TOTAL = 0
210 READ NUMBER,ITEM$,PRICE
220 IF NUMBER = 000 THEN 270
230     LET TOTAL = TOTAL + NUMBER
240     PRINT NUMBER,ITEM$,PRICE
250     READ NUMBER,ITEM$,PRICE
260 GOTO 220
270 PRINT
280 PRINT "TOTAL NUMBER OF ITEMS PROCESSED";TOTAL
290 REM    DATA
300 DATA 13,CANDLES,1.19,23,VASE 7 INCH,3.99
310 DATA 3,PLATE HANGER,1.19,45,COASTER,1.29
320 DATA 8,PLACEMAT OVAL,4.98,000,X,0
999 END
```

```
RUN

13               CANDLES          1.19
23               VASE 7 INCH      3.99
3                PLATE HANGER     1.19
45               COASTER          1.29
8                PLACEMAT OVAL    4.98

TOTAL NUMBER OF ITEMS PROCESSED 92
```

Notice that the end-of-file processing, which prints the total number of items processed, does not occur until the trailer record (000,X,0) at the end of the file is read and equals the IF condition in line 220 (NUMBER = 000). Also note that the number of trailer values—three—is the same as the number of variables in the READ statement.

The program in Example 67 illustrates the use of an INPUT statement to provide the end-of-file indicator. Report titles are printed as part of the output.

**Example 67**

```
110 REM THIS PROGRAM ALLOWS THE USER TO ENTER INVENTORY AND
120 REM SALES INFORMATION AND, AT THE END OF PROCESSING,
```

*Example 67 continues*

*Example 67, continued*

```
130 REM PRINTS TOTALS FOR NUMBER OF ITEMS PROCESSED AND
140 REM THE SALES FOR THE SESSION.
150 REM
160 REM        VARIABLE NAMES:
170 REM
180 REM            ITEM$ = NAME OF ITEM
190 REM            NUMBER = NUMBER OF ITEM
200 REM            PRICE = PRICE OF ITEM
210 REM            QUANTITY = QUANTITY SOLD
220 REM            TOTAL = TOTAL ITEMS SOLD
230 REM            SALES = SALES PRICE
240 REM            VOLUME = TOTAL SALES VOLUME
250 REM            MORE$ = YES OR NO ANSWER
260 REM
270 LET TOTAL = 0
280 LET VOLUME = 0
290 PRINT "THIS PROGRAM PRINTS A LISTING OF THE TOTAL NUMBER"
300 PRINT "OF ITEMS PROCESSED AND THE SALE VALUE OF ITEMS"
310 PRINT "PROCESSED. YOU WILL BE ASKED TO ENTER THE"
320 PRINT "ITEM NAME, ITEM NUMBER, PRICE, AND QUANTITY SOLD."
330 PRINT "SEPARATE EACH WITH A COMMA."
340 PRINT "YOU WILL BE ABLE TO END PROCESSING BY ENTERING"
350 PRINT "YES OR NO TO THE QUESTION, 'MORE ITEMS TO BE"
360 PRINT "PROCESSED?'"
370 PRINT
380 PRINT "ENTER NAME, ITEM NUMBER, PRICE, QUANTITY"
390 INPUT ITEM$,NUMBER,PRICE,QUANTITY
400      LET TOTAL = TOTAL + QUANTITY
410      LET SALES = PRICE * QUANTITY
420      LET VOLUME = VOLUME + SALES
430      PRINT "MORE ITEMS TO BE PROCESSED?"
440      INPUT MORE$
450      IF MORE$ = "NO" THEN 470
460 GOTO 370
470 PRINT
480 PRINT "TOTAL ITEMS PROCESSED";TOTAL
490 PRINT "TOTAL SALES            ";VOLUME
999 END

RUN

THIS PROGRAM PRINTS A LISTING OF THE TOTAL NUMBER
OF ITEMS PROCESSED AND THE SALE VALUE OF ITEMS
PROCESSED. YOU WILL BE ASKED TO ENTER THE
ITEM NAME, ITEM NUMBER, PRICE, AND QUANTITY SOLD.
SEPARATE EACH WITH A COMMA.
YOU WILL BE ABLE TO END PROCESSING BY ENTERING
YES OR NO TO THE QUESTION, 'MORE ITEMS TO BE
PROCESSED?'

ENTER NAME, ITEM NUMBER, PRICE, QUANTITY
?TABLES,2321,15.00,2
MORE ITEMS TO BE PROCESSED?
?YES

ENTER NAME, ITEM NUMBER, PRICE, QUANTITY
?LAMP,104,13.98,3
MORE ITEMS TO BE PROCESSED?
?YES

ENTER NAME, ITEM NUMBER, PRICE, QUANTITY
?CHAIR,4576,39.95,4
MORE ITEMS TO BE PROCESSED?
?NO

TOTAL ITEMS PROCESSED 9
TOTAL SALES            231.74
```

### Logical Operators within the IF-THEN Statement

The IF-THEN statement is a logical expression because the comparison within the condition tested is either true or false. In addition to the six relational operators that were introduced, three **logical operators—AND, NOT,** and **OR**—can also be used to form logical expressions. Example 68 illustrates the use of the logical operator AND.

*Example 68*

```
300 IF NAMES$ = "STEVE" AND AGE > 30 THEN 530
```

When using the logical operator AND in an IF-THEN statement, both comparisons joined by AND must be true for the instruction or line number of the statement following THEN to be executed.

Example 69 illustrates the use of the logical operator OR.

*Example 69*

```
400 IF A < 1 OR A > 50 THEN 500
```

The logical operator OR requires that only one of the comparisons joined by OR be true for the compound expression to be true. In Example 69 either A must be less than 1 or A must be greater than 50 for line 500 to be executed.

Example 70 illustrates the use of the logical operator NOT.

*Example 70*

```
420 IF NOT X > Y THEN 600
```

In Example 70 if it is not true that X > Y, the condition following IF is true, and line 600 is executed. If it is true that X > Y, then the condition following IF is false, and the line after line 420 is executed.

It is possible to use more than one logical operator in a logical expression. Just as there is a hierarchy of mathematical operations, there is a hierarchy of logical operators. Parentheses affect the order in which the steps in a logical expression are performed just as they do with mathematical operations. The computer performs comparisons in logical expressions containing more than one logical operator in the following order: The logical operator NOT is performed first, the logical operator AND is performed second, the logical operator OR is performed last. Example 71 illustrates the priority of operations in a compound logical expression.

*Example 71*

### Hierarchy of Operations

| Operation | Symbol |
|---|---|
| Parentheses | ( ) |
| Arithmetic Operators | +, -, *, / |
| Relational Operators | =, >, <, >=, <=, < > |
| Logical Operators | NOT, AND, OR |

Example 72 demonstrates the order in which the computer solves a compound logical expression.

*Example 72*

```
300 LET A = 1
310 LET B = 5
320 LET C = 2
330 LET D = 3
340 LET E = 4

350 IF A > B OR C = D AND (C < D + E) THEN 490
```

1. The expression within parentheses is evaluated.

```
(C < D + E)
(2 < 3 + 4)
    TRUE
```

2. The relational operators are considered next.

```
A > B
1 > 5
FALSE

C = D
2 = 3
FALSE
```

3. The computer considers the logical operators last.

```
C = D and C < (D + E)
2 = 3      2 < (3 + 4)
FALSE AND      TRUE
      FALSE

A > B OR C = D AND C < (D + E)
1 > 5    2 = 3    2 < (3 + 4)
FALSE OR FALSE AND    TRUE
FALSE OR         FALSE
      FALSE
```

4. The complete IF expression is false, so control passes to line 360, the statement following the IF statement, rather than to line 490.

### The IF-THEN-ELSE Statement

Many systems allow the use of an IF-THEN-ELSE statement. With the IF-THEN statement program logic is transferred only when the condition following IF is true. The IF-THEN-ELSE statement transfers program logic when the condition is either true or false. If the condition is true, logic transfers to the statement or line number following THEN; if the condition is false, logic transfers to the statement or line number following ELSE.

*Example 73*

**Statement Format:**
Line number IF Condition THEN Statement(s) or line number
          ELSE Statement(s) or line number

*Example 73 continues*

**Sample Statement:**

```
400 IF A = B THEN LET C = C + 1
    ELSE 600
410 . . .
```

The statement format in Example 73 illustrates that more than one BASIC statement or a line number can follow THEN and ELSE. In the sample statement if it is true that A equals B, then the LET statement is executed. Because there is not a line number following THEN, after the LET statement is executed, control passes to line 410. If A does not equal B, the program logic transfers to line 600, the line number following ELSE.

An advantage of the IF-THEN-ELSE statement is that fewer programming statements are required. Although the IF-THEN statement could be used to accomplish the same tasks as the sample statement, an IF-THEN would require more than one statement.

## Exercises

1. What would be the output of the program below? (Hint: In line 180 the T on the left is assigned the current value of T, plus 3.)

```
170 LET T = 2
180     LET T = T + 3
190     PRINT T;
200 GOTO 170
999 END
```

2. What would be the output in the program in question 1 if line 200 were changed to:

```
200 GOTO 180
```

3. Write a program to count by twos and produce the following output. Note that the output is all on one line, each output value in a new zone.

```
2          4          6          8          10
```

4. True or false? If A is greater than B in the statement that follows, the line following line 200 would be executed.

```
200 IF A > B THEN 340
```

5. True or false? Numeric value A is being compared with numeric value B in the statement that follows.

```
410 IF A$ = B$ THEN 500
```

6. Look at the IF-THEN-ELSE statement that follows. What is executed if the condition is true? What is executed if the condition is false?

```
460 IF T > S THEN 500 ELSE PRINT T
```

## Answers to Exercises

1. 5 5 5 5 5 5 5...     (endless loop)

2. 5 8 11 14 17...     (endless loop)

```
3.  100 LET N = 0
    110 IF N > 10 THEN 999
    120     LET N = N + 2
    130       PRINT N,
    140 GOTO 110
    999 END
```

4. False—statement 340 would be executed.

5. False—A\$ and B\$ are alphanumeric variables.

6. If it is true that T > S, program logic transfers to line 500. If it is false that T > S, the PRINT statement following the ELSE is executed, and program logic transfers to the line after the IF-THEN-ELSE statement.

## The FOR/NEXT Statement

Another looping structure, the FOR/NEXT statement, has wide application in BASIC programming and offers some distinct advantages. The statement format for the FOR/NEXT looping structure is shown in Example 74.

*Example 74*

**Statement Format:**
Line number FOR variable = Initial value TO Test value [STEP Variable increment]
        NEXT Variable

**Sample Statement:**
```
150 FOR X = 1 TO 20 STEP 5
.
.
.
200 NEXT X
```

In Example 74 the initial value in the sample statement is the numeric constant 1. The test value is the numeric constant 20. The value of the initial value or the test value can be a constant, a variable, or an arithmetic expression. The loop performed by the FOR/NEXT statements will be terminated when the value of the FOR variable is greater than the test value. The STEP parameter of the statement format is an optional parameter. If no STEP increment is specified in the program statement, an increment value of 1 is implied.

It is important to understand that when using the FOR/NEXT statements, the words FOR and NEXT must be used together.

An application of the sample statement in Example 74 is shown in Example 75. Any BASIC statements can be used within the body of a FOR/NEXT loop. Statements between the FOR and NEXT statements are indented. In this program the PRINT statement is used in the body of the loop. The flowchart is shown on page 582.

*Example 75*

```
100 REM THIS PROGRAM CALCULATES THE VALUE OF VARIABLE X.
110 REM
120 FOR X = 1 TO 20 STEP 5
130     PRINT X;
140 NEXT X
999 END

RUN

 1   6   11   16
```

***Flowchart for***
***Example 75***

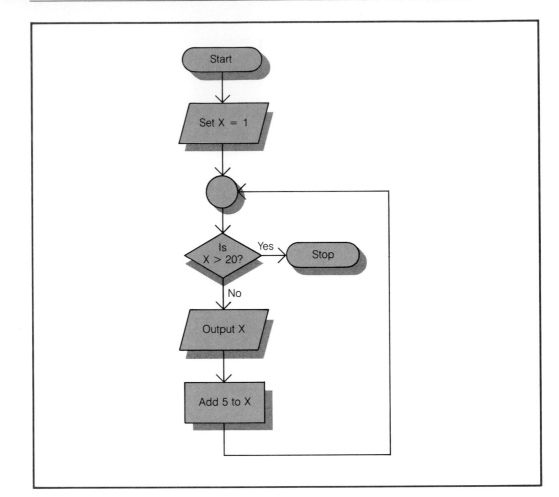

Variable X is assigned the initial value of 1 by the FOR statement in line 120. The value 20 is the test value following the word TO, and the STEP increment 5 indicates that 5 is to be added to the value of X with each pass through the loop. The semicolon after the PRINT statement in line 130 causes the output to be printed across the page. If 5 is added to the last value, 16, one more time, the final value would exceed the test value of 20. The loop, therefore, executes four times and terminates when the value of X is 21. After the loop is terminated, the line number following the NEXT statement, which in this case is line 999, is executed.

### The Step Parameter with FOR/NEXT

Example 76 uses the same values as Example 75 but does not include the STEP parameter. Notice the difference in the output.

***Example 76***

```
100 REM THIS PROGRAM CALCULATES THE VALUE OF VARIABLE X.
110 REM
120 FOR X = 1 TO 10
130     PRINT X;
140 NEXT X
999 END
```

*Example 76 continues*

*Example 76, continued*    RUN

```
1   2   3   4   5   6   7   8   9   10
```

A negative value is used as the STEP increment of the FOR statement in the program shown in Example 77.

**Example 77**

```
100 REM THIS PROGRAM CALCULATES THE VALUE OF VARIABLE T USING
110 REM A NEGATIVE VALUE IN THE STEP PARAMETER.
120 REM
130 FOR T = 15 TO 5 STEP -5
140      PRINT T,
150 NEXT T
999 END
```

RUN

```
15              10              5
```

When using a negative increment, the initial value must be greater than the test value. It is not possible to descend to a number from a lower number. For example, the statement

```
200 FOR T = 1 TO 15 STEP -5
```

would not be executed by the computer.

It is also possible to use a decimal value for the STEP increment. Example 78 illustrates a STEP increment of .5.

**Example 78**

```
100 REM THIS PROGRAM CALCULATES THE VALUE OF VARIABLE C IN
110 REM STEP INCREMENTS OF .5.
120 REM
130 FOR C = 1 TO 3 STEP .5
140      PRINT C,
150 NEXT C
999 END
```

RUN

```
1              1.5              2              2.5              3
```

A decimal STEP increment can also be negative. In Example 78 if the initial value had been 3, the test value had been 1, and the increment had been −.5, the output for the program would have been reversed, as shown below.

```
3              2.5              2              1.5              1
```

### Advantages of FOR/NEXT

The flowchart in Example 79 illustrates the flow of logic for the two programs that follow in Examples 80 and 81. The program in Example 80 uses GOTO and IF-THEN statements; the program in Example 81 uses FOR/NEXT statements. The two programs produce identical output. Notice that the decision symbol in the flowchart checks both the IF-THEN and the FOR/NEXT statements.

***Example 79***
*(Flowchart for Examples 80 and 81)*

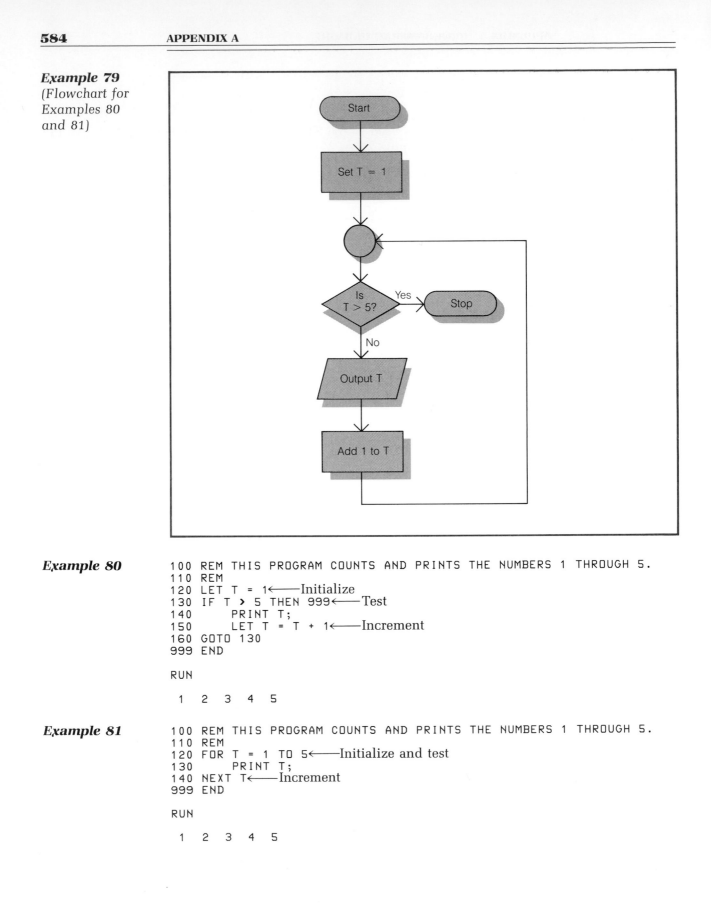

***Example 80***

```
100 REM THIS PROGRAM COUNTS AND PRINTS THE NUMBERS 1 THROUGH 5.
110 REM
120 LET T = 1←——Initialize
130 IF T > 5 THEN 999←——Test
140     PRINT T;
150     LET T = T + 1←——Increment
160 GOTO 130
999 END

RUN

 1  2  3  4  5
```

***Example 81***

```
100 REM THIS PROGRAM COUNTS AND PRINTS THE NUMBERS 1 THROUGH 5.
110 REM
120 FOR T = 1 TO 5←——Initialize and test
130     PRINT T;
140 NEXT T←——Increment
999 END

RUN

 1  2  3  4  5
```

It is easy to see that the program in Example 81 uses fewer statements. Both programs are counting applications. The advantage of using FOR/NEXT statements is that they perform loops with fewer coding lines than IF-THEN statements. The FOR/NEXT loop has three elements: (1) initialization of the variable to be used, (2) calculation of the value of the variable according to the STEP increment, and (3) the test of the counter to see if the test value has been reached. Examples 80 and 81 illustrate these three steps.

### The INPUT Statement with FOR/NEXT

The INPUT statement can be used to set the test value in a FOR/NEXT loop. The program in Example 82 illustrates this capability. This program converts the number of laps swum to feet and calculates the cumulative distance to hundredths of a mile for each lap processed in the program loop. The user enters the test value using an INPUT statement. The flowchart is shown on page 586.

*Example 82*

```
100 REM THIS PROGRAM CALCULATES THE DISTANCE OF EACH 64-FOOT LAP
110 REM SWUM BY THE USER WITH THE MAXIMUM NUMBER OF LAPS
120 REM BEING ENTERED BY THE USER.  THE PROGRAM ALSO CALCULATES
130 REM THE DISTANCE OF LAPS SWUM IN MILES TO THE HUNDREDTH
140 REM DECIMAL PLACE.
150 REM
160 REM           VARIABLE NAMES:
170 REM
180 REM           C = COUNTER FOR FOR/NEXT LOOP
190 REM           N = TEST VALUE INPUT BY USER
200 REM           FEET = LAPS SWUM IN FEET
210 REM           MILES = LAPS SWUM IN MILES
220 REM
230 PRINT "THIS PROGRAM WILL PRINT A LISTING OF EACH LAP"
240 PRINT "SWUM, THE DISTANCE IN FEET, AND DISTANCE TO"
250 PRINT "HUNDREDTHS OF A MILE. YOU WILL BE ASKED TO"
260 PRINT "ENTER THE HIGHEST NUMBER OF LAPS SWUM."
270 PRINT
280 PRINT "ENTER THE HIGHEST NUMBER OF LAPS SWUM."
290 INPUT N
300 PRINT
310 PRINT "LAPS","FEET","MILES"
320 PRINT
330 FOR C = 1 TO N
340      LET FEET = C * 64
350      LET MILES = FEET/5280
360      PRINT C,FEET,
370      PRINT USING "##.##";MILES
380 NEXT C
999 END

RUN

THIS PROGRAM WILL PRINT A LISTING OF EACH LAP
SWUM, THE DISTANCE IN FEET, AND DISTANCE TO
HUNDREDTHS OF A MILE. YOU WILL BE ASKED TO
ENTER THE HIGHEST NUMBER OF LAPS SWUM.

ENTER HIGHEST NUMBER OF LAPS SWUM.

?6
```

*Example 82 continues on page 587.*

*Flowchart for
Example 82*

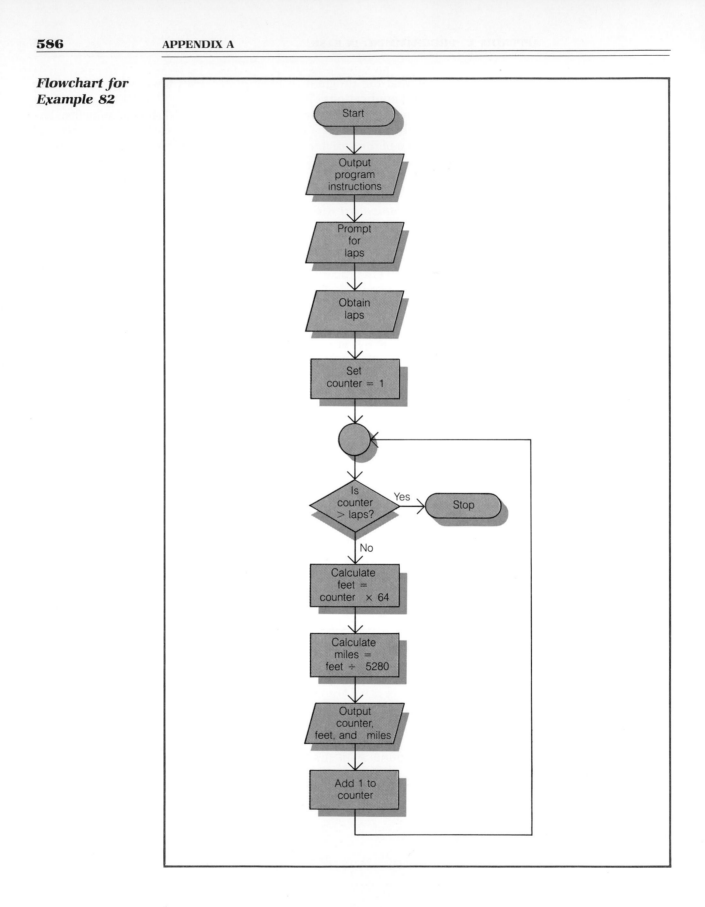

*Example 82, continued*

```
LAPS    FEET    MILES

 1       64     0.01
 2      128     0.02
 3      192     0.04
 4      256     0.05
 5      320     0.06
 6      384     0.07
```

The advantage of using an INPUT statement to set the test value is that the user can enter any number to be processed.

### Arithmetic Expressions in the FOR Statement

As noted earlier, arithmetic expressions can be used for the initial value or test value in the FOR statement. The program in Example 83 uses an arithmetic expression as the test value.

*Example 83*

```
100 REM THIS PROGRAM USES AN ARITHMETIC EXPRESSION AS THE
110 REM TEST VALUE.
120 REM
130 LET A = 2
140 LET B = 3
150 FOR I = 1 TO A * B
160      PRINT I
170 NEXT I
180 PRINT
190 PRINT "TOTAL NUMBERS PRINTED =";I - 1
999 END

RUN

 1
 2
 3
 4
 5
 6

TOTAL NUMBERS PRINTED = 6
```

The value of I represents the value that, after the final loop, is equal to 7. When the value 7 is compared with the test value of A * B, or 2 × 3, it is found to exceed the test value; therefore, the FOR/NEXT loop terminates and the statement following the NEXT I, line 180, is executed. Line 190 causes the total line to print. The total of numbers printed is one less than the final value of variable I. The subtraction of 1 is necessary to remove the last addition of 1 from the variable I—this last addition is the one that causes the value to exceed the test condition.

### The READ/DATA Statements with FOR/NEXT

The use of the INPUT statement to enter a variable amount in the FOR statement has already been demonstrated. The program in Example 84 on page 588 illustrates the use of the READ/DATA statements to set the test value in the FOR statement.

*Example 84*

```
100 REM THIS PROGRAM USES THE READ/DATA STATEMENTS TO PROVIDE
110 REM THE TEST VALUE IN THE FOR STATEMENT.
120 REM
130 REM     VARIABLE NAMES:
140 REM
150 REM     TOTAL = TOTAL NUMBER PROCESSED
160 REM     N = TEST VALUE
170 REM     A = FIRST VALUE TO BE READ
180 REM     B = SECOND VALUE TO BE READ
190 REM     C = LOOP COUNTER
200 REM
210 LET TOTAL = 0
220 READ N
230 FOR C = 1 TO N
240     READ A,B
250     PRINT A,B
260     LET TOTAL = TOTAL + 2
270 NEXT C
280 PRINT
290 PRINT "TOTAL NUMBERS PROCESSED";TOTAL
300 REM        DATA
310 DATA 8
320 DATA 1,2,3,4,5,6,7,8
330 DATA 9,10,11,12,13,14,15,16
999 END

RUN

1                2
3                4
5                6
7                8
9                10
11               12
13               14
15               16

TOTAL NUMBERS PROCESSED 16
```

The READ statement in line 220 obtains the value of 8 from the DATA statement in line 310, thus providing the value for the test value in the FOR statement in line 230. The READ statement in line 240 provides the data to be processed as variables A and B within the FOR/NEXT loop. The value 8 in line 310 could have been included as part of the DATA statement on line 320, but when it is set apart as it is here, it is easily seen by the reader. The FOR/NEXT loop is repeated eight times, the value of N. There are, however, a total of 16 numbers processed, as shown in the output. This is because the READ statement in line 240 directs the reading of two variables at a time, not one; therefore, the eight loops read a total of 16 numbers. The total of numbers processed, variable TOTAL, is incremented by 2 in line 260. Two is added to the value of TOTAL each time a loop is performed because two variables, A and B, are read by the READ statement in line 240.

The program in Example 85 uses READ/DATA statements to supply values for scores that are added, then it prints the sum.

*Example 85*

```
100 REM THIS PROGRAM USES THE READ/DATA STATEMENTS TO SUPPLY VALUES
110 REM FOR VARIABLES WITHIN THE FOR/NEXT LOOP AND PRINTS THE SUM.
120 REM
130 REM          VARIABLE NAMES:
140 REM          C = COUNTER FOR FOR/NEXT LOOP
```

*Example 85 continues on page 590.*

*Flowchart for*
*Example 85*

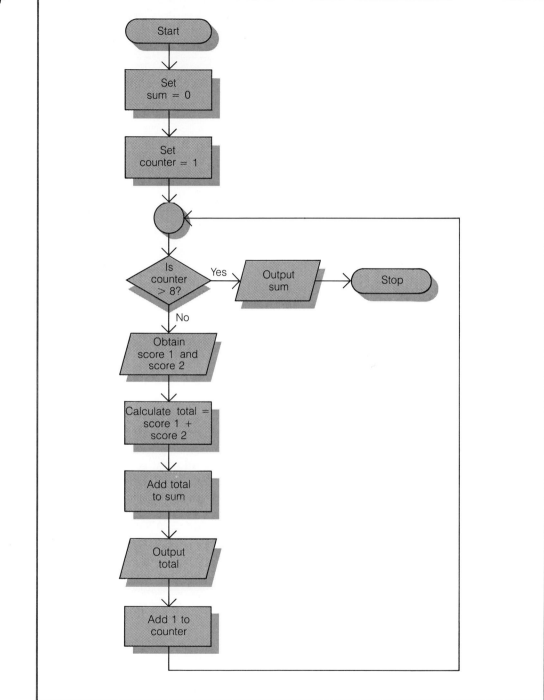

*Example 85, continued*

```
150 REM          SUM = SUM OF NUMBERS
160 REM          TOTAL = TOTAL OF TWO NUMBERS READ
170 REM          SCORE1 = FIRST SCORE READ
180 REM          SCORE2 = SECOND SCORE READ
190 REM
200 LET SUM = 0
210 REM
220 FOR C = 1 TO 8
230     READ SCORE1,SCORE2
240     LET TOTAL = SCORE1 + SCORE2
250     LET SUM = SUM + TOTAL
260     PRINT TOTAL
270 NEXT C
280 PRINT
290 PRINT "SUM OF NUMBERS IS";SUM
300 REM     DATA
310 DATA 85,43,23,33,22,99,78
320 DATA 67,45,32,76,51,22,89
330 DATA 28,71
999 END

RUN

 128
 56
 121
 145
 77
 127
 111
 99

SUM OF NUMBERS IS 864
```

### Control within a FOR/NEXT Loop

It is possible to transfer control within a FOR/NEXT loop using an IF-THEN statement. The program in Example 86 demonstrates this technique. This program prints a listing of names and total scores. A row of asterisks is printed for those people with scores over 250.

**Example 86**

```
100 REM THIS PROGRAM TRANSFERS CONTROL WITHIN THE FOR/NEXT
110 REM LOOP USING THE IF-THEN STATEMENT.  OUTPUT CONSISTS
120 REM OF A LIST OF NAMES AND TOTAL SCORES, THOSE TOTAL
130 REM SCORES OVER 250 WILL HAVE A ROW OF ASTERISKS AFTER
140 REM THE SCORE.
150 REM
160 REM          VARIABLE NAMES:
170 REM          NAMES$ = NAMES
180 REM          SCORE1 = FIRST SCORE READ
190 REM          SCORE2 = SECOND SCORE READ
200 REM          SUM = SUM OF TWO SCORES
210 REM          C = FOR/NEXT LOOP COUNTER
220 REM
230 FOR C = 1 TO 4
240     READ NAMES$,SCORE1,SCORE2
250     LET SUM = SCORE1 + SCORE2
260     IF SUM > 250 THEN 290
270     PRINT NAMES$,SUM
280     GOTO 300
290     PRINT NAMES$,SUM;" *****"
300 NEXT C
```

*Example 86 continues*

*Example 86, continued*

```
310 REM       DATA
320 DATA TED,190,231,LEE,189,90
330 DATA JACK,110,130,MICKEY,200,110
999 END

RUN

TED               421 *****
LEE               279 *****
JACK              240
MICKEY            310 *****
```

Example 86 illustrates an appropriate transfer of control with the FOR/NEXT loop using the IF-THEN statement. Some transfer techniques, however, are not correct. Example 87 illustrates a similar program but shows an incorrect transfer.

**Example 87**

```
250 FOR C = 1 TO 4
260     READ NAMES$,SCORE1,SCORE2
270     LET SUM = SCORE1 + SCORE2
280     IF SUM > 250 THEN 300
290     PRINT NAMES$,SUM
300     GOTO 250
310 NEXT C
```

The GOTO statement in line 300 bypasses the NEXT statement in line 310. This is incorrect programming procedure. The NEXT C statement causes variable C to be incremented. The program would be correctly written if the IF-THEN statement directed the program to the NEXT statement in line 310.

Likewise, it is incorrect to transfer into a FOR/NEXT loop. Example 88 is an outline of a program that illustrates an incorrect programming procedure using a GOTO statement to transfer into a FOR/NEXT loop.

**Example 88**

```
220 GOTO 300
230 -------
240 -------
250 -------
260 FOR C = 1 TO 10
270     ----------
280     ----------
290     ----------
300     PRINT NAMES$
310     ----------
320 NEXT C
```

The program statements in Example 89 illustrate transferring out of a loop with an IF-THEN statement. Although this program will run, it does not represent good programming technique.

**Example 89**

```
230 FOR C = 1 TO 30
240     LET T = A + B
250     IF T > 100 THEN 290
260     PRINT T
270 NEXT C
280 ----------
290 ----------
```

Examples 87 through 89 illustrate this general rule: Do not transfer into or out of FOR/NEXT loops except through the FOR and NEXT statements.

### Nested FOR/NEXT Loops

It is possible to place a FOR/NEXT loop within another FOR/NEXT loop. Multiple FOR/NEXT loops are called nested loops and are referred to as inner and outer loops. Example 90 illustrates nested FOR/NEXT loops.

**Flowchart for Example 90**

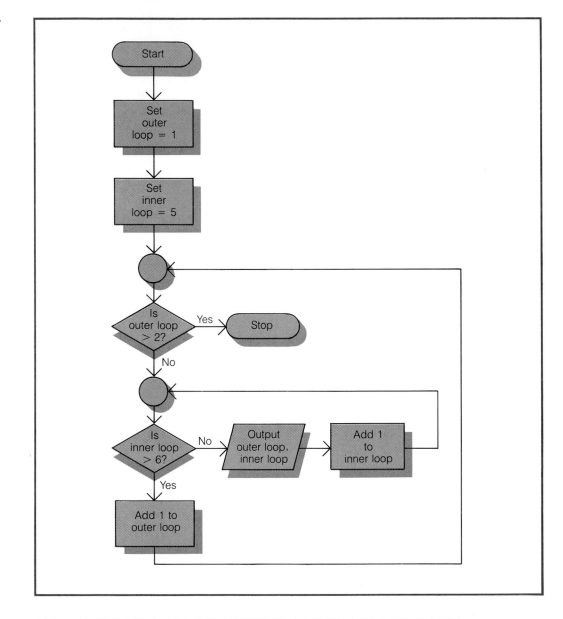

**Example 90**

```
100 REM THIS PROGRAM DEMONSTRATES A NESTED FOR/NEXT LOOP.
110 REM
120 FOR OUTER = 1 TO 2
130     FOR INNER = 5 TO 6
140         PRINT OUTER,INNER
150     NEXT INNER
160 NEXT OUTER
999 END
```

*Example 90 continues*

*Example 90, continued*    RUN

```
1                    5
1                    6
2                    5
2                    6
```

Notice the spacing of the FOR/NEXT loops in the program. The inner loop, lines 130 through 150, is contained and executed within the outer loop, lines 120 through 160. Initially, variable Outer in the outer loop is given a value of 1, and variable Inner in the inner loop is given a value of 5. The inner loop is performed repeatedly until the condition of the FOR statement in line 130 is satisfied, which means that the test value of 6 is reached. Then the NEXT statement in line 160 is executed, giving variable Outer the value of 2. The inner loop is repeated again with the values of 5 and 6 for the values of variable Inner.

The large brackets in Example 91 indicate an important point: The inner loop cannot intersect the outer loop; completion of the inner loop must be totally within the outer loop structure. It is possible to have more than one nested loop, but the loops cannot intersect each other. Notice that the structures are labeled "Correct" and "Incorrect." The incorrect structure contains intersecting loops.

*Example 91*

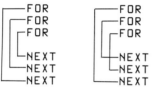

    Correct       Incorrect

### The PRINT Statement with FOR/NEXT

The program in Example 92 uses PRINT statements within both the inner and outer loops to illustrate the logical progression of nested FOR/NEXT loops.

*Example 92*

```
100 REM THIS PROGRAM CONTAINS NESTED FOR/NEXT LOOPS INCLUDING A
110 REM PRINT STATEMENT WITHIN BOTH THE INNER AND OUTER LOOPS.
120 REM
130 FOR OUTER = 1 TO 3
140     PRINT "OUTER LOOP"
150     FOR INNER = 1 TO 3
160         PRINT TAB(5);"INNER LOOP"
170     NEXT INNER
180 NEXT OUTER
999 END

RUN

OUTER LOOP
     INNER LOOP
     INNER LOOP
     INNER LOOP
OUTER LOOP
     INNER LOOP
     INNER LOOP
     INNER LOOP
OUTER LOOP
     INNER LOOP
     INNER LOOP
     INNER LOOP
```

### Calculations with FOR/NEXT

As mentioned, calculations can be made within FOR/NEXT loops. This is true for both inner loops and outer loops. The program in Example 93 illustrates this concept by calculating variable N within the inner loop.

***Example 93***

```
100 REM THIS PROGRAM USES THE VALUES OF VARIABLES IN BOTH
110 REM FOR STATEMENTS FOR CALCULATIONS WITHIN THE INNER LOOP.
120 REM
130 FOR O = 1 TO 4
140     FOR I = 2 TO 5
150         LET N = O * I
160         PRINT N;
170     NEXT I
180 NEXT O
999 END

RUN

 2   3   4   5   4   6   8   10   6   9   12   15   8   12   16   20
```

The use of the IF-THEN statement to transfer control within a FOR/NEXT loop has already been discussed. The program in Example 94 uses the IF-THEN statement to transfer control within an inner FOR/NEXT loop.

***Example 94***

```
100 REM THIS PROGRAM USES THE INPUT STATEMENT TO INPUT TWO
110 REM VARIABLE VALUES AND USES THE IF-THEN STATEMENT TO
120 REM TRANSFER CONTROL WITHIN THE INNER FOR/NEXT LOOP TO
130 REM PRINT NO RESULTING NUMBERS LARGER THAN 10.
140 REM
150 PRINT "ENTER FIRST VALUE"
160 INPUT VALUE1
170 PRINT "ENTER SECOND VALUE"
180 INPUT VALUE2
190 REM
200 FOR O = 1 TO VALUE1
210     PRINT "LOOP";O
220     FOR I = 1 TO VALUE2
230         LET S = (O + I) * 2
240         IF S > 10 THEN 260
250         PRINT S
260     NEXT I
270 NEXT O
999 END

RUN

ENTER FIRST VALUE
?3
ENTER SECOND VALUE
?4
LOOP 1
 4
 6
 8
 10
LOOP 2
 6
 8
 10
LOOP 3
 8
 10
```

The value of S is calculated on line 230. Line 240 checks the value of S to determine if, after calculations, it has exceeded 10. If so, control within the inner FOR/NEXT passes to line 260, NEXT I, without the value of variable S being printed. Therefore, no numbers greater than 10 are printed in the output.

## Exercises

1. Look at the following statements. How many times would the loop be performed?
```
450 FOR M = 1 TO 5 STEP 2
460     PRINT M
470 NEXT M
```

2. What would be the output from the following statements?
```
330 FOR N = 10 TO 5 STEP -1
340     PRINT N;
350 NEXT N
```

3. What would be the output from the following statements?
```
220 PRINT "T MULTIPLIED BY 3 AND 4"
230 FOR T = 2 TO 8
240     PRINT T * 3,T * 4
250 NEXT T
```

4. What would be the output from the following statements?
```
350 FOR B = 5 TO 10 STEP -1
360     PRINT B
370 NEXT B
```

5. What would be the output from the following statements?
```
220 LET T = 5
230 LET N = 10
240 LET S = 1
250 FOR C = T TO N STEP S
260       PRINT C
270 NEXT C
```

## Answers to Exercises

1. The loop will be performed three times, with M = 1, 3, and 5.

2.    10   9   8   7   6   5

3. T MULTIPLIED BY 3 AND 4
```
   6              8
   9              12
   12             16
   15             20
   18             24
   21             28
   24             32
```

4. The statements would not execute because you cannot go from a lesser number to a greater number with a negative STEP increment.

5.    5
      6
      7
      8
      9
      10

## Sample Program: Price Markups

The sample program that follows illustrates concepts presented thus far. The program uses nested FOR/NEXT loops to calculate markup percentages on prices. The flowchart in Example 95 is labeled to highlight three major steps. It corresponds to the BASIC program in Example 97.

*Example 95*
*(Flowchart for*
*Example 97)*

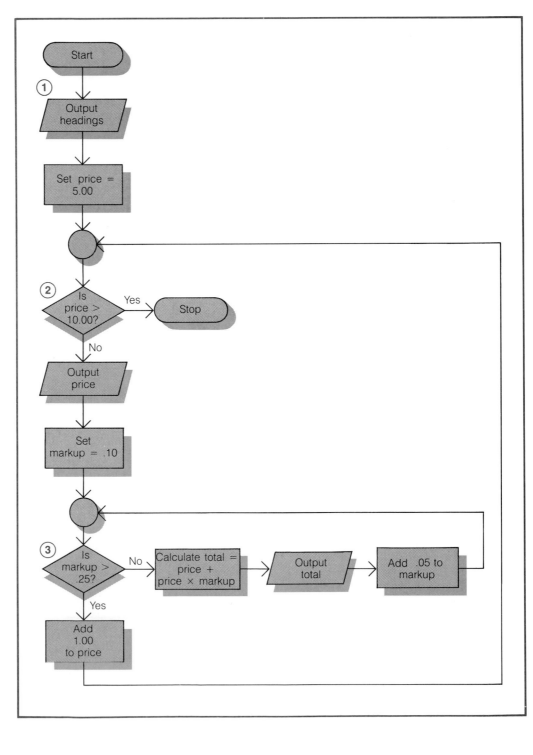

① Step 1 in the flowchart uses an input/output symbol to indicate that headings must be printed first.

② Step 2 uses a decision symbol to check the value of the price to determine if it exceeds 10.00. If it does, the program terminates as indicated with the Stop in the terminal symbol. If the computer determines that the price does not exceed the test value of 10.00, the outer loop is performed. This loop begins with an input/output symbol that prints the current value of the variable assigned to price.

③ Step 3 involves another decision symbol; this one checks the value of the markup to determine if the amount exceeds 25%. If the value does not exceed 25%, the inner loop is performed. A total is calculated and printed as indicated in the processing and input/output symbols in the flowchart. When the value of the markup exceeds the test value of 25%, the loop is completed and control passes to the decision symbol in step 2.

The pseudocode for the sample program is also provided. Compare the two design tools. Which would be easier to modify and maintain?

**Example 96**
*(Pseudocode for Example 97)*

**Pseudocode:**

```
Begin price markup program
    Output headings
    Set price to 5.00
    DOWHILE price is not greater than 10.00
        Output price
        Set markup to .10
        DOWHILE markup is not greater than .25
            Calculate total = price + (price X markup)
            Output total
            Add .05 to markup
        ENDDO
        Add 1.00 to price
    ENDDO
End price markup program
```

**Example 97**

```
100 REM CALCULATION OF PRICE MARKUPS
110 REM
120 REM THIS PROGRAM CALCULATES MARKUP PERCENTAGES ON PRICES
130 REM FROM $5.00 TO $10.00 IN INCREMENTS OF 10%, 15%, 20%,
140 REM AND 25%.  OUTPUT CONSISTS OF A LISTING OF THE PRICES
150 REM AND THE VALUES OF THE PRICES WITH THE MARKUP INCLUDED.
160 REM
170 REM         VARIABLE NAMES:
180 REM          PRICE = PRICE OF ITEM
190 REM          MARKUP = MARKUP AMOUNT
200 REM          TOTAL = PRICE + MARKUP
210 REM
220 PRINT "PRICE","10%","15%","20%","25%"
230 PRINT
240 FOR PRICE = 5.00 TO 10.00
250     PRINT USING "###.##";PRICE,
260     FOR MARKUP = .10 TO .25 STEP .05
270         LET TOTAL = PRICE + (PRICE * MARKUP)
280         PRINT USING "###.##";TOTAL,
```

*Example 97 continues*

```
290        NEXT MARKUP
300 NEXT PRICE
999 END

RUN

PRICE          10%            15%            20%            25%

  5.00           5.50           5.75           6.00           6.25
  6.00           6.60           6.90           7.20           7.50
  7.00           7.70           8.05           8.40           8.75
  8.00           8.80           9.20           9.60          10.00
  9.00           9.90          10.35          10.80          11.15
 10.00          11.00          11.50          12.00          12.50
```

As in previous programs, this program begins with the important REM section in lines 100 through 210, which includes the description of the program, definitions of variable names, and spacing to make the program easier to read.

Lines 220 and 230 accomplish the printing of the headings allowing for a blank line between the heading line and the first detail line of the report. Line 220, ① on the flowchart, carries out the processing for printing the report headings, as indicated in the input/output symbol.

Lines 240 through 310 form the outer FOR/NEXT loop. The beginning of this loop corresponds with the decision symbol in the flowchart, ②. This loop processes the prices in the range of prices from 5.00 to 10.00. If it is determined, when the value is checked, that the value does not exceed 10.00, then line 250 is executed. Line 250 codes the printing of the line with the PRINT USING statement.

The inner FOR/NEXT loop is coded in lines 260 through 290. On the flowchart the beginning of the inner FOR/NEXT loop is depicted by the decision symbol ③. The inner loop processes the markup percent that is to be added to the price. Calculation of the total of the price plus the markup is coded on line 270. This corresponds to the first processing symbol within the inner loop on the flowchart. Line 280 prints the value of the total with the PRINT USING statement. This statement precedes the NEXT statement on line 290, which transfers processing of the loop to line 260, the FOR statement.

The PRINT statement on line 300 causes the output to be double spaced. The NEXT statement on line 310 continues the processing of the outer loop, directing control to the FOR statement in line 240. Once the test value of 10.00 has been exceeded, the computer executes the line following the NEXT statement, which is line 999, the END statement.

This program illustrates a distinct advantage of FOR/NEXT statements: The values contained within the FOR/NEXT statements can be adjusted easily. If a different range of prices is to be computed using the same markup percentages, changes can easily be made in the outer FOR statement. Likewise, if a different set of percentages is to be used within the inner FOR/NEXT loop, it is simple to insert those values in the inner FOR statement.

## Arrays

So far, in dealing with variable names, we have understood that the computer establishes a storage location in memory and gives the location the variable name. The computer is able to retrieve the data from that location when it encounters the variable name. This method has been sufficient for all the programs we have written thus far, but occasionally, we shall find that it limits the techniques we can use to manipulate the data.

In particular, we may want to manipulate data in groups such as all the grades for a class, or all the days in a calendar month, or all the completion times of a marathon. In each group there are too many data values to juggle individually; at the very least it would be inconvenient to give each item a separate variable name. But like data can be processed as a group. As you will see, the FOR/NEXT statement is especially suited to this purpose. We begin with single-dimensional arrays—lists of data—then move to two-dimensional arrays.

## Single-Dimensional Arrays

To provide manipulation capabilities to process arrays, you will use **subscripted variables.**

Let us look at the difference between a variable and a subscripted variable. As mentioned, a variable name designates one location in memory. A subscripted variable, however, references multiple locations used to store similar items. Example 98 illustrates this concept.

*Example 98*

In ① the variable name A references one storage location, represented by the single block. In ② *each* of the blocks represents one storage location. Each of these storage locations is referenced by a variable of the form A(X), where the value of X determines the specific block being referenced. Values can be placed into and retrieved from these storage locations. You are probably wondering how one variable name can be used to reference multiple locations. This is made possible by **subscripts.**

The group of similar items referenced by a subscripted variable is called an **array.** Each item within an array is called an element of the array. To reference one particular element within an array, the variable name should be followed by a value in parentheses. This variable followed by a value in parentheses is called a **subscripted variable,** and the value within the parentheses is a subscript. In number ② of Example 98, the subscript is the value X. A subscript can be a numeric constant, a numeric variable, or an arithmetic expression. The value of the subscript cannot be negative, and it should not be larger than the size of the array. The subscripted variable may be either alphanumeric or numeric. Example 99 demonstrates various forms of subscripted variables.

*Example 99*       A(1)        NAME$(X)        A(T + 4)

To demonstrate the use of a subscripted variable, let us consider the ages of five children: 5, 14, 7, 12, and 2. Perhaps we want the ages of all the children to be available at the same time to determine the age of the oldest child. We could give each of these ages its own variable name—such as AGE1, AGE2, AGE3, AGE4, and AGE5—as illustrated in Example 100.

*Example 100*

| A1 | A2 | A3 | A4 | A5 |
|---|---|---|---|---|
| 5 | 14 | 7 | 12 | 2 |

This method limits the manipulation capabilities we have. On the other hand, we could also give the array of ages one variable name by subscripting that variable name, as shown in Example 101. We shall return to this data in Example 103.

*Example 101*

A(X)

| 5 | 14 | 7 | 12 | 2 |
|---|---|---|---|---|

### *The DIM Statement*

If you use a subscripted variable, most versions of BASIC automatically set up an array with ten elements. If, however, you want a larger number of storage locations for any particular list in your program, you have to instruct the computer to reserve those locations. For this purpose you use a **DIM** statement. DIM stands for dimension, and Example 102 illustrates the format of the dimension statement.

*Example 102*

**Statement Format:**
Line number DIM Variable name (Number of locations needed for this variable)

**Sample Statement:**
220 DIM NET(15)

The sample statement tells the computer to reserve 15 storage locations for the array named NET. When determining the size of the array, make sure you reserve enough locations to meet your needs. If you attempt to use an array with an inadequate number of storage locations reserved, you will receive an error message like "SUBSCRIPT OUT OF RANGE." Do not, however, arbitrarily reserve an unreasonably large number of locations because you will use up too much memory needlessly.

The DIM statement may be placed anywhere within the program as long as it precedes any statement that uses the subscripted variable. Quite often, programmers place the DIM statements toward the beginning of the program. Although it is necessary to give a dimension to any list that has more than ten elements, many programmers automatically dimension all arrays, even those with less than ten elements. The use of DIM statements for all arrays, regardless of size, provides additional internal documentation. This documentation increases the ease of debugging by demonstrating which variables are subscripted and how many elements the array contains.

A single-dimensional array is known as a **list.** You have already seen how a DIM statement is used to reserve memory locations for the elements in a list. You have also seen how a variable is subscripted to reference an element within that list. We now need to see how we can actually place data into those storage locations and how we can manipulate and retrieve data from them.

Data can be placed into the storage locations reserved for an array by using LET, READ, or INPUT statements.

### Using LET Statements to Load an Array

Remember, the purpose of the subscript following a variable is to identify which element of the array is being referenced. A(1) will reference the first element in the list named A; A(2) will reference the second element in the list named A; and so on. To place values in the storage locations—that is, to load the array—we can use the LET statement as shown in Example 103. The LET statement in this example gives the subscripted variable A(1) the value of 7.

*Example 103*

```
30 LET A(1) = 7
```

Consider our example of an array with children's ages in Example 101. To place the ages 5, 14, 7, 12, and 2 into the appropriate storage locations, we could use the following LET statements:

```
200 LET A(1) = 5
210 LET A(2) = 14
220 LET A(3) = 7
230 LET A(4) = 12
240 LET A(5) = 2
```

After executing these statements, the array is loaded and the values can be referenced by using the subscripted variable names.

### Using READ Statements to Load an Array

Just as we can use READ/DATA statements to assign values to variables, we can also use them to assign values to subscripted variables. We could load the age array with the following statements:

```
200 READ A(1),A(2),A(3),A(4),A(5)
500 DATA 5,14,7,12,2
```

### Using INPUT Statements to Load an Array

The INPUT statement may also be used to assign values to variables. The following statements would load the age array with the ages of the children.

```
250 PRINT "ENTER THE AGES OF THE CHILDREN, EACH SEPARATED"
260 PRINT "BY COMMAS."
270 INPUT A(1),A(2),A(3),A(4),A(5)
```

### Variables as Subscripts

Remember, a subscript can be a numeric constant, a numeric variable, or an arithmetic expression. The advantage of using subscripted variables to increase the manipulation capabilities of data within an array has been mentioned. The ability to subscript a variable with a variable provides the means of obtaining this increased manipulation capability.

Look again at the process of loading an array using READ/DATA statements.

```
200 READ A(1),A(2),A(3),A(4),A(5)
500 DATA 5,14,7,12,2
```

Notice that each subscript value is increased by 1 to reference the next element in the age array. By using a variable as the subscript, we can use a FOR/NEXT loop to increment the subscript value and, therefore, perform the identical process of referencing each element. The FOR/NEXT loop instructions are as follows:

```
200 FOR I = 1 TO 5
210    READ A(I)
220 NEXT I
230 DATA 5,14,7,12,2
```

Statements 200 and 220 instruct the computer to perform statement 210 five times, each time increasing the value of I by 1. The following READ statements will be executed in this loop.

```
READ A(1)
READ A(2)
READ A(3)
READ A(4)
READ A(5)
```

These instructions will perform the same process as the original READ statement:

```
200 READ A(1),A(2),A(3),A(4),A(5)
```

Although these examples demonstrate how a variable subscript can be used to load arrays, you may not yet see the advantages inherent in using the variable subscript over using the numeric constant subscript. However, if we had been processing the ages of a large number of children instead of only five, the advantages would be much more apparent. For example, you can write a FOR/NEXT loop with the READ statement to obtain the ages of 100 children using variables as subscripts:

```
200 FOR I = 1 TO 100
210    READ A(I)
220 NEXT I
```

These statements demonstrate that the ability to use a variable subscript can save a great deal of time and effort. Later we shall see additional examples of the advantages of variable subscripts.

Variable subscripts also can be used to PRINT information. Using the FOR/NEXT loop, the ages of the five children can be printed as shown in Example 104.

*Example 104*

```
250 FOR I = 1 TO 5
260    READ A(I)
270 NEXT I
280 FOR I = 1 TO 5
290    PRINT A(I)
300 NEXT I
310 DATA 5,14,7,12,2
999 END

RUN

 5
14
 7
12
 2
```

These two FOR/NEXT loops can be combined into one FOR/NEXT loop that accomplishes the same results, as shown below.

```
250 FOR I = 1 TO 5
260      READ A(I)
270      PRINT A(I)
280 NEXT I
290 DATA 5,14,7,12,2
```

How do you think the output would appear if you replaced the PRINT instruction with the following statement?

```
270 PRINT A(I);
```

The output would look like that shown in Example 105.

*Example 105*        5   14   7   12   2

### Two-Dimensional Arrays

So far, our discussion concerning subscripted variables has been dealing with single-dimensional arrays, or lists. But we are also able to store information in two-dimensional arrays, which are frequently referred to as **tables.** Example 106 illustrates the difference between a single-dimensional array and a two-dimensional array.

*Example 106*     Array A(X)

| A(1) | A(2) | A(3) | A(4) | A(5) |
|------|------|------|------|------|

. . .

Array A(X,Y)

| A(1,1) | A(1,2) | A(1,3) | A(1,4) | A(1,5) | A(1,6) |
|--------|--------|--------|--------|--------|--------|
| A(2,1) | A(2,2) | A(2,3) | A(2,4) | A(2,5) | A(2,6) |
| A(3,1) | A(3,2) | A(3,3) | A(3,4) | A(3,5) | A(3,6) |

. . .

The single-dimensional array, or list, is arranged with one element next to the other. The two-dimensional array is arranged in a rectangle composed of rows and columns. The variable names for single-dimensional arrays are subscripted with one subscript, which references a particular element within the list. The variable names for two-dimensional arrays are subscripted with two subscripts to reference a particular element within the table. Example 107 illustrates the difference between subscripts for single-dimensional arrays and subscripts for two-dimensional arrays.

*Example 107*

**Single-Dimensional Array Variable Names**:

N(1)         N(Y)         N(Y+4)

**Two-Dimensional Array Variable Names**:

N(1,4)        N(Y,D)        N(Y+3,4)

The first subscript for the two-dimensional array is the number of the element's row, and the second subscript is the number of the element's column. Therefore, NAME$(1,4) refers to an element named NAME$ in the first row of the fourth column of the table. This concept is illustrated in Example 108.

*Example 108*

NAME$(1,4)

*Dimensioning a Two-Dimensional Array*

With a two-dimensional array most versions of BASIC automatically reserve ten row locations and ten column locations for each row—hence, 100 locations. If more locations are needed, it is necessary to dimension the table according to the statement format illustrated in Example 109.

*Example 109*

**Statement Format:**

Line number DIM Array name(X,Y) where X is the row element and Y is the column element

**Sample Statement:**

200 DIM P(12,26)

As with the single-dimensional arrays, good programming practices dictate dimensioning all two-dimensional arrays, regardless of size.

Multiple single-dimensional and/or two-dimensional arrays may be dimensioned with one DIM statement as illustrated in Example 110.

*Example 110*

230 DIM X(5,20),Y(6),R(3),T(4,16)

*Using FOR/NEXT to Load a Two-Dimensional Array*

To place values into tables, process the values, and print them, it is necessary to use nested FOR/NEXT loops. The following statements are used to load a two-dimensional array of three rows and five columns:

```
300 FOR ROW = 1 TO 3
310     FOR COLUMN = 1 TO 5
320           READ A(ROW,COLUMN)
330     NEXT COLUMN
340 NEXT ROW
350 REM    DATA
360 DATA 2,4,6,8,10
370 DATA 3,5,7,9,11
380 DATA 16,15,14,13,12
999 END
```

Line 300 instructs the computer to repeat the instructions from line 300 through line 340 three times. Another FOR/NEXT loop is located within these statements. When one FOR/NEXT loop is nested within another FOR/NEXT loop, the computer increments the value of the outer loop one time, then the inner FOR/NEXT loop is repeated until the test value, in this case 5, is reached. As the computer performs the inner FOR/NEXT loop, the variable COLUMN is incremented once for each pass through the loop. Therefore, the first time the computer reads a DATA statement, the subscript values are 1 for the row (variable ROW) and 1 for the column (variable COLUMN). This is because the outer FOR/NEXT loop set the row subscript to 1 and the inner FOR/NEXT loop set the column subscript to 1. When the computer reads the first DATA element, it is given the variable name A(1,1). The second time the computer reads a DATA element, the element is given the variable name A(1,2) because the subscript COLUMN has increased in value by 1. The third time the computer reads a DATA element, the element is given the variable name A(1,3) because the subscript COLUMN has again increased in value by 1. When the computer has completed the inner FOR/NEXT loop, the value of the subscript referenced by the outer FOR/NEXT loop increases by 1; thus, the variable name becomes A(2,1). This process continues, with the value of COLUMN increasing by 1 for every pass through the inner loop (as indicated by the FOR statement in line 310), and the value of ROW increasing by 1. Upon completion of the nested FOR/NEXT loops, the following variables have values as shown:

| | | | | |
|---|---|---|---|---|
| A(1,1) = 2 | A(1,2) = 4 | A(1,3) = 6 | A(1,4) = 8 | A(1,5) = 10 |
| A(2,1) = 3 | A(2,2) = 5 | A(2,3) = 7 | A(2,4) = 9 | A(2,5) = 11 |
| A(3,1) = 16 | A(3,2) = 15 | A(3,3) = 14 | A(3,4) = 13 | A(3,5) = 12 |

### Processing Variables in a Two-Dimensional Array
Variables in a two-dimensional array are processed using the same nested FOR/NEXT loop techniques just presented. Let us say we want to add all the elements that have already been placed in a table for a final total value. Examine the following statements:

```
190 LET TOTAL = 0
200 FOR ROW = 1 TO 3
210     FOR COLUMN = 1 TO 5
220           LET TOTAL = TOTAL + A(ROW,COLUMN)
230     NEXT COLUMN
240 NEXT ROW
250 PRINT TOTAL
```

The computer will perform line 220, changing the value of COLUMN five times before it changes the value of ROW. Thus, the LET statement is performed 15 times, and each time the value of the next element in the table is added to the already accumulating total.

### Printing Two-Dimensional Arrays

Printing two-dimensional arrays also requires nested FOR/NEXT loops. The statements in Example 111 produce the table shown when they are RUN.

*Example 111*

```
200 FOR ROW = 1 TO 3
210     FOR COLUMN = 1 TO 5
220         READ AMOUNT(ROW,COLUMN)
230         PRINT AMOUNT(ROW,COLUMN),
240     NEXT COLUMN
250     PRINT
260 NEXT ROW
270 DATA 1,15,2,44,51,43,12,74,5,123,4,9,1,2,6
999 END

RUN
```

| | | | | |
|---|---|---|---|---|
| 1 | 15 | 2 | 44 | 51 |
| 43 | 12 | 74 | 5 | 123 |
| 4 | 9 | 1 | 2 | 6 |

## 7 Exercises

Answer questions 1 through 5 using the following program.

```
200 FOR X = 1 TO 10
210     READ N(X)
220     PRINT N(X)
230     LET A = N(X) + X
240     PRINT A
250 NEXT X
260 DATA 20,83,6,14.2,18,92.4,3,1,100,813
999 END
```

1. What output will result from the first pass through the FOR/NEXT loop?

2. How many times will the computer execute the READ statement?

3. What output will result from the last pass through the FOR/NEXT loop?

4. Is a DIM statement required for the program?

5. Write a DIM statement for the program.

6. Write a single DIM statement to reserve storage locations for an array named T with five rows and six columns and an array named C with seven elements.

7. Write a nested FOR/NEXT loop to place values into a table as shown.

| | | |
|---|---|---|
| 6 | 7 | 13 |
| 2 | 5 | 9 |

8. Add two statements to your program in exercise 7 that will add all the values and PRINT the total.

## Answers to Exercises

1. 20
   21

2. Ten times

3. 813
   823

4. A DIM statement is not required because the computer automatically reserves ten storage locations for an array.

5. `150 DIM N(10)`

6. `200 DIM T(5,6),C(7)`

7.
```
180 FOR O = 1 TO 2
190     FOR I = 1 TO 3
200         READ S(O,I)
210         PRINT S(O,I),
220     NEXT I
230     PRINT
240 NEXT O
250 REM DATA
260 DATA 6,7,13,2,5,9
```

8.
```
170 LET T = 0
201 LET T = T + S(O,I)
241 PRINT T
```

## Menus and Subroutines

A **menu** is not a list of food dishes and prices, but it is like a restaurant menu in the sense that it is a list of *choices*. A menu offers an easy way for users to interact with the computer, particularly users who are only minimally trained to use existing software. For instance, a menu for a word processing program might appear on the CRT screen as follows:

```
MENU

1 CREATE A DOCUMENT
2 UPDATE A DOCUMENT
3 PRINT A DOCUMENT

ENTER YOUR CHOICE:
```

To make a selection for, say, printing a document, you would type in the number 3. The computer system would then give you other options related to printing the document.

Now let us see how menu choices are used within the program.

## ON GOTO

Let us now look at menus used with the ON GOTO statement, which is a statement used with the CASE structure that we studied in Chapter 8. Instead of having an IF statement, where there are two choices (yes and no), a CASE statement gives you several choices—a format that fits very nicely into a menu.

The format of the ON GOTO statement is as follows:

*Example 112*

**Statement Format:**
Line number ON <u>n</u> GOTO Line number, Line number, Line number,...

**Sample Statement:**
```
200 ON N GOTO 330, 340, 350
```

The value in location <u>n</u>—a BASIC variable—will be whatever the user places in it by typing in the menu choice. The program in turn will place that menu choice in location N by using an input statement: INPUT N. For instance, if the value in location N is 1, then the program transfers to the first line number—330—in the list of line numbers that we separated with commas. If it has a value of 2, it goes to 340. If 3, it goes to 350. If the value is none of these numbers, then the next statement in the series of BASIC statements is executed.

This ON GOTO concept can appear complicated in the abstract; after the subroutine discussion, read on to the hot tub example to see how it really works.

## GOSUB and RETURN

A **subroutine** in BASIC is a sequence of statements grouped as a unit within the program. The transfer to the subroutine is made from the GOSUB statement. The GOSUB statement specifies the line number of the statement that starts the subroutine. At the end of the subroutine, the RETURN statement transfers control back to the statement after the GOSUB. Note how these work in the following program segment:

*Example 113*

```
                 .
                 .
                 .
 ┌─200 GOSUB 900
 │ ┌►210  .
 │ │      .
 │ │      .
 │ └►900 REM SUBROUTINE PROFIT COMPUTATION
 │        .
 │        .
 │        .
 └──970 RETURN
```

The GOSUB statement causes transfer to line 900, where the subroutine is located in the program. Line 970 is the last line of the subroutine; the RETURN statement causes a transfer to line 210.

Subroutines are particularly useful when program coding is executed more than once. Instead of repeating the code, it can be written in a subroutine; the subroutine is invoked (GOSUB) each time it is needed. After each use, the computer carries on from the line following the GOSUB.

## Menus and Subroutines: The Hot Tub Example

Which hot tub salesperson has the hottest sales? As the remarks section (lines 120 through 130) of Example 114 indicates, we are demonstrating a program that uses a menu selection to call subroutines to produce information—such as top salesperson—related to hot tub sales data.

*Example 114*

```
100 REM   HOT TUB SALES MENU                        J. HARRIS
110 REM
120 REM THIS PROGRAM USES A MENU SELECTION TO CALL SUBROUTINES
130 REM TO PRODUCE OUTPUT RELATED TO HOT TUB SALES DATA.
140 REM
150 REM            VARIABLE NAMES
160 REM            NAMES$  - SALESPERSON NAME ARRAY
170 REM            UNITS   - UNITS SOLD ARRAY
180 REM            NUMBER  - NUMBER OF ITEMS IN ARRAY
190 REM            MENU    - MENU SELECTION
200 REM            HIGH    - HIGH SALES HOLD AREA
210 REM            HIGHSP$ - HIGH SALESPERSON HOLD AREA
220 REM            TOTAL   - TOTAL SALES
230 REM            AVG     - AVERAGE SALES
240 REM
250 DIM NAMES$(100),UNITS(100)
260 REM READ IN ARRAYS
270 READ NUMBER
280 FOR S = 1 TO NUMBER
290     READ NAMES$(S),UNITS(S)
300 NEXT S
310 REM PRINT MENU
320 PRINT
330 PRINT "HOT TUB SALES MENU"
340 PRINT
350 PRINT " CODE   FUNCTION"
360 PRINT
370 PRINT "1 - TOP SALESPERSON"
380 PRINT "2 - AVERAGE SALES"
390 PRINT "3 - TOTAL SALES"
400 PRINT "4 - STOP"
410 PRINT
420 PRINT "ENTER A NUMBER, 1 THROUGH 4: ";
425 INPUT MENU
430 REM TRANSFER TO CORRECT SUBROUTINE, BASED ON MENU SELECTION
440 ON MENU GOTO 450, 470, 490, 510
450 GOSUB 540
460 GOTO 320
470 GOSUB 650
480 GOTO 320
490 GOSUB 740
500 GOTO 320
510 PRINT "END OF PROGRAM"
520 STOP
530 REM TOP SALESPERSON ROUTINE
540 LET HIGH = 0
550 FOR S = 1 TO NUMBER
560     IF UNITS(S) > HIGH THEN 580
570     GOTO 600
580     LET HIGH = UNITS(S)
590     LET HIGHSP$ = NAMES$(S)
600 NEXT S
610 PRINT
620 PRINT "TOP SALESPERSON IS ";HIGHSP$
630 RETURN
640 REM AVERAGE SALES SUBROUTINE650 LET TOTAL = 0
650 LET TOTAL = 0
660 FOR S = 1 TO NUMBER
670     LET TOTAL = TOTAL + UNITS(S)
680 NEXT S
690 LET AVG = TOTAL/NUMBER
700 PRINT
710 PRINT "AVERAGE SALES: ";AVG
720 RETURN
```

*Example 114 continues*

*Example 114, continued*

```
730 REM TOTAL SALES SUBROUTINE
740 LET TOTAL = 0
750 FOR S = 1 TO NUMBER
760     LET TOTAL = TOTAL + UNITS(S)
770 NEXT S
780 PRINT
790 PRINT "TOTAL SALES: ";TOTAL
800 RETURN
810 REM     DATA
820 DATA 6
830 DATA BOORD,176,DREY,185,FITZPATRICK,150
840 DATA GERAMI,152,MCGAHEY,120,METZGER,166
850 END
```

Each record of data (see lines 830 through 840) consists of the name of a salesperson followed by the number of hot tubs sold by that person in this fiscal year. The program (see lines 260 through 300) reads that data into two arrays: one for salespeople's names and one for the corresponding number of hot tubs sold. As lines 160 and 170 show, NAMES$ is the variable name for the salesperson name array and UNITS is the variable name for the units sold array. The program is flexible because it first reads in (on line 270) the number of salespeople (six in this example, as indicated by the data on line 820), then (on line 280) establishes a READ loop to read exactly that many salespeople.

Now that the data is available, we can print a menu, starting on line 320, to give users choices of what to do with the data. The menu gives us four choices: 1 - TOP SALESPERSON, 2 - AVERAGE SALES, 3 - TOTAL SALES, 4 - STOP. The user looking at the menu can then type in one of the codes, 1 through 4, which is placed in the variable MENU. Then, as line 440 shows, it is used with an ON GOTO statement. The ON GOTO causes the program to transfer to a line that calls the appropriate subroutine.

For instance, if the user types in 1, then the value of MENU is 1, and on line 440 the program transfers to line 450 because that is the first one in the list of statement numbers. At line 450 the program transfers to the subroutine that begins on line 540, which determines who the top salesperson is. When that routine is complete, the RETURN statement at line 630 causes the program to transfer back to the place where it was called.

The output for the menu is shown in Example 115. (The top salesperson is Drey, with 185 hot tubs.)

**Example 115**

```
HOT TUB SALES MENU

CODE    FUNCTION

1 - TOP SALESPERSON
2 - AVERAGE SALES
3 - TOTAL SALES
4 - STOP

ENTER A NUMBER, 1 THROUGH 4: 1

TOP SALESPERSON IS DREY
```

The program will keep looping back to allow the user to make a selection from the menu. To stop the program, the user must type in 4, which indicates STOP.

# Functions

Functions are precoded portions of programs. Some standard functions are available with BASIC; these are listed in Table A-1. The X in parentheses next to each function name is the argument of the function. The argument is the place holder for the data sent to the function. Functions are used either in arithmetic expressions or alone on the right side of an assignment statement. Let us look at some examples of functions to see how they work.

## SQR

Consider the first function shown in the table, SQR(X), which stands for "the square root of X" (X can represent any nonnegative number).

For example, the hypotenuse C of a right triangle, as related to sides A and B, is

$$C = \sqrt{A^2 + B^2}$$

*In BASIC this would be expressed as*

```
200 LET C = SQR(A**2+B**2)
```

## RND

Suppose you want to find a random integer between 1 and 13 (to represent the dealing of a card in a deck):

```
200 LET C = INT(RND(X)*13)+1
```

In this example the RND function returns a value between 0 and 1. Multiplying that value by 13, then taking only the integer part of it by using INT yields a number between 0 and 12. The added 1 makes the number between 1 and 13, as desired.

*Table A-1*

**Some standard BASIC functions**

| Function | Meaning |
| --- | --- |
| SQR(X) | Square root of X |
| RND(X) | A random number between 0 and 1 |
| INT(X) | The integer less than number X |
| ABS(X) | The absolute value of X |
| SGN(X) | The sign of X |
| LOG(X) | The natural logarithm (base E) of X |
| EXP(X) | E raised to the X power |
| SIN(X) | Trigonometric sine of X |
| COS(X) | Trigonometric cosine of X |
| TAN(X) | Trigonometric tangent of X |
| COT(X) | Trigonometric cotangent of X |
| ATN(X) | Trigonometric arctangent of X |

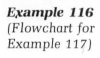

*Example 116*
(Flowchart for
Example 117)

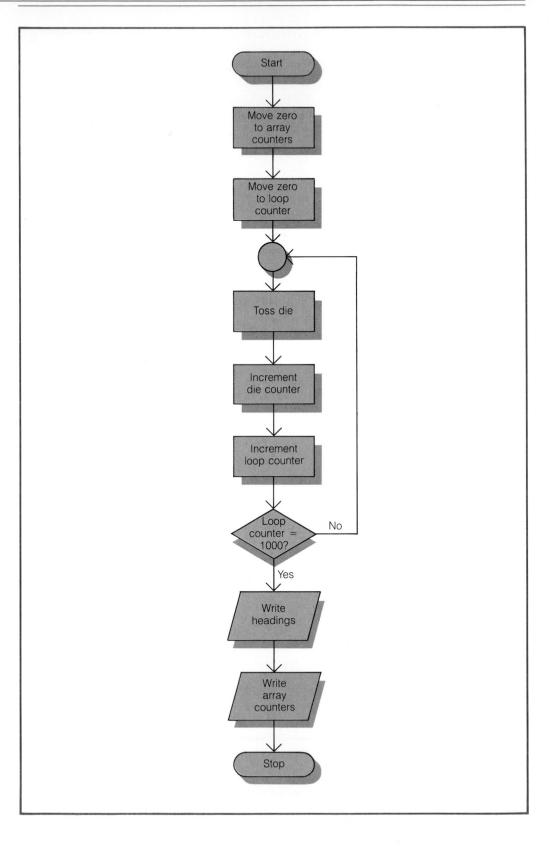

## INT

INT gives you the value of the largest integer less than or equal to the argument. When the argument is 6.41, INT(6.41) = 6. However, for negative numbers it is not so obvious. For instance, INT(−2.44) = −3.

## Die Toss Example

This example uses two functions—the INT and the RND functions—which are combined to test the randomizing formula to see if the results really are equally distributed. We shall simulate the tossing of a six-sided die. If we have a good randomizing program. the chances should be about equal that any one of the six sides (1, 2, 3, 4, 5, or 6) could appear when we toss the die. If, as the flowchart in Example 116 indicates, we are going to toss the die 1000 times, then the number of times we get any of the six numbers should be about equal. We shall test this proposition with our program.

Notice in Example 117 that we have set up a FOR/NEXT loop to toss the die. In simulating the toss of the die, we shall follow the formula shown on line 330 of the program in Example 117: INT(RND(X)*6) + 1. The RND function returns a number between 0 and 1; when we multiply this by 6, the result is between 0 and 5.999. When we take the INT function, that makes the number an integer between 0 and 5. When we add 1 to it, then it is an integer between 1 and 6. These two functions together deliver some integer between 1 and 6, and that integer is placed in location DIE.

To illustrate how this works, suppose the RND function yields .61. Multiply this number by 6 to get 3.66. The INT function reduces it to 3. Add 1, and the final result in DIE is 4.

Or: If RND returns .981, then 6 times .981 is 5.886, INT(5.886) is 5, 5 + 1 is 6, and the result is placed in DIE.

In either case we got a number between 1 and 6. Try other examples yourself, but be sure your original value from the RND function is *between* 0 and 1.

Note that on line 340 DIE is used as a subscript to add to the proper counter. For example, if 2 appeared on a particular turn, 1 would be added to the counter for 2s. The idea is that when we are done we shall have six counters with six numbers corresponding to the number of times the numbers 1 through 6 were thrown by the toss of the die.

*Example 117*

```
100 REM USING RND TO TOSS DIE          L. ALBAND
110 REM
120 REM THIS PROGRAM USES THE RND FUNCTION TO SIMULATE THE
130 REM TOSSING OF A DIE 1000 TIMES. FOR EACH DIE TOSS, A NUMBER
140 REM BETWEEN 1 AND 6 WILL BE GENERATED. THE PROGRAM WILL COUNT
150 REM THE NUMBER OF TIMES EACH RESULT (1 THROUGH 6) APPEARS
160 REM AND PRINT THE FINAL COUNTS.
170 REM
180 REM     VARIABLE NAMES
190 REM          COUNT - COUNTER ARRAY
200 REM          DIE   - DIE TOSS
210 REM
220 DIM COUNT(6)
230 REM INITIALIZE COUNT ARRAY
```

*Example 117 continues*

*Example 117,*
*continued*

```
240 FOR S = 1 TO 6
250    COUNT(S) = 0
260 NEXT S
270 REM DIE TOSS LOOP
280 PRINT
290 PRINT "BEGINNING DIE TOSSES...PLEASE WAIT"
300 PRINT
310 X = 1
320 FOR S = 1 TO 1000
330    DIE = INT(RND(X)*6) + 1
340    COUNT(DIE) = COUNT(DIE) + 1
350 NEXT S
360 REM PRINT RESULTS
370 PRINT "DIE","COUNT"
380 PRINT
390 FOR S = 1 TO 6
400    PRINT S,COUNT(S)
410 NEXT S
420 PRINT
430 END
```

Example 118 shows the output for this program. If you run this program, you will find the results will probably vary from the results shown here. The only thing that will be the same is that the numbers probably will not vary much from each other and that they should add up to 1,000.

**Example 118**

```
BEGINNING DIE TOSSES...PLEASE WAIT

DIE          COUNT

1            155
2            159
3            160
4            198
5            162
6            166
```

## / Programming Exercises

The following are programming exercises in the BASIC language arranged in order of increasing difficulty and complexity. Notice that in some of the problems we provide both the input and the expected output. In others we leave it to you to determine the output.

1. Write a program to figure the difference between 33 and 13 and print the following output.

   ```
   THE DIFFERENCE BETWEEN 33 AND 13 IS 20
   ```

2. Write a program using the INPUT statement to give the following output.

   ```
   ENTER 3 NUMBERS
   ?
   THE SUM OF THESE THREE NUMBERS IS
   ```

3. Write a program using the INPUT statement to give the following edited output.

```
ENTER ITEM
?
ENTER PRICE
?1.98
THE PRICE FOR SHOELACES IS $1.98
```

4. Use PRINT TAB to print your initials with a selected character such as X. For example:

```
XXXXX      X        X   X
    X      X        XX XX
    X      X        X X X
    X      X        X   X
    X      XXXXX     X   X
```

5. Write a program to prepare a student honor roll. There are five sets of students' grades to be averaged. Any student with an average of 92 or higher is eligible for the honor roll. Input consists of the following names and grades:

| Name | Grades |
|---|---|
| CATHY CARY | 92,99,94,98,94 |
| PAULETTE RACKOW | 81,80,72,92,90 |
| KITTIE STEWART | 95,96,97,96,96 |
| NORMAN LEE | 71,85,88,90,89 |
| DELORIS PUSINS | 85,85,89,90,89 |
| BRENDA WOODARD | 95,94,99,96,95 |

6. The following inventory items are to be sold at a 15 percent discount. Read the item name and current price. Display the item name and discounted price. Use the following input data:

| Item Name | Current Price | Item Name | Current Price |
|---|---|---|---|
| BRUSH | 2.98 | SHAMPOO | 1.35 |
| CURLERS | 4.00 | CONDITIONER | 1.60 |
| PINS | 1.89 | | |

Expected output:

| | |
|---|---|
| BRUSH | 2.53 |
| CURLERS | 3.40 |
| PINS | 1.61 |
| SHAMPOO | 1.15 |
| CONDITIONER | 1.36 |

7. Write a program to list several activities and the number of calories they expend in time intervals of 15, 30, 45, and 60 minutes. Input should consist of:

| Activity | Calories Burned per Minute |
|---|---|
| Sleeping | 2.3 |
| Sitting | 1.7 |
| Swimming | 6.0 |
| Jogging | 15.0 |

8. Read data for instructor name and three class sizes for each instructor. Display the name of any instructor with an average class size larger than 30 students. Also display the total number of students in all classes. Use the following input data:

| Instructor | Class 1 | Class 2 | Class 3 |
|---|---|---|---|
| CLAYTON LONG | 30 | 30 | 25 |
| JACK MUNYAN | 35 | 31 | 30 |
| TED BAHN | 40 | 41 | 30 |
| JOYCE FOY | 25 | 30 | 35 |
| MICKEY PERLOW | 30 | 31 | 26 |

Show how the expected output should appear.

9. Using single-dimensional arrays, write an interactive program to input names of contributors for the local charity drive and the amount of their contributions. The program should also print a list of the names and the amounts. Include a report title, column headings, and lines that give the total number of contributors and the total contributions.

10. Write a program to read a three-by-five array (3 rows, 5 columns) and display it by column.
Input is as follows:

```
14        6        11        3        10
1         5        8         16       20
7         4        2         18       9
```

Output is as follows:

```
14        1        7
6         5        4
11        8        2
3         16       18
10        20       9
```

# Appendix B

## Number Systems

Data can be represented in the computer in one of two basic ways: as **numeric data** or as **alphanumeric data.** The internal representation of alphanumeric data—letters, digits, special characters—was discussed in Chapter 4. Recall that alphanumeric data may be represented using various codes; EDCDIC and ASCII are two common codes. Alphanumeric data, even if all digits, cannot be used for arithmetic operations. Data used for arithmetic calculations must be stored numerically.

Data stored numerically can be represented as the binary equivalent of the decimal value with which we are familiar. That is, values such as 1050, 43218, and 3 that we input to the computer will be converted to the binary number system. In this appendix we shall study the binary number system (base 2) and two related systems, octal (base 8) and hexadecimal (base 16).

## Number Bases

A number base is a specific collection of symbols on which a number system can be built. The number base familiar to us is base 10, upon which the **decimal** number system is built. There are ten symbols—0 through 9—used in the decimal system.

Since society uses base 10, that is the number base most of us understand and can use easily. It would theoretically be possible, however, for all of us to learn to use a different number system. This number system could contain a different number of symbols and perhaps even symbols that are unfamiliar.

### Base 2: The Binary Number System

Base 2 has exactly two symbols: 0 and 1. All numbers in the **binary** system must be formed using these two symbols. As you can see in column 2 of Table B-1, this means that numbers in the binary system become long quickly; the number

1000 in base 2 is equivalent to 8 in base 10. (When different number bases are being discussed, it is common practice to use the number base as a subscript. In this case we could say $1000_2 = 8_{10}$.) If you were to continue counting in base 2, you would soon see that the binary numbers were very long and unwieldy. The number $5000_{10}$ is equal to $10011100010000_2$.

The size and sameness—all those zeros and ones—of binary numbers make them subject to frequent error when they are being manipulated by humans. To improve both convenience and accuracy, it is common to express the values represented by binary numbers in the more concise octal and hexadecimal number bases.

## Base 8: The Octal Number System

The **octal** number system uses exactly eight symbols: 0, 1, 2, 3, 4, 5, 6, and 7. Base 8 is a convenient shorthand for base 2 numbers because 8 is a power of 2: $2^3 = 8$. As you will see when we discuss conversions, one octal digit is the equivalent of exactly three binary digits. The use of octal (or hexadecimal) as a shorthand for binary is common in printed output of main storage and, in some cases, in programming.

Look at the column of octal numbers in Table B-1. Notice that, since 7 is the last symbol in base 8, the following number is 10. In fact, we can count right through the next seven numbers in the usual manner, as long as we end with 17. Note, however, that $17_8$ is pronounced *one-seven*, not *seventeen*. The octal number 17 is followed by 20 through 27, and so on. The last double-digit number is 77, which is followed by 100. Although it takes a little practice, you can see that it would be easy to learn to count in base 8. However, hexadecimal, or base 16, is not quite as easy.

*Table B-1*    **Number bases 10, 2, 8, 16: First values**

| Base 10 (decimal) | Base 2 (binary) | Base 8 (octal) | Base 16 (hexadecimal) |
|---|---|---|---|
| 0 | 0000 | 0 | 0 |
| 1 | 0001 | 1 | 1 |
| 2 | 0010 | 2 | 2 |
| 3 | 0011 | 3 | 3 |
| 4 | 0100 | 4 | 4 |
| 5 | 0101 | 5 | 5 |
| 6 | 0110 | 6 | 6 |
| 7 | 0111 | 7 | 7 |
| 8 | 1000 | 10 | 8 |
| 9 | 1001 | 11 | 9 |
| 10 | 1010 | 12 | A |
| 11 | 1011 | 13 | B |
| 12 | 1100 | 14 | C |
| 13 | 1101 | 15 | D |
| 14 | 1110 | 16 | E |
| 15 | 1111 | 17 | F |
| 16 | 10000 | 20 | 10 |

## Base 16: The Hexadecimal Number System

The **hexadecimal** number system uses exactly 16 symbols. As we have just seen, base 10 uses the familiar digits 0 through 9, and bases 2 and 8 use a subset of those symbols. Base 16, however, needs those ten symbols (0 through 9) and six more. The six additional symbols used in the hexadecimal number system are the letters A through F. So the base 16 symbols are: 0, 1, 2, 3, 4, 5, 6, 7, 8, 9, A, B, C, D, E, and F. It takes some adjusting to think of A or D as a digit instead of a letter. It also takes a little time to become accustomed to numbers such as 6A2F or even ACE. Both of these examples are legitimate numbers in hexadecimal.

As you become familiar with hexadecimal, consider the matter of counting. Counting sounds simple enough, but it can be confusing in an unfamiliar number base with new symbols. The process is the same as counting in base 10, but most of us learned to count when we were too young to think about the process itself. Quickly—what number follows 24CD? The answer is 24CE. We increased the right-most digit by one—D to E—just as you would have in the more obvious case of 6142 to 6143. What is the number just before $1000_{16}$? The answer is $FFF_{16}$; the last symbol (F) is a triple-digit number. Compare this with $999_{10}$, which precedes $1000_{10}$; 9 is the last symbol in base 10. As a familiarization exercise, try counting from 1 to 100 in base 16. Remember to use A through F as the second symbol in the teens, twenties, and so forth ( . . . 27, 28, 29, 2A, 2B, and so on).

## Conversions Between Number Bases

It is sometimes convenient to use a number in a base different from the base currently being used—that is, to change the number from one base to another. Many programmers can nimbly convert a number from one base to another, among bases 10, 2, 8, and 16. We shall consider these conversion techniques now. Table B-2 summarizes the methods.

*Table B-2*    **Summary conversion chart**

| From Base | To Base | | | |
|---|---|---|---|---|
| | **2** | **8** | **16** | **10** |
| **2** | —— | Group binary digits by 3, convert | Group binary digits by 4, convert | Expand number and convert base 2 digits to base 10 |
| **8** | Convert each octal digit to 3 binary digits | —— | Convert to base 2, then to base 16 | Expand number and convert base 8 digits to base 10 |
| **16** | Convert each hexadecimal digit to 4 binary digits | Convert to base 2, then to base 8 | —— | Expand number and convert base 16 digits to base 10 |
| **10** | Divide number repeatedly by 2; use remainders as answer | Divide number repeatedly by 8; use remainders as answer | Divide number repeatedly by 16; use remainders as answer | —— |

## To Base 10 from Bases 2, 8, and 16

We present these conversions together because the technique is the same for all three.

Let us begin with the concept of positional notation. **Positional notation** means that the value of a digit in a number depends not only on its own intrinsic value but also on its location in the number. Given the number 2363, we know that the appearance of the digit 3 represents two different values, 300 and 3. Table B-3 shows the names of the relative positions.

*Table B-3*

**Digit positions**

| Digit | 2 | 3 | 6 | 3 |
|---|---|---|---|---|
| Position | Thousand | Hundred | Ten | Unit |

Using these positional values, the number 2363 is understood to mean:

$$\begin{array}{r} 2000 \\ 300 \\ 60 \\ \underline{\phantom{00}3} \\ 2363 \end{array}$$

This number can also be expressed as:

$(2 \times 1000) + (3 \times 100) + (6 \times 10) + 3$

We can express this expanded version of the number another way, using powers of 10 (note that $10^0 = 1$).

$2363 = (2 \times 10^3) + (3 \times 10^2) + (6 \times 10^1) + (3 \times 10^0)$

Once you understand the expanded notation, the rest is easy: You expand the number as we just did in base 10, but use the appropriate base of the number. For example, follow the steps to convert $61732_8$ to base 10:

1. Expand the number, using 8 as the base:

   $61732 = (6 \times 8^4) + (1 \times 8^3) + (7 \times 8^2) +$
   $(3 \times 8^1) + (2 \times 8^0)$

2. Complete the arithmetic:

   $61732 = (6 \times 4096) + (1 \times 512) + (7 \times 64) +$
   $(3 \times 8) + 2$
   $= 24576 + 512 + 448 + 24 + 2$

3. Answer: $61732_8 = 25562_{10}$

The same expand-and-convert technique can be used to convert from base 2 or base 16 to base 10. As you consider the following two examples, use Table B-1 to make the conversions. (For example, A in base 16 converts to 10 in base 10.)

Convert $C14A_{16}$ to base 10:

$$C14A_{16} = (12 \times 16^3) + (1 \times 16^2) + (4 \times 16^1) + 10$$
$$= (12 \times 4096) + (1 \times 256) + (4 \times 16) + 10$$
$$= 49482$$

So $C14A_{16} = 49482_{10}$.

Convert $100111_2$ to base 10:

$$100111_2 = (1 \times 2^5) + (1 \times 2^2) + (1 \times 2) + 1$$
$$= 39$$

So $100111_2 = 39_{10}$.

## From Base 10 to Bases 2, 8, and 16

These conversions use a simpler process but more complicated arithmetic. The process, often called the *remainder method*, is basically a series of repeated divisions by the number of the base to which you are converting. You begin by using the number to be converted as the dividend; succeeding dividends are the quotients of the previous division. The converted number is the combined remainders accumulated from the divisions. There are two points to remember:

1. Keep dividing until you reach a zero quotient.

2. Use the remainders in reverse order.

Consider converting $6954_{10}$ to base 8:

```
8|6954
 8|869     2
  8|108    5
   8|13    4
    8|1    5
     0     1
```

Using the remainders backwards, $6954_{10} = 15452_8$.

Now use the same technique to convert $4823_{10}$ to base 16:

```
16|4823
 16|301    7
  16|18    13 (=D)
   16|1    2
     0     1
```

The remainder 13 is equivalent to D in base 16. So $4823_{10} = 12D7_{16}$.

Convert $49_{10}$ to base 2:

```
2|49
 2|24     1
  2|12    0
   2|6    0
    2|3   0
     2|1  1
       0  1
```

Again using the remainders in reverse order, $49_{10} = 110001_2$.

## To Base 2 from Bases 8 and 16

To convert a number to base 2 from base 8 or base 16, convert each digit separately to three or four binary digits, respectively. Use Table B-1 to make the conversion. Leading zeros may be needed in each grouping of digits to fill out each to three or four digits.

Convert $4732_8$ to base 2:

| 4 | 7 | 3 | 2 |
|---|---|---|---|
| 100 | 111 | 011 | 010 |

So $4732_8 = 100111011010_2$.

Now convert $A046B_{16}$ to base 2:

| A | 0 | 4 | 6 | B |
|---|---|---|---|---|
| 1010 | 0000 | 0100 | 0110 | 1011 |

Thus $A046B_{16} = 10100000010001101011_2$.

## From Base 2 to Bases 8 and 16

To convert a number from base 2 to base 8 or base 16, group the binary digits from the right in groups of three or four, respectively. Again use Table B-1 to help you make the conversion to the new base.

Convert $111101001011_2$ to base 8 and base 16:

In the base 8 conversion, group the digits three at a time, starting on the right:

| 111 | 101 | 001 | 011 |
|---|---|---|---|
| 7 | 5 | 1 | 3 |

So $111101001011_2 = 7513_8$.

For the conversion to base 16, group the digits four at a time, starting on the right:

| 1111 | 0100 | 1011 |
|---|---|---|
| F | 4 | B |

$111101001011_2 = F4B_{16}$.

Sometimes the number of digits in a binary number is not exactly divisible by 3 or 4. You may, for example, start grouping the digits three at a time and finish with one or two "extra" digits on the left side of the number. In this case, just add as many zeros as you need to the front of the binary number.

Consider converting $1010_2$ to base 8. By adding two zeros to the front of the number to make it $001010_2$, we now have six digits, which can be conveniently grouped three at a time:

| 001 | 010 |
|---|---|
| 1 | 2 |

So $1010_2 = 12_8$.

/ **Summary and Key Terms**

- Data can be represented in the computer as **numeric data** or **alphanumeric data.** Data to be used for arithmetic calculations must be represented numerically.

- The number system familiar to us is base 10, the **decimal** number system; it uses symbols 0 through 9.

- Base 2, the **binary** number system, uses the two symbols 0 and 1.

- Base 8, the **octal** number system, uses the symbols 0 through 7.

- Base 16, the **hexadecimal** number system, uses the symbols 0 through 9 and A through F.

- The concept of **positional notation** means that the value of a digit in a number depends on its location in the number as well as on its own intrinsic value.

- Octal and hexadecimal are convenient shorthand number systems for representing data converted from base 2.

- There are techniques for converting numbers from one number base to another. See the summary of conversion methods in Table B-2.

/ **Review Questions**

1. Count as follows: 25 to 61 in base 8, 10001 to 100010 in base 2, CDF to D00 in base 16.

2. Convert as follows:

   $100111_2$ to base 10; $671_8$ to base 10; $ACED_{16}$ to base 10;
   $1101010_2$ to base 10; $43_8$ to base 10; $1023B_{16}$ to base 10.

   Check your work by performing each conversion in reverse.

3. Convert as follows:

   $9073_{10}$ to base 2; $614_{10}$ to base 8; $591_{10}$ to base 16;
   $61_{10}$ to base 2; $3146_{10}$ to base 8; $157_{10}$ to base 16.

   Check your work by performing each conversion in reverse.

4. Convert as follows:

   $461_8$ to base 2; $F16C_{16}$ to base 2;
   $2107_8$ to base 2; $1A046_{16}$ to base 2;
   $111101_2$ to base 8; $110101100101_2$ to base 16;
   $10011001_2$ to base 8; $10101100010101_2$ to base 16.

# Credits

We are indebted to the many people and organizations who contributed excerpts, illustrations, and photos to this book. The page numbers and contributors are listed below.

## Text Credits

8. Margin note entitled "The Age Machine" based on "Age Machine Evolves from Artist's Idea," *Computerworld*, 4/23/84, p. 27.

34. Margin note entitled "What's a 'Microsuper'?" excerpted from "What's a 'Microsuper'?," *Computerworld*, 10/21/85, p. 39. Copyright 1985 by CW Communications/Inc., Framingham, MA 01701. Reprinted from *Computerworld*.

64. Margin note entitled "The Computer Museum" courtesy of The Computer Museum.

67. Margin note entitled "Japan's Persistent Software Gap" based on "Japan's Persistent Software Gap," *Fortune*, 10/15/84, pp. 150–160.

185. Margin note entitled "*USA Today*: Newspaper in Space" based on "*USA Today*: Satellite Network Delivers Daily," *Computerworld*, 10/14/85, p. 1.

253. Margin note entitled "Egoless Programming" excerpted from *The Psychology of Computer Programming* by Gerald M. Weinberg. Copyright © 1971 by Litton Educational Publishing, Inc. Reprinted by permission of Van Nostrand Reinhold Company.

274. Quotes in the margin note entitled "The Reports of My Death Have Been Greatly Exaggerated" excerpted from "Here's What's On Your Mind," *Computerworld*, 3/11/85, pp. ID 10+. Copyright 1985 by CW Communications/ Inc., Framingham, MA 01701. Reprinted from *Computerworld*.

309. Quote in the margin note entitled "A Happy UNIX Customer" excerpted from "The Fate of UNIX," *Business Computer Systems* 2/85, pp. 42+. Reprinted by permission of Cahners Publishing Company.

321. Box entitled "On the Road" based on "PC Rocks and Rolls," *PC Magazine*, 1/24/84.

379. Box entitled "The Shape of Things to Come" excerpted from "The Shape of Things to Come," *PC World*, 1/86, pp. 143–151. Reprinted by permission of *PC World*, Volume 4, Issue 1 (January, 1986). Published at 501 2nd Street, Suite 600, San Francisco, CA 94107.

## Illustration Credits

487. F17-6 Art and legend adapted from *Potential Health Hazards of Video Display Terminals* by National Institute for Occupational Safety and Health, Cincinnati, Ohio, 1981, p. 23.

495. F17-11b Redrawn from *InfoWorld*, 12/18/85, p. 1. Copyright © 1985 by Popular Computing Inc., a subsidiary of CW Communications, Inc. Reprinted from *InfoWorld*, 1060 Marsh Road, Menlo Park, CA 94025.

## Text Photo Credits

ii-iii. Photos courtesy of Hewlett-Packard.

v. J. Gilderoy–Photo Graphics.

vi. Top, Courtesy of Apple Computers, Inc.
Middle, Courtesy of Cray Research, Inc.
Bottom, Courtesy of Control Data Corporation.

vii. Top, Wayland Lee.
Middle, Photo courtesy of Hewlett-Packard.

viii. Left, Photo courtesy of Hewlett-Packard.
Right, Photo courtesy of International Business Machines.

ix. Photo courtesy of Hewlett-Packard.

x. Top left, IBM Archives.
Bottom left, Sperry Corporation.
Top right, Courtesy of Motorola, Inc.

xi. Top, Apollo Computer Inc.
Bottom, Photo courtesy of Digital Equipment Corporation.

xii. Top, BASF Systems Corporation.
Middle, Courtesy of Apple Computers, Inc.

xiii. Top left, Courtesy of Radio Shack, a division of Tandy Corporation.
Top right, Sperry Corporation.
Bottom, NASA.

xiv. Photo courtesy of Hewlett-Packard.

xv. Photos courtesy of Hewlett-Packard.

xvi. Photo courtesy of Hewlett-Packard.

xvii. Top, Sperry Corporation.
Bottom, Photo courtesy of Hewlett-Packard.

xviii. Top left, Courtesy of Apple Computers, Inc.
Top right, Photo courtesy of Borland International, Inc.
Bottom, Photo courtesy of Hewlett-Packard.

xix. Top, Produced with 35mm Express™ from BPS.
Bottom, Courtesy of Texas Instruments.

xx. Top, Dow Jones and Company, Inc.
Bottom, CompuServe, Inc.

xxi. Top, Courtesy of Bell Laboratories, AT&T.
Bottom, Photo courtesy of Hewlett-Packard.
xxii. Left, Sperry Corporation.
Right, Courtesy of Bell Laboratories, AT&T.
xxiii. Sperry Corporation.
xxiv. See gallery opener credits.
4. NASA.
5. ©Steven M. Caras.
6. F1-1, top left and right Courtesy of Apple Computers, Inc.
F1-1, bottom left and right Photos courtesy of Hewlett-Packard.
8. ©Nancy Burson with Richard Carling and David Kramlich.
9. F1-2 ©Terry Hourigan.
10. F1-3 Sperry Corporation.
11. Photo: Jeffrey Aaronson/Aspen.
13. F1-4 ©Terry Hourigan.
14. Left, General Motors Corporation.
F1-5 Pacific Gas and Electric Company.
15. F1-6 Dr. Roy Harrell, University of Florida.
16. F1-7 Photo by Bill Boyle/Purdue University.
17. F1-8 NOAA.
F1-9 Courtesy of International Business Machines Corp.
18. F1-10 Courtesy of Apple Computer, Inc.
22. Breeder Software Specialists.
24. Courtesy of International Business Machines Corp.
26. F2-3(a) Sperry Corporation.
F2-3(b) Recognition Equipment Incorporated.
F2-3(c) Photo courtesy NCR Corporation.
28. F2-4 Photo courtesy of International Business Machines Corp.
29. F2-5(a,b) Sperry Corporation.
30. F2-6(a,c) BASF Systems Corporation.
F2-6(b) Sperry Corporation.
32. F2-8(a) Photo courtesy of International Business Machines Corp.
F2-8(b) Courtesy of Cray Research Inc.
F2-8(c) Photo courtesy of Digital Equipment Corporation.
F2-8(d) Photo courtesy of Hewlett-Packard.
50. F3-1 Culver Pictures.
51. F3-2 Both, IBM Archives.
52. F3-3 Both, IBM Archives.
53. F3-4 Culver Pictures.
54. F3-5(a-c) IBM Archives.
55. F3-6 IBM Archives.
56. Both, IBM Archives.

57. F3-8 Both, Iowa State University of Science and Technology.
58. F3-9 IBM Archives.
59. F3-10 Courtesy of Princeton University Communications.
60. F3-11 Sperry Corporation.
61. F3-12, F3-13 Both, IBM Archives.
63. F3-14 Photo courtesy of Hewlett-Packard.
64. The Computer Museum, Boston, MA.
65. F3-15 IBM Archives.
66. F3-16 Wide World Photos.
69. F3-17(a,b) Courtesy of Margaret and Jerry Wozniak.
F3-17(c) Courtesy of Apple Computer, Inc.
71. Upper left, Courtesy of NeXT, Inc. Center, Microsoft Corporation. Upper right, ©Lotus Development Corporation 1986. Used with permission.
72. F3-18 Photo courtesy of International Business Machines Corp.
73. Photo courtesy of International Business Machines Corp.
75. F3-19 COMPAQ Computer Corporation.
102. F5-1 Courtesy of International Business Machines Corp.
104. F5-2 Sperry Corporation.
105. F5-3 Courtesy of Texas Instruments.
108. Photo courtesy NCR Corporation.
109. Cauzin Systems, Inc.
110. F5-6 Photo courtesy NCR Corporation.
113. F5-8 Sperry Corporation.
114. F5-9 Photo courtesy NCR Corporation.
115. Courtesy of Texas Instruments.
117. F5-10(a) Wayland Lee.
F5-10(b,c) Photo courtesy of Hewlett-Packard.
118. F5-11(a,c) Computer Graphics Research Group, Ohio State University.
F5-11(b) The Graphic Systems Research Group at the IBM U.K. Scientific Centre.
119. F5-11(d,e) ©Melvin Prueitt/Photo Researchers, Inc.
F5-11(f) Copyright 1986 Pixar. All rights reserved.
120. F5-12 Courtesy of International Business Machines Corp.
F5-13 Matrix Instruments, Inc.
121. Left, Casio, Inc.
F5-14 Copyright 1986 Pixar. All rights reserved.
122. F5-15(a,b) Chrysler Corporation.
123. F5-16 CALCOMP.
F5-17 Photo courtesy of Hewlett-Packard.

124. F5-18(a) Courtesy of Apple Computer, Inc.
F5-18(b) Electronic Arts.
125. F5-19(a,b) Courtesy of Apple Computer, Inc.
F5-20 Photo courtesy of Hewlett-Packard.
126. F5-21(a,b) Photo courtesy of Hewlett-Packard.
129. F5-23 Both, ITT Qume, San Jose, CA.
131. F5-25 Courtesy of International Business Machines Corp.
133. F5-26 Photo courtesy of Hewlett-Packard.
134. F5-27 Photo courtesy of NCR Corporation.
147. F6-2 Sperry Corporation.
150. F6-4 Courtesy of International Business Machines Corp.
153. F6-6(a), F6-7 Sperry Corporation.
156. F6-10(a) Courtesy of Texas Instruments.
F6-10(b) Nashau Computer Products.
F6-10(c) BASF Systems Corporation.
157. F6-12 Photo courtesy NCR Corporation.
159. F6-13(a,c) Amcodyne Inc.
166. F6-19 Courtesy of International Business Machines Corp.
168. Polaroid.
169. F6-20(a) Courtesy of Apple Computer, Inc.
170. F6-21(a) ©James Schnepf.
F6-21(b) Microscience International Corporation.
171. F6-22(a,b) Plus Development Corp.
173. Left, Wayland Lee/Courtesy LifeCard International, Inc.
F6-23 Mark Joseph/Chicago.
183. F7-1 Apollo Computer Inc.
184. F7-2 Sperry Corporation.
185. USA TODAY/Gannett Co., Inc.
187. F7-4(b,c) Inmac.
F7-4(d) CompuServe, Inc.
191. Photo: Jeffrey Aaronson/Aspen.
192. F7-8 Inmac.
218. Department of the Navy.
244. ©Ian Yeomans/Susan Griggs Agency Ltd.
272. Department of the Navy.
359. F13-1 Courtesy of International Business Machines Corp.
360. F13-2(a,c) Photo courtesy of Hewlett-Packard.
F13-2(b) Wayland Lee.
361. F13-3 Courtesy of Apple Computer, Inc.
F13-4 Inmac.
363. F13-5, F13-6 Courtesy of Apple Computer, Inc.
365. F13-7 CompuServe, Inc.

366. Ed Kashi.
367. F13-8 Photo courtesy of Addison-Wesley Publishing Company.
    F13-9 Courtesy of Apple Computer, Inc.
368. Left, Human Edge.
    Right, CBS Interactive Learning.
369. Left, MECA.®
    Center, Electronic Arts.
    Right, Microsoft Corporation.
370. F13-10 Courtesy of Apple Computer, Inc.
    Lower left, Electronic Data Systems.
371. F13-11 Courtesy of Apple Computer, Inc.
372. Courtesy of Apple Computer, Inc.
373. F13-12(a–c) Courtesy of Apple Computer, Inc.
    F13-13 Courtesy of International Business Machines Corp.
374. F13-14 Courtesy of Bell Laboratories, AT&T.
375. Top, COMPAQ Computer Corporation.
    F13-15(a) Courtesy of Radio Shack, a division of Tandy Corporation.
    F13-15(b) COMPAQ Computer Corporation.
376. F13-16(a) Courtesy of International Business Machines Corp.
    F13-16(b) Photo courtesy of Hewlett-Packard.
377. F13-17(a) Zenith Electronic Corporation.
    F13-17(b) Courtesy of International Business Machines Corp.
378. F13-18(a) Courtesy of Apple Computer, Inc.
    F13-18(b) INFOMART.
379. ©Human Touch Computer Products, Cherry Hill, NJ.
381. ©Michael Salas.
384. F13-19 Inmac.
    F13-20 Courtesy of Radio Shack, a division of Tandy Corporation.
431. Paul Ambrose Studios, 1985. All rights reserved.
432. F15-11 Wayland Lee.
435. F15-15(a) Microsoft Corporation.
    F15-15(b) Courtesy of International Business Machines Corp.
436. F15-16(a–c) Software Publishing Company.
437. F15-17(a,c) ©Lotus Development Corporation 1986. Used with permission.
    F15-17(b) Mouse Systems.
    F15-17(d) Polaroid.
    F15-17(e,f) Produced with 35mm Express™ from BPS.
439. F15-19 Produced with 35mm Express™ from BPS.

440. F15-20(a–c) Courtesy of Grafix Partner by Brightbill Roberts.
441. F15-21 Decision Resources.
    F15-22(a–c) Courtesy of International Business Machines Corp.
443. F15-23 Polaroid.
452. Both, Dow Jones and Company, Inc.
483. F17-3 left, Photo courtesy of Hewlett-Packard.
    F17-3 right, Courtesy of Texas Instruments.
486. F17-5 Courtesy of AT&T.
491. F17-7(a) Photo courtesy of Digital Equipment Corporation.
    F17-7(b) Chrysler Corporation.
    F17-7(c) Photo courtesy of Hewlett-Packard.
492. ©Malcolm S. Kirk.
493. F17-8(a) Courtesy of Cincinnati Milacron.
    F17-8(b) Courtesy of Hitachi, Ltd.
494. F17-9 Printed with permission from Automatix, the adaptive automation company.
495. F17-10 Courtesy of International Business Machines Corp.
    F17-11 Photo courtesy of Hewlett-Packard.
506. Photo courtesy of Borland International, Inc.
509. Sperry Corporation.
511. F18-3 Courtesy of International Business Machines Corp.

# Gallery Photo Credits

## Gallery 1

Opener: Rockwell International.
1. Art: George Samuelson.
2. Courtesy of International Business Machines Corp.
3. Photo Courtesy of Mentor Graphics.
4. TRW.
5. Courtesy of Motorola, Inc.
6. Courtesy of AT&T.
7. Courtesy of International Business Machines Corp.
8. Sperry Corporation.
9. TRW.
10. Courtesy of Motorola, Inc.
11. Courtesy of International Business Machines Corp.
12. Courtesy of Advanced Micro Devices, Inc., Sunnyvale, CA.
13. Courtesy of AT&T.
14. Sperry Corporation.
15–17. Photo courtesy of Hewlett-Packard.

18. Courtesy of Motorola, Inc.
19. Courtesy of Advanced Micro Devices, Inc., Sunnyvale, CA.
20. National Semiconductor.
21. Courtesy of Advanced Micro Devices, Inc., Sunnyvale, CA.
22. Photo ©Peter Poulides.
23. Courtesy of Apple Computers, Inc.
24. Courtesy of AT&T.

## Gallery 2

Opener: Cardiff University/Australian Information Service.
1. Copyright 1986 Pixar. All rights reserved.
2. Courtesy of International Business Machines Corp.
3. ©Peter Tenzer/Wheeler Pictures.
4. Apollo Computer Inc.
5. Courtesy of Apple Computer, Inc.
6. Six Flags Over Texas.
7. Bluth Group Ltd.
8–9. Copyright 1986 Pixar. All rights reserved.
10. ©1985 Paramount Pictures Corporation. All rights reserved.
11. Ed Kashi.
12. Photo courtesy of Hewlett-Packard.
13. ©The Walt Disney Company.
14. ©Zoological Society of San Diego.
15. Courtesy of International Business Machines Corp.
16. Courtesy of Apple Computer, Inc.
17. Photo courtesy of Hewlett-Packard.
18. Richard J. Feldman, NIH.
19. Evans & Sutherland.
20. The Graphic Systems Research Group at the IBM U.K. Scientific Centre.
21. National Centre for Atmospheric Research/National Science Foundation.
22. NASA/Ames Research Center.
23–24. Jet Propulsion Laboratory.
25. COMPAQ Computer Corporation.
26. ©Maria Karras.
27. Images courtesy of Henry N. Wagner, Jr., M.D., The Johns Hopkins Medical Institution, Baltimore, Maryland.
28. COMPAQ Computer Corporation.

29. Courtesy of the Smith-Kettlewell Eye Research Foundation.
30. Cranston/Csuri Productions, Inc.
31–32. Evans & Sutherland.
33. Photo courtesy of Hewlett-Packard.
34. Howard Sochurek from Woodfin Camp & Associates.
35. Courtesy of International Business Machines Corp.
36. Courtesy of Apple Computer, Inc.
37. Courtesy of National Computer Camp, Orange, Connecticut.
38. Courtesy of the Smith-Kettlewell Eye Research Foundation.
39–41. Courtesy of International Business Machines Corp.
42. Courtesy of Apple Computer, Inc.
43. Eugene Richards/Magnum Photo, Inc.
44. Photo ©Peter Poulides.
45. Courtesy of International Business Machines Corp.
46. ©Chuck O'Rear/West Light.
47. Cadam Inc.
48. Kim Steele.
49. Andy Freeberg.
50. ©Chuck O'Rear/West Light.
51. USDA.
52–53. American Resources Corp.
54. Photo courtesy of Hewlett-Packard.
55. Kim Steele.
56. Courtesy of Texas Instruments.
57. Courtesy of Norand Corporation, 550 Second St SC, Cedar Rapids, Iowa 52401.
58. Bureau of Reclamation, U.S. Department of the Interior.
59. Courtesy of International Business Machines Corp.
60–61. ©Chuck O'Rear/West Light.
62. P.R. Cavanaugh, Pennsylvania State University.
63. Doug Wilson ©Discover Magazine 6/82, Time, Inc.

## Gallery 3

Opener: Photo courtesy of Hewlett-Packard.
1–5. Courtesy of International Business Machines Corp.
6. Learning and Epistemology Group, MIT.
7–8. Courtesy of International Business Machines Corp.
9. With compliments of the Australian Information Service.

10. Kurt D. Moses.
11. Courtesy of International Business Machines Corp.
12. Peter Ryan, Photo Researchers.
13–14. Courtesy of International Business Machines Corp.
15. ©1985 R. Ressmeyer/One Day In The Life, Inc.
16. Courtesy of International Business Machines Corp.
17. ©Malcolm S. Kirk.
18. Courtesy of International Business Machines Corp.
19. Chuck O'Rear/West Light.
20. Cap Gemini DASD.
21. Courtesy of International Business Machines Corp.
22–23. Courtesy of Apple Computer, Inc.

## Gallery 4

Opener: John Madere.
1. Photo courtesy NCR Corporation.
2–3. Courtesy of Texas Instruments.
4. Sperry Corporation.
5. EnerGraphics/Enertronics Research, Inc.
6. Kim Steele.
7. Kim Steele.
8. Courtesy of Texas Instruments.
9–14. Illustrator's Stock Photos.
15. Carroll Touch, Inc.
16. Contact Press/Louis Psihoyos ©1986.
17. Photo courtesy NCR Corporation.
18. Courtesy of Texas Instruments.
19. Courtesy of Apple Computer, Inc.
20. Photo courtesy NCR Corporation.
21. Courtesy of Texas Instruments.
22–23. Photo courtesy NCR Corporation.
24–25. COMPAQ Computer Corporation.
26. Courtesy of International Business Machines Corp.
27. Courtesy of Apple Computer, Inc.
28. Courtesy of AT&T.
29. Bud Lee Picturemaker.
30. ©Chuck O'Rear/West Light.
31. IEEE/NEC Information Systems, Inc.
32. Kevin Horan/Time.

## Gallery 5

Opener: GE Robotics & Visions Systems.
1–8. Courtesy of Control Data Corporation.
9. Courtesy of AT&T.
10. Rockwell International.
11. Courtesy of 3M.
12. Courtesy Andrew Lippman, Massachusetts Institute of Technology, Media Laboratory, Movie-Map Project. Cambridge, MA.
13. Richard Sobol/Time Magazine.
14–16. Courtesy Conrac Division.
17. Tom Tracy.
18–21. Photo courtesy SRI International.
22. Courtesy of Texas Instruments.
23–24. The PROTEAN project, Knowledge Systems Laboratory, Computer Science Department, Stanford University, Stanford, CA, 1986. Russell Altman, photographer.
25. David M. Doody/UNIPHOTO.
26. Sperry Corporation.
27. Courtesy of International Business Machines Corp.
28–30. Courtesy of ViewData Corporation.

## Buyer's Guide

The photos in the Buyer's Guide are unnumbered; they are referenced below by page number.

BG-1    Wayland Lee/Era Electronics.
BG-2    Wayland Lee/ComputerCraft.
BG-3    Top, Courtesy AST Research. Bottom, Courtesy of Uarco, Inc.
BG-4    ©Nita Winter.
BG-5    Top left, Courtesy of Uarco, Inc. Top right, Photo courtesy of INMAC, Santa Clara, CA. Bottom, Wayland Lee.
BG-6    Upper left, Photo courtesy of INMAC, Santa Clara, CA. Upper right, Microscience International Corporation. Lower left, Courtesy of Sentinel Technologies, Inc., Hyannis, MA. Lower right, Courtesy of Plus Development Corporation.
BG-7    Top, Courtesy of Texas Instruments.

Middle, Courtesy of Apple
Computer, Inc.
Bottom, Photo courtesy of
INMAC, Santa Clara, CA.

BG-8 Photo courtesy of INMAC,
Santa Clara, CA.

BG-9 Top, Photo courtesy of Hew-
lett-Packard.
Bottom left and right, Hayes
Microcomputer Products.

BG-10 Top, Courtesy of Apple Computer, Inc.
Bottom, Wayland Lee.

BG-11 Top, Courtesy AST Research.
Bottom left, Software Publishing Co.
Bottom right, Produced with
35mm Express™ from BPS.

BG-13 Courtesy of International Business Machines Corp.

BG-14 Top, Wayland Lee.
Bottom, Courtesy of Interna-
tional Business Machines
Corp.

BG-15 Wayland Lee.

BG-16 Wayland Lee.

# Glossary

**Access arm**  A mechanical device that can access all the tracks of one cylinder in a disk storage unit.

**Accumulator**  A register that collects the results of computations.

**Acoustic coupler**  A modem that connects to a telephone receiver rather than directly to a telephone line.

**Ada**  A structured programming language, named for Countess Ada Lovelace, that encourages modular program design.

**Address**  A number used to designate a location in memory.

**Address register**  Locates where instructions and data are stored in memory.

**ALGOL (ALGOrithmic Language)**  A language, developed primarily for scientific programming, that has limited file processing capabilities.

**Amplitude**  The height of the carrier wave form in analog transmission; it indicates the strength of the signal.

**Amplitude modulation**  A change of the amplitude of the carrier wave in analog data transmission to represent either the 0 bit or 1 bit.

**Analog transmission**  The transmission of computer data as a continuous electric signal in the form of a wave.

**Analytical engine**  A mechanical device of cogs and wheels, designed by Charles Babbage, that embodied the key characteristics of modern computers.

**Analytical graphics**  Traditional line graphs, bar charts, and pie charts used to illustrate and analyze data.

**ANS-COBOL**  A version of COBOL standardized in 1974 by the American National Standards Institute (ANSI).

**APL (A Programming Language)**  A powerful, interactive, easily learned language introduced by IBM.

**Arithmetic/logic unit (ALU)**  The electronic circuitry in a computer that executes all arithmetic and logical operations.

**Arithmetic operations**  Mathematical calculations performed on data by the ALU.

**Artificial intelligence**  The field of study that explores computer involvement in tasks requiring intelligence, imagination, and intuition.

**ASCII (American Standard Code for Information Interchange)**  A coding scheme using 7-bit characters to represent data characters.

**Assembler**  A translator program used to convert assembly language programs to machine language.

**Assembly language**  A second generation language that uses abbreviations for instructions.

**Asynchronous transmission**  Data transmission in which each group of message bits is preceded by a start signal and ended with a stop signal.

**Atanasoff-Berry Computer (ABC)**  The first electronic digital computer, designed by John V. Atanasoff and Clifford Berry in the late 1930s.

**Attribute**  Column of a relation in a relational database.

**Audio-response units**  See *Voice synthesizers*

**Audit trail**  A method of tracing data from the output back to the source documents.

**Auto-answer**  Automatic answering by a modem of incoming calls from another modem.

**Auto-dial**  Automatic calling by a modem of another modem.

**Auto-disconnect**  Automatic disconnecting by a modem of a call when the other party hangs up or a disconnect message is received.

**Automated teller machine (ATM)**  Input/output device connected to a computer used by bank customers for financial transactions.

**Automatic redial**  Automatic redialing by a modem when a busy signal is encountered.

**Auxiliary storage**  See *Secondary storage*

**Background**  In large computers, the memory area for programs with low priorities.

**Band printer**  An impact printer using a horizontally rotating band containing characters that are struck by hammers through paper and ribbon.

**Bar code reader**  A stationary photoelectric scanner that reads bar codes by means of reflected light.

**Bar codes**  Standardized patterns (Universal Product Code) of vertical marks that identify products.

**BASIC (Beginners' All-purpose Symbolic Instruction Code)**  A high-level programming language that is easy to learn and use.

**Batch processing**  A data processing technique in which transactions are collected into groups, or batches, for processing.

**Binary system**  A system in which data is represented by combinations of 0s and 1s, which correspond to the two states off and on.

**Biometrics**  The science of measuring individual body characteristics; used in some security systems.

**Bit**  A binary digit.

**Bit-mapped display**  See *Dot-addressable display*

**Block**  See *Physical record*

**Blocking factor**  The number of logical records in one physical record.

**Boilerplate**  An electronically produced form letter.

**Boldface**  Printing of characters or words in darker type than the surrounding characters or words.

**Booting**  Loading the operating system into memory.

**Bulletin board systems (BBSs)**  Telephone-linked personal computers that provide public-access message systems.

**Bursting**  The separation of continuous-form computer paper into individual sheets.

**Bus lines**  Collections of wires connecting the parts of a computer.

**Bus network**  A local area network topology that allows you to add nodes (microcomputers) anywhere in the system.

**Bypass**  A communications alternative that does not use the local telephone company.

**Byte**  Strings of bits (usually 8) used to represent one character of data—letter, digit, or special character.

**Bytes (bpi) per inch**  An expression of the amount (density) of data stored on magnetic tape.

**C**  A sophisticated programming language invented by Bell Labs in 1974.

**Candidates**  Alternative plans offered in the preliminary design phase of a project.

**Carrier wave**  An analog signal used in the transmission of electric signals.

**Carterfone decision**  The Federal Communications Commission decision allowing competitors in the formerly regulated domain of AT&T.

**Cassette tape**  An inexpensive data storage device used in home computer systems.

**Cathode ray tube (CRT)**  The most common type of computer screen.

**Cell**  The intersection of a row and a column in a spreadsheet.

**Centralized data processing**  The placement of all processing, hardware, software, and storage in one central location.

**Central processing unit (CPU)**  Electronic circuitry that executes stored program instructions. It consists of two parts: the control unit and the arithmetic/logic unit.

**Chain printer**  An impact printer consisting of characters on a chain that rotate past all print positions.

**Change agent**  The role of the systems analyst in overcoming resistance to change within an organization.

**Channel**  In communications, the path over which data travels. See also *Track*.

**Character**  A letter, number, or special character (such as $).

**Character addressable**  Refers to computers that address data as a series of single characters.

**Character-oriented**  Refers to word processing programs that display special characters on the screen that do not appear when the text is printed.

**Character printers**  Impact printers, similar to typewriters, that print character by character.

**Characters (cpi) per inch**  An expression of the amount (density) of data stored on magnetic tape.

**Check bit**  See *Parity bit*

**Classify**  To categorize data according to characteristics that make it useful.

**Client**  An individual or organization contracting for systems analysis.

**Clock**  A component of the CPU that produces pulses at a fixed rate to synchronize all computer operations.

**Clone**  A personal computer that closely imitates the operation and architecture of the IBM Personal Computer.

**Closed architecture**  Personal computer design that limits add-ons to those that can be plugged into the back of the machine.

**Coaxial cable**  Bundles of insulated wires within a shield enclosure that can be laid underground or undersea.

**COBOL (COmmon Business-Oriented Language)**  An English-like programming language used primarily for business applications.

**CODASYL (COnference of DAta SYstem Languages)**  The organization of government and industrial representatives that introduced COBOL.

**Cohesion**  A measure of the inner strength of a program module.

**Cold site**  An environmentally-suitable empty shell in which a company can install its own computer system.

**Command menu**  The menu of commands in an applications software program such as Lotus 1-2-3.

**Common carrier**  An organization approved by the FCC to offer communications services to the public.

**Compact disk read-only memory (CD-ROM)**  Optical data storage technology using disk formats identical to audio compact disks.

**Compare operation**  An operation in which the computer compares two numbers and performs alternative operations based on the comparison.

**Compatible**  Personal computer that can run software designed for the IBM Personal Computer.

**Compiler**  A translator that converts the symbolic statements of a high-level language into computer-executable machine language.

**Computer**  A machine that accepts data (input) and processes it into useful information (output).

**Computer-aided design (CAD)**  The use of computers and interactive graphic displays to design products.

**Computer-aided design/computer-aided manufacturing (CAD/CAM)**  The use of computers to provide a bridge between design and manufacturing.

**Computer-aided engineering (CAE)**  The use of computers and special software by engineers to verify that product designs will work and can be made economically.

**Computer-aided manufacturing (CAM)**  The use of computers to control machine tools, robots, and other automated factory equipment.

**Computer anxiety**  Fear of computers.

**Computer conferencing**  A method of sending, receiving, and storing typed messages within a network of users.

**Computer doctor**  Jargon for a computer repairperson.

**Computer Fraud and Abuse Act**  A law passed by Congress in 1984 to fight computer crime.

**Computer-integrated manufacturing (CIM)**  The integration of all automated machines and computers in the factory and elsewhere in the company.

**Computer literacy**  The awareness and knowledge of, and interaction with, computers.

**Computer marts**  Large buildings designed to house dozens of high-tech vendors.

**Computer operator**  A person who monitors the console screen, reviews procedures, and keeps peripheral equipment running.

**Computer output microfilm (COM)**  Computer output produced as very small images on sheets or rolls of film.

**Computer phobia**  See *Computer anxiety*

**Computer programmer**  A person who designs, writes, tests, and implements programs.

**Conditional replace**  A word processing function that queries the user whether to replace or not each time the program finds an instance of a particular item.

**Connector**  A symbol used in flowcharting to connect paths.

**Console**  The front panel of a computer system that alerts the operator when something needs to be done.

**Console terminal**  A terminal that allows the operator to communicate with the computer system.

**Consortium**  A joint venture to support a complete computer facility to be used in an emergency.

**Contention**  The method in which a terminal determines when a shared data transmission line is free for its use.

**Continuous word system**  A speech recognition system that can understand sustained speech, so users can speak normally.

**Control structures**  Patterns for controlling the flow of logic in a program. The three basic control structures are sequence, selection, and iteration.

**Control unit**  The circuitry that directs and coordinates the entire computer system in executing stored program instructions.

**Copy command**  A word processing command that allows the user to place a copy of one or more words, lines, or paragraphs in another location in the document.

**Copy protection**  A software or hardware block that makes it difficult or impossible to make unauthorized copies of software.

**Coupling**  A measure of the strength of the relationship between program modules.

**Cursor**  A flashing indicator on the screen that indicates where the next character will be inserted.

**Cursor control keys**  Special keys on the keyboard that allow the user to move the cursor on the screen.

**Cut and paste**  Copy and move commands in word processing programs.

**Cyberphobia**  See *Computer anxiety*

**Cylinder**  A set of tracks on a magnetic disk that can be accessed by one positioning of the access arm.

**Cylinder method**  A method of organizing data on a magnetic disk. Data organization is vertical, which minimizes seek time.

**Daisy wheel printer**  A letter quality character printer that has a removable wheel with a set of spokes, each containing a raised character.

**Data**  Raw material to be processed by a computer.

**Database**  A collection of interrelated files stored together with minimum redundancy.

**Database administrator (DBA)**  A person or group of persons responsible for monitoring and coordinating all activities related to the database.

**Database management system (DBMS)** A set of programs that create, manage, protect, and provide access to the database.

**Database model** A model that represents data relationships found in the real world.

**Data buses** See *Bus lines*

**Data collection device** A device that allows direct data entry in such places as factories and warehouses.

**Data communications** The process of exchanging data over communications facilities.

**Data communications systems** Computer systems that transmit data over communications lines, such as public telephone lines or private network cables.

**Data dictionary** A DBMS tool that contains an on-line description of all the items contained in the database.

**Data Encryption Standard (DES)** The standardized public key by which senders and receivers can scramble and unscramble their messages.

**Data entry operator** A person who prepares data for computer processing.

**Data flow diagram (DFD)** A diagram that shows the flow of data through an organization.

**Data transfer** The transfer of data between memory and secondary storage.

**Data value** The value of each attribute of each tuple in a relational database model.

**Deadlock** The condition in which each of two programs operating at the same time need resources held captive by the other, and neither program is willing to release the resource it is holding until it gets the one the other is holding.

**Debugging** The process of detecting, locating, and correcting mistakes in a program.

**Decision box** The standard diamond-shaped box used in flowcharting to indicate a decision.

**Decision logic table** See *Decision table*.

**Decision support system (DSS)** A computer system that supports managers in nonroutine decision-making tasks.

**Decision table** A standard table of the logical decisions that must be made regarding potential conditions in a given system.

**Decollating** The process of removing carbon paper from between the layered copies of multiple-copy computer paper.

**Dedicated word processor** A machine specifically designed for word processing.

**Demand-pull** A manufacturing procedure in which parts are not made until there is a request for them downstream in the factory process.

**Demodulation** Reconstruction of the original digital message after analog transmission.

**Density** The amount of data stored on magnetic tape expressed in number of characters per inch (cpi) or bytes per inch (bpi).

**Dependent variables** Outputs of a model, so called because they depend on the inputs.

**Desk-checking** A programming phase in which the logic of the program is mentally checked, to ensure that it is error-free and workable.

**Desktop publishing** See *Electronic publishing*

**Detail design** A systems design subphase in which the system is planned in detail.

**Detail report** A report that provides complete, specific information on routine operations.

**Diagnostic message** A message that informs the user of programming language syntax errors.

**Diagnostics** Error messages provided by the compiler as it translates a program.

**Difference engine** A machine designed by Charles Babbage to solve polynomial equations by calculating the successive differences between them.

**Digital transmission** The transmission of data as distinct pulses.

**Digitizer** A graphics input device that converts images into digital data that the computer can accept.

**Digitizing tablet** A graphics input device that allows the user to create images. It has a special stylus that can be used to draw or trace images, which are then converted to digital data that can be processed by the computer.

**Direct access** See *Direct file processing*

**Direct-access storage device (DASD)** A storage device in which a record can be accessed directly.

**Direct-connect modem** A modem connected directly to the telephone line.

**Direct conversion** A system conversion in which the user simply stops using the old system and starts using the new one.

**Direct file organization** Organization of records so each is individually accessible.

**Direct file processing** Processing that allows the user to access the record wanted directly by using a record key.

**Director of information management** A person who oversees the MIS department and must understand the goals and operations of the entire organization.

**Disaster recovery plan** A method of restoring data processing operations if those operations are halted by major damage or destruction.

**Discrete word system** A speech recognition system limited to understanding isolated words.

**Disk cartridge** A cartridge containing a single magnetic disk.

**Disk drive** A device that allows data to be read from a disk and written on a disk.

**Diskette** A single magnetic disk on which data is recorded as magnetic spots.

**Disk pack** A stack of magnetic disks assembled together.

**Distributed data processing (DDP)** A data processing system in which processing is decentralized, with the computers and storage devices in dispersed locations.

**Documentation** A detailed written description of the programming cycle and specific facts about the program. Also refers to the instruction manual for packaged software.

**Dot-addressable display** A graphics display screen that is divided into dots, each of which can be illuminated.

**Dot-matrix printer** A printer that constructs a character by activating a matrix of pins to produce the shape of a character on paper.

**Download** The transfer of data from a mainframe or large computer to a smaller computer.

**Drum plotter** A graphics output device in which paper is rolled on a drum with a computer-controlled pen poised over it.

**Drum printer** A printer consisting of a cylinder with embossed rows of characters on its surface. Each print position has a complete set of characters around the circumference of the drum.

**Dumb terminal** A terminal that does not process data. It is merely a means of entering data into a computer and receiving output from it.

**Early defect removal** Review by programming team members of each other's work, especially at the design level.

**EBCDIC** (Extended Binary Coded Decimal Interchange Code) Established by IBM and used in IBM mainframe computers.

**Editing program** See *Grammar and style program*

**EDVAC** (Electronic Discrete Variable Automatic Computer) A computer, proposed by John von Neumann, that successfully used the stored program concept.

**Egoless programming** Programming with the attitude that the program is not personal property but benefits from inspection by other programmers.

**Electronically altered PROM (EAPROM)** A programmable read-only chip that can be electronically erased and reprogrammed.

**Electronically erased PROM (EEPROM)** A programmable read-only chip that can be electronically erased and reprogrammed.

**Electronic disk** See *RAM disk*

**Electronic fund transfers (EFTs)** Payment for goods and services using funds transferred from accounts electronically.

**Electronic mail** The process of sending messages directly from one terminal or computer to another. The messages may be sent and stored for later retrieval.

**Electronic publishing** Use of a personal computer, special software, and a laser printer to produce very high quality documents that combine text and graphics.

**Electronic spreadsheet** An electronic worksheet used to organize data into rows and columns for analysis.

**Encryption** The process of encoding communication.

**End-user revolution** Trend that computer users are becoming more knowledgeable about computers and less reliant on computer professionals.

**ENIAC** (Electronic Numerical Integrator And Computer) The first general-purpose electronic computer, which was built by Dr. John Mauchly and J. Presper Eckert, Jr. and was first operational in 1946.

**Erasable optical disk** An optical disk on which data can be stored, moved, changed, and erased, just as on magnetic media.

**Erasable PROM (EPROM)** Programmable read-only memory that can be erased and then reprogrammed.

**Erase head** The head in a magnetic tape unit that erases any previously recorded data on the tape.

**Ergonomics** The study of human factors related to computers.

**E-time** The execution portion of the machine cycle.

**Event-driven** Refers to multiprogramming; programs share resources based on events that take place in the programs.

**Exception report** A report that shows only data reflecting unusual circumstances.

**Expansion slots** The slots inside a computer that allow a user to insert additional circuit boards.

**Expert shell** Software having the basic structure to find answers to questions; the questions themselves can be added by the user.

**Expert system** A software package that presents the computer as an expert on some topic.

**External direct-connect modem** A modem that is separate from the computer, allowing it to be used with a variety of computers.

**External label** Paper placed on the side of a tape reel for identification purposes.

**Facsimile technology** The use of computer technology to send digitized graphics, charts, and text from one facsimile machine to another.

**Fair Credit Reporting Act** Legislation passed in 1970 allowing individuals access to and the right to challenge credit records.

**Feasibility study** See *Preliminary investigation*

**Federal Communications Commission (FCC)** The federal agency that regulates communications facilities.

**Federal Privacy Act** Legislation passed in 1974 stipulating that no secret personal files can be kept by government agencies and that individuals can have access to all information concerning them stored in government files.

**Fiber optics** Technology that uses light instead of electricity to send data.

**Field** A set of related characters.

**Fifth generation** A term coined by the Japanese referring to new forms of computer systems involving artificial intelligence, natural language, and expert systems.

**File** A collection of related records. In word processing, a document created on a computer.

**File directory** A list of files saved on disk.

**File management program** A program that allows the user to enter data on forms and make requests for particular types of data items.

**File protection ring** The plastic ring on a tape reel used for writing data on the tape.

**Firmware** Read-only memory used to store programs that will not be altered.

**Fixed length** A term indicating that all records in a file are of the same length.

**Fixed-length words** Words whose size depends on the word length of the computer. Used by word-addressable computers, which process data one word at a time.

**Flatbed plotter** A graphics output device that resembles a table with a sheet of paper on it and a mechanical pen suspended over it. The pen moves around on the paper under control of the computer program.

**Floppy disk** A flexible magnetic disk on which data is recorded as magnetic spots.

**Flowchart** The pictorial representation of an orderly step-by-step solution to a problem.

**Footmouse** A mouse controlled by foot.

**Footnoting program** A word processing program that inserts and numbers footnotes automatically.

**Foreground** An area in memory for programs that have a high priority.

**Form letter program** A word processing program that can be designed to send out "personalized" letters that look like letters produced on a typewriter.

**FORTH** A language released by Charles Moore in 1975 that was designed for real-time control tasks, as well as business and graphics applications.

**FORTRAN (FORmula TRANslator)** The first high-level language, introduced in 1954 by IBM; it is scientifically oriented.

**Fragment** A portion of real memory that is too small to hold even a segment and is therefore unusable.

**Freedom of Information Act** Legislation passed in 1970 that allows citizens access to personal data gathered by federal agencies.

**Frequency** The number of times an analog signal repeats during a specific time interval.

**Frequency modulation** The alteration of the carrier wave frequency to represent 0s and 1s.

**Front-end processor** A communications control unit designed to relieve the central computer of some communications tasks.

**Full-duplex transmission** Data transmission in both directions at once.

**Function keys** Special keys programmed to execute commonly-used commands.

**Gallium arsenide** Speedy material used as a substitute for silicon in chipmaking.

**Gantt chart** A bar chart commonly used to depict schedule deadlines and milestones.

**General-purpose register** A register used for several functions, such as arithmetic and addressing purposes.

**Generic operating system** An operating system that works with different computer systems.

**Gigabyte (GB)** One billion bytes.

**GIGO** Garbage in, garbage out: The quality of the output is directly dependent on the quality of the input.

**Grammar and style program** A word processing program that identifies unnecessary words and wordy phrases in a document.

**Graphics adapter board** A circuit board that enables an IBM Personal Computer to display pictures or graphs as well as text.

**Graphics card** See *Graphics adapter board*

**Graphics printer** A printer that can produce graphics output, such as dot-matrix, ink-jet, and laser.

**Gray market** Unauthorized dealers of computer equipment.

**Greater than (>) condition** A comparison operation that determines if one value is greater than another.

**Green-bar paper** Shaded-band computer paper.

**Hacker**  A person who gains access to computer systems illegally, usually from a personal computer.

**Half-duplex transmission**  Data transmission in either direction, but only one way at a time.

**Hardcard**  10 or 20 megabytes of hard disk on a board that fits into an expansion slot inside a personal computer.

**Hard copy**  Printed paper output.

**Hard disks**  5-inch or 3½-inch Winchester disks in sealed modules.

**Hard magnetic disk**  A metal platter coated with magnetic oxide and used for magnetic disk storage.

**Hard-sectored disk**  A disk with a hole in front of each sector, near the center of the diskette.

**Hardware**  The computer and its associated equipment.

**Hashing**  The process of applying a formula to a key to yield a number that represents the address.

**Header label**  The internal label on a magnetic tape that contains identifying information.

**Head switching**  Activation of a particular read/write head over a particular track.

**Hexadecimal number system**  A number system that uses 16 symbols to represent data.

**Hierarchical model**  A database model in which records in a file are associated in a one-to-many, or parent-child, relationship.

**Hierarchy chart**  See *Structure chart*

**High-level languages**  English-like programming languages developed after the development of symbolic languages.

**HIPO**  Hierarchy plus Input-Process-Output: A set of diagrams that describes program functions from the general to the detailed level.

**Home controls**  Personal computer-controlled devices that receive their instructions over existing household wiring and perform some household tasks.

**Host computer**  The central computer in a star network.

**Hot site**  A fully equipped computer center with hardware, communications facilities, environmental controls, and security, for use in an emergency.

**Hybrid**  A computer with its own unique design that will also stimulate another computer manufacturer, notably IBM.

**Icon**  A small figure on the computer screen that represents a computer activity.

**Impact printer**  A printer that forms characters by physically striking the paper.

**Implementation**  The phase of systems analysis that includes training, equipment conversion, file conversion, system conversion, auditing, evaluation, and maintenance.

**Independent variables**  Inputs to a model, so called because they can change.

**Indexed file organization**  Combination of sequential and direct file organization.

**Indexed file processing**  A method of file organization representing a compromise between sequential and direct methods.

**Indexed processing**  See *Indexed file processing*

**Index files**  Files that allow the same data to be presented in different sequential orders. They also allow the user quickly to search a database for a record.

**Index generator program**  A word processing program that marks important terms in the text and automatically generates an index when the document is completed.

**Information**  Processed data; data that is organized, meaningful, and useful.

**Information center**  A company center that offers employees computer and software training, help in getting data from other computer systems, and technical assistance.

**Information utilities**  Commercial consumer-oriented communications systems, such as The Source and CompuServe.

**Initialize**  To set the starting values of certain program variables.

**Ink-jet printer**  A printer that sprays ink from jet nozzles onto the paper.

**Input**  Data that is input to the computer system for processing.

**Input device**  A device that puts data in machine-readable form and sends it to the processing unit.

**Inquire**  To ask questions about data in a mainframe computer through a computer terminal.

**Inquiry**  A request for information.

**Integrated circuit**  A complete electronic circuit on a small chip of silicon.

**Integrated package**  An all-in-one package of programs joining word processing, spreadsheet, database, and graphics.

**Intelligent terminal**  A terminal that can be programmed to perform a variety of processing tasks.

**Interactive**  Data processing in which the user communicates directly with the computer, maintaining a dialogue.

**Interblock gap (IBG)**  See *Interrecord gap (IRG)*

**Internal labels**  Labels on the magnetic tape itself: *header label* appears on the tape right after the load point and before the first data record and contains identifying information; *trailer label* is at the end of the file, before the end-of-file marker, and includes a count of the number of records in the file.

**Internal modem**  A modem on a circuit board that can be installed in a computer by the user.

**Internal storage**  See *Memory*

**International Consultative Committee on Telegraphy and Telephony (CCITT)**  A United Nations agency involved in development of communications standards.

**Interpreter**  A program that translates and executes high-level languages one instruction at a time.

**Interrecord gap (IRG)**  The blank space on magnetic tape that separates records.

**Interrupt**  Condition that causes normal program processing to be suspended temporarily.

**Interview**  The data gathering operation in systems analysis.

**Iteration**  See *Loop*

**Iteration control structure**  A looping mechanism.

**I-time**  The instruction portion of the machine cycle.

**Join relational operation**  An operation used to combine two relations based on common attributes into a new relation.

**Joy stick**  A graphics input device that allows fingertip control of figures on a CRT screen.

**Just-in-time (JIT)**  See *Demand-pull*

**Key**  Unique identifier for a record.

**Keyboard**  A common input device similar to the keyboard of a typewriter.

**Kilobyte (KB)**  1024 bytes.

**Knowledge-based system**  The use of a natural language to access a knowledge base.

**Laptop computer**  A small, portable computer weighing as little as 9 pounds.

**Large-scale integration (LSI)**  A chip containing a large number of integrated circuits.

**Laser printer**  A printer that uses a light beam to transfer images to paper.

**Leader**  The first 10- to 15-foot portion of a magnetic tape that has no data recorded on it.

**Leading decision**  The loop-ending decision that occurs at the beginning of a DOWHILE loop.

**Leased lines**  See *Private lines*

**Less than (<) condition**  A logical operation in which the computer compares values to determine if one is less than another.

**Letter-quality printer**  A printer, such as a daisy wheel, that produces high-quality output.

**Librarian**  A person who catalogs processed disks and tapes and keeps them secure.

**Light pen**  A graphics input device that allows the user to interact directly with the computer screen.

**Line printer**  A printer that assembles all characters on a line at one time and prints them out practically simultaneously.

**Link**  Physical data communications medium.

**Link fields**  The common data items included in the database relations that are to be acted upon by a relational operation.

**Link/load phase**  The phase during which prewritten programs may be added to the object module by means of a link/loader.

**Liquid crystal display (LCD)**  The flat display screen found on laptop computers.

**LISP (LISt Processing)**  A language designed to process nonnumeric data; popular for writing artificial intelligence programs.

**Load module**  Output from the link/load step.

**Load point**  The beginning of data on a magnetic tape.

**Local area network (LAN)**  A network designed to share data and resources among several computers.

**Logical operations**  Comparing operations. The ALU is able to compare numbers, letters, or special characters and take alternative courses of action.

**Logical record**  A record written by an applications program.

**Logic chip**  See *Microprocessor*

**Logic flowchart**  A flowchart that represents the flow of logic in a program.

**Logo**  A language developed at MIT by Seymour Papert that features commands that move a ''turtle'' on the CRT screen.

**Loop**  Repetition of program instructions under certain conditions.

**Machine cycle**  Combination of I-time and E-time.

**Machine language**  The lowest level of language that represents information as 1s and 0s.

**Magnetic core**  Flat doughnut-shaped metal used as an early memory device.

**Magnetic disk**  An oxide-coated disk on which data is recorded as magnetic spots.

**Magnetic-ink character recognition**  A method of machine-reading characters made of magnetized particles.

**Magnetic tape**  A magnetic medium with an iron oxide coating that can be magnetized. Data is stored on the tape as extremely small magnetized spots.

**Magnetic tape unit**  A data storage unit used to record data on and retrieve data from magnetic tape.

**Mainframe**  A large computer that has access to billions of characters of data and is capable of processing data very quickly.

**Main memory**  See *Memory*

**Main storage**  See *Memory*

**Management information system (MIS)**  A set of formal business systems designed to provide information for an organization.

**Manufacturing Automation Protocol (MAP)**  Protocol for a local area network that provides communications between the equipment of all factory automation vendors that support it.

**Manufacturing resource planning (MRP) software**  Software that maintains needed inventory levels, tracks billing for materials, and keeps track of parts needed for given production schedules.

**Mark I**  Early computer built in 1944 by Harvard professor Howard Aiken.

**Mass storage devices**  Devices able to store enormous volumes of data.

**Master file**  A semipermanent set of records.

**Megabyte (MB)**  One million bytes.

**Memory**  The electronic circuitry that temporarily holds data and program instructions needed by the CPU.

**Memory management**  The process of allocating memory programs and of keeping the programs in memory separate from one another.

**Memory protection**  The process of keeping a program from straying into other programs and vice versa.

**Menu**  An on-screen list of commands and the keystrokes necessary to execute those commands.

**Menu cursor**  A cursor used to select commands in the command menu of a program.

**Menu-driven**  Feature of a program that presents an on-screen menu, a list of commands and the keystrokes necessary to execute those commands.

**MICR inscriber**  A device that adds magnetic characters to a document.

**Microcode**  Permanent instructions inside the control unit that are executed directly by the machine's electronic circuits.

**Microcomputer manager**  The manager in charge of personal computer use.

**Microcomputer**  The smallest and least expensive class of computer.

**Microdisk**  A 3½-inch diskette.

**Microfiche**  4- by 6-inch sheets of film that can be used to store computer output.

**Microfloppy**  See *Microdisk*

**Micro-to-mainframe link**  Connection between microcomputers and mainframe computers.

**Microprocessor**  A general-purpose processor on a chip, developed in 1969 by an Intel Corporation design team headed by Ted Hoff.

**Microsecond**  One millionth of a second.

**Microwave transmission**  Line-of-sight transmission of data signals from relay station to relay station through the atmosphere.

**MICR reader/sorter**  A machine that reads and sorts documents imprinted with magnetic characters.

**Millisecond**  One thousandth of a second.

**Minicomputer**  A computer smaller than a mainframe in storage capacity.

**Minifloppy**  A 5¼-inch floppy disk.

**MIS manager**  The manager of the MIS department.

**MITS Altair**  The first microcomputer kit, offered to computer hobbyists in 1975.

**Model**  An image of something that actually exists, or mathematical representation of a real-life system.

**Modem**  A device that converts a digital signal to an analog signal or vice versa.

**Modula-2**  A Pascal-like language designed to write systems software.

**Modulation**  The process of converting a signal from digital to analog.

**Module**  A set of logically related statements that perform a specific function.

**Monochrome**  A computer screen that displays information in only one color on a black background.

**Monolithic**  Refers to the inseparable nature of memory chip circuitry.

**Mouse**  A computer input device that repositions the cursor on the screen by its movement on a flat surface.

**Move command**  In word processing, a command that moves one or more words, lines, or paragraphs from one location to another.

**MSX machine**  A microcomputer based on Microsoft Extended Basic. Most of these machines are of Japanese manufacture.

**Multipoint line**  A line configuration in which several terminals are connected to one computer.

**Multiprogramming**  Concurrent execution of two or more programs on a computer and the sharing of the computer's resources.

**Multistar network**  A network in which several host computers are tied together and each host has its own star network of smaller computers.

**Multiuser, multitasking personal computer**  A supermicro with a high-speed microprocessor and significantly increased memory and hard-disk capacity.

**Nanosecond**  One billionth of a second.

**Natural language** Programming language that resembles natural human language.

**NCR paper** Multiple-copy computer paper that does not use carbon paper.

**Near-letter-quality** Printing produced by dot-matrix printers with 24-pin printheads, or by printing each letter twice.

**Network** A computer system that uses communications equipment to connect two or more computers and their resources.

**Network model** A database model similar to a hierarchical model except that a child record can be associated with more than one parent record.

**Node** A microcomputer in a network.

**Nonimpact printer** A printer that uses a nonimpact printing method.

**Nonprocedural language** Language that simply states what task is to be accomplished but does not state the steps needed to accomplish it.

**Object module** Machine-language version of a program produced by a compiler or assembler.

**Observation** A technique of systems analysis in which the subject organization is simply observed.

**OCR-A** Standard typeface for optical characters.

**Octal number system** A number system based on eight symbols.

**Office automation** The use of technology to help achieve the goals of the office.

**On-demand report** Report providing information in response to an unscheduled demand from a user.

**On-line** Refers to processing in which terminals are directly connected to the computer.

**Open architecture** Personal computer design that allows additional circuit boards to be inserted in expansion slots inside the computer to support add-ons.

**Open Systems Interconnection (OSI)** A set of communications protocols defined by the International Standards Organization (ISO).

**Operating environment** A comfortable operating system environment in which the user does not have to memorize or look up commands.

**Operating system** A set of programs through which a computer manages its own resources.

**Optical-character recognition (OCR) devices** Input devices that use a light source to read special characters and convert them to electrical signals to be sent to the CPU.

**Optical-mark recognition (OMR) devices** Input devices that use a light beam to recognize marks on paper.

**Optical read-only memory (OROM)** Optical storage media that cannot be written to but can be used to supply software or data.

**Optical-recognition system** A system that converts optical marks, optical characters, handwritten characters, and bar codes into electrical signals to be sent to the CPU.

**Organization chart** A hierarchical diagram depicting management by name and title.

**Orphans** Personal computers that have been discontinued and are no longer supported by their manufacturers.

**Output** Raw data that has been processed into usable information.

**Output devices** Devices, such as printers, that make processed information available for use.

**Overlapped processing** Multiprogramming in which two or more programs are operating concurrently and are sharing the resources of the computer.

**Packaged software** Software that is packaged and sold in stores.

**Page frame** Space in main memory in which to place a page.

**Pages** Equal-sized blocks into which a program is divided.

**Paging** The process of keeping program pages on disk and calling them into memory as needed.

**Parallel conversion** A method of systems conversion in which the old and new systems are operated simultaneously until the users are satisfied that the new system performs to their standards.

**Parallel processing** Refers to the use of many processors, each with its own memory unit, working at the same time to process data.

**Parity bit** An extra bit added to each byte to alert the computer if a bit is incorrect.

**Participant observation** A form of observation in which the systems analyst temporarily joins the activities of the group.

**Pascal** A structured, high-level programming language named for Blaise Pascal, the seventeenth-century French mathematician.

**Periodic report** A report produced on a regular schedule and preplanned to produce detail, summary, or exception data.

**Peripheral equipment** Hardware devices attached to a computer.

**Personal computer** See *Microcomputer*

**Phantom disk** See *RAM disk*

**Phase** The relative position in time of one complete cycle of a wave.

**Phased conversion** A systems conversion method in

which the new system is eased into gradually by all users.

**Physical record** A collection of logical records.

**Picosecond** One trillionth of a second.

**PILOT** A programming language invented in 1973; used most often to write computer-aided-instruction in various subjects.

**Pilot conversion** Systems conversion method in which a designated group of users try the system first.

**Pipelining** The sending of one program's output, as produced, to be processed as another program's input.

**Pixel** Picture element on a computer display screen.

**PL/I (Programming Language One)** A free-form and flexible programming language designed as a compromise for scientific and business use.

**Point-to-point line** A direct connection between each terminal and the computer or between computers.

**Point-of-sale terminal** A terminal used as a cash register in a retail setting. It may be programmable or connected to a central computer.

**Polling** A method of line control in which the computer asks each terminal if it has a message to send and coordinates the transmission accordingly.

**Portable computer** A self-contained computer that can be easily carried and moved.

**Preliminary design** The subphase of systems design in which the new system concept is developed.

**Preliminary investigation** The first phase of a systems analysis project in which it is determined if and how a project should proceed.

**Presentation graphics** High-quality business graphics designed to allow the user to share information with others.

**Primary memory** See *Memory*

**Primary storage** See *Memory*

**Priming read** The first Read statement in a program.

**Printer spacing chart** A chart used to determine and show a report format.

**Private line** A communications line dedicated to one customer.

**Procedural language** A language used to present a step-by-step process for solving a problem.

**Process box** The rectangular box that indicates actions to be taken.

**Processes** Actions taken on data—comparing, checking, stamping, authorizing, filing, etc.

**Processor** The central processing unit (CPU) of a computer.

**Production-push** A manufacturing style in which

machines are run at their full potential, building up parts for more advanced production steps and stock for customers.

**Program** A set of step-by-step instructions that directs a computer to perform specific tasks and produce certain results.

**Programmable read-only memory (PROM)** Chips that can be programmed with specialized tools called ROM burners.

**Programming language** A set of rules that instructs a computer what operations to perform.

**Programming team** A group of people working on the same programming project.

**Project relational operation** An operation that selects certain attributes from a relation.

**PROLOG (PROgramming in LOGic)** An artificial intelligence programming language invented in 1972 by Alan Colmerauer at the University of Marseilles.

**Prompt** A signal that the computer or operating system is waiting for a command from the user.

**Protocol** A set of rules for the exchange of data between a terminal and a computer or between two computers.

**Prototype** A limited working system or subset of a system that is developed quickly.

**Pseudocode** An English-like way of representing structured programming control structures.

**Query language** A high-level, nonprocedural language, included in most database management systems, for people with no formal programming training to use to specify requirements.

**Questionnaire** A source of information in the data-gathering phase of systems analysis.

**Queues** Areas on disk in which programs waiting to be run are kept.

**Ragged right** The uneven right edge of a document.

**RAM disk** A chip that lets the computer regard part of its memory as a third disk drive.

**RAM-resident program** A program that stays in memory background, ready to be activated when needed.

**Random access** See *Direct file processing*

**Random-access memory (RAM)** Memory that provides volatile temporary storage for data and program instructions.

**Randomizing** See *Hashing*

**Raster-scan** Video display technology in which electronic beams cause the CRT screen to emit light to produce a screen image.

**Read** To bring data outside the computer into memory.

**Read-only media** Media recorded on by the manufacturer that can be read from but not written to by the user.

**Read-only memory (ROM)** Memory that can be read only and remains after the power is turned off.

**Read/write head** An electromagnet that reads the magnetized areas on magnetic media and converts them into the electrical impulses that are sent to the processor.

**Real-time processing** Processing in which the results are available in time to affect the activity at hand.

**Record** A collection of related fields.

**Reduced instruction set computer (RISC)** A computer that offers only a small subset of instructions.

**Reformatted** Refers to the reformatting of paragraphs that have been altered during word processing.

**Refreshed** Refers to the maintenance of the image on a CRT screen.

**Register** A temporary storage area for instructions or data.

**Relation** A table in a relational database model.

**Relational model** A database model that organizes data logically in tables.

**Relational operations** Processes that manipulate relations.

**Relational schema** A description of the types of data a file will contain in a relational database management system.

**Report form** A form created by a user in response to prompts from a database management system.

**Report generator** A feature of a database management system that allows the user to prepare common types of business reports without using a programming language.

**Resolution** Clarity of a video display screen.

**Resource allocation** The process of assigning resources to certain programs for their use.

**Response time** The time between a typed computer request and the response of the computer.

**Retrieval** Recovery of data stored in a computer system.

**Right-justified** Refers to an even right margin in a computer document.

**Ring network** A circle of point-to-point connections of computers at local sites, with no central host computer.

**Robot** A computer-controlled device that can physically manipulate its surroundings.

**ROM burner** A specialized device used to program read-only memory chips.

**Rotational delay** For disk units, the time it takes for a record on a track to revolve under the read/write head.

**Round-robin scheduling** System of having users take turns using the processor.

**RPG (Report Program Generator)** A problem-oriented language designed to produce business reports.

**Sampling** Collecting a subset of data relevant to a system.

**Satellite transmission** Data transmission from earth station to earth station via communications satellites.

**Scan rate** The number of times a CRT screen is refreshed in a given time period.

**Schema** The logical organization of data in a database.

**Screen** A television-like output device that displays data and output.

**Screen-oriented** Refers to a word processing program that displays on the screen exactly what will be printed on paper.

**Scrolling** A word processing feature that allows the user to view any part of the document on the screen in 20-line chunks.

**Search and replace** A word processing function that finds and changes each instance of a repeated item.

**Secondary storage** Additional storage for data and programs that is separate from the CPU and memory.

**Secondary storage devices** Auxiliary units outside the CPU that can store additional data and programs.

**Sector method** A method of organizing data on a disk in which each track is divided into sectors that hold a specific number of characters.

**Security** A system of safeguards designed to protect a computer system and data from deliberate or accidental damage or access by unauthorized persons.

**Seek time** The time required for an access arm to position over a particular track on a disk.

**Segmentation** The process of dividing a program into blocks of various sizes and placing these blocks in noncontiguous memory locations.

**Selection control structure** A control structure used to make logic decisions.

**Select relational operation** An operation that forms a new relation by selecting certain tuples from a given relation.

**Semiconductor** A crystalline substance that conducts electricity when it is "doped" with chemical impurities.

**Semiconductor storage** Data storage on a silicon chip.

**Sequence control structure** A control structure in which one statement follows another in sequence.

**Sequential file organization** Organization of records in sequential order by key.

**Sequential file processing** Processing in which records are usually in order according to a key field.

**Serial processing** Processing in which one program must finish running before another can begin.

**Server** A device that performs specific functions for other devices in a network.

**Shell** An operating environment layer that separates the operating system from the user.

**Simplex transmission** Transmission of data in one direction only.

**Simulation** The use of computer modeling to reach decisions about real-life situations.

**Sink** In a data flow diagram, a destination for data going outside an organization.

**Site license** A license permitting a customer to make multiple copies of a piece of software.

**Smalltalk** An object-oriented language in which text is entered into the computer using the keyboard but all other tasks are performed using a mouse.

**Smart terminal** A terminal that can do some processing, usually to edit data it receives.

**SNOBOL** A powerful string processing language used by text editors and language processors.

**Soft-sectored disk** A disk whose sectors are determined by the software.

**Software** Instructions that tell a computer what to do.

**Software piracy** Unauthorized copying of computer software.

**Sort** An operation that arranges data into a particular sequence.

**Source** In a data flow diagram, an origin outside the organization.

**Source data automation** The use of special equipment to collect data and send it directly to the computer.

**Source document** Original paper containing data to be prepared as input to the computer.

**Source module** A program as originally coded, before being translated into machine language.

**Source program listing** A list of a program as the programmer wrote it.

**Speech recognition** The process of presenting input data to the computer through the spoken word.

**Speech recognition device** A device that accepts the spoken word through a microphone and converts it into digital code that can be understood by the computer.

**Speech synthesis** The process of enabling machines to talk to people.

**Spelling checker program** A word processing program that checks the spelling in a document.

**Spooling** A process in which files to be printed are placed temporarily on disk.

**Spreadsheet** A worksheet divided into rows and columns that can be used to organize and present business data.

**Stand-alone programs** Individual programs, such as word processing and spreadsheet programs.

**Star network** A network consisting of one or more smaller computers connected to a central host computer.

**Start/stop transmission** Asynchronous data transmission.

**Stock tab** Inexpensive newsprint printer paper.

**Storage register** A register that temporarily holds data taken from or about to be sent to memory.

**Structure chart** A chart that illustrates the top-down design of a program and is often used to either supplement or replace a logic flowchart.

**Structured flowcharting** Flowcharting in which a limited number of control structures is used to minimize program complexity.

**Structured interview** An interview in which planned questions are used.

**Structured programming** A set of programming techniques that includes a limited number of control structures, top-down design, and module independence.

**Structured walkthrough** A formal process among members of a programming team in which the design or code of an individual programmer is evaluated.

**Subschema** The logical organization of data in a database for a particular user application.

**Summarize** To reduce data to a more concise, usable form.

**Summary report** A management information system report limited to totals or trends.

**Supercomputer** The largest and most powerful category of computers.

**Supermicro** A multiuser, multitasking microcomputer that has a high-speed microprocessor, increased memory, and hard-disk storage.

**Supermini** A minicomputer at the top end of size and price.

**Supervisor program** An operating system program that controls the entire operating system and calls in other operating system programs from disk storage as needed.

**Supply reel** A reel that has tape with data on it or on which data will be recorded.

**Surge protector** A device that prevents electrical problems from affecting data files.

**Switched line** A communications line that connects through a switching center to a variety of destinations.

**Symbolic language** See *Assembly language*

**Synchronous transmission** Data transmission in which characters are transmitted together in a continuous stream.

**Synonyms** Records with duplicate disk addresses.

**Syntax errors** Errors in use of programming language.

**Synthesis by analysis** Speech synthesis in which the device analyzes the input of an actual human voice, stores and processes the spoken sounds, and reproduces them as needed.

**Synthesis by rule** Speech synthesis in which the device applies linguistic rules to create an artificial spoken language.

**System** An organized set of related components established to perform a certain task.

**System journal** A file whose records represent transactions made at the terminal.

**System survey** See *Preliminary investigation*

**System testing** A testing process in which the development team uses test data to test programs to determine whether they work together satisfactorily.

**Systems analysis** The process of studying an existing system to determine how it works and how it meets user needs.

**Systems analyst** A person who plans and designs individual programs and entire computer systems.

**Systems design** The process of developing a plan for a system, based on the results of the systems analysis.

**Systems development** The process of programming and testing to bring a new system into being.

**Systems flowchart** A drawing that depicts the flow of data through a computer system.

**Systems life cycle** A systems cycle consisting of preliminary investigation, systems analysis, systems design, systems development, and systems implementation phases.

**Systems Network Architecture (SNA)** A set of communications protocols made commercially available by IBM.

**Table of contents program** With a word processing program, this program allows the user to mark chapter headings in a document and automatically generates a table of contents when the document is completed.

**Tab settings** Right and left margin settings in a word processing program.

**Take-up reel** A reel that always stays with the magnetic tape unit.

**Tape drives** Drives on which reels of magnetic tape are mounted when their data is ready to be read by the computer system.

**Tariff** A list of services and rates to be charged for data communications services.

**Telecommunications** Merger of communications and computers.

**Telecommuting** Refers to the home use of telecommunications and computers as a substitute for the commute to work.

**Teleconferencing** A system of holding conferences by linking geographically disbursed people together through computer terminals or personal computers.

**Teleprocessing** A system in which terminals are connected to the central computer via communications lines.

**Terminal** A device that consists of an input device, an output device, and a communications link to the main terminal.

**Thermal printer** A printer that produces characters using heat in the pins in the print head.

**Thesaurus program** With a word processing program, this program provides a list of synonyms and antonyms for an overused word in a document.

**Time-delay** A modem feature that allows a computer to call another computer and transfer a file at a future time.

**Time-driven** Refers to time-sharing, a special case of multiprogramming.

**Time-sharing** Concurrent use of one machine by several people, who are give time slices by turns.

**Time slice** In time-sharing, a period of time—usually a few milliseconds or microseconds—during which the computer works on a user's tasks.

**Top-down design** A design technique that identifies basic program functions before dividing them into subfunctions called modules.

**Topology** The physical layout of a local area network.

**Touch screen** A computer screen that accepts input data by letting the user point at the screen to select a choice.

**Track** On tape, a channel that runs the entire length of a magnetic tape. On most modern computer tapes, one cross section of the tape, representing one character, contains 9 bits, one on each track. On disk, one of many data-holding concentric circles.

**Trailer label** The internal label on a magnetic tape that appears at the end of the file, before the end-of-file marker, and includes a count of the number of records in the file.

**Trailing decision** The loop-ending decision that occurs at the end of a DOUNTIL loop.

**Transaction file** A file that contains all changes to be made to the master file: additions, deletions, and revisions.

**Transaction processing** The technique of processing transactions in random order.

**Transistor** A small device that transfers electrical signals across a resistor.

**Translator** A program that translates programming language into machine language.

**Transponder** A device in a communications satellite that receives a transmission from earth, amplifies the signal, changes the frequency, and retransmits the data to a receiving earth station.

**Tuple** A row in a relational database model.

**Ultra large-scale integration (ULSI)** A 10-megabit chip.

**Ultramicro disk** A 2½-inch 500K diskette.

**Unit testing** The individual testing of a program using test data.

**UNIVAC I** (Universal Automatic Computer) The first computer built for business purposes.

**Universal manager program** A program that uses a common interface to coordinate separate stand-alone programs.

**Universal Product Code (UPC)** A code number unique to a product that is represented on the product's label in the form of a bar code.

**UNIX** A generic multiuser, time-sharing operating system developed in 1971 at Bell Labs.

**Unstructured interview** An interview in which questions are planned in advance, but the systems analyst can deviate from the plan.

**Update** Keeping files current by changing data as appropriate.

**User friendly** Refers to software that is easy for a novice to use.

**User involvement** Involvement of users in the systems life cycle process.

**Users** People who buy and use computer software or have contact with computer systems.

**Utility programs** Programs that perform routine file conversions and sort/merge operations.

**Vacuum tube** An electronic tube used as a basic component in the first generation of computers.

**Value-added network (VAN)** A communications system in which a value-added carrier leases lines from a common carrier. The lines are then enhanced by adding error detection and faster response time.

**Vaporware** Products, both hardware and software, that are marketed before they exist.

**Variable length** Refers to records containing different numbers of characters.

**Vectors** The arrows—lines with directional notation—used in data flow diagrams.

**Vertical markets** Markets consisting of groups of similar customers.

**Very high-level language** Fourth-generation language.

**Very large-scale integration (VLSI)** A 1-megabit chip.

**Videoconferencing** Computer conferencing combined with cameras and wall-size screens.

**Video display terminal (VDT)** A terminal with a screen.

**Video graphics** Computer-produced animated pictures.

**Videotex** Data communications merchandising.

**Virtual memory** See *Virtual storage*

**Virtual storage** A condition in which part of the program is stored on disk and is brought into memory only as needed.

**VisiCalc** The first electronic spreadsheet for personal computers, written by Daniel Bricklin and Robert Frankston.

**Vision system** A set of computer-controlled machines that can take automatic action based on what is seen.

**Voice input** See *Speech recognition*

**Voice mail** A system in which the user can dictate a message into the voice mail system, where it is digitized and stored into the recipient's voice mailbox. Later the recipient can dial the mailbox, and the system delivers the message in audio form.

**Voice-output device** See *Voice synthesizer*

**Voice synthesizer** A device that converts data in main storage to vocalized sounds understandable to humans.

**Volatile** Refers to the loss of data in semiconductor storage when the current is interrupted or turned off.

**Volume testing** Testing of a program by using real data in large amounts.

**von Neumann machine** A serial processing computer.

**Wand reader** An input device that scans the special letters and numbers on price tags in retail stores.

**Winchester disk** A disk drive in which the disks, access arms, and read/write heads are combined in a sealed module.

**Word** The number of bits that constitute a common unit of data, as defined by the computer system.

**Word addressable** Refers to computers that move data one word at a time.

**Word processing** Computer-based creation, editing, formatting, storing, and printing of text.

**Word wrap**  A word processing feature that automatically starts a word at the left margin of the next line if there is not enough room on the line.

**Write-enable ring**  See *File protection ring*

**Write-once media**  Media that can be written to only once.

**Written documents**  Procedures manuals, reports, forms, and other material used in the data gathering phase of systems analysis.

**WYSIWYG**  "What you see is what you get," an acronym referring to screen-oriented word processing programs.

# Index

Page numbers that appear in italics contain figures and may also contain related text.